THE FUTURE OF SOCIAL MOVEMENT RESEARCH

Social Movements, Protest, and Contention

Series Editor Bert Klandermans, VU-University, Amsterdam

Associate Editors Ron R. Aminzade, University of Minnesota
David S. Meyer, University of California, Irvine
Verta A. Taylor, University of California, Santa Barbara

Volume 39 Jacquelien van Stekelenburg, Conny Roggeband, and Bert Klandermans, editors, *The Future of Social Movement Research: Dynamics, Mechanisms, and Processes*

Volume 38 Ashley Currier, *Out in Africa: LGBT Organizing in Namibia and South Africa*

Volume 37 Gregory M. Maney, Rachel V. Kutz-Flamenbaum, Deana A. Rohlinger, and Jeff Goodwin, editors, *Strategies for Social Change*

Volume 36 Zakia Salime, *Between Feminism and Islam: Human Rights and Sharia Law in Morocco*

Volume 35 Rachel Schurman and William A. Munro, *Fighting for the Future of Food: Activists versus Agribusiness in the Struggle over Biotechnology*

Volume 34 Nella Van Dyke and Holly J. McCammon, editors, *Strategic Alliances: Coalition Building and Social Movements*

Volume 33 Stefaan Walgrave and Dieter Rucht, editors, *The World Says No to War: Demonstrations against the War on Iraq*

Volume 32 Rory McVeigh, *The Rise of the Ku Klux Klan: Right-Wing Movements and National Politics*

Volume 31 Tina Fetner, *How the Religious Right Shaped Lesbian and Gay Activism*

Volume 30 Jo Reger, Daniel J. Myers, and Rachel L. Einwohner, editors, *Identity Work in Social Movements*

(continued on page 471)

THE FUTURE OF SOCIAL MOVEMENT RESEARCH

Dynamics, Mechanisms, and Processes

Jacquelien van Stekelenburg,
Conny Roggeband, and
Bert Klandermans, editors

Social Movements, Protest, and Contention
Volume 39

University of Minnesota Press
Minneapolis • London

Copyright 2013 by the Regents of the University of Minnesota

All rights reserved. No part of this publication may be reproduced, stored in a retrieval system, or transmitted, in any form or by any means, electronic, mechanical, photocopying, recording, or otherwise, without the prior written permission of the publisher.

Published by the University of Minnesota Press
111 Third Avenue South, Suite 290
Minneapolis, MN 55401-2520
http://www.upress.umn.edu

A Cataloging-in-Publication record for this book is available from the Library of Congress.
ISBN 978-0-8166-8651-3 (hc)
ISBN 978-0-8166-8654-4 (pb)

Printed in the United States of America on acid-free paper

The University of Minnesota is an equal-opportunity educator and employer.

20 19 18 17 16 15 14 13   10 9 8 7 6 5 4 3 2 1

Contents

Acknowledgments   ix

Introduction: The Future of Social Movement Research   xi
   Jacquelien van Stekelenburg and Conny Roggeband

I. Grievances and Identities: The Demand Side of Participation

1. The Dynamics of Demand   3
   Bert Klandermans

2. Is the Internet Creating New Reasons to Protest?   17
   Francesca Polletta, Pang Ching Bobby Chen,
   Beth Gharrity Gardner, and Alice Motes

3. Social Movement Participation in the Global Society: Identity, Networks, and Emotions   37
   Verta Taylor

4. "Protest against Whom?": The Role of Collective Meaning Making in Politicization   59
   Marjoka van Doorn, Jacomijne Prins, and Saskia Welschen

Discussion: Opening the Black Box of Dynamics in Theory and Research on the Demand Side of Protest   79
   Martijn van Zomeren

II. Organizations and Networks: The Supply Side of Contention

5. The Changing Supply Side of Mobilization: Questions for Discussion   95
   Conny Roggeband and Jan Willem Duyvendak

6. Bringing Organizational Studies Back into Social Movement Scholarship   107
   Sarah A. Soule

7. Organization and Community in Social Movements 125
   Suzanne Staggenborg

8. Organizational Fields and Social Movement Dynamics 145
   Mario Diani

9. Social Movement Structures in Action: Conceptual Propositions and Empirical Illustration 169
   Dieter Rucht

Discussion: The Changing Supply Side of Mobilization: Impressions on a Theme 191
Debra Minkoff

III. Dynamics of Mobilization

10. Changing Mobilization of Individual Activists? 205
    Stefaan Walgrave

11. Mobilizing for Change in a Changing Society 217
    Jacquelien van Stekelenburg and Marije Boekkooi

12. Ethnicity, Repression, and Fields of Action in Movement Mobilization 235
    Pamela E. Oliver

13. Identity Dilemmas, Discursive Fields, Identity Work, and Mobilization: Clarifying the Identity–Movement Nexus 263
    David A. Snow

14. Movements of the Left, Movements of the Right Reconsidered 281
    Swen Hutter and Hanspeter Kriesi

Discussion: Mobilization and the Changing and Persistent Dynamics of Political Participation 299
Christopher Rootes

IV. The Changing Context of Contention

15. The End of the Social Movement as We Know It? Adaptive Challenges in Changed Contexts 315
    Ruud Koopmans

16. Social Movements and Elections: Toward a Broader
    Understanding of the Political Context of Contention   325
    Doug McAdam and Sidney Tarrow

17. Social Movements, Power, and Democracy:
    New Challenges, New Challengers, New Theories?   347
    Donatella della Porta

18. Recent Trends in Public Protest in the United States:
    The Social Movement Society Thesis Revisited   369
    John D. McCarthy, Patrick Rafail, and Ashley Gromis

19. The "Contentious French" Revisited   397
    Nonna Mayer

Discussion: Meaning and Movements in the
    New Millennium: Gendering Democracy   419
    Myra Marx Ferree

Afterword   429
Bert Klandermans

Contributors   439

Index   443

Acknowledgments

The editors are grateful to the colleagues who served as reviewers of the chapters: Kenneth Andrews, Ed Amenta, Rob Benford, John Campbell, Xenia Chryssochoou, Frank den Hond, John Drury, Jennifer Earl, Bob Edwards, Doug Imig, Olivier Fillieule, Dana Fisher, Bill Gamson, Marco Giugni, Jim Jasper, Craig Jenkins, Christian Lahusen, Holly McCammon, David Meyer, Dan Myers, Belinda Robnett, Jackie Smith, Nella Van Dyke, Jeroen van Laer, Joris Verhulst, Edward Walker, Nancy Whittier, and Mayer Zald.

Introduction: The Future of Social Movement Research

Jacquelien van Stekelenburg and Conny Roggeband

In 2001, *Dynamics of Contention* appeared. McAdam, Tarrow, and Tilly made an attempt to synthesize the approaches in the field, to assess where we were and what the major unanswered questions were at that moment. The decade that has passed since the appearance of *Dynamics of Contention* has been a vigorous one in the social movement academic field and in the activist field. Take the year 2011, which was a major one for social movements: the Arab Spring; precarity demonstrations in southern Europe; the Israeli urban camp demonstrations, culminating in the largest demonstration in the history of the country; and finally, the Occupy movement. What is remarkable, however, is that everything came together in so many parts of the world.[1] Are the dynamics of contention changing? Worldwide, we see an increasing number of citizens who stand up against authorities. Although this alludes to a growing demand for protest, such a growing demand would not have materialized had there not been a growing supply of protest opportunities that appealed to people and sophisticated mobilization techniques that brought demand and supply together. In an ever more globalizing world, streams of migration make populations of Western societies increasingly diverse, while the establishment of ever more transnational and supranational political institutions and multinationals has changed contentious politics fundamentally. At the same time, a new social fabric has emerged, and loosely coupled networks have become the prime mode of organization and structure of society, while the Internet, social media, and cell phones have given the world a virtual outlook and facilitated other forms of communication and transnational ties. These societal processes of globalization, individualization–diversification, and virtualization imply significant changes in movement dynamics and the context of mobilization that call for a revision of theory. One can see this volume—*The Future of Social Movement Research*—as an attempt to integrate the efforts of scholars and update assessments of where we are based on these fundamental changes in the political game, which, as has been argued, have made contentious politics more important, while traditional political parties have lost support.

In October 2009, a group of American and European sociologists, political scientists, and social psychologists met in Amsterdam to discuss challenges in the future of social movement research. The occasion of Bert Klandermans's so-called retirement—obviously, he never stopped working!—was seized to bring together an exceptional combination of experts in the field of social movements. In short, the core question of the symposium asked,

> How are dynamics of contention influenced by the development toward globalization, the diversification of societies, the more diffuse mobilizing structures, and the emergence of new communication techniques?

In a unique preparatory trajectory—we will come back to this later—four teams comprising six interdisciplinary scholars from the United States and Europe each developed the state of the art and suggested possible research agendas.

This endeavor was motivated by past experiences of fruitful transatlantic cooperation, which were key to significant advances in social movement theory in the 1980s and 1990s. Around 1980, the study of social movements in Europe was completely separated from that in the United States. Both continents attempted to answer the question why social movements in the 1960s had started to grow explosively. In the United States, the question was answered through structural approaches such as *resource mobilization*, with an emphasis on the extent to which organizations are able to mobilize resources, and the *political process approach*, which focuses on political conditions. In Europe, the answer lay in cultural approaches, with an emphasis on conflict between lifestyles and identities, the so-called *New Social Movements* approach. In that setting, Klandermans and Tarrow took the initiative to bring scholars from the United States and Europe together at workshops in Ithaca, New York, in 1985 and in Amsterdam in 1986. These workshops resulted in the volume *From Structure to Action: Comparing Social Movement Research across Cultures* (Klandermans, Kriesi, and Tarrow 1988), which by now is a classic in the field. Several conferences and symposia followed, each of which was turned into a book: 1988 in Ann Arbor, Michigan (*Frontiers in Social Movement Theory*; Morris and Mueller 1992); 1992 in Washington, D.C. (*Comparative Perspectives on Social Movements*; McAdam, McCarthy, and Zald 1996); 1992 in San

Diego, California (*Social Movements and Culture*; Johnston and Klandermans 1995); and 1995 in Mont Pelerin, Switzerland (*Social Movements in a Globalizing World*; della Porta, Kriesi, and Rucht 1999). Another result was the prestigious book series *Social Movements, Protest, and Contention* published by the University of Minnesota Press and edited by Bert Klandermans, Ron R. Aminzade, David S. Meyer, and Verta A. Taylor.

The effort of the network was to make a theoretical connection between the structural and cultural factors identified; they worked toward a synthetic theoretical model that linked political opportunity structures and mobilizing networks as structural requirements and framing as a mediating mechanism, as laid out in *Comparative Perspectives in Social Movements* (McAdam, McCarthy, and Zald 1996). In 1999, della Porta, Kriesi, and Rucht concluded that political opportunities, mobilizing structures, and framing processes had become consensus.

Yet this classic agenda of political opportunity structures, mobilizing structures, and collective action frames that emerged from the international cooperation has gradually lost its central position (Klandermans and Roggeband 2007; McAdam, Tarrow, and Tilly 2001). It has been criticized and reelaborated from various angles both by insiders (e.g., McAdam, Tarrow, and Tilly 2001) and outsiders (e.g., Goodwin and Jasper 2004; see also *Sociological Forum* 1999), but so far, no successful new paradigm has replaced the classic triad.

Precisely in these times of a paradigm vacuum and significant changes in contentious politics awaiting theoretical and empirical scrutiny, the established collaboration between interdisciplinary scholars in the United States and Europe gradually eroded. At the turn of the millennium, the network seems to have moved into a state of abeyance (cf. Taylor 1989). Regular contacts between individual members do still exist and have resulted, for instance, in *The Blackwell Companion to Social Movements,* edited by Snow, Soule, and Kriesi (2004); *Transnational Protest and Global Activism,* edited by della Porta and Tarrow (2005); *Social Movements and Networks: Relational Approaches to Collective Action,* edited by Diani and McAdam (2003); and *The Blackwell Encyclopedia of Social and Political Movements,* edited by Snow and colleagues (2013). However, the transatlantic network did not continue its regular thematic meetings and symposia and, as such, has not developed a new research agenda—arguably because transatlantic cooperation is nowadays less flexible. Protectionist funding in the United States and Europe directs research funds mainly to researchers from the same continent, but also the War on Terror and the recent economic crises have led research on social movements in the United States and Europe to once again grow apart.

The 2009 Amsterdam workshop intended to revitalize the once-so-successful transatlantic and interdisciplinary network and to explore the implications of a changing context for collective action and protest.

Changing Movement Dynamics

Since the 1990s, the context of contentious politics has changed significantly. We asked our contributors to reflect on the influences of three inseparably intertwined processes: *globalization, individualization–diversification,* and *virtualization.*

Globalization has resulted in establishing ever more transnational and supranational political institutions that have had a rapidly growing impact on people's daily lives. Economic globalization—production transfer, increased international trade, and the growth of transnational corporations—has generated new issues of mobilization. Social movement activity evolves in response to globalization processes and has become increasingly transnational (e.g., della Porta, Kriesi, and Rucht 1999; della Porta and Tarrow 2005; Tarrow and McAdam 2005). Scholars have identified mechanisms and processes related to this change such as scale shift (Tarrow and McAdam 2005); the tight relationship between global governance institutions, nation-states, and transnational social movements (Keck and Sikkink 1998); and the multilayered opportunity structures in which movements now operate (Keck and Sikkink 1998).

Contemporary societies are increasingly individualized and more diverse. People have become disembedded from their old communal modes of life and reembedded in new ones, in which they must assemble new lifestyles and identities (Beck 1992). Bauman (2000) highlights the decline of traditional institutions and the fluid and fragmentary nature of social bonds and individual identities, which he coined as a move from solid to liquid societies. Networks have become the prime mode of organization and structure of society (Castells 1996). Formal organizations have turned into networks of networks, which in turn are intersected with informal networks rooted in the personal lifeworld and more diffuse interpersonal group settings. In a network society, political participation is increasingly rooted in everyday networks of participants, and the social movement actor involved is likely to be a diffuse and decentralized network rather than an organization (Duyvendak and Hurenkamp 2004; Melucci 1996; Taylor 2000). Della Porta and Tarrow (2005) observed that activists increasingly have "multiple belongings" (overlapping memberships linked with polycentric networks) and "flexible or tolerant identities" (characterized by inclusiveness and a positive emphasis on diversity and cross-fertilization).

A third related process can be coined *virtualization* and is related to the spread of new communication technologies such as the Internet, social media, e-mail, and cell phones. New information and communication technologies are changing the ways in which activists communicate, collaborate, and demonstrate. Some scholars have argued that modern mass media make it possible to fabricate new connections among people from various backgrounds, resulting in mobilizing structures that have the potential to be more diverse and inclusive on the basis of gender, race and ethnicity, and nationality (Taylor 2000), whereas others argue that inequalities in real life are reproduced in the virtual world, resulting in the so-called digital divide (e.g., Norris 2001). The Internet creates its own venues and demand for action but also lowers the threshold for participation. The increased attention to the virtual dimensions of social movement organizing and mobilizing does not take away the strong emphasis on the organizational aspects of social movements yet draws more attention to relations, networks, and communities (real and virtual).

These processes have important temporal and spatial consequences for mobilization. As many authors in this volume argue, globalization, individualization–diversification, and virtualization create new venues for action, new forms, and new structures, whereas older structures, repertoires, and organizational forms have kept their importance.

In terms of time, globalization and the use of new communication technologies have increased the speed by which information spreads and at which social movement actors can respond to issues and incidents. They have affected the timing of protest, as it is now relatively easy to coordinate (almost) simultaneous actions at a global scale. In terms of time investment, activists now have a wide range of options available between being a longtime engaged and a one-shot, press-the-button activist. Yet this timescale shift may also lead to more fleeting and momentary commitments and actions, resulting in short-term actions and rapidly shifting issues.

In terms of space, virtualization has created a new spatial protest dimension. The World Wide Web is increasingly used as a new globalized space to articulate new issues, to protest, to search for bystanders, and to mobilize adherents. Also, it has become more common to orchestrate multispace actions that share one goal and specific protest form but that are staged at different places. The recent Occupy movement is a good example of this. We see more and more dislocated or diasporic forms of protest, that is, protest actions organized in a random location but directed at adversaries in another location. The fluidity of social bonds and the Internet is blurring the boundaries between public and private spaces of mobilization. Although public spaces are still the most common places to protest, you can now also protest from your bedroom or stage protests at the kitchen table.

How this changing societal context influences the dynamics of contention is both a theoretical and empirical question that the authors in this volume try to answer. We borrow the economic metaphor of demand and supply to explore how the different aspects and processes of mobilization are affected by these changes in context (Klandermans 2004). *Demand* refers to the potential in a society for protest; it relates to the interest in a society in what a movement stands for. Is the movement addressing a problem about which people are worried? Is there a need for a movement on these issues? What personal grievances politicize and translate into political claims, and how? *Supply* refers, conversely, to the opportunities staged by organizers to protest. It relates to the characteristics of the movement. What organizational forms are used? What is the movement's strength? Is it a movement with which people can identify? Does it stage activities that are appealing to people?

Demand and supply do not automatically come together. *Mobilization* is the *process* that links demand and supply and can thus be seen as the marketing mechanism of the movement domain. Mobilization campaigns attempt to bring demand and supply together. The mobilizing structure organizers assemble is the connecting tissue between the supply side of organizers and their appeals and the demand side of participants and their motives. This makes it highly dynamic: a fit—or misfit—between motives and appeals makes for successful or failed mobilization and, as such, affects movement outcomes and effects.

The Symposium: Search for New Theoretical and Empirical Terrain

In their search for new theoretical and empirical terrain, the participants of the workshop—including the initiators of the transatlantic network (Klandermans, Tarrow, Rucht, Kriesi, McAdam, and Snow—sadly, without the late Melucci) and scholars who became involved in the extended network that had formed through joint research and book projects over the years—were invited to reflect on four domains of contention: demand, supply, mobilization, and the context of mobilization.

The symposium was an extraordinary occasion with unique preparatory activities. In brief, the participants were assigned to virtual discussion groups clustered around the four themes. One year before the symposium, the four chairs designed preambles with theoretical and empirical questions relating to each chair's assigned theme. The participants of every team responded to their respective preambles in short essays. The chairs wrote responses to these essays. In the subsequent round, the participants had the opportunity to react to the response of their chair and the other essays of the first round within their theme. Finally, the discussants of each team provided an overview of where the respective teams stood and how they envisioned to proceed. These preambles, essays, and reactions for all four themes—the discussion threads—functioned as input for the symposium itself. The papers were presented during the actual symposium, and minutes were taken of the discussions. After the symposium, our authors were asked to draft position papers based on the collected material. This whole process eventually resulted in 23 essays.[2] The four central themes in the volume are as follows:

- grievances and identities: the dynamics of demand
- organizations and networks: the dynamics of supply
- the dynamics of mobilization
- the changing context of contention

The format of the volume closely follows the format of the symposium. That is to say, every theme starts with an introductory essay and contains a collection of additional essays and a concluding essay, in which the discussant reflects on the state of the art of the discussant's theme. Bert Klandermans agreed to write the volume's afterword.

This Volume: Theoretical and Empirical Developments

One of the aims behind this endeavor has been to generate theoretical insights based on sound empirical research. The diverse case studies and approaches provide an overview of the field in a multitude of dimensions, from micro-processes to mesoanalysis to macro-overviews. The different parts in this volume not only map the theoretical and empirical state of the art in social movement studies but also engender new urgent questions for research and point to interesting new theories and fields of research. The contributors examine how changes in the sociopolitical context of contentious politics affect the demand and supply of the movement domain and mobilization. In this introduction, we highlight three of the mechanisms that the authors of this volume identify in relation to the changes in context: boundary work, the dual dynamics of politicization and privatization, and brokerage–frame alignment and methodological implications linked to contextual changes. These mechanisms mediate between supply and demand and so influence mobilization processes.

Boundary Work

Various authors in this volume (Taylor, Diani, Snow, Soule) point to the importance of clear identities for collective action and the central role of boundaries to secure this. Verta Taylor, in her contribution, argues that collective identity formation is a necessary precondition for action and that activists deploy identity strategies with the goal of changing individuals, culture, institutions, and the state. Diani holds that mechanisms of boundary construction are crucial both to secure the continuity of collective action over time and space and to provide participants with the necessary motivations to act. As Snow notes, such boundaries may be symbolic, but boundary activities may also include the construction and display of physical settings and props such as protest placards, specific clothing, and bodily markings. Soule suggests that organizations with unclear, diffuse identities may draw fewer participants to their events or receive less media attention than those organizations with coherent identities. Yet, as Christopher Rootes notes in his discussion, "where identities have, under the impact of social and technological change, become unprecedentedly multiple, fluid, and/or fragmented, it may be doubted whether identity is still a glue capable of holding social movements together." Identity boundaries have become blurry, as Marjoka van Doorn, Jacomijne Prins, and Saskia Welschen argue. The Internet both plays a role in this blurring, as Francesca Polletta, Pang Ching Bobby Chen, Beth Gharrity Gardner, and Alice Motes contend, but also facilitates new identities, some of the virtual, as the example of the Pirate Party makes clear. The fluid and fragmented character of new identities may obstruct the formation of strong and enduring identities, which seems a precondition for building and sustaining enduring social movements.

Politicization and Privatization

The authors examine the processes of politicization and nonpoliticization of collective identities. Bert Klandermans, Verta Taylor, and Martijn van Zomeren all point to the role emotions play in the politicization of collective identity. Taylor, Polletta and collaborators, and Jacquelien van Stekelenburg and Marije Boekkooi highlight the growing importance of virtual networks in the politicization of collective identity. Van Doorn and collaborators examine a case in which identity, against all odds, is not politicized. Their study points to the importance of consensus building at the microlevel and how the blurring of identity boundaries is a central obstacle to mobilization. Polletta and collaborators point out that the Internet has eroded the lines between the public and the private and has turned movement participation into one among a repertoire of activities that include leisure and consumption activities as well as political ones. This interesting observation points to a dual dynamic of politicization and privatization. Private issues, such as individual consumption, become a domain of contention, whereas political identity is increasingly seen as something that is similar to musical taste or food preferences, traditionally seen as personal or private. Also, groups—virtually—organized around issues like cooking, parenting, or pets may transform themselves into (temporary) action platforms. Authors, in particular the contributions of Suzanne Staggenborg and Dieter Rucht, point to the importance of such preexisting networks and prior campaigns for processes of politicization. Rucht points out that in diffuse and broad protest coalitions, "tolerant identities" may help to overcome differences in worldviews and make consensus formation less necessary for politicization. Yet, although this may work for campaigns, both Diani and Soule point out that for enduring mobilizations, identity work remains a central asset.

Brokerage and Frame Alignment

In solid or more traditional organizational structures, mobilizing processes were easier and often more top down compared to networklike or coordination-structured mobilization. Movement participants cannot be easily located around solid organizational structures, as Van Stekelenburg and Boekkooi argue, but move flexibly within liquid networks. The Occupy movement is a good example here. This makes brokerage a more necessary mechanism. In the politicizing process, leaders, as "entrepreneurs of identity," play a central role. Soule points to the role of "bridge builders" or "coalition brokers," who have multiple organizational affiliations and are able to foster coalitions between movement organizations, even those that are not within the same movement industry. Rootes argues that groups and individuals whose identities are relatively diffuse or fluid are better placed to play the brokerage roles by which movements may be held together and by which effective collective action may be achieved.

Methodological Implications

Finally, many of the contributions contend that social processes like individualization and virtualization have important methodological consequences for the study of collective action. Attention to relations (Diani), networks (Rucht), and communities both real and virtual (Staggenborg) instead of organizations requires a different, more processual and dynamic approach. This implies that we have to find different ways of tracing protest behavior and understand the ties, motivations, and identities of both individual protesters and the structure of their actions. The contributors come up with different solutions for this problem of location. Taylor points out that attention to the dynamics of the politicization of collective identity provides insight into how social movement tactics and performances, if not repertoires, diffuse, vary, and change. In a similar vein, Van Doorn and colleagues direct our attention to identity narratives and the role these play in organizing and mobilizing. Rucht proposes to study specific campaigns to explore the constellation of actors and organizations involved. Van Stekelenburg and Boekkooi suggest that we should pay more attention to the key role of organizers and how they move in different network constellations. Diani argues that we should take a more relational approach to social movements. Although some of these methods may work well for case study research, they are rather difficult to apply in comparative research. Burt (2000) pointed to the very limited evidence that we have on the dynamics of networks over time; collecting measures of even one type of network tie at one point in time for a large, loosely bounded system is a time-consuming and difficult task, and this fact limits our ability to study networks over time. Social change thus begs for methodological innovation, but there is still little consensus over what methods may be most appropriate to deal with dispersing collective action patterns. Yet considerable progress in developing new tools, methods, and approaches to social movements has been made. Arguably, the most progress has been made in terms of what Bert Klandermans describes in chapter 1 as "the virtue of comparison." Be it a comparison over time, a comparison between movements or demonstrations, or a cross-national comparison, comparative research teaches us that what counts for one context doesn't have to count for another context and, as such, furthers our theorizing on social movements. This volume demonstrates that by now, some impressive, large longitudinal and cross-national data sets have been gathered, which enables such comparative studies. Swen Hutter and Hanspeter Kriesi (chapter 14) use an extended version of the Kriesi and colleagues (1995) data set. John D. McCarthy, Patrick Rafail, and Ashley Gromis (chapter 18) use the Dynamics of Collective Action data set, which contains all of the protest events reported in the *New York Times* between 1960 and 1995.

Our goal in undertaking this endeavor was to reflect on challenges for future social movement research. In 2008, at the start, we could not have envisioned how quickly and fluidly the dynamics of contention were changing. This made our endeavor a fascinating and adventurous journey. We traveled in a turbulent period with an all-star team (as our reviewers noted) discussing these contentious political events. We could not have wished ourselves better company! We believe that the book provides sufficient food for thought and discussion. It is our hope that it spurs new cross-national and interdisciplinary research initiatives to make social movement studies flourish, just as our topic of research does.

Notes

1. We asked our contributors to reflect on contentious 2011; this quotation is from Suzanne Staggenborg.
2. All chapters have been peer reviewed. The list of peer reviewers can be found in the acknowledgments. We are grateful for the time and attention the peer reviewers devoted to specific chapters and are sure that all chapters gained strength by their comments.

References

Bauman, Zygmunt. 2000. *Liquid Modernity.* Cambridge: Polity Press.
Beck, Ulrich. 1992. *Risk Society: Towards a New Modernity.* New Delhi: Sage.
Burt, Ronald S. 2000. "The Network Structure of Social Capital." In *Research in Organizational Behavior,* edited by Robert I. Sutton and Barry M. Staw, 345–423. Greenwich, Conn.: JAI Press.
Castells, Manuel. 1996. *The Rise of the Network Society.* Oxford: Blackwell.
Della Porta, Donatella, Hanspeter Kriesi, and Dieter Rucht. 1999. *Social Movements in a Globalizing World.* New York: Macmillan.
Della Porta, Donatella, and Sidney Tarrow. 2005. *Transnational Protest and Global Activism.* New York: Rowman and Littlefield.
Diani, Mario, and Doug McAdam. 2003. *Social Movements and Networks: Relational Approaches to Collective Action.* Oxford: Oxford University Press.
Duyvendak, Jan Willem, and Menno Hurenkamp. 2004. *Kiezen voor de kudde: Lichte gemeenschappen en de nieuwe meerderheid.* Amsterdam: Van Gennep.
Goodwin, Jeff, and James M. Jasper. 2004. *Rethinking Social Movements: Structure, Meaning, and Emotion.* Lanham, Md.: Rowman and Littlefield.
Johnston, Hank, and Bert Klandermans. 1995. *Social Movements and Culture.* Minneapolis: University of Minnesota Press.
Keck, Margaret E., and Kathryn Sikkink. 1998. *Activists beyond Borders: Advocacy Networks in International Politics.* Ithaca, N.Y.: Cornell University Press.
Klandermans, Bert. 2004. "The Demand and Supply of Participation: Social–Psychological Correlates of Participation in Social Movements." In *The Blackwell Companion to Social Movements,* edited by David A. Snow, Sarah A. Soule, and Hanspeter Kriesi, 360–79. Oxford: Blackwell.
Klandermans, Bert, Hanspeter Kriesi, and Sidney Tarrow. 1988. *From Structure to Action: Comparing Social Movement Research across Cultures.* Vol. 1. Greenwich, Conn.: JAI Press.
Klandermans, Bert, and Conny Roggeband. 2007. *Social Movements across Disciplines.* New York: Springer.

Kriesi, H., R. Koopmans, J. W. Duyvendak et al. 1995. *New Social Movements in Western Europe: A Comparative Analysis.* Minneapolis: University of Minnesota Press.

McAdam, Doug, John D. McCarthy, and Mayer N. Zald. 1996. *Comparative Perspectives on Social Movements.* New York: Cambridge University Press.

McAdam, Doug, Sidney Tarrow, and Charles Tilly. 2001. *Dynamics of Contention.* Cambridge: Cambridge University Press.

Melucci, Alberto. 1996. *Challenging Codes: Collective Action in the Information Age.* Cambridge: Cambridge University Press.

Morris, Aldon D., and Carol M. Mueller. 1992. *Frontiers in Social Movement Theory.* New Haven, Conn.: Yale University Press.

Norris, P. 2001. *Digital Divide? Civic Engagement, Information Poverty, and the Internet Worldwide.* Cambridge: Cambridge University Press.

Snow, David, Doug McAdam, Donatella della Porta, and Bert Klandermans. 2013. *Blackwell Encyclopedia of Social and Political Movements.* Oxford: Blackwell.

Snow, David A., Sarah A. Soule, and Hanspeter Kriesi. 2004. *The Blackwell Companion to Social Movements.* Oxford: Blackwell.

Sociological Forum. 1999. "Mini-Symposium: Social Movements." 14:27–136.

Tarrow, Sidney, and Doug McAdam. 2005. "Scale Shift in Transnational Contention." In *Transnational Protest and Global Activism,* edited by D. della Porta and S. Tarrow, 121–47. Lanham, Md.: Rowman and Littlefield.

Taylor, Verta. 1989. "Social Movement Continuity: The Women's Movement in Abeyance." *American Sociological Review* 54:761–75.

———. 2000. "Mobilizing for Change in a Social Movement Society." *Contemporary Sociology* 29:219–30.

I
Grievances and Identities: The Demand Side of Participation

1

The Dynamics of Demand

Bert Klandermans

The demand side of protest concerns the characteristics of a social movement's mobilization potential. A movement's mobilization potential can be characterized in terms of its demographic and political composition; in terms of collective identities, shared grievances, and shared emotions; in terms of its internal organization; and in terms of its social and virtual embeddedness in the society at large. Speaking of the dynamics of demand, I refer to the process of the formation of mobilization potential: grievances and identities politicize, environments turn supportive, and emotions are aroused.

Scholarly attention to the dynamics of demand has been limited. Perhaps social movement scholars do not bother too much about how mobilization potential is formed, as they tend to study contention when it takes place and mobilization potential is formed and mobilized already. Hence little is known about the formation of mobilization potential in the ebb and flow of contentious politics. Basic questions, such as how consensus is formed; how individuals come to feel, think, and act in concert; why and how some grievances turn into claims, while others don't; and why and how some identities politicize, while others don't, remain unanswered.

In the following paragraphs, I will briefly discuss each of these aspects. The contributors to this section all elaborate on pieces of the puzzle.

Demographic and Political Composition

For a long time it was taken for granted that political protest more frequently attracted males, youths, students, and workers. Meyer and Tarrow's (1998) review of the literature, however, suggests that the demographic composition of the crowds participating has become more diverse (see also McCarthy, Rafail, and Gromis, chapter 18; Mayer, chapter 19). Moreover, owing to streams of immigration, the ethnic composition of the population of European democracies has become more diverse, which reflects the composition of mobilization potentials. At the same time, the process of globalization has made questions about the transnational composition of mobilization potential more relevant.

Demographic characteristics of mobilization potential commonly deemed of interest are age, gender, class, ethnicity, religion, and nationality. Mobilization potential can be more heterogeneous or homogeneous in terms of these characteristics. Marwell and Oliver's (1993) mathematical simulations suggest that heterogeneous mobilization potential is more likely turned into action than is homogeneous potential. Obviously, the mobilization potential of movements varies with regard to these characteristics. Such variation is not random but rather is related to the issues a movement addresses. Poor-quality education more likely bothers younger people and their parents, whereas retirement age is more a matter of concern of the elderly; regulations that restrict wearing veils are more likely to worry Muslims than non-Muslims; and so on.

As for the political composition of a movement's mobilization potential, I have in mind the ideological left–right distinction. Unlike in the 1960s and 1970s, today's movements are no longer exclusively oriented to the left. Indeed, over the last few decades, Western democracies have witnessed viable, sometimes vicious movements from the extreme right (For Europe, see Klandermans and Mayer 2006; Hutter and Kriesi, chapter 14; for the United States, see McCarthy et al., chapter 18). The political extreme right provides the mobilization potential for protests regarding abortion, xenophobia, racism or religious fundamentalism, and, most recently in the United States, the Tea Party movement.

The Formation of Mobilization Potential

Little is known about how exactly mobilization potential is formed. A few decades ago, I introduced the distinction between *consensus mobilization* and *consensus formation* (Klandermans 1984). Whereas consensus mobilization concerns "the deliberate attempts to spread the view of a social actor among parts of the population," consensus formation concerns "the unplanned convergence of meaning in social networks and subcultures" (Klandermans 1988, 175). Gamson (1992), in his *Talking Politics,* shows that people use any kind of information source if they talk with their friends about politics. In chapter 2, Polletta and colleagues discuss the question of the role of the Internet in this regard. Employing time series analysis, Vliegenthart (2007) demonstrated for the issue of immigration and integration that in a complex interplay between real-life events, media attention, debates in the parliament, and debates between politicians, public opinion is formed and converted into anti-immigrant party support in the Netherlands.

Grievances, Identities, and Emotions

Consensus formation encompasses the formation of grievances, the formation of collective identity, and emotion work. Taylor (chapter 3) and Van Doorn, Prins, and Welschen (chapter 4) extensively discuss these processes.

Grievance Theory

Grievances concern "outrage about the way authorities are treating a social problem" (Klandermans 1997, 38). In *The Social Psychology of Protest,* I made the distinction between illegitimate inequality, suddenly imposed grievances, and violated principles. Much social psychology literature on grievance formation is about illegitimate inequality, which deals with relative deprivation and social justice.

Relative deprivation theory assumes that feelings of relative deprivation result from a comparison of one's situation with a certain standard—one's past, someone else's situation, or an ideological standard such as equity or justice (Folger 1986). If a comparison results in the conclusion that a person is not receiving what she deserves, the person experiences relative deprivation. The literature distinguishes between relative deprivation based on personal comparisons (individual deprivation) and relative deprivation based on group comparisons (group deprivation) (Kelly and Breinlinger 1996). Research demonstrates that group relative deprivation is particularly important for engagement in collective action (Major 1994), but the work of Foster and Matheson (1999) suggests that so-called double deprivation, which is a combination of group and individual deprivation, is even more effective. On the basis of a meta-analysis, Van Zomeren, Postmes, and Spears (2008) conclude that the cognitive component of relative deprivation (i.e., the observation that a person receives less than the standard of comparison) has less influence on action participation than does the affective component (i.e., such feelings as indignation and discontent about outcomes).

Social psychologists have applied social justice theory to the study of social movements (Tyler and Smith 1998). The social justice literature distinguishes between two classes of justice judgments: distributive and procedural. Distributive justice is related to relative deprivation in that it refers to the fairness of outcome distributions. Procedural justice, conversely, refers to the fairness of decision-making procedures and the relational aspects of the social process, that is, whether authorities treat people with respect and can be trusted to act in a beneficial and unbiased manner (Tyler and Lind 1992). Research has found that people care more about how they are treated than about outcomes. On the basis of these findings, Tyler and Smith (1998) propose that procedural justice might be a more powerful predictor of social movement participation than distributive justice; that is what we found indeed in our research both in South Africa and among migrants in the Netherlands and New York (cf. Klandermans, Roefs, and Olivier 2001; Klandermans, Van der Toorn, and Van Stekelenburg 2008).

Political trust and political cynicism further influence the formation of grievances. Folger (1986) argues that perceived inequalities will not turn into discontent if people trust responsible actors (mostly authorities) to deal with the problem. Indeed, we found in our research in South Africa that relative deprivation is reduced when people trust government (Klandermans, Roefs, and Olivier 2001). Conversely, if people are cynical about politics, feelings of injustice are more likely to turn into contestation (Klandermans, Van der Toorn, and Van Stekelenburg 2008).

Efficacy

People who are part of a movement's mobilization potential are aggrieved, but as we know, grievances do not provide a sufficient reason to participate in collective action. Therefore the key question for any grievance theory to address is, why do some aggrieved people protest, whereas others do not? Resource mobilization and political process theory proposed that the availability of resources and the presence of opportunities play a key role. Numerous studies have demonstrated that groups with more resources and more opportunities are more likely to mobilize for collective action. At a social psychological level, this translates into the finding that people are more likely to participate in movement activities when they believe this will help to redress their grievances at affordable costs. Simon and colleagues (1998) have called this the *instrumental pathway* to movement participation. The key component for the instrumental pathway is efficacy—an individual's expectation that collective action participation can make a difference. The formation of mobilization potential, therefore, very much concerns the generation of such feelings of efficacy.

Identity

Identity, specifically collective identity, became an important concept in the social movement literature in the past twenty-five years. Indeed, at our conference in Amsterdam in 1986 (see Van Stekelenburg and Roggeband in the introduction to this volume), we began to conceive of collective identity as a significant factor in movement participation. Alberto Melucci (1981), who took part in that conference, was among the first to emphasize the significance of collective identity in the social movement context. In the years to follow the concept began to gain prominence in the social movement literature (see Stryker, Owens, and White 2000). Meanwhile, social psychologists began to explore the role of group identification in movement participation (Kelly and Breinlinger 1996; Simon et al. 1998; De Weerd and Klandermans 1999; Stürmer 2000; Simon and Klandermans 2001; Klandermans, Sabucedo, and Rodriguez 2002) and concluded that the more a person identifies with a group involved in a protest activity, the more likely the person is to take part in that activity.

Recent work draws attention to the fact that people simultaneously hold several identities that may come into conflict and guide behavior in different directions (cf. Kurtz 2002). Individuals might find themselves under cross-pressure (Oegema and Klandermans 1994) when two groups with which they identify are on opposite sides of a controversy. Indeed, movement activists who challenge their government are often accused of being disloyal to the country. This problem is especially relevant in the case of protest participation by immigrants, specifically Muslim immigrants, which is easily deemed disloyalty to their country of residence. González and Brown (2003) coined the term *dual identity* to point to the concurrent workings of a subordinate identity (e.g., ethnic identity) and a supraordinate identity (e.g., national identity). They claim that dual identity is desirable as it implies sufficient identification with one's subgroup to experience basic security and sufficient identification with the overarching group to preclude divisiveness.

Evidence suggests that, indeed, people who hold a dual identity are more satisfied with their situation than people who do not (González and Brown 2003; Simon 2011). Furthermore, studies of South African citizens and Spanish and Dutch farmers suggest that holding a dual identity stimulates subgroup mobilization (Klandermans, Roefs, and Olivier 2001; Klandermans, Sabucedo, and Rodriguez 2004). If people are dissatisfied, holding a dual identity makes them more likely to participate in collective action (Klandermans, Van der Toorn, and Van Stekelenburg 2008).

Emotions

Recent work in sociology and social psychology has brought emotions to the study of social movements (Jasper 1998; Goodwin, Jasper, and Polletta 2000; Van Zomeren et al. 2004; Van Stekelenburg 2006). Emotions can be avoidance or approach oriented. Fear, which makes people refrain from taking action, is an example of an avoidance-oriented emotion. Anger is an approach-oriented emotion and is known to be an antecedent of protest participation (Van Zomeren et al. 2004). There appears to be a relation between emotions and efficacy. When people do not feel efficacious, they are more likely to experience fear; feeling efficacious, conversely, is associated with experiencing anger (Mackie, Devos, and Smith 2000). Van Zomeren and colleagues (2004) show that anger is an important stimulant of protest participation, and they describe a pathway to participation based on anger. Mobilization potential grows if people feel efficacious, not only because that makes them feel more effective, but also because it makes them feel angrier.

An Integrating Framework

Strikingly, a framework integrating identities, grievances, and emotions into a single model was lacking. With Jacquelien van Stekelenburg, I developed such a model (Van Stekelenburg and Klandermans 2007, 2009, 2012). The model we developed assigns a central, integrating role to processes of identification. To develop the shared grievances and shared emotions that characterize a movement's mobilization potential, a shared identity is needed (see Figure 1.1).

The dependent variable of the model (the strength of the motivation to participate in collective action) results from emotions and grievances shared with a group with which the individual identifies. Grievances may originate from interests and/or principles that are felt to be threatened. The more people feel that interests of the group and/or principles that the group values are threatened, the angrier they are and the more they are prepared to take part in collective action to protect their interests and/or to express their anger.

The Dynamics of Demand

A weakness of the social movement literature is the lack of theorizing and research into the dynamics of the demand side. As mentioned, this is partly due to the fact that research on social movements usually starts too late to study the formation of mobilization potential, as the demand for protest has already materialized. Mobilization presupposes actors that set out to organize and mobilize. Such actors put a lot of effort into *consensus mobilization,* that is, into disseminating their views and gaining support for it, but whether the frame resonates, that is, whether people are susceptible to the frame that organizers try to disseminate, depends also on the more diffuse process of *consensus formation.*

The formation of mobilization potential entails three processes: the politicization of grievances, the politicization of collective identity, and the amplification of motivation by emotion. Grievances must be translated into demands. This is a process that is more complicated than one would imagine.

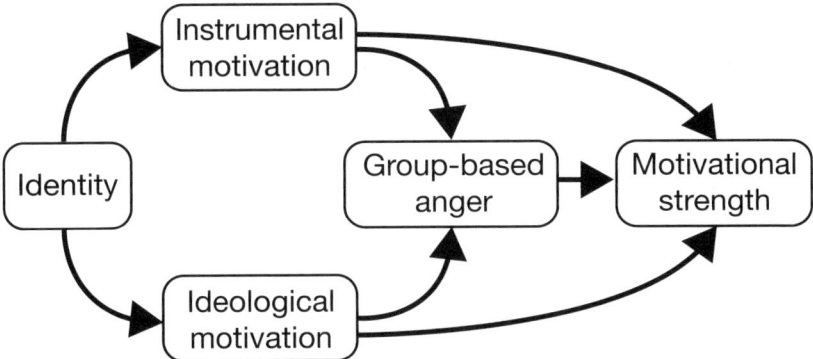

Figure 1.1. An integrated framework.

Take the demonstrations against the war in Iraq. We observed that next to the proximate goal of protesting the imminent war per se, broader dissatisfaction with the functioning of politics was at stake (Klandermans 2010). The level of mobilization in the countries we studied appears for obvious reasons to be dependent on the degree of opposition against the war but also on the degree of dissatisfaction with the functioning of the incumbent government.

Or take the fact that grievances can be translated into demands of interest or demands of principle. Van Stekelenburg, Klandermans, and Van Dijk (2011) demonstrate that in case of the former, people are more likely to develop instrumental motives to participate, whereas they are more likely to develop ideological motives in case of the latter.

Bernd Simon and I (2001) have elaborated on the dynamics of politicization of collective identity. A process of politicization implies that support of third parties is sought and that the social environment becomes divided into allies and opponents (see also Van Doorn, Prins, and Welschen, chapter 4). The more polarized the relationship between allies and opponents becomes, the less deviation from the group's opinions and actions is accepted, and the more opinions and acts of the opponents are rejected. Eventually, this results in radicalization (Simon 2011).

As mentioned, fear and anger are two possible correlates of grievances. Rather than being a separate motivational pathway, emotions mute or amplify existing motivations. Fear has a muting effect and anger has an amplifying effect. Polarization and radicalization and the role of emotions in that process warrant elaborate investigation, including the study of other emotions such as hope and despair (Gould 2009; Simon 2011; Taylor, chapter 3).

The Conduits of Consensus Formation

A movement's mobilization potential is not a collection of isolated individuals, nor is it isolated from other parts of society. Individuals are embedded in formal, informal, and virtual networks, which in turn are embedded in multiorganizational fields. A movement's mobilization potential can be described in terms of the *social capital* accumulated in it. Paxton (2002, 257) argued that associational life accumulates social capital, which "provides space for the creation and dissemination of discourse critical of the present government, and ... provides a way for active opposition to the regime to grow."

Taylor, in her essay, proposes the concept of *discursive communities* to signify these settings in which consensus formation takes place. Understanding of the formation of mobilization potential in a society requires insight into these processes of consensus formation. A possible mechanism is suggested by findings of our migrant study: apparently, grievances generate fear or anger, depending on whether they are discussed in people's networks and the characteristics of those networks. People's informal, formal, and virtual embeddedness seems a key factor in the formation of mobilization potential.

Part of the infrastructure of a movement's mobilization potential consists of the communication networks that connect individuals. Open and closed communication channels and weak and strong ties weave a web of connections that influence how easy or difficult it is to reach a movement's mobilization potential. Francesca Polletta and her collaborators allude to the role of the Internet in that respect. This corroborates Van Stekelenburg and Klandermans's (2012) observation that technologies such as mobile phones, the Internet, and Facebook played a crucial role in the mobilization of high school students in the Netherlands in a protest campaign against educational policy (see also Van Stekelenburg and Boekkooi, chapter 11).

The Virtue of Comparison

Note that I discussed a cluster of context variables. Only comparisons of place and time can tell us how contextual variation works. Such comparison may involve *nation*, that is, the national political system in which protest is staged; *mobilizing context*, that is, the demand and supply of protest and the techniques of mobilization; and *protest*, that is, the characteristics of the protest event. At a specific point in time, a specific national context generates a specific mobilizing context; the interaction of nation and mobilizing context produces a specific type of collective action; and a specific type of collective action brings a specific group of people up in arms.

Conclusion

The core of my argument is (1) that we need to study processes, that is, the formation of demand and its transition into action; (2) that the characteristics of mobilization potential I discussed are mutable and vary over time and place; and (3) that comparative studies are needed to register this variation and its impact on collective action participation.

The composition of mobilization potential has all kinds of implications for the chances of the supply side of protest and the process of mobilization to be successful. Depending on the composition of mobilization potential, matters such as communication channels, multiorganizational fields, and action repertoires vary. Consumers boycott producers, workers strike, antineoliberals block world summits, and the French stage street demonstrations.

Insight into the composition of mobilization potential is needed to assess which part of a movement's potential ends up in the demonstration. Mobilization potential never fully converts into action. My work on the peace movement with Dirk Oegema (Klandermans and Oegema 1987; Oegema and Klandermans 1994) demonstrated that nonconversion and erosion—as we labeled it—is not random. The challenge of the study of the supply side of protest and of the mobilization process is to try to understand who of the mobilization potential ends up participating, how he is mobilized, and why he takes part (see also Boekkooi, Klandermans, and Van Stekelenburg 2011). Note that I take the mobilization potential, *not* the general population, as my point of reference. The mobilization potential is the result of the combined impact of *consensus formation* and *mobilization*. *Action mobilization,* that is, the transformation of potential into action, is a process that is both analytically and empirically to be distinguished from the formation of that potential.

About This Section

Martijn van Zomeren, the discussant in this section, takes my call for the study of processes one step further in his plea to open the black box of dynamics. He comments on the essays in this section and alludes to what current social psychology has to offer to the study of movements, protest, and contention. Polletta and colleagues take us back to where it all begins—the formation of grievances—and wonder how the Internet and other digital technologies might create new reasons for protesting: new identities and grievances, new stakes in and motivations for protest. Taylor takes the argument further by conceptualizing social movements as discursive communities and discussing the role such communities play in the construction of politicized collective identity. She examines the role of emotions in this respect and highlights the significance of emotions in contentious performances. Van Doorn, Prins, and Welshen take the conceptual frameworks of Taylor and Whittier and Simon and Klandermans as their point of departure in an attempt to further conceptualize the process of politicization. They argue that, at the end of the day, such politicization takes place in interpersonal interaction. They present quotations from focus group discussions with young Moroccan Dutch to illustrate their argument.

References

Boekkooi, Marije, Bert Klandermans, and Jacquelien van Stekelenburg. 2011. "Quarreling and Protesting: How Organizers Shape a Demonstration." *Mobilization* 16, no. 2: 223–42.

De Weerd, Marga, and Bert Klandermans. 1999. "Group Identification and Social Protest: Farmer's Protest in the Netherlands." *European Journal of Social Psychology* 29:1073–95.

Folger, Robert. 1986. "A Referent Cognition Theory of Relative Deprivation." In *Relative Deprivation and Social Comparison: The Ontario Symposium*, edited by M. Olson James, C. Peter Herman, and Mark P. Zanna, 33–56. Hillsdale, N.J.: Lawrence Erlbaum.

Foster, Mindy D., and Kimberly Matheson. 1999. "Perceiving and Responding to the Personal/Group Discrimination Discrepancy." *Personality and Social Psychology Bulletin* 25:1319–29.

Gamson, William. 1992. *Talking Politics*. Cambridge, Mass.: Cambridge University Press.

González, Roberto, and Rupert Brown. 2003. "Generalization of Positive Attitudes as a Function of Subgroup and Superordinate Group Identifications in Intergroup Conflict." *European Journal of Social Psychology* 33:195–214.

Goodwin, Jeff, James M. Jasper, and Francesca Polletta. 2000. "The Return of the Repressed: The Fall and Rise of Emotions in Social Movement Theory." *Mobilization* 5, no. 1: 65–82.

Gould, Deborah. 2009. *Moving Politics: Emotion and ACT UP's Fight against AIDS*. Chicago: University of Chicago Press.

Jasper, James. 1998. "The Emotions of Protest: Affective and Reactive Emotions in and around Social Movements." *Sociological Forum* 13:397–424.

Kelly, Caroline, and Sarah Breinlinger. 1996. *The Social Psychology of Collective Action*. Basingstoke, U.K.: Taylor and Francis.

Klandermans, Bert. 1984. "Mobilization and Participation in a Social Movement: Social Psychological Expansions of Resource Mobilization Theory." *American Sociological Review* 49:583–600.

———. 1988. "The Formation and Mobilization of Consensus." In *From Structure to Action: Comparing Social Movement Research across Cultures,* edited by Bert Klandermans, Hanspeter Kriesi, and Sidney Tarrow, 173–96. Greenwich, Conn.: JAI Press.

———. 1997. *The Social Psychology of Protest.* Oxford: Blackwell.

———. 2010. "Peace Demonstrations or Anti-government Marches: The Political Attitudes of the Protestors." In *The World Says No to War: Demonstrations against the War in Iraq,* edited by Stefaan Walgrave and Dieter Rucht, 98–118. Minneapolis: University of Minnesota Press.

Klandermans, Bert, and Nonna Mayer. 2006. *Extreme Right Activists in Europe: Through the Magnifying Glass.* London: Routledge.

Klandermans, Bert, and Dirk Oegema. 1987. "Potentials, Networks, Motivations, and Barriers: Steps towards Participation in Social Movements." *American Sociological Review* 52:519–31.

Klandermans, Bert, Marlene Roefs, and Johan Olivier. 2001. *The State of the People: Citizens, Civil Society, and Governance in South Africa, 1994–2000.* Pretoria: Human Science Research Council.

Klandermans, Bert, Jose Manuel Sabucedo, and Mauro Rodriguez. 2002. "Politicization of Collective Identity: Farmer's Identity and Farmer's Protest in the Netherlands and Spain." *Political Psychology* 23:235–52.

———. 2004. "Multiple Identities among Farmers in the Netherlands and Spain." *European Journal of Social Psychology* 34:229–364.

Klandermans, Bert, Jojanneke van der Toorn, and Jacquelien van Stekelenburg. 2008. "Embeddedness and Identity: How Immigrants Turn Grievances into Action." *American Sociological Review* 73:992–1012.

Kurtz, Sharon. 2002. *Workplace Justice: Organizing Multi-identity Movements.* Minneapolis: University of Minnesota Press.

Mackie, Diane N., Thierry Devos, and Eliot R. Smith. 2000. "Intergroup Emotions: Explaining Offensive Action Tendencies in an Intergroup Context." *Journal of Personality and Social Psychology* 79:602–16.

Major, Brenda. 1994. "From Social Inequality to Personal Entitlement: The Role of Social Comparisons, Legitimacy Appraisals, and Group Membership." *Advances in Experimental Social Psychology* 26:293–355.

Marwell, Gerald, and Pamela Oliver. 1993. *The Critical Mass in Collective Action: A Micro-social Theory.* Cambridge: Cambridge University Press.

Melucci, Alberto. 1981. "Ten Hypotheses for the Analysis of New Movements." In *Contemporary Italian Sociology,* edited by Diana Pinto, 173–94. Cambridge: Cambridge University Press.

Meyer, David S., and Sidney R. Tarrow. 1998. "A Movement Society: Contentious Politics for a New Century." In *The Social Movement Society: Contentious Politics for a New Century,* edited by David S. Meyer and Sidney R. Tarrow, 1–28. Lanham, Md.: Rowman and Littlefield.

Oegema, Dirk, and Bert Klandermans. 1994. "Why Social Movement Sympathizers Don't Participate: Erosion and Nonconversion of Support." *American Sociological Review* 59:703–22.

Paxton, Pamela. 2002. "Social Capital and Democracy: An Interdependent Relationship." *American Sociological Review* 67:254–77.

Simon, Bernd. 2011. "Collective Identity and Political Engagement." In *Identity and Participation in Culturally Diverse Societies,* edited by Assad E. Azzi, Xenia Chryssochoou, Bert Klandermans, and Bernd Simon, 137–57. Malden, Mass.: Wiley-Blackwell.

Simon, Bernd, and Bert Klandermans. 2001. "Politicized Collective Identity: A Social Psychological Analysis." *American Psychologist* 56:319–31.

Simon, Bernd, Michael Loewy, Stefan Stürmer, Ulrike Weber, Peter Freytag, Corinna Habig, Claudia Kampmeier, and Peter Spahlinger. 1998. "Collective Identification and Social Movement Participation." *Journal of Personality and Social Psychology* 74:646–58.

Stryker, Sheldon, Timothy J. Owens, and Robert White, eds. 2000. *Self, Identity, and Social Movements.* Minneapolis: University of Minnesota Press.

Stürmer, Stefan. 2000. "Soziale Bewegungsbeteiligung: Ein psychologisches Zwei-Wege Modell." PhD diss., University of Kiel.

Tyler, Tom R., and Allen E. Lind. 1992. "A Relational Model of Authority in Groups." *Advances in Experimental Social Psychology* 25:115–91.

Tyler, Tom R., and Heather Smith. 1998. "Social Justice and Social Movements." In *Handbook of Social Psychology,* 4th ed., edited by Daniel Gilbert, Susan T. Fiske, and Gardner Lindzey, 595–626. New York: McGraw-Hill.

Van Stekelenburg, Jacquelien. 2006. "Promoting or Preventing Social Change: Instrumentality, Identity, Ideology, and Group-Based Anger as Motives of Protest Participation." PhD diss., VU-University.

Van Stekelenburg, Jacquelien, and Bert Klandermans. 2007. "Individuals in Movements: A Social Psychology of Contention." In *Handbook of Social Movements across Disciplines,* edited by Bert Klandermans and Conny Roggeband, 157–204. New York: Kluwer.

———. 2009. "Social Movement Theory: Past, Presence, and Prospects." In *Movers and Shakers: Social Movements in Africa,* edited by S. Ellis and I. Kessel, 17–43. Leiden, Netherlands: Brill.

———. 2012. "Collective versus Connective Action: Mobilization and Participation in Two Types of Campaigns Compared." Unpublished manuscript.

Van Stekelenburg, Jacquelien, Bert Klandermans, and Wilco W. Van Dijk. 2011. "Combining Motivations and Emotion: The Motivational Dynamics of

Collective Action Participation." *Revista de Psicología Social* 26:91–104.

Van Zomeren, Martijn, Tom Postmes, and Russell Spears. 2008. "Toward an Integrative Social Identity Model of Collective Action: A Quantitative Research Synthesis of Three Socio-psychological Perspectives." *Psychological Bulletin* 134:504–35.

Van Zomeren, Martijn, Russell Spears, Agneta H. Fischer, and Collin W. Leach. 2004. "Put Your Money Where Your Mouth Is! Explaining Collective Action Tendencies through Group-Based Anger and Group Efficacy." *Journal of Personality and Social Psychology* 87:649–64.

Vliegenthart, Rens. 2007. "Framing Immigration and Integration: Facts, Parliament, Media, and Anti-immigrant Party Support in the Netherlands." PhD diss., VU-University.

2

Is the Internet Creating New Reasons to Protest?

Francesca Polletta, Pang Ching Bobby Chen,
Beth Gharrity Gardner, and Alice Motes

Social movement scholars have been wary of granting the Internet transformative political power. To be sure, the Internet and other digital technologies have changed the form and probably the amount of protest. Movement scholars have documented activists' use of cell phones, e-mail, text messages, chat rooms, blogs, and Twitter to mobilize rapid and massive demonstrations in places as far-flung as Maldova, Iran, and China. New digital technologies have made possible novel tactics of protest such as culture jamming and hactivism (Lievrouw 2006; Van Laer and Van Aelst 2009); new forms of mobilization such as smart mobs (Rheingold 2002) and networked affinity groups (Juris 2008); and new targets such as advertisers and corporate brands (Lievrouw 2006; Micheletti and Stolle 2008). Digital mobilizing tools have undoubtedly affected the *supply* of protest, to use Klandermans's (2004, 360) phrase. But when it comes to accounting for the *demand* for protest, social movement scholars have been cautious. The Internet only "amplifies existing impulses and forces" (Bakardjieva 2009, 102); it does not produce them. "Yes, activists adopt new technologies when those technologies serve their purposes," Charles Tilly wrote in 2006, "but purposes override techniques" (42; see discussion in Earl et al. 2010).[1]

In this chapter, we ask whether new digital technologies are also *creating* impulses, forces, and purposes. Is the Internet fostering new identities, new grievances, new stakes in protest, and/or new terrains of contention? Is it contributing not only to the supply of protest but also to the demand for it? We argue that it is. When thousands of Chinese visited a website to register their opposition to Google's Chinese name change, they were motivated by an issue that did not exist before the rise of the Internet (Yang 2009). The impulse to protest restrictions on online gaming time obviously did not exist before online gaming. These may seem minor changes. Other changes, however, are further reaching. We focus on two whose importance lies in part in the fact that they force us to rethink two assumptions that have underpinned theorizing about movements. One is that protest is hard work; the other is that protest requires moving issues and people from the private sphere to the public.

With respect to the first, the Internet has transformed the typical calculus of individual participation. Participation has become easier—as easy, in some cases, as pressing a button. We explore the consequences of that development for our understanding of mobilization. Among them, we suggest that standard models centered on the mobilizing role, variously, of collective identity and friendship may be off the mark. Friendship in the Facebook era may mobilize less by levying emotional obligations on intimates to participate and more by providing information to weakly linked acquaintances. It may, moreover, produce not just the motivation to act on one's interests but the interests themselves. Collective identity, for its part, may be politically effectual, even if transient or centered on consumption choices, and more powerful by being virtual.

To some extent, the lower costs of mobilization on their own have changed the issues on behalf of which people mobilize. But new digital technologies have also altered the relations between the public and private in ways that have produced whole new classes of contentious issues. This is the second development, or set of developments, we want to discuss, as we turn from the motivations behind people's participation to the goals on behalf of which they participate. We are not the first to note that consumption has become a major site of contemporary contention. The Internet has contributed to that shift, in part by making consumption-based activism easier and by rendering corporations more vulnerable to such activism. But we focus on how the prominence of Internet technologies in people's lives, and especially in the lives of young people, is creating new perceptions of the sociopolitical context (Klandermans, chapter 1). The Internet is creating new notions of privacy and entitlement and new boundaries between the realms of consumption and politics. In particular, the Internet may be destabilizing ideas about intellectual and artistic production that have long held the status of common sense. As a result, young people may perceive laws around copyright more as an immediate and mobilizing threat than as one more front in a long-running battle for radical artistic freedom. In other words, the Internet is affecting the demand for protest by naturalizing new boundaries between the worlds of public use and private ownership.

When we say that the Internet has helped to create the demand for protest, we emphasize that it has done so in conjunction with other developments, for example, the spread of movement forms and strategies to areas outside politics in what Meyer and Tarrow (1998) call the contemporary "movement society," capitalist production's increasing dependence on brand status (Micheletti and Stolle 2008), and young people's alienation from electoral politics (Zukin et al. 2006). Nevertheless, we believe the Internet's role deserves its own scrutiny. We do not provide anything like the kind of scrutiny we have in mind in this essay; instead, our purpose is programmatic. We ask how we might use scholarship on social movements to evaluate the possibilities claimed for the Internet, and we ask how developments associated with the Internet may require us to rethink our models of mobilization. We will be more speculative than we would like. Given the lightning fast speed at which digital technologies are changing, moreover, we suspect that some of the hunches we raise will soon be proven either wrong or beside the point. Still, it strikes us as worthwhile to pit what we know about mobilization offline against what seems to be happening online as a way to potentially rethink both.

Why Participate? Theories of Micromobilization

Social movement theorizing about why people participate has long been animated by the assumption that protest is hard work. It is often rewarding work, but is hard nonetheless. It takes time, energy, and sometimes money. It is often risky: participants may be insulted, beaten, arrested or may lose their jobs, be expelled, or lose their immigration status. The kicker, according to Olson (1965), is that participation is also irrational because participants will gain access to whatever collective good is secured even if they do not participate.

What accounts, then, for people's willingness to participate? Contra Olson, social movement scholars have shown that strong solidary bonds, a motivating frame, and/or a powerful collective identity trump people's narrow calculations of rational self-interest. For example, friends recruit friends to participate. This is in part because friends provide a conduit of information about protest opportunities (Kitts 2000; Diani 2004) and because spending time with your friends, whether protesting or doing something else, is appealing. It is also, says Klandermans (2004, 371), because "it is your friends who keep you to your promises." Friendship imposes an obligation to participate. Collective identity, for its part, provides a sense of shared fate. "If I know who I am, then I also know what I have to do," as Simon (2004, 169) puts it. Collective identities are not invented at will; they are nurtured in structural contexts rather than individually chosen (McAdam and Paulsen 1993). Of course, we all have multiple identities. To participate, however, our movement identity must become most salient, while we retain a sense of identity with a superordinate entity (the nation, say, or Catholics) (Simon 2004). Compelling frames, for their part, make protest seem possible, necessary, and urgent (Snow 2004).

Numerous studies have shown that these factors motivate people to engage in the hard work, and often high risk, of activism. Now, however, imagine that protest is not hard work; at least, it is not necessarily hard work. Participating may mean simply clicking on a link contained in an e-mail message, skimming the content of a petition, filling in one's name and address, and pressing "send." It may mean getting an e-mail message about the location of a public demonstration, with information about the action's legal status, the likelihood that there will be arrests, and provisions for support to those arrested, then learning from one's Facebook page which friends are going to the demonstration and who has room in her car. It may mean getting an invitation from a Facebook friend to add the application "Causes" to one's page and then displaying the friend's cause: "Animal Rights," sponsored by PETA (with 3.4 million subscribers), or "Stop Global Warming," sponsored by the Alliance for Climate Protection (with 3.1 million subscribers). It may mean clicking on a link in a Cause message or in any of the other messages one receives by e-mail requesting donations to a political cause. It may mean donating one's Facebook status to a cause so that the status update line reads, "Francesca is donating her status to tackle Climate Change: http://amnhblogs.org/donate-status," or updates daily: "In 17 Days 919 palestinians killed by Israel including 284 children and 100 women, 4260 injured." We will talk later about whether all these forms of participation can be considered "real" protest, or at least political in any meaningful sense. For now, though, we emphasize simply the diverse opportunities for protest participation offered by the Internet (see also Van Stekelenburg and Boekkooi, chapter 11).

As numerous observers have pointed out, new digital technologies have made it much easier to form, join, and coordinate groups (Earl and Kimport 2011; Van Laer and Van Aelst 2009; Van Stekelenburg and Boekkooi, chapter 11; Shirky 2008). According to Internet scholar Clay Shirky, this means that you may not have to care deeply about an issue to mobilize. For example, when passengers on an American Airlines flight waited on the tarmac for a gate in Austin for eight hours, with toilets overflowing and food supplies exhausted, they were understandably furious. They were probably no more furious than the many airline passengers who, from the beginning of airline travel, have experienced equally annoying delays. But when one of their members, a Californian real estate agent, used the Internet to start a petition, this group of passengers launched a national movement for airline reform. They lobbied Congress for the passage of an Airline Passengers' Bill of

Rights and succeeded in getting airlines to voluntarily accept such standards.

According to Shirky (2008, 181), "the old model for coordinating group action required convincing people who care a little to care more, so that they would be roused to act." But in this new model, "people who cared a little could participate a little, while being effective in the aggregate." To be sure, social movement theorists never thought that simply caring about an issue was sufficient motivation to participate. After all, many people who care deeply about an issue still do not participate (Klandermans and Oegema 1987). But the factors that social movement theorists have identified as getting people over the hump from concern to participation may not be the right ones either. Presumably not many people on the stranded American Airlines flight were connected by prior bonds of friendship. They probably developed a sense of solidarity with their fellow passengers during the long wait on the tarmac, but it is hard to imagine that they developed a collective identity that was encompassing enough to motivate action on behalf of all airline passengers. It seems unlikely that it was the rhetorical power of the e-mail sent by the real estate agent who launched the petition that moved passengers from inaction to action.

It is not that people did not experience solidary bonds or read a persuasive message so much as that those factors seem beside the point. Imagine that you are mad and you can do something about it in five minutes at your keyboard in the privacy of your own home without incurring any costs other than those minutes of time. That seems to have been enough. Does this mean, then, that when it comes to Internet protest, we need completely new models of participation? Do friendship, collective identity, and persuasive frames have no place in shaping individuals' decisions to participate? One possibility is that those factors still operate, but differently.

Friendship

Contrary to some early expectations, people use social networking sites like Friendster, MySpace, and Facebook to communicate with their offline friends. People are not using these sites to network with strangers (Pempek, Yermolayevaa, and Calvert 2009; Livingstone 2008). However, at least two features of online "friendship" make it distinctive. One is the size of friendship networks. People strike up relationships with friends of friends. One study showed that networking site users had, on average, more than double the number of friends online as offline (Pempek, Yermolayevaa, and Calvert 2009, 236; see also Tufeki 2008). Along with the size of these networks of acquaintances, their visibility is striking. Users know who knows whom. They know what members of their network are doing and thinking about, and they know that if they post information about their own opinions or activities, others may well comment on it.

What do these features of online friendship mean for protest? Movement scholars have long recognized that people are more likely to participate when they know that a critical mass of other people will also participate (Oliver and Marwell 1988). That knowledge was hard to come by before friendship networks were made visible on social networking sites; now it is easily obtained. You know who is going to a demonstration, who is considering going to a demonstration, and who likes the fact that someone is considering going to a demonstration. Online friends may also get people to pay attention to a cause that they would otherwise ignore. E-mail petitions have an option that allows the user to instruct that the petition be forwarded to a list of e-mail addresses. For petition sponsors, the fact that the petition comes not out of the blue but from a friend makes it more likely to be read. The friend's endorsement also makes it more likely to be signed. As one observer puts it, "this 'tell a friend' phenomenon is key to how organizing happens on the net. It gives people who feel alienated from politics something valuable to contribute: their unique credibility within their particular circle of acquaintances. A small gesture to these friends can contribute to a massive multiplier effect" (Boyd 2003, 2). In this scenario, one participates not for the pleasure of spending time with a friend and not necessarily because one feels an obligation to the particular friend, whom one may not even know well, but rather because the friend has vouched for the worth of participation (see, e.g., Melber 2006).

Indeed, more than helping people to get over the hump from concern to participation, online friends may help to create the concern in the first place. Groups on social networking sites form around users rather than around common interests (boyd 2006). When I send you a news story about a demonstration, a petition, or a link to a cause, I presume, boyd writes, "that anyone who is interested in being Friends should also be interested in receiving such content." Combine this with the fact that users of social networking sites enact a "hoped-for self" in their profiles—they perform the identity of whom they want to be in the consumption preferences they record, photos they post, and political views they list (Pempek, Yermolayevaa, and Calvert 2009; Zhao, Grasmuck, and Martin 2008; boyd 2006; Liu, Maes, and Davenport 2006)—and one can see the potential for people to adopt political causes because a charismatic friend has done so.

Collective Identity

Note that in the scenario we just sketched, collective identity operates differently than it does in older models of participation. In their analysis of the students who went south in 1964 for Freedom Summer, McAdam and Paulsen (1993) found that people who had a strong identification with a particular collective actor—say, teachers or the civil rights movement or the Democratic Party—were also deeply embedded in that structural context; that is, they were teachers or members of the NAACP or Democratic Party youth activists. In the age of the Internet, by contrast, subjective identifications need not be anchored in structural contexts. In other words, you can develop solidarity with people protesting a rigged election and act on behalf of that solidarity, even though you are not old enough to vote. As Abrams and Hogg (2004, 148) put it, "the 'group,' or more particularly the ingroup, is no longer restricted to specific social networks of known others." It is also not clear that the two components of politicized identity described by Simon and Klandermans (2001)—the identification both with the challenging group and the superordinate entity of which the group is a part—are necessary. It may be that mobilizing identifications are with distant groups (Lea, Spears, and Watt 2007) or are recent and transient (Langman 2005).

Indeed, the virtual collective identity fostered online may be, in some respects, more mobilizing than a collective identity forged in church basements by people holding hands and singing "We Shall Overcome." Social psychological research has shown that, while in some circumstances, being able to see other members of one's group strengthens one's sense of collective identity and makes cooperation more likely, in other circumstances, visibility does not have that effect (Lea, Spears, and Watt 2007). To the contrary, when it comes to cooperating with people whose identity is not visually obvious, for example, their nationality or their political allegiance, one is more likely to feel a common bond if one does not see them. Why? Because the less anonymous the people with whom one is interacting, the more likely one is to be distracted by the other identities they have—identities that make them different rather than the same. So a collective identify forged online may be mobilizing precisely insofar as it is virtual and therefore partial and even ambiguous. In the case of the Occupy movements of 2011, consider not the small number of people who camped out but the much larger number of people who came to the protest site for a rally, or made a donation online, or sent a petition supporting activists' right to remain on the site. These people shared a sense of collective identity with the protesters, one they gained from blog entries, Facebook posts, YouTube videos, online newspaper stories, and television reports. Would that sense of collective identity have been stronger if potential supporters had spent substantial time interacting with the protesters in the Occupy sites? Perhaps a middle-aged administrative assistant or a building trades union member would have appreciated the radicalism of many young occupiers, would have enjoyed the long conversations about veganism, anarchism, and legalizing marijuana, would have found compelling the long meetings and the endless drumming—but perhaps not. Digital media may make possible an imagined community that is in some ways closer to what supporters want it to be than what it really is. The virtual character of the community makes it easier to project one's aspirations onto it.

Now, one might ask whether some of the collective actions we have been describing, especially the online petitions and the Facebook postings, really count as protest. Numerous observers have wondered whether online protest is evanescent, unlikely to translate into sustained mobilization. "Commitment levels are opaque," a consultant to grassroots activists worries. "Maybe a maximum of 5 percent are going to take action, and maybe it's closer to 1 percent.... In most cases of Facebook groups, members do nothing" (Hesse 2009). The point is a reasonable one. Why should displaying markers of a political self translate into anything resembling effective protest?

Perhaps for two reasons. One is that targets often do not know what to make of the huge numbers of people signing an e-petition or joining a Facebook group or a Twitter feed. That uncertainty can translate into impact. Maybe thousands of people signed an e-petition because it was easy to do so, but if the petition is ignored, will they take more drastic action? Will a significant portion of the five thousand bank customers who recently signed an e-petition against new ATM fees now pick up and move their accounts to another bank? Another source of uncertainty lies in just whom those five thousand represent. Are they the sum total of discontent or the tip of the iceberg? Finally, is five thousand an impressive number to reporters who may or may not choose to make it a story? To be sure, what the numbers mean will likely become clearer as e-tactics become institutionalized, returning some advantage to the targets of protest. But for now, the virtual character of online protest may confer strategic advantages on the movement.

The other possibility for more enduring impact is that online friends may press people to be consistent with their displayed identities. The fact that friendship networks are visible is a source of information but also may be one of constraint. To be sure, behaving consistently with one's identity may mean something as banal as not expressing a preference for fur coats while displaying an animal rights cause. But it may also require more active participation, especially if active participation is not very demanding.

Frames

With respect to the third mobilizing variable, collective action framing, effective frames are probably still those that combine diagnostic, prognostic, and motivational features; that develop a clear sense of "us" and "them"; and that create a "fire in the belly and iron in the soul" (Gamson 1992, 32).[2] The difference in the Internet age may be in how effective frames are arrived at. Despite framing theory's origins in a symbolic interactionism, work on frames since then has tended to treat frames as stable objects produced by organizations with an expertise in persuasive communication. But the lowered costs of mobilization mean that formal organizations are less necessary to protest (Bimber, Flanagin, and Stohl 2005). To be sure, much of Internet protest is still coordinated by formal organizations, but much of it, like the bank and airline protests we described, is not. In these cases, whatever framing is necessary to motivate people to participate is accomplished by participants themselves. This suggests that we shift the analytic focus back to those more emergent processes of meaning making, among actors with varying levels of political involvement in the issue.

In sum, the proliferation and visibility of online social networks, like the growth of the Internet generally, have undoubtedly lowered the motivational threshold for protest participation. They have probably contributed to protest animated by expressive, performative, and consumption-oriented identities (see Taylor, chapter 3). But the visibility of online social networks may also exercise a constraining force: insofar as social networks constitute a public, they may compel members to act in line with their professed identities. Insofar as they constitute a public, too, they may be treated as an influential voice in political decision making.

What Are We Fighting For? The Emergence of New Issues

Theories about the emergence of new movements are undergirded by a second set of assumptions, again commensensical on their face, about the relations between protest, politics, and the public sphere. Resource mobilization and political process theories were motivated by the recognition that groups turned to protest when they were unable to press their claims through regular political channels. This was the challenge to the older pluralist models: those who were excluded from the structure of political bargaining had no choice but to turn to extrainstitutional protest. Issues did not have to begin as recognizably public and political to become the objects of contention. To the contrary, activists often sought to get issues seen as private (e.g., segregation, or domestic abuse, or abortion) recognized as public. That recognition would compel the government to take action, to give claimants access to political decision making. The assumption, though, was that there was a public sphere that could be distinguished from the spheres both of the market and of private life. We argue that the Internet has not only shifted protest more to the market and private life but has also eroded the lines between the public and the private in at least two ways, with real import for the demand side of protest. One, it has begun to transform people's ideas about private property and public use in a way that has helped to generate a new class of contentious issues. Two, it has turned movement participation into one among a repertoire of activities that include leisure and consumption as well as political action.

Consumption and Public Use

Consumption, not politics, has become a major site of contention. Zukin and colleagues (2006) found that in 2002, more Americans aged twenty to twenty-eight had engaged in consumer activism—either not buying a product or buying a product for ethical reasons—in the last twelve months than had engaged in any other kind of political behavior. Stolle, Hooghe, and Micheletti (2005) found that 72 percent of the Belgian, Swedish, and Canadian students they surveyed had bought something based on ethical considerations in the last twelve months, and 63 percent said they had boycotted a product. Shopping has become social activism. Activist groups have protested genetically modified foods, forced corporations to respond to charges of using sweatshop labor by implementing monitoring schemes, created labeling schemes for organic and fair trade food products, and won parliamentary seats based on their opposition to restrictions on music and movie downloading. Consumption-based activism has not ignored the state, but it has resolutely intervened in arenas that were formerly viewed as the purview of the market. Boycotts and buycotts have centuries-old precedents, and consumer activism came of age in the 1970s, but the Internet has contributed to the scale both of consumption-based activism and the demand for it.

The Internet figures prominently in today's consumption-based activism as a potent tool. "Hacktivists" disable corporate websites (Lievrouw 2006) and "culture jammers" use online visual and textual parody to spoof brand logos and images (Harold 2007; Lievrouw 2006; Micheletti and Stolle 2008; Klein 2000). What makes these strategies so attractive, and, sometimes, effective, is that they capitalize on the virtual character of commodities in late capitalism. Manufacturing giants today market not products but brands. Buyers choose products based on the image associated with them; marketers offer "identities and pleasures that can be accessed only through their brands" (Holt 2002, 72). Maintaining a variously hip, attractive, and socially responsible image thus becomes essential to the bottom line (Harold 2007; Micheletti and Stolle 2008). Insofar as the Internet, along with television, film, and print media, is one of the places where companies seek to hone and preserve their images, the Internet becomes a critical site of contention. In this sense, the Internet generates not just tactics of protest but also vulnerabilities in the system and thus opportunities for protest.

More important, possibly, than either of these—a tool or terrain of activism—the Internet may figure in people's daily lives in a way that is changing their commonsensical understandings of the boundary between private ownership and common use. In this sense, the Internet may have contributed to producing new grievances by eroding the understandings of legal ownership that have structured consumption in the past. By new grievances, we mean the demands for open access to art, images, and ideas that have roiled the music industry but have also begun to affect the fields of journalism, science, publishing, and government (Electronic Frontier Foundation 2011; Hess and Ostrom 2006). Activists have challenged existing copyright laws by taking cases to court (Broussard 2007), engaging in civil disobedient collective acts of downloading music illegally or displaying copyrighted art (Harold 2007), launching initiatives to produce and promote alternative forms of copy agreements among artists and intellectual themselves (Broussard 2007; Harold 2007), and forming political parties aimed at securing legislative representation for a pro-file-sharing platform (Prodger 2009).

Of course, there have always been groups advocating for the freer dissemination of music, texts, and visual images, and there have long been collective challenges to the institution of private property. What may be new, however, is that the Internet is eroding the conceptual linchpins of intellectual property doctrine and law. In other words, the Internet is making such challenges increasingly commonsensical. As Yar (2008) points out, intellectual property law is based on several myths. One is that intangible goods, such as particular arrangements of words or images, are the same as tangible goods. But stealing a tangible object, say, a pair of shoes, deprives the owner of using those shoes herself, whereas stealing an image does not deprive the image's creator of its continued use. That has always been the case, of course, but in a digital age, the possibilities for reproducing content are endless and extend across vast sweeps of space and media. If it was not clear before that ideas and images have a different status than material objects, for those who have grown up in a digital age, it has become increasingly so. Copyright law also rests on a nineteenth-century notion of the individual creator, a myth insofar as intellectual and artistic works have always drawn on prior works, whether credited or not. Today, however, the myth is challenged by forms of musical and visual bricolage that have become commonplace: mash-ups, memes, and image macros (a picture with superimposed text that makes a joke of the picture's meaning); bricolage art; and sound collages (Harold 2007). In this context, the idea that a melody composed of a few notes belongs to only one author, no matter how the notes are integrated into a new piece, becomes increasingly anachronistic. As the ideal of openness becomes easier to realize, it becomes more important to protect (for a similar argument about humanitarianism, see Haskell 1985).

Do we have evidence that this is the case? We know that young people increasingly see downloading music as acceptable; 70 percent do not feel guilty about it, with even higher numbers among younger respondents (Marrakesh Records 2009). The question, though, is whether this common sense is translating into politicized grievances and collective action. Our evidence here is fragmentary. Recent legislative battles over more stringent protections against online piracy were followed more closely by young people, with 23 percent of eighteen- to twenty-nine-year-olds reporting that they followed the bills closely, compared to just 7 percent of the population as a whole (Pew Research Center for the People and the Press 2012). We also know that protests that have encouraged people to engage in coordinated illegal music downloading have secured wide participation. Although many of organizations that advocate for open access (groups like the Electronic Frontier Foundation, Free Software Foundation, Creative Commons, and Public Knowledge) are made up of professionals like computer programmers and academics, others are dominated by young people. The Pirate Party, which was formed to reform patent, copyright, and privacy laws shortly before the 2006 parliamentary elections in Sweden, is currently the fifth largest political party in Sweden, with the second largest youth branch. Although it did not follow up its unexpected victory in the 2009 European parliamentary elections with a win in the Swedish national election, it did inspire efforts by the mainstream parties to woo youth back (Wikileaks 2010a). And diplomatic cables released by Wikileaks reveal Swedish officials trying to persuade U.S. officials to take seriously the message of the Pirate Party's 2009 electoral victory in crafting legislation around copyright infringement. Whereas U.S. officials insisted that file sharing was theft, Swedish officials countered that the Pirate Party's appeal showed that young people had a different understanding of intellectual property and law, and that legislation should be responsive to that (Wikileaks 2010b). Internationally, the Pirate Party has created spin-offs in Germany, Spain, Austria, Poland, Finland, France, and at least twenty other countries (Prodger 2009). In the United States, Students for Free Culture has chapters at thirty colleges.

The notion that the Internet is leading people to think about private property differently—and about ideas of privacy based on private property—is also supported by the curious compatibility in protest discourse of principles of open access with those of privacy. One might think that the advocacy of unrestrained access to information would be in tension with the advocacy of controls on corporations' ability to collect information on consumers. If "information just wants to be free," as the clever slogan animating anticopyright mobilizations goes, then how can one justify disallowing it to anyone? Yet activists today tend not to recognize that tension. As a twenty-year-old explained his vote for Sweden's Pirate Party, "Civil rights. Everybody has a right of privacy for their own e-mails, SMS messages and phone calls. File-sharing is just a small bit of the whole cake" (Prodger 2009). Advocacy groups like Public Knowledge, the Electronic Frontier Foundation, and Free Press variously litigate and lobby around issues of both privacy and openness. The fact, then, that for many activists the causes of privacy and informational freedom are not in any tension speaks to changes in how each of these terms—privacy, information, and freedom—is being understood.

Again, these trends are merely suggestive. Mainly, they call for much more research on whether people's use of the Internet is changing their expectations about privacy, property, and public use. The possibility is that the Internet does not so much create new issues altogether—people have always advocated against the ownership of ideas—as it gives people a new stake in those issues.

Protest in a Repertoire of Sociable Action

We want to sketch a second way in which the Internet may be redrawing the line between private, nonpolitical issues and public, political ones. Here we go back to the questionably political status of much contemporary collective action around consumption. Earl and Schussman (2008) found that the vast majority of online petitions are targeted to entertainment entities. Sometimes garnering signatures in the thousands, online petitioners call variously for their favorite pop group to tour their country, for a cancelled television show to be brought back on air, and for a baseball manager to be fired. It is hard to see this as political or as protest in the sense of a challenge to institutional authority. And indeed, Earl and Schussman's point is that movement tactics have become both institutionalized and, thanks to the Internet, accessible. This has made them an attractive vehicle for consumption-oriented demands.

It is tempting, therefore, to draw a line between politicized consumption and nonpolitical consumption. But doing so is not so easy. We referred earlier to Zukin and colleagues' (2006) finding that nearly half of all Americans reported having boycotted or buycotted a product in the last twelve months and that, for those aged twenty to twenty-eight, consumer activism was their preferred form of politics. However, when the researchers interviewed people about their consumer activism, they found that fewer than half could give an appropriate example of boycotting or buycotting. In many cases, they cited poor service, bad product quality, or, in the case of one young man who boycotted Busch beer, "'cause it doesn't do anything for me." Conversely, many of those engaged in music downloading do see themselves as mounting a political challenge to an oligopolistic industry (Lievrouw 2006, 5). And such efforts, whether motivated by a political consciousness or not, have proved more of a threat to the industry than the parodic efforts of small groups of activists.

One alternative is that people may move from consumption-based collective action to more traditional forms of political engagement and protest. You may download music, realize it is illegal, and then join a group protesting current copyright laws. You may protest restrictions on your gaming time and then from there go on to other civil liberties issues. But no researcher has adduced evidence that this is in fact occurring. We believe that the evidence suggests something different: people may move among spheres of leisure, consumption, and politics without recognizing boundaries among them. The decisive change, here, is that the sphere of "real" politics is not experienced as separate from other spheres. Alternatively, activism is not even thought of as part of the sphere of real politics, associated, as the latter is, with the domination of special interests, party orthodoxy, and boring incrementalism (Zukin et al. 2006). Fully 51 percent of college Facebook users include their political views in their profiles—most commonly, they said, "to express who I am" (Pempek, Yermolayevaa, and Calvert 2009). On one hand, the fact that political identity is put on par with what band you listen to, how many friends you have, and who you think is cute suggests a kind of devaluation of political identity. On the other hand, if acting on your political identity is as easy as acting on your musical tastes, then the fact that your profession of political commitment is one more accoutrement of an appealing self may not make it any less politically effective.

Go back for a moment to Earl and Schussman's (2008) online petitions. Although the largest category of petitions—over twelve thousand—targeted entertainment entities, almost ten thousand petitions fell into the combined categories of local, state, national, and international politics. Were the same people launching and signing these petitions? We do not know. The possibility exists, though, that someone drawn to the site to demand the continuation of his favorite TV show might also click on a petition for a political issue, or that a friend might notify him both of the petition for the TV show and the petition for the political cause. Given the fact that the means of acting in public political spheres and private nonpolitical ones are equally accessible—and, in the case of e-petitions, are the same—the divide between them may be eroding. In other words, protest may be becoming one strategy of action in a repertoire of social and sociable actions rather than civic or political ones.

More evidence comes from Bakardjieva's (2009) study of Internet use in Calgary. The people she interviewed were confused when she asked them whether they used the Internet for purposes of "civic engagement." In most cases, they had no idea what she meant; in others, they interpreted the phrase to mean using civic services such as public libraries. They were enthusiastic about their participation in social groups online, groups that were dedicated to things like parenting, pets, and jogging. What is interesting, however, is that those groups also engaged in political activism. A joggers' group was "responsive to environmental issues, a pet-lover forum to calls for defense of animal rights, a parenting group to debates around day-care policies and funding (and ultimately, gender equity), the patient advocates to health care reform initiatives" (Bakardjieva 2009, 101).

Similarly blurred boundaries between the worlds of leisure and consumption, on one hand, and politics, on the other, are evident in data from the Annenberg School's national Digital Future survey. In the last three years, 15 percent of respondents have identified themselves as members of an "online community," defined as "a group that shares thoughts or ideas, or works on common projects, through electronic communication only." In 2008, nearly half of these groups were devoted to members' hobbies. Large numbers were also social (41 percent) and professional (33 percent). Only 11 percent of the groups were described as political. Yet fully three-quarters of online community members said they used the Internet to participate in "communities related to social causes" (this was up 30 percent from 2006) (Lebo 2008). Eighty-seven percent of online community members said they were participating in at least some social causes that were new to them since their involvement in online communities began (Lebo 2008, 117).

This suggests that online communities dedicated to leisure, professional, or social activities also occasionally turn their attention to political issues and protest activities. People do not carry their political commitments into their nonpolitical online communities; to the contrary, most of the Digital Futures respondents became involved in political causes through their participation in the nonpolitical online community. Rather, it seems that online groups engaged in an array of activities, some of which involved just talk, others action, some of which were not political, others political. Just as Bakardjieva's Internet users saw their activities more in terms of their group focus than in terms of a commitment to civic engagement, so the Digital Futures respondents were unwilling to call their groups political, even though they connected them to political causes.

Conclusion

In this essay, we have focused on the demand side of protest, asking how the Internet and other digital technologies have created new reasons for protesting: new identities and grievances, new stakes in and motivations for protest.

One way to sum up our answers is to say that the Internet has created new publics. This is true in several respects. New digital technologies, and especially social networking sites, have created new networks of sociability. These have provided not only new conduits of information about protest issues and events but also the compelling force of group attention. With *public* understood here in its sense as visible or open (as in "publicity"), social networking sites make public people's political identities in a way that creates pressures to consistency. People may signal their political commitments in such banal ways as modifying their status updates online or turning their Twitter pages green, but they may also encounter pressures to act further on those commitments. At the same time, social networking sites have created a public that, at least for the moment, media and political actors pay attention to. The sheer fact that thousands, sometimes hundreds of thousands, of people have signed on to a cause, whether or not social movement scholars would call it "political," makes it newsworthy. And media coverage, we know, is one of the most effective (perhaps necessary) routes to political impact (Ferree et al. 2002; Gamson 1990).

New digital technologies have also redrawn the line between the public and what is *not* public. This is in two senses. The Internet and other new digital technologies have made it possible to engage in political action with much less risk, even less inconvenience. Combined with the fact that in a "movement society," people increasingly use movement tactics to register consumer preferences (Earl and Kimport 2008), participating in protest has become increasingly like registering consumer preferences. Protest may be located more in a repertoire of social activities than in one of political or even civic activities.

In a second change, new digital technologies may be mainstreaming radical notions of collective ownership. Here the line is being drawn between public and private, not in the sense of personal, but in the sense of properly controlled by the market. The traction of movements for the more open dissemination and use of intellectual, artistic, and technical materials may rest less on those movements' superior mobilizing abilities than on the fact that the Internet is increasingly eroding the common sense that made those movements unthinkable. In this sense, too, the Internet is creating the basis for new grievances.

Notes

1. Earl et al. (2010) show that scholars arguing for and against the transformative power of the Internet are actually studying different kinds of e-tactics. Some scholars focus on web pages that do little more than provide information, whereas others focus on online organizing strategies such as e-petitioning. But the e-tactics that are associated with less substantial changes in mobilization tend to be less common—although they are the most researched.

2. Conversely, the ease of protest may mean that impassioned justifications for participation are less necessary. It would be an irony if, at a time when social movement scholars have turned enthusiastically to recognizing the importance of emotions in protest, emotions may be less important in protest.

References

Abrams, Dominic, and Michael Hogg. 2004. "Collective Identity: Group Membership and Self-Conception." In *Self and Social Identity*, edited by Marilyn Brewer and Miles Hewstone, 147–81. New York: John Wiley.

Bakardjieva, Maria. 2009. "Subactivism: Lifeworld and Politics in the Age of the Internet." *Information Society* 25, no. 2: 91–104.

Bimber, Bruce, Andrew J. Flanagin, and Cynthia Stohl. 2005. "Reconceptualizing Collective Action in the Contemporary Media Environment." *Communication Theory* 15:365–88.

Boyd, Andrew. 2003. "The Web Rewires the Movement." *The Nation*. http://www.thenation.com/doc/20030804/boyd.

boyd, danah. 2006. "Friends, Friendsters, and MySpace Top 8: Writing Community into Being on Social Network Sites." *First Monday* 11, no. 12. http://www.firstmonday.org/issues/issue11_12/boyd/index.html.

Broussard, Sharee. 2007. "The Copyleft Movement: Creative Commons Licensing." *Communication Research Trends*. http://www.highbeam.com/doc/1G1-169411830.html.

Diani, Mario. 2004. "Networks and Participation." In *The Blackwell Companion to Social Movements,* edited by David A. Snow, Sarah A. Soule, and Hanspeter Kriesi, 337–59. Oxford: Blackwell.

Earl, Jennifer, and Katrina Kimport. 2008. "The Targets of Online Protest: State and Private Targets of Four Online Protest Tactics." *Information, Communication, and Society* 11:449–72.

———. 2011. *Digitally Enabled Social Change: Activism in the Internet Age*. Cambridge, Mass.: MIT Press.

Earl, Jennifer, Katrina Kimport, Greg Prieto, Carly Rush, and Kimberly Reynoso. 2010.

"Changing the World One Webpage at a Time: Conceptualizing and Explaining 'Internet Activism.'" *Mobilization* 15, no. 4: 425–46.

Earl, Jennifer, and Alan Schussman. 2008. "Contesting Cultural Control: Youth Culture and Online Petitioning." In *Civic Life Online: Learning How Digital Media Can Engage Youth,* edited by W. Lance Bennett, 71–96. Cambridge, Mass.: MIT Press.

Electronic Frontier Foundation. 2011. "About EFF." https://www.eff.org/about.

Ferree, Myra Marx, William Gamson, Jurgen Gerhards, and Dieter Rucht. 2002. *Shaping Abortion Discourse: Democracy and the Public Sphere in Germany and the United States.* Cambridge: Cambridge University Press.

Gamson, William. 1990. *The Strategy of Social Protest.* Homewood, Ill.: Dorsey Press.

———. 1992. *Talking Politics.* Cambridge, Mass.: Cambridge University Press.

Harold, Christine. 2007. *OurSpace: Resisting the Corporate Control of Culture.* Minneapolis: University of Minnesota Press.

Haskell, Thomas. 1985. "Capitalism and the Origins of the Humanitarian Sensibility." *American Historical Review* 90:551–60.

Hess, Charlotte, and Elinor Ostrom. 2006. "A Framework for Analysing the Microbiological Commons." *International Social Science Journal* 58, no. 29: 335–49.

Hesse, Monica. 2009. "Facebook's Easy Virtue: 'Click-through Activism' Broad but Fleeting." *Washington Post.* http://www.washingtonpost.com/wp-dyn/content/article/2009/07/01/AR2009070103936.html.

Holt, Douglas. 2002. "Why Do Brands Cause Trouble? A Dialectical Theory of Consumer Culture and Branding." *Journal of Consumer Research* 29:70–90.

Juris, Jeffrey. 2008. *Networking Futures: The Movements against Corporate Globalization.* Durham, N.C.: Duke University Press.

Kitts, James A. 2000. "Mobilizing in Black Boxes: Social Networks and Social Movement Organizations." *Mobilization* 5, no. 2: 241–57.

Klandermans, Bert. 2004. "The Demand and Supply of Participation: Social-Psychological Correlates of Participation in Social Movements." In *The Blackwell Companion to Social Movements,* edited by David A. Snow, Sarah A. Soule, and Hanspeter Kriesi, 360–79. Oxford: Blackwell.

Klandermans, Bert, and Dirk Oegema. 1987. "Potentials, Networks, Motivations, and Barriers: Steps towards Participation in Social Movements." *American Sociological Review* 52:519–31.

Klein, Naomi. 2000. *No Logo: No Space, No Choice, No Jobs.* New York: Picador.

Langman, Lauren. 2005. "From Virtual Public Spheres to Global Justice: A Critical Theory of Internetworked Social Movements." *Sociological Theory* 23:42–74.

Lea, Martin, Russell Spears, and Susan E. Watt. 2007. "Visibility and Anonymity Effects on Attraction and Group Cohesiveness." *European Journal of Social Psychology* 37:761–73.

Lebo, Harlan. 2008. *The 2008 Digital Future Report: Surveying the Digital Future, Year*

Seven. Los Angeles, Calif.: Center for the Digital Future, USC Annenberg School.

Lievrouw, Leah A. 2006. "Oppositional and Activist New Media: Remediation, Reconfiguration, Participation." In *Proceedings of the Participatory Design Conference, PDC 2006: Expanding Boundaries in Design,* edited by G. Jacucci, F. Kensing, I. Wagner, and J. Blomberg, 115–24. Palo Alto, Calif.: Computer Professionals for Social Responsibility and Association for Computing Machinery.

Liu, Hugo, Pattie Maes, and Glorianna Davenport. 2006. "Unraveling the Taste Fabric of Social Networks." *International Journal on Semantic Web and Information Systems* 2, no. 1: 42–71.

Livingstone, Sonia. 2008. "Taking Risky Opportunities in Youthful Content Creation: Teenagers' Use of Social Networking Sites for Intimacy, Privacy, and Self-Expression." *New Media and Society* 10:393–411.

Marrakesh Records. 2009. *Youth and Music Survey 2009 by Human Capital for Marrakesh Records.* London: Marrakesh Records.

McAdam, Doug, and Ronnelle Paulsen. 1993. "Specifying the Relationship between Social Ties and Activism." *American Journal of Sociology* 99:640–67.

Melber, Ari. 2006. "MySpace, MyPolitics." *The Nation.* http://www.thenation.com/doc/20060612/melber.

Meyer, David S., and Sidney R. Tarrow. 1998. "A Movement Society: Contentious Politics for a New Century." In *The Social Movement Society: Contentious Politics for a New Century,* edited by David S. Meyer and Sidney R. Tarrow, 1–28. Lanham, Md.: Rowman and Littlefield.

Micheletti, Michele, and Dietlind Stolle. 2008. "Fashioning Social Justice through Political Consumerism, Capitalism, and the Internet." *Cultural Studies* 22: 749–69.

Oliver, Pamela E., and Gerald Marwell. 1988. "The Paradox of Group Size in Collective Action: A Theory of the Critical Mass II." *American Sociological Review* 53:1–8.

Olson, Mancur. 1965. *The Logic of Collective Action: Public Goods and the Theory of Groups.* Cambridge, Mass.: Harvard University Press.

Pempek, Tiffany A., Yevdokiya A. Yermolayevaa, and Sandra L. Calvert. 2009. "College Students' Social Networking Experiences on Facebook." *Journal of Applied Developmental Psychology* 30:227–38.

Pew Research Center for the People and the Press. 2012. "Cruise Ship Accident, Election Top Public's Interest: Young People Track Web Protests over Online Piracy Bills." Washington, D.C.: Pew Research Center. http://www.people-press.org/2012/01/24/cruise-ship-accident-election-top-publics-interest/.

Prodger, Matt. 2009. "Why the Pirates Are on the Rise in Sweden." *BBC Newsnight.* http://news.bbc.co.uk/2/hi/programmes/newsnight/8140895.stm.

Rheingold, Howard. 2002. *Smart Mobs: The Next Social Revolution.* Cambridge, Mass.: Basic Books.

Shirky, Clay. 2008. *Here Comes Everybody: The Power of Organizing without Organizations.* New York: Penguin.
Simon, Bernd. 2004. *Identity in Modern Society: A Social Psychological Perspective.* Oxford: Blackwell.
Simon, Bernd, and Bert Klandermans. 2001. "Politicized Collective Identity: A Social Psychological Analysis." *American Psychologist* 56:319–31.
Snow, David. 2004. "Framing Processes, Ideology, and Discursive Fields." In *The Blackwell Companion to Social Movements,* edited by David A. Snow, Sarah A. Soule, and Hanspeter Kriesi, 380–412. Oxford: Blackwell.
Stolle, Dietland, Marc Hooghe, and Michelle Micheletti. 2005. "Politics in the Supermarket: Political Consumerism as a Form of Political Participation." *International Political Science Review* 26:245–69.
Tilly, Charles. 2006. *Regimes and Repertoires.* Chicago: University of Chicago Press.
Tufeki, Zeynep. 2008. "Grooming, Gossip, Facebook, and Myspace." *Information, Communication, and Society* 11:544–64.
Van Laer, Jeroen, and Peter Van Aelst. 2009. "Cyber-Protest and Civil Society: The Internet and Action Repertoires in Social Movements." In *The Handbook of Internet Crime*, edited by Yvonne Jewkes and Majid Yar, 230–54. Cullompton, U.K.: Willan.
Wikileaks. 2010a. "US Embassy Cables: Pirate Party Rides an Electoral Wave in Sweden." http://www.guardian.co.uk/world/us-embassy-cables-documents/211229?INTCMP=SRCH.
———. 2010b. "US Embassy Cables: Pirate Party Success Shows Young People Don't Trust Us, Says Swedish Government." http://www.guardian.co.uk/world/us-embassy-cables-documents/223962?INTCMP=SRCH.
Yang, Guobin. 2009. *The Power of the Internet in China: Citizen Activism Online.* New York: Columbia University Press.
Yar, Majid. 2008. "The Rhetoric and Myths of Anti-piracy Campaigns: Criminalization, Moral Pedagogy, and Capitalist Property Relations in the Classroom." *New Media Society* 10:605–23.
Zhao, Shanyang, Sherri Grasmuck, and Jason Martin. 2008. "Identity Construction on Facebook—Digital Empowerment in Anchored Relationships." *Computers in Human Behavior* 24:1816–36.
Zukin, Cliff, Scott Keeter, Molly Andolina, Krista Jenkins, and Michael X. Delli Carpini. 2006. *A New Engagement? Political Participation, Civic Life, and the Changing American Citizen.* Oxford: Oxford University Press.

3

Social Movement Participation in the Global Society: Identity, Networks, and Emotions

Verta Taylor

Research interest in the social psychology and motivational dynamics of social movements has changed dramatically over the last thirty years. The 1970s and 1980s saw the rise of the resource mobilization and political process perspectives. These approaches shifted attention away from the social psychological and group processes involved in collective action that had concerned collective behavior theorists and toward structural, political, and organizational analyses that stressed the similarity and links between movements and more routine forms of organizational and political life. As a result, questions pertaining to the emergence of shared beliefs, solidarity, group consciousness, and micromobilization were given short shrift by social movement researchers. This began to change in the mid- to late 1980s, when some scholars in the United States began to ask whether resource mobilization and political process approaches had gone too far in abandoning social psychological analyses of movements (Ferree and Miller 1985; Snow et al. 1986; Gamson 1992a, 1992b). About the same time, European scholars loosely grouped under the rubric "new social movement" theorists (Cohen 1985; Klandermans 1985; Melucci 1985; Touraine 1985) proposed the concept of collective identity as a way of understanding people's motivations to act collectively, and some sociologists sympathetic to mobilization and process theory began to use collective identity to explain how "structural inequality gets translated into structural discontent" (Taylor and Whittier 1992, 104; also Morris and Mueller 1992).

Attention to the social and psychological dynamics of collective action has increased over the past decade (Van Zomeren and Iyer 2009). Bert Klandermans (chapter 1), arguably the leading social psychologist of collective action, recently joined scholars (Melucci 1989; Giddens 1991; Castells 1997; Taylor 2000a; Chryssochoou 2010) who have suggested that structural and cultural processes may be transforming the repertoires and dynamics of contentious politics in Western societies, specifically, the transnational nature of political and economic institutions; the diversification of group identities that has resulted from immigration and shifting demographics; the network structure or "liquidity"(Bauman 2000; Roggeband and Duyvendak, chapter 5) of relationships in modern Western societies; and the rise of new media, especially the Internet.

In this essay, I offer some preliminary observations about how these changes might affect key social psychological processes related to mobilization. Specifically, I focus on the importance of collective identity theory for understanding how shared grievances and identities are politicized and deployed in contentious politics in the modern world. I begin by discussing my conception of collective identity as dynamic, interactive, and socially constructed. The analysis focuses on the performative aspects of identity and the importance of tactics for the construction of a politicized collective identity. The core of my argument is that attention to the social psychological dynamics of the politicization of collective identity provides insight into how social movement tactics and performances, if not repertoires, diffuse, vary, and change. Next, I discuss my view of social movements as discursive communities, highlighting the significance of network ties, multiple identities, and contentious performances or protest for the construction of collective identity. Finally, I examine the role emotions play in the politicization of grievances. I highlight the significance of emotions in public performances of protest and argue that social movements have played an important role in redefining emotion norms and expression rules, which may contribute to the ubiquity of social movements in Western societies.

Collective Identity, Contentious Performances, and Repertoires

Constructing, maintaining, and renegotiating collective identity is an essential social psychological dynamic of mobilization that affects all aspects of social movement activity from emergence to outcomes (Melucci 1989; Taylor and Whittier 1992; Gamson 1992a; Klandermans 1992, 1994; Polletta and Jasper 2001; Bernstein 2005; Reger, Myers, and Einwohner 2008). Over the past fifteen years, scholars of social movements have used the concept of collective identity to respond to the limitations of resource mobilization and political process approaches that treated status (class, race, gender, nationality) or structurally based interests as the basis of collective grievances and relied upon rational choice models to explain protest participation and the tactical choices of social movement actors. Elsewhere, I have defined collective identity as the shared definition of a group that derives from members' common interests and solidarity (Taylor 1989). Polletta and Jasper's (2001, 285) definition as "an individual's cognitive, moral, and emotional connection with a broader community, category, practice, or institution" emphasizes comparable aspects and processes. Klandermans and De Weerd (2000) point out that although collective identity and social identity are related concepts, it is important to keep in mind that collective identity is a mesolevel concept; collective identity concerns cognitions shared by a group, whereas social identity concerns cognitions of a single individual about membership in one or more groups (Tajfel and Turner 1979). Definitions of collective identity among social movement scholars are consistent with the new social movement tradition (Melucci 1989, 1996) that has sought to extend the Marxist concept of class consciousness, which is the central mechanism of political mobilization, to understand solidarities and politicized identities formed to resist other structures of power besides strictly economic or class inequalities. New social movement scholars argue that in postindustrial societies, social movements are efforts to regain control over decisions and arenas of life increasingly subject to state control, to resist the colonization of the lifeworld, and to transform civil society (Habermas 1984, 1995; Melucci 1989). If people participate in social movements to change society, they also become involved in collective action to gain recognition, alter self-conceptions, and challenge negative group representations (Taylor 2000b; Bernstein 1997). Politics is always, in some sense, about identity.

In an earlier formulation, Nancy Whittier and I (1992) drew on Melucci's (1985, 793) formulation of collective identity as a "shared definition of the field of opportunities and constraints offered to collective action" to distinguish three distinct but overlapping processes that contribute to the formation of collective identity: (1) *boundaries* that mark differences between a category of persons and dominant groups, (2) *consciousness* of the criteria that explain a group's structural position and common interests, and (3) the politicization of a group's commonalities and differences through the *negotiation* and re-creation of new self-affirming identities. Bernstein's (1997, 2005) concept of "identity deployment" furthers our understanding of collective identity by emphasizing the importance of public identity disclosure both for internal group definitions of collective identity and as a movement strategy. Her research on the gay and lesbian movement advances our understanding of identity performances by demonstrating that movement identities do not always emphasize a challenging group's *differences*; activist identities sometimes accentuate *sameness,* or a group's commonalities with the dominant group, suppressing rather than celebrating the boundaries between "us" and "them."

Collective identities are (Klandermans 1994) "transient" in the sense that they change over the life cycle of a movement as a result of historical context (Whittier 1995; Bernstein 1997), the organizational characteristics of movements (Gamson 1996; Reger 2002), internal identity disputes (Taylor and Rupp 1993; Gamson 1995a, 1995b), and a movement's targets (Bernstein 1997; Einwohner 2002; Rupp and Taylor 2003; Taylor and Leitz 2010). Constructing and maintaining collective identity, or a sense of "we" in opposition to some collectively defined "they," requires a great deal of *identity work* (Snow and McAdam 2000; Reger, Myers, and Einwohner 2008), and the collective identities that mobilize movement participants are typically contested and contentious (Taylor and Rupp 1993; Gamson 1995, 1996; Ward 2008). Some scholars have argued that in late modern societies, participation in social movements is becoming a key factor in the social constitution of personal identities and biographies (Giddens 1991; Cerulo 1997). Castells argues, for example, that globalization, the network society, and new forms of communication, especially the Internet, have made it easier for people to organize around a common identity (see Polletta et al., chapter 2). *Liquid modernity* is the term Bauman (2000) uses to describe modern societies characterized by provisional networks and negotiated forms of community and identity, no longer stable but loose and subject to change.

A recent body of work calls attention to the performative aspects of identity in contention (Bernstein 1997, 2005; Taylor and Rupp 2003; Taylor and Van Dyke 2004; Whittier 2012), which allows us to understand how identity relates to tactics, strategies, and repertoires of contention (Taylor, Rupp, and Gamson 2004; Taylor et al. 2009). Contentious politics approaches increasingly view social movements not as groups or organizations but as interactive performances in which collective actors make claims against elites, authorities, or some other group (Tilly 2008). Contentious performances and repertoires are critical to the emergence, endurance, and outcomes of social movements because they are occasions for collective actors to demand recognition, signal numerical strength, promote movement goals, and build solidarity. For example, drag queen performances—that is, shows in which biological men dress and perform songs as women—are an important tactical repertoire of the gay and lesbian movement that meld politics and entertainment to challenge conventional understandings of gender and sexuality and to illuminate gay life for mainstream heterosexual audiences (Rupp and Taylor 2003). Drag performances contribute to the formation of collective identities by building a sense of solidarity among diverse (gay and straight) audiences (Kaminski and Taylor 2008).

Although political process theorists have tended to view identity politics as a retreat into culture that does not engage institutionalized structures of political power (Tilly 1995; McAdam, Tarrow, and Tilly 2001), social movement scholars who have been interested in the role of collective identity in mobilization argue that activists deploy identity strategies with the goal of changing individuals, culture, institutions, and the state (Whittier 2011). In health and self-help movements, for example, demands for recognition of illness, psychological conditions, or victimization experiences are intertwined with material and policy objectives (Taylor 1996; Taylor and Zald 2010; Brown 2007; Klawiter 2008; Whittier 2009; Taylor and Leitz 2010). Similarly, Rios and Lopez-Aguado (2012) suggest that Chicano gang-associated young men perform "cholo style"—that is, they embrace visible tattoos, baggy clothes, and shaved heads—as a collective response and form of resistance to racial stigmatization, class subordination, and criminalization.

Social movements, however, are more than contentious performances. As Staggenborg and Lecomte (2009) find in their study of the Canadian women's movement, contentious episodes influence subsequent campaigns and repertoires by creating social movement communities, submerged networks, and collective identity among participants, which become a basis for further mobilization (Taylor et al. 2009). Contentious performances do not, in other words, simply morph into repertoires. Rather, people's ability to come together to engage in collective action requires explanation. Research on the 2004 same-sex marriage protest in San Francisco demonstrates how an activist collective identity acquired through participation in a prior social movement can influence forms of claim making or tactical repertoires used in subsequent episodes of political contention (Taylor et al. 2009). After Mayor Gavin Newsome defied the Defense of Marriage Act by ordering officials to issue marriage licenses to same-sex couples, 4,037 couples married at city hall, creating a monthlong public spectacle that came to be known as the "winter of love," until the courts shut down the marriages. Couples who received marriage licenses in the wedding protest, which drew wide media attention, fully expected that the marriages would be halted and overturned by the courts.

The use of "marriage counter protests" as a tactic to promote the legalization of same-sex marriage originated in 1998 when cofounders of Marriage Equality California went to the assessor-recorder's office in San Francisco City Hall on Valentine's Day to request a marriage license. They returned each year, joined by more and more lesbian and gay couples, until the assessor-recorder's office began issuing licenses to same-sex couples. As the initiators of this action explain, this claim-making performance drew on participants' prior experience and identification with other episodes of contention:

> We were very inspired by the grassroots organizers in Greensboro, North Carolina, the four college students that sat in at the lunch counters, and

rendered visible segregation and the ugliness of white-only lunch counters. And we thought the only way to render visible the discrimination that crosses across the marriage counter every single day is to go and request a marriage license. We'll do it with dignity. We'll do it very peacefully.

One of the organizers explained further that marriage counter protests were "a moment of civil disobedience where anyone can participate because there's a marriage license counter in every town no matter how big or small." This tactical innovation set off a campaign for marriage equality across the United States. We find clear evidence in this case that politicized collective identity is a necessary antecedent of protest participation and that politicized collective identity shapes tactical choice. Participants in the 2004 San Francisco same-sex wedding protest arrived with a history of activism in a variety of other movements, including the feminist, gay and lesbian, civil rights, and pro-choice movements. These prior movements supplied the collective identities, network linkages, and tactical repertoires that fueled the campaign for marriage equality in California. Similarly, Occupy movements, which originated on Wall Street and spread to every continent, mobilized out of prior social movements, both transnational and local.

Network Embeddedness: Discursive Communities, Multiple Identities, and Identity Strategies

Social psychologists (Simon and Klandermans 2001; Simon 2011; Chryssochoou 2010) have suggested that the politicization of identity may be endemic to the increasingly network-based and multicultural nature of Western democracies. Attention to the social psychological processes related to collective identification, signification, and politicization is essential to understanding how globalization, cultural diversity, the network society, and new communication technologies beckon new identities, forms of community, and contentious performances in which identity is enacted and deployed to achieve standing and make claims on authorities.

Studies of the relationship between social movement participation and networks find that embeddedness within primary groups and social networks in small communities is a strong predictor of individual participation (Snow, Zurcher, and Ekland-Olson 1980; McAdam 1986; Diani 2004; della Porta and Diani [1999] 2006). Scholars concerned with the relationship between networks and social movement participation have focused mainly on the structural properties of networks such as the number and intensity of ties, degree of homogeneity, and communication flows. Although these strands of research have generated important findings, it is necessary to pay greater attention to the cultural dimension of networks that supply the themes, worldviews, ideologies, and practices used to articulate collective identity. Here I emphasize the way networks supply the cultural context, strategies, and symbolic repertoires that facilitate the politicization of identity. I draw on Nancy Whittier's (2012) concept of *identity strategies*—or strategies and tactics that include public identity disclosure and emotion-laden expressions of identity—to understand how collective identity is articulated.

As Bert Klandermans (1992; 1997, 49) has argued, "consensus mobilization," which is necessary for mobilization, "is a matter of symbolic politics." And politics is as much a discursive struggle as it is a contest over resources. Following Wuthnow (1989; see also Rochon 1998), it is useful to think of social movements as *discursive communities* held together not only by common action and bonds of solidarity but also by identities, symbols, shared identity discourse, and practices of everyday life that attribute participants' experiences to particular forms of social injustice. If social movement actors create their own idiocultures, or systems of knowledge, belief, behaviors, and customs (Fine 1979), it is also true that they are constrained or facilitated in this by the symbolic tools, conventions, and identities in the larger societal context as well as the cultural context of the networks from which social movement identities are drawn. Almost all scholars who have sought to explain the emergence and dynamics of social movements have been interested in the small-scale settings or networks removed from the direct control of dominant groups that generate the counterhegemonic ideas and identities associated with political mobilization (Polletta 1999; Tilly 2000; Futrell and Simi 2004; Reed and Foran 2002). These have been referred to variously as "free spaces," "cultures of solidarity," "safe spaces," "submerged networks," "social movement communities," "movement halfway houses," "political cultures of opposition," "beloved communities," and "abeyance structures." Katzenstein (1998), for example, discusses the role that "feminist habitats" have played in sustaining feminist activism within broader institutions since the retrenchment of the mass women's movement of the late 1960s and 1970s. Church congregations, which are localized cultural groups with particular visions of morality and social life, can also serve as a site for the construction of politicized identities (Morris 1984; Williams 2002).

One way of thinking about the relationship between these preexisting networks and movement participation is to conceive of that relationship as the link between individuals—that is, their identities—and group memberships. This means that the identities of social movement activists are influenced by a participant's configuration of group memberships. There is a growing awareness among social movement scholars that participation in multiple organizations and personal networks creates webs of links that can, at times, converge, but, at other times, counteract each other, making it all the more important to pay attention to the role of multiple identities in mobilization (Rosenthal et al. 1997: Van Stekelenburg and Klandermans 2009). Some scholars argue that *dual identities* resulting from immigration and cultural diversification are playing a larger role in political contention in Western Europe (Klandermans, Van der Toorn, and Van Stekelenburg 2008; Azzi et al. 2010). In the United States, dual identities, such as race, class, ethnicity, gender, religion, and sexuality, have sometimes facilitated mobilization within the civil rights, gay and lesbian, and women's movements (McAdam 1992; Kurtz 2002; Roth 2004; Ghaziani 2008), and at other times, identity disputes have contributed to factionalization and demobilization (Rupp and Taylor 1987; Gamson 1995a, 1995b; Robnett 1997; Breines 2006). It can be difficult for individuals to hold on to numerous identities simultaneously; inevitably some will be more salient than others, especially the transient identities that result from social movement participation. Some movements, however, have been successful at mobilizing activists with *multiple identities*. Scholars of the women's movement find that despite national, religious, and racial–ethnic differences, transnational feminist networks have used the opportunities afforded by globalization, such as information and computer technologies, to network, forge solidarity, create organizations, and build coalitions to advance the goals of feminism (Rupp 1998; Rupp and Taylor 1999; Taylor and Rupp 2002; Moghadam 2005; Ferree 2007).

When activists work to create solidarity among diverse constituencies and struggle to represent themselves as similar to or different from those they oppose or seek to influence, there is always the potential for disagreement and conflict, making the construction of collective identity challenging. Reger, Myers, and Einwohner (2008) propose an intersectional approach to collective identity that moves beyond singular attention to gender, race, ethnicity, nationality, sexuality, and other identities to understand how multiple identities influence activist self-conceptions, solidarity, and tactics.

The body of writings on cycles of mobilization and movement-to-movement influence (Meyer and Whittier 1994) suggests that scholars should examine a wider range of dual or multiple identities in addition to status and class. In the United States, the movement-based collective identities formed by participants in the women's, civil rights, gay and lesbian, peace, environmental, and other movements of the 1960s and 1970s have spilled over to influence the collective identities of a host of social movements that have permeated virtually every institutional sector, including health, education, the military, religion, the workplace, and corporations (Brown 2007; Epstein

2007). Some movements, such as queer movements (Gamson 1995, 1996) and multiracial movements (Bernstein and De la Cruz 2008), mobilize around the destabilization of fixed gender and sexual identities and monoracial identities to secure social recognition. Research on women's and gay and lesbian movements emphasizes how these movements have used cultural repertoires, such as performance, everyday resistance, and ritual, to challenge and destabilize fixed gender and sexual identity categories (Gamson 1995a, 1995b; Taylor and Rupp 2003; Taylor, Rupp, and Gamson 2004).

Research on networks and social movement participation has recently begun to examine the impact of virtual links, as new web-based technologies have changed the social contexts within which identity can be constructed (Cerulo 1997; Futrell and Simi 2004). Scholars debate whether political contention that relies on the Internet and other new media is able to produce the social psychological elements necessary for consensus mobilization. Some researchers who have explored media-generated communities argue that such communities create the kind of "pseudo-gemeinschaft" experiences that are conducive to collective identity formation (Cerulo 1997; Meyrowitz 1997; McCaughey and Ayers 2003). In a study of two opposing Dutch web forums (ethnic Dutch vs. Dutch Muslims), Van Stekelenburg, Oegema, and Klandermans (2010) found that participating in online debates radicalizes and polarizes intergroup relations, which suggests that web-based protest can create opportunities for the formation of collective identity. Other researchers of Internet activism are more guarded in their predictions regarding the impact of new communication technologies on community, solidarity, and identity (Earl and Kimport 2011).

In assessing the role of networks in consensus mobilization, it is necessary to keep in mind the importance of contentious performances in identification processes (Taylor and Van Dyke 2004; Tilly 2008). Protest actions are one of the means by which challenging groups forge solidarity and construct collective identity. In movements that frame injustice in terms of identity politics, *identity strategies* provide a crucial link between individual and collective identity. The use of identity disclosure as a social movement tactic emerged in the 1970s in the "coming out" strategies of the gay and lesbian movements. According to Whittier (2012, 147), "identity strategies include individual or group disclosure of identity with the aim of producing change in how individuals understand and feel about their identity, in how the group is defined in the larger culture, or in the politics of the state and other institutions." The pervasiveness of politicized collective identities and identity strategies in Western societies, which have seen an abundance of social movements since the 1960s, creates new linkages and cultural meanings among social movement participants.

These linkages, in turn, facilitate the diffusion of social movement identities and contentious performances. To return to my original point, social movements are embedded in dense relational settings, and these networks supply not only the social ties but the cultural context, the strategies, and the tactical repertoires that facilitate the construction of politicized collective identities.

Emotions and Perceptions of Grievances

In the last decade, there has been a flurry of scholarship in search of an empirically grounded explanation for the common emotional patterns associated with protest participation (Jasper 1998; Aminzade and McAdam 2001; Goodwin, Jasper, and Polletta 2001; Taylor 2010). As Jim Jasper (1997, 127) argues, "emotions give ideas, ideologies, identities, and even interests their power to motivate." A host of emotions, such as anger, shame, fear, hate, anxiety, and depression, as well as love, pride, happiness, satisfaction, and joy, arise from the structural inequalities in power and status associated with protest (Kemper 1978). Scheff (1990) argues that emotions are so critical to the exercise of power that shame and pride are at the heart of conflict between groups and even nations. While structural factors can give rise to any number of emotions, the expression, management, and regulation of emotions is ultimately a social matter governed by cultural and interactional processes (Hochschild 1983). A goal of many social movements is to create and pass on new self-conceptions and societal conceptions of previously stigmatized groups, replacing feelings of shame and loneliness with pride and solidarity. Numerous studies have shown that participants often engage in considerable emotion labor to merge their personal identities with the collective identity of a social movement community (Snow and McAdam 2000; Klandermans and De Weerd 2000; Whittier 2001; Dunn 2004; Taylor and Leitz 2010). Social movements work to harness participants' emotions and to transform what might be negative or counterproductive emotions, such as depression, sadness, grief, and anger, into feelings of hope, joy, righteous indignation, efficacy, and group pride that are conducive to the formation of a politicized collective identity. A great deal of the emotional change associated with collective identity transformation occurs through the use of identity strategies and other tactics that produce change in how individuals understand and feel about themselves. For example, through consciousness raising, feminist movements transform guilt, shame, and depression, all of which are passive feelings associated with gender subordination, into anger or righteous indignation (Taylor 1995; Taylor and Whittier 1995; Summers-Effler 2002; Lyman 2004; Reger 2004; Hercus 2005). In their study of a pen-pal network of women imprisoned for committing infanticide while suffering postpartum psychiatric illness, Taylor and Leitz (2010) found that participating in the social movement network triggered profound emotional transformation. Participants used a psychiatric illness collective action frame to remake their identities as good mothers, replacing guilt and shame with pride and anger toward medical authorities and the legal system that failed to acknowledge their illness. In health and self-help movements, emotions play an important role in politicizing the illness experience (Taylor 1996; Brown 2007; Whittier 2009).

Social movements mobilize, in part, by fostering distinctive *emotion cultures* that specify "feeling rules" and "expression rules" that include expectations about how members should feel about themselves and dominant groups as well as how they should manage and express feelings evoked by day-to-day encounters with dominant groups and targets they seek to influence (Taylor and Whittier 1995; Taylor 2000a). Social movements use emotion-laden rituals to create solidarity and self-change among participants, to nurture and sustain activists, and to challenge and influence elites and authorities. In their study of the transnational women's movement that mobilized from the late nineteenth century to the Second World War, Taylor and Rupp (2002) found that the emotion culture of the international women's movement created a community that was able to transcend national boundaries and identities. Social movements also use emotion strategically to influence targets of change (Whittier 2001, 2009; Taylor and Leitz 2010). Movements oriented toward transformations of collective identity attempt to broker sympathy by reframing participants as members of oppressed classes or as sympathetic victims (Taylor 2000b; Whittier 2001; Dunn 2004). In culturally diverse societies, there has been a burgeoning of "survivor" movements, and Dunn (2004) argues that social movements are increasingly becoming what Clark (1997) terms "sympathy brokers," which mobilize, in part, by constructing sympathy-worthy victims.

The 1960s and 1970s cycle of protest created a changed context for contentious politics by amplifying participants' feelings of efficacy through the creation of new emotional framings and collective identities conducive to protest. Although the relationship between emotions and perceptions of injustice is complicated (Jasper 1998), a substantial body of research on the women's and gay and lesbian movements demonstrates that anger, when framed as righteous indignation, motivates individuals and groups to participate in protest (Summers-Effler 2002; Lyman 2004; Reger 2004; Hercus 2005; Guenther 2009; Gould 2009). Anger moves people to adopt a more challenging relationship to authorities than subordinate emotions, such as fear, shame, sadness, and despair, which can lead people to avoid participation in collective action (Klandermans, Van der Toorn, and Van Stekelenburg 2008). Organizers of the 2004 San Francisco wedding protest, for example, described the monthlong protest as an opportunity to channel participants' anger over passage of the federal Defense of Marriage Act that defines marriage as a legal union between a man and a woman.

Because emotion is central to the construction of collective identity, it seems logical to conclude that the new collective identities that allow people to make their own histories in culturally diverse societies may result in polarization and radicalization. This may result from the fact that identity strategies often include emotion-laden public identity disclosure. For example, the most eye-catching aspect of the Tea Party's protest against health care reform in the United States was the group's consistent use of anger and hate, expressed in anti-elitist and racist rhetoric, to oppose universal health care. There is some preliminary evidence that online activism may provoke emotions that contribute to radicalization and polarization. In their study of ethnic Dutch and Dutch Muslim web forums, Van Stekelenburg, Oegema, and Klandermans (2010) found that the anonymity of interactions and the absence of effective social control mechanisms that characterize Internet activism enhance the extremity of people's expressions.

In considering the importance of emotion to the politicization of collective identity, it is important to keep in mind that the concept of "movement" refers, after all, to the everyday actions of hundreds of individuals, many of whom never belong to a social movement organization (Oliver 1989). Everyday activism, which does not involve the same kind of consciousness coordination that organized actions do, is often provoked by the emotion of the moment. Given the centrality of the concept of the "personal as political" to the women's movement, it should come as no surprise that a recent study by Mansbridge and Flaster (2008) finds that women who reported having called someone a "male chauvinist pig" were motivated, in most cases, by righteous anger at a perceived proximate injustice and by a sense of duty based on feminist identity and solidarity.

Emotion and emotion-laden tactics are central to the construction and deployment of collective identity. Meyer and Tarrow (1998, 4) have argued that, in Western societies, "protest behavior is employed with greater frequency, by more diverse constituencies, and is used to represent a wider range of claims than ever before." It is conceivable that social movements themselves might be playing a major role in changing norms and rules for the expression of emotions such as anger and righteous indignation.

Conclusion

I have drawn on recent research advances in the study of social movements to reflect on some of the ways that globalization, culturally diverse network societies, and the Internet are influencing the social psychological dynamics of contention. The evidence is clear that, as modernization theorists predicted, social movements are instrumental in the politicization of collective identities in Western democratic societies. My analysis calls attention to the relationship between identity and tactics to highlight the significance of politicized collective identities for collective action oriented toward institutional and cultural change as well as for understanding the role of collective identity in the innovation and diffusion of social movement identities, identity strategies, and tactical repertoires. I argue that the abundance of social movements and the spread of contentious processes into virtually every institutional sector of U.S. society can be explained, at least in part, by the pervasiveness of identity politics in postindustrial democratic societies (Taylor 2010).

I have also reviewed the body of work that calls attention to the importance of networks for motivating social movement participation, highlighting recent advances in collective identity theory that attend to the mobilization dilemmas created by the dual and multiple identities associated with liquid modernity. Research demonstrates that previous social movement cycles are also a significant influence on the collective identities of social movement actors. Many recent movements combine prior movement collective identities with current politicized identities such as feminist breast cancer activists, gay and lesbian employee networks, and black feminist writing collectives. I have also highlighted the growing importance of virtual networks in the politicization of collective identity and discussed promising new lines of work that suggest that virtual networks may create new but distinct forms of community and identity.

The question of multiple identities brings immediately to mind the kinds of identity conflict, disputes, and contests that have plagued many movements in the United States in recent decades. One of the most significant advances of collective identity theory has been to bring emotions and group processes squarely into the analysis of the social psychology of social movements. Prior attempts to incorporate culture and social psychological processes into models of social movement participation relied heavily on cognitive approaches to meaning as spelled out by the frame alignment perspective (Snow et al. 1986). Researchers have made considerable advances in understanding the role of emotion in the politicization of collective identity, especially the importance of emotion-laden tactics that rely on identity disclosure, whether through organized forms of protest or everyday activism. It may be that the use of public disclosure of individual and collective identities to change both participant and societal conceptions of groups makes it more acceptable for aggrieved groups to express and harness the anger and righteous indignation necessary for the politicization of collective identity.

This may be the appropriate moment to ask whether the nature and dynamics of political contention are undergoing seismic change in light of the global economic crisis, the increased cultural diversification of Western democratic societies, and the role of the Internet and new media in protest. There can be little doubt that in Western societies, social movements increasingly serve as sources of identity, solidarity, and meaning. For some groups, social movement communities have replaced traditional forms of community and identity, and for others, traditional forms of community and identity are becoming politicized (Taylor 2000a). Social movements also mirror the fragmentation of late modern society in their divisions of race, ethnicity, nationality, class, gender, and sexuality, which necessitates an intersectional approach to understanding the construction of collective identity. Although globalization, diversification, the rise of the network society, and new communication technologies may be changing the context of contention, I conclude by arguing that there nevertheless remains considerable continuity in forms of political contention because, as Charles Tilly (1978, 1986) suggests, fundamental changes in repertoires of contention occur slowly and are constrained not only by the cultural context but by limits set by the established repertoires. As recent research advances demonstrate, a full understanding of the origins, forms, and dynamics of social movements requires that our theories and models pay closer attention to how the structural and cultural changes taking place in postindustrial democratic societies may be affecting the motivational dynamics, network and group processes, and emotions that explain individual participation in social movements.

References

Aminzade, Ronald, and Doug McAdam. 2001. "Emotions and Contentious Politics." In *Silence and Voice in the Study of Contentious Politics*, edited by Ronald Aminzade, Jack A. Goldstone, Doug McAdam, Elizabeth J. Perry, William H. Sewell Jr., Sidney Tarrow, and Charles Tilly, 14–50. Cambridge: Cambridge University Press.

Azzi, Assaad E., Xenia Chryssochoou, Bert Klandermans, and Bernd Simon, eds. 2010. *Identity and Participation in Culturally Diverse Societies: A Multidisciplinary Perspective*. Malden, Mass.: Wiley-Blackwell.

Bauman, Zygmunt. 2000. *Liquid Modernity*. Cambridge: Polity Press.

Bernstein, Mary. 1997. "Celebration and Suppression: The Strategic Uses of Identity by the Lesbian and Gay Movement." *American Journal of Sociology* 103:531–65.

———. 2005. "Identity Politics." *Annual Review of Sociology* 31:47–74.

Bernstein, Mary, and Marcie De la Cruz. 2008. "What Are You? Explaining Identity

as a Goal of the Multiracial Hapa Movement." *Social Problems* 56:722–45.
Breines, Winifred. 2006. *The Trouble between Us: An Uneasy History of White and Black Women in the Feminist Movement.* New York: Oxford University Press.
Brown, Phil. 2007. *Contested Illnesses and the Environmental Health Movement.* New York: Columbia University Press.
Castells, Manuel. 1997. *The Power of Identity.* Malden, Mass.: Blackwell.
Cerulo, Karen A. 1997. "Identity Construction: New Issues, New Directions." *Annual Review of Sociology* 23:385–409.
Chryssochoou, Xenia. 2010. "Development, (Re) Construction, and Expression of Collective Identities." In *Identity and Participation in Culturally Diverse Societies: A Multidisciplinary Perspective,* edited by Assaad E. Azzi, Xenia Chryssochoou, Bert Klandermans, and Bernd Simon, 5–7. Malden, Mass.: Wiley-Blackwell.
Clark, Candace. 1997. *Misery and Company in Everyday Life.* Chicago: University of Chicago Press.
Cohen, Jean L. 1985. "Strategy or Identity: New Theoretical Paradigms and Contemporary Social Movements." *Social Research* 52:663–716.
Della Porta, Donatella, and Mario Diani. (1999) 2006. *Social Movements.* 2nd Rev. and Exp. ed. Malden, Mass.: Blackwell.
Diani, Mario. 2004. "Networks and Participation." In *The Blackwell Companion to Social Movements,* edited by David A. Snow, Sarah A. Soule, and Hanspeter Kriesi, 339–59. Oxford: Blackwell.
Dunn, Jennifer. 2004. "The Politics of Empathy: Social Movements and Victim Repertoires." *Sociological Focus* 37:235–50.
Earl, Jennifer, and Katrina Kimport. 2011. *Digitally Enabled Social Change: Activism in the Internet Age.* Cambridge, Mass.: MIT Press.
Einwohner, Rachel L. 2002. "Bringing the Outsiders In: Opponents' Claims and the Construction of Animal Rights Activists' Identity." *Mobilization* 7, no. 3: 253–68.
Epstein, Steve. 2007. *Inclusion: The Politics of Difference in Medical Research.* Chicago: University of Chicago Press.
Ferree, Myra Marx. 2007. "On-line Identities and Organizational Connections: Networks of Transnational Feminist Websites." In *Gender Orders Unbound? Globalization, Restructuring, and Reciprocity,* edited by Ilse Lenz, Charlotte Ullrich, and Barbara Fersch, 141–66. Leverkusen, Germany: Barbara Budrich.
Ferree, Myra Marx, and F. D. Miller. 1985. "Mobilization and Meaning: Some Social Psychological Contributions to the Resource Mobilization Perspective on Social Movements." *Sociological Inquiry* 55, no. 1: 38–61.
Fine, Gary Alan. 1979. "Small Groups and Culture Creation: The Idioculture of Little League Baseball Teams." *American Sociological Review* 44:733–45.
Futrell, Robert, and Pete Simi. 2004. "Free Spaces, Collective Identity, and the Persistence of US White Power Activism." *Social Problems* 51:16–42.

Gamson, Joshua. 1995. "Must Identity Movements Self-Destruct? A Queer Dilemma." *Social Problems* 42:390–407.

———. 1996. "The Organizational Shaping of Collective Identity: The Case of Lesbian and Gay Film Festivals in New York." *Sociological Forum* 11:231–61.

Gamson, William A. 1991. "Commitment and Agency in Social Movements." *Sociological Forum* 6:27–50.

———. 1992a. "The Social Psychology of Collective Action." In *Frontiers in Social Movement Theory*, edited by Aldon Morris and Carol Mueller, 53–76. New Haven, Conn.: Yale University Press.

———. 1992b. *Talking Politics*. New York: Cambridge University Press.

Ghaziani, Amin. 2008. *The Dividends of Dissent: How Conflict and Culture Work in Lesbian and Gay Marches on Washington*. Chicago: University of Chicago Press.

Giddens, Anthony. 1991. *Modernity and Self-Identity: Self and Society in the Late Modern Age*. Stanford, Calif.: Stanford University Press.

Goodwin, Jeff, James M. Jasper, and Francesca Polletta. 2001. *Passionate Politics: Emotions and Social Movements*. Chicago: University of Chicago Press.

Gould, Deborah. 2009. *Moving Politics: Emotion and ACT UP's Fight against AIDS*. Chicago: University of Chicago Press.

Guenther, Katja M. 2009. "The Impact of Emotional Opportunities on the Emotion Cultures of Feminist Organizations." *Gender and Society* 23:337–62.

Habermas, Jürgen. 1984. *The Theory of Communicative Action: Reason and the Rationalization of Society*. Boston: Beacon.

———. 1995. *Moral Consciousness and Communicative Action*. Cambridge, Mass.: MIT Press.

Hercus, Cheryl. 2005. *Stepping Out of Line: Becoming and Being a Feminist*. New York: Routledge.

Hochschild, Arlie. 1983. *The Managed Heart: The Commercialization of Human Feeling*. Berkeley: University of California Press.

Jasper, James. 1997. *The Art of Moral Protest: Culture, Biography, and Creativity in Social Movements*. Chicago: University of Chicago Press.

———. 1998. "The Emotions of Protest: Affective and Reactive Emotions in and around Social Movements." *Sociological Forum* 13:397–424.

Kaminski, Elizabeth, and Verta Taylor. 2008. "'We're Not Just Lip-Synching Up Here': Music and Collective Identity in Drag Performances." In *Identity Work: Negotiating Sameness and Difference in Activist Environments*, edited by Rachel Einwohner, Dan Myers, and Jo Reger, 47–75. Minneapolis: University of Minnesota Press.

Katzenstein, Mary Fainsod. 1998. *Faithful and Fearless: Moving Feminist Protest Inside the Church and Military*. Princeton, N.J.: Princeton University Press.

Kemper, Theodore D. 1978. "Toward a Sociology of Emotions: Some Problems and Some Solutions." *American Sociologist* 13:30–41.

Klandermans, Bert. 1985. "Individuals and Collective Action: Rejoinder to Schrager." *American Sociological Review* 50:860–91.

———. 1992. "The Social Construction of Protest and Multi-Organization Fields." In *Frontiers in Social Movement Theory*, edited by Aldon Morris and Carol Mueller, 77–103. New Haven, Conn.: Yale University Press.

———. 1994. "Transient Identities: Changes in Collective Identity in the Dutch Peace Movement." In *New Social Movements: From Ideology to Identity*, edited by Hank Johnston, Joseph Gusfield, and Enrique Llarana, 168–85. Philadelphia: Temple University Press.

———. 1997. *The Social Psychology of Protest*. Oxford: Blackwell.

Klandermans, Bert, and Marga De Weerd. 2000. "Group Identification and Political Protest." In *Self Identity and Social Movements*, edited by Sheldon Stryker, Timothy Owens, and Robert W. White, 68–92. Minneapolis: University of Minnesota Press.

Klandermans, Bert, Jojanneke van der Toorn, and Jacquelien van Stekelenburg. 2008. "Embeddedness and Identity: How Immigrants Turn Grievances into Action." *American Sociological Review* 73:992–1012.

Klawiter, Maren. 2008. *The Biopolitics of Breast Cancer: Changing Cultures of Disease and Activism*. Minneapolis: University of Minnesota Press.

Kurtz, Sharon. 2002. *Workplace Justice: Organizing Multi-Identity Movements*. Minneapolis: University of Minnesota Press.

Lyman, Peter. 2004. "The Domestication of Anger: The Use and Abuse of Anger in Politics." *European Journal of Social Theory* 7, no. 2: 133–47.

Mansbridge, Jane, and Katerine Flaster. 2008. "The Cultural Politics of Everyday Discourse: The Case of 'Male Chauvinist.'" *Critical Sociology* 33:627–60.

McAdam, Doug. 1986. "Recruitment to High Risk Activism: The Case of Freedom Summer." *American Journal of Sociology* 92:64–90.

———. 1992. "Gender as a Mediator of Activist Experience: The Case of Freedom Summer." *American Journal of Sociology* 97:1211–49.

McAdam, Doug, Sidney Tarrow, and Charles Tilly. 2001. *Dynamics of Contention*. Cambridge: Cambridge University Press.

McCaughey, Martha, and Michael D. Ayers, eds. 2003. *Cyberactivism: Online Activism in Theory and Practice*. New York: Routledge.

Melucci, Alberto. 1985. "The Symbolic Challenge of Contemporary Movements." *Social Research* 52:781–816.

———. 1989. *Nomads of the Present: Social Movements and Individual Needs in Contemporary Society*. Philadelphia: Temple University Press.

———. 1996. *Challenging Codes: Collective Action in the Information Age*. New York: Cambridge University Press.

Meyer, David, and Sidney Tarrow, eds. 1998. *The Social Movement Society: Con-

tentious Politics for a New Century. Lanham, Md.: Rowman and Littlefield.
Meyer, David S., and Nancy Whittier. 1994. "Social Movement Spillover." *Social Problems* 41:277–98.
Meyrowitz, Joshua. 1997. "Shifting Worlds of Strangers: Medium Theory and Changes in 'Them' vs. 'Us.'" *Sociological Inquiry* 67, no. 1: 59–71.
Moghadam, Valentine. 2005. *Globalizing Women: Transnational Feminist Networks.* Baltimore: Johns Hopkins University Press.
Morris, Aldon. 1984. *The Origins of the Civil Rights Movement: Black Communities Organizing for Change.* New York: Free Press.
Morris, Aldon, and Carol Mueller, eds. 1992. *The Frontiers of Social Movement Theory.* New Haven, Conn.: Yale University Press.
Oliver, Pamela E. 1989. "Bringing the Crowd Back In: The Nonorganizational Elements of Social Movements." *Research in Social Movements, Conflict, and Change* 11:1–30.
Polletta, Francesca. 1999. "Free Spaces in Collective Action." *Theory and Society* 28:1–38.
Polletta, Francesca, and James Jasper. 2001. "Collective Identity in Social Movements." *Annual Review of Sociology* 27:283–305.
Reed, Jean-Pierre, and John Foran. 2002. "Political Cultures of Opposition: Exploring Idioms, Ideologies, and Revolutionary Agency." *Critical Sociology* 28:335–70.
Reger, Jo. 2002. "Organizational Dynamics and Construction of Multiple Feminist Identities in the National Organization for Women." *Gender and Society* 16:710–27.
———. 2004. "Organizational 'Emotion Work' through consciousness-raising: An analysis of a feminist organization." *Qualitative Sociology* 27:205–22.
Reger, Jo, Daniel J. Myers, and Rachel L. Einwohner, eds. 2008. *Identity Work in Social Movements.* Minneapolis: University of Minnesota Press.
Rios, Victor M., and Patrick Lopez-Aguado. 2012. "Pelones y Matones: Chicano Cholos Perform for a Punitive Audience." In *Performing the U.S. Latina and Latino Borderlands,* edited by Arturo J. Aldama, Chela Sandoval, and Peter Garcia, 382–400. Bloomington: Indiana University Press.
Robnett, Belinda. 1997. *How Long? How Long? African American Women in the Struggle for Civil Rights.* New York: Oxford University Press.
Rochon, Thomas R. 1998. *Culture Moves: Ideas, Activism, and Changing Values.* Princeton, N.J.: Princeton University Press.
Rosenthal, Naomi, David McDonald, Michele Ethier, Meryl Fingrutd, and Roberta Karant. 1997. "Structural Tensions in the Nineteenth-century Women's Movement." *Mobilization* 2, no. 1: 21–46.
Roth, Benita. 2004. *Separate Roads to Feminism: Black, Chicana, and White Feminist Movements in America's Second Wave.* Cambridge: Cambridge University Press.
Rupp, Leila J. 1998. "Feminisms and Internationalism: A View from the Centre." *Gender and History* 10:535–38.
Rupp, Leila J., and Verta Taylor. 1987. *Survival in the Doldrums: The American*

Women's Rights Movement 1945 to the 1960s. New York: Oxford University Press.
———. 1999. "Forging Feminist Identity in an International Movement: A Collective Identity Approach to Twentieth-century Feminism." *Signs* 24:363–86.
———. 2003. *Drag Queens at the 801 Cabaret.* Chicago: University of Chicago Press.
Scheff, Thomas. 1990. *Microsociology: Emotion, Discourse, and Social Structure.* Chicago: University of Chicago Press.
Simon, Bernd. 2011. "Collective Identity and Political Engagement." In *Identity and Participation in Culturally Diverse Societies,* edited by Assad E. Azzi, Xenia Chryssochoou, Bert Klandermans, and Bernd Simon, 137–57. Malden, Mass.: Wiley-Blackwell.
Simon, Bernd, and Bert Klandermans. 2001. "Politicized Collective Identity: A Social Psychological Analysis." *American Psychologist* 56:319–31.
Snow, David A., E. Burke Rochford, Steven K. Worden, and Robert D. Benford. 1986. "Frame Alignment Processes, Micromobilization, and Movement Participation." *American Sociological Review* 51:464–81.
Snow, David, and Doug McAdam. 2000. "Identity Work Processes in the Context of Social Movements: Clarifying the Identity/Movement Nexus." In *Self, Identity, and Social Movements,* edited by S. Stryker, T. Owens, and R. White, 41–67. Minneapolis: University of Minnesota Press.
Snow, David, Louis Zurcher, and Sheldon Ekland-Olson. 1980. "Social Networks and Social Movements: A Microstructural Approach to Differential Recruitment." *American Sociological Review* 45:787–801.
Staggenborg, Suzanne, and Josee Lecomte. 2009. "Social Movement Campaigns: Mobilization and Outcomes in the Montreal Women's Movement Community." *Mobilization* 14, no. 2: 37–52.
Summers-Effler, Erika. 2002. "The Micro Potential for Social Change: Emotion, Consciousness, and Social Movement Formation." *Sociological Theory* 20:41–60.
Tajfel, Henri, and John C. Turner. 1979. "An Integrative Theory of Intergroup Conflict." In *The Social Psychology of Intergroup Relations,* edited by W. G. Austin and S. Worchel, 33–47. Monterey, Calif.: Brooks/Cole.
Taylor, Verta. 1989. "Social Movement Continuity: The Women's Movement in Abeyance." *American Sociological Review* 54:761–75.
———. 1995. "Watching for Vibes: Bringing Emotions into the Study of Feminist Organizations." In *Feminist Organizations: Harvest of the New Women's Movement,* edited by Myra Marx Ferree and Patricia Yancey Martin, 223–33. Philadelphia: Temple University Press.
———. 1996. *Rock-a-by Baby: Feminism, Self-Help, and Postpartum Depression.* New York: Routledge.
———. 2000a. "Mobilizing for Change in a Social Movement Society." *Contemporary Sociology* 29:219–30.

———. 2000b. "Emotions and Identity in Women's Self-Help Movements." In *Self, Identity, and Social Movements,* edited by Sheldon Stryker, Timothy J. Owens, and Robert W. White, 271–99. Minneapolis: University of Minnesota Press.

———. 2010. "Culture, Identity, and Social Movements: Studying Protest as If People Really Matter." *Mobilization* 15, no. 2: 113–34.

Taylor, Verta, Katrina Kimport, Nella Van Dyke, and Ellen Andersen. 2009. "Culture and Mobilization: Tactical Repertoires, Same-Sex Weddings, and the Impact on Gay Activism." *American Sociological Review* 74:865–90.

Taylor, Verta, and Lisa Leitz. 2010. "From Infanticide to Activism: Emotions and Identity in Self-Help Movements." In *Social Movements and the Transformation of American Health Care,* edited by Jane Banaszak-Holl, Sandra Levitsky, and Mayer N. Zald, 266–83. New York: Oxford University Press.

Taylor, Verta, and Leila J. Rupp. 1993. "Women's Culture and Lesbian Feminist Activism: A Reconsideration of Cultural Feminism." *Signs* 19:32–61.

———. 2002. "Loving Internationalism: The Emotion Culture of Transnational Women's Organizations, 1888–1945." *Mobilization* 7, no. 2: 125–44.

Taylor, Verta, Leila J. Rupp, and Joshua Gamson. 2004. "Performing Protest: Drag Shows as Tactical Repertoires of the Gay and Lesbian Movement." *Research in Social Movements, Conflict, and Change* 25:105–37.

Taylor, Verta, and Nella Van Dyke. 2004. "'Get Up, Stand Up': Tactical Repertoires of Social Movements." In *The Blackwell Companion to Social Movements,* edited by David A. Snow, Sarah A. Soule, and Hanspeter Kriesi, 262–93. Oxford: Blackwell.

Taylor, Verta, and Nancy E. Whittier. 1992. "Collective Identity in Social Movement Communities: Lesbian Feminist Mobilization." In *Frontiers in Social Movement Theory,* edited by Aldon Morris and Carol Mueller, 104–29. New Haven, Conn.: Yale University Press.

———. 1995. "Analytical Approaches to Social Movement Culture: The Culture of the Women's Movement." In *Social Movements and Culture,* edited by Hank Johnston and Bert Klandermans, 163–87. Minneapolis: University of Minnesota Press.

Taylor, Verta, and Mayer N. Zald. 2010. "Conclusion: The Shape of Collective Action in the U.S. Health Sector." In *Social Movements and the Transformation of American Health Care,* edited by Jane Banaszak-Holl, Sandra Levitsky, and Mayer N. Zald, 300–17. Oxford: Oxford University Press.

Tilly, Charles. 1978. *From Mobilization to Revolution.* Reading, Mass.: Addison-Wesley.

———. 1986. *The Contentious French.* Cambridge, Mass.: Belknap Press.

———. 1995. *Repertoires and Cycles of Collective Action.* Durham, N.C.: Duke University Press.

———. 2000. "Spaces of Contention." *Mobilization* 5, no. 2: 135–59.

———. 2008. *Contentious Performances.* New York: Cambridge University Press.

Touraine, Alain. 1985. "An Introduction to the Study of Social Movements." *Social Research* 52:749–87.

Van Stekelenburg, Jacquelien, and Bert Klandermans. 2009. "Social Movement Theory: Past, Presence, and Prospects." In *Movers and Shakers: Social Movements in Africa*, edited by Stephen Ellis and Ineke Kessel, 17–43. Leiden, Netherlands: Brill.

Van Stekelenburg, Jacquelien, Dirk Oegema, and Bert Klandermans. 2010. "No Radicalization without Identification: How Ethnic Dutch and Dutch Muslim Web Forums Radicalize over Time." In *Identity and Participation in Culturally Diverse Societies*, edited by Assad E. Azzi, Xenia Chryssochoou, Bert Klandermans, and Bernd Simon, 256–74. Malden, Mass.: Wiley-Blackwell.

Van Zomeren, Martijn, and Aarti Iyer. 2009. "Introduction to the Social and Psychological Dynamics of Collective Action." *Journal of Social Issues* 65:645–60.

Ward, Jane. 2008. "Diversity Discourse and Multi-Identity Work in Lesbian and Gay Organizations." In *Identity Work in Social Movements*, edited by Jo Reger, Daniel J. Myers, and Rachel L. Einwohner, 233–55. Minneapolis: University of Minnesota Press.

Whittier, Nancy. 1995. *Feminist Generations: The Persistence of the Radical Women's Movement*. Philadelphia: Temple University Press.

———. 2001. "Emotional Strategies: The Collective Restriction and Display of Oppositional Emotions in the Movement against Child Sexual Abuse." In *Passionate Politics: Emotions and Social Movements*, edited by Jeff Goodwin, James Jasper, and Francesca Polletta, 233–50. Chicago: University of Chicago Press.

———. 2009. *Healing for Justice: The Politics of Child Sexual Abuse*. Oxford: Oxford University Press.

———. 2012. "The Politics of Coming Out: Visibility and Identity in Activism against Child Sexual Abuse." In *Strategies for Social Change*, edited by Gregory M. Maney, Rachel V. Kutz-Flamenbaum, Deana A. Rohlinger, and Jeff Goodwin, 145–69. Minneapolis: University of Minnesota Press.

Williams, Rhys H. 2002. "From the 'Beloved Community' to 'Family Values': Religious Language, Symbolic Repertoires, and Democratic Culture." In *Social Movements: Identity, Culture, and the State*, edited by David S. Meyer, Nancy Whittier, and Belinda Robnett, 247–65. New York: Oxford University Press.

Wuthnow, Robert. 1989. *Communities of Discourse*. Cambridge, Mass.: Harvard University Press.

4

"Protest against Whom?": The Role of Collective Meaning Making in Politicization

Marjoka van Doorn, Jacomijne Prins, and Saskia Welschen

The process of politicization of collective identities is crucial for our understanding of collective action. Research has demonstrated that the more a collective identity politicizes, the more willing group members will be to act collectively on behalf of their group (for a complete review, see Van Stekelenburg and Klandermans 2007, 2010). Politicized collective identity can be understood as "a form of collective identity that underlies group members' explicit motivations to engage in . . . a power struggle" (Simon and Klandermans 2001, 323). But what exactly is involved in this process of politicization? Are there certain conditions under which politicization is bound to occur? Not less important, when does politicization hold off against the odds? What methods can we use to study this process in practice?

To date, theoretical understanding of the politicization of collective identities is shaped by the frameworks of Taylor and Whittier (1992) and Simon and Klandermans (2001). Although with different points of departure and emphases, both frameworks offer analytical tools for studying the process of politicization of collective identities. What both frameworks share is the idea that politicization is a dynamic and multilevel process rather than a stable outcome, as the term *politicized collective identity* would suggest.

The two frameworks were formulated by their authors to set the agenda for future research. Extensive empirical studies of processes of politicization of collective identities have not yet followed suit. Taylor and Whittier (1992) included a case study in their 1992 publication, but the emphasis is on the changing content of lesbian feminism as an ideology rather than the concrete process of politicization. Klandermans and Simon (2001, 331) explicitly emphasize the need for future empirical research into the "hypothesized process of politicization and its various stages."

In this chapter, we take up that challenge by examining one of the stages of the processes of politicization in practice: the process of intragroup meaning making. Central to our approach is a combined focus on content and process.

In addition to earlier theorizing in social movement literature on the process of collective identity formation (see, e.g., Melucci 1989, 1995), we argue that processes of microlevel meaning making are equally central to the politicization process. Whether a collective identity politicizes ultimately depends on whether group members come to share certain perceptions and interpretations of their own position as a group, its relation with other groups, and the broader societal context. An in-depth examination of this process of shared meaning making may also help us understand why some collective identities do, and others do not, politicize.

In our empirical case study, we demonstrate that processes of meaning making can be studied convincingly on the microlevel of concrete, interpersonal interactions in talk. This level of analysis requires a qualitative approach. We argue that the focus group, by creating a setting in which group members are actively involved in the co-construction of meaning, offers an excellent site to capture interactions in talk.

However, before moving on to this empirical study, we first discuss the concept of politicized collective identity as formulated in the works of Taylor and Whittier (1992) and Simon and Klandermans (2001). Following their work, we will argue that three levels of analysis are relevant for the study of politicization: the macro-, the meso-, and the microlevels. We describe how, on a macrolevel, social cleavages in society set the stage for intergroup conflict. On the mesolevel, organizers of protest try to mobilize groups in society by offering interpretative frameworks for struggle and thereby act as engineers of politicized collective identity (Benford and Snow 2000; Gamson 1992; for an elaborate discussion of the "identity–movement nexus," see Snow, chapter 13).

At the end of the day, however, politicization depends on whether individuals at the microlevel develop a sense of collective identity and a shared understanding of the relevant social cleavages, and whether they are convinced by the call to action of organizers. In processes of intragroup meaning-making, all three levels come together. The case study in the third part of the chapter illustrates the complex microdynamics of politicization of collective identity among young Moroccan Dutch. We will argue that a lack of consensus on meanings on the microlevel is an important obstacle in the process of politicization of this collective identity.

Theoretical Frameworks of Politicized Collective Identity

We first need to come to grips with the notion of *collective identity*, which is defined by Taylor and Whittier (1992, 170) as "the shared definition of a group that derives from members' common interests, experiences and solidarity." Politicized collective identities are central in spurring groups into collective action (see Van Stekelenburg and Klandermans 2010).

But how does a collective identity politicize? New social movement theory attributes a key role to collective identity, as is evident inter alia in the work of Melucci (1989, 1995). However, as Taylor and Whittier (1992, 170) observe, there is a lack of attention to "the way that constituencies involved in defending their rights develop politicized group identities." To date, the theoretical frameworks of Taylor and Whittier (1992) and Simon and Klandermans (2001) are the most important attempts to fill this vacuum. Taylor and Whittier describe the process of politicization in terms of the concepts of boundaries, political consciousness development, and negotiation (see also Taylor, chapter 3).

Boundaries

Boundary drawing is a key element in the process of politicization of collective identities. In Taylor and Whittier's (1992, 175) terms, *boundaries* refer to the "social, psychological and physical structures that establish differences between challenging and dominant groups." First, individuals come to see themselves as part of a group when some shared characteristic becomes salient and is defined as important. As a result, boundaries are drawn between "a challenging and a dominant group" (175). In their use of the concept of boundaries, Taylor and Whittier draw from work in symbolic and anthropological interactionism, specifically that of Barth (1969). This author emphasizes that it is not essentialist characteristics that define groups but socially and politically constructed boundaries.

Importantly, boundaries can be internally and externally defined. Internal definition takes place when boundaries are the result of group members' self-definition. The recognition of in-group similarity automatically evokes the group's differentiation from other groups. External definition is about boundaries being recognized, constructed, or imposed onto the group from the outside, by others (Jenkins 2004, 40).

Of key importance is the idea that boundaries are not clear-cut, stable, and objectively visible (see Taylor, chapter 3). Instead, they exist in the shared meanings attributed to group membership by group members and are by consequence dynamic. This dynamic character would be captured best by speaking of processes of boundary drawing.

Consciousness

As the second component of politicized collective identity, Taylor and Whittier (1992) refer to Cohen's (1985) term *consciousness* and what Morris (1990) calls *political consciousness*. Consciousness raising consists of both the awareness of group membership and the realization of the group's position within society, in comparison to other groups. This position must be perceived as illegitimate or unjust to make group membership politically relevant. Often the *own group* is perceived as oppressed and in opposition to the dominant order. While "boundaries locate persons as members of a group, . . . it is group consciousness that imparts larger significance to a connectivity" (Taylor and Whittier 1992, 178). Quantitative research in the 1970s indicated a relationship between a lack of group consciousness, or "awareness among group members of their status as a deprived group" (Miller et al. 1981, 494), and nonengagement in collective action. Consciousness raising is thus a crucial step in the process of politicization of collective identity. An understudied aspect remains, however, the process leading to group consciousness and the negotiations that it involves.

Like boundary drawing, the construction of collective consciousness can be understood as a dynamic process. In continuation, we discuss collective consciousness in terms of processes of consciousness raising.

Negotiation

The third component of politicizing collective identities is what Taylor and Whittier (1992) call (referring to Margolis 1985) *negotiation*. Negotiation involves the process by which groups work to change symbolic meanings, for instance, the meaning of the group's position in society, which is commonly defined in terms of members' common interests in opposition to dominant groups.

Negotiation takes place on two levels. The first level is the private setting, between members of the collectivity. The second level is the public setting, the negotiations between the collectivity and a larger audience. An example might be attempts to free the group from dominant representations or to undermine the status quo in the power balance between groups in society.

Shared Grievances, Adversarial Attributions, and Triangulation of the Conflict

The second theoretical framework that provides us insight in politicization is Simon and Klandermans's (2001) model of politicized collective identity. Simon and Klandermans argue that politicization begins with the awareness of shared grievances within a group. Klandermans (1997) defines *illegitimate inequality, suddenly imposed grievances,* and *violated principles* as important grievances. For these grievances to lead to politicization of a collective identity, they should be experienced as widely shared among in-group members (Simon and Klandermans 2001).

Subsequently, blame for these grievances needs to be attributed to an external enemy. When groups or individuals blame themselves for the inferior position they hold in society, there is no external enemy to oppose. On the contrary, when adversarial attributions are made, collective action becomes an option as "a group that holds an external enemy or opponent responsible is likely to demand corrective action or compensation from that opponent" (Simon and Klandermans 2001, 325).

When the opponent does not comply with the group's corrective claims, the interaction becomes more confrontational. Simon and Klandermans (2001) argue that a collective identity "fully politicizes" when attempts are made to involve a third party (e.g., national government or the general public) in the conflict. They denominate this last step to politicization as *triangulation*: the conflict is triangulated as third parties are forced to take sides in the conflict.

Simon and Klandermans (2001, 319) proposed that people evince politicized collective identity to the extent that they "engage as self-conscious group members in a power struggle on behalf of their group knowing that it is the more inclusive societal context in which this struggle has to be fought out." At the same time, identification with the "more inclusive societal context" is a central condition for politicization: "a politicized collective identity presupposes identification with the more inclusive social entity that provides the context for shared grievances, adversarial attributions, and the ensuing power struggles for social change (or resistance to such change)" (326).

Differences and Similarities between Conceptualizations

Different Perspectives on Collective Identity

The two frameworks depart from a different perspective on collective identity. In line with common approaches in sociology, Taylor and Whittier (1992) conceptualize collective identity as a group characteristic, whereas Simon and Klandermans (2001), informed by a more social psychological perspective, depart from an individual point of view. Their emphasis is on the identity of a person as a group member rather than the identity of a group "as a sui generis entity" (320).

We believe that to understand processes of politicization of collective identity, both the collective and the individual levels need to be taken into account (see Chryssochoou 2003). The collective level is important because this is where the shared definition of the group is formed and becomes a symbolic resource for group members. However, a focus on the individual level sensitizes us to the fact that each individual relates to the group in his own, idiosyncratic way (Klandermans and De Weerd 2000, 76).

The challenge is to develop an approach that is able to integrate both levels of the process of identification (e.g., Welschen 2010, 3). We believe that studying identity construction within the in-group, in the interactions between group members, can help us overcome the theoretical distinction between collective group identity and individual identification with a group.

Similarities: Politicized Collective Identity as a Multilevel Process

An important similarity in both frameworks is that politicization of collective identities is conceived of as a multilevel process, involving intra- and intergroup processes as well as the wider societal context. For the sake of our analysis, we believe it is helpful to make a distinction between three different levels that are relevant for processes of politicization of collective identities: the macro-, meso-, and microlevels.

Macrolevel: Social Cleavages Define the Political Significance of Collective Identities

The macrolevel concerns intergroup power relations within the broader societal context. The concept of *social cleavages* offers a useful tool to analyze central power relations in society.

Social cleavages traditionally have been a source of sociopolitical conflict, the fault lines along which opposing identities emerged (Lipset and Rokkan 1967; Kriesi et al. 1995). Categorizations or macrosocial indicators such as class, gender, religion, ethnicity, and socioeconomic position divide groups in society and demarcate the distribution of power between groups. Imbalanced power relations between groups give rise to potential grievances of—underprivileged—groups and give political significance to collective identities.

Both frameworks of politicization discussed earlier place a strong emphasis on unequal power relations between groups. The in-group consists of an oppressed or aggrieved group that demands compensation from a dominant out-group. In Taylor and Whittier's (1992) framework, boundaries are drawn between a "challenging" in-group and a "dominant" out-group; in Simon and Klandermans's (2001) framework, the aggrieved group attributes its grievances to a well-defined out-group.

Social cleavages offer the raw material used in the process of boundary drawing, as they can convincingly be used as boundary markers. However, whether a social cleavage shapes politicization of identities depends on the meaning given to that cleavage by the different groups in society. An important intermediary role in this meaning-making process can be played by mesolevel actors.

Mesolevel: Organizers as the Engineers of Politicized Collective Identity

On the mesolevel, political leaders and organizers of protest try to manipulate the significance of social cleavages. They try to steer the attention to certain opposing collective identities and not to others (Boekkooi, Klandermans, and Van Stekelenburg 2011). Simon and Klandermans (2001, 326) stress the importance of leaders in the politicizing process, quoting Reicher and Hopkins (1996), who argue that leaders can be understood as "entrepreneurs of identity."

Organizers play a key role in how people determine who they are and who they are not and what political meaning they should attach to their identity (see literature on "framing," e.g., Benford and Snow 2000; Gamson 1992; Snow, chapter 13). By framing a conflict in a particular way, they play a crucial role in convincing people to act on behalf of their group. They make an effort to raise consciousness among those who might be sympathetic to the cause of protest. They frame grievances in terms of an intergroup conflict, influencing us–them distinctions, and they make attributions about who is to blame.

Although individuals may already be sympathetic to a certain cause, they may not be unified through the sheer existence of a collective identity, until organizers attach meaning to it in politicized terms.

Microlevel: Co-construction of Meaning within Groups

The microlevel is about meaning-making processes taking place in interpersonal interactions that strengthen or weaken the ties between group members. It is at this level that people attribute meaning to their social world and develop (shared) interpretations of the wider social context.

In both frameworks, shared understanding plays a crucial role in the politicization of collective identity. Group members must have a shared understanding of what the identity of the group is, who the opponent is, how to interpret the position of the group in society, and so on. With their focus on boundaries, consciousness, and negotiation, Taylor and Whittier (1992, 171) emphasize the importance of cultural components, subjective experiences, values, and symbolic understandings created by discontented groups in their struggle for change. They convincingly highlight the role of meaning and ideology in the mobilization and maintenance of collective action.

Of specific importance for our argument is the point, reiterated by Taylor and Whittier (1992, 174), that "collective political actors do not exist de facto by virtue of individuals sharing a common structural location; they are created in the course of social movement activity." What this suggests is that a macrosocial indicator such as a deprived position in society in itself is not enough for a collective identity to politicize. It is only when actors reach consensus about meaning and ideology that identities actually politicize. In a similar vein, Simon and Klandermans (2001, 324) argue that politicized group members are "mindful of their shared group membership, their common enemy or opponent, and especially the wider societal struggle that is affected by and affects this power struggle."

Although sharing meaning is deemed important, neither framework provides further detail on how this process should be conceptualized or how it can be observed. Nor is it made clear how processes on the microlevel interact with processes on both macro- and mesolevels. It is this internal process of meaning making between members of the in-group that has our interest here. Investigating this process can give us insight into how people interpret the sociopolitical context and thus make sense of their place in society and the political relevance of their collective identity.

It is crucial to emphasize that in this process, consensus is not a given. Instead, group members debate, contest, and negotiate the meaning of the group identity, the identity of relevant out-groups, the position of the own group in society, grievances, and claims to be made. This is a point to which both frameworks in our view pay insufficient attention. The strong emphasis in both frameworks on intergroup power relations implies a degree of predictability of and consensus about the identity and position of the own group as well as intergroup relations in the wider social context (but see Taylor, chapter 3).

In similar vein, whereas *negotiation* for Taylor and Whittier (1992) predominantly refers to interaction between in-group members and a dominant out-group, in this chapter, we focus on negotiation as an intra-group process, taking place in the interaction between in-group members. In our illustrative case study, we show that when individuals fail to reach consensus about the identity of the in-group and its relation with out-groups, politicization is hampered.

Dynamics of Nonpoliticization: The Moroccan Dutch Case

In this section, we use the thoughts developed in the previous section as a point of departure for explaining how a lack of consensus at a microlevel may prevent collective identities from politicizing. In particular, we study dynamics of (non)politicization in a group of second-generation immigrants in the Netherlands. We argue that young Moroccan Dutch, based on macrolevel context, have ample reason to mobilize against a deprived position in the Netherlands. However, on a mesolevel, few attempts have been made to mobilize Moroccan Dutch for collective action. We make use of the concepts described by Taylor and Whittier (1992) and Simon and Klandermans (2001) to demonstrate, on a microlevel, how the collective identity of young Moroccan Dutch is negotiated and constructed in interaction. Moreover, we show how intragroup negotiation about the collective identity hampers the process of politicization.

To support our argument that politicization can be studied effectively on a microlevel, we shortly present data from focus group discussions collected for research on collective identity construction among young Moroccan Dutch (Prins, Van Stekelenburg, and Klandermans 2010).[1] Focus groups provide an ideal setting in which to study the social construction of meaning (Gamson 1992): when talking about their identity with peers, young Moroccan Dutch search for a common basis of understanding. At the same time, differences arise: notwithstanding a shared ethnic and religious identity, not all young Moroccan Dutch give meaning to these identities in a similar way. Central to our analysis is the construction and negotiation of collective identity among group members.

Macrolevel Dynamics

Young Moroccan Dutch in the Netherlands deal with a negatively evaluated ethnic and religious identity: Moroccan immigrants in the Netherlands are lowest in the "ethnic hierarchy" (Hagendoorn and Pepels 2003; Van Praag 2006), and research consistently indicates that the Moroccan Dutch are seen as criminal, unadjusted, and lazy (Gordijn, Koomen, and Stapel 2001; Harchaoui and Huinder 2003; De Jong 2007). Following the September 11 attacks in 2001, the public debate regarding the socioeconomic and cultural integration of Moroccan immigrants in Dutch society shifted to their religious background, Islam, and its alleged threat to Dutch society (Harchaoui and Huinder 2003; Vliegenthart 2007; De Koning and Meijer 2010). From 9/11 onward, Islam has been increasingly associated with violence and intolerance and is considered to be undermining "modern" Dutch values, in particular, gender equality, acceptance of homosexuality, and the embracement of modern thought and lifestyles (Sniderman and Hagendoorn 2007; De Koning and Meijer 2010). The Netherlands Institute for Social Research reports that prejudices regarding both the ethnic and religious backgrounds of young Moroccan Dutch hamper their influx into the job market (Nievers and Andriessen 2010).

Although most young Moroccan Dutch are born and raised in the Netherlands, in the media and in public, they are called to account by native Dutch as members of the Moroccan or Muslim community (Ersanilli and Scholten 2009; Ketner 2009). On the basis of supposed value conflicts between Dutch identity, on one hand, and Moroccan and Muslim identity, on the other, membership in the latter two groups is often perceived as mutually exclusive with being Dutch (Sniderman and Hagendoorn 2007; Ghorashi 2010). The prevailing assumption is that to become "Dutch," one needs to distance oneself from one's own ethnic and/or religious background (Ghorashi 2010). Ghorashi argues that this remains an impossible task when migrants are continuously addressed as "absolute others" (Ghorashi 2010, 80). Both their ethnic and religious identities have gained salience for young Moroccan Dutch (De Koning 2008). In our focus groups, we found that young Moroccan Dutch readily refer to shared grievances (exclusion, discrimination, injustice, deprivation, etc.). However, contrary to what we expected based on the macrolevel context, very few attempts have been made among young Moroccan Dutch to undertake collective action.

Mesolevel Dynamics

As was argued earlier, organizers play an important role in the politicization of identity. Organizers attempt to determine the boundaries of a group, raise consciousness of alleged group members, and frame a message that appeals to those who identify with the cause. Although several individuals and many organizations have stepped forward as representatives of the Moroccan and/or Muslim community, until now, none of them has been able to formulate a claim that resonated within these communities and spurred collective action.

A notable exception was the Arab European League (AEL), which, originating in Antwerp, founded in 2002 a Dutch counterpart. The AEL was founded to represent the interests of the Arab minority in Europe, with its main goal being to eradicate discrimination of Muslims. The announcement that a Dutch counterpart of the AEL would be set up initially led to enthusiasm among young Moroccan Dutch, who saw the AEL as a "Moroccan pride" or "Muslim pride" organization (De Koning and Meijer 2010). However, hopes that the AEL would be able to express their grievances were soon dashed. Despite the movement's initial success, it collapsed owing to external pressure by politicians, the police, and the Dutch security agency (AIVD). Internally, the movement suffered from lack of leadership, especially when the popular theologist Mohammed Cheppih refused chairmanship of the Dutch AEL in 2003 (De Koning and Meijer 2010). Although the mobilization attempt died out, the enthusiasm with which the AEL was met shows potential for politicization of both the ethnic Moroccan and the Muslim identities.

Since the demise of the AEL in 2003, young Moroccan Dutch have taken various initiatives to express discontent about and counter the group's negative image. However, none of these initiatives was met with the level of support the AEL initially received. An example are the—mostly—higher educated Moroccan Dutch girls who use both online and traditional media to improve the image of girls wearing headscarves. They present themselves in playful ways as individuals who are well integrated into Dutch society (e.g., "Headscarf Brigade" or the "Real Dutch" campaign by Al Nisa, advertising a Muslim girl eating a raw herring, a typical Dutch delicacy). Another, very different example are the young Moroccan Dutch boys who stirred up a riot in a neighborhood in Gouda, a Dutch provincial town, in 2008. Allegedly, discontent about the negative portrayal of Moroccan Dutch in the media catalyzed this riot. Because of the violent character of the protest, representatives of the Moroccan community rushed to distance themselves from it, emphasizing that the culprits were part of a small group, not representative of the Moroccan Dutch community (e.g., as expressed in a blog post by Naima El Yaakoubi, "A Mirror for the Moroccan Community," *Veiliggouda*, May 24, 2011).

In short, whereas the AEL was successful in articulating a common grievance and a message that resonated throughout the entire community, other initiatives failed to attract broad and sustained support. Internal disagreement on the group's boundaries and grievances seemed to nip the process of politicization in the bud. In the next paragraph, we describe how microlevel dynamics play a pivotal role in the politicization of collective identities.

Microlevel Dynamics

In this section, we describe, based on microlevel interactions among young Moroccan Dutch in focus groups, why the collective Moroccan identity fails to politicize. We show how the analytic concepts provided by Simon and Klandermans (2001) and particularly by Taylor and Whittier (1992) can be interpreted on the microlevel: interpretations of the sociopolitical context; adversarial attributions; boundary work, consciousness raising, and negotiations—all these characteristics of politicization can be observed when studying actual interactions between group members.

Boundary Drawing

In our focus group data, we found many references to the construction of group boundaries. Group boundaries were sometimes internally defined, but more often, participants referred to boundaries as imposed by native Dutch. Young Moroccan Dutch in our focus groups almost unanimously expressed that they felt addressed by native Dutch as "Moroccans":

> KHADIJA: I agree with her, but I think this whole Moroccan–Dutch thing... it is kind of imposed on you by the outside world because

> people tell you, "Hey, you are a Moroccan, oh, no, you are Dutch." You hear it in school, in the media, "You are a Moroccan, you are 'allochthonous.'"[2] (girl, academic-level education)

In Jenkins's (2004) terms, the Moroccan identity in this quotation is externally defined rather than internally. Although we found different strategies to deal with this imposed identity (cf. Eijberts and Roggeband 2008), the existence of boundaries defined by others is recognized among young Moroccan Dutch:

> MUSA: It's just subconscious and when you hear certain people talk then it becomes activated, and then you think hey, keep in mind which group you belong to, because either way, polarization is ongoing and at a certain moment you will have to choose to which group you belong, there will be no gray areas anymore. And that's just true. (boy, academic-level education)

This quotation shows that Moroccan and Dutch identities are experienced as mutually exclusive. The us–them distinction, vital for the politicization of a collective identity, is certainly present according to this respondent.

The politicizing effect of such an us–them distinction is also illustrated in the following fragment:

> SAID: I think integration will take a while. . . . The longer Moroccans are here, the more it fades away.
> SAMIR: I don't think so.
> SAID: They'll get used to different things.
> HASSAN: I don't think so because ten or fifteen years ago, nobody would talk about Moroccans and now . . .
> SAID: That's true.
> HASSAN: Then it would have to be better by now, then it should have become less . . .
> SAMIR: I think we are all coming to a certain climax, that things will really get out of hand. (boys, higher vocational training)

Here Said forwards his expectation that the us–them distinction between the Moroccan Dutch and the native Dutch will slowly fade away and that Moroccan Dutch will be accepted in Dutch society. Samir, on the contrary, tries to convince the group that the increasing negative attention on Moroccan Dutch will cause "a climax, that things will really get out of hand," possibly referring to a (violent) confrontation between Moroccan Dutch and native Dutch.

Despite initial contestation, in the course of this short interaction, Hassan and Said accept the politicized meaning given to Moroccan identity by Samir.

Although broad consensus is reached among young Moroccan Dutch regarding their excluded position in Dutch society and the salience of their ethnic and religious identities, it seemed difficult for group members to reach consensus on what Moroccan identity entails. Whereas many participants indicated "feeling Moroccan," they also often expressed "feeling Dutch" or expressed feelings of belonging to Dutch society:

> DRISS: I feel Moroccan, mainly Moroccan. It's more Moroccan in the Netherlands and in Morocco you are Dutch, that's always the same, but I mainly feel Moroccan, I'm also Dutch, I was raised here so . . . (boy, academic-level education)
>
> NAJET: We live here, we live our lives here, our family is here, of course. Even when we go to Antwerp for the weekend, I feel Dutch, because where do I go at the end of the weekend? We're going home. Where is my home? In [Dutch town]. (girl, higher vocational training)

In other words, the Moroccan identity as imposed by native Dutch is not and cannot be embraced by young Moroccan Dutch. The ambiguity of belonging to both groups causes the boundaries between identities to become unclear. Moreover, when discussing "typically Moroccan" attributes, no consensus was reached on whether these were actually Moroccan or Muslim, or neither:

> SALIMA: What does it mean for you to be a Moroccan?
> VIKRI: Speak the language, spend your holidays in Morocco.
> NASSIM: Family, family is important.
> VIKRI: Yeah, family is central, but I think that is true for other cultures as well, that is just, I think that it is something Islamic that family is really central and important.
> SALIMA: That is a difference with the Dutch culture, they put their parents in homes much more easily than we do, we don't do that so often.
> AMIR: Well, I see . . . I don't agree with you entirely. I mean, I know enough Dutch people who don't want to know about that either. . . . I also know many Surinamese families that really . . . appreciate family ties, so I don't really think it's something Islamic. (boys and girls, academic-level education and higher vocational training)

This extract illustrates that although young Moroccan Dutch readily refer to existing macrolevel cleavages, there is little agreement on the boundaries or content of their own collective identity. Despite the notion of mutual exclusiveness of Dutch and Moroccan identity on a macrolevel, the Moroccan Dutch identity as discussed on the microlevel does contain elements of the Moroccan and the Dutch. Where one identity ends and the other begins is often blurry. All in all, the clear us–them distinction imposed by the native Dutch becomes problematic when participants in our focus groups draw group boundaries in interaction with each other.

Consciousness Raising

In our focus groups, we found that young Moroccan Dutch often recount experiences in which they refer to the position of Moroccan Dutch in society. The following excerpt shows how interviewees reach consensus about the disadvantaged position in the labor market of the Moroccan Dutch as a group:

> HAKIM: There are just too many things to your disadvantage.
> NAJIM: Yeah, you've got to work twice as hard as a regular person, try twice as hard, it has got to do with many things.
> INTERVIEWER: Can you give an example?
> NAJIM: Like working, for example, you have to be able to prove yourself to your boss.
> HAKIM: Yeah, like he says, you have to be better than someone else to be as good, to have as many rights. You really have to be better than him. (boys, lower vocational training)

In this fragment, two boys share their perceptions of the deprivation of Moroccan Dutch in the job market. They feel Dutch employers will make Moroccan Dutch work harder than native Dutch to get the same recognition. The boys describe themselves as relatively deprived, reflecting macrolevel cleavages: they will have to work hard but are granted no securities about receiving equal treatment as their Dutch colleagues. The fact that a hypothetical experience is recounted, rather than a real one, tells us that the awareness of group membership is high. Moreover, the co-construction of this story by two participants points out that deprivation is not necessarily an individual but rather a collective experience shared by young Moroccan Dutch in the Netherlands (Prins, Van Stekelenburg, and Klandermans 2010).

Nevertheless, experiences of deprivation were not consistently agreed on. In the following extract, the discussion turns to Moroccan employers. One of the participants uses his personal experience to renegotiate the discriminative experience put forward previously:

IMRAAN: Yeah, but if you get hired by a Moroccan. He will not make a fuss when you are five minutes late.
ALI: Listen to me, . . . what he is saying, is not right.
INTERVIEWER: What is not right?
ALI: He says that when you get hired by a Moroccan you can come in late and that he will say yeah that's OK. . . . I got hired by a Moroccan last year and he really got mad and said, "You've got to show up in time, pal," and this year I got hired by a Dutch man and . . . when I'm late it's no problem, "Sure it can happen, no problem."
IMRAAN: It depends on the person.
NAJIM: Yeah, it depends on the person.
HAKIM: It has got nothing to do with whether you are a Moroccan or not.
ALI: It hasn't got anything to do with Moroccans. (boys, lower vocational training)

Here the deprived position of young Moroccan Dutch on the work floor, put forward earlier, is questioned by one of the participants. Ali instigates the other participants to reconsider the link between ethnic identity and the group's societal position: "It has got nothing to do with being Moroccan." Disagreement on the interpretation of the sociopolitical context, stemming from contradicting experiences on group and individual levels, seems to hamper consciousness raising, a prerequisite for politicization of collective identity.

Participants went as far as to accuse Moroccan Dutch of "playing the role of the victim":

SOUMAYA: What really annoys me is that allochthonous people among themselves, we often play the role of the victim. Very often they will say like "yeah, because we are allochthonous we have to prove ourselves more." Says who? You see, I am not different from any other Dutch student. I don't feel I have to prove myself more because I'm allochthonous.
HANAN: Yeah, we're just the same. (girls, academic-level education)

In many instances, we found that participants strongly expressed that "everybody has the chance to make it," stressing individual agency rather than collective deprivation. This indicates that, rather than using collective strategies that would signal politicization of Moroccan Dutch identity, Moroccan Dutch prefer individual mobility strategies to improve their position. Moreover, the awareness of belonging to a deprived group is not uncontested among group members. The lack of agreement on one of the group's central grievances reduces potential for the politicization of the Moroccan Dutch identity.

Negotiation

The preceding analyses show that before even involving third parties to negotiate the status quo in society at large (*triangulation* in Simon and Klandermans's terms), young Moroccan Dutch internally disagree on the boundaries of their identity and their position in society. The meanings of both the Moroccan and the Muslim identity are negotiated among in-group members rather than between in- and out-group members.

Internal contestation on the meaning and boundaries of Moroccan Dutch identity as well as on the interpretation of the sociopolitical context makes it difficult for young Moroccan Dutch to formulate a collective claim:

> INTERVIEWER: Would you consider taking action? Make a statement about discrimination in the media, at school, or at work?
> DRISS: Yeah, I think we would be number such-and-such or so and, yeah. What for exactly, and how?
> NAJET: Protest against whom?
> HAFIDA: Do you feel involved in student protests now that the new government is announcing cutbacks?
> EVERYONE: Yeah.
> HAFIDA: I really think that when all the students go demonstrate, that something will change.
> NAJET: But that isn't about Muslims.
> MUSA: But then you really have a goal. (boys and girls, academic-level education and higher vocational training)

This extract illustrates participants' willingness to join in collective action—as Dutch students. They feel they could make a difference when demonstrating against educational cutbacks. Evidently, a collective identity as students, as well as a shared grievance and an external enemy, are readily recognized among participants. At the same time, collective action on behalf of the Moroccan or Muslim identity seems inconceivable: "What for exactly, and how?" Moreover, the lack of adversarial attributions is manifested here: "Protest against whom?"

The negotiation by young Moroccan Dutch about the boundaries of the group's identity and the group's position in Dutch society prevents them from developing a clear sense of shared identity, shared grievances, and a shared adversary to blame. Although specific incidents may occasionally spark politicization among some Moroccan Dutch, without a mesolevel initiative to channel common grievances and make a collective claim, it remains improbable that young Moroccan Dutch will engage in collective action on behalf of their group.

Conclusion

In this chapter, we demonstrated that an analysis on the microlevel of concrete interactions in talk can shed light on the process of politicization of collective identities. The main frameworks regarding the politicization of collective identities (Taylor and Whittier 1992; Simon and Klandermans 2001) both emphasize the importance of group members' shared understanding of the collective identity, relevant out-groups, grievances felt, and claims to make. What they fail to make clear, however, is how group members arrive at these shared understandings, or contrarily, how they might fail to reach consensus.

Our argument has been that these processes of internal meaning making within groups are a crucial element in the politicization of collective identities and should be examined in detail if we want to better understand this process. We suggest that interviewing focus groups is a research method tailored for exactly this kind of examination. In focus groups, we can capture the process of joint meaning making—including negotiations on boundaries, shared grievances, and claims to make—on the spot.

Examining this process may also help us find answers to the puzzling question of why some collective identities—though all macrosocial indicators would predict them to—fail to politicize. An interesting question for future research would be what the contribution of organizers could be in facilitating consensus building in groups that struggle with the construction of a collective identity. After all, politicization of collective identities depends on whether individuals at the microlevel develop a sense of collective identity and a shared understanding of the relevant social cleavages and whether they are convinced by the call to action of mesolevel organizers. The case of young Moroccan Dutch shows us that politicization can be hampered by the lack of consensus on these key issues. Although the native Dutch still consider this group as mainly Moroccan, the negotiation among group members themselves on the boundaries of their collective identity and on the group's position in Dutch society can explain the failure of politicization to occur in a macrolevel context, which would predict the contrary.

Notes

1. Data presented here were collected between 2008 and mid-2010. Jacomijne Prins is currently conducting focus groups in which participants reflect on contentious events in the Arab countries since 2011. For this chapter, we could not take into account how solidarity with protest in the Arab world affects politicization of Muslim identity in the Netherlands.

2. Common Dutch word meaning "originating from another country."

References

Barth, Frederik. 1969. *Ethnic Groups and Boundaries.* Boston: Little, Brown.

Benford, Robert D., and David Snow. 2000. "Framing Processes and Social Movements: An Overview and Assessment." *Annual Review of Sociology* 26:611–39.

Boekkooi, Marije, Bert Klandermans, and Jacquelien van Stekelenburg. 2011. "Quarrelling and Protesting: How Organizers Shape a Demonstration." *Mobilization* 16, no. 2: 221–39.

Chryssochoou, Xenia. 2003. "Studying Identity in Social Psychology: Some Thoughts on the Definition of Identity and Its Relation to Action." *Journal of Language and Politics* 2:221–42.

Cohen, Anthony P. 1985. *The Symbolic Construction of Community.* London: Ellis Horwood.

De Jong, Jan Diederik Allard. 2007. *Kapot Moeilijk: Een Etnografisch Onderzoek naar Opvallend Delinquent Gedrag van "Marokkaanse" Jongens.* Amsterdam: Uitgeverij Aksant.

De Koning, Martijn. 2008. *Zoeken naar een "zuivere" islam: Geloofsbeleving en identiteitsvorming van jonge Marokkaans-Nederlandse moslims.* Amsterdam: Bert Bakker.

De Koning, Martijn, and Roel Meijer. 2010. "Going All the Way: Politicization and Radicalisation of the Hofstad Network in the Netherlands." In *Identity and Participation in Culturally Diverse Societies,* edited by Assaad E. Azzi, Xenia Chryssochoou, Bert Klandermans, and Bernd Simon, 220–38. West Sussex, U.K.: Wiley-Blackwell.

Eijberts, Melanie, and Conny Roggeband. 2008. "The Five Cs (Concealing, Conciling, Circumventing, Compensating, Confronting): How Muslim Migrant Women in the Netherlands Deal with Stereotypes about Them." Paper presented at the 10th International Interdisciplinary Conference about Women, Women's Worlds, Madrid.

Ersanilli, Evelyn, and Peter Scholten. 2009. "Inleiding." *Migrantenstudies* 1:2–6.

Gamson, William A. 1992. *Talking Politics.* New York: Cambridge University Press.

Ghorashi, Halleh. 2010. "From Absolute Invisibility to Extreme Visibility: Emancipation Trajectory of Migrant Women in the Netherlands." *Feminist Review* 94:75–92.

Gordijn, Ernestine H., Willem Koomen, and Diederik A. Stapel. 2001. "Level of Prejudice in Relation to Knowledge of Cultural Stereotypes." *Journal of Experimental Social Psychology* 37:150–57.

Hagendoorn, Louk, and José Pepels. 2003. "Why the Dutch Maintain More Social Distance from Some Ethnic Minorities Than Others: A Model Explaining the Ethnic Hierarchy." In *Integrating Immigrants in the Netherlands: Cultural versus Socio-economic Integration,* edited by Louk Hagendoorn, Justus Veenman, and Wilma Vollebergh, 41–61. Aldershot, U.K.: Ashgate.

Harchaoui, Sadik, and Chris Huinder, eds. 2003. *Stigma: Marokkaan! Over afstoten en insluiten van een ingebeelde bevolkingsgroep.* Utrecht: Forum, Instituut voor Multiculturele Ontwikkeling.

Jenkins, Richard. 2004. *Social Identity.* London: Routledge.

Ketner, Susan. 2009. "'Ik denk niet in culturen . . . ik denk eigenlijk meer in mijn geloof.' Waarom jongeren van Marokkaanse afkomst in Nederland de Moslimidentiteit zo sterk benadrukken. *Migrantenstudies* 1:73–87.

Klandermans, Bert. 1997. *The Social Psychology of Protest.* Oxford: Basil Blackwell.

Klandermans, Bert, and Marga de Weerd. 2000. "Group Identification and Social Protest." In *Self, Identity, and Social Movements,* edited by Sheldon Stryker, Timothy J. Owens, and Robert W. White, 68–90. Minneapolis: University of Minnesota Press.

Kriesi, Hanspeter, Ruud Koopmans, Jan Willem Duyvendak, and Marco G. Giugni. 1995. *New Social Movements in Western Europe.* Minneapolis: University of Minnesota Press.

Lipset, Seymour M., and Stein Rokkan. 1967. "Cleavage Structures, Party Systems, and Voter Alignments: An Introduction." In *Party Systems and Voter Alignments: Cross-National Perspectives,* edited by Seymour M. Lipset and Stein Rokkan, 1–64. New York: Free Press.

Margolis, Diane Rothbard. 1985. "Redefining the Situation: Negotiations on the Meaning of Woman." *Social Problems* 32:332–47.

Melucci, Alberto. 1989. *Nomads of the Present: Social Movements and Individual Needs in Contemporary Society.* London: Hutchinson Radius.

———. 1995. "The Process of Collective Identity." In *Social Movements and Culture,* edited by Hank Johnston and Bert Klandermans, 41–63. Minneapolis: University of Minnesota Press.

Miller, Arthur H., Patricia Gurin, Gerald Gurin, and Oksana Malanchuk. 1981. "Group Consciousness and Political Participation." *American Journal of Political Science* 25:494–511.

Morris, Aldon D. 1990. "Consciousness and Collective Action: Towards a Sociology of Consciousness and Domination." Paper presented at the annual meeting of the American Sociological Association, San Fransisco.

Nievers, Eline, and Iris Andriessen. 2010. *Discriminatiemonitor niet-westerse migranten op de arbeidsmarkt 2010.* The Hague: Netherlands Institute for Social Research.

Prins, Jacomijne, Jacquelien van Stekelenburg, and Bert Klandermans. 2010. "Storytelling and Identity Construction among Moroccan Adolescents in the Netherlands." Paper presented at the ISPP Annual Meeting, San Francisco.

Reicher, Stephen, and Nick Hopkins. 1996. "Seeking Influence through Characterizing Self-Categories: An Analysis of Anti-abortionist Rhetoric." *British Journal of Social Psychology* 35:297–311.

Simon, Bernd, and Bert Klandermans. 2001. "Politicized Collective Identity: A Social Psychological Analysis." *American Psychologist* 56:319–31.

Sniderman, Paul M., & Louk Hagendoorn. 2007. *When Ways of Life Collide: Multiculturalism and Its Discontents in the Netherlands.* Princeton, N.J.: Princeton University Press.

Taylor, Verta, and Nancy Whittier. 1992. "Collective Identity in Social Movement Communities: Lesbian Feminist Mobilization." In *Frontiers of Social Movement Theory,* edited by Aldon D. Morris and Carol Mueller, 104–29. New Haven, Conn.: Yale University Press.

Van Praag, C., ed. 2006. *Marokkanen in Nederland: een profiel.* The Hague: Nederlands Interdisciplinair Demografisch Instituut.

Van Stekelenburg, Jacquelien, and Bert Klandermans. 2007. "Individuals in Movements: A Social Psychology of Contention." In *Handbook of Social Movements across Disciplines,* edited by Bert Klandermans and Conny Roggeband, 157–204. New York: Springer.

———. 2010. "The Social Psychology of Protest." *Sociopedia.isa.* http://www.sagepub.net/isa/admin/viewPDF.aspx?&art=Protest.pdf.

Vliegenthart, Rens. 2007. "Framing Immigration and Integration: Facts, Parliament, Media, and Anti-immigrant Party Support in the Netherlands." PhD diss., VU-University.

Welschen, Saskia. 2010. "Making Sense of Being South African: The Analysis of National Identity Construction in Talk." Paper presented at the World Congress on Sociology, Gothenburg.

Discussion: Opening the Black Box of Dynamics in Theory and Research on the Demand Side of Protest

Martijn van Zomeren

Discussing the chapters in this section of this book has been an inspiring enterprise. As an experimental social psychologist studying collective action against collective disadvantage, I particularly appreciate the broad, diverse, and insightful contributions that all chapters make to our knowledge of when, why, and how people protest. For instance, Klandermans (chapter 1) provides a thoughtful overview of the dynamic demand side of protest, whereas Taylor (chapter 3) discusses important social–psychological dynamics such as the role of emotions in the politicization of grievances. The dynamics of the politicization of identity similarly play a large role in Van Doorn, Prins, and Welschen's (chapter 4) discussion of how narratives can reveal insights about the content of disadvantaged group members' identity. Finally, Polletta and colleagues (chapter 2) discuss how the advent of the Internet (and, in particular, the dynamic nature of social media) might alter the very practice of mobilization.

I found all contributions to be thought provoking, yet I could not escape the sense that something was lacking from all contributions. The word *dynamics* united these contributions by making visible a considerable gap in their collective focus: a lack of explicit theorizing about the psychological processes that constitute these dynamics. This resembles a black box: something goes in (e.g., identity, grievances, emotion), and something comes out (e.g., mobilization, protest), but too little is said about the psychological processes in between. This box is not Pandora's—in fact, I believe that opening it will be fruitful rather than destructive.

For instance, many approaches still focus implicitly or explicitly on individuals' instrumental motivations to protest, assuming an underlying cost–benefit calculus (e.g., Polletta et al., chapter 2). However, individuals are often unable and/or unwilling to carefully calculate thus (Tversky and Kahneman 1974). Instrumentality is just one way by which situations can become psychologically self-relevant—a precondition for any motivated action (Lazarus 1991). Events can also become self-relevant through individuals' identity, emotion, and morality concerns (Lazarus 1991). Yet a clear theory of how self-relevance translates into different motivations for action is typically missing from the literature. As such, important aspects of the demand side of contention are not yet sufficiently grounded in psychological theories. It thus remains unclear whether often implicit assumptions about what makes individuals tick accurately and comprehensively reflect what actually makes them tick.

Therefore I suggest that more *integration* is needed between different approaches and that scholars should more strongly ground their models in psychological theory and research. A beneficial consequence of this development would be that psychological research will then also be better equipped to learn from different approaches because they share similar assumptions about what makes humans tick. These recommendations fit with the ideas that explaining individuals' motivation to participate in collective action requires an understanding of their psychology and that a key challenge for the field is to integrate psychological explanations with social and political explanations (Van Zomeren, Postmes, and Spears 2008). This requires an accurate understanding of what makes individuals tick, and therefore we need to open the black box of dynamics.

The Need to Open the Black Box

I start with arguing that there is such a thing as a black box of dynamics and that it needs to be opened. For instance, Van Doorn, Prins, and Welschen note that the concept and operationalization of politicized identity is often ambiguous. This is unfortunate because it has become a key concept in predicting social movement participation and collective action more generally (Simon and Klandermans 2001; Van Zomeren et al. 2008). This theoretical fuzziness is traceable to a lack of psychological theorizing because identity scholars in the social movement tradition typically do not differentiate between *self* and *identity*. As a consequence, they rely on the assumption that individuals are motivated to protect and maintain established identities (e.g., Simon et al. 1998; Stürmer and Simon 2004), which in fact makes it hard to explain how such established identities change or transform (e.g., McGarty et al. 2009). This is somewhat ironic because the transformation of an established identity (e.g., being gay) into a politicized identity (e.g., being a member of the gay movement) should increase participation in collective action.

Research suggests that identity formation and transformation start with an individual's changing *self-definition* as a group member (e.g., Postmes et al. 2005; Drury and Reicher 2009; McGarty et al. 2009). This is because, relatively independently of individuals' established identities, their *personal* or *group* selves can become salient in response to an event (i.e., subjectively defining the self as "I" or "we"; Turner et al. 1987). This is important if we want to explain how identities politicize because the self is viewed as more strongly context dependent than an established identity (yet an equally rich source of motivation). In fact, individuals do not act on events that are not psychologically self-relevant (Lazarus 1991). A focus on the personal or group self in response to events is thus more appropriate than a focus on established identities when we want to explain the dynamics of identity formation and transformation processes.

This strong situational perspective is grounded in the self-categorization theory (Turner et al. 1987), which conceptualizes personal and group levels of self that motivate individuals' behavior (see also Simon et al. 1998). Both selves are made salient by situations—for instance, being emerged in a crowd easily makes salient the group self. The group self is motivationally concerned with group desires and goals (which may or may not fit a particular established group identity), whereas the personal self is motivationally concerned with personal desires and goals (which often do not fit with a particular established group identity). In narrative approaches to group identity, such as the approach of Van Doorn, Prins, and Welschen, where Dutch Moroccans talk about their group, one could therefore wonder whether it is the "I" or the "we" that is talking about one's established identity. Is it the *personal self* viewing group identity as a tool to fulfill personal desires or achieve personal goals? Or is it the *group self* seeking to fulfill group desires and achieve group goals (e.g., as Dutch Moroccans or as Muslims)? We can only know if we clearly differentiate between situational selves and established identities.

The practical implication of a clear differentiation between self and identity is to focus on the group self (if possible, in conjunction with an established group identity) in framing and other mobilization attempts. This should be effective because (1) one can thus motivate both higher and lower identifiers with the group (whereas a focus on an established identity would only resonate with those already highly identified) and (2) one can focus on the content of the event rather than the content of individuals' group identity (which is notoriously difficult to describe). I am not suggesting here that established identities are unimportant in explaining collective action (on the contrary, see Simon et al. 1998; Van Zomeren et al. 2008), but I believe that to open the black box of dynamics, we need a dynamic rather than a static conceptualization of self at the center of our explanations (see also Drury and Reicher 2009; McGarty et al. 2009).

A second indication that the black box of dynamics exists and should be opened comes from Polletta and colleagues, who explore how the advent of the Internet might have changed the dynamics of mobilization. They suggest that online protest decreases the threshold for participation and undermines the assumption that protest occurs in the public domain. As such, they claim that collective action has become less costly, which implies that it has become easier to mobilize individuals. After all, clicking a button to sign an online petition in private does not take much effort, and despite its low cost, online action may still be effective given the potential power in numbers that can be wielded over the Internet. However, Polletta and colleagues seem to lean heavily on the assumption that individuals instrumentally calculate the costs and benefits of collective action. Although the literature suggests that (some) individuals have instrumental motivations for participating, we also know that individuals are often unable or unwilling to carefully calculate the pros and cons of participation (Tversky and Kahneman 1974). Moreover, although individuals might often seem to engage in such a calculus, they are actually rationalizing their unconscious motivations (e.g., Haidt and Kesebir 2010). For these and other reasons (see Van Zomeren and Spears 2009), it is doubtful whether individual cost–benefit calculation is as important as many believe. Furthermore, Polletta and colleagues do not engage with the question whether the lowered costs of protest might have effects on other psychological motivations for protest. How does online mobilization affect psychological self-relevance? How does it affect individuals' emotional experiences? These questions emphasize that individuals' motivations requires that individuals see an event as psychologically self-relevant and that this can translate into different motivations for action (e.g., instrumental and identity-based motivation; Simon et al. 1998; Stürmer and Simon 2004).

Different from approaches like that of Simon et al. (1998), however, individuals' motivations to engage in collective action are also strongly linked with the *emotion process*. Indeed, Klandermans and Taylor both emphasize the importance of emotions (in particular, anger), but both are also less clear about their conceptualization of emotions and the psychological processes by which individuals come to experience these emotions. A good example comes from Taylor's chapter in this volume, where it is noted that righteous indignation, as a form of anger, is a potent emotion with respect to motivating protest because it leads individuals to challenge those in power. However, how it is evoked, how it is different from nonrighteous indignation, and why exactly it leads to challenge (rather than, for instance, powerless rumination) all remain unclear. Psychological theory and research on emotion have much to say on these issues. This work views emotion as a continuous psychological process, with anger, for instance, following the cognitive appraisal of self-relevance and blame for unfairness (Frijda 1986; Lazarus 1991, 2001). It views the experience of anger, unlike many other negative emotional states, as including a distinct *approach* motivation with a physiology that discerns anger from other negative emotions (Carver and Harmon-Jones 2009; in the context of social movements, see Klandermans et al. 2008; Klandermans, chapter 1). This should be important to social movement scholars if one assumes that evoking particular emotional states facilitates mobilization. Indeed, according to Lazarus (1991), any analysis of motivation has to include psychological processes concerning the self, emotion, and other types of motivation. In this sense, the influential and pioneering work of Simon et al. (1998) seems incomplete to the extent that it does not provide a clear theoretical account of emotions in the context of collective action.

Klandermans comes much closer to proposing an explicit psychological process model that includes identity, emotion, and instrumental motivation (see also Van Stekelenburg et al. 2009, 2011). In this model, collective identity underlies instrumental, emotional, but also ideological antecedents of individuals' motivational strengths to participate. The model suggests that a sense of collective identity underlies instrumental and ideological reasons for collective action, both of which are amplified by group-based anger. This model is broad in its scope, and I have no doubt about its strong predictive power. However, unlike the Simon et al. (1998) model, Klandermans's model predicts the motivational strength of people who have already participated in collective action. This implies that the model may not be as general as Simon et al.'s (1998) model (despite being more complete in an analytic sense). Furthermore, it is doubtful whether individuals' senses of collective identity causally affect individuals' instrumental and/or ideological motivations (e.g., Van Zomeren, Spears, and Leach 2008, study 2). An alternative (but not mutually exclusive) hypothesis would be that threats to group interests or ideology are the very reason why individuals experience increased group identification (Van Zomeren et al. 2004, Experiment 1; Van Zomeren, Postmes, and Spears 2011). In fact, this is the case because of the resonance between the group self that is made salient by such threats and the established group identity. Moreover, because of the causal primacy of identity, the Klandermans model does not allow for individuals to act collectively on the basis of their personal selves. For instance, individuals sometimes protest because of violated personal convictions (Van Zomeren, Postmes, and Spears 2011) or as the outcome of a personal cost–benefit calculus (Klandermans 1984). This illustrates how easily assumptions about human motivation slip into the predictive models we have about collective action and social movement participation and therefore why it would be a good idea to acknowledge that there is a black box of dynamics that should be opened.

Opening the Black Box

In the following, I outline an integrative perspective on the psychological processes that might reside inside the black box of dynamics. The dynamic dual-pathway model of coping with collective disadvantage (for a detailed discussion, see Van Zomeren, Leach, and Spears 2012) aims to identify the different psychological processes that explain why individuals become motivated to protest, whether and how these different processes relate to each other, and how undertaking collective action feeds back into the motivations that led them to act. In contrast to other models (Simon et al. 1998; Klandermans, chapter 1), this model aims to be explicitly dynamic in a psychological sense. To meet this aim, the model is grounded in psychological theory and research about coping (e.g., Lazarus 1991, 2001), which can be viewed as a system of psychological mechanisms that helps the individual adaptively respond to events by, for instance, motivating action (Lazarus 1991, 2001).

According to Lazarus (1991), individuals deal with situational threats to the self (which include, but are not restricted to, established identities) by focusing on their *cognitive appraisals* of the situation, which helps them to adapt to the situation. These attempts at adaptation are called *coping* and are integral to how individuals manage threats in their daily lives. Collective action is thus viewed as one out of many ways to cope with situational threats to individuals' personal or group interests, identities, and moral standards (see also Ellemers 1993; Wright 2009). The added value of a coping approach is that it suggests that what follows from perceiving one's group to be threatened is far from simple and straightforward—individuals may act on the threat individually or collectively, they may remain indifferent, or they may try to avoid it altogether (physically, but also psychologically in terms of denial). This is reminiscent of the idea that grievances per se might not predict collective action (Klandermans, chapter 1)—in fact, a coping approach identifies important factors that facilitate such approach coping and offers a psychological process model of the dynamics in the black box.

The input for coping is, first and foremost, the appraisal of *self-relevance*—is this event sufficiently relevant to the self (Lazarus 1991)? The role of established identities here is that they lower the threshold for which events become self-relevant (e.g., feminists are more likely to respond collectively to events about women's disadvantage), but situational aspects might make the personal or a different group self salient (i.e., "I" as a unique person, "we" as social movement scholars). Thus self-relevance includes the dynamic and situational self as described by self-categorization theory as well as established identities. If an event is appraised as self-relevant, a select number of different cognitive appraisals guide how individuals cope with the self-relevant event (Lazarus 1991). In the context of collective action, coping is directed at activating adaptive responses to the environment as a function of appraisals of *external blame for unfairness* (e.g., the government or other authorities) and *coping potential* (e.g., in-group support, power, efficacy, resources). The more strongly individuals appraise external blame for their unfair situation, the more strongly they experience group-based anger and a strong motivation to act collectively. This psychological process, with group-based anger at its core, is called *emotion-focused approach coping* (see Folkman and Moskowitz 2004). It aims to redress the disrupted balance in the self-environment relationship through emotional approach.

In addition, theory and research show that the more coping potential individuals appraise, the more strongly they perceive the efficacy of their group to achieve its goal, which leads to their motivation to act collectively. This psychological process, with group efficacy beliefs at its core, is called *problem-focused approach coping*. It aims to redress the disrupted balance in the self–environment relationship to solve the problem at hand through unified effort. Both types of coping can be activated after a threat to individuals' personal or group interests, identities, and moral standards makes the situation self-relevant. The dynamic part of the model is that engaging in collective action, or any outcome of coping for that matter, can feed back into these cognitive appraisals of self-relevance, blame for unfairness, and group efficacy. This implies that individuals continuously monitor their situations and thus also monitor their need to cope. This elaborate line of thought adds to our understanding of what makes humans tick and moves theoretically beyond the Simon et al. (1998) and Klandermans models.

The empirical evidence for the coping model is fairly solid (as it is for the broader coping perspective; for reviews, see Folkman and Moskowitz 2004; Lazarus 1991, 2001). This is particularly true for the causal arrows in the model. For instance, Van Zomeren et al. (2004) experimentally manipulated theorized antecedents of group-based anger and group efficacy (i.e., appraised unfairness and in-group support, respectively). As predicted, they found that appraisals that the group was unfairly treated increased group-based anger and that appraisals that the group supported collective action increased group efficacy beliefs. In turn, both group-based anger and group efficacy increased individuals' willingness to engage in collective action.

Furthermore, Van Zomeren, Spears, and Leach (2008) investigated the role of self-relevance in how individuals cope through emotion- or problem-focused approaches. Following up a field study that showed that group identification affected willingness to act through group-based anger, they asked participants in one experimental condition to describe a day in their lives as a "student" or as a "unique individual." Results showed that this manipulation increased individuals' group-based anger and their willingness to engage in student action in the student relative to the unique individual condition. Thus self-relevance facilitated emotion-focused approach coping. However, both studies showed that self-relevance moderated problem-focused approach coping; that is, group efficacy beliefs were of particular importance for those who perceived the situation as self-relevant for their personal selves. These findings support the view that the psychological self-relevance of a situation is key to activating coping and that different forms of approach coping are promoted by the experience of group-based anger and group efficacy. Through a coping approach, we thus move beyond a distinction between instrumental and identity-based motivations for collective action (Simon et al. 1998; Stürmer and Simon 2004). This also allows both the personal and group selves to be involved in motivations to undertake collective action.

Van Zomeren, Postmes, and Spears (2011) also found empirical evidence for the dynamic nature of the model. Multiple experiments found that individuals who signed a petition had stronger group efficacy beliefs than those who did not sign or did not have the opportunity to do so (see also Van Stekelenburg and Klandermans 2007; Drury and Reicher 2009). By contrast, they did not evince a stronger sense of group identification. This is important in thinking about how action changes actors in general and, more specifically, about how identities politicize (Van Doorn, Prins, and Welschen, chapter 4), how the Internet affects individuals' motivations to protest (Polletta et al., chapter 2), and how positive emotions might be important to consider (Klandermans, chapter 1; Taylor, chapter 3).

Implications of Opening the Black Box

What is the added value for social movement scholars to open the black box of dynamics? Although other frameworks, such as those of Simon et al. (1998) and Klandermans, have strong merits of their own, the dynamic dual-pathway model is broader than Simon and colleagues' model because it focuses on appraised self-relevance as well as on established identities; it specifies the consequences of self-relevance in terms of different coping strategies; it specifically views emotions as integral to the coping process; and it is explicitly dynamic in terms of feedback loops. The dynamic dual-pathway model is also more general than Klandermans's model because it does not restrict itself to predicting the behavior of those already participating in collective action and allows for motivated action based in the personal self. Therefore this model provides a good basis for individuals' motivations to undertake collective action. This has implications for work on collective action and social movements.

For instance, an interesting missing aspect in the work by Van Doorn, Prins, and Welschen is at which level of self (personal or group) established identities are discussed when individuals engage in identity talk. Which self is talking? Recent work by Postmes and colleagues (2005) on the psychological process of *inductive identity formation* suggests that identities can form and transform through interpersonal interactions that make salient both the personal and group selves. When an individual thinks about her personal self as a unique part of the group, the individual's identification with the group becomes grounded in the idea that "everyone can be herself." This avoids the feeling of interchangeability of group members (e.g., anyone could do this) and promotes thinking about one's own unique contribution to the group. Perhaps this is one reason why the Moroccan Dutch engaged in identity talk in the chapter by Van Doorn, Prins, and Welschen did not politicize—they were thinking about themselves *only* as group members but not as individuals that could contribute to their group's efforts to fight discrimination. Discussing their established identity from this point of view will actually be more effective in changing and transforming that identity (in terms of politicization) because it will allow individuals to connect to both the group and their personal contributions to it. This nicely illustrates the point that scholars need to differentiate between self and identity.

The importance of self-relevance, emotion, and the multifaceted nature of motivation becomes particularly pronounced when thinking about Polletta and colleagues' ideas about the instrumental benefits of online protest. The argument that online actions have lower thresholds particularly applies to those who perceive collective disadvantage as personally self-relevant—in fact, such persons rely on instrumental motivation more than those who view it as relevant to their group selves. There is certainly a healthy rationale for focusing on lower identifiers given that these typically constitute the vast majority of any mobilization potential. However, there might be other motivational consequences too—for instance, social psychological research on online versus offline communication reveals that online communication easily makes the group self-salient because individuals are not distracted by personal cues such as in face-to-face communication (Spears et al. 2002). Thus online mobilization strategies might lower the costs of action but also speak to the group self, which might culminate in emotion-focused approach coping (Van Zomeren, Postmes, and Spears 2008). Moreover, Polletta and colleagues' argument actually suggests that online mobilization should also facilitate problem-focused approach coping if lowering the costs of action translates psychologically into increased group efficacy beliefs. In this sense, Polletta and colleagues' argument about the facilitating nature of online mobilization illustrates the enormous potential of the Internet to facilitate mobilization and social change.

It is important to emphasize that emotions are an integral part of any coping framework. An interesting question is which emotions are relevant to approach coping in terms of collective action. Although there is an understandable and strong focus in the literature on anger and related emotional labels (e.g., outrage, indignation, resentment), both Taylor and Klandermans suggest that *positive emotions,* such as pride and hope, might be important as well. These suggestions raise the question whether hope and pride constitute unique motivational pathways and whether it is possible to integrate hope and pride within a coping framework. This is not a rhetorical question—in fact, Lazarus (1991, 282) suggested that hope is a "problematic emotion" because most key appraisals do not seem to predict it. I hypothesize that group-based pride is associated with the psychological self-relevance of the group and thus with emotion-focused approach coping (e.g., stronger pride, stronger anger). Hope, however, should be associated with strong group efficacy beliefs and thus be part of problem-focused approach coping. This integration could easily be tested, for example, in the context of the emotion rituals and emotional resonance that Taylor discusses in the context of social movements.

I have focused thus far on how psychological process models might inform social movement scholars in terms of what makes humans tick. Of course, this is not to say that psychological researchers cannot learn much from approaches that focus on social movements and, more broadly, politics. For example, political process models (e.g., McAdam 1982; McAdam, Tarrow, and Tilly 2001) force psychological process models to specify how *political* processes may or may not be mediated by *psychological* processes, and vice versa. For instance, political process models suggest that grievances, organizational strength, and political opportunities are necessary for mobilization to occur. One could argue that these factors first need to be translated into individual motivation (i.e., become psychologically self-relevant) before individuals will engage in any action. Thus grievances and organizational strength need to be felt and experienced—which fits nicely with the experience of emotion- and problem-focused types of approach coping. The proof of the pudding here would be to test whether indicators of grievances and organizational strength *only* predict mobilization when individuals experience them as such.

Similarly, resource mobilization models could focus on the largely undiscovered country of psychological resources that have not yet attracted much attention beyond psychology. For instance, positive emotions can be viewed as resources because they build up a reservoir of psychological and social resources (energy, self-esteem, networks; Frederickson 2001). Such a reservoir can turn threats into challenges ("yes we can!"), which should lead to approach behavior (see also Drury and Reicher 2009). Similarly, sharing positive emotions, such as hope and pride, binds groups and communities together, which enables powerful co-action (Van Zomeren et al. 2008). In fact, it might be the experience of these positive emotions that plays a large role in the politicization of identities (Drury and Reicher 2009).

There is much to learn about how the politicization of identity occurs (Van Doorn, Prins, and Welschen, chapter 4; Taylor, chapter 3). Theory and research employing different approaches may shed different light on this issue. For instance, if we view politicized identity as just another established identity and thus just another indicator of self-relevance, then the dynamic dual-pathway model does not require any change. Yet, if a politicized identity is something special, then the dynamic dual-pathway model forces scholars to specify how it is special in terms of individuals' multifaceted motivations. Does a politicized identity include a chronic sense of group-based anger (e.g., related to shared grievances and adversarial attributions; Simon and Klandermans 2001) and/or group efficacy beliefs? If so, the model can accommodate this construct. But if there is something special about the construct, the model should be adapted to integrate this unique quality of a politicized identity. It is therefore up to future theory and research, be it in psychology or sociology or political science, to show what this unique quality is.

An undertheorized aspect of politicized identity might relate to Klandermans's ideology variable (see Van Stekelenburg et al. 2009). Klandermans focuses specifically on violated values as core determinants of individuals' motivational strengths. Although Lazarus (1991) views the violation of values as increasing appraised self-relevance, this motivation is not yet made explicit in the dynamic dual-pathway model. We have reason to believe from correlational data (Van Zomeren et al. 2011) that violations of individuals' moral convictions uniquely politicize individuals' identities. This is because moral convictions carry strong self-relevance and imply strong and absolute norms that resonate with the strong and absolute norms that we believe are often part of the content of a politicized identity. Indeed, moral convictions are extremely self-relevant and thus easily initiate the coping process. This tells us something new about the psychological process of politicization—that it is the powerful combination of violated moral convictions and politicized identities that unleashes a strong motivation to participate in collective action.

Conclusion

In this discussion chapter, I identified a black box called "dynamics" indicative of the larger literature on collective action and social movements. I challenged scholars to get more specific in terms of what makes humans tick (with a focus on self-relevance and the multifaceted nature of human motivation). I believe, too, that little note is taken from psychological theorizing that suggests that collective disadvantages are not simply threats but threats with which one needs to cope; that self does not equate to identity; and that insights from theory and research on coping provide insights into the psychological processes by which individuals manage their changing environments such as the changing demand side of protest. I hope that scholars from different disciplines will rise up collectively to meet this challenge.

Note

This discussion chapter was supported by VENI-grant 451-09-003 from the Netherlands Organisation for Scientific Research (NWO).

References

Carver, Charles S., and Eddie Harmon-Jones. 2009. "Anger Is an Approach-Related Affect: Evidence and Implications." *Psychological Bulletin* 135:183–204.

Drury, John, and Stephen Reicher. 2009. "Collective Psychological Empowerment as a Model of Social Change: Researching Crowds and Power." *Journal of Social Issues* 65:707–25.

Ellemers, Naomi. 1993. "The Influence of Socio-structural Variables on Identity Management Strategies." *European Review of Social Psychology* 4:22–57.

Folkman, Susan, and Judith T. Moskowitz. 2004. "Coping: Pitfalls and Promise." *Annual Review of Psychology* 55:745–74.

Frederickson, Barbara L. 2001. "The Role of Positive Emotions in Positive Psychology: The Broaden-and-Build Theory of Positive Emotions." *American Psychologist* 56:218–26.

Frijda, Nico H. 1986. *The Emotions.* Cambridge: Cambridge University Press.

Haidt, Jonathan, and Selin Kesebir. 2010. "Morality." In *Handbook of Social Psychology,* 5th ed., edited by Susan Fiske, Daniel Gilbert, and Graham Lindzey, 797–832. Hoboken, N.J.: John Wiley.

Klandermans, Bert. 1984. "Mobilization and Participation: Social-Psychological Expansions of Resource Mobilization Theory." *American Sociological Review* 49:583–600.

Klandermans, Bert, Jojanneke van der Toorn, and Jacquelien van Stekelenburg. 2008. "Embeddedness and Identity: How Immigrants Turn Grievances into Action." *American Sociological Review* 73:992–1012.

Lazarus, Richard S. 1991. *Emotion and Adaptation.* New York: Oxford University Press.

———. 2001. "Relational Meaning and Discrete Emotions." In *Appraisal Processes in Emotion,* edited by Klaus R. Scherer, Angela Schorr, and Tom Johnstone, 37–67. Oxford: Oxford University Press.

McAdam, Doug. 1982. *Political Processes and the Development of Black Insurgency.* Chicago: University of Chicago Press.

McAdam, Doug, Sidney Tarrow, and Charles Tilly. 2001. *Dynamics of Contention.* Cambridge: Cambridge University Press.

McGarty, Craig, Ana-Maria Bliuc, Emma F. Thomas, and Renata Bongiorno. 2009. "Collective Action as the Material Expression of Group Membership." *Journal of Social Issues* 65:839–57.

Postmes, Tom, Russell Spears, Antonia T. Lee, and Rosemary J. Novak. 2005. "Individuality and Social Influence in Groups: Inductive and Deductive Routes to Group Identity." *Journal of Personality and Social Psychology* 89:747–63.

Simon, Bernd, and Bert Klandermans. 2001. "Politicized Collective Identity: A Social-Psychological Analysis." *American Psychologist* 56:319–31.

Simon, Bernd, Michael Loewy, Stefan Stürmer, Ulrike Weber, Peter Freytag, Corinna Habig, Claudia Kampmeier, and Peter Spahlinger. 1998. "Collective Identification and Social Movement Participation." *Journal of Personality and Social Psychology* 74:646–58.

Spears, Russell, Martin Lea, Rolf A. Corneliussen, Tom Postmes, and Wouter Ter Haar. 2002. "Computer-Mediated Communication as a Channel for Social Resistance: The Strategic Side of SIDE." *Small Group Research* 33:555–74.

Stürmer, Stefan, and Bernd Simon. 2004. "Collective Action: Towards a Dual-Pathway Model." In *European Review of Social Psychology,* edited by Wolfgang Stroebe and Miles Hewstone, 59–99. Hove, U.K.: Psychology Press.

Turner, John C., Michael A. Hogg, Penelope J. Oakes, Stephen D. Reicher, and Margaret S. Wetherell. 1987. *Rediscovering the Social Group: A Self-Categorization Perspective.* Oxford: Basil Blackwell.

Tversky, Amos, and Daniel Kahneman. 1974. "Judgment under Uncertainty: Heuristics and Biases." *Science* 27, no. 1974: 1124–31.

Van Stekelenburg, Jacquelien, and Bert Klandermans. 2007. "Individuals in Movements: A Social Psychology of Contention." In *Handbook of Social Movements,* edited by Bert Klandermans and Conny M. Roggebrand, 157–204. New York: Kluwer.

Van Stekelenburg, Jacquelien, Bert Klandermans, and Wilco W. van Dijk. 2009. "Context Matters: Explaining How and Why Mobilizing Context Influences Motivational Dynamics." *Journal of Social Issues* 65:815–38.

———. 2011. "Combining Motivations and Emotion: The Motivational Dynamics of Collective Action Participation." *Revista de Psicología Social* 25:131–44.

Van Zomeren, Martijn, Colin W. Leach, and Russell Spears. 2012. "A Dynamic Dual Pathway Model of Coping with Collective Disadvantage." *Personality and Social Psychology Review* 16:180–99.

Van Zomeren, Martijn, Tom Postmes, and Russell Spears. 2008. "Toward an Integrative Social Identity Model of Collective Action: A Quantitative Research Synthesis of Three Socio-psychological Perspectives." *Psychological Bulletin* 134:504–35.

———. 2011. "Can Moral Convictions Motivate the Advantaged to Challenge Social Inequality? Extending the Social Identity Model of Collective Action." *Group Processes and Intergroup Relations* 14:735–54.

Van Zomeren, Martijn, and Russell Spears. 2009. "Metaphors of Protest: A Classification of Motivations for Collective Action." *Journal of Social Issues* 65:661–80.

Van Zomeren, Martijn, Russell Spears, Agneta H. Fischer, and Colin W. Leach. 2004. "Put Your Money Where Your Mouth Is! Explaining Collective Action Tendencies through Group-Based Anger and Group Efficacy." *Journal of Personality and Social Psychology* 87:649–64.

Van Zomeren, Martijn, Russell Spears, and Colin W. Leach. 2008. "Exploring Psychological Mechanisms of Collective Action: Does the Relevance of Group Identity Influence How People Cope with Collective Disadvantage?" *British Journal of Social Psychology* 47:353–72.

Wright, Stephen C. 2009. "The Next Generation of Collective Action Research." *Journal of Social Issues* 65:859–79.

II
Organizations and Networks: The Supply Side of Contention

5
The Changing Supply Side of Mobilization: Questions for Discussion

Conny Roggeband and Jan Willem Duyvendak

Social Change and How It Affects the Supply Side of Contention

Three interrelated processes of social change described by social analysts of (post)modernity and globalization affect the supply side of contention: (1) the emergence of "light" communities, which result from processes of individualization and globalization and are facilitated by the proliferation of the Internet; (2) the shift from identity politics to light identities and issue-oriented politics; and (3) the homogenization of light communities, which may lead to processes of exclusion and the reproduction of inequalities. We think these sociological processes raise a number of relevant and urgent questions for debate among social movement scholars. By focusing on larger sociological processes, we aim to provide insight into developments regarding individual and collective identities as well as possible consequences for mobilization efforts.

The Emergence of Light Communities

Traditional networks and organizations (political parties, unions, churches) have lost their mobilizing force in many Western countries. Empirical sociological research and theory (Wuthnow 1994, 1998; Putnam 2000; Putnam et al. 2002; Brint 2001) show changing engagement of individuals with traditional networks and organizations. According to scholars like Putnam (2000; Putnam et al. 2002) and Skocpol (2003), people are less willing to create and maintain meaningful collectives such as civic associations. Other scholars, such as Etzioni (1996) and Wuthnow (1994), contend that communities are eroding and that in mass society, communities of individuals become fragmented into atomized units. Bauman (2001) argues that new forms of light or liquid communities are emerging, which are able to generate more expressive, temporal, and issue-oriented forms of participation. More and more people avoid heavy, long-term engagements and leave more formal institutions for looser engagements in informal, sometimes temporarily, or issue-specific networks (Schudson 2006; Zukin et al. 2006; Dalton 2008). More "porous" bonds (Wuthnow 1998) and a dissolving civil society (Dekker 2002) produce lighter communities. Sociopolitical participation is increasingly rooted in everyday networks of participants, and (potential) actors are likely to be involved in diffuse and decentralized networks rather than in formal organizations (Taylor 2000; Duyvendak and Hurenkamp 2004). Whereas greedy or heavier institutions and communities were time consuming, created strong bonds and loyalties, and promoted strong socialization processes resulting in profiled collective identities, these light communities are far more informal, open, temporary, and flexible, resulting in loose ties, short-term engagements, and lower identification (Duyvendak and Hurenkamp 2004). The different chapters in this section, in particular, those of Rucht (chapter 9) and Staggenborg (chapter 7), provide nice examples of such loosely coupled activist networks (see also Van Stekelenburg and Boekkooi, chapter 11).

Although networks as such are certainly not new, globalization may be enhancing their prevalence and scope (Smith and Fetner 2007). The macrosociological process of globalization has altered the landscape of mobilization and created new, more fluid *socioscapes* (Urry 2005), in which people acting on the basis of local information and relationships may initiate action that, through cyberspace and other channels, may impact distant places and peoples. As Urry states, such fluid structures demonstrate no clear point of departure and no necessary end state or purpose. These fluid systems "create over time their own context for action rather than being 'caused' by such contexts" (246). The clearest example of such a global fluid system is the Internet, which has resulted in an increasing pervasiveness of virtual networks in sociopolitical life. We think that these are one of the clearest examples of the new light communities to which we refer (Wellman and Giulia 1999; Wellman et al. 2001). The Internet facilitates forms of electronically mediated participation that have created conditions for the emergence of new kinds of highly fluid, mobilizing structures that tend to be far less structured, with networks that are more open and participatory and articulated across a wide variety of issues (see also Polletta et al., chapter 2, and Van Stekelenburg and Boekkooi, chapter 11). Another, nonvirtual contemporary example of a light community is the Occupy movement, with its fluid and changing constellations. These movements cannot be easily understood within existing frameworks. Chadwick (2007) argues that the Internet encourages "organizational hybridity." Established interest groups, parties, and social movement organizations are experiencing processes of hybridization. New organizational forms are emerging that exist only in hybrid form and that could not function in the ways they did without the Internet and the complex spatial and temporal interactions it facilitates. Individuals now create loose networks based on online forums, blogs, and open databases. This results in self-organized protests and political action in the absence of an interest group or other central coordination or affiliation. Yet more formal organizations with solid structures, such as classic political parties and trade unions, are also increasingly active on the Internet and make use of social media such as Facebook and Twitter. These organizations simultaneously use diverse ways of organizing and mobilizing, blending online and offline efforts, using virtual spaces, and crossing national boundaries. Collective action space thus becomes more diverse and invaded by a wide range of different actors, organizational forms, and repertoires. Rucht, in his contribution to this section, provides a useful taxonomy for mapping the diverse and sometimes hybrid structural components used in action mobilization.

Globalization may alter the scale of existing networks. The increasing importance of transnational institutions such as the United Nations or the European Union urges national groups and networks to create international links for joint mobilization. This may result in loose international connections between national organizations and networks to campaign or protest together on the transnational level (Roggeband 2010). Such transnational constellations of different domestic actors play an important role in knowledge transfer, policy learning, and norm diffusion (Roggeband 2007, 2010). Feminists, for instance, have used transnational networks when national governments are unwilling to respond to the demands of local feminist organizations or if channels of access to the state are blocked. In such cases, feminists have sought to enhance their local political leverage via what Keck and Sikkink (1998, 12–13) call the "boomerang pattern of influence," whereby loose coalitions of groups and activists from different countries put pressure on more powerful states and supranational organizations to bring pressure to bear in turn on a particular government that violates rights or resists desired policy changes. Such loose networks are often temporary and issue specific and do not necessarily replace local preexisting networks.

Of course, we need more longitudinal and comparative research to see if traditional social movement organizations are indeed substituted by more loose, ad hoc forms of organizing. But if we take the claims of sociologists such as Bauman, Wuthnow, and Putnam seriously, what, then, are the implications for the multiorganizational field of social movements, which turn into a fluid configuration of loosely connected groups and individuals? And what are the consequences of the digitalization and hybridization of networks for (collective) identities, forms of participation, and strategies of social movements? Will this lead to fragmentation and/or will it eventually even result in an evaporation of the overarching network?

From Identity Politics to Light Identities?

Both the old and new social movements were strongly identity based (workers, women, ethnic minorities, gays and lesbians) and therefore, unintentionally, reinforced ethnic, gender, sexual, and class boundaries. New networks such as the global justice movement (GJM) are more often issue based and allow for a more diverse constituency. As della Porta (chapter 17) notes, many of the cosmopolitan activists in the GJM have some shared characteristics such as global and cross-issue framing and overall tolerant identities. An emerging question is whether this change from identity politics to issue politics also implies a change from strong (collective and organization) identities and more greedy and intensive forms of participation toward lighter identities and looser, less obliging forms of participation and strategy. One consequence of lighter communities may be that activists are less inclined to engage in heavier tactics or more demanding forms of action and will, therefore, be less effective in those circumstances that ask for that repertoire. If we again take the case of the GJM, this in fact appears to prove the opposite, as it combines new organizational forms and quite confrontational action repertoires. Is this example enough of an argument against the idea that the loosening of ties among (potential) participants is necessarily weakening the impact of social movements since their action repertoires have become more limited in scope? Or is it in our day perhaps a *conditio sine qua non* to be light to attract people and, overall, this indeed constrains action repertoire options?

Identity politics, central to many new and older social movements, such as the labor movement and women's movement, appears to be under pressure from processes of individualization. One of the leading theorists of individualization, Ulrich Beck, launched the *individualization of class* thesis. In his view, class struggles have lost their central place and role in contemporary societies. In response to Beck's thesis, Bagguley (2005) argues that there still are significant class-related grievances but that class struggle is no longer dominated by collective action. Instead, protest related to class grievances has become increasingly individualized. This author shows that although there has been a dramatic decline in trade union membership and strike action since the early 1980s, there has been an even more dramatic increase in the pursuit of individual grievances by employees. Interestingly, Bagguley also demonstrates that individual cases for sex, race, and disability jurisdictions have increased. This shift from collective to individual action has consequences for social movements but does not necessarily point to a decline in collective identities; people still mobilize on the basis of a collective notion such as class. There is a question, however, whether all these individual acts add up to a collective social movement. Soule, in chapter 6, suggests that social movement theory should turn to organizational theory to address the question of how changes in identity affect the trajectory of various kinds of organizational actors.

Sociological processes resulting in lighter identities and people less willing to engage in very obliging forms of participation were taken more seriously by new social movement (NSM) theorists such as Melucci, Touraine, and Castells than by protagonists of the political process approach, who tend to put more emphasis on the (political) elite. A culturalist NSM approach would claim that in a network society, political participation is increasingly rooted in everyday networks of participants and that (potential) actors are likely to be involved in diffuse and decentralized networks rather than in formal organizations. Organizations become looser, less formalized, and more dynamic. Conversely, scholars using political process approaches to social movements have convincingly showed that collective (and individual) identities are strongly influenced by political context. Their approach would claim that it depends on political factors if changes in the way (post)modern people relate and engage translate into shifts in the supply side of mobilization.

What are the challenges that identity-based social movement organizations face as a result of these developments? Hensby, Sibthorpe, and Driver (2009) contend that social movement organizations need to adopt different organizational forms and structures that allow for more "choice" and "voice" for individual activists. The multiple affinities and involvements of movement supporters make it more difficult to tie activists to their organizations but, at the same time, provide the opportunity to create new collaborative activity across or between different groups and organizations. According to Hensby, Sibthorpe, and Driver, new, more loose organizations—which are often Internet based—better fit the needs of the more individually oriented activist because of their flexibility and openness.

Literature on the rise of Internet-facilitated networks suggests that these may act as "identity-granting subcultures" that foster collective identities in the long run (Langman 2005, 57; see also Polletta et al., chapter 2). New interpersonal networks, generated by Internet-based discussions, are places where people may construct, negotiate, and articulate new identities that are decoupled from national, ethnic, or religious categories. This is, for instance, claimed by Moghadam (2000), who shows how new network-based movements, such as the Muslim feminist movement, may link older groups dealing with various issues such as labor, feminism, ecology, peace, and anticapitalism and create a new encompassing or multi-interpretable identity that transcends boundaries between the groups that constitute the network. Yet Norris (2001), in contrast, indicates that the Internet reinforces and may even intensify traditional social cleavages. Parker and Song (2006, 590) make a similar claim, maintaining that "new media forms update rather than delete existing collective affiliations, no matter how individualistically they are felt and expressed." Their research on the Internet activity of young people in two British ethnic minority communities demonstrates how participants in debates and forums are constantly redefining and negotiating identity categories and labels, which results in an ongoing reconfiguration of personal and collective identities. The empirical question here is how virtual networking affects collective identities and to what extent these collective identities still function as a fundamental asset for mobilization.

Light Communities, Closed Communities?

The more open and fluid collective identity of light communities may allow for more inclusion than movements with strong and therefore more exclusive identities would. This is an argument brought forward about the GJM, which is organized around a common issue, criticizing globalization processes, rather than a clear common identity. Different authors argue that this might result in a more plural rank and file, the assumption being that the GJM creates a more open democratic space. But is this indeed the case? As Polletta (2006) indicates, participatory democracy has gained renewed popularity among social movement activists, especially in the anticorporate globalization and social justice movements, yet this organizational form risks alienating working-class people and activists of color. Apparently some actors, notably Western middle-class actors, are better positioned and equipped to voice their opinions, concerns, interests, and emotions. Although informal networks that foster protest may seem more open and inclusive, they may also exclude certain segments of society, leading to silencing or marginalizing of dissent voices (Walgrave and Klandermans 2010). Research in the Netherlands demonstrates that light communities tend to be of a rather homogeneous nature (Duyvendak and Hurenkamp 2004; Hurenkamp, Tonkens, and Duyvendak, 2011).

The access to and interaction patterns in informal networks have been studied and compared in various settings. These studies point to tendencies toward homogenization, instead of diversification. Social psychological theories such as homophily and the similarity attraction paradigm explain why individuals tend to interact more frequently and to like others who resemble themselves on characteristics such as age, class, gender, occupation, sexuality, politics, family status, where they live, or interests (Marsden 1987). Both theories agree that groups have the tendency to reproduce themselves by the selective recruitment of similar people in the group and by facilitating the turnover of dissimilar people. As people tend to develop network ties with other people sharing similar sociodemographic characteristics, people joining to form groups are relatively similar. This similarity is perpetuated owing to conservative selection of new members (McPherson, Smith-Lovin, and Cook 2001). Strong homophily mechanisms are visible in a wide array of relationships, ranging from friendship to the limited networks of discussion about a particular topic or more loose social contacts (McPherson, Smith-Lovin, and Cook 2001). This points to the exclusionary mechanisms of informal networks, which may result in unequal access to the instrumental resources (such as advice, sponsorship, mentoring, and information) and social resources (friendship and support) that informal networks provide (Boogaard and Roggeband 2010). Literature on organizational behavior as well as gender and ethnicity studies indicate that access and voice are very unevenly distributed in organizations and that more informal and horizontal organizations are no exceptions to this rule (Acker 2006). An additional concern here can be derived from sociological literature on networks and organizational behavior research on diversity in organizations. This research indicates that increased diversity of members often reinforces processes of exclusion (Acker 2006). The by now classic study of Kanter (1977) showed that variation in the proportions of people of different social types affects contact across categories. In highly skewed (as opposed to balanced and slightly skewed) groups, the numerically dominant type has a greater capacity to get things done or to mobilize resources. Overall, the research generally finds that heterogeneity in salient categories contributes to increased conflict, reduced communication, and lower performance (Boogaard and Roggeband 2010). Yet, on the positive side, it can contribute to a broader range of contacts, information sources, and creativity.

The role of the Internet in this aspect appears to be ambiguous. The Internet has been a key factor in creating new connections and networks across the globe and, to some extent, has resulted in the democratization of information and participation. Some early optimistic analyses envisioned the Internet as a "decentralizing, globalizing, harmonizing, and empowering" medium (Negroponte 1995, 229), as a new communication technology that would bring about a smaller and more open world. According to the cyber-optimists, the Internet can create a public sphere in Habermas's (1984) sense, one that is not regulated by the state or by commercial interests but rather is owned and controlled by the participants themselves (Schneider 1996). Yet others have noted that the Internet tends to reinforce existing class and social relations both within and across countries. Access to this medium is not equally distributed across the globe. The Internet has developed unevenly throughout the world, creating what has become known as the *global digital divide* (Castells 2001; Norris 2001). Castells (2001, 247) contends that "the heralding of the internet's potential as a means of freedom, productivity, and communication comes hand in hand with the denunciation of the 'digital divide' induced by inequality on the internet." Many countries in the global South lag behind in the development of information and communication technologies, causing large disparities in access to information and relevant networks. But also technological opportunities are often unevenly distributed with societies (Norris 2001). This digital divide may result in a democratic divide, as Norris (2001) contends. Diani (chapter 8) argues that if we look beyond indicators of presence and access and focus on capabilities and conditions of use, differences probably are significant. So, although the Internet has been able to bridge divides and create new virtual communities across the globe, it is not necessarily a more inclusive space with equal access for all.

This brings us to the question of whether more open and looser networks like the GJM or virtual networks like MoveOn are less prone to exclusionary tendencies, or whether they, to a large extent, reproduce existing inequalities. What kind of organizations or networks and what media guarantee space and voice to marginalized and less resourceful actors?

As social movement scholars, we need to address these pertinent research questions and further develop a research agenda and research strategy. So far, we lack enough longitudinal and comparative data to answer the central question about the position of formal organizations vis-à-vis looser groups with respect to transforming potentiality into action. The authors in this section argue that we indeed need more longitudinal data, not just about protest events, but also data that look closer at the supply side of contention, that is, at the development of social movement organizations, networks, and communities and the relations (coalitions, alliances) that exist between organizations within organizational fields. Diani, Rucht, and Staggenborg all address the important methodological question of how changes in organizational and mobilization patterns over time may be studied. Diani argues that we need to complement our effort to measure events or study single organizations with examining systematic relational patterns within organizational fields or social movement sectors, whereas Rucht suggests better distinguishing between types of organizations. Though we fully agree that these are urgent tasks, here we have emphasized taking broader sociological developments into account as well, because changing identities owing to processes of individualization—and how this may affect collective identities—is of decisive importance for the supply side of political protest in the long run.

References

Acker, Joan. 2006. "Inequality Regimes." *Gender and Society* 20:441–64.

Bagguley, Paul. 2005. "The Individualisation of Class Struggle." Unpublished manuscript. http://www.sociology.leeds.ac.uk/about/staff/bagguley.php.

Bauman, Zygmunt. 2001. *Community: Seeking Safety in an Insecure World.* Cambridge: Polity Press.

Beer, Paul de. 2007. "How Individualized Are the Dutch?" *Current Sociology* 55:389–413.

Boogaard, Brendy, and Conny Roggeband. 2010. "Paradoxes of Intersectionality: Theorizing Inequality in the Dutch Police Force through Structure and Agency." *Organization* 17:53–75.

Brint, Steven. 2001. "Gemeinschaft Revisited: A Critique and Reconstruction of the Community Concept." *Sociological Theory* 19:1–23.

Castells, Manuel. 2001. *Internet Galaxy: Reflections on the Internet, Business, and Society.* Oxford: Oxford University Press.

Chadwick, Andrew. 2007. "Digital Network Repertoires and Organizational Hybridity." *Political Communication* 24:283–301.

Dalton, Russell. 2008. *The Good Citizen: How a Younger Generation Is Reshaping American Politics.* Washington, D.C.: CQ Press.

Duyvendak, JanWillem, and Menno Hurenkamp, eds. 2004. *Kiezen voor de kudde.* Amsterdam: Van Gennep.

Etzioni, Amitai. 1996. "The Responsive Community: A Communitarian Perspective." *American Sociological Review* 61:1–11.

Habermas, Jürgen. 1984. *The Theory of Communicative Action: Reason and the Rationalization of Society.* Boston: Beacon.

Hensby, Alexander, Joanne Sibthorpe, and Steven Driver. 2009. "Together, Alone? Reflexive Leadership and Political Activism in Membership-Based Social Movement Organizations." http://www.psa.ac.uk/journals/pdf/5/2009/hensby.pdf.

Hurenkamp, Menno, Evelien Tonkens, and JanWillem Duyvendak. 2011. "Citizenship in the Netherlands: Locally Produced, Nationally Contested." *Citizenship Studies* 15:205–25.

Kanter, Rosabeth Moss. 1977. *Men and Women of the Corporation.* New York: Basic Books.

Keck, Margaret E., and Kathryn Sikkink. 1998. *Activists beyond Borders: Advocacy Networks in International Politics.* Ithaca, N.Y.: Cornell University Press.

Langman, Lauren. 2005. "From Virtual Public Spheres to Global Justice: A Critical Theory of Internetworked Social Movements." *Sociological Theory* 23:42–74.

McPherson, Miller, Lynn Smith-Lovin, and James M. Cook. 2001. "Birds of a Feather: Homophily in Social Networks." *Annual Review of Sociology* 27:415–44.

Moghadam, Valerie. 2000. "Transnational Feminist Networks: Collective Action in an Era of Globalization." *International Sociology* 15:57–85.

Negroponte, N. 1995. *Being Digital.* New York: Alfred A. Knopf.

Norris, Pippa. 2001. *Digital Divide? Civic Engagement, Information Poverty, and the Internet Worldwide.* Cambridge: Cambridge University Press.

Parker, David, and Miri Song. 2006. "New Ethnicities Online: Reflexive Racialisation and the Internet." *Sociological Review* 54:575–94.

Polletta, Francesca. 2006. *It Was Like a Fever: Storytelling in Protest and Politics.* Chicago: University of Chicago Press.

Putnam, Robert. 2000. *Bowling Alone: The Collapse and Revival of the American Community.* New York: Simon and Schuster.

Putnam, Robert M., and Lewis M. Feldstein. 2002. *Better Together: Restoring the American Community.* New York: Simon and Schuster.

Roggeband, Conny. 2007. "Translators and Transformers: International Inspiration and Exchange in Social Movements." *Social Movement Studies* 6:247–61.

———. 2010. "Transnational Networks and Institutions: How Diffusion Shaped the Politicization of Sexual Harassment in Europe." In *The Diffusion of Social Movements: Actors, Mechanisms, and Political Effects,* edited by Rebecca Kolins Givan, Kenneth M. Robers, and Sarah A. Soule, 19–33. Cambridge: Cambridge University Press.

Schneider, Steven. 1996. "Creating a Democratic Public Sphere through Political Discussion." *Social Science Computer Review* 14:373–93.

Schudson, Michael. 2006. "The Varieties of Civic Experiences." *Citizenship Studies* 10:591–606.

Skocpol, Theda. 2003. *Diminished Democracy: From Membership to Management in American Civic Life.* Rothbaum Series. Norman: University of Oklahoma Press.

Smith, Jackie, and Tina Fetner. 2007. "Structural Approaches to Social Movements." In *Handbook of Social Movements across Disciplines,* edited by Bert Klandermans and Conny Roggeband, 1–12. New York: Springer.

Taylor, Verta. 2000. "Mobilizing for Change in a Social Movement Society." *Contemporary Sociology* 29:219–30.

Urry, John. 2005. "The Complexities of the Global." *Theory, Culture, and Society* 22:235–54.

Walgrave, Stefaan, and Bert Klandermans. 2010. "Open and Closed Mobilization Patterns: The Role of Channels and Ties." In *The World Says No to War: Demonstrations against the War on Iraq,* edited by Stefaan Walgrave and Dieter Rucht, 169–93. Minneapolis: University of Minnesota Press.

Wellman, Barry, and Milena Giulia. 1999. "Virtual Communities as Communities: Net-Surfers Don't Ride Alone." In *Communities in Cyberspace,* edited by Mark Smith and Peter Kollock, 167–94. London: Routledge.

Wellman, Barry, Anabel Quan Haase, James Witte, and Keith Hampton. 2001. "Does the Internet Increase, Decrease, or Supplement Social Capital?" *American Behavioral Scientist* 45:436–55.

Wuthnow, Robert. 1994. *Sharing the Journey: Support Groups and America's New Quest for Community.* New York: Free Press.

———. 1998. *Loose Connections: Joining Together in America's Fragmented Communities.* Cambridge, Mass.: Harvard University Press.

Zukin, Cliff, Scott Keeter, Molly Andolina, Krista Jenkins, and Michael X. Delli Carpini. 2006. *A New Engagement? Political Participation, Civic Life, and the Changing American Citizen.* New York: Oxford University Press.

6
Bringing Organizational Studies Back into Social Movement Scholarship

Sarah A. Soule

Since at least the 1970s, organizations and social movement scholars have recognized the complementary nature of their respective fields, and as a result, many of the central questions in each field have been enriched via cross-pollination between these two distinct areas. For example, some of the most important questions asked by resource mobilization scholars of social movements have drawn on imagery from scholars of organizations. As well, social movement researchers have borrowed insights from organizational ecologists to help explain the dynamics of population change in social movement industries and sectors. Likewise, social movement scholars have drawn on neoinstitutional theories to explain core questions related to organizational forms and fields as well as the diffusion of social movements. Finally, social movement scholars have drawn on insights from the embeddedness approach to organizations to help explain a number of central questions related to network dynamics of social movements (see Diani, chapter 8).

On the other side, scholars of organizations associated with the neoinstitutional tradition have drawn on social movement theory to describe how politics and movements (and the sociopolitical field more broadly) impact basic organizational processes. Furthermore, organizational ecologists have drawn on social movement theories to describe some of the factors that affect the emergence and legitimization of new organizational populations, noting that social movement activities are often generative of new organizational forms. Finally, scholars of organizations interested in the effects of social movements on firms and industries have drawn on the body of research on social movement consequences, noting that some of the same factors that explain the consequences of movements on states also help us understand the impact of movements on firms, corporations, and industries (for a literature review, see Soule 2009). Historically, the nexus of organizations and social movement theories has been a rich area of inquiry, and each of these two fields has learned a great deal from the other.

However, in recent years, this once mutual relationship has grown imbalanced, with scholars of organizations embracing social movement scholarship and, at the same time, social movement scholars turning a cold shoulder to organizational scholars. I base this claim on a proliferation of workshops, conferences, edited volumes, and special issues of journals, all of which have been organized primarily by scholars of organizations with the explicit goal of learning from social movement scholars at the same time that movement scholarship that *explicitly* embraces organizational studies has seemingly declined (for similar observations about this, see Clemens and Minkoff 2004; Caniglia and Carmin 2005; Minkoff and McCarthy 2005).[1] Perhaps this is not an entirely fair representation. In fact, *Mobilization* dedicated a special issue to the topic of organizations in 2005 (Caniglia and Carmin 2005), and as I review later, some movement scholars are still explicitly engaging organizational theory. However, I assert that this relationship has become lopsided, with scholars of organizations wholeheartedly welcoming and engaging social movement scholarship, while social movement scholarship has moved away from explicitly utilizing organizational scholarship.

It is beyond the scope of this chapter to fully analyze why this is the case, but it is worth speculating briefly about some of the possible reasons. First, this may be because many movement scholars have become interested in loosely structured networks of social movement participants that seem to deliberately eschew formal organizations. Thus it could be that organizational theories (or at least those that focus on formal organizational processes) are perceived as less relevant to the current substantive topics of interest in the field. Related to this, many social movement scholars have become interested in online activism, which may be possible without traditional social movement organizations (SMOs) (Earl 2010; see Polletta et al., chapter 2). Again, here it could be that the substantive areas of interest of many in the social movement field dictate that organizational theory is less important than it once was to understanding social movements. Finally, there has always been a tension in the social movement literature between those who think organization promotes mobilization (e.g., McCarthy and Zald 1977) and those who think organization is disastrous for mobilization (e.g., Piven and Cloward 1977). Thus it could be that this tension and debate have made some scholars leery of studying the organizations (at least the formal ones) that comprise social movements.

Whatever the reasons may be, I argue that this is a shame for at least two reasons. First, despite the fact that many social movements may be eschewing formal organization, formal SMOs remain a critical aspect of social movements and should not be overlooked simply because we are also intrigued by informal movement networks, affinity groups, and online networks of activists. Consider, for example, a recent data collection effort by Andrews and Edwards (2005) that shows that there are nearly five hundred environmental organizations active in the state of North Carolina alone. Similarly, in their study of more than five thousand environmental organizations in the United States, Brulle and colleagues (2007) find that the founding rate of new environmental movement organizations was still remarkably high in 2000. Or consider Walker, McCarthy, and Baumgartner's (2011) study of formal organizations associated with three different U.S. social movements (peace, women's, and human rights movements), which shows that although there may have been some declines in the number of organizations since the 1980s, the numbers are still startlingly high (and much higher than those of the 1960s). Finally, in a European context, consider Vermeulen's (2006) study of immigrant organizations in several cities, which shows growth (and not decline) in the number of formal organizations associated with immigrant groups. Thus, despite the claim by some social movement scholars that formal SMOs are a thing of the past, data seem to indicate that formal SMOs are far from moribund.

In fact, the continued existence of these more formal SMOs alongside less formal networks of activists and affinity groups may be explained by organizational theories. In particular, *resource partitioning theories* seek to explain such heterogeneity in organizational populations. Like large macrobreweries that exist alongside the rapidly multiplying microbreweries in many countries, social movements comprise many different kinds of organizations, some formal, some not. The simple observation that many movements today seem to prefer less formal organizations is not necessarily borne out in the data, and even if it were, it does not necessarily follow that this means that formal organizations are a thing of the past.

A second reason for my lament that social movement scholars have lately been less interested in organizational sociology is that there are several new lines of inquiry in organizational studies that have direct bearing on social movement processes and issues central to the field yet have thus far been underutilized by social movement scholars. In particular, recent work on *organizational population diversity, organizational identity and categories*, and *organizational learning* should be of interest to social movement scholars. My aim is to discuss each of these, with the hope of stimulating some ideas for how social movement scholars can bring organizations back into their analyses.

Organizational Population Diversity and Social Movement Outcomes

One of the key questions of research by social movement scholars working in the organizational ecology tradition is how various population-level characteristics impact the survival rates of individual SMOs (e.g., Minkoff 1993, 1994, 1995, 1997, 1999; Edwards and Marullo 1995; McLaughlin and Khawaja 2000; Edwards and Foley 2003; Murphy 2005; Levitsky 2007; Soule and King 2008). In a series of papers and a book drawing on her important data collected from *The Encyclopedia of Associations,* Minkoff examines the dynamics of competition, legitimacy, and mutualism among advocacy organizations associated with the women's and race and ethnic civil rights movements.

Minkoff's work inspired a number of others both to collect data on populations of organizations and to use the principles of organizational ecology to understand population dynamics associated with social movements in the United States (e.g., Edwards and Marullo 1995; McLaughlin and Khawaja 2000; Edwards and Foley 2003). A recent example is Murphy's (2005) research on the population of transnational environmental organizations. Interested mainly in the emergence of these organizations, Murphy's analysis draws on concepts core to organizational ecology (e.g., density dependence, legitimacy, and mutualism) and statistical modeling techniques associated with the organizational ecology perspective to study the rates of founding of environmental organizations operating at the transnational level.

In another recent treatment, Soule and King (2008) look at how interorganizational competition and organizational concentration, two facets of organizational populations often examined by organizational ecologists (especially those associated with resource partitioning theories), impact levels of movement organizational disbanding. These scholars find that specialist SMOs—that is, those that have a very narrow and specialized tactical repertoire—tend to survive and even thrive under conditions of high movement industry concentration. Finally, Vermeulen (2006) studies immigrant organizations in several European cities using classic organizational ecology to explain the growth and persistence of these organizations, even during times of anti-immigrant sentiment.[2]

This research is obviously important. But recent work in organizational ecology has moved beyond questions related to the impact of competition, legitimation, and mutualism on the founding and disbanding of organizations and has started to study the effects of *population diversity*. Social movement scholars should begin to look more closely at the impact of SMO *population diversity* on various movement-related outcomes (see also Taylor and Van Dyke 2004; Clemens and Minkoff 2004).

One type of diversity that might be of interest to social movement scholars is tactical diversity. Several researchers have examined the independent effects of "insider" versus "outsider" tactics on policy change (e.g., Soule et al. 1999; McCammon et al. 2001) and on organizational survival (Edwards and Marullo 1995). However, it could be that the mix of tactics used by a given movement or movement organization might be a stronger predictor of policy change, as it could be that it is not insider versus outsider tactics that matter to policy change but rather the diversity of tactics used. This is, in fact, what has been found in a recent study by Olzak and Ryo (2007), which accurately notes that social movement scholars assert that organizational diversity is important to movement processes but that few have actually studied this. Their paper offers a corrective to this gap. They study the impact of both tactical and goal diversity of civil rights movement organizations and find that goal diversity increases the rate of protest, whereas tactical diversity increases the passage of desired policies.

Another promising paper examines the impact of social movement organizational population diversity on the enactment of gay rights ordinances in the United States. In this paper, Negro, Peretti, and Carroll (2012) show that the structure of an organizational population plays an important role in sociolegal change. They find that net of the political opportunity structure, level of movement resources, and countermobilization, an important predictor of the passage of gay rights ordinances in the United States is the presence of movement organizations that bridge between movement organizations using either insider or outsider tactical forms. Similarly, they find that the presence of organizations that mirror those in the straight community is important to securing gay rights ordinances. Their findings demonstrate the utility of looking seriously at the effect of the *diversity* of SMOs on policy change (as opposed to the somewhat standard operating procedure of measuring organizational strength with metrics such as counts of organizations, members, or levels of funding).

In addition to affecting policy change (Olzak and Ryo 2007; Negro, Peretti, and Carroll 2012) or protest rates (Olzak and Ryo 2007), the diversity of tactics used by a movement ought to impact the level of repression of that movement. There is some evidence for this claim at the protest event level, as recent research shows that police are more likely to respond to events at which protesters use multiple tactics (e.g., Soule and Davenport 2009; Davenport, Soule, and Armstrong 2011). At the event level, the argument is that multiple tactics are more difficult for police to control. However, one might expect that the particular mix of tactics (rather than just the sheer number of tactics) deployed by a movement will also impact how police and other agents of repression will react to that movement. For example, it might be the case that police and other state agents are more likely to repress movements that use a broad and diverse repertoire of tactics because such movements may be perceived as appealing to many constituents and thus may be assumed to be more threatening because of the potential to mobilize greater numbers of protesters.

Thus I agree with Olzak and Ryo (2007) that despite claiming that organizational diversity is important, few social movement scholars have actually looked at this empirically. Examining the effects of diversity on social movement processes would not only enrich our understanding of these processes but would also enrich the organizational studies literature by assessing whether population diversity arguments hold in different populations of organizations.

Organizational Identities and Categories

Another area of organizational sociology that remains underexplored by movement scholars is the literature on organizational identity and categories. Organizational ecologists have recently begun to emphasize identity as a fundamental basis for the conceptualization and identification of organizational forms, and they have begun to identify categories and the process of categorization as key questions for empirical research (see the review in Negro, Koçak, and Hsu 2010).

One of the key questions in this growing body of empirical work is in regard to the effects of organizational identity on the trajectory of various kinds of organizational actors. Empirical studies of the identity of organizations, individuals, and firms have established that there are various kinds of penalties associated with unclear identities; that is, organizations that do not fit well into established categories have been found to suffer a variety of penalties. For example, Zuckerman and colleagues (2003) find that feature film actors who are typecast into particular genres fare better in securing future work because they exhibit a more cohesive and clear identity than do actors who span different film genres. In a similar vein, Hsu (2006) finds that feature films that fall into multiple genres (e.g., Western musicals) have lower appeal (as measured by film ratings) than do films that are categorized into a single genre. Finally, Hsu, Hannan, and Koçak (2009) find that eBay sellers who auction goods in single categories are able to close more sales than are eBay sellers whose goods span different categories on the website.

It is curious that this line of research has yet to be picked up on by social movement scholars, especially given the importance of identity to social movement processes (e.g., Stryker, Owens, and White 2000; also see part I of this volume). Are SMOs that present an unclear identity similarly penalized?

Will they draw fewer participants to their events or receive less media attention than those organizations with coherent identities? Will they have lower survival rates or be more likely to be repressed? These kinds of questions have scarcely been picked up on by social movement scholars.

One exception is a paper by Fassiotto and Soule (2012) that examines whether boundary spanning at protest events impacts congressional attention to a movement's issues. Focusing on the women's movement in the United States, these authors measure the clarity of the identity of an event by the distance between claims that are made at an event (where claims that are often used together in the past are considered relatively close, whereas claims that are infrequently used together in the past are considered relatively distant). They find that events that clearly fit into the women's movement category received more congressional attention than those that did not. These findings suggest that the research on organizational identity and categories is applicable to social protest events. Future research should similarly bring the organizational literature on identities into the study of SMOs and events in other settings.

In addition to the interest in categories and questions about any penalties that may accrue to organizations and events that span established categorical identities, organizational sociologists have recently begun to focus on the concept of *authenticity* (Carroll and Wheaton 2010; Carroll and O'Connor 2012). In the growing literature on authenticity, scholars find that organizations and products that are perceived as authentic accrue various types of benefits. For example, Carroll and O'Connor find that people are willing to pay more for authentic goods and that this willingness to pay more is above and beyond any perception of quality of the goods. In other words, in the marketplace for (in their case) specialty food items and luxury leather goods, authentic goods command a higher price and higher praise. Others observe that perceived authenticity of goods increases their appeal in music (Peterson 1997; Grazian 2003), restaurants (Fine 2004), wines (Negro et al. 2006), and cuisine (Rao, Monin, and Durand 2005).

The issue of authenticity ought to be of interest to social movement scholars because of its connection to the phenomena of movements "selling out" or "being channeled" or of cooptation. For example, Chasin (2001) studies the evolution of the gay and lesbian niche market alongside the evolution of the gay and lesbian movement, noting that corporations responded to the movement by making donations to major gay and lesbian organizations. Through Chasin's work, which is critical of the gay and lesbian movement, we see that as the movement began to accept corporate funding, it was channeled into less confrontational tactics. Similarly, Jenkins and Ekert (1986) have demonstrated how foundation and philanthropic funding defused some of the more confrontational tactics of the civil rights movement, perhaps lowering the efficacy of that movement.

We might think of the trajectories of such movements in terms of a loss of authenticity, as all these phenomena might signal that a movement has become somehow distanced from its original vision or basis; that is, when a movement or movement organization is channeled by its funders into using different kinds of tactics or articulating different kinds of goals (Jenkins and Ekert 1986; Chasin 2001), we might consider this a loss of authenticity. We may say that as a movement becomes less radical because of its desire to obtain funding, it somehow loses its connection to its roots and to its original reason for being. Or when movement leaders and organizations are coopted by their targets, we might speak of them as losing authenticity (Gamson 1990).[3]

These observations may lead us to wonder what a loss of authenticity does to some basic social movement processes. For example, to what extent does a loss of authenticity impact the ability of a movement to recruit participants or to secure its desired goals? Is a loss of authenticity associated with less media attention? Does it spurn schisms and factions, which then give birth to new organizations that are somehow more true to the origins of the original organization or movement (see Kretschmer 2009)?

One study that begins to examine these questions is that of so-called heretical social movements (Hipsher 2007). Heretical social movements are those in which the identity of core activists is out of sync with the issue of the movement. Hipsher (2007) studies two such organizations working on either side of the abortion issue in the United States: Catholics for a Free Choice (a pro-choice, Catholic organization) and Feminists for Life of America (a pro-life, feminist organization). Her study examines how identity communities demarcate boundaries of authentic group membership and make "heretics" out of organizations that violate these boundaries. Hipsher's analysis points to the benefits of remaining authentic (and, conversely, the penalties associated with a loss of authenticity).

Organizational Learning via Coalitions

Owing to the increasing interest in social movement coalitions (e.g., Van Dyke and McCammon 2010), we have learned a great deal about what kinds of factors impact the probability that two or more SMOs will enter a coalition. This research points to the importance of three kinds of factors that impact social movement coalitions. First, scholars have examined how the structure of political opportunities (including threats) and the broader economic context affect the decision of groups to form a coalition (Van Dyke 2003; Van Dyke and McCammon 2010; Almeida 2010; Wiest 2010). For example, Reese et al.

(2010) show that SMOs activated interpersonal ties to form antiwar coalitions when the Bush administration threatened war in Iraq, and Okamoto (2010) shows that Asian American groups formed pan-Asian organizations when they were threatened with hate crimes. Second, this literature also points to the importance of interpersonal social ties across various movement organizations (see Diani, chapter 8). Referred to as "bridge builders" or "coalition brokers," we know that individuals with multiple organizational affiliations are able to foster coalitions between movement organizations, even those that are not within the same movement industry (e.g., Rose 2000; Grossman 2001). In their study of the Win without War coalition, Corrigall-Brown and Meyer (2010) show that the interpersonal ties between five key activists inspired the formation of this particular coalition.

Finally, this research looks at the importance of ideology, identity, and interests in forging coalitions (e.g., Cornfield and McCammon 2010). For example, Van Dyke (2003) notes that on college campuses, multi-issue organizations are important because such organizations are able to forge coalitions with more specialized organizations. Some researchers point to the fact that there are many missed opportunities for coalitions because groups have difficulty putting aside differences to work together (e.g., Ferree and Roth 1998). Others chronicle the difficulties that successful coalitions face in trying to find common ideological and/or identity-based ground (e.g., Lichterman 1995; Roth 2010).

This research on coalitions is critically important to understanding the dynamics of collaboration between SMOs. However, to date, this research has focused on coalitions as a key *dependent variable,* asking what kinds of factors facilitate the formation of coalitions (and what factors hinder formation of coalitions). Few scholars interested in coalitions have looked at *coalitions as an independent variable* (for notable exceptions, see Jones et al. 2001; Murphy 2005; Larson and Soule 2009). The question of the *effect* of coalitions on some relevant social movement outcome should be of great interest to social movement scholars.

On this point, *organizational learning theorists* provide excellent theoretical insights and methodological tools for understanding what happens once organizations collaborate. Organizational learning theory argues that one important outcome of organizational collaboration is knowledge sharing (March 1991; Cohen and Levinthal 1990; Grant 1996). We might argue that one important piece of knowledge that is shared by SMOs is knowledge about how to deploy specific protest tactics. Thus we might assume that one effect or consequence of movement organizational collaboration is the sharing of tactics via diffusion processes.

Wang and Soule (2012) take these insights into account as they focus on the question of whether collaboration between SMOs facilitates the transfer of knowledge between the organizations. These authors study the entire social movement sector of the United States (1960–95), looking carefully at the ties between all organizations mentioned as protesting in newspaper articles. Interorganizational ties, in their study, are determined by the copresence of organizations at protest events. Wang and Soule find that tactics (an essential element of social movement knowledge) do, in fact, diffuse via organizational collaboration. They also show that organizations with more diverse tactical repertoires adopted more tactics, but only up to a certain point (beyond which an organization simply has too many tactics in its quiver and cannot absorb more). Finally, they show that more prominent (measured by network centrality) organizations are more likely to "send" tactics to other organizations, whereas less prominent organizations are more likely to "receive" tactics. This kind of analysis is important to fostering the connection between organizational studies and social movements because it addresses an issue important to social movement scholars: diffusion (e.g., Givan, Roberts, and Soule 2010). However, it does this by drawing on organizational learning theory, something that social movement scholars have not previously done. Future research might examine the effect of frame or issue diffusion via organizational collaboration and/or examine these processes cross-nationally and over time.

Conclusions

Social movement scholarship has historically benefited from insights from organizational theory. Organizational ecology, neoinstitutional, and embeddedness accounts have provided important theoretical insights about basic movement organizational processes. Moreover, social movement scholars have borrowed methods of data collection and data analysis from these traditions. And this relationship has not been one-sided, as scholars of organizations have drawn heavily on social movement theories and methodological techniques to answer questions about how movements matter to the creation of new organizational forms and fields, to changes in organizational policy and practices, and to processes of field structuration.

I have argued in this essay that despite this mutual borrowing and learning from one another, in recent years, social movement scholarship has moved away from embracing organizational theories. I am not the first to note this trend (see also Caniglia and Carmin 2005; Minkoff and McCarthy 2005; Diani, chapter 8), however, I may be the first to note that this has happened at the same time that organizational scholars are ramping up their attempts to engage social movement scholarship. Thus, as I said at the outset, I fear that this once mutual relationship has grown lopsided. This is a shame because formal SMOs remain an important facet of social movements and because new lines of theory and research in organizational studies have direct bearing on basic social movement questions and processes.

The ultimate goal of this essay was not to analyze why social movement scholars have moved away from organizational studies but rather to briefly review several new lines of inquiry and theory initiated by organizational scholars and to suggest some of the ways in which these should be of interest to social movement scholars. I focused here on three different lines of research and theory that I hope will capture the imagination of social movement scholars. First, I suggested that the recent attention to population diversity by (primarily) organizational ecologists can inform work on social movement outcomes. For example, rather than comparing the effects of different tactics on some desired outcome, we might begin to look at the effect of the particular *mix* of tactics on some outcome. Are movements and movement organizations that use a diverse array of tactics more successful than those that have a narrow repertoire? Are they more likely to be repressed? Answering such questions would inform not only theory on movement outcomes but also activist strategy.

Second, I noted that recent work on organizational identity ought to be of interest to social movement scholars, especially because of our long-standing interest in issues related to identity. Here I noted that questions about the effect of unclear organizational identities on mobilization potential and other key outcomes should be of interest to social movement scholars and activists alike. I also discussed related research on organizational authenticity and noted that this is an issue that movement scholars have barely touched. That is, are movements that are deemed more authentic more likely to win success and/or mobilize participants?

Finally, I highlighted work on organizational learning, which uses network ideas and methodology, and suggested that this approach could be useful to movement scholars interested in the interorganizational transfer of knowledge. For example, I noted that such an approach could be useful in studies of tactical diffusion, an area of great interest to social movement scholars (Givan, Roberts, and Soule 2010).

My treatment of these new areas of inquiry was not designed to be exhaustive, and I am quite certain that there is additional research by organizational scholars that will be of import to social movement scholars. I hope, though, that my discussion of these issues will inspire future research on SMOs that draws explicitly on these developments in organizational studies.

Notes

1. See, e.g., the special issue of *Administrative Science Quarterly*, edited by Davis et al. (2008), the special issue of *Business and Society*, edited by de Bakker and den Hond (2008), and the forthcoming special issue of *Organizational Studies*, edited by de Bakker et al.

2. Other movement research drawing on organizational ecology examines outcomes *other than* founding and disbanding rates of organizations. For example, Olzak and Uhrig (2001) use ideas about niche overlap to understand how tactical overlap of protest organizations influences subsequent rates of protest. Likewise, Larson and Soule (2009) study how interorganizational competition (also measured by tactical overlap) influences aggregate levels of protest in the United States. King, Bentele, and Soule (2007) look at how congressional hearings are affected by both social movements *and* the ecological dynamics of congressional hearings such that hearings about rights-related issues legitimate each other at first, and then compete with one another later, for congressional attention.

3. A specific example may be illustrative. Several leaders of the American civil rights movement, for example, Stokely Carmichael, argued that whites ought to be excluded from that movement. Typically, their argument was that whites could not understand the true struggles of African Americans and that their presence in the movement thus would somehow undermine this struggle. Although, to the best of my knowledge, these leaders did not use the word *authenticity*, such argumentation hints at the importance of authenticity to social movements. In this case, allowing whites into key civil rights organizations and events would damage the legitimacy of the movement because it would somehow be inauthentic to include whites, because most white Americans had not experienced the plight of African Americans firsthand.

References

Almeida, Paul. 2010. "Social Movement Partyism: Collective Action and Oppositional Political Parties." In *Strategic Alliances: Coalition Building and Social Movements*, edited by Nella Van Dyke and Holly J. McCammon, 170–97. Minneapolis: University of Minnesota Press.

Andrews, Andrew, and Bob Edwards. 2005. "The Organizational Structure of Local Environmentalism." *Mobilization* 10, no. 2: 213–34.

Brulle, Robert, Liesel Hall Turner, Jason Carmichael, and J. Craig Jenkins. 2007. "Measuring Social Movement Organization Populations: A Comprehensive Census of U.S. Environmental Movement Organizations." *Mobilization* 12, no. 3: 255–70.

Caniglia, Beth Schaefer, and Joann Carmin. 2005. "Scholarship on Social Movement

Organizations: Classic Views and Emerging Trends." *Mobilization* 10, no. 2: 201–12.

Carroll, Glenn R., and Kieran O'Connor. 2012. "Authenticity and Consumer Choice: Tests of a Sociological Theory." Unpublished manuscript.

Carroll, Glenn R., and Dennis Wheaton. 2010. "The Organizational Construction of Authenticity: An Examination of Contemporary Food and Dining in the U.S." *Research in Organizational Behavior* 29:255–82.

Chasin, Alexandra. 2001. *Selling Out: The Gay and Lesbian Movement Goes to Market.* New York: Macmillan.

Clemens, Elisabeth S., and Debra C. Minkoff. 2004. "Beyond the Iron Law: Rethinking the Place of Organizations in Social Movement Research." In *The Blackwell Companion to Social Movements,* edited by David A. Snow, Sarah A. Soule, and Hanspeter Kriesi, 155–70. Oxford: Blackwell.

Cohen, Wesley M., and Daniel A. Levinthal. 1990. "Absorptive Capacity: A New Perspective on Learning and Innovation." *Administrative Science Quarterly* 35:128–52.

Cornfield, Daniel B., and Holly J. McCammon. 2010. "Approaching Merger: The Converging Public Policy Agendas of the AFL and CIO, 1938–1955." In *Strategic Alliances: Coalition Building and Social Movements,* edited by Nella Van Dyke and Holly J. McCammon, 79–98. Minneapolis: University of Minnesota Press.

Corrigall-Brown, Catherine, and David S. Meyer. 2010. "The Prehistory of a Coalition: The Role of Social Ties in Win without War." In *Strategic Alliances: Coalition Building and Social Movements,* edited by Nella Van Dyke and Holly J. McCammon, 3–21. Minneapolis: University of Minnesota Press.

Davenport, Christian, Sarah A. Soule, and David A. Armstrong III. 2011. "Protesting While Black? The Differential Policing of American Activism, 1960–1990." *American Sociological Review* 76:152–78.

Davis, Gerald F., Calvin Morrill, Hayagreeva Rao, and Sarah A. Soule, eds. 2008. "Social Movements in Organizations and Markets." Special issue, *Administrative Science Quarterly* 53, no. 3.

De Bakker, Frank, and Frank den Hond, eds. 2008. "Introducing the Politics of Stakeholder Influence." Special issue, *Business and Society* 47, no. 1.

De Bakker, Frank, Frank den Hond, Brayden King, and Klaus Weber. Forthcoming. "Social Movements, Civil Societies, and Corporations." Special issue, *Organization Studies.*

Earl, Jennifer. 2010. "Spreading the Word versus Shaping the Conversation: The Use of Web 2.0 Tools in Protest Websites." Paper presented at the Annual Meeting of the American Sociological Association, Atlanta, Ga.

Edwards, Bob, and Michael W. Foley. 2003. "Social Movement Organizations beyond the Beltway: Understanding the Diversity of One Social Movement Industry." *Mobilization* 8, no. 1: 87–107.

Edwards, Bob, and Sam Marullo. 1995. "Organizational Mortality in a Declining

Social Movement: The Demise of Peace Movement Organizations in the End of the Cold War Era." *American Sociological Review* 60:908–27.

Fassiotto, Magali, and Sarah A. Soule. 2012. "The Consequences of Boundary Spanning: Congressional Attention to Women's Protest in the United States." Unpublished manuscript.

Ferree, Myra Marx, and Silke Roth. 1998. "Gender, Class, and the Interaction between Social Movements: A Strike of West Berlin Day Care Workers." *Gender and Society* 12:626–48.

Fine, Gary A. 2004. *Everyday Genius: Self-Taught Art and Culture of Authenticity.* Chicago: University of Chicago Press.

Gamson, William. 1990. *The Strategy of Social Protest.* 2nd ed. Belmont, Calif.: Wadsworth.

Givan, Rebecca Kolins, Kenneth M. Roberts, and Sarah A. Soule. 2010. *Diffusion of Social Movements: Actors, Mechanisms, and Political Effects.* Cambridge: Cambridge University Press.

Grant, Robert M. 1996. "Toward a Knowledge-Based Theory of the Firm." *Strategic Management Journal* 17:109–22.

Grazian, D. 2003. *Blue Chicago: The Search for Authenticity in Urban Blues Clubs.* Chicago: University of Chicago Press.

Grossman, Zoltan. 2001. "'Let's Not Create Evilness for This River': Interethnic Environmental Alliances of Native Americans and Rural Whites in Northern Wisconsin." In *Forging Radical Alliances across Difference: Coalition Politics for the New Millennium,* edited by Jill M. Bystydzienski and Steven P. Schact, 146–59. London: Rowman and Littlefield.

Hipsher, Patricia. 2007. "Heretical Social Movement Organizations and Their Framing Strategies." *Sociological Inquiry* 77:241–63.

Hsu, Greta. 2006. "Jacks of All Trades and Masters of None: Audiences' Reactions to Spanning Genres in Feature Film Production." *Administrative Science Quarterly* 51:420–50.

Hsu, Greta, Michael T. Hannan, and Ö. Koçak. 2009. "Multiple Category Memberships in Markets: An Integrated Theory and Two Empirical Tests." *Administrative Science Quarterly* 74:150–69.

Jenkins, J. Craig, and Craig M. Ekert. 1986. "Channeling Black Insurgency: Elite Patronage and Professional Social Movement Organizations in the Development of the Black Movement." *American Sociological Review* 51:812–29.

Jones, Andrew W., Richard N. Hutchinson, Nella Van Dyke, Leslie Gates, and Michelle Companion. 2001. "Coalition Form and Mobilization Effectiveness in Local Social Movements." *Sociological Spectrum* 21:207–31.

King, Brayden G., Keith Bentele, and Sarah A. Soule. 2007. "Protest and Policy Making: Explaining Fluctuation in Congressional Attention to Rights Issues, 1960–1986." *Social Forces* 86:137–64.

Kretschmer, Kelsy. 2009. "Contested Loyalties: Dissident Identity Organizations, Institutions, and Social Movements." *Sociological Perspectives* 52:433–54.

Larson, Jeff A., and Sarah A. Soule. 2009. "Sector-Level Dynamics and Collective Action in the United States, 1965–1975." *Mobilization* 14, no. 3: 293–314.

Levitsky, Sandra R. 2007. "Niche Activism: Constructing a Unified Movement Identity in a Heterogeneous Organizational Field." *Mobilization* 12, no. 3: 271–86.

Lichterman, Paul. 1995. "Piecing Together Multicultural Community: Cultural Differences in Community Building among Grass-Roots Environmentalists." *Social Problems* 42:513–34.

March, James G. 1991. "Exploration and Exploitation in Organizational Learning." *Organization Science* 2:71–87.

McCammon, Holly J., Karen E. Campbell, Ellen M. Granberg, and Christine Mowery. 2001. "How Movements Win: Gendered Opportunity Structures and U.S. Women's Suffrage Movements, 1866–1919." *American Sociological Review* 66:49–70.

McCarthy, John D., and Mayer N. Zald. 1977. "Resource Mobilization and Social Movements: A Partial Theory." *American Journal of Sociology* 82:1212–41.

McLaughlin, Paul, and Marwan Khawaja. 2000. "The Organizational Dynamics of the U.S. Environmental Movement: Legitimation, Resource Mobilization, and Political Opportunity." *Rural Sociology* 65:422–39.

Minkoff, Debra C. 1993. "The Organization of Survival: Women's and Racial-Ethnic Voluntarist and Activist Organizations, 1955–1985." *Social Forces* 71:887–908.

———. 1994. "From Service Provision to Institutional Advocacy: The Shifting Legitimacy of Organizational Forms." *Social Forces* 72:943–69.

———. 1995. "Interorganizational Influences on the Founding of African American Organizations, 1955–1985." *Sociological Forum* 10:51–79.

———. 1997. "The Sequencing of Social Movements." *American Sociological Review* 62:779–99.

———. 1999. "Bending with the Wind: Strategic Change and Adaptation by Women's and Racial Minority Organizations." *American Journal of Sociology* 6:1666–1703.

Minkoff, Debra C., and John D. McCarthy. 2005. "Reinvigorating the Study of Organizational Processes in Social Movements." *Mobilization* 10, no. 2: 289–308.

Murphy, Gillian. 2005. "Coalitions and the Development of the Global Environmental Movement: A Double-Edged Sword." *Mobilization* 10, no. 2: 235–50.

Negro, Giacomo, Michael T. Hannan, Hayagreeva Rao, and Ming Leung. 2006. "No Barrique, No Berlusconi: Conflict and Terroir among Italian Wine Producers." Paper presented at the Workshop on Organizational Ecology, Sintra, Portugal.

Negro, Giacomo, O. Özgecan Koçak, and Greta Hsu. 2010. "Research in Categories in the Sociology of Organizations." *Research in the Sociology of Organizations* 31:3–35.

Negro, Giacomo, Fabrizio Peretti, and Glenn Carroll. 2012. "'We Are Everywhere': Organizational Diversity and the Enactment of Gay Rights Ordinances in U.S. Communities, 1972–2008." Unpublished manuscript.

Okamoto, Dina G. 2010. "Organizing across Ethnic Boundaries in the Post–Civil Rights Era: Asian American Panethnic Coalitions." In *Strategic Alliances: Coalition Building and Social Movements*, edited by Nella Van Dyke and Holly J. McCammon, 143–69. Minneapolis: University of Minnesota Press.

Olzak, Susan, and Emily Ryo. 2007. "Organizational Diversity, Vitality, and Outcomes in the African American Civil Rights Movement." *Social Forces* 85:1561–92.

Olzak, Susan, and Noah Uhrig. 2001. "The Ecology of Tactical Overlap." *American Sociological Review* 66:694–717.

Peterson, R. A. 1997. *Creating Country Music: Fabricating Authenticity.* Chicago: University of Chicago Press.

Piven, Francis Fox, and Richard Cloward. 1977. *Poor People's Movements.* New York: Vintage Books.

Rao, Hayagreeva, P. Monin, and R. Durand. 2005. "Border Crossing: Bricolage and the Erosion of Categorical Boundaries in French Gastronomy." *American Sociological Review* 70:968–91.

Rose, Fred. 2000. *Coalitions across the Class Divide: Lessons from the Labor, Peace, and Environmental Movements.* Ithaca, N.Y.: Cornell University Press.

Roth, Benita. 2010. "Organizing One's Own as Good Politics: Second Wave Feminists and the Meaning of Coalition." In *Strategic Alliances: Coalition Building and Social Movements*, edited by Nella Van Dyke and Holly J. McCammon, 99–118. Minneapolis: University of Minnesota Press.

Soule, Sarah A. 2009. *Contention and Corporate Social Responsibility.* Cambridge: Cambridge University Press.

Soule, Sarah A., and Christian Davenport. 2009. "Velvet Glove, Iron Fist, or Even Hand? Protest Policing in the United States, 1960–1990." *Mobilization* 14, no. 1: 1–22.

Soule, Sarah A., and Brayden G. King. 2008. "Competition and Resource Partitioning in Three Social Movement Industries." *American Journal of Sociology* 113:1568–1610.

Soule, Sarah A., Doug McAdam, John McCarthy, and Yang Su. 1999. "Protest Events: Cause or Consequence of State Action? The U.S. Women's Movement and Federal Congressional Activities, 1956–1979." *Mobilization* 4, no. 2: 239–50.

Stryker, Sheldon, Timothy J. Owens, and Robert W. White. 2000. *Self, Identity, and Social Movements.* Minneapolis: University of Minnesota Press.

Taylor, Verta, and Nella Van Dyke. 2004. "'Get Up, Stand Up': Tactical Repertoires of Social Movements." In *The Blackwell Companion to Social Movements*, edited by David A. Snow, Sarah A. Soule, and Hanspeter Kriesi, 262–93. Oxford: Blackwell.

Van Dyke, Nella. 2003. "Crossing Movement Boundaries: Factors That Facilitate Coalition Protest by American College Students, 1930–1990." *Social Problems* 50:226–50.

Van Dyke, Nella, and Holly J. McCammon. 2010. *Strategic Alliances: Coalition Building and Social Movements.* Minneapolis: University of Minnesota Press.

Vermeulen, Floris. 2006. *The Immigrant Organizing Process: Turkish Organizations in Amsterdam and Berlin and Surinamese Organizations in Amsterdam, 1960–2000.* Amsterdam: Amsterdam University Press.

Walker, Edward T., John D. McCarthy, and Frank R. Baumgartner. 2011. "Replacing Members with Managers? Mutualism among Membership and Non-membership Advocacy Organizations in the U.S." *American Journal of Sociology* 116:1284–1337.

Wang, Dan, and Sarah A. Soule. 2012. "Networks of Learning: The Diffusion of Protest Claims and Tactics among Social Movement Organizations, 1960–1995." *American Journal of Sociology* 117:1674–1722.

Wiest, Dawn. 2010. "Interstate Dynamics and Transnational Social Movement Coalitions: A Comparison of Northeast and Southeast Asia." In *Strategic Alliances: Coalition Building and Social Movements,* edited by Nella Van Dyke and Holly J. McCammon, 50–76. Minneapolis: University of Minnesota Press.

Zuckerman, E. W., T.-Y. Kim, K. Ukanwa, and J. von Rittman. 2003. "Robust Identities or Non-entities? Typecasting in the Feature Film Labor Market." *American Journal of Sociology* 108:1018–74.

7
Organization and Community in Social Movements

Suzanne Staggenborg

Social movement scholars influenced by resource mobilization theory and the seminal work of McCarthy and Zald (1973, 1977) have long focused on *social movement organizations* (SMOs) as the major organizational structures in social movements. SMOs remain important to the study of social movements, and recent scholarship confirms the critical role of organizations in the mobilization of collective action (Sampson et al. 2005). Yet scholars recognize that SMOs are not the only organizational forms that support movement mobilization; other important mobilizing structures include social networks, cultural groups, movement habitats within institutions, movement-related commercial establishments, coalitions, alternative institutions, and more established organizations that become movement allies at times, such as unions and community organizations. Moreover, there may be changes over time in the types of structures employed by social movements. Some scholars suggest that movement structures might currently be changing from more organized ones, with more formalized SMOs, to less formal issue networks and groups, owing in part to the influence of globalization and improved communication technologies (Roggeband and Duyvendak, chapter 5; Van Stekelenburg and Boekkooi, chapter 11). If such a shift is in fact occurring, changes in movement structures are expected to have important implications for mobilization, collective identity, and strategies.

In this essay, I argue that the concept of *social movement community* (SMC) is useful in conceptualizing the diffuse nature of social movements and their changing structures (Buechler 1990; Taylor and Whittier 1992; Lichterman 1995; Stoecker 1995; Staggenborg 1998). Particularly at the grassroots level, where much of the activity of social movements takes place, the concept allows us to consider how a range of mobilizing structures, including decentralized and informal structures as well as formal SMOs, affect the mobilization, collective identity, and strategies of social movements. Depending on how centralized they are, and what types of organizations and networks exist within them, movement communities can support different types of collective action campaigns, which in turn affect the organizational shape of the movement. By examining changes in movement communities over time, we can see how the structures of movements are changing in the wake of new movement campaigns and in response to developments such as new communications technologies. We can then see how changes in the structures of movement communities affect subsequent movement mobilization and collective campaigns.

I begin with a discussion of SMCs and three related components: organization and culture, collective identity, and movement campaigns. Next, I discuss a methodological approach to the study of movement communities. I then draw on case studies of two campaigns, the World March of Women (WMW) and the Pittsburgh G20 protests, to explore the analytic benefits of focusing on movement communities.

Social Movement Communities

Social movements and their organizational structures have been conceptualized in a variety of ways. Tilly (2008; Tilly and Wood 2009) and Tarrow (2011) view movements as "sustained interactions" with authorities, elites, or opponents, consisting of a series of collective action campaigns. McCarthy and Zald (1977) conceptualize social movements as "preferences" for social change that are mobilized by SMOs within a "social movement industry" (SMI) consisting of all SMOs that share a general goal. Melucci (1989) describes enduring movements as consisting of "submerged networks" that emerge from time to time for collective actions. Diani (1992) sees movements as "networks of informal interaction" among individuals and groups that engage in political or cultural conflict and share a collective identity. The concept of a "multiorganizational field" refers to all of the organizations with which a movement organization interacts, including opponents as well as supporters (Klandermans 1992). The concept of "ideologically structured action" (Zald 2000) emphasizes that movements engage in a variety of movement-inspired actions besides contentious politics in many different arenas, ranging from schools and families to government agencies and political parties.

The concept of a SMC is broader than the concepts of a SMI and a multiorganizational field in that it includes various types of movement contributors such as individuals, informal groups, and networks as well as SMOs and other organizations. Like multiorganizational fields, SMCs contain different types of organizations, including SMOs, cultural groups, alternative organizations, and established organizations that lend support to movement activities. As in Melucci's and Diani's conceptions of social movements, movement communities include networks of individual activists, who may belong to different groups at different times and participate in movement campaigns from time to time. Diani and Bison's (2004) conception of movement processes as involving informal networks of exchange among various types of movement actors, collective identity, and social or political conflict is akin to the idea of a SMC. Diani (chapter 8) examines different "modes of coordination" of collective action, including those of movements, organizations, coalitions, and subcultures or communities. Whereas this typology specifies the logics of distinct forms of coordination, the SMC concept differs in that it directs us to focus on interactions among the different types of actors and spaces that maintain grassroots movements. Thus coalitions and organizations, as well as individuals and other entities, are part of SMCs.

Although the concept is particularly useful in examining local movement communities, it might also be employed at regional, national, and international levels (Aunio and Staggenborg 2011). At any level, we can look at the characteristics of movement communities that affect their ability to engage in collective action. Some communities have central organizations or movement centers, which bring community members together on a regular basis, and SMCs vary in the extent to which they overlap with other communities. In a *general* movement community, activists from multiple *specific* movement communities interact; for example, a general progressive movement community might include activists from environmental, labor, and women's groups, who are tied together by social networks and participation in a movement center (Staggenborg 1998, 183).

Thinking about movements as communities leads to a number of research questions regarding organization and culture, collective identity, and movement campaigns. In the following sections, I elaborate on these issues before discussing methodological issues in studying movement communities and providing examples from my case studies.

Organization and Culture

How do some movements endure for many years and continue to mobilize campaigns? Movement organizations often decline, yet people continue to participate in, and identify with, the movement. Movement communities typically contain cultural groups and other "abeyance" structures (Taylor 1989) that keep like-minded individuals in contact and identified with the movement. When a particular movement is in a period of lull, activists from specific movement communities, such as the women's movement, may become active in overlapping SMCs such as the peace movement community (Meyer and Whittier 1994). Individuals may engage in ideologically structured action in different venues, such as families and workplaces, disseminating a movement's ideas and advancing its goals. One research question, then, concerns the types of cultural and organizational structures in a SMC and the opportunities that they provide for ideologically structured action.

Some movement communities are better able to sustain ideology and activism than others, depending on organizational structures and culture. Lichterman (1995) notes that movement communities have different cultural bases, affecting their ability to form and sustain alliances even when there is ideological agreement. Communities that build on the *communitarian* ties and practices of preexisting communities, such as racial or ethnic groups, are likely to see themselves as part of unified groups with leaders who can speak for them, whereas *personalized* communities emphasize individual responsibility within collective efforts (516). Lichterman finds that cultural practices such as the intensive individual participation in lengthy meetings associated with personalized communities limit multicultural alliances, raising the question of how common cultural practices and ties can be created within and across diverse movement communities (see Rose 2000; Obach 2004).

SMCs include formal and informal "free spaces" that allow activists to connect with one another and develop movement frames and ideology. These spaces may be more or less integrated into traditional communities and may have dense local ties and/or extralocal ties that reach into other movement communities, geographic places, and levels of action (Polletta 1999). One question is how ties to outside communities might expand the cultural frames and ideological perspectives of activists in local movement communities. Polletta argues that weak ties to outside networks in the national civil rights movement and the northern Left allowed rural southern civil rights activists and feminists in the civil rights movement to expand their behavioral expectations and collective identities (21–22). In looking at movement communities, we can ask how spaces and networks facilitate conversations among local and extralocal activists and how these exchanges affect ideologies, identities, and collective actions. In some movement communities, informal gathering places may offer free spaces in which community conversations occur. In other communities, activists may have to create deliberately the structures and networks that enable them to exchange ideas and develop movement ideology and strategy. As Lichterman (1995) and Polletta (1999) argue, the structure and culture of a movement community can inhibit or facilitate movement alliances and actions.

By specifying the characteristics of movement communities, we can examine changes over time in their structures and cultures, and we can compare different movement communities to one another. Movement communities vary with regard to their cultural bases; the extent of overlap among activists from specific movements; the types of formal and informal structures they contain; the density of network connections among organizations and individuals; and the extent of centralization in the community created by movement centers and other means of uniting activists. Depending on how general and centralized they are, and what types of organizations, cultures, and networks exist within them, movement communities can support different types of collective actions and movement campaigns. We can look at the effectiveness of different types of mobilizing structures across communities and campaigns over time.

Collective Identity

Related to the nature of organization and culture in social movement communities is the question of how collective identity gets created, maintained, and expanded. Because actions and campaigns are not continuous, and organizations often decline, collective identity is an important glue for movement communities. Individuals and groups must internalize a movement identity to remain prepared to contribute to the movement and join campaigns as they arise. Collective identity involves "cognitive, moral, and emotional connection with a broader community, category, practice, or institution," which "may be imagined rather than experienced directly" (Polletta and Jasper 2001, 285). For example, Whittier (1995, 1997) finds that generations of feminist activists continue to feel connected to the women's movement; even when no longer regularly active in women's movement organizations, they maintain a collective identity and participate in the movement through occasional feminist campaigns, their workplaces, their daily lives, and other social movements. The structures of the women's movement community affect the ways in which collective identity is maintained and the opportunities for participation. Taylor and Whittier (1992) argue that collective identity is nurtured within movement communities via the creation of group boundaries through alternative institutions and ritual events, the fostering of oppositional consciousness, and the politicization of everyday life.

Collective identity develops within different types of organizational structures and contexts, and the nature of those structures and contexts in movement communities affects the nature of the identity and its potential expansion. For example, Valocchi (2001) found that the "organizational centralization" of the Old Left prevented gay activists in the Communist Party

(CP) from extending the collective identity of the Left to issues of same-sex oppression, whereas the "organizational fluidity" of the New Left allowed for this expansion of identity. Interactions among activists, who bring their individual identities to organizations, are critical to collective identity, but some organizational contexts, such as the cell-like structure of the CP, prevent the interactions between new recruits and organizational founders needed to expand collective identity (Valocchi 2001, 455). The ideologies of some movements and organizations are also more flexible and easily expanded than those of others.

Within movements, the structures that nourish collective identity may depend on the nature of movement goals and the extent to which a larger movement of preferences exists in the mainstream society. Futrell and Simi (2004) argue that collective identity is essential to the persistence of the white power movement (WPM); building on Polletta (1999), they show that both "indigenous" and "transmovement" spaces are prefigurative ones in which the collective identity of this marginal movement is nourished. Indigenous spaces consist of "small locally-bound, interpersonal networks where members engage in political socialization, boundary marking, and other cultural practices," whereas transmovement spaces create connections between local movement communities and broader movement networks (Futrell and Simi 2004, 17). In the WPM, identity is developed in structures, such as the family, that are "small in size, exclusive, intimate, and rooted in enduring relationships—all qualities that encourage members to safely and openly express their radical racial ideologies" (23). Intramovement structures, such as white power music festivals and websites, provide opportunities for broadening networks and collective identity in relatively risk-free spaces. Thus one important question is how movement community structures are matched to ideology, with some types of structures allowing identities with little support in the broader culture to spread. The question of how cyberspace can be used to recruit activists and reinforce identity, and how this might be changing the structures of movements, is also a critical one (see Polletta et al., chapter 2).

Rituals and narratives are essential to collective identity in a wide variety of movements. Narratives or stories can be used strategically to foster collective identity, but they might also "precede and make possible the development of a coherent community or collective actor" (Polletta 2006, 12). In the case of the WPM, "identity talk" includes the telling of elaborate morality tales and stories about racial dispossession, often as a part of ritual performances at informal gatherings such as parties (Futrell and Simi 2004, 28–29). In more formal settings, such as Aryan Nation congresses, Futrell and Simi find that rituals such as commitment ceremonies and the singing of racialized hymns create emotion and commitment to the collective identity of the WPM. Although surveillance and repression of Aryan Nation congresses decreased their frequency, white power music festivals substituted as new gathering places for the WPM (33). How movement communities create and maintain free spaces for ritual performances of movement narratives is an important question for movement community research.

Some movement communities are unable to maintain themselves or may weaken over time. The population of organizations and institutions connected to a movement community changes as some organizational movement identities become attenuated. Gamson (1996) found that two different lesbian and gay film festivals in New York fostered different types of collective identities and that both festivals became more oriented toward the film community and less connected to the movement community over time. Thus we need to look at the types of organizational structures within movement communities and how they shape collective identity, as well as the ways in which the organizations and institutions associated with movement communities change over time. Organizations may loosen or dissolve their ties to the *movement* ideology and goals that are central to a movement community. Over time, movement communities may be absorbed into the mainstream community or may transform into subcultures that have lost their ties to movement preferences (Buechler 1990, 43).

Movement Campaigns

To maintain their connections to social movements, movement communities need to engage in periodic campaigns, which mobilize activists for collective action and advance movement goals (Marwell and Oliver 1984; Tilly 2008; Staggenborg and Lecomte 2009). A *movement campaign* is "a sustained, organized public effort making collective claims on target authorities" (Tilly and Wood 2009, 3). Campaigns extend beyond a single event or collective action and demonstrate that a movement is capable of a large, public display of unity and commitment. Movement communities consist of mobilizing structures that can be activated for collective action; during the course of movement campaigns, the structures of movement communities and the connections of groups within and across movement communities become visible.

One important set of research questions concerns how the structure and culture of a movement community affect the nature of the campaigns that the community can mount and how campaigns, in turn, affect the shape of the movement community. We might expect movement communities that have dense networks, active SMOs, and central meeting places to mount campaigns most easily. Highly decentralized movement communities, and those with networks that are deeply submerged, can be expected to have a difficult time mobilizing extensive campaigns featuring large public demonstrations. Communities that lack dense networks, SMOs capable of acting as movement centers, and centralized meeting places may fail to mobilize some elements of a movement community, and disconnected groups may lack a shared preference for particular strategies within campaigns.

Leadership is critical to the mobilization of movement campaigns, and the organizational structures of movement communities affect the development of movement leadership. Depending on the types of organizations and networks within the movement community, effective leadership may or may not be available to campaigns. Ganz (2000) argues that organizational structures that permit "regular, open, and authoritative deliberation" and those with ties to multiple constituencies are most likely to develop and support "leadership teams" and "strategic capacity." While organizational structures and networks affect the quality of leadership available to movement communities, effective leaders in turn help to expand networks and build "bridges" within movement communities (Robnett 1997). During a campaign, it is possible to draw more members of the movement community into active participation and to expand leadership roles in the community (Downton and Wehr 1991).

While the structures and cultures of SMCs influence campaigns, movement campaigns also bring about changes in the structures of movement communities. Campaigns build organizations, create coalitions, and expand or strengthen networks both within and across movement communities. Tilly (2008, 89–90) argues that campaigns affect subsequent campaigns in three ways: they alter the political opportunity structure, they create new models for "contentious performances," and they create new networks and alliances. Campaigns typically involve coalitions, often cross-movement ones, and bonds of trust and successful outcomes from alliances in one campaign—as well as conflicts and coalition failures—typically carry over to subsequent coalitions and campaigns. Even when campaigns do not succeed in changing public policies, they may strengthen (or weaken) movement communities, thereby affecting future campaign prospects (Staggenborg and Lecomte 2009). In a study of the same-sex wedding campaign in California, which was a deliberate political strategy of "contentious cultural performance," Taylor et al. (2009) found that an initial campaign not only increased solidarity and identity within the movement but also spurred subsequent collective action.

Campaigns may involve "scale shift" among levels of action (Tarrow 2005), and connections may be made among different types of activists such as grassroots activists working on local campaigns and professional activists working in international nongovernmental organizations or transnational governmental organizations. For example, international networks of activists have been created within movements such as the global justice movement and the international women's movement. Activists interact with one another during collective campaigns, such as protests at United Nations–sponsored meetings, and at movement forums, such as the World Social Forums (Smith et al. 2008). These activists are likely to return to their local movement communities after participating in international campaigns and events (Tarrow 2005), but they stay in touch through e-mail and other information and communication technologies. Important research questions concern how structures, including Internet-based ones, can be devised to allow extralocal movement communities to sustain themselves and to mount ongoing campaigns.

Methods of Studying Movement Communities

Scholars have used multiple approaches in studying social movements (Klandermans and Staggenborg 2002), and various methods can be used to study movement communities, including surveys of participants, in-depth interviews of activists, and documentary analyses of movement literature. To study past campaigns and communities, it is necessary to use techniques such as content analysis of documents and newspaper accounts and interviews with any past and present activists who are available. Obviously, the further in the past organizational activities and campaigns are, the more difficult it will be to locate surviving activists, and the more memories will have faded. Sometimes we are lucky enough to witness movement communities and campaigns in action. When no campaign is in progress, an observer can attend meetings and observe events such as cultural performances in a movement community, interview participants about various community groups and activities, and employ documents and interviews to study changes over time. When a campaign is under way, participant observation can be used to observe the planning and execution of the collective campaign, followed by in-depth interviews with activists and analysis of available documents and news accounts. Participant observation in movement communities and campaigns allows the researcher to experience directly a number of processes such as the construction of collective identity through interactions, the formation of alliances, and the mobilization of campaigns. By watching, and perhaps participating in, the planning and performance of protests, we can see just how the structures and cultures of movement communities affect mobilization and strategies. For instance, a lack of strong ties between activists working in different organizations may lead to a lack of coordination on strategies.

The following are two examples of research using this methodological approach. First, the case of the World March of Women (WMW) campaign provides insights into the ways in which movement identities can be expanded and local and international linkages can be created. This research began with a study that mapped the various elements of the Montreal women's movement with the use of documents, secondary sources, informal discussions with activists and academics knowledgeable about the local women's movement, and theoretical ideas about movement communities. This led to a focus on feminism within universities, unions, community organizations, women's centers, and cultural groups and events as well as women's movement organizations. While researching the local movement community in the late 1990s, I learned of planning under way for the 2000 WMW and realized that a focus on this campaign would make visible the "submerged networks" of the movement community.

To study the campaign in Montreal, my students and I used participant observation, in-depth interviews, and analysis of documents such as minutes of meetings and literature collected during participant observation. Most of the participant observation was done by Josée Lecomte, a young francophone PhD student, who gained an insider's perspective through participant observation in the regional WMW coalition. Over a period of eleven months, she spent over eight hundred hours in the field, attending meetings and organizing activities with other members of the Montreal coalition, which was open to all who attended its public meetings. She wrote detailed field notes based on her observations, describing the networks and interactions of activists and groups, organizational structures, strategies, framing and ideology, and other campaign dynamics. Following this period of participant observation, we interviewed twenty-five activists involved in various organizations and activities associated with the campaign (see Staggenborg and Lecomte 2009).

The second case, the protests against the G20 in Pittsburgh in September 2009, demonstrates how local structures limit and facilitate the organization of a movement campaign. After the announcement that the G20 meetings would be held in Pittsburgh, it was obvious that protests would be staged in response. It was not obvious exactly how these protests would be organized, but the situation offered an excellent opportunity to watch the networks of the progressive movement community in action. Before long, public meetings were called to plan the protests, and along with other members of a research team, I was able to attend meetings that were held either weekly or biweekly up until the week of the summit and follow-up meetings that continued into October and November 2009. We also attended the demonstrations and other events held during the week of the G20 meetings. We surveyed activists at four major events, and we attended and took field notes at many of the other events. After this participant observation, we interviewed twenty-six activists involved in different groups and protest activities. Our observations allowed us to witness dynamics such as the framing of issues, efforts to create alliances, and interactions of activists and authorities. By interviewing activists after these observations, we were able get the perspectives of a variety of informants about statements and events that we witnessed during our field observations.

The World March of Women

With the expansion of the international women's movement in recent years, grassroots activists are increasingly connected to one another through advocacy networks, conferences on women sponsored by the United Nations, international women's movement organizations, and a growing list of unifying concerns that includes poverty and violence against women (Keck and Sikkink 1998; Antrobus 2004; Ferree and Mueller 2004). The WMW, which was initiated by the Fédération des femmes du Québec (FFQ), held international events in October 2000 and subsequently became an ongoing international organization, again holding events around the globe in 2005 and 2010 (Dufour and Giraud 2007a, 2007b). Leaders of the FFQ, a long-standing Quebec feminist organization founded in 1966, began to expand the group's mobilizing activities and agenda in the early 1990s (interview with Françoise David in Rebick 2005, 246–50). In 1995, the FFQ organized the Quebec Women's March against Poverty, known as the Bread and Roses March. This march was a highly successful province-wide campaign that united feminists and community organizers around the issue of poverty, enlarging the organizational infrastructure of the women's movement community in Quebec and strengthening collective identity among feminists.

The United Nations World Women's Conference in Beijing, which was held soon after the Bread and Roses March in 1995, then provided an opportunity for scale shift. Hoping to create an international campaign, members of the FFQ traveled to Beijing and gave a very well received workshop on the Bread and Roses March (Rebick 2005, 245). FFQ organizers were able to create an international coalition that subsequently organized the 2000 WMW. Influenced by both local and international women's movement communities, the WMW adopted the two issues of poverty and violence against women as the overriding themes of the campaign.

The FFQ worked with the international coalition on worldwide organization of the campaign, coordinated the organization of the event in Quebec, and participated in the Canadian World March committee. Local and regional organizing committees were formed to organize the campaign in cities and municipalities. After many months of planning, more than 5,500 coalitions from 163 countries and territories led marches in villages, neighborhoods, and cities around the world in October 2000 as part of the WMW. In

Montreal, activists were recruited through various types of mobilizing structures in the movement community, which became visible as the campaign was mounted. Elements of overlapping movement communities (labor, community, and feminist) came together during the campaign, particularly through the participation of women's centers, community organizations, and union women's committees, and the campaign helped to strengthen these structures (Staggenborg and Lecomte 2009).

The culture and organization and collective identity of the Montreal movement community, impacted by the prior campaign, were critical to the mobilization of the WMW in Montreal. Community organizations and centers that were not previously associated with feminism became part of the women's movement community with the Bread and Roses March, which framed poverty as a women's issue. Other organizations in the general movement community were ideologically flexible and willing to move into new issue territory; most important, the unions in Quebec were already active on issues beyond traditional labor issues and were easily brought into the WMW campaign. Women's centers in Montreal were already part of a province-wide coalition organization, and many women's centers and union women's committees were members of the FFQ. Both the women's center coalition and the FFQ acted as movement community centers that brought their members into active participation in the WMW (Staggenborg and Lang 2007, 187).

The collective identities of activists, together with the agendas of organizations, were expanded by the WMW campaign. A number of individuals and members of organizations reported in interviews that they made connections with activists in other types of organizations for the first time. Activists in unions, community and ethnic organizations, women's centers, religious groups, and other organizations came to know one another better through the campaign and came to identify with a broader and more diverse movement community. As a union activist said, "We expanded our network of women.... We had a common project that linked, in the end, all the women" (personal interview, April 2001). Perhaps most important, women reported expanding their consciousness of international feminist issues. Through campaign alliances, different groups within movement communities can begin to overcome cultural differences as they strengthen and enlarge their networks. The WMW campaign not only expanded networks in Quebec but FFQ leaders were instrumental in creating an ongoing organization that connected feminists around the world (Dufour and Giraud 2007a, 2007b).

In sum, the WMW campaign in Montreal was influenced by the organization and culture of the local movement community and by the collective identity of its participants. A previous campaign, the 1995 Bread and Roses

March, had created new networks and expanded identities in the community, bringing community centers and antipoverty organizers into the feminist community through the framing of poverty as a feminist issue. The movement community contained organizations, such as the FFQ, that were important in bringing different elements of the movement community together. It also included ideologically flexible structures, such as the union women's committees and women's centers in Montreal, that provided essential resources and participants to the campaign. The WMW campaign then led to further changes in the movement community as well as to scale shift in the form of greater involvement by participants such as the FFQ in the international women's movement.

The Pittsburgh Protests against the G20

When the White House announced on May 28, 2009, that Pittsburgh, Pennsylvania, had been chosen to host the G20 meetings from September 24 to 25, 2009, local activists began at once to plan protests. They ended up organizing a wide range of activities before and during the G20 summit, including a People's Summit; a March for Jobs and tent city; a rally and march by an interfaith group calling itself the "G-6 Billion"; a Women's Tent City put together by local women's peace groups; another tent city set up by a coalition called the Three Rivers Climate Convergence to emphasize climate justice and sustainable living; and two large-scale marches—one unpermitted march called the People's Uprising on the first day of the G20 summit and another, permitted People's March on the second day of the summit.

To understand how these events were organized, and to assess the successes and limitations of the protests, we need to look at the nature of the local movement community. Many activists in the movement community were connected through the Thomas Merton Center (TMC), which was founded in 1972 by antiwar activists as a peace and justice center. The TMC provided a center for the progressive movement community in Pittsburgh, including an active Anti-War Committee (AWC) formed in January 2003 to oppose the U.S. invasion of Iraq. The AWC planned and staged a large antiwar protest in Pittsburgh in late January 2003, attracting thousands of participants; following this success, the group organized another large march against the war in April 2003 and, in subsequent years, on the March anniversary of the invasion of Iraq. When the White House announced the Pittsburgh G20 meetings, the AWC immediately decided to use its experience to organize a large permitted march against the G20.

The TMC hosted a series of public meetings of activists prior to the G20 week, intended to create some coordination of effort and to allow the different groups organizing protests to share information about their efforts with one another. In addition to the TMC-based alliance, another center of organization for the G20 protests was a loose coalition of local anarchist and other antiauthoritarian groups called the Pittsburgh G20 Resistance Project (PGRP). There were connections between these two centers of activity in that a few activists participated in both alliances and there were prior network connections among the groups, but much of the organizing work for the G20 protests took place separately in the two alliances. The PGRP met weekly and organized working groups to plan its activities, including the People's Uprising. Anarchists within the PGRP were well connected to other anarchists around the country, and some traveled to other places during the summer to report on plans for the G20 and to encourage nationwide participation. Members of the PGRP and the TMC-based alliance collaborated to produce a statement of respect for diversity within the movement, known as the Pittsburgh Principles, which helped activists from different movement communities achieve a fair measure of unity.

The accomplishments and limitations of the Pittsburgh G20 protests reflect the organization and culture of the movement community. Although the TMC was a movement center for some groups, it did not encompass all activists in the community and lacked sufficient resources. Because the movement community had no single center at the time of the G20 protests, two separate alliances organized most of the G20 protests. Nevertheless, it is useful to conceive of a single progressive movement community with fluid boundaries that includes the multiple organizations, individuals, cultural groups, and events contributing to the G20 protests. Many activists outside the TMC had network connections to TMC activists, and some key participants in anarchist groups were former volunteers or staff at the Merton Center. The progressive movement community consists of a large number of groups and individuals, some well connected to one another and others only weakly tied together. Progressive or leftist activists in Pittsburgh share some ideological positions, but there are also areas of disagreement. These features of the general movement community help to explain the ability of specific communities (e.g., anarchists, peace activists) to mobilize, and they also affect the ability of different groups to work together. In looking at networks and bridge leaders, we can see how cooperative efforts, such as the Pittsburgh Principles, emerge. While Diani conceives of coalitional processes of coordination as distinct from community processes, I view coalitions as part of the broader movement community.

Activists in Pittsburgh succeeded in organizing a wide variety of protests and events during the week of the G20 meetings, despite frustrating months spent trying to secure permits for various events and fighting ordinances meant to restrict protest. During the G20 week, there was a huge police presence in Pittsburgh, and the police arrested many protesters and bystanders, including students, especially on the evening of September 25, 2009, at the University of Pittsburgh. Nevertheless, relations among protesters were respectful, and protesters worked together to support arrestees and fight for accountability from the city and police after the G20.

Activists were able to mobilize protests because the SMC contained many preexisting organizations, networks, and experienced activists. Participants used their skills to mobilize through websites as well as to attract a great deal of mainstream media attention to the protests. Pittsburgh's Indymedia Center, originating out of the 1999 Seattle protests, along with other Indymedia centers around the world, provided continual coverage of the protests during the G20 week. The PGRP and the TMC alliances provided places for both individuals and groups in the movement community to come together and plan protests against the G20. Local activists also had extralocal movement connections, and some national and international groups provided resources to local groups. But the protests were largely organized by local activists, though many activists from outside Pittsburgh attended the protests.

Along with its successes in mobilization and strategy, the movement community also experienced important limitations in planning and carrying out the protests. Given the short notice that the G20 would be held in Pittsburgh, activists were under a great deal of time pressure. The delays in obtaining permits made planning extremely difficult, and many plans had to be changed at the last minute as protesters were denied permits for sites close to the convention center where the summit was held. The TMC, which was doing much of the coordinating work, suffered from severe resource limitations and could not meet all the demands placed on it by the G20 plans. Given the resource shortages and other constraints, cooperation to avoid duplication of effort and to present a united front to authorities was critical.

Yet it was very difficult to expand cooperation among protesters. One reason was that activists had multiple identities and no unified collective identity as G20 protesters. Because activists had different ideas about how to organize politically, there was little agreement about the type of coalition or alliance that was desired or needed. Most PGRP activists saw themselves as having quite different politics than the TMC-based alliance, and some participants in the TMC-based alliance associated coalitions with hierarchy and exclusion, whereas others wanted more structure and coordination. Because there was little agreement on the structure and goals of the alliance, it became a kind of information-sharing space, where different groups and individuals reported on their plans. Although some joint strategizing was done in the public meetings, a fair amount of duplication of effort and lack of coordination resulted from the deference paid to individual organizations and differing approaches, much to the evident frustration of some participants.

Duplication of effort led to low turnout and logistical difficulties for a number of events. For instance, there were no fewer than three tent cities in different locations, and as a result, visitors to the tent cities were relatively few in number despite the huge amount of work involved in setting them up. Some participants in the planning meetings questioned early on why there should be three different tent cities, but each group had its own identity that it wanted to highlight. In another example of lack of coordination, the G6 Billion held a march and rally on September 20 at the same time that Bail Out the People was holding its March for Jobs at another location. Although both groups had representatives at the public planning meetings, each group had its own agenda, identity, and ideology, and the lengthy battle for permits also made planning difficult. But despite these limitations, Pittsburgh activists considered the protests successful overall, and changes in the local SMC created by the campaign can be expected to influence subsequent campaigns. In 2011, many of the same activists who protested the G20 became active in Occupy Pittsburgh, the local offshoot of Occupy Wall Street, and it is likely that networks and bonds of trust carried over from one campaign to the next.

Conclusion

The organization and culture of SMCs and the collective identities of activists affect the ability to carry out campaigns such as the WMW and the Pittsburgh G20 protests. Movement communities are often decentralized and may encompass a wide variety of individuals and groups. Over time, they may shrink or expand, and they may experience scale shift. During a campaign, we can observe the impacts of mobilizing structures, and processes of mobilization, in action. Afterward, we can examine the impact of the campaign on the movement community; it may build organizations, collective identity, and networks or create new divisions and burnout among activists.

In the case of the WMW, preexisting networks in the movement community were strengthened by a prior campaign, the Bread and Roses March, and used by a long-standing movement organization, the FFQ, to mobilize the 2000 campaign. The campaign then further expanded networks and collective identity in the local movement community and, at the international level, produced an ongoing organization that strengthened the global women's movement. In the case of the Pittsburgh G20 protests, existing groups and activists allowed the community to mobilize relatively quickly. Connections among different groups in the community, and the presence of the TMC as a movement center, allowed for a certain degree of unity, enough to formulate the Pittsburgh Principles and to organize public planning meetings of activists. However, G20 protesters had no unifying collective identity, and individual groups maintained their own agendas. Connections among activists were not strong enough to avoid substantial duplication of effort.

This analysis provides mixed support for the contention that the organization of social movements is becoming more decentralized and informal and that coalitions are giving way to less formal modes of coordination. In the case of the WMW, a movement organization, the FFQ, played a central role in organizing the campaign, but various formal and informal groups and networks also emerged in Montreal. Globally, a decentralized international network has been relatively successful in sustaining the WMW and carrying out campaign activities every five years (Dufour and Giraud 2007b). In Pittsburgh, the progressive movement community is fairly decentralized, with numerous groups acting on their own, and some activists clearly did not want to participate in a formal coalition. Conflicting ideas about organizations and coalitions are one of the obstacles to ongoing coordinated protest campaigns.

Although this essay provides no firm evidence of the changing nature of movements, the concept of a SMC does provide a tool for empirical research on changes in social movements. In thinking about the structural changes that may be occurring in movements, we have to go beyond thinking about changes in the formality of SMOs and networks. Movements consist of diffuse, often decentralized communities of diverse actors. To understand movement structures and cultures, we need to look for movements in a wide variety of places, including cultural groups, political movement organizations, alternative institutions, movements within institutions, and individuals engaged in ideologically structured actions. To understand how movements are changing over time, we need more studies of how these structures emerge during movement campaigns and how the campaigns then affect subsequent campaigns through their impacts on local communities and their linkages to national and international movement communities.

References

Antrobus, Peggy. 2004. *The Global Women's Movement: Origins, Issues, and Strategies.* London: Zed Books.

Aunio, Anna-Liisa, and Suzanne Staggenborg. 2011. "Transnational Linkages and Movement Communities." *Sociology Compass* 5:364–75.

Buechler, Steven M. 1990. *Women's Movements in the United States.* New Brunswick, N.J.: Rutgers University Press.

Diani, Mario. 1992. "The Concept of Social Movement." *Sociological Review* 40:1–25.

Diani, Mario, and Ivano Bison. 2004. "Organizations, Coalitions, and Movements." *Theory and Society* 33:281–309.

Downton, James V., Jr., and Paul E. Wehr. 1991. "Peace Movements: The Role of Commitment and Community in Sustaining Member Participation." *Research in Social Movements, Conflicts, and Change* 13:113–34.

Dufour, Pascale, and Isabelle Giraud. 2007a. "The Continuity of Transnational Solidarities in the World March of Women, 2000 and 2005: A Collective Identity-Building Approach." *Mobilization* 12, no. 3: 307–22.

———. 2007b. "Globalization and Political Change in the Women's Movement: The Politics of Scale and Political Empowerment in the World March of Women." *Social Science Quarterly* 88:1152–73.

Ferree, Myra Marx, and Carol McClurg Mueller. 2004. "Feminism and the Women's Movement: A Global Perspective." In *The Blackwell Companion to Social Movements*, edited by David A. Snow, Sarah A. Soule, and Hanspeter Kriesi, 576–607. Oxford: Blackwell.

Futrell, Robert, and Pete Simi. 2004. "Free Spaces, Collective Identity, and the Persistence of U.S. White Power Activism." *Social Problems* 51:16–42.

Gamson, Joshua. 1996. "The Organizational Shaping of Collective Identity: The Case of Lesbian and Gay Film Festivals in New York." *Sociological Forum* 11:231–61.

Ganz, Marshall. 2000. "Resources and Resourcefulness: Strategic Capacity in the Unionization of California Agriculture, 1959–1966." *American Journal of Sociology* 105:1003–62.

Keck, Margaret E., and Kathryn Sikkink. 1998. *Activists beyond Borders: Advocacy Networks in International Politics.* Ithaca, N.Y.: Cornell University Press.

Klandermans, Bert. 1992. "The Social Construction of Protest and Multiorganizational Fields." In *Frontiers in Social Movement Theory*, edited by Aldon D. Morris and Carol McClurg Mueller, 77–103. New Haven, Conn.: Yale University Press.

Klandermans, Bert, and Suzanne Staggenborg, eds. 2002. *Methods of Social Movement Research.* Minneapolis: University of Minnesota Press.

Lichterman, Paul. 1995. "Piecing Together Multicultural Community: Cultural Differences in Community Building among Grass-Roots Environmentalists." *Social Problems* 42:513–34.

Marwell, Gerald, and Pamela Oliver. 1984. "Collective Action Theory and Social Movements Research." In *Research in Social Movements, Conflicts, and Change*, edited by Louis Kriesberg, 1–27. Greenwich, Conn.: JAI Press.

McCarthy, John D., and Mayer N. Zald. 1973. *The Trend of Social Movements in America: Professionalization and Resource Mobilization.* Morristown, N.J.: General Learning Press.

———. 1977. "Resource Mobilization and Social Movements: A Partial Theory." *American Journal of Sociology* 82:1212–41.

Melucci, Alberto. 1989. *Nomads of the President: Social Movements and Individual Needs in Contemporary Society.* Philadelphia: Temple University Press.

Meyer, David S., and Nancy Whittier. 1994. "Social Movement Spillover." *Social Problems* 41:277–98.

Obach, Brian K. 2004. *Labor and the Environmental Movement: The Quest for Common Ground.* Cambridge, Mass.: MIT Press.

Polletta, Francesca. 1999. "'Free Spaces' in Collective Action." *Theory and Society* 28:1–38.

———. 2006. *It Was Like a Fever: Storytelling in Protest and Politics.* Chicago: University of Chicago Press.

Polletta, Francesca, and James M. Jasper. 2001. "Collective Identity and Social Movements." *Annual Review of Sociology* 27:283–305.

Rebick, Judy. 2005. *Ten Thousand Roses: The Making of a Feminist Revolution.* Toronto, Ont.: Penguin Canada.

Robnett, Belinda. 1997. *How Long? How Long? African-American Women in the Struggle for Civil Rights.* New York: Oxford University Press.

Rose, Fred. 2000. *Coalitions across the Class Divide: Lessons from the Labor, Peace, and Environmental Movements.* Ithaca, N.Y.: Cornell University Press.

Sampson, Robert J., Doug McAdam, Heather MacIndoe, and Simon Weffer-Elizondo. 2005. "Civil Society Reconsidered: The Durable Nature and Community Structure of Collective Civic Action." *American Journal of Sociology* 111:673–714.

Smith, Jackie, Marina Karides, Marc Becker, Dorval Brunelle, Christopher Chase-Dunn, Donatella della Porta, Rosalba Icaza Garza, et al. 2008. *Global Democracy and the World Social Forums.* Boulder, Colo.: Paradigm.

Staggenborg, Suzanne. 1998. "Social Movement Communities and Cycles of Protest: The Emergence and Maintenance of a Local Women's Movement." *Social Problems* 45:180–204.

Staggenborg, Suzanne, and Amy Lang. 2007. "Culture and Ritual in the Montreal Women's Movement." *Social Movement Studies* 6:177–94.

Staggenborg, Suzanne, and Josée Lecomte. 2009. "Social Movement Campaigns: Mobilization and Outcomes in the Montreal Women's Movement Community." *Mobilization* 14, no. 2: 405–22.

Stoecker, Randy. 1995. "Community, Movement, Organization: The Problem of Identity Convergence in Collective Action." *Sociological Quarterly* 36:111–30.

Tarrow, Sidney. 2005. *The New Transnational Activism.* New York: Cambridge University Press.

———. 2011. *Power in Movement: Social Movements and Contentious Politics.* Rev. and Updated 3rd ed. New York: Cambridge University Press.

Taylor, Verta. 1989. "Social Movement Continuity: The Women's Movement in Abeyance." *American Sociological Review* 54:761–75.

Taylor, Verta, Katrina Kimport, Nella Van Dyke, and Ellen Ann Andersen. 2009. "Culture and Mobilization: Tactical Repertoires, Same-Sex Weddings, and the Impact on Gay Activism." *American Sociological Review* 74:865–90.

Taylor, Verta, and Nancy E. Whittier. 1992. "Collective Identity in Social Movement Communities: Lesbian Feminist Mobilization." In *Frontiers in Social Movement Theory,* edited by A. D. Morris and C. M. Mueller, 104–29. New Haven, Conn.: Yale University Press.

Tilly, Charles. 2008. *Contentious Performances.* New York: Cambridge University Press.

Tilly, Charles, and Lesley J. Wood. 2009. *Social Movements, 1768–2008.* 2nd ed. Boulder, Colo.: Paradigm.

Valocchi, Steve. 2001. "Individual Identities, Collective Identities, and Organizational Structure: The Relationship of the Political Left and Gay Liberation in the United States." *Sociological Perspectives* 44:445–67.

Whittier, Nancy. 1995. *Feminist Generations: The Persistence of the Radical Women's Movement.* Philadelphia: Temple University Press.

———. 1997. "Political Generations, Micro-cohorts, and the Transformation of Social Movements." *American Sociological Review* 62:760–78.

Zald, Mayer N. 2000. "Ideologically Structured Action: An Enlarged Agenda for Social Movement Research." *Mobilization* 5, no. 1: 1–16.

8
Organizational Fields and Social Movement Dynamics

Mario Diani

Some time ago, Minkoff and McCarthy (2005, 290–92) identified the study of movements as organizational fields as a key area of research in the recent past, yet one in which the link between social movement and organizational studies had not been exploited as it might and should have been (see also McAdam and Scott 2005). Part of our current difficulty derives from our persistent tendency to treat social movements as aggregates of discrete elements (be they individual or organizational actors or events) rather than as systems of relations. I will address this problem by introducing a typology of "modes of coordination" of collective action. Building on both my earlier work (Diani 1992; Diani and Bison 2004) and broader debates on organizational and governance networks (see, e.g., Ouchi 1980; Powell 1990; Sørensen and Torfing 2007), I suggest that the responses to basic organizational dilemmas of resource allocation and boundary definition differentiate social movement, coalitional, organizational, and subcultural–communitarian modes of coordination (see, e.g., Laumann, Galaskiewicz, and Marsden 1978). Then, I discuss the relationship between social movements and network forms of organization in organizational studies (Podolny and Page 1998; Borgatti and Foster 2003; Provan and Kenis 2007). Finally, I show how this typology may help to reformulate some core questions of social movement analysis.

A qualification is in order before proceeding. I regard work on concepts as an essential component of a scientific enterprise; in particular, I think that we should neither use new terms to refer to phenomena or processes for which we already have available concepts nor, conversely, overstretch existing concepts to denote empirical phenomena that differ on some important

145

analytic dimensions (Sartori 1970). This is even more important when the boundaries of the phenomena under observation are extremely fluid, as in the case of social movements.

One should keep a neat line between empirical conceptions of social movements (i.e., the set of observable phenomena that we conventionally associate with social movements) and analytic conceptions (i.e., the properties of a concept that enable us to identify specific mechanisms and processes).

When exploring the relation between social movement and organizational studies, we must identify as clearly as possible the distinctive analytic properties of social movements, differentiating them from other instances of collective action, if necessary, at the cost of charges of narrowness. Instead, we have to be very inclusive in the range of empirical phenomena analyzed and look within them for specific, social movement–type mechanisms. Since the early 2000s, the "contentious politics" perspective (McAdam, Tarrow, and Tilly 2001) has stimulated important progress on this ground, encouraging the search for similar mechanisms across a larger variety of episodes of political contention. However, this has happened somehow to the cost of diverting attention from the distinctiveness of the concept of social movement (Diani 2003). For example, in the empirical cases of contention McAdam, Tarrow, and Tilly (2001) analyze, social movement actors are just one set of the protagonists of much more complex contentious processes. In fairness, McAdam and colleagues do not deny the specificity of social movements; however, having long criticized a strategy of research that treated movements as self-contained entities, they are not particularly interested in placing the differences between movements and other instances of contentious politics at the center of their agenda. Nonetheless, my own research on interorganizational networks (Diani 1995; Diani and Bison 2004; Diani, manuscript in preparation) has convinced me that focusing on such differences may still be a valuable exercise.

The Structure of Social Movements: Aggregations or Relations?

The lack of attention to organizational fields is at the same time a cause and an outcome of the tendency to conflate an empiricist and an analytic view of social movements. In turn, this may be seen as a reflection of a much larger inclination in the social sciences to think of structure in aggregative rather than relational terms—or, if we prefer, to treat collectivities as aggregates of actors (in the case of social movements, also events, actions, etc.) rather than as systems of relations between the same elements (on aggregative vs. relational views of social structure, see Kontopoulos 1993).

In an aggregative perspective, the collective properties of movements are ultimately given not by relations but by means and percentages, that is, by the distribution of the traits commonly associated with it. For example, we assess the relative strength of new social movements in different European countries by looking at the incidence of protest events, linked to their core issues, out of all protest events taking place in a country during a certain period (e.g., Kriesi et al. 1995); we make claims about the structure of environmentalism based on the distribution of the traits of the organizations active in the environmental organizational field (e.g., Andrews and Edwards 2005); or we draw the profile of social movements in light of the average profile of their activists and sympathizers (e.g., Dalton 2008). Accordingly, when we think of changes taking place in social movements and, more generally, in patterns of political participation, we focus on variations in the quantities of certain properties. For example, we test the movement society thesis by exploring variations in the aggregate numbers and features of protest events over time (e.g., Soule and Earl 2005; McCarthy, Rafail, and Gromis, chapter 18) or by looking at changes in the share of the population that claims to have participated in demonstrations (e.g., Snow, Soule, and Kriesi 2004, 4, drawing on Norris 2002).

These are valuable exercises that have enabled us to go beyond the limitations of interpretations based on speculation or, at best, anecdotal evidence. However, they imply focusing on the presence or absence and on the weight of certain elements in a given instance of collective action rather than on how such elements shape specific relational patterns. It's important to know how many organizations interested in a given set of issues operate in a given country at a given time and what their main traits are, but it's also important to know whether and how those organizations are connected to each other: whether they collaborate, mutually supporting their respective initiatives, blending them into broader agendas, or whether they do work independently, trying to secure themselves a specific niche.

For example, comparative evidence suggests that animal rights issues may or may not be linked to more classic political ecology or conservationist agendas, depending on the traditions of different countries (Rootes 2003); only in the former case could we meaningfully treat animal rights campaigns as indications of a burgeoning environmental movement. Likewise, specific urban mobilizations on polluting factories, new urban bypasses, the preservation of green commons, or the like do not necessarily suggest the presence of an environmental movement. They may be mere instances of single-issue collective action, narrowly defined, or they may be linked by their proponents into much larger campaigns, through the connecting role of individuals and/or organizations mobilizing on several issues as well as through symbolic processes. Only the latter may be taken as indications of the existence of a broader environmental movement (Diani 1995).

Overlooking relational patterns may also prove, at times, positively misleading. For example, a comparison of civil society organizations active in Bristol and Glasgow in the early 2000s (Diani 2009) shows that although the number of organizations promoting radical protest tactics and displaying other classic traits of protest organizations is very similar in the two cities, the relational patterns in which they are involved are totally different. In Glasgow, they form a densely knit cluster; in Bristol, they are scattered across the whole civic network and occupy no distinct positions. If we were to apply the criteria used to test the movement society thesis and focus on percentages and means, we would be tempted to conclude that we are facing two similar local movement societies; an analysis based on relational patterns shows exactly the opposite.

These examples suggest that when it comes to understanding the features of collective action, the configuration of networks is at least as important, and at times more important, than the properties of single actors, be they individuals or organizations. Although social movement analysts generally agree that movements are best conceived as complex systems involving multiple actors, they have not paid enough attention to the methodological dimension of the problem, namely, how to theorize movement dynamics and connect theories to specific research operations. Limiting ourselves to the study of organizations, which is the focus of this chapter, we are indeed swinging between data collection strategies, such as those based on surveys, that enable the treatment of multiple cases but are basically of the aggregative type (e.g., Andrews and Edwards 2005; Brulle et al. 2007) and in-depth qualitative case studies that enable the reconstruction of the logics of networking by a small group of actors but are not particularly effective at capturing the overall structure of even a local network (e.g., Armstrong 2005).

The first strategy provides a complete account of the profile of an organizational field but falls short of specifying in any reasonable detail the relational dynamics within it: do organizations interested in the same issues work together in sustained campaigns? Or do they operate mainly on their own? And even if the former applies, do they operate as an integrated movement, or are they divided into noncommunicating factions? These and similar questions can hardly be addressed by standard surveys only. This leaves a number of issues open. For example, in chapter 6, Soule refers to studies documenting the persistent high number of U.S. organizations working on environmental issues as proof of the persistent relevance of social movement organizations (more specifically, environmental movement organizations). However, neither Soule nor the authors she cites offer any criteria to differentiate environmental movement organizations from other types of political and voluntary organizations. They simply treat all organizations promoting collective action on environmental issues as environmental movement organizations. However, many of the organizations to which they refer work in ways that render them totally indistinguishable from what other intellectual traditions call public interest groups, as has been repeatedly and correctly noted (e.g., Jordan and Maloney 1997; Burstein and Linton 2002). The only way to capture differences between social movement and interest group processes is, as I argue in the next pages, by looking at the different relational patterns in which organizations are involved.

The second strategy, that of in-depth qualitative studies of specific organizational fields, has generated impressive accounts of social movement milieus, especially those with strong (sub)cultural dimensions such as gay and lesbian or women's movements (e.g., Staggenborg 1998, 2001; Armstrong 2005). Normally, this approach implies an aprioristic selection of the organizations relevant to the mobilization process and a focus on strategic action. It generates great insight into the organizations most directly linked to a given cause, their logics of alliance building, and their relations to core external actors. However, while it is undoubtedly relational in its attention to interactions between a selected number of actors, it is less effective at locating them within broader organizational populations and at providing systematic reconstructions of the structure of fields. What is, for instance, the role of militant feminist groups within organizational populations in which the range and number of organizations addressing issues linked to women's conditions from different cultural and ideological perspectives is much larger? We cannot assume them to be the same, but we cannot rule out possible overlaps either. To map relational patterns within an organizational field more clearly, we need to specify the peculiarity of social movements as relational processes and differentiate them on this ground from other forms of collective action. To this task I now turn.

Social Movements and Other Modes of Coordination of Collective Action

Social movement scholars broadly agree that "social movements are only one of numerous forms of collective action" (Snow, Soule, and Kriesi 2004, 6). *Collective action* indeed includes all "social phenomena in which social actors engage in common activities for demanding and/or providing collective goods" (Baldassarri 2009, 391), namely, uncontentious activities aimed at service delivery, mutual and self-help, and so on, as well as contentious actions promoted and coordinated by formal organizations such as parties, unions, or interest groups (Tarrow 1998, 3). Introducing the concept of *modes of coordination* helps us to differentiate between social movements and other forms in a more systematic way.

By "mode of coordination" I mean a specific combination of the mechanisms through which resources are allocated within a certain collectivity, decisions are made, collective representations are elaborated, and feelings of solidarity and mutual obligation are forged (for earlier uses of this expression, see, among others, Camerer and Knez 1996; Thevenot 2001; Mayntz 2003). We can identify at least two broad classes of mechanisms, associated with *resource allocation* and *boundary definition*. Resource allocation (*resource transfers* for Laumann, Galaskiewicz, and Marsden 1978) includes the whole set of procedures through which decisions are made regarding the use of organizational resources—from choice of agendas, strategies, and tactics to selection of leadership and resource mobilization. Within specific organizations, such decisions may be made and implemented through formal as well as informal procedures, although in most cases, they are made through a combination of the two (e.g., March and Simon 1958). We can extend this logic, however, to organizational fields by noting that resource allocation may also take place through informal exchanges between groups and organizations that maintain their independence and autonomy. In some cases, organizations may concentrate most of their resources on their own project and devote a very limited amount of resources to collaborative projects, which results in fairly sparse interorganizational networks. In other cases, resources invested in collaboration may be substantial and are more likely to lead to fairly dense interorganizational networks.

At the same time, mechanisms of *boundary definition* (*boundary interpenetration* for Laumann, Galaskiewicz, and Marsden 1978) are relevant not only for specific organizations (Lawrence and Lorsch 1967) but also, and possibly more, for broader organizational fields. Although processes of boundary definition may also be primarily associated with ideational elements, social representations, framing processes, and the creation and reproduction of boundaries are also supported by relational mechanisms. Boundaries are criteria that classify elements of social life into different groups and categories, while shaping the relations between elements both within and between those groups (Abbott 1995; Tilly 2005). They are an essential component of processes of identity building, helping to establish connections across time and space, for example, between phases in individual lives, or between different generations, or between events occurring simultaneously in different locations (Somers 1994; Melucci 1996; Pizzorno 2008).

Processes of boundary definition and identity building are embedded in relational structures. Among the different types of ties that contribute to boundary definition, those consisting of individuals' multiple memberships and affiliations play a crucial role, as identities are defined by their intersection

(Simmel 1995). Within organizational fields promoting collective action, this means pointing at the role that "latent" networks (Melucci 1996; see also Taylor and Whittier 1992), connecting different organizations through activists' multiple involvements and personal connections, play in generating broader collective identities and specific boundaries. Joint membership is an adequate proxy for boundary defining ties as it is diffuse rather than specific and expressive rather than instrumental: people join multiple organizations (in voluntary associations) to express their support for them all and to participate generically in their activities rather than for very specific, ad hoc purposes. This sets in motion processes of boundary definition that often cut across organizational boundaries. Many others have also looked at organizational memberships as one of the bases for the ties that make up the fabric of a collectivity (Breiger 1974; Carroll and Ratner 1996). Their role seems particularly important in accounting for links between collectivities in which the basis of interpersonal linkages is clearly not kin or friendship such as epistemic communities or communities of practice.

Looking at movements from the perspective of these two types of mechanisms makes it explicit that having many people interested in a given cause, many protest events occurring on issues that seem more or less related to a set of common problems, and/or a set of organizations mobilizing on similar issues does not warrant per se the existence of a social movement. It is certainly difficult to think of a movement in the absence of such elements, but the reverse does not automatically apply. For a movement to be in place, we need a particular form of coordinating those elements. In my earlier work, I have identified such forms as networks of informal exchanges between a multiplicity of actors on the basis of a shared collective identity (Diani 1992). In this perspective, strongly influenced by anthropologist Luther Gerlach's (2001) earlier work, networks do not simply represent one instance of the "social movement bases" that, according to Tilly and Tarrow (2007, 114), provide the infrastructure necessary for the promotion of social movement campaigns. Instead, networks constitute social movements in that they represent a distinctive mode of coordinating collective action (although it goes without saying that not all network forms of organization constitute social movements—more on this in the third section).

Organizations mobilizing on behalf of broad public causes may engage in extensive interorganizational collaborations for several reasons. Very few of them actually command enough resources to conduct mobilizations on their own; moreover, actions promoted by broad coalitions are more likely to attract public attention, be perceived as worthy, and gain political legitimacy. The format and composition of those cooperative efforts is variable. Although some organizations may work together on a recurrent basis on different campaigns, not all the organizations that identify with a given movement collaborate simultaneously on every single project. Taken together, however, these collaborations result in relatively dense—at times, very dense—interorganizational networks.

It is important to stress the heterogeneity—if to varying degrees—of the actors involved in these networks. When looked at individually, they display a huge variety of organizational forms, ranging from the highly formal to the totally loose and spontaneous; they also differ substantially in the amount and types of resources and skills they command, and they articulate in different issue priorities and specific agendas the broad goals of the movement in which they are active. Their urge to develop broader alliances and large-scale cooperation always needs to find a balance with the aspiration to preserve their autonomy and specificity.

From this it follows that in a social movement mode of coordination, the terms of interorganizational collaboration are informal and have to be renegotiated each time a new issue, opportunity, or threat emerges. In other words, each collective action event is the product of a specific negotiation. This does not mean that practices of repeated collaboration between different organizations may not generate informal routines that reduce the costs of the negotiation; however, these routines are not formalized. Negotiations between movement actors refer to several aspects of mobilization campaigns, including the articulation of their specific goals, the choice of the most appropriate tactics and mobilizing messages, the identification of the social sectors from which to search for support, and the contributions that each coalition partner is expected to give.

Mechanisms of *boundary definition*[1] are crucial in social movements for a number of reasons, the most obvious being that movements have no formal boundaries and no formally defined criteria for inclusion or exclusion. There are no formal social movement members, as the only criterion for "membership"—better, "for being part"—is direct involvement with activities and/or organizations that are associated with the movement. By "associated," I mean that they are socially constructed as linked to a broader collective experience called "movement." Therefore the boundaries of a movement are defined by processes of mutual recognition whereby social actors recognize different elements as part of the same collective experience and identify some criteria that differentiate them from the rest. Those elements may be individuals or organizations but also events.

Individuals may be associated with a movement to the extent that they recognize each other, and are recognized by other actors, as a part of that particular movement. It does not suffice that they adopt certain lifestyles, hold certain values and opinions, or show willingness to engage in certain actions as individuals. It is necessary that they represent themselves and be represented by others as protagonists of a broader collective process. Organizations, likewise, do not belong in a movement because of their issue priorities, their strategies and tactics, or their organizational profiles but rather because they define themselves as part of that movement and are perceived as such by significant others. There is nothing in an association for the protection of birds that makes it part of the environmental movement; this depends at the very least on the inclusion of bird protection in a broader environmental agenda and on a recognition of the affinity between that particular organization's goals, agendas, and policies and those of the organizations associated with the environmental movement. Finally, the same logic can be applied to events: we do not get a movement out of the sum of the events on issues with similar characteristics but out of processes of meaning construction that associate the specific events with a specific project. A protest against industrial pollution in a working-class neighborhood may be an instance of the environmental movement if certain representations of reality prevail, but it may also be equally plausibly regarded as an example of class struggle and associated with working-class movements or with localistic, not-in-my-backyard mobilizations, if other narratives prevail.

Mechanisms of boundary construction are also essential because they secure the continuity of collective action over time and space. Social movements exist, in other words, because both actors mobilized in them and observers are capable of locating in a broader picture actors and events that operate in different points in space and time. For example, environmentalism exists to the extent that people are capable of providing a common interpretation for actions on nuclear energy, industrial pollution, and animal protection, occurring in different localities and at different time points. Moreover, boundary definition helps in providing participants with the necessary motivations to act. Although participation in collective action may be driven by a range of factors, including instrumental calculations, sanctions, and/or incentives coming from one's personal networks, contingent opportunities, and so on, identity plays an essential role in supporting actors' decisions to undertake long-term, sometimes dangerous, always uncertain projects. This applies not only at the individual level, on which analysts have focused (Melucci 1996; McAdam 2003; Pizzorno 2008), but also at the organizational level: though interorganizational exchanges are subject to constant negotiation, new alliances are easier if there are routines and recurrent practices that also reflect in particular identities and definitions of boundaries.

Like resource coordination, boundary definition also often takes a multidimensional, complex form. We only rarely have clear-cut identities and boundaries, neatly separating movements from their environments (including other movements; Beamish and Luebbers 2009); rather, we have boundaries that are often permeable, more or less dense areas of mutual recognition, and possibly chains of recognition (Pizzorno 2008). It is important to stress the dual nature of boundary definition, at the organizational level and the movement level. The fact that there is a movement-level identity, that is, a boundary encompassing all the actors associated with a movement, does not mean a demise of organizational identity. To the contrary, feelings of belongingness, solidarity, and obligation may be, and often are, addressed to both specific organizations and a movement taken as a whole (Lofland 1996, 11). This does not rule out the possibility that some individuals identify exclusively with a movement, without developing loyalty and affiliations to any specific organization (think, for example, of the affinity groups in the global justice movement described by McDonald 2002). In general, however, there is some kind of balance between organizational and broader identities. Such tension reflects in activists' multiple affiliations and involvements in several experiences through organizational membership, personal connections, and participation in specific activities. Accordingly, boundary definition takes place through intense multiple membership and personal connections cutting across organizational boundaries (e.g., Carroll and Ratner 1996).

Summing up this discussion, it is precisely the coupling of informal resource exchanges and boundary definitions encompassing multiple actors that defines the analytical properties of a social movement mode of coordination. However, many collective activities that we associate with movements actually occur through other modes of coordination. I distinguish here between coalitional, organizational, and subcultural–communitarian modes (see Figure 8.1).

Let us start with *coalitional* modes of coordination. *Coalitions* and *movements* are often used interchangeably (e.g., Meyer and Corrigall-Brown 2005; Van Dyke and McCammon 2010). In terms of resource allocation, they are actually very similar, as both consist of multiple, often heterogeneous, independent actors sharing resources in pursuit of some common goal. However, these two modes of coordination differ in the nature and scope of boundary definition mechanisms. In contrast to social movements, the boundary work taking place in coalitions is temporary and locally circumscribed. Given their instrumental, goal-oriented nature, coalitions exhaust their function either when their goal is achieved or when it is clear that the cause has been lost. It is certainly true that coalitions, originally set up by organizations each focusing on its own identity, may gradually see the emergence of broader feelings of

		Focus of boundary definition	
		Collective identity includes multiple actors	Collective identity is focused on specific organizations
Focus of resource allocation	Dense exchanges between actors in an organizational field	Social movement	Coalition
	Most decisions made within organizations	Subculture/ community	Organization

Figure 8.1. Modes of coordination of collective action.

solidarity among their proponents and thus contribute to the formation of broader social movements. However, at the analytic level, the idea of coalition may be brought down to "temporary, means oriented alliances among individuals or groups which differ in goals... [with] little value consensus... [and] tacit neutrality on matters which go beyond the immediate prerogatives" (Gamson 1961, 374).[2]

It is also important to remember that a huge chunk of protest activity as well as voluntary action (actually the largest part of it) follows the logic of *organizational processes*. These consist of modes of resource allocation and boundary definition that do not involve systematic interorganizational networking and take place largely within specific groups or organizations. This model accommodates organizational forms ranging from the extremely hierarchical and formalized (such as twentieth-century mass parties) to the extremely decentralized and informal (such as alternative communes or grassroots groups), from the extremely endowed with resources (such as business associations) to the extremely deprived (such as neighborhood action groups). What matters here is that action is promoted and coordinated by units that have an autonomous decisional capacity, whether this comes from formally appointed leaders or officers or from the grassroots, participatory deliberations of activists' meetings. Admittedly, boundary definition is by no means less relevant to organizations than to social movements. However, in this model, loyalties and attachments are primarily focused on specific groups and organizations rather than on broader collectivities. The exclusiveness and rigidity of these boundaries may vary substantially. The more they are permeable, the less we have an organizational mode of coordination in place.

Finally, it is also possible to think of *subcultures–communities* as a distinct mode of coordination of collective action. By this I mean a process in which interorganizational linkages are sparse, yet there are widespread feelings of identification, with a much broader collectivity than the one represented by specific organizations, and a set of practices that support it. These include individuals' multiple affiliations in different forms of community life. In authoritarian regimes, where associational life is severely constrained, people may mobilize through the contacts developed in the context of legitimate activities. In Czechoslovakia before the Velvet Revolution, these were often theaters (Glenn 1999); in mid-nineteenth-century France, "informal centers of sociability like cafés, vintners, and cabarets" (Aminzade 1995, 42) hosted French republicans at times of intensifying repression. Community structures such as the mosque or the bazaar in Islamic countries of North Africa and the Middle East have played an important role in facilitating collective action not only during the Arab Spring but also in earlier uprisings (Bennani-Chraïbi and Fillieule 2003). Even in democratic countries, dense subcultural networks may strengthen identity feelings and facilitate spontaneous, informal mobilization when dense organizational structures are not in place or available, for whatever reason. For example, participating in reading groups, patronizing the same cafes or bookshops, being active in the same cultural milieu or scene generates connections on which people may draw to promote collective action when necessary. The feminist and lesbian communities studied in the United States by Staggenborg (1998, 2001; Staggenborg and Lecomte 2009) and Taylor and Whittier (1992; Whittier 1995), the submerged interpersonal networks explored by Melucci (1996) in 1980s Milan, and the cultural scenes investigated by Haunss and Leach (2009) all provide illustrations of this phenomenon. So do the epistemic communities mobilizing on a transnational scale on issues such as Internet governance (Padovani and Pavan 2007; Pavan 2012) or creative commons (Fuster Morell 2010). These networks seem to have been massively involved in the promotion of the 2011 protest activities around the world: not only did they facilitate enormously the organization of coordinated events, such as the October 15 demonstrations,[3] but the very structure of connections promoting the activities has been equated to the Internet itself for its polycentric and territorially decontextualization (Friedersdorf 2011).

Integrating Social Movement and Organizational Theory

The typology of modes of coordination introduced in the previous section presents more than passing analogies to what has been elaborated by analysts of economic organizations. Following earlier contributions (Powell 1990; Baker 1992; Mizruchi and Galaskiewicz 1993), massive attention has been paid to network forms of organization and interorganizational relations (Kenis and Knoke 2002; Brass et al. 2004; Provan, Fish, and Sydow 2007; Provan and Kenis 2007). Although it is debatable whether it makes sense to speak of specific network organizations rather than applying the network model of governance to the exploration of organizational networks in general (Borgatti and Foster 2003, 995–96; Podolny and Page 1998), there is widespread consensus on some of the fundamental traits and advantages of network modes of organizations. Subsequently, I refer to them rather than to the network organization model, which seems to me a hybrid between networks and bureaucratic modes of coordination.

First of all, and analogously to what happens in the case of social movements, "in network modes of resource allocation, transactions occur neither through discrete exchanges nor by administrative fiat, but through networks of individuals engaged in reciprocal, preferential, mutually supportive actions.... Individual units exist not by themselves, but in relation to other units" (Powell 1990, 303; see also Podolny and Page 1998). More broadly, networks are characterized by patterned forms of interaction between formally independent units, whether individuals or organizations (Jones, Hesterly, and Borgatti 1997, 914; Monge and Contractor 2003, 219–21). The forms and contents of interactions are flexible, and there is no necessarily formalized division of labor and tasks. They may imply the exchange of information, resources, solidarity, and so on. Integration and differentiation combine both horizontally, across formal organizational boundaries, and vertically (Baker 1992, 401). Network organizations are actually highly integrated, regardless of formal divisions.

While organizational theorists identify different types of network governance, including some that are fairly centralized, the form closest to the social movement mode of functioning is *shared governance* (Provan and Kenis 2007). This entails some degree of involvement for all network members and is more diffuse among organizations in health and social services, also as a form of capacity building, than in the private sector. This form of governance does not usually produce binding decisions, as the major mechanism to secure compliance is moral suasion (Provan and Kenis 2007, 233–35). In business networks as well as in social movements, social control passes largely through relational mechanisms such as mutuality, reciprocity, and so on, rather than through contract: "[implicit and open-ended] contracts are socially—not legally—binding" (Jones, Hesterly, and Borgatti 1997, 914; see also Ouchi 1980; Powell 1990, 304–5). The presence of shared macrocultures strongly contributes to this particular form of governance by facilitating the convergence of expectations and norms. This happens through specific socialization processes, the sharing of specific languages, and tacitly understood rules (Jones,

Hesterly, and Borgatti 1997, 930). Actors' mutual reputation is also essential in situations of uncertainty (Jones, Hesterly, and Borgatti 1997, 932–33).

The network model in business also shares with the social movement model a number of advantages and disadvantages vis-à-vis more hierarchical forms of organization. They both represent a flexible way of acquiring resources, attaining collective goals, enhancing participants' legitimacy, and reducing uncertainty (Brass et al. 2004, 802). The multiplicity of the actors involved in social movements is actually functionally comparable to the disaggregation of firms into autonomous units, meant to increase their capacity to deal with uncertain environments (Jones, Hesterly, and Borgatti 1997, 918). Network forms of organization also facilitate the mobilization of the resources better suited to specific tasks and goals, a capability particularly important in contexts in which (as put in business language, easily adaptable to collective action) "products or projects are unique, require input from various experts, and must be solved creatively, [so that] an integrated organization is more effective" (Baker 1992, 402). Moving to the disadvantages, some of the problems usually attributed to network organizations, such as risks of propinquity or of oligarchy, or the problem of overembeddedness, that is, of overreliance on the most solid ties (Krackhardt 1994), all apply significantly to social movements too.

Some important differences also separate the network organizational model developed in business and organizational studies from the model of social movement proposed here. First, although a network organization does not develop in linear forms, as its final format is rarely anticipated (Powell 1990, 322–23), by comparison to movement networks, network organizations in business seem to involve a higher degree of deliberate planning and design (Baker 1992; Provan, Fish, and Sydow 2007). Second, whereas the role of mutual social control is important in both movement and business networks, movement integration relies virtually entirely on it, while business networks are often also kept together by contracts (Provan, Fish, and Sydow 2007, 482).

Finally, an open issue shared by both research fields revolves around the difference between a *network mode of organization* and a *network organization*. In the business and management literature, there is considerable variation in the focus of analysis, which stretches from networks of formally independent organizations within a broader organizational field (e.g., in Kenis and Knoke's 2002 concept of *field-net*) to clearly bounded organizations in which the network component refers to the pattern of organizing between different units (e.g., Baker 1992). Such extension in its use has prompted some to question the analytic value of the concept of network organization (Borgatti and Foster 2003).

In the case of social movements, it is likewise essential to stress the difference between *social movement networks* and *social movement network organizations*. In other words, within broader movement networks, one can frequently identify network organizations proper, which operate as autonomous decision-making units. Examples include global organizations such as Attac (Kolb 2005) or CRIS, the Communication Rights in the Information Society campaign (Thomas 2006), networks originated from national or local independent groups and associations to coordinate specific campaigns, or even the councils for voluntary sector setup in British cities to provide services to the voluntary sector. Analytically, however, the network organization seems to me a spurious intermediate form between a social movement and an organizational mode of coordination.

The typology of modes of coordination proposed here substantially enriches existing attempts to integrate social movement and organization theory by firmly locating the analysis at the interorganizational level. More specifically, it enables a thorough reconstruction of organizational fields as distinctive network structures rather than as aggregates of actors with specific interests and activities (for an early example, see Di Maggio 1986). Pointing in the same direction, Kenis and Knoke (2002) have more recently proposed the concept of field-nets to stress the noncoincidence of the notion of field with the notion of a system of interorganizational relations. Although attention to networks in and between organizations has grown massively, applications of network analytical tools to the study of whole fields are still remarkably limited. This remark does not apply only to social movements (Ansell 1997; Boudourides and Botetzagias 2007; Saunders 2007; Cinalli and Füglister 2008) but indeed to organizational theory (Betts and Stouder 2003; Provan, Fish, and Sydow 2007). Although this may be partially due to the lack of resources necessary to conduct these inquiries, this framework facilitates research by placing the multiplexity of networks center stage.

Conclusions: Modes of Coordination and Social Movement Research

Adopting the concept of modes of coordination is not just functional to a better integration of social movement and organization theory; it may also prompt a useful reformulation of some classic themes of social movement research. First, we can reinterpret the *emergence of social movements* as transformations in relational patterns. There is no denying that periods of high political mobilization correspond to high organizational formation rates (Minkoff 1995) and to variable combinations of new agendas, tactical innovations, new organizations, and new organizational models (Tarrow 1989). But we can also look, from a relational perspective, to the emergence of a social movement first and foremost as a process of strengthening the connections between actors that previously acted mainly independently from each other, privileging organizational modes of coordination or, at best, engaging in ad hoc instrumental coalition. There are not (only) new actors, then, but new ties and solidarities between existing actors, which enable recognition as a coherent unit what before appeared as fragmented (Kriesi 1988). Even the newness of a movement can actually be regarded as the extent to which it is capable of building boundaries and sustained collaborations that cut across the established cleavages of a given society (Diani 2000). In this perspective, and consistently with research on network governance (Jones, Hesterly, and Borgatti 1997, 927), changes in network composition through a relaxation or tightening of the boundaries and criteria for inclusion become a central issue; so do the conditions for alliance building (Borland 2008; Heaney and Rojas 2008). The comparative assessment of the Arab revolts of spring 2011 illustrates, for example, the shifting facilitators and constraints on coalition building across countries and phases and the difficulty of keeping together internally diverse coalitions (Diani and Moffatt 2012).

A focus on modes of coordination may also bring us beyond the limitations of recurring controversies about the (presumed) distinctiveness of social movement organizations vis-à-vis public interest groups (Jordan and Maloney 1997; Burstein and Linton 2002; Andrews and Edwards 2004). To date, social movement analysts have shifted between arguing the case for diversity based on a comparison of the characteristics of social movements and interest groups in terms of major orientations of their action, tactics, and so on (Snow, Soule, and Kriesi 2004, 7–8), and acknowledging that "social movements [assume] various organizational forms, . . . including hierarchy, decentralized networks, and a spontaneous, leaderless form without much organization at all—a form that may bear some resemblance to a market" (Campbell, 2005, 67). I think it would be more accurate and useful to say that a social movement mode of coordination may regulate the relations between a multiplicity of actors, the heterogeneity of which, in terms of organizational properties, may vary considerably depending on phase and context, and that accounting for the composition of movement networks becomes a central focus for investigation. Under what conditions do social movements include only actors close to the grassroots model of participatory organization, inclined to protest and weary of negotiating with institutions? And under what conditions do they, in contrast, display high internal heterogeneity of forms and/or greater variation of ideological stances? Following this approach, a social movement organization becomes simply any organization involved in a social movement mode of coordination with other organizations. The identification of the specific traits of the organizations involved in specific movements at specific times becomes an empirical question, not a theoretical one. Even the October 2011 anticapitalist demonstrations saw the convergence of fairly heterogeneous groups and organizations; what made them a movement was not the informal internal structure of each group mobilized (unions were there, for example) but the informal nature of the ties between those groups.[4]

Third, the passage from one to another mode of coordination may represent a useful way to interpret the *transformation of social movements*. This is usually analyzed in light of the transformation of the actors involved in them. Social movements may institutionalize, meaning that movement organizations change their profiles and become more bureaucratized, more professional, less kin on using confrontational tactics and more inclined to follow pressure strategies. Or social movements may dissolve because of their radicalization, with their different organizations turning into sects unwilling to compromise and to engage in sustained collaborations and a shared boundary definition (e.g., della Porta 1995). In either case, and irrespective of the specific content that the process takes, from a relational point of view, we have the reduction of social movement dynamics and the prevalence of other modes of coordination. These may be of the organizational or, at best, coalitional type and reflect a situation in which identities and boundaries are defined primarily in relation to specific organizations rather than to broader collectivities like movements. Or organizations may lose their capacity to cooperate in a sustained way, but still their members or sympathizers may share in the same cultural and community experiences, reproducing a sense of collective identity even in the absence of large-scale, coordinated mobilization. For example, the evolution of feminist movements since the 1960s provides empirical evidence of both dynamics (Whittier 1995; Staggenborg 1998), while the passage from a coalitional to an organizational mode of coordination—through the merger of previously independent coalition partners—is exemplified by the case of the labor organizations American Federation of Labor and Congress of Industrial Organizations in the United States (Cornfield and McCammon 2010).

Finally, looking at modes of coordination may help us reorient discussions on the properties of a *movement society*. It is certainly correct to argue that movements are no longer the expression of the disenfranchised but are a form of action among others (Goldstone 2004), available to different types of social groups. The studies that support this or similar statements through the systematic analysis of diachronic data (e.g., Soule and Earl 2005; McCarthy, Rafail, and Gromis, chapter 18) are certainly important. At the same time, there is no reason why we should restrict our explorations to the analyses of changes in properties measured at the individual level (i.e., as variations in the properties of individual people, individual organizations, or individual protest events). For example, it's certainly important to know what percentage of civic organizations in a given society is prepared to use protest tactics, and whether this percentage has changed over time, but it would also be important to know about the prevailing modes of coordination. Are organizations prepared to use protest linked in dense relational exchanges, which also imply a shared collective identity? In such cases, it might be plausible to view the movement society as characterized by deep political cleavages, salient enough to generate sustained conflict. In contrast, if organizations prepared to use protest were to operate mainly through an organizational mode of coordination, that is, as autonomous actors, this would support a view of the movement society as largely dominated by an instrumental and pragmatic conception of politics, in which protest simply increases the range of tactical options available to individual actors. My work on civic networks in Glasgow and Bristol exemplifies precisely these two ideal-typical situations (Diani, in preparation).

Notes

1. Tilly (2005, 137–46) lists a number of specific mechanisms associated with boundary definition (see also Diani 2007, 319–20).

2. See Diani, Lindsay, and Purdue (2010, 220–22) and Diani (in preparation) for more systematic discussions of these issues.

3. See, e.g., http://15o.democraciarealya.es/ and Friedersdorf (2011).

4. See, e.g., Hilary Wainwright, "Resistance Takes Root in Barcelona," *Red Pepper* blog, October 16, 2011, http://www.redpepper.org.uk/resistance-takes-root-in-barcelona/.

References

Abbott, Andrew. 1995. "Things of Boundaries." *Social Research* 62:857–82.
Aminzade, Ronald. 1995. "Between Movements and Party: The Transformation of Mid-nineteenth-century French Republicanism." In *The Politics of Social Protest*, edited by Craig Jenkins and Bert Klandermans, 39–62. Minneapolis: University of Minnesota Press.
Andrews, Kenneth, and Bob Edwards. 2004. "Advocacy Organizations in the US Political Process." *Annual Review of Sociology* 30:479–506.
———. 2005. "The Organizational Structure of Local Environmentalism." *Mobilization* 10, no. 2:213–34.
Ansell, Christopher K. 1997. "Symbolic Networks: The Realignment of the French

Working Class, 1887–1894." *American Journal of Sociology* 103:359–90.

Armstrong, Elizabeth A. 2005. "From Struggle to Settlement: The Crystallization of a Field of Lesbian/Gay Organizations in San Francisco, 1969–1973." In *Social Movements and Organizations,* edited by Gerald F. Davis, Doug McAdam, Richard W. Scott, and Mayer N. Zald, 161–87. New York: Cambridge University Press.

Baker, Wayne E. 1992. "The Network Organization in Theory and Practice." In *Networks and Organizations,* edited by Nitin Nohria and Robert Eccles, 397–429. Boston: Harvard Business School Press.

Baldassarri, Delia. 2009. "Collective Action." In *Oxford Handbook of Analytic Sociology,* edited by Peter Hedstrom and Peter Bearman, 391–418. Oxford: Oxford University Press.

Beamish, Thomas, and Amy Luebbers. 2009. "Alliance Building across Social Movements: Bridging Difference in a Peace and Justice Coalition." *Social Problems* 56:647–76.

Bennani-Chraïbi, Mounia, and Olivier Fillieule, eds. 2003. *Résistances et protestations dans les sociétés musulmanes.* Paris: Presses de Sciences Po.

Betts, Stephen C., and Michael Stouder. 2003. "The Network Perspective in Organization Studies: Network Organizations or Network Analysis?" *Proceedings of the Academy of Strategic Management* 2:1–6.

Borgatti, Stephen P., and Pacey Foster. 2003. "The Network Paradigm in Organizational Research: A Review and Typology." *Journal of Management* 29:991–1013.

Borland, Elizabeth. 2008. "Social Movement Organizations and Coalitions: Comparisons from the Women's Movement in Buenos Aires, Argentina." *Research in Social Movements, Conflicts, and Change* 28:83–112.

Boudourides, Moses, and Iosif A. Botetzagias. 2007. "Networks of Protest on Global Issues in Greece 2002–2003." In *Civil Societies and Social Movements,* edited by Derrick Purdue, 109–23. London: Routledge.

Brass, Daniel J., Joseph Galaskiewicz, Heinrich R. Greve, and Wenpin Tsai. 2004. "Taking Stock of Networks and Organizations: A Multilevel Perspective." *Academy of Management Journal* 47:795–817.

Breiger, Ronald L. 1974. "The Duality of Persons and Groups." *Social Forces* 53:181–90.

Brulle, Robert J., Liesel H. Turner, Craig J. Jenkins, and Jason Carmichael. 2007. "Measuring SMO Populations: A Comprehensive Census of U.S. Environmental Movement Organizations." *Mobilization* 12, no. 3: 195–211.

Burstein, Paul, and April Linton. 2002. "The Impact of Political Parties, Interest Groups, and Social Movement Organizations on Public Policy." *Social Forces* 75:135–69.

Camerer, Colin, and Marc Knez. 1996. "Coordination, Organizational Boundaries, and Fads in Business Practices." *Industrial and Corporate Change* 5:89–112.

Campbell, John L. 2005. "Where Do We Stand? Common Mechanisms in Organizations and Social Movement Research." In *Social Movements and Organizations,*

edited by Gerald F. Davis, Doug McAdam, Richard W. Scott, and Mayer N. Zald, 41–68. New York: Cambridge University Press.
Carroll, William K., and Robert S. Ratner. 1996. "Master Framing and Cross-Movement Networking in Contemporary Social Movements." *Sociological Quarterly* 37:601–25.
Cinalli, Manlio, and Katharina Füglister. 2008. "Networks and Political Contention over Unemployment: A Comparison of Britain, Germany, and Switzerland." *Mobilization* 13, no. 3: 259–76.
Cornfield, Daniel, and Holly McCammon. 2010. "Approaching Merger: The Convergence Policy Agendas of the AFL and CIO, 1938–1955." In *Strategic Alliances*, edited by Nella van Dyke and Holly McCammon, 79–98. Minneapolis: University of Minnesota Press.
Dalton, Russell. 2008. *Citizen Politics*. 5th ed. Washington, D.C.: CQ Press.
Della Porta, Donatella. 1995. *Social Movements, Political Violence, and the State*. Cambridge: Cambridge University Press.
Diani, Mario. 1992. "The Concept of Social Movement." *Sociological Review* 40:1–25.
———. 1995. *Green Networks: A Structural Analysis of the Italian Environmental Movement*. Edinburgh: Edinburgh University Press.
———. 2000. "Simmel to Rokkan and Beyond: Elements for a Network Theory of (New) Social Movements." *European Journal of Social Theory* 3:387–406.
———. 2003. "The Terrestrial Emporium of Contentious Knowledge." *Mobilization* 8, no. 1: 109–12.
———. 2007. "The Relational Element in Charles Tilly's Recent (and Not So Recent) Work." *Social Networks* 29:316–23.
———. 2009. "Social Movement Organizations: A Relational View." Paper presented at the ASA Annual Meeting, San Francisco.
Diani, Mario, and Ivano Bison. 2004. "Organizations, Coalitions, and Movements." *Theory and Society* 33:281–309.
Diani, Mario, Isobel Lindsay, and Derrick Purdue. 2010. "Sustained Interactions? Social Movements and Coalitions in Local Settings." In *Strategic Alliances: New Studies of Social Movement Coalitions*, edited by Nella Van Dyke and Holly McCammon, 219–38. Minneapolis: University of Minnesota Press.
Diani, Mario, and Caelum Moffatt. 2012. "Modes of Coordination of Collective Action in the Middle-East: Has the Arab Spring Made a Difference?" Unpublished manuscript.
Di Maggio, Paul. 1986. "Structural Analysis of Interorganizational Fields." *Research in Organizational Behavior* 8:335–70.
Friedersdorf, Conor. 2011. "How Occupy Wall Street Is Like the Internet." *The Atlantic*. October 17. http://www.theatlantic.com/technology/archive/2011/10/how-occupy-wall-street-is-like-the-internet/246759/.
Fuster Morell, Mayo. 2010. "Participation in Online Creation Communities: Eco-

systemic Participation?" *Journal of Information Technology and Politics.* http://politicsofopensource.jitp.net/sites/politicsofopensource.jitp.net/files/papers/Fuster_1.pdf.

Gamson, William. 1961. "A Theory of Coalition Formation." *American Sociological Review* 26:373–82.

Gerlach, Luther. 2001. "The Structure of Social Movements: Environmental Activism and Its Opponents." In *Networks and Netwars: The Future of Terror, Crime, and Militancy,* edited by John Arquilla and David Ronfeldt, 289–310. Santa Monica, Calif.: RAND.

Glenn, John K. 1999. "Competing Challengers and Contested Outcomes to State Breakdown: The Velvet Revolution in Czechoslovakia." *Social Forces* 78:187–211.

Goldstone, Jack. 2004. "More Social Movements or Fewer? Beyond Political Opportunity Structures to Relational Fields." *Theory and Society* 33:333–65.

Haunss, Sebastian, and Darcy Leach. 2009. "Scenes and Social Movements." In *Culture, Social Movements, and Protest,* edited by Hank Johnston, 255–76. Burlington, Vt.: Ashgate.

Heany, Michael, and Fabio Rojas. 2008. "Coalition Dissolution, Mobilization, and Network Dynamics in the U.S. Antiwar Movement." *Research in Social Movements, Conflicts, and Change* 28:39–82.

Jones, Candace, Williams S. Hesterly, and Stephen P. Borgatti. 1997. "A General Theory of Network Governance: Exchange Conditions and Social Mechanisms." *Academy of Management Review* 22:911–945.

Jordan, Grant, and William Maloney. 1997. *The Protest Business?* Manchester, U.K.: Manchester University Press.

Kenis, Patrick, and David Knoke. 2002. "How Organizational Field Networks Shape Interorganizational Tie-Formation Rates." *Academy of Management Review* 27:275–93.

Kolb, Felix. 2005. "The Impact of Transnational Protest on Social Movement Organizations: Mass Media and the Making of ATTAC." In *Transnational Protest and Global Activism,* edited by Donatella della Porta and Sidney Tarrow, 95–120. Lanham, Md.: Rowman and Littlefield.

Kontopoulos, Kyriakos. 1993. *The Logics of Social Structure.* Cambridge: Cambridge University Press.

Krackhardt, David. 1994. "Graph Theoretical Dimensions of Informal Organizations." In *Computational Organizational Theory,* edited by Kathleen M. Carley and Michael J. Prietula, 89–111. Hillsdale, N.J.: Lawrence Erlbaum.

Kriesi, Hanspeter. 1988. "The Interdependence of Structure and Action: Some Reflections on the State of the Art." In *From Structure to Action,* edited by Bert Klandermans, Hanspeter Kriesi, and Sidney Tarrow, 349–68. Greenwich, Conn.: JAI Press.

Kriesi, Hanspeter, Ruud Koopmans, Jan Willem Duyvendak, and Marco Giugni.

1995. *New Social Movements in Western Europe.* Minneapolis: University of Minnesota Press.

Laumann, Edward O., Joseph Galaskiewicz, and Peter V. Marsden. 1978. "Community Structure as Interorganizational Linkages." *Annual Review of Sociology* 4:455–84.

Lawrence, Paul, and Jay Lorsch. 1967. "Differentiation and Integration in Complex Organizations." *Administrative Science Quarterly* 12:1–30.

Lofland, John. 1996. *Social Movement Organizations.* New York: Aldine de Gruyter.

March, James, and Herbert Simon. 1958. *Organizations.* New York: John Wiley.

Mayntz, Renate. 2003. "New Challenges to Governance Theory." In *Governance as Social and Political Communication,* edited by Henrik P. Bang, 27–40. Manchester, U.K.: Manchester University Press.

McAdam, Doug. 2003. "Beyond Structural Analysis: Toward a More Dynamic Understanding of Social Movements." In *Social Movements and Networks,* edited by Mario Diani and Doug McAdam, 281–98. Oxford: Oxford University Press.

McAdam, Doug, and Richard Scott. 2005. "Organizations and Movements." In *Social Movements and Organizations,* edited by Gerald F. Davis, Doug McAdam, Richard W. Scott, and Mayer N. Zald, 4–40. New York: Cambridge University Press.

McAdam, Doug, Sidney Tarrow, and Charles Tilly. 2001. *Dynamics of Contention.* Cambridge: Cambridge University Press.

McDonald, Kevin. 2002. "From Solidarity to Fluidarity: Social Movements beyond 'Collective Identity': The Case of Globalization Conflicts." *Social Movement Studies* 1:109–28.

Melucci, Alberto. 1996. *Challenging Codes.* Cambridge: Cambridge University Press.

Meyer, David S., and Catherine Corrigall-Brown. 2005. "Coalitions and Political Context: U.S. Movements against War in Iraq." *Mobilization* 10, no. 2: 327–44.

Minkoff, Debra. 1995. *Organizing for Equality: The Evolution of Women's and Racial–Ethnic Organizations in America.* New Brunswick, N.J.: Rutgers University Press.

Minkoff, Debra, and John D. McCarthy. 2005. "Reinvigorating the Study of Organizational Processes in Social Movements." *Mobilization* 10, no. 2: 289–308.

Mizruchi, Mark S., and Joseph Galaskiewicz. 1993. "Networks of Interorganizational Relations." *Sociological Methods and Research* 22:46–70.

Monge, Peter R., and Noshir S. Contractor. 2003. *Theories of Communication Networks.* Oxford: Oxford University Press.

Norris, Pippa. 2002. *Democratic Phoenix.* Cambridge: Cambridge University Press.

Ouchi, William G. 1980. "Markets, Bureaucracies, and Clans." *Administrative Science Quarterly* 25:129–41.

Padovani, Claudia, and Elena Pavan. 2007. "Diversity Reconsidered in a Global Multi-Stakeholder Environment: Insights from the Online World." In *The Power of Ideas,* edited by Wolfgang Kleinwächter, 99–109. Berlin: Germany Land of Ideas.

Pavan, Elena. 2012. *Frames and Connections in the Governance of Global Communication.* Lanham, Md.: Rowman and Littlefield.

Pizzorno, Alessandro. 2008. "Rationality and Recognition." In *Approaches in the Social Sciences,* edited by Donatella della Porta and Michael Keating, 162–74. Cambridge: Cambridge University Press.

Podolny, Joel M., and Karen L. Page. 1998. "Network Forms of Organization." *Annual Review of Sociology* 24:57–76.

Powell, Walter W. 1990. "Neither Markets nor Hierarchy: Network Forms of Organization." *Research in Organizational Behavior* 12:295–336.

Provan, Keith G., Amy Fish, and Joerg Sydow. 2007. "Interorganizational Networks at the Network Level: A Review of the Empirical Literature on Whole Networks." *Journal of Management* 33:479–516.

Provan, Keith G., and Patrick Kenis. 2007. "Modes of Network Governance: Structure, Management, and Effectiveness." *Journal of Public Administration Research and Theory* 18:229–52.

Rootes, Christopher, ed. 2003. *Environmental Protest in Western Europe.* Oxford: Oxford University Press.

Sartori, Giovanni. 1970. "Concept Misformation in Comparative Politics." *American Political Science Review* 64:1033–52.

Saunders, Claire. 2007. "Using Social Network Analysis to Explore Social Movements: A Relational Approach." *Social Movement Studies* 6:227–43.

Simmel, Georg. 1995. *Conflict and the Web of Group Affiliations.* New York: Free Press.

Snow, David, Sarah Soule, and Hanspeter Kriesi. 2004. "Mapping the Terrain." In *The Blackwell Companion to Social Movements,* edited by David A. Snow, Sarah A. Soule, and Hanspeter Kriesi, 3–16. Oxford: Blackwell.

Somers, Margaret R. 1994. "The Narrative Constitution of Identity: A Relational and Network Approach." *Theory and Society* 23:605–49.

Sørensen, Eva, and Jacob Torfing. 2007. *Theories of Democratic Network Governance.* Cheltenham, U.K.: Edward Elgar.

Soule, Sarah, and Jennifer Earl. 2005. "A Movement Society Evaluated: Collective Protest in the United States, 1960–1986." *Mobilization* 10, no. 3: 345–64.

Staggenborg, Suzanne. 1998. "Social Movement Communities and Cycles of Protest: The Emergence and Maintenance of a Local Women's Movement." *Social Problems* 45:180–204.

———. 2001. "Beyond Culture versus Politics—A Case Study of a Local Women's Movement." *Gender and Society* 15:507–30.

Staggenborg, Suzanne, and Josée Lecomte. 2009. "Social Movement Campaigns: Mobilization and Outcomes in the Montreal Women's Movement Community." *Mobilization* 14, no. 2: 163–80.

Tarrow, Sidney. 1989. *Democracy and Disorder.* Oxford: Clarendon Press.

———. 1998. *Power in Movement.* New York: Cambridge University Press.

Taylor, Verta, and Nancy Whittier. 1992. "Collective Identity in Social Movement Communities: Lesbian Feminist Mobilization." In *Frontiers of Social Movement*

Theory, edited by Aldon Morris and Carol Mueller, 104–32. New Haven, Conn.: Yale University Press.

Thevenot, Laurent. 2001. "Organized Complexity: Conventions of Coordination and the Composition of Economic Arrangements." *European Journal of Social Theory* 4:405–25.

Thomas, Pradip. 2006. "The Communication Rights in the Information Society (CRIS) Campaign: Applying Social Movement Theories to an Analysis of Global Media Reform." *Gazette* 68:291–312.

Tilly, Charles. 2005. *Identities, Boundaries, and Social Ties*. Boulder, Colo.: Paradigm.

Tilly, Charles, and Sidney Tarrow. 2007. *Contentious Politics*. Boulder, Colo.: Paradigm.

Van Dyke, Nella, and Holly McCammon, eds. 2010. *Social Movement Coalitions*. Minneapolis: University of Minnesota Press.

Whittier, Nancy. 1995. *Feminist Generations: The Persistence of the Radical Women's Movement*. Philadelphia: Temple University Press.

9

Social Movement Structures in Action: Conceptual Propositions and Empirical Illustration

Dieter Rucht

Time and again, it has been shown that social movements are not amorphous masses but rest on some sort of organization. This insight was shared, with the exception of early mass psychologists, by almost all students of social movements, as exemplified by Lewis Killian's (1964, 442) definition: "A social movement is a collectivity acting with some continuity, not short-lived collectivity like a crowd. Over its life span it must develop some sort of structures." Curtis and Zurcher (1973) referred to this structural basis and its supportive environment as the "alliance structure" of a broader "multiorganizational field." In the context of the resource mobilization approach that has taken shape since the second half of the 1970s, social movement organizations (SMOs) and their aggregate, dubbed "social movement industries," moved to the center of attention. Most of the work carried out in this line of research is descriptive, focusing on a particular SMO, a set or an alliance of organizations in a particular campaign, or providing a broad overview of the organizational basis of a specific movement. Also, some conceptual work has been published on structure as a precondition for action, types of organizations, the role of networks, leadership in social movements, and so on (see, e.g., Gerlach and Hine 1970; Curtis and Zurcher 1974; Breines 1980; Klandermans 1989; Lofland 1996; Kriesi 1996; Barker, Johnson, and Lavalette 2001; Clemens and Minkoff 2004). Still, these conceptual endeavors, and even more so theoretical work on the structural basis of social movements, are underdeveloped. This is my starting point.

Instead of applying indiscriminately the term SMO to all sorts of structural elements in a social movement, I rather suggest laying out a more refined conceptional framework that takes into account different structures and linkages to grasp an extremely complex reality. Hence the first section of this chapter focuses on concepts and tools to grasp the structural basis of social movements. Second, I apply these tools in an illustrative manner to a recent social movement campaign in Germany. My intention here is to put some flesh on the conceptional bones and to show the multitude of both more stable and more volatile structural elements. To some extent, these illustrations might also help to document the usefulness and limits of the proposed framework and probably also show the need to complement and refine it. Finally, I discuss the empirical material and relate it to more general trends in both social movements and social movement research.

Toward a Conceptual Framework

Social movements, though often, and for the most part correctly, described as fuzzy phenomena or moving targets, may occasionally appear as "masses." In fact, however, they always rely on a structure. The term *structure,* to put it in very general terms, is meant here as a pattern of more or less stable relationships within and between various elements of a larger entity. Structure implies some degree of regularity and therefore predictability.

Structure is an abstract category covering an extremely wide range of social and nonsocial phenomena. In the case of social movements, it could refer, for example, to an informal hierarchy within a group, a weekly or annual meeting, a steering committee composed of delegates, a mode of decision making, tacit or explicit rules that regulate communication, an umbrella organization composed of dozens of informal or formal organizations, or a set of different ideological strands. Because of its vagueness, the term *structure* may serve as a convenient denominator to emphasize the nonamorphous character of social movements. Yet this term is not suited to grasp the variety of different elements or substructures that are part and parcel of a social movement.

When trying to make a social movement structure identifiable and tangible, most researchers apply the term SMO. Some use this category in a very broad sense, referring to any kind of "group" that can be attributed to a social movement. Others understand SMO in a more narrow sense, setting it apart, for example, from informal circles. Still others distinguish between groups and/or organizations, on one hand, and networks of individuals or groups and organizations, on the other.

Organizations defined in a narrow way are usually associated with characteristics such as a formal membership, a clear division of roles and internal functions, a mission statement, and probably even a legal status. Collective entities with such features, though probably in a less distinct way when compared to corporations or bureaucracies, can be found in almost all social movements. Their number and significance, however, may be overestimated because they are easier to identify and usually more accessible to outsiders, especially when SMOs have offices, spokespeople, newsletters, and websites; hold regular meetings; keep minutes; and launch declarations. Accordingly, researchers tend to underestimate the number of small, local and/or informal groups, which are more difficult to overview and study.

In the context of the resource mobilization approach, SMOs and processes related to them move to the center of analysis. In empirical studies, there is even a tendency to equate the ensemble of SMOs in a particular social movement with the movement itself, though it has been repeatedly stressed that social movements are not identical with their organizations: "The organized aspects of a social movement never entirely encompass it. . . . There is no completely organized social movement" (Lang and Lang 1961, 495).

Ironically, leading proponents of this approach, when defining a social movement, did not directly refer to SMOs as a constitutive element but characterized a social movement, in its most general form, as a "set of opinions and beliefs in a population which represents preferences for changing some elements in the social structure and/or reward distribution of a society" (McCarthy and Zald 1977, 1217–18).

Resource mobilization theorists' emphasis on movement structures has not led to an elaborated conceptual mapping of these structures. "This lack of attention to organizations is curious given the centrality of organizational structure in resource mobilization theories of collective action" (Olzak 1989, 123). Therefore a few basic categories will be suggested to capture a reality whose complexity cannot be adequately grasped with the term SMO only. When leaving aside the role and functions of individuals with regard to and within a social movement (McCarthy and Zald 1977, 1221–22) and concentrating on collectivities, a limited set of forms can be postulated:

1. Probably the most elementary collective unit of a social movement is the small and locally based circle of activists. It encompasses rarely more than twenty people. Sometimes these groups are completely informal. In other cases, they may have a formal status as a registered association. For the most part, this status tends to be only a superficial feature without profound consequences for the life of the group. In Germany, for example, these groups are usually called *citizen initiatives*. I suggest calling these collectivities *basic action groups*.
2. A second kind of collectivity is to a considerable degree marked by formal rules that define collective aims, membership, leadership,

decision making, financial and other accountability, and so on. Here it seems fully appropriate to speak of a *movement organization*. The size of these organizations may vary considerable, ranging from several dozens of individuals to hundreds of thousands. Large organizations are usually divided into local, regional, state, and probably even national chapters. Besides movement organizations based on individual membership, there also exist *umbrella organizations* composed of more specific organizations. Some umbrella organizations include both individuals and organizations as members.

3. Groups and organizations in social movements coordinate and even collaborate on an ad hoc basis or in a more enduring way. Provided that the participating collectivities maintain a horizontal relationship, thereby keeping their autonomy, the generic term *network* seems appropriate. When coordination is fairly limited in time and thematic range, we can refer to it as a *campaign network* (or campaign alliance). In addition, there also exist more permanent collaborative structures of autonomous groups and networks, which I call *enduring networks*. Typically, these enduring networks, at least when considered over a large time span, raise a multitude of issues. Quite often, they represent a specific ideological strand within a given social movement. But there are also cases of both campaign networks and enduring networks that include a multitude of ideological strands. For example, the German peace movement in the first half of the 1980s was directed by a coordination committee, the *Koordinationsausschuss,* in which ten different political strands and/or kinds of groups held thirty seats according to their estimated size (Leif 1985). Networks sometimes become internally differentiated, establishing subgroups, task forces, committees, and so on, and focusing on specific thematic aspects or functions, thereby forming an extremely complex structure.

4. Besides the various collectivities mentioned thus far, it is also important to take into account structural elements that, unlike the former structures, do not primarily and directly serve the purpose of consensus mobilization and action mobilization (Klandermans 1984). Rather, they are shells, spaces, or forums in which certain kinds of social movement activity can unfold. In this regard, two types elements can be discerned. First are *material service structures.* This term may apply to certain physical structures, for example, educational or training centers set up by social movements or small presses and bookshops that serve the needs of one or several movements. Second, there may be also more *immaterial service structures*

that provide technical know-how and/or factual expertise, or rather, cultural goods, such as music and theater, in direct support of social movements. More recently, groups in the wider context of social movements have been set up to enhance both internal and external communication processes, mainly relying on the Internet. A well-known example is the network of Indymedia groups in support of global justice movements.

5. In addition to these movement-oriented service structures, it is also important to consider the role of publicly accessible spaces that are not geared per se toward movement activities but nevertheless may play an important role in these. Such spaces can be street corners, coffeehouses, parental groups running a self-organized kindergarten, universities, centers for adult education, factories, and the like. Ohlemacher (1996) referred to them as *social relais,* emphasizing their importance for informal discussions among movement activists and bystanders and as recruitment pools for new activists. Obviously, these spaces cannot be understood as part of a social movement structure. Nevertheless, they should be taken into account to the extent that they are populated by social movement activists and actually used by these to promote their cause.

6. Finally, and probably most neglected in contemporary movement research, is the role of *supportive social milieus,* out of which social movements may grow or which especially long-lived movements may produce. These milieus are characterized by distinct lifestyles and behaviors that manifest themselves in cultural and political preferences, consumer choices, use of language and jargon, dress codes, and numerous other expressive symbols. These behaviors allow the insiders to intuitively recognize each other in their sameness but correspondingly can be decoded by outsiders belonging to another milieu. Social milieus, of course, have no clear-cut contours and may overlap to some degree. Yet there are also milieus that differ so widely that they are incompatible with each other. Social milieus imply their own infrastructures, for example, coffeehouses, bars, and cultural facilities. These facilities can overlap or almost become identical with the material and immaterial service structures of social movements.

Among the six basic structural components described, the first four are ultimately geared toward action mobilization, whereas the last two provide a ground for consensus mobilization. As an overview, the taxonomic framework presented so far is condensed in Table 9.1.

Table 9.1. Structural components of social movements and their immediate environments

Component	Main characteristics	Examples
Basic action groups	Small, local, informal, face-to-face interaction	Local antinuclear groups, feminist consciousness-raising groups, citizen initiatives
Movement organizations	Greatly varying size, from local to international levels, importance of formal rules	Robin Wood, National Organization for Women, Campaign for Nuclear Disarmament, Greenpeace, Attac
Networks • campaign network • enduring network	Nonhierarchical relationship; components can be basic action groups, organizations, task forces, service structures	Climate Alliance, Preparatory Assembly of the European Social Forum, Global People's Movement
Service structures • material • immaterial	Run by volunteers and/or employees, usually offering "political" instead of market prices for their goods and services in support of social movements	Halfway houses, Ruckus training center for civil disobedience, press houses, Indymedia, informal advisory groups for social movements
Social *relais*	Open access, not oriented toward movement activity but populated to some extent by activists	Parental group running a kindergarten, educational center for adults, factories, universities
Social milieus	Marked by similar lifestyles and cultural and political tastes	Left-alternative milieu of the 1970s, politicized urban-black communities, rural farmer communities, worker communities

Empirical Illustration: The Anti-Castor Campaign of 2010

In the following, an attempt will be made not only to apply the concepts presented earlier to an outstanding protest campaign but also to demonstrate their coexistence and entanglement. This case may illustrate the variety and complexity of social movement structures.

The Setting and the Issue

Gorleben, a small village in a remote and scarcely populated district, the Wendland, at the eastern margin of Lower Saxony in Germany, has gained a nationwide reputation. In 1977, this area was declared to be the future site not only of a large plant to reprocess burned nuclear fuel but also for the final storage *(Endlager)* of high-radioactivity waste from all nuclear reactors in Germany. Mainly because of fierce resistance in the concerned region, the plans for the reprocessing facility in Gorleben were abandoned in 1979. However, the intention to install the nuclear waste deposits in the nearby salt dome is still being pursued today. Because of a number of technical and political problems, the process for testing the waste deposits was slowed and temporarily even halted. Therefore the government, together with the large electricity companies, decided to build temporary storage facilities on the surface, the largest of which was erected in Gorleben. There the containers should remain for several decades to cool and lose some of their radioactivity. However, a large proportion of burned nuclear fuel was not stored directly in Gorleben and temporary facilities elsewhere in Germany but rather was sent to the reprocessing plant in La Hague in Brittany. After reprocessing, and later without reprocessing, the nonuseable nuclear waste was transported back to Gorleben in large steel containers, known as the Castor transport. This happened for the most part once a year starting in 1995. From the first until the twelfth transport in November 2010,[1] antinuclear groups from the Wendland region and beyond protested against the Castor transport. In addition, they opposed the continuing operation of nuclear reactors. Even more so, they rejected the storage plans for Gorleben because, in the eyes of the protesters, the planned waste deposits were inherently unsafe and had been pushed forward without the participation and consent of the citizenry.

Although the protesters knew that they could not stop but, at best, only delay the transport, they still used it as an opportunity to express their dissent against German nuclear policy and to publicize the worldwide unsolved problem of developing safe and ready nuclear waste storage. Though these protests have been far from insignificant since their inception in 1994–95, they reached an unprecedented level in 2010 for a number of reasons. Most important was a decision—later canceled—of the federal conservative-liberal government coalition to significantly delay the phasing out of nuclear electricity production, as was decided by contract and a subsequent law in 2002.

In the following, I describe the anti-Castor campaign that culminated in early November 2010. Special attention is paid to the various structural components of this campaign. Along its route, the transport of the eleven Castor containers, lasting for several days, provided different access points that were chosen by different components of the overall protest movement.

Already on its way from La Hague to the northern part of Germany, the transport train was met by protests and blockades in both France and Germany, causing a delay of a few hours. The bulk of protests, however, occurred along the two final segments: first, the last fifty-two kilometers of the railroad journey from the medium-sized city of Lüneburg to the small city of Dannenberg, in the center of the Wendland area; second, the final nineteen kilometers, with the Castor containers traveling on large trucks to their destination at the intermediary storage facility in Gorleben.

Castor transport over the final two legs of the journey was not an easy endeavor. During the days of the transport, several tens of thousands of protesters opposed the transport in various and sometimes ingenious ways. Conversely, approximately twenty thousand police officers tried to channel and, partly, repress the protest activities. What kinds of structures were involved in which kinds of protest? Among the many components that came into play, I have selected a few that may serve as empirical examples of the formal categories introduced previously.

Basic Action Groups

First, the transport was challenged by a considerable number of basic action groups of different shapes. One was a small and completely informal group centered around a young French activist living in Lüneburg. As a former champion sports climber, she engaged, as she had practiced on various other occasions, in a kind of stunt act, hanging on a rope from a high bridge over the railroad along which the Castor transport was expected to pass. Because of the electric wires above the railway, she could not hang down far enough to effectively block the train. The train, as it approached the spot, came only to a brief stop and then slowly passed underneath the activist hanging from the rope.

An example of a second and equally informal action group comprised a dozen locals who, closely watched and controlled by some thirty police officers accompanied by water cannons, gathered with banners and placards on both sides of a small road crossing the railway on which the Castor train was expected to pass. According to one of the locals, this kind of gathering at this particular place occurred previously on the occasion of several earlier Castor transports. Such small and unspectacular events could be seen in may other places in the Wendland. For instance, local residents installed X-signs, the regional symbol of resistance against nuclear power transport and facilities, at numerous crossroads, mounted straw puppets on fences and trees, and burned small fires in barrels during the days surrounding the Castor transport.

Social Movement Organizations

A classical example of a SMO is the Bürgerinitative Lüchow-Dannenberg (Regional Citizen Initiative, or the BI), which was created in 1977 and, since then, has remained a key actor in regional protests. It has a formal and legal structure with an elected president, a press speaker, a regular budget, and almost one thousand members adhering to various local subgroups. The BI was involved in a broad range of activities during the campaign. One of these was to organize a large rally on a field near the city of Dannenberg on Saturday, November 6. This event was attended by twenty-five thousand (according to the police) to fifty thousand (according to the organizers) protestors and was supported by numerous other groups and SMOs. An introductory speech was delivered by a representative of the BI, followed by a range of other speakers, including representatives from the local farmer alliance against nuclear energy, members of direct action networks, the current president of Greenpeace International, and a trade union activist. Part of the program comprised performances by well-known singers. Though it was clear that this rally would be peaceful, access roads to the site were crowded with police, who possessed several water cannons, an armored car, and hundreds of other police cars that formed, along a distant road, a huge semicircle around the crowd of protesters. In addition to the organization of this rally and a few other protests, the BI was also strongly engaged in setting up infrastructures for various camps in the area, providing food, offering sleeping room in the houses of local residents, maintaining contact with the press, and so on.

A second important regionally based SMO is the so-called Bäuerliche Notgemeinschaft (Farmers Emergency Alliance). It has very close links to the BI but relies on its own constituency and structure. Like the BI, it had already emerged in the early phase of the struggles against nuclear facilities in the Gorleben area. On many occasions, the Farmers Alliance made public appearances with dozens of tractors equipped with protest placards and banners. The tractors were used not only as a symbol but also as a very effective tool for road blockades. On the occasion of the 2010 anti-Castor campaign, members of the Farmers Alliance conducted several blockades to prevent police cars from accessing the road the Castor would take. Altogether, around six hundred tractors were used in these actions. Some of these blockades, as has happened in the past, will result in legal prosecutions. Another blockade was initiated by a woman who supposedly is a member of or sympathizer with the Farmers Alliance. She led a flock of twelve hundred sheep and five hundred goats onto the road. This unexpected action caused some trouble for the police before they eventually managed to clear the road.

A third SMO contributing to the anti-Castor campaign was Greenpeace Germany. As in most other cases, Greenpeace was not involved in any preparatory meeting but acted on its own with a spectacular coup. After the Castor containers had been shifted from the train wagons onto the trucks and were ready to head toward Gorleben, a big commercial truck, disguised as a transporter for beverages, crossed the road close to Dannenberg, stopped there, and lowered its large container. Inside the container was a group of Greenpeacers, who immediately fixed the container with large screws onto the road. This action came as a complete surprise to the police. They first had to figure out what was going on, and then they were forced to bring heavy equipment to the spot and engage in a cumbersome procedure to separate the container from the road. It took them approximately three hours to clear the road. As is their usual tactic, Greenpeace had given vague hints of its plans to selected journalists, who came to the scene to report this action nationwide.

Social Movement Networks

Another key activity promoted by political groups from outside the region was the so-called *schottern,* an artificial, thus far unknown verb derived from the substantive *Schotter,* the German technical term for the layer of rocks underneath iron rails. The activists' plan was to pull away as many rocks as possible so that rails would no longer rest on solid ground and the Castor train, for reasons of security, would not be able to pass. This idea only became widespread in the months preceding the 2010 Castor transport. Eventually, approximately seventeen hundred people publicly declared their intention to take part in this illegal activity and, accordingly, were threatened with prosecution just for their declaration of intent. Although the event promoters promised to refrain from the use of any kind of violence against people and, notably, police, the *schottern* campaign was met with some suspicion by many other groups, including the local BI and those action networks that were strictly committed to nonviolence.

The major recruitment base for the *schottern* campaign consisted of political groups, including many student committees, especially in the cities of Berlin, Hamburg, and Hanover. The campaign was not promoted by any distinct committee, let alone a SMO. Rather, it was announced, and effectively organized, by a few loosely coupled experienced activists who advertised the *schottern* concept in various gatherings, called a number of leftist intellectuals to sign a supportive declaration, and arranged bus rides, based on the purchase of tickets, to the Wendland area. Thus it was based on an extremely loose network. To my knowledge, its key figures did not physically meet before the actual action took place.

Altogether, some twenty-five hundred *schottern* activists assembled at various segments of the railroad between Lüneburg and Dannenberg. Attempts to pull away parts of the track bed underneath the rails largely failed, partly because of violent police intervention. This resulted in a substantial number of injuries due to the use of tear gas and batons. A few among the protesters resorted to violence, engaging in physical skirmishes with the police and burning a police car—an event that was widely reported in the news, with some media, notably the infamous tabloid *BILD,* suggesting that this was exactly the kind of protest that characterized the activists in general.

Some kilometers away from the *schottern* activity and closer to the city of Dannenberg, another contingent of protesters adhering to the activist network Widersetzen (Resist) took part in an additional blockade on the railroad tracks. Some four thousand to five thousand determined activists eventually reached the tracks near the village of Harlingen. A part of this blockade proved to be relatively successful because of the clever selection of the site. This was an area marked by a steep upward slope on both sides of the track. Although a great police presence was at the site during the nightly blockade, they were unable to pull most of the demonstrators uphill. After desperate attempts, they gave up. Accordingly, the Castor train came to an effective halt for several hours. Only in the morning, and with the help of additional and fresh police contingents, was the blockade disbanded so that the train could proceed toward the fortified Dannenberg railway station where the trucks were waiting to pick up the heavy load.

In addition, two more large antinuclear networks had called for road blockades very close to the intermediary storage facility in Gorleben. The network X-tausendmal quer has firm roots in the region but reaches far beyond, with a constituency spread mainly over northern Germany. This network, aside from the regional SMOs, was the most important organizer of past activities against the Castor transports. It is strongly committed to nonviolent direct action and adheres to the classic concept of civil disobedience. The second network, ausgestrahlt, is an offspring of X-tausendmal quer and follows a similar political and tactical line. In contrast to the latter, however, ausgestrahlt does not focus mainly on transports and nuclear waste deposits but rather has a broader and more strategically oriented perspective on nuclear power in general. Also, ausgestrahlt tries to mobilize people from all over Germany. It makes clever use of modern means of communication and puts much emphasis on influencing mass media (see later). For example, ausgestrahlt was the main organizer of a "human chain" covering a distance of 120 kilometers between two old nuclear reactors in northern Germany in April 2010. This event, in which approximately 140,000 people participated, was widely reported by mass media, including the major television channels. Also, the anti-Castor activities made their way into the mainstream media in both Germany and abroad. In the Netherlands, for example, they were reported on several occasions on the eight o'clock television news.

Together, the two networks mobilized probably some four thousand activists for a road blockade lasting forty-four hours. On Tuesday, November 9, starting two hours before dawn, it took police forces about four hours to end the blockade in a nonviolent manner. As an eyewitness, I observed that both sides treated each other in a respectful way so that no serious acts of aggression occurred. Only when this last hindrance was cleared did the eleven Castors leave the Dannenberg station and, after a two-hour ride under heavy police protection, eventually reach their destination at the Gorleben facility.

Additional Structural Elements of the Campaign

The previously described groups, organizations, and networks were complemented by many more, of which just a few are mentioned to provide a comprehensive picture of the campaign. One further element were various local groups that chose their own activities. For example, five hundred local residents, among them many high school students, equipped with hand lanterns, organized their own rally in Dannenberg on the evening before the general and big rally on Saturday, November 5. This points to the fact that schools serve as social *relais* to recruit protesters. Another example were some twenty-five members of a protestant parish who gathered at the spot between the tail of the blockade and the police presence in front of gated corridor leading to the waste facility. The parish group formed a circle and sang songs for hours, accompanied by a harp player. At the other end of the long blockade line on the road, though at some distance, a few hundred fans of techno music danced by a truck on which a DJ was commanding a mighty sound system plus a light show. These young people referred to themselves as the *hedonists*. They are part of a social milieu mainly concentrated in the larger cities. Apparently, this milieu has some overlap with the urban left-alternative milieu, which served as a recruitment base for the more politically than culturally oriented protesters.

```
Lüneburg •————————• railway •————————• Dannenberg •————• road •————• Gorleben
```

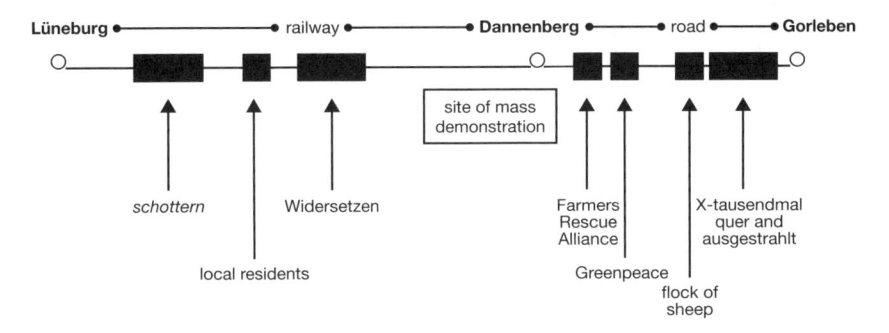

                                  site of mass
                                  demonstration

   schottern   Widersetzen   Farmers   X-tausendmal
                                         Rescue   quer and
                                         Alliance   ausgestrahlt
            local residents   Greenpeace
                                         flock of
                                         sheep

Figure 9.1. Selected groups and activities along the transport route.

Between the fairly distant poles of the church group and the hedonist dancers, a samba band, and later on a brass orchestra, entertained the activists sitting around or lying in their sleeping bags in the midst of the road.

In support of the blockade, unnamed self-organized local support groups were offering hot beverages and food. In addition, various regional groups and organizations, including the local Social Democratic Party, had set up camps with large tents, mobile kitchens, information centers, and so on. Other locals hosted and fed protesters in their homes. Taken together, these components provided a fully decentralized but very effective material service structure.

Last but not least, one should also mention a group of elderly people who, equipped with portable chairs, organized their own sit-in to protest the Castor transport. By coining their action *Stuhlgang*, a play of words difficult to translate, they made reference not only to carrying chairs but also to sitting on the toilet bowl.

The Spatial and Temporal Chain of Resistance

The lengthy transport route and the expected or actual schedule of the transport train and subsequent trucks provided numerous access points for different kinds of groups and activities. In a way, these offered, both spatially and temporally, a range of opportunities. On one hand, they physically and temporally separated the activities of various groups. On the other hand, this constellation served as an overarching framework or, more precisely, a kind of storyline that could be watched from day to day, and even hour to hour, by not only the activists involved but also the public at large. Figure 9.1 provides an overview of the access points for selected activities along the transport route.

Widening the Perspective

Obviously the anti-Castor campaign described here composed an extraordinary chain of events that varied considerably in terms of range, breadth, duration, intensity, specific form, and location. Accordingly, the campaign was resting on a complex underlying structure. All the components that were laid out in the introductory conceptual framework—basic action groups, movement organizations, networks, service structures, social *relais,* and social milieus—could be found in different variants. And as usual, in reality, not only clear-cut cases but also hybrids of these structures could be observed. For example, the Farmers Alliance ranges somewhere between an SMO and a network. As a whole, the structures of the anti-Castor campaign imply features that are of a more general significance and can be related both to other empirical cases and to theoretical considerations.

No Overarching Coordination

Interestingly, the various structural components of the campaign somehow complemented each other and partly interacted without any centralized coordination. Although some examples of such a decentralized mobilization and action structure can be found in the past, the anti-Castor campaign epitomizes a more general trend of progressive movement taking place over the last few decades, namely, to refrain from intense and long disputes about the one and only correct theory, strategy, and appropriate tactic. This could be also observed in the context of global justice movements' activities, for example, the three different marches—each associated with one specific color—undertaken by different ideological tendencies in the Prague protests against the International Monetary Fund and World Bank meeting in September 2000 (Chesters and Welsh 2004).

It appears that major contemporary protest campaigns, and probably broader social movement settings in general, provide a space that is filled by strikingly different structures and corresponding tactics. These structures sometimes compete for scarce resources but, for the most part, act in an implicit division of labor. This is opposite to the Leninist concept of avant-garde and elitist leadership engaged in directing the masses. Yet it is also different from the concept of a full-blown grassroots structure or the "segmented, polycentric, ideologically integrated network" described by Gerlach and Hine (1970). The latter assumes, or at least aims at, a loose coordination of small, informal, overlapping, similarly minded and tactically similarly oriented groups as they could be observed in the nonviolent direct action movement of the United States (Epstein 1988). Instead, in the anti-Castor campaign, grassroots networks acted side by side with other groups based on a different structure: a hierarchical SMO such as Greenpeace; a well-organized regional antinuclear initiative; a stable protest group of local farmers; newly engaged urban hedonists; politicized pupils; local residents who chose to express their dissent in their immediate environment; other locals providing logistical support and/or inviting a bunch of unknown demonstrators to spend one or several nights for free.

This pattern of fully autonomous or only loosely coupled structures exempts the actors from what, in other contexts, and especially with regard to large and unified actors, have been described as organizational dilemmas. One typical example of such a dilemma is to meet the affective, moral, and cognitive expectations of a specific constituency, on one hand, and, on the other, to conform to the need for quick and effective decision making and strategic intervention. Moreover, this pattern also frees the collective actors to a large extent from the cumbersome "coalition work" (Staggenborg 1986) that characterizes many other movements.

Spontaneity versus Routine–Organization–Institution

Another theoretically interesting aspect of the anti-Castor campaign is the relationship between, and combination of, spontaneity and organization (on this topic, see Killian 1984; Rosenthal and Schwartz 1989; Turner 1991). As mentioned before, the 2010 campaign was, in principle, a repeat of similar but smaller campaigns in the past. Accordingly, many of the groups involved had developed a firm routine in practicing resistance. Over the years, the Castor protest has even become ritual. It is noteworthy that the *Streckenkonzept*, the concept of attributing different groups to different sections along the transport route, was already applied in 2001 (Leach and Haunss 2011, 85). For example, the X-tausendmal quer and the ausgestrahlt networks blocking the last section of the road to Gorleben knew perfectly well what to do. With explicit agreement from the heads of police, they were able to transport material and facilities to the site of the blockade. This included a station wagon with loudspeakers, a mobile kitchen, portable toilets, and bales of straw to protect the demonstrators from the cold. Even the nightly eviction of the blockade by police appeared a matter of routine. The police worked their way along the road in a sophisticated division of labor that reminded me of an assembly line. Actually, those front men who carried away the bodies were lined up in a queue and, after having served for a short time, went back to the end of the queue to wait patiently for their next carrying job. Routinization could be equally observed among many of the demonstrators, who did not actively resist being carried away and, based on an agreement with the police, never tried to get back to the road once they had been evicted.

At the same time, almost every Castor transport, and especially the one in 2010, includes a few surprising elements. Some of the actions of the police and demonstrators remind one of a cat-and-mouse game in which each side tries to prove its cleverness by outsmarting its opponents. The *schottern* activity, for example, was an unprecedented tactic that was deliberately announced before the actual activity. However, because the number of participants and the access points along the railroad were unknown before the action took place, this tactic caused considerable headaches on the side of the police. Other surprising acts were the blockade by sheep and goats and the Greenpeace container fixed onto the road. A further new element was the participation of the techno hedonists, who had already joined a major antinuclear rally in Berlin in summer 2010. These partly creative acts of resistance were not only cheered by thousands of activists but also admired more or less openly by sympathizing journalists. No wonder reports about the events could also be found abroad in foreign newspapers and other media.

Political Tendencies and Movement Identity

The anti-Castor campaign also illustrates the possibilities and limits of bringing together quite different ideological tendencies or segments. As in many other cases, there was a clear-cut common negative denominator: against the use of nuclear power in general and the extension of phasing it out; against the nuclear waste deposits as planned for the salt dome in Gorleben; against the Castor transport to the intermediary waste facility. These aims, in both a symbolic and physical sense, united demonstrators from very different social and cultural backgrounds and political leanings, ranging from radical leftists to conservatives. The differences in worldviews and political visions were essentially bracketed in a spirit that has been dubbed "tolerant identities" (della Porta 2005). At least to some extent, differences and tensions came to the fore only when the appropriateness of confrontational and potentially violent activities was discussed. According to a broad consensus, violence against people is not tolerated; however, other forms of resistance, potentially including low-profile property damage, are not necessarily rejected. Consider a call to action by a key player, the regional Bürgerinitiative, in the year 2000, claiming that "imagination is called for. Out of diversity, complementarity should emerge rather than mutual impediment. The best place [to be] is wherever there are not a lot of police" (as cited by Leach and Haunss 2011, 85).

In the Castor campaign of 2010, these discussions about appropriate tactics seemed to occur within and not between the various groups and tendencies. There was no place, apart from the large Saturday rally, where most of them physically came together. Also, there was a suspicious lack of mesomobilization actors, as were to be found in other movement campaigns (see, e.g., Gerhards and Rucht 1992). In this sense, the territorial and temporal separation of the main activities of different ideological tendencies as well as the absence of an overarching coordinating body or joint call for action helped to avoid friction and open conflict.

What from an external viewpoint might be perceived as *the* anti–nuclear power movement or, more specifically, *the* anti-Castor movement is by no means conducted by a unified actor. Accordingly, it would be hard to speak in this case of a clear movement identity, although the enthusiastic atmosphere at the mass demonstration near Dannenberg might suggest otherwise. Instead, there is a strong identification with specific groups, organizations, networks, and tendencies that are socially and/or ideologically relatively coherent, each favoring its own form of action and risk taking. Because this structural and tactical menu was broadly known prior to the main activities, protest novices had to decide which activities they wanted to join. Because such a choice was not an easy one for politically inexperienced people, the left-alternative daily *Die Tageszeitung* provided a kind of political map in which various tendencies and their corresponding activities were described. Activists who, for example, were attracted by the *schotterer* tactics could learn from both the newspaper and more specifically from websites where to buy the bus ticket and how to get to one of the two camps related to this specific tactic.

The Struggle for Public Resonance and Recognition

When comparing the anti-Castor campaign with protest campaigns from the 1960s to the 1980s, one is struck by the different attitudes and behaviors toward all kinds of mass media. While in earlier times, most groups, with some notable exceptions, such as Greenpeace, devoted little attention and resources to influence media coverage, this has become an important concern for many, but not all, of the groups involved in the Castor campaign. The regional Bürgerinitiative had its own press bus to be driven to the spot where action took place so that journalists could get information, advice, interviews, and other kinds of support.

Even more sophisticated was the public relations work carried out by the networks X-tausendmal quer and ausgestrahlt. Some twelve volunteers worked for several days in a press center that was established in a former restaurant located in the main street of Dannenberg. Most were very experienced. They knew the editorial lines of different newspapers; they took into account news values and interests of specific journalists and media; they distributed information via Twitter, text messages, and other means to both journalists and activists around the clock; they issued press releases and organized press conferences; and they constantly watched and critically discussed media coverage of ongoing events. More impressive than the provision of these facilities and services, however, was the media activists' conscious way of framing the protesters' motivation, aims, and activities. In internal meetings, they discussed the appropriateness of attractive formulas and slogans, potential answers to tricky questions, and the appropriate timing of messages and declarations.

Whereas in the past, journalists sympathizing with the cause of a protest movement were often confronted with a naive attitude among organizers toward mass media, today they are rather surprised to see the level of protestor sophistication. Accordingly, speakers of some groups had no problem making an appearance on the evening news shows of almost all relevant TV channels at the height of the conflict. Equally, the police are fully aware of the crucial role of the media in reporting on the conflict. A very elaborate and well-resourced system of public relations work could already be seen during the protests against the G8 meeting in Heiligendamm in summer 2007 (Rucht and Teune 2008). And even in the Castor campaign, which could hardly be perceived as an event of primary international interest, the efforts of the police to allow friendly and supportive coverage were stunning. It suffices to note that more than a hundred police officers were in charge of arranging accreditation and serving journalists' demands and needs.

As already stressed in a number of previous scholarly works, the activities of protest groups and social movements cannot be understood only with reference to their opponents. In addition, it is crucial to take into account the direct and indirect presence of an audience who, even in the era of the Internet, is largely informed by conventional mass media such as newspapers, radio, and TV (Gamson 2004; Rucht 2004). One can even go a step further in claiming that the decisive battleground for contemporary conflicts involving social movements is not the physical site of protest but rather the way the struggle is presented in the mass media. In this regard, both in the case of the anti-G8 campaign in summer 2007 and the anti-Castor campaign in 2010, the protesters were fairly successful. Not only were they able to get ample media coverage but, for a large part, they received neutral or even supportive coverage. Why this was the case would be worthy of study in its own right. The general lesson, however, is that in the analysis of contemporary social movements and their opponents, more attention should be paid to the struggle for public attention and support in which mass media play a crucial and sometimes decisive role.

Conclusion

As epitomized in the book *From Structure to Action* (Klandermans, Kriesi, and Tarrow 1988), larger campaigns, let alone more enduring social movements, would not exist without a structural base. However, the generic notion of social movement structure needs to be unpacked. This was the aim of the first section of this chapter, in which I distinguished six specific components ranging from basic action groups to social milieus. Furthermore, for some of these components, subtypes or variants were identified.

To illustrate the existence, interplay, and overlap of more specific structures, the campaign against the transport of nuclear waste in Germany in November 2010 served as a telling case. Though this campaign is rather narrow in its thematic focus, time frame, and geographic scope, it exhibited a stunning complexity of structural forms and related activities. These elements worked hand in hand in a kind of implicit division of labor without any central coordination. The surprising smoothness of the campaign was facilitated by the temporal and spatial setting of a transport over a considerable distance and lasting for several days. This setting provided different direct access points and other spaces that could be filled by various movement activities. Some of these, based on a strong regional tradition of protest, were a matter of routine, while others were added as new, and partly surprising, elements of resistance.

In several respects, this case is outstanding. For instance, very few short-lived mass campaigns rest on such variegated structure with a fairly low level of internal tension and ideological rivalry. Furthermore, the scope of this campaign was extraordinary. It led to the thus far largest acts of civil disobedience in the history of the Federal Republic of Germany.

Conversely, this case also exhibits some features and trends that seem to be typical for progressive social movements in our times. Besides the absence of overarching bodies of coordination that also characterize contemporary global justice movements, this campaign exhibited a number of features to be found elsewhere: the blending of routine and spontaneity; the coexistence of fairly different ideological tendencies that, probably only at the symbolic level, are bound together into an "imagined community"; the high sensitivity for the struggle of recognition in which mass media and their audiences play a crucial role; the emergence of sophisticated public relations work based on both the conscious use of framing strategies and the use of modern tools of communication, including telephone conferences, action alerts via mobile phones, and various Internet facilities such as live streams of ongoing activities. The opportunities for communication from many to many—instead of few to many—are not supportive only of a decentralized campaign such as the one studied here. They also foster a more enduring decentralized structure of progressive social movements with very different components, ranging from informal circles of friends to campaign-oriented task forces to highly formalized nationwide or even international organizations.

In part, these elements are the crystallized result of previous protest activities which, especially in this case, have a history of more than thirty years. This campaign activated both organizational and cultural resources that were preexisting: material resources, experiences, technical skills, action repertoires, symbols and slogans, trust and friendship, and so on. These resources had both an enabling and a restricting effect. They facilitated certain kinds of activities as part of "a limited set of routines that are learned, shared, and acted out through a relatively deliberate process of choice" (Tilly 1995, 26). Yet they also prevented the use of the full range of the theoretically available action repertoire, for example, the use of outright violence. At the same time, during the course of action, new activists, new experiences, and new tactics were incorporated and partly merged with preexisting elements so that these become affected and probably subject to change. In this sense, we are confronted with a phenomenon that Anthony Giddens (1984), in his general sociological theory, called the "duality of structure," and that I prefer to call *structure in action*—an aspect of social reality of which social movements and protest campaigns are perfect examples.

Note

1. The most recent transport was in November 2011. In structural terms, the 2011 campaign was very similar to that of the previous year, but smaller in size. This can be mainly explained by the fact that the German government had decided to phase out nuclear power earlier than initially planned.

References

Barker, Colin, Alan Johnson, and Michael Lavalette, eds. 2001. *Leadership in Social Movements*. Manchester, U.K.: Manchester University Press.
Breines, Wini. 1980. "Community and Organization: The New Left and Michels 'Iron Law.'" *Social Problems* 27:419–29.
Chesters, Graeme, and Jan Welsh. 2004. "The Rebel Colours of S26: Social Movement: 'Frame-work' during the Prague IMF/WB protests." *Sociological Review* 52:314–35.
Clemens, Elizabeth S., and Debra C. Minkoff. 2004. "Beyond the Iron Law: Rethinking the Place of Organizations in Social Movement Research." In *The Blackwell*

Companion to Social Movements, edited by David A. Snow, Sarah A. Soule, and Hanspeter Kriesi, 155–70. Oxford: Blackwell.

Curtis, Russell L., and Louis A. Zurcher. 1973. "Stable Resources of Protest Movements: The Multiorganizational Field." *Social Forces* 52:53–61.

———. 1974. "Social Movements: An Analytical Exploration of Organizational Forms." *Social Problems* 21:356–70.

Della Porta, Donatella. 2005. "Multiple Belongings, Tolerant Identities, and the Construction of 'Another Politics': Between the European Social Forum and the Local Social Fora." In *Transnational Protest and Global Activism,* edited by Donatella della Porta and Sidney Tarrow, 175–202. Lanham, Md.: Rowman and Littlefield.

Epstein, Barbara. 1988. "The Politics of Prefigurative Community: The Non-violent Direct Action Movement." In *Reshaping the US Left: Popular Struggles in the 1980s,* edited by Mike Davis and Michael Sprinker, 63–92. London: Verso.

Gamson, William A. 2004. "Bystanders, Public Opinion, and the Media." In *The Blackwell Companion to Social Movements,* edited by David A. Snow, Sarah A. Soule, and Hanspeter Kriesi, 242–61. Oxford: Blackwell.

Gerhards, Jürgen, and Dieter Rucht. 1992. "Mesomobilization: Organizing and Framing in Two Protest Campaigns in West Germany." *American Journal of Sociology* 98:555–95.

Gerlach, Luther P., and Virginia P. Hine. 1970. *People, Power, Change: Movements of Social Transformation.* Indianapolis, Ind.: Bobbs-Merill.

Giddens, Anthony. 1984. *The Constitution of Society: Outline of the Theory of Structuration.* Berkeley: University of California Press.

Killian, Lewis M. 1964. "Social Movements." In *Handbook of Modern Sociology,* edited by Robert R. Faris, 426–55. Chicago: Rand McNally.

———. 1984. "Organization, Rationality and Spontaneity in the Civil Rights Movement." *American Sociological Review* 49:770–83.

Klandermans, Bert. 1984. "Mobilization and Participation: Social Psychological Expansions of the Resource Mobilization Theory." *American Sociological Review* 4:583–600.

———. 1989. *Organizing for Change: Social Movement Organizations in Europe and the United States.* International Social Movement Research 2. Greenwich, Conn.: JAI Press.

Klandermans, Bert, Hanspeter Kriesi, and Sidney Tarrow, eds. 1988. *From Structure to Action: Comparing Social Movement Participation across Cultures.* Greenwich, Conn.: JAI Press.

Kriesi, Hanspeter. 1996. "The Organizational Structure of New Social Movements in a Political Context." In *Comparative Perspectives on Social Movements: Political Opportunities, Mobilizing Structures, and Cultural Framings,* edited by Doug

McAdam, John D. McCarthy, and Mayer N. Zald, 152–84. Cambridge: Cambridge University Press.

Lang, Kurt, and Gladys E. Lang. 1961. *Collective Dynamics.* New York: Crowell.

Leach, Darcy K., and Sebastian Haunss. 2011. "'Wichtig ist der Widerstand': Rituals of Taming and Tolerance in Movement Responses to the Violence Question." In *Prevent and Tame: Protest under (Self-)Control,* edited by Florian Heßdörfer, Andrea Pabst, and Peter Ullrich, 73–98. Berlin: Dietz.

Leif, Thomas. 1985. *Die professionelle Bewegung: Friedensbewegung von innen.* Bonn, Germany: Forum Europa.

Lofland, John. 1996. *Social Movement Organizations.* New York: Aldine de Gruyter.

McCarthy, John, and Mayer N. Zald. 1977. "Resource Mobilization and Social Movements: A Partial Theory." *American Journal of Sociology* 81:1212–41.

Ohlemacher, Thomas. 1996. "Bridging People and Protest: Social Relays of Protest Groups against Low-Flying Military Jets in West Germany." *Social Problems* 43:197–218.

Olzak, Susan. 1989. "Analysis of Events in the Study of Collective Action." *Annual Review of Sociology* 15:119–41.

Rosenthal, Naomi, and Michael Schwartz. 1989. "Spontaneity and Democracy in Social Movements." *International Social Movement Research* 2:33–59.

Rucht, Dieter. 2004. "Movement Allies, Adversaries, and Third Parties." In *The Blackwell Companion to Social Movements,* edited by David A. Snow, Sarah A. Soule, and Hanspeter Kriesi, 198–216. Oxford: Blackwell.

Rucht, Dieter, and Simon Teune, eds. 2008. *Nur Clowns und Chaoten? Die G8-Proteste in Heiligendamm im Spiegel der Massenmedien.* Frankfurt, Germany: Campus.

Staggenborg, Susanne. 1986. "Coalition Work on the Pro-Choice Movement: Organizational and Environmental Opportunities and Obstacles." *Social Problems* 33:374–90.

Tilly, Charles. 1995. "Contentious Repertoires in Great Britain, 1758–1834." In *Repertoires and Cycles of Collective Action,* edited by Mark Traugott, 15–42. Durham, N.C.: Duke University Press.

Turner, Ralph H. 1991. "The Use and Misuse of Rational Models in Collective Behavior and Social Psychology." *Archives Européennes de Sociologie* 32, no. 1: 84–108.

Discussion:
The Changing Supply Side of Mobilization: Impressions on a Theme

Debra Minkoff

The chapters in this section, including the introductory comments by Roggeband and Duyvendak (chapter 5), demonstrate the continued importance of organizations (loosely defined) in our theoretical models of social movement processes as well as in the actual trajectories of social movements themselves. At the same time, they also highlight the fact that the meaning and conceptual status of *organization* is quite varied, even among some of the top scholars in the field, which potentially limits the development of a shared vocabulary for moving the field forward. Without reprising long-standing debates in the study of the organizational aspects of social movements, my goal here is to use these contributions as a starting point for offering some general impressions for advancing theory and research on the "changing supply side of mobilization."

Impression 1

There is a clear trend toward locating social movements in their broader organizational and structural contexts, moving us beyond earlier conflations of social movements with social movement organizations (SMOs). Widening our perspective in this way has provided the chance to refocus the kinds of questions we ask with respect to the "supply side of mobilization," which I take to mean "the 'supply' of social movement activities to aggrieved people" (Klandermans 2001, 273), or what Staggenborg (chapter 7) refers to as "movement contributors." As Diani (chapter 8) argues, there are many forms of collective action that could be of interest to us, but our focus is (or should be) on those structures and mechanisms that are productive of *social movements*, that is, that provide the material (or, matériel—we are talking about the stuff of fighting, if not a war, then a set of broad-based institutional challenges) for coordinated and sustained collective mobilization.

To start, we know that some degree of organization is a "structural necessity to step up from loosely-related protest events to sustained collective action, one of the distinguishing features of social movements" (Klandermans 2001, 273). We also know that the available vehicles for temporally and spatially bounded protest events are distinct from those needed for more durable and broad challenges in and against the state, market, and societal sectors. The introductory chapter by Roggeband and Duyvendak focuses our attention on formal organizations and informal networks; the chapters themselves broaden the discussion to social movement communities (Staggenborg, chapter 7), organizational populations and fields (Soule, chapter 6; Diani, chapter 8), and social movement structures (Rucht, chapter 9). There is not much new here, but I think it is important to note that there are multiple modes of organizing under each general form that vary in their ability to provide "movement activities" to participants, particularly over the long haul.

Social movement organizations, commercial enterprises, community-based organizations, nonprofit service agencies, and political parties are all formal organizations, but some are explicitly dedicated to social movement mobilization, whereas others can be considered "secondary contributors"—creating collective identities that promote protest involvement, providing information about relevant issues and events, sharing resources and acting in coalition for specific campaigns, or bringing folks together to participate in discrete events (what Rucht designates as material and immaterial service structures). Similarly, various kinds of networks—face-to-face, interorganizational, and virtual—may also be explicitly concerned with social movement goals or may function as "cooptable" (Freeman 1973) networks for involvement in specific events or campaigns. In Diani's suggested conceptualization, networks themselves may be constitutive of social movements, to the extent that linked actors are involved in informal resource exchanges and active boundary definition and identity building.

Impression 2

Every so often, someone takes inventory of various "movement mobilizing structures" (McCarthy 1996), but this kind of work doesn't seem to cumulate in ways that facilitate a collective research agenda around the structures necessary to transform "potentiality into action" (Klandermans 2001, 280). Rucht's effort to provide a conceptual map of relevant social movement structures is in this spirit, although its wider applicability will have to be honed by additional empirical studies. As a more general point, the contributions to this section demonstrate the importance of documenting both the *composition* and *structure* of the social movement field, that is, the distribution of organizational forms and their connections to each other. As Staggenborg's chapter demonstrates, characteristics such as the degree of centralization at the community or field level as well the heterogeneity of organizational actors in terms of how well established they are, the characteristics of their members, identities, and ideological commitments, and so forth, determine the prospects for mounting successful movement campaigns—as well as whether groups with shared interests choose to work together or independently. Drawing from Diani's chapter, a focus on the composition of movement networks enables us to ask questions such as whether (or to what extent) the field is dominated by grassroots groups committed to a direct-action, participatory model that inclines the movement against negotiation with authorities, for example.

I would suggest, however, that we need a combined relational (network) *and* an aggregative (demographic) approach as a foundation for asking the question explicitly advocated by Diani and implicitly posed by the empirical cases described by Rucht and Staggenborg: what are the dominant relational dynamics, or modes of coordination, within fields? Although I agree with Diani that we need to be reflective about which organizations we designate as SMOs, I think we also need to know something about the set of partners available for collaboration or collective action before we evaluate the relational linkages between them. And although Diani makes a strong argument that there must be at least some informal resource sharing and shared boundary definition to designate some collective action as a social movement, the anti-Castor campaign and aspects of the G20 and other global justice protests suggest that movements—or at least discrete movement campaigns—can take place with very loose or no coordination (or failed efforts at coordination, for that matter). In a narrow sense, using Diani's criteria, we may not want to call these campaigns social movements, but more discussion about how much active coordination and shared collective identity–boundary maintenance is needed to constitute a social movement is important. How to do this without getting bogged down in definitional disputes, however, is less than obvious.

Impression 3

One important common theme across the chapters is the role of a shared collective identity in structuring the networks of exchange that constitute sustained collective action. Such networks may be latent or activated, serving as a necessary precondition for, and consequence of, the construction of salient group boundaries. Such concepts as social *relais,* supportive social milieus, and latent networks all imply some socially structured action potential that may remain dormant or incoherent without intervention by movement organizers or political activists. As Diani and Soule both suggest, mechanisms of boundary construction, or processes of categorization, are not only fundamental aspects of collective identities but have important consequences for the trajectories of social movements. As Diani notes,

> mechanisms of boundary construction are also essential because they secure the continuity of collective action over time and space. Social movements exist, in other words, because both actors mobilized in them and observers are capable of locating in a broader picture actors and events that operate in different points in space and time.

There is, I think, an interesting link here to Soule's discussion of organizational identities and processes of categorization, in that the ability of members and supporters to identify—and identify with—a social movement or movement organization depends on the clarity of the group identity. Furthermore, the notion that there are penalties associated with unclear identities, whether conceptualized at the organizational or movement level, provides a novel way of understanding the prospects for mobilization as well as the "continuity of collective action" and the direction it takes. As Soule notes, unclear identities may influence levels of participation, media attention, and the risk of repression as well as the chance for successful collaboration (whether in enduring or event coalitions; Levi and Murphy 2006). As Rucht argues in reference to the anti-Castor campaign in particular and to the global justice movement more generally, bringing together groups with different ideological tendencies may be possible for discrete events, but longer-term movement building may not be feasible (or may create unintended exclusions, a concern raised by Roggeband and Duyvendak in their introductory comments).

Impression 4

As valuable as documenting and describing the organizational–structural landscape is, the harder task is analyzing which organizational forms may be more productive of shorter- or longer-term mobilization, for example, to understand (1) the mechanisms by which demand is translated into sustained (and sustainable) collective action; (2) how the distribution of (primary and secondary, for lack of better terms) mobilizing structures has changed over time; and (3) what consequences this has for protest potentials (note use of the plural) across social groups and political contexts. Not surprisingly, I think that Soule's advocacy of greater reliance on organizational theory and research as well as Diani's integration of network approaches to organizations provide the most fruitful directions for theorizing field-level changes in the supply side of mobilization.

In this regard, the relevance of diversity or heterogeneity in organizational fields and movement communities becomes strikingly clear when reading the contributions to this section. The chapters by Rucht, Staggenborg, and Diani demonstrate the importance of variation in documenting field- or community-level characteristics (both aggregative and relational) and evaluating whether heterogeneity might influence the dynamics of the kind of short-lived campaigns described by Rucht and Staggenborg differently than for long-lived movement or organizational survival. More important, Soule's contribution moves us in the direction of actively theorizing the relevance of such population diversity for social movement dynamics and outcomes. As she illustrates, research streams informed by organizational ecology demonstrate the payoffs of population-level diversity for policy outcomes in the civil rights and gay rights arenas, whereas her own work with Braydon King provides a promising theoretical approach to understanding how processes of resource partitioning influence movement trajectories by shaping organizational survival.

Soule's contribution further demonstrates that organizational theories enable us to go further in understanding what happens when movement actors collaborate, which is another central theme throughout each of the chapters in this section. Organizational learning theory posits that above and beyond the kind of resource sharing and identity work that Diani emphasizes, collaborators very tangibly learn from each other, which facilitates the further diffusion of tactics as well as ideas and critical resources. Staggenborg's analysis likewise points to the generative effect of collaboration on consolidating collective identities in local movement communities, which has positive consequences for subsequent collective action. However, an organizational perspective might also suggest the hypothesis that collaborators can also exploit each other by extracting scarce resources or creating dependencies that ultimately weaken one or more partners, thereby influencing their longer-term viability and, at least potentially, the diversity of actors with whom they can collaborate in the first place. Here we see the potentially important link between collaboration and diversity: the dynamics of collaboration within and across fields are shaped by the heterogeneity of existing actors and networks, at the same time that such dynamics shape movement fields and thus the prospects for collaboration over time.

Impression 5

We need more longitudinal research before we make strong claims about significant shifts in the supply side of mobilization such as in the mix of formal organizations and networks, or greedy membership structures being supplanted by less demanding ones, or strong(er) identities by weak(er) ones. It is not at all clear, however, what are the appropriate units of analysis, or the baseline, from which to measure change. So, to determine whether formal SMOs have been supplanted by looser groups within social movements or movement networks, we need to know "since when" and be able to justify the time frame of analysis, whether substantively or theoretically. To illustrate, Roggeband and Duyvendak more or less explicitly emphasize movement-related trends in the post-1980s period (substantive justification?), locating the evolution of movement forms within processes of globalization and individualization (theoretical justification?), but my sense is that this could be discussed at some length.

Even more vexing is the unit of analysis question. Some suggestions (loosely derived from the chapters) include the following:

- start with *events or campaigns* and identify and categorize relevant "contributors" (SMOs, community groups, coalitions, etc.) and then select earlier or later comparison cases to examine changes in "mix" over time and variation in expressions of collective identities
- start with a *place* (Glasgow, Gorleben, Montreal, Pittsburgh) and examine the differential involvement of actors embedded in a variety of mobilizing structures and/or linked in a web of relationships (generative of identities, events, etc.) and trace over time
- start with *broad issues or social cleavages* and see where the action or organization is and how it has changed over time (locally, nationally, transnationally)
- start with *individuals* and measure associational involvement over time

There are some models out there to structure such research, so it is not as though we need to start from scratch. In fact, research conducted by any of the contributors to this section provides as good a starting point as any. But we still need to address the question of time frames and levels of analysis and, I think, to consider more creative, if demanding, research designs that are intentionally multilevel and longitudinal.

Even if we can identify the objects of empirical research, we need to be more explicit about the mechanisms of transformation. If we do observe a shift in the dominance of more formal movement organizations to informal and loose networks, how do we account for that change? An important distinction, not explicitly addressed in the chapters in this section, is that between exogenous and endogenous dynamics. Do processes of organizational expansion and interorganizational competition exhaust the space for more formal organizing or promote development of new, potentially innovative organizational forms (exogenous mechanisms of change)? Do certain organizational forms face greater repression such that they cannot survive over the long haul (endogenous explanation)? Is the presumed turn to more informal structures a response to the dominance of more hierarchical, less participatory forms of organization, or have the social bases of protest shifted such that they make more "sense" for aggrieved groups (i.e., a mix of endogenous and exogenous pressures)?

My earlier work on the evolution of the American civil rights and feminist organizational fields was intended to sensitize social movement scholars to the importance of endogenous dynamics (see, e.g., Minkoff 1995), a theme echoed by Koopmans (2004) in his subsequent efforts to specify evolutionary mechanisms in waves of contention. Rucht, in an earlier version of the chapter included here, suggested some testable hypotheses that also seem to privilege internal, field-level dynamics. Focusing on the relationship between "old" and "new" groups, for example, he offered these hypotheses: (1) the existing organizational infrastructure increases the founding rate of new groups by providing resources, skills, and legitimacy (what my early work refers to as *positive density dependence*); (2) existing groups restrict the demand and space for new actors (competition or negative density dependence); (3) prior density promotes innovation or radicalization in an effort to create a new niche; and (4) older groups are likely to absorb or integrate newly formed groups. The assumption here is that there is a limited amount of space for multiple forms of organizing and a great deal of competition among organizing forms, which may promote or constrain social movement development.

Diani also suggests some provocative reconceptualizations of classic questions in social movement studies in relational terms. Following his approach, the issue of social movement emergence can be understood as the creation of new collaborative ties and solidarities, or strengthening of existing ones, between actors around a shared social movement project. Likewise, the question of movement transformation can be understood as a shift in the dominant mode of coordination among actors—moving, for example, from a situation of structural interdependence to an unwillingness to collaborate as repression intensifies and groups radicalize (as one example). Movement cycles thus become interpretable as shifts in dominant modes of coordination, and the question then becomes what conditions privilege coalitional, organizational, social movement, or subaltern collaborative models and how this might vary across time and space.

These represent just a few possible theoretical perspectives on changing supply-side dynamics that emphasize field-level processes; alternative approaches might give primacy to exogenous factors such as patterns of political repression or variations in resource availability across societal sectors. For now, however, my main point is that we need theories to get leverage on the trends we observe, not just documenting or describing them.

Coda

Roggeband and Duyvendak's introductory comments highlight a number of other important issues that are not explicitly addressed in the chapters reviewed here. Most centrally, the very topic that initially motivated the discussion on which these chapters were based was an interest in the *changing* supply side of mobilization. Most of the contributions allude to changes in the field of action in recent decades, but the relevance of such changes for "transforming potentiality into action" continues to merit greater specification. Whereas Roggeband and Duyvendak posit the idea of a secular shift from the dominance of formal organizations to more informal or loose networks, with an attendant move from strong collective and/or organizational identities coupled with more greedy and/or intensive forms of participation to "lighter" identities and looser and/or lower cost kinds of involvement (note the many analytic conflations), there is by no means a consensus on this issue—or agreement about how this might matter for "structure in action," to use Rucht's terminology.

There is, in contrast, more agreement that the spread and increased deployment of information and communication technologies (ICTs) by social movements need to be taken into account in theorizing contemporary activism. But if we are focusing on the supply side of mobilization, the relevant question seems to be, how do ICTs function with respect to "supplying social movement activities to aggrieved groups"? Do they serve as a unique infrastructure for mobilizing individuals, creating new or reinforcing existing collective identities and/or providing new opportunities for engagement and forms of action? Furthermore, are the mechanisms by which they serve these functions substantially different from the mechanisms by which informal networks and formal SMOs promote collective identities and political action, either via face-to-face interactions or more mediated ones?

I've argued in a much earlier paper that even (oft-maligned) national SMOs can provide meaningful connections and collective identities to otherwise disconnected individuals—especially those who may not have access to dense, face-to-face activist networks and social movement communities (Minkoff 1997). Although virtual networks are unlikely to create solidarity and purposive commitment to the same extent as being in the trenches, they can get people there, a starting point for the processes of grievance definition, collective identity formation, and joint action, which are integral to sustained social movement activity. This seems to be one of the lessons learned by MoveOn.org, which added house parties to their repertoire after

George W. Bush was reelected. Furthermore, in the absence of access to the trenches, direct (e.g., Facebook, Twitter) and mediated (e.g., MoveOn.org) ICTs can provide meaningful, if primarily symbolic, opportunities for affiliation and creation of activist identities. The link between such collective identities and collective action, and the role that ICTs play in mobilization, remain critical areas of comparative analysis.

There is also a pressing need for systematic empirical studies on exactly how new technologies matter. Jennifer Earl has one of the most comprehensive and innovative studies under way (see Earl and Kimport 2011, among other publications). Earl does a couple of important things. First, she draws a distinction between online support of offline protests (information, coordination, logistics) and online protest actions (e.g., petitions and denial of service actions, i.e., legal and illegal ones) and develops hypotheses regarding the mix of forms and how they are likely to change over time. Second, she directly examines whether what she calls "traditional organizers," such as formal SMOs, remain as central in organizing online opportunities for protest involvement as they have been in organizing offline protests. Most important, she has developed a strategy for sampling websites over time to get at the kinds of longitudinal questions in which we are interested here. Hers is a rigorous and innovative agenda that is also likely to provide a model for comparative research.

As a last point, despite the centrality of macrolevel considerations in the preamble, the chapters themselves are fairly silent on this important topic. However, I want to echo Roggeband and Duyvendak's insistence that to understand the changing supply side of mobilization and its consequences, we need to be willing to connect our interest in the mesolevel to macrolevel theories of social structure and social change. This impulse is reflected in Roggeband and Duyvendak's emphasis on such concepts as "network society," "globalization," and "individualization" in their introductory comments. However, it is critical to remember that the social bases of interaction and political mobilization are structured by macrolevel inequalities in access to resources and opportunities to organize for social and political change. Although the mesolevel configuration of movement networks and organizations has the potential to destabilize existing power relations, it may also reinforce them. And as I have suggested, the field of action is also subject to its own endogenous constraints that may undermine the best of inclusive and participatory intentions among activists, as is also the case within activist and advocacy organizations themselves (see Strolovitch 2007).

Here, then, is a final question that remains insufficiently addressed by the contributions to this section: what kinds of organizations or networks and what kinds of media guarantee space and voice to more marginalized and less resourceful actors? (Roggeband and Duyvendak, chapter 5). The rather loosely coordinated protest campaign documented by Rucht as well as the more intentional mobilizations of progressive communities in Montreal and Pittsburgh that Staggenborg describes give the impression that there are multiple points of access for even less well organized or resourced groups and/or that the costs of participation are relatively low for many different constituencies. However, we know that even intendedly participatory groups, such as the World Social Fora or various segments of the global justice movement, have to work hard to offset the unintentional reproduction of inequality (Polletta 2002; Smith 2004; della Porta 2007; Doerr 2008). Groups and individuals bring different resources with them to the table, so to speak, and without some reflection and accountability, the kinds of collaborations and negotiations that constitute what Diani refers to as a social movement mode of coordination may be ineffective with respect to truly transformative social change.

These final observations point to the intersection of the demand side along with the supply side of contention and are intended to remind us of the distinctive contribution of Bert Klandermans's corpus: not only has he challenged us to interrogate the link between micro-, meso-, and macrolevel processes and how they structure the demand and supply sides of sustained collective action, but he has also provided us with integrative models of how to do so, both theoretically and empirically.

References

Della Porta, Donatella, ed. 2007. *The Global Justice Movement: Cross-National and Transnational Perspectives.* Boulder, Colo.: Paradigm.

Doerr, Nicole. 2008. "Deliberative Discussion, Language, and Efficiency in the WSF Process." *Mobilization* 13, no. 4: 395–410.

Earl, Jennifer, and Katrina Kimport. 2011. *Digitally Enabled Social Change: Activism in the Internet Age.* Cambridge, Mass.: MIT Press.

Freeman, Jo. 1973. "The Origins of the Women's Liberation Movement." *American Journal of Sociology* 78:792–811.

Klandermans, Bert. 2001. "Why Social Movements Come into Being and Why People Join Them." In *The Blackwell Companion to Sociology,* edited by Judith Blau, 268–81. Malden, Mass.: Blackwell.

Koopmans, Ruud. 2004. "Movements and Media: Selection Processes and Evolutionary Dynamics in the Public Sphere." *Theory and Society* 33:367–91.

Levi, Margaret, and Gillian H. Murphy. 2006. "Coalitions of Contention: The Case of the WTO Protests in Seattle." *Political Studies* 54:651–70.

McCarthy, John D. 1996. "Mobilizing Structures: Constraints and Opportunities in Adopting, Adapting, and Inventing." In *Comparative Perspectives on Social Movements,* edited by Doug McAdam, John D. McCarthy, and Mayce N. Zald, 141–51. Cambridge: Cambridge University Press.

Minkoff, Debra. 1995. *Organizing for Equality: The Evolution of Women's and Racial-Ethnic Organizations in America, 1955–85.* ASA Rose Monograph Series. New Brunswick, N.J.: Rutgers University Press.

———. 1997. "Producing Social Capital: National Social Movements and Civil Society." *American Behavioral Scientist* 40:606–19.

Polletta, Francesca. 2002. *Freedom Is an Endless Meeting: Democracy in American Social Movements.* Chicago: University of Chicago Press.

Smith, Jackie. 2004. "The World Social Forum and the Challenges of Global Democracy." *Global Networks* 4:413–21.

Strolovitch, Dara. 2007. *Affirmative Advocacy: Race, Class, and Gender in Interest Group Politics.* Chicago: University of Chicago Press.

III
Dynamics of Mobilization

10

Changing Mobilization of Individual Activists?

Stefaan Walgrave

Mobilization is the process through which a demand for collective action present in a certain community is met by a supply of collective action events staged by social movements. As participation by individuals is a necessary condition for the existence of social movements and protest, mobilization of participants is key to understanding social movements. The centrality of the mobilization process appears clearly from the existing literature. We see two main distinctions in a large body of work that has tackled mobilization using different concepts, theories, and methods.

A first stream focuses on the social movement organizations (SMOs) staging collective action and on how organizations try to reach out beyond their constituencies and try to influence individual-level participation decisions. Mainstream mobilization research, therefore, has focused primarily on the *structural* preconditions of participation. Probably the strongest and most robust finding emerging from the bulk of scholarly work on mobilization is that network embeddedness increases the chances of being asked to participate (Schussman and Soule 2005). People who are embedded in conducive social networks are more likely to be reached by mobilizing messages, and their participation decision is more likely to meet approval by their peers (McAdam and Paulsen 1993; Passy 2002). The type and flavor of these conducive social networks are a subject of discussion. Formal organization membership, in most studies, emerges as a strong predictor of participation. Members of organizations are sometimes mobilized en bloc, as organizations mobilize their members in a top-down fashion. But also informal, interpersonal ties have been identified as channels of mobilization, whether or not these ties are part of formal structures

(McAdam 1988). Hence individuals have the agency to mobilize as well, and not all mobilization is organizational in nature. In sum, *structuralists* contend that the key aspect of mobilization is what Klandermans and Oegema (1987) have called *action mobilization* and that inciting people to take part in a concrete movement or event is mainly affected by the structural location of the individual.

A second stream of work has dealt with the *cultural* paths to participation. The basic idea is that people engage not only because they are being asked or targeted but also because they agree with the causes put forward by the movement. The main object of debate among *culturalists* has been to what extent there is what Klandermans and Oegema (1987) calls *consensus mobilization*, the consequence of top-down efforts by SMOs, or rather whether there is *consensus formation*, or autonomous individuals independently attributing meaning to real-world problems. The former take is exemplified by the frame-alignment approach of Snow and colleagues (1986). These scholars state that people participate when SMOs succeed in aligning their messages with the beliefs of potential constituents by adapting their own messages or by changing their constituents' beliefs. A contradictory version of cultural mobilization sketches a picture of more active individual participants not just embracing the ideas postulated by SMOs but behaving as active attributors of meaning constructing their own ideas and searching for opportunities to put these ideas into practice (Jasper 1998).

Summarizing, the existing literature on mobilization can be categorized along two axes: structure versus culture and bottom up (individuals) versus top down (organizations). Naturally, most work recognizes that mobilization is a matter of structure *and* culture and that both top-down and bottom-up processes are at work. But in practice, most studies have worked within one of these four theoretical approaches of mobilization.

This volume addresses the future of social movement research. What is new regarding mobilization? We do not dispose of the necessary longitudinal studies to convincingly show that anything has changed and that mobilization anno 2012 is substantially different from mobilization a few decades ago. It appears that all traditional ways of mobilizing people are still common. For example, in many countries, trade unions are still large organizations that, at times, transform into mobilizing machines that, via formal recruitment, are able to produce protest events with massive attendance; some unions literally drive their constituents to the protest venue, provide lunch packages, negotiate with the employer the day of labor lost, and encapsulate the participants in a strong structure of local trade union representatives. This type of structural, top-down mobilization is still very much in use. What seems to be happening, though, is that structural top-down mobilization is *complemented* with other types of mobilization in which individuals play a larger role and formal organizations are to some extent bypassed. This is not to say that such bottom-up mobilizations did not exist earlier. Yet I suggest, in line with other contributions in this volume (see, e.g., Van Stekelenburg and Boekkooi, chapter 11), that they may have become more frequent.

In the remainder of this preamble to part III, I first speculate about two potential changes in mobilization dynamics: SMOs have partially lost their grip on the mobilization process, and mobilization is challenged by an increased diversity of potential participants. Second, I raise a number of methodological challenges and sketch some preliminary avenues for further research. Third, I briefly introduce the four chapters of the section on mobilization and show how they are connected to the changes outlined in this introduction.

Changing Mobilization?

A first challenge to mobilization theory seems to be the shifting balance between organizations and individuals. Key in this respect is the more reticent and reserved position of potential participants vis-à-vis SMOs. It appears that sustained activism with fully committed people organizing their personal lives around their activism (Downton and Wehr 1998) has become increasingly rare (see also Mayer, chapter 19). Especially among the young, more variable and changing engagements are the rule. This does not imply that people would be less willing to engage or spend less time in social movements or protest—in fact, studies show that aggregate protest participation is on the rise in many countries—but rather that many potential participants do not commit themselves to one cause but act as wavering protest consumers jumping from one cause to another, temporarily picking a SMO or protest event as they see fit. Information and communication technology (ICT) use allows these multiple activists to manage their complex identities, to follow several causes at a distance, and to jump on the bandwagon when they feel like it (Walgrave et al. 2012). Linked to that, some observers also see an increasing reliance on loosely coupled networks and informal ties (also called *light communities*) rather than formal connections as the basis of mobilization (see Roggeband and Duyvendak, chapter 5; Van Stekelenburg and Boekkooi, chapter 11). Also, dramatic focusing events appear to have become more important as people engage more in a reactive and temporary way, depending on what attracts their attention on the public agenda, rather than in a persistent and planned way. As a consequence of all these changes, top-down en bloc recruitment is complemented, and individuals appear to be more empowered and less dependent on organizational supply of protest. Just like the customer, the (potential) participant has become king.

My own work about protest participation in Belgium cannot substantiate these claims as I lack longitudinal data, but it highlights some of the correlates of the detachment of participants from formal SMO structures. On the basis of a series of ten protest surveys on Brussels's demonstrations (2003–8), one can observe that a substantial number of participants do not seem to follow the top-down organizational logic (for a description of the research and data, see Walgrave and Verhulst 2011). For example, quite a large number of protesters report to be attending the demonstration "on their own" (±15 percent), which indirectly challenges the idea that people need supportive networks to enable participation. Also, many demonstrators indicate to have decided to participate only during the very last days (±30 percent), implying that SMOs are dependent on late deciders, who must be convinced until the very end. A majority of respondents claim *not* to have been asked by others to participate (±65 percent)—even at typical trade union events—suggesting that many activists, at least in their own perception, are not mobilized by others but have mobilized themselves. Finally, a sizeable group of demonstrators reports participating for the first time (during the last five years) in a protest event (±30 percent); these first-timers are by definition not committed, long-term activists but possibly one-shot participants.

Most interesting, however, are the immense differences between protest events staged by different types of social movements dealing with different issues. The mobilization processes associated with newer types of movements are very different from those of traditional movements. Distinguishing typical old social movement (OSM) events (trade unions), new social movement (NSM) events (peace and environmental movements), and consensual movement events (against random violence or for the unity of the country), one encounters quite dramatic differences. Participants in the four OSM events in our sample overwhelmingly refer to organizations as the most important information channel for the demonstration (68 percent), and NSM participants mention these formal channels somewhat less (55 percent), but people participating in the three consensual movement events hardly mention organizations at all (7 percent). The latter group records that especially the mass media has been important (43 percent), while press coverage was as good as absent among OSM (4 percent) and NSM (3 percent) participants. Our questionnaire also contains questions on membership of the protest-staging organizations. Again, differences between movement types are striking. Seventy-five percent of the OSM demonstrators report such membership, against 43 percent for NSM protesters and only one in ten consensual movement participants.

A possible consequence of increasing individualized mobilization may be that in the long run, SMOs get weaker. As enduring activists are difficult to find, and as people tune in and out again, SMOs lose resources, and their infrastructures may crumble. Continuity is problematic, expertise is not permanent, and pressure on decision makers is not persisting.

Although the typical structural top-down model of mobilization is still very much alive, there are thus signs that some recent movements do mobilize in a different way (provided one can still speak of a "movement" in those cases). Note again that this evidence does not prove that mobilization processes are changing across the board. The data do suggest, however, that mobilization is definitely more bidirectional than structural (and cultural) top-down theories seem to suggest. Mobilization theory could benefit from more explicitly recognizing the plurality of mobilization processes and investigating their complementarity. We know that both structure and culture play a role, and we know that mobilization is a matter not just of top-down activation but also of self-mobilization by individuals. The key question becomes what types of mobilization occur under which circumstances and what explains the variance in mobilization processes. These questions call for comparative research designs.

I will more briefly deal with a similar, second challenge to mobilization theory. This second challenge as well relates to fundamental societal shifts affecting how movements mobilize and relate to their constituency. Societies become increasingly diverse and "liquid" (Bauman 2000; see also Van Stekelenburg and Boekkooi, chapter 11). Functional differentiation implies that people play increasingly different roles in different subsystems, leading to complex and layered identities (Luhmann 1995; see also Snow, chapter 13). Globalization and denationalization, together with immigration and mobility, lead to increasing heterogeneity and conflict. In chapter 12, Oliver elaborates on this increasing diversity and points toward differences between the different social carriers of social movements. Differentiation implies that interests and correlated beliefs are increasingly fragmented. Consequently, social movements are confronted with a more diverse potential constituency. For example, trade unions seem to have more trouble uniting workers as they are diverse and have conflicting interests. How can SMOs mobilize large groups when the common ground between their potential supporters is withering? Again, I do not claim that traditional mobilization of homogenous groups no longer exists. In case of massive layoffs or company restructuring, for instance, large homogenous groups of workers still take to the streets in traditional bread-and-butter marches. But with increasing fragmentation, how can SMOs mobilize on issues that go beyond immediate and clearly defined interests?

Part of the answer is via staging the consensual, and mostly "reactive," mobilizations that I mentioned earlier. Evidence shows that protest events reacting to highly publicized focusing events are characterized by a large degree of internal diversity. For example, in many countries, dramatic random killings have led to massive demonstrations expressing outrage and pressing for policy measures; evidence suggests that these events are mostly very diverse and that people from all walks of life participate (often for the first time). Such a kind of short-lived and issue-based engagement can be used by protest organizers to reach out to a large and diverse constituency. The event, and the media attention for it, creates a temporary opportunity for recruitment of heterogeneous crowds. The event itself temporarily increases the salience of a specific identity that was only latently present and allows SMOs to appeal to that identity (see Snow, chapter 13). Roggeband and Duyvendak speak about a shift from "identity-based" to "issue-based" social movements. A way to overcome increased fragmentation and interest diversity is to capitalize on external events powerfully highlighting specific issues and to surf the wave of saliency.

Aggregate-level evidence suggests that increasingly different sorts of people resort to protest participation to defend their interests and express their opinions (Meyer and Tarrow 1998). Protest has become "normalized" (Van Aelst and Walgrave 2001). This observation seems to contradict my earlier argument that interest fragmentation makes it more difficult to mobilize; however, I do not think it does. The specialization of participation is growing, while at the same time, joining protest and social movements has become more widespread. Workers, employers, firefighters, nurses, peace activists, police officers, ecologists, lawyers, students, and so on, all take to the streets, but they do so in separate, small events drawing on narrow identities and very specific claims. In their essay in this book, Roggeband and Duyvendak point toward trends toward homogenization within social movements and decreasing heterogeneity. If this were true, it would indicate a growing disintegration of the social movement sector. Regarding mobilization, it would imply that differences in mobilization strategies and processes between movements and events are substantial. I earlier hinted in that direction. Once more, this calls for research systematically comparing mobilization processes across movements and issues.

Methodological Challenges and Future Research

As suggested earlier, I believe that the empirical study of mobilization would be served by using standardized measures and by drawing on comparative designs. The conceptual fragmentation in the field would not be really problematic as long as scholars agreed on how to measure mobilization empirically. But this is not the case. As a consequence, we know relatively little about differences and similarities in mobilization processes across nations, across time, across issues, and across types of participation. Of course, we know, for example, that strong ties and mutual trust are more required for risky and involved types of participation (e.g., violent action) compared to less demanding types of collective action (e.g., signing petitions) (Della Porta 1988). But apart from these extreme cases, we are ignorant about the extent to which weak ties suffice to produce similar action repertoires. I showed previously that there are striking differences between the mobilization of participants in the same type of action (legal street demonstrations) staged by different movements and addressing different issues. Mobilization theory stays largely silent on how to make sense of these differences; we make general references to different types of movements with alleged differences in internal structure, as I did here, but that is as far as we get. Preliminary evidence suggests that even when action form and issue are controlled for, there are substantial differences in how participants are recruited in different nations (Walgrave and Verhulst 2009). So the opportunity structure in a country, both at general and issue-specific levels, seems to affect how participants are mobilized. Finally, time is a variable as well. Movements' mobilization goes in cycles; active periods and latent phases alternate. Here, too, we expect the mobilization process to substantially vary between periods of reaching out and shrinking in.

To compare across action forms, nations, issues, and time, we need better—that is, standardized—measures that enable us to systematically assess how mobilization varies. Only standardization allows for comparison. This is no plea to get rid of case studies, nor is it an attack on qualitative, in-depth work; but to gain more empirical leverage and understand variations in mobilization, we need more cases and systematic observation.

Two other methodological challenges for the study of mobilization are worth mentioning. First, the large majority of studies sample on the dependent variable and examine joiners only (with some notable exceptions; Oegema and Klandermans 1994). Key differences between participants and nonparticipants are unexplored, and we often remain ignorant about the precise causal mechanism generating participation. Interestingly, political scientists drawing on general population surveys do tend to incorporate both categories—participants and nonparticipants—but owing to the general nature of these surveys, the mobilization mechanisms they can explore are entirely decontextualized (Verba, Schlozman, and Brady 1995).

Second, probably one of the most tricky issues in social sciences in general and the study of social movements in particular is bridging the microlevel of individual participation and the mesolevel of mobilization by SMOs. How can we couple mesolevel evidence on the mobilization efforts and strategies of organizations with microlevel evidence regarding the motives, networks, and beliefs of individual participants? The frame-alignment approach yields a plausible narrative stating that participation is the result of the "resonance" of the "frames" of participants and SMOs. Yet, according to my knowledge, no study has ever empirically tested to what extent participants' beliefs and SMOs' messages correspond and, most critically, to what extent there is less correspondence between nonparticipants and SMOs. So far, we seem to lack established methods to connect micro- and macrodata on mobilization.

How This Volume Contributes

This introduction attempted to highlight some debates and problems standing out in mobilization theory and research. This book's section on mobilization offers four different chapters addressing some of these issues.

Van Stekelenburg and Boekkooi's essay directly tackles the shifting balance between formal organizations and participants. They coin the concept of *mobilizing structures* and speak of a continuum from formal organizational to informal mobilization via social networks. They explicitly address the micro–meso bridge by showing that the decisions by formal peace movement organizations in the Netherlands, namely, their internal division and late agreement, negatively affected the turnout and mobilization processes for the major antiwar (Iraq) demonstrations in 2003. Individual participants also decided relatively late to participate because there simply was no earlier information about the event available. Van Stekelenburg and Boekkooi contend that the boom of new media, and especially Web 2.0, has shifted the burden of mobilization from organizations to small groups and individuals; new media access is cheap and allows relatively resource-poor individuals or groups to create content and disseminate it widely. These authors claim that it is especially new media that allow mobilization to become a bottom-up process: through ICT use, individuals initiate protest rather than being just the targets of mobilization efforts of organized actors; the necessity to line up with large organizations has disappeared.

In chapter 13, Snow tackles the shift in contemporary mobilization processes from a cultural perspective. He introduces the idea of a *dilemma of multiple identities*. The different roles people play and the groups to which they belong generate distinct social identities. Mobilization, Snow claims, is the consequence of an alignment between one of those identities and the grievances experienced, or claims made, by social movements. Snow's essay directly speaks to the idea that interests and beliefs have become multiple and, as a consequence, fragmented. People can be mobilized based on an identity that previously was not salient at all and only existed latently. He explicitly underscores the importance of focusing events that are able to activate an underlying identity and supports the idea that successful mobilization may in some way be reactive to those events.

Hutter and Kriesi (chapter 14) criticize students' of social movement neglect of alternative channels of influencing (political) decision making. Their basic claim is that mobilization also happens via the electoral channel (parties) and via the channel of interest intermediation (interest groups). By only focusing on the protest channel, social movement scholars overlook the most important contemporary mobilization, that is, the electoral mobilization of the populist Right against the consequences of globalization. Some (right-wing) groups prefer—because of their different values—the electoral channel above the movement–protest channel to voice their grievances and to affect policy. By limiting their focus to mobilization for protest (or movements), social movement scholars have missed the most important contemporary mobilization, Hutter and Kriesi hold. Instead, they have focused on relatively marginal contemporary phenomena such as the protest staged by the global justice movement. So if we want to study the changing dynamics of mobilization, we also need to take the electoral channel into account. The key point of this contribution is that different issues lead to different types of mobilization. As I argued earlier, movements mobilize differently depending on the issue at stake. I contended that this is the reason we need comparative research comparing mobilization for protest over time, across nations, across issues, and across different types of collective action. Hutter and Kriesi take this argument a step further. They claim that issues, and the groups caring about them, not only determine the type of collective action employed but even whether the protest channel is chosen at all. Disaffected groups have several ways to influence politics, and mobilization for protest is only one of those. A large number of the grievances people hold are never translated in protest but are transformed in votes or in support for interest groups.

Oliver, in a similar vein, elaborates on the idea that mobilization differs across movements and issues, and especially across the different "social carriers" of a movement. Limiting herself to the protest arena, she argues that the context within which movements operate can be very different within the same country and even when it comes to the same issue. Fighting for a similar cause, some groups within a movement may experience repression, whereas others' actions are facilitated. So whereas Hutter and Kriesi claim that different issues lead to mobilization in different arenas, Oliver states that even within the same issue, groups may be compelled to follow different strategies. Oliver's main claim is that the mobilization decisions by groups are affected by the prevailing regime and its strategies of repression but also by the positions and actions of other social groups making similar claims and by the actions of other movements.

References

Bauman, Zygmunt. 2000. *Liquid Modernity*. Oxford: Blackwell.

Della Porta, Donatella. 1988. "Recruitment Processes in Clandestine Political Organizations: Italian Left-Wing Terrorism." In *From Structure to Action,* edited by B. Klandermans, H. Kriesi, and S. Tarrow, 155–69. Greenwich, Conn.: JAI Press.

Downton, James, and Paul Wehr. 1998. "Persistent Pacifism: How Activist Commitment Is Developed and Sustained." *Journal of Peace Research* 35:531–50.

Jasper, James. 1998. "The Emotions of Protest: Affective and Reactive Emotions in and around Social Movements." *Sociological Forum* 13:397–424.

Klandermans, Bert, and Dirk Oegema. 1987. "Potentials, Networks, Motivations, and Barriers: Steps toward Participation in Social Movements." *American Sociological Review* 52:519–31.

Luhmann, Niklas. 1995. *Social Systems*. Stanford, Calif.: Stanford University Press.

McAdam, Doug. 1988. "Micromobilization Contexts and the Recruitment to Activism." In *From Structure to Action,* edited by B. Klandermans, H. Kriesi, and S. Tarrow, 125–54. Greenwich, Conn.: JAI Press.

McAdam, Doug, and Ronnelle Paulsen. 1993. "Specifying the Relationship between Social Ties and Activism." *American Journal of Sociology* 99:640–67.

Meyer, David, and Sydney Tarrow, eds. 1998. *The Social Movement Society*. Lanham, Md.: Rowman and Littlefield.

Oegema, Dirk, and Bert Klandermans. 1994. "Why Social Movement Sympathizers Don't Participate: Erosion and Nonconversion of Support." *American Sociological Review* 59:703–22.

Passy, Florence. 2002. "Social Networks Matter, but How?" In *Social Movements and Networks: Relational Approaches to Collective Action,* edited by M. Diani and D. McAdam, 21–49. Oxford: Oxford University Press.

Schussman, Alan, and Sarah A. Soule. 2005. "Process and Protest: Accounting for Individual Protest Participation." *Social Forces* 84:1083–1108.

Snow, David A., R. Burke Rochford, Steven K. Worden, and Robert B. Benford. 1986. "Frame Alignment Processes, Micromobilization, and Movement Participation." *American Sociological Review* 51:464–82.

Van Aelst, Peter, and Stefaan Walgrave. 2001. "Who Is That (Wo)man in the Street? From the Normalisation of Protest to the Normalisation of the Protester." *European Journal of Political Research* 39:461–86.

Verba, Sydney, Kay Schlozman, and Henri Brady. 1995. *Voice and Equality: Civic Voluntarism in American Politics*. Cambridge, Mass.: Harvard University Press.

Walgrave, Stefaan, Lance Bennett, Jeroen Van Laer, and Christian Breunig. 2012.

"Multiple Engagements and Network Bridging in Contentious Politics: Digital Media Use of Protest Participants." *Mobilization* 16, no. 3: 325–49.

Walgrave, Stefaan, and Joris Verhulst. 2009. "Government Stance and Internal Diversity of Protest: A Comparative Study of Protest against the War in Iraq in Eight Countries." *Social Forces* 87:1355–87.

———. 2011. "Selection and Response Bias in Protest Surveys." *Mobilization* 16, no. 2: 489–500.

11
Mobilizing for Change in a Changing Society

Jacquelien van Stekelenburg and Marije Boekkooi

To explain the occurrence of protest events, social movement research has focused on external structural factors such as resource mobilization or political opportunities. However, protest events do not appear out of the blue. Some people have to take the initiative to start organizing and mobilizing an event to offer a supply of protest (Klandermans 2004). For protest to occur, a critical mass is needed that is especially motivated, resourceful, and willing to put in time, energy, and resources (Oliver, Marwell, and Teixeira 1985). Not many studies focus on these *organizers* of protest and how their mobilization efforts influence the dynamics of protest (Goodwin and Jasper 1999; but for an exception, see Boekkooi, Klandermans, and Van Stekelenburg 2011). However, to understand what happens at the macrolevel of movements, we need to know what happens at the microlevel of organizers (Lichbach 1998; Jasper 2004).

It is this understudied role of the organizers of protest on which this chapter focuses. The mobilization of an event is a two-step process comprising initiators mobilizing other organizers and organizers mobilizing participants (Boekkooi 2012). By *initiators,* we mean those people who mobilize other activists to help them organize; by *organizers,* we refer to those people who are involved in the decision making about the organization of the event and the mobilization of the participants.

This contribution focuses on how organizers build a mobilizing structure (with an emphasis on networks) in which special attention is paid to how new developments, such as the transformation from solid to liquid society (Bauman 2000), "personalism" (Lichterman 1996), and information and communication technologies (ICTs), shape new types of mobilizing structures, thereby changing both mobilizing strategies and the forms protests take. We hold that *who* starts organizing and mobilizing and *how* they do so shapes the mobilizing structure, which has important implications for the mobilization campaign and the dynamics of protest. A continuum of types of mobilizing structures is developed, and illustrative evidence is provided that shows how different types of mobilizing structures generate different dynamics of protest.

Individualization

Late modern societies are changing. Solid societal patterns are eroding, and we are moving toward a liquid society (Bauman 2000) or a network society (Castells 1996), in which bonds between people are looser and more flexible. Individuals in late modern societies prefer less binding and more flexible relationships with organizations over traditional rigid and hierarchical ones (Bennett, Breunig, and Givens 2008). In late modern societies, people become increasingly connected as *individuals* rather than as members of a community or group; they operate their own personal community networks. Traditional greedy institutions, such as trade unions and churches, which made significant demands on members' time, loyalty, and energy (Coser 1967), are replaced by light groups and associations that are loose, easy to join, and easy to leave (Roggeband and Duyvendak, chapter 5). Society is thus becoming organized around networked individuals (Wellman et al. 2003) rather than groups or local solidarities, and connections are loose and flexible rather than fixed.

Despite this process of individualization, people in late modern societies *are* still committed to collective causes (Norris 2002). Underlying this is what Lichterman (1996) calls *personalism*: people are politically active because they feel a personal sense of political responsibility rather than an obligation to a community or group. Personalism thus affects the greediness of organizations and groups because an organization or group can only act greedy when the individual feels a strong attachment to the group. Hence concepts such as traditional versus new, formal versus informal, and offline versus online do not automatically align with organizations or networks being either light or greedy. In fact, some informal groups, such as anarchist subcultures, can be greedy, whereas membership in some formal traditional groups, such as so-called checkbook membership of a political party, can be light. Some new online groups, such as Facebook friends, can be greedy, whereas other traditional offline groups, such as sports associations, can be light. So what matters is not whether a group is traditional or new, formal or informal, or online or offline but how strong the bond is: how much one identifies with it, how much time is invested, the emotional intensity, intimacy, and mutual trust involved in membership (cf. Granovetter 1973). It is thus not the organization or network per se that determines the greediness but an interaction between an individual and the organization or network.

Information and Communication Technologies

Although the process of individualization has evolved since the late 1950s and 1960s, it accelerated and moved to a new level with the rise of new communication technologies, especially the Internet. Without ICTs, the network society we know now would not have been possible.

ICTs progress quickly, quickly enough to distinguish between the older generation (Web 1.0) and the newer generation (Web 2.0) (Bekkers et al. 2008). Whereas Web 1.0, for example, classical websites, was about one sender attempting to reach many receivers via one medium, where receivers read, viewed, and consumed information, Web 2.0, for example, Twitter, wikis, blogs, and social media, is about many senders attempting to exchange information with many receivers via multiple media, where people write, produce, and influence the information. Whereas Web 1.0 was—like classical media—still based on a top-down approach by institutionalized organizations, Web 2.0 offers people the possibility to coproduce relevant content. Every citizen is able to start a blog to communicate specific political ideas. Web 2.0 applications also changed communication from one to one to many to many (Boulos and Wheeler 2007). Instant messaging via Twitter but also blogs and wikis facilitate fast and inexpensive many-to-many communication. Moreover, Web 2.0 applications let people form groups effortlessly. Obviously, social connections existed under Web 1.0 as well, but mainly in the form of one-to-one e-mail communication. Various social media, such as LinkedIn, MySpace, and Facebook, make it easy to be linked in a virtual network, while previously, this was time consuming and effortful and thus costly. Whether people find online networks as beneficial as offline networks is a question to be answered, but Web 2.0 applications have given people a set of tools that allow them to create and find groups with ease.

Obviously, the distinction between classical media, Web 1.0, and Web 2.0 is blurred because organizers almost never use just a single mobilization channel but instead draw on myriad channels both offline and online. Like for activism, Internet activism is seldom exclusively Internet centered (Meikle 2002), and contemporary offline actions are almost always accompanied by online tactics.

Consequences for Organizers

These developments—individualization processes amplified by ICTs—are, of course, not without consequences for organizers. How important are ICTs for contentious politics? Political leaders seem to be convinced by their effectiveness—Egypt's President Mubarak decided to cut of the Internet and mobile phone providers when the Jasmine Revolution set off, while Chinese leaders chose to ban searches for "Egypt" on the Internet. However, ICTs' influence on contentious performances is subject to much scholarly controversy. For example, it is argued that they change the ways in which activists communicate and collaborate and perform their contentious acts. Several authors have shown that social movements—being networks of diverse groups and activists—are especially keen on using the Internet because of its fluid, nonhierarchical structure, which fits their ideological and organizational needs (Bennett 2003; Van de Donk et al. 2004), and because of the low costs of organizing and communicating (Earl and Kimport 2011). Bimber (1998), however, is critical about the assertion that increasing communication capacity heightens political participation. He observes that political participation among U.S. citizens has not changed significantly since the 1950s, despite the increase in opportunities to communicate resulting from the expansion of television (Bimber 1998) or the Internet (Bimber 2001). The effects of Web 1.0 indeed were limited to reinforcing existing mobilization processes and routines and the positions of already well-established actors (Norris 2001; Boekkooi, Klandermans, and Van Stekelenburg 2011). Rather than a qualitatively different way of mobilizing, Web 1.0 brought quantitative changes in the form of "supersizing effects" on the proliferation of information, reach, and speed (see, e.g., Norris 2001; Earl and Schussman 2003). Web 2.0, however, does change the dynamics of contention fundamentally. The literature describes four ways in which ICTs—especially Web 2.0—change the dynamics of mobilization: reduction of mobilization and participation costs, expansion of organizers' tactical repertoire, promotion of collective identity, and the creation of networks.

Reduction of Costs

By lowering communication and coordination costs, ICTs facilitate group formation, recruitment, and retention, which facilitates the formation of mobilizing structures, reduces the cost of conventional forms of mobilization and participation, and creates new low-cost forms of participation. ICTs make organizing without organizations feasible (cf. Earl and Kimport 2011).

Expansion of Tactical Repertoire

The tactical repertoire available to organizers ranges from real actions that are supported and facilitated by the Internet to virtual actions that are Internet based (Van Laer and Van Aelst 2009). Internet-supported actions involve the Internet as a device that reinforces the traditional tools of organizers by making it easier to organize and coordinate. Smart phones, for instance, make it possible to continuously document activists on the spot about actions and interactions with the police and thereby change the tactics of groups like the Black Bloc (McPhail and McCarthy 2005). Internet-based action involves the Internet's function of creating new and modified tactics, as, for instance, online petitions, e-mail bombings, and hacktivism, expanding the action tool kit of social movements.

Promotion of Collective Identity

ICTs can foster collective identity across a dispersed population as ICTs can encourage the perception among individuals that they are members of a larger community by virtue of the emotions, grievances, and feelings of efficacy they share (Brainard and Siplon 2000; Arquilla and Ronfeldt 2001). Social media sites offer several opportunities to display an identity, for instance, by adopting or donating a site or by placing a *twibbon*—a logo specifically designed to place on social media sites. Such twibbons offer people the chance to visibly display these cases to the virtual networks with which they identify (see also Polletta et al., chapter 2).

Creation of Networks

ICTs' capability to create networks has arguably the greatest effects for organizers because it impacts on social embeddedness, which is a key factor for mobilization (Klandermans, Van der Toorn, and Van Stekelenburg 2008; Van Stekelenburg and Klandermans 2010a; 2010b). Social media sites such as Facebook and MySpace—which have attracted millions of users worldwide since their introduction—make it possible to be connected with hundreds of people who share interests and activities across political and geographic borders. Furthermore, social media sites not only allow individuals to meet and connect to strangers, virtually or in reality, they also enable users to publicly display their connections (boyd and Ellison 2007). This public display of connections is a crucial component of social network sites, which can result in connections between individuals that would not otherwise be made. As such, the Internet created an additional public sphere; people are nowadays embedded in *virtual* networks in addition to (in)formal *physical* networks. This is important and relevant in the context of mobilization because the more people are socially embedded—formally, informally, and virtually—the higher the chances are that they will be targeted with a mobilizing message and keep to their promises to participate (Klandermans and Oegema 1987), and the more they will participate in protest (Klandermans, Van der Toorn, and Van Stekelenburg 2008). As such, individualization processes amplified by ICTs made *virtual embeddedness*—in addition to formal and informal embeddedness—a key factor for mobilization (Van Stekelenburg and Klandermans 2013).

Mobilizing Structures

The mobilizing structure is the connecting tissue between organizers and participants. Despite their name, mobilizing *structures* are not static or preexisting. It is the organizers' task to combine, rearrange, and activate these relational configurations and form mobilizing structures through which to mobilize participants. Organizers thus need to build a network of networks, which may be formal or informal, virtual or physical, and part of the movement or not. Organizers may use any relationship they have at their disposal. They may build a mobilizing structure entirely from formal organizations or entirely from informal social relationships or any combination thereof, depending on their choice and existing relationships. There is no preset recipe; organizers may assemble and combine anything they are able to, be it formal or informal, broad or narrow. We will use the term *mobilizing structure* to refer to all the organizers' different assemblages of relational structures.

Many studies have shown that networks are important in explaining differential recruitment and mobilization (e.g., Snow, Zurcher, and Ekland-Olson 1980; Klandermans and Oegema 1987; Tarrow 1994; Diani 2004), and which organizations join the mobilizing coalition is an important predictor of who will participate in the protest (e.g., McAdam and Paulsen 1993; Kitts 2000; Fisher et al. 2005). Most studies are based on organizational affiliations, showing that organizations predominantly mobilize their own members to take to the streets. Some scholars have also looked at membership in civil society organizations (Baldassarri and Diani 2007; Klandermans, Van der Toorn, and Van Stekelenburg 2008) or embeddedness in a community (Gould 2003). Other studies have shown that it is not only organizations mobilizing their members; members themselves are important vehicles to bring new people to the streets and into the organization because they often ask people in their environments to join too (Gould 2003; Snow, Zurcher, and Ekland-Olson 1980).

But even networks with the primary goal of movement mobilization (e.g., social movement organizations) might need hard work to be activated to participate in a particular campaign. Many times, social movement organizations decline to participate in a campaign and thus to become part of the mobilizing structure. In fact, no network automatically functions as a mobilizing structure; organizers need to adapt, appropriate (McAdam, McCarthy, and Zald 1996), assemble, and activate networks for them to function as mobilizing structures. A process of mesomobilization (Gerhards and Rucht

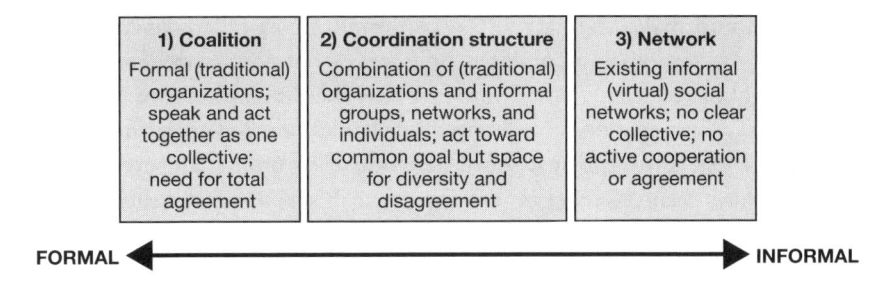

1) Coalition	2) Coordination structure	3) Network
Formal (traditional) organizations; speak and act together as one collective; need for total agreement	Combination of (traditional) organizations and informal groups, networks, and individuals; act toward common goal but space for diversity and disagreement	Existing informal (virtual) social networks; no clear collective; no active cooperation or agreement

FORMAL ←——————————————————————→ INFORMAL

Figure 11.1. Continuum of mobilizing structures.

1992) is necessary to build the mobilizing structure. Groups must make a strategic decision to join (Van Dyke 2003). Joining a mobilizing structure may be costly—a person needs to put in time, energy, and resources, which are also needed for the maintenance of the person's own group and attainment of his own goals (Staggenborg 1986). Furthermore, participation in a joint campaign may obscure the person's own identity and visibility (Gerhards and Rucht 1992; Meyer and Corrigall-Brown 2005), and groups may lose some of their autonomy (Levi and Murphy 2006). But cooperation also enables (especially small) groups to achieve matters they cannot achieve on their own (Staggenborg 1989), it increases visibility, and importantly, it increases the range of people who can be reached (Meyer and Corrigall-Brown 2005; see also Heaney and Rojas 2008).

A Continuum of Mobilizing Structures: From Formal Organizational to Informal Social Networks

The existence of different types of networks in society—from formal to informal and inside and outside a social movement—and the possibility for organizers to include any and all of these types into their mobilizing structure mean that mobilizing structures can take diverse forms. We propose a continuum of mobilizing structures ranging from consisting of only formal networks to only informal networks and any combination in between (as developed in the dissertation of Boekkooi 2012).

On the formal end of the continuum, Boekkooi (2012) places formal coalitions (see Box 1 in Figure 11.1): organizers try to mobilize the combined membership bases of organizations, often ones specifically designed for protest activity. Formal coalitions mostly present themselves as a single collective that speaks and acts uniformly. On the other end of the continuum, we find the most informal type of mobilizing structure, consisting of only informal social networks, not necessarily designed for protest activity (see Box 3 in Figure 11.1).

The use of informal social networks was common in so-called old-fashioned bread-and-butter uprisings, where people went from door to door to call on their neighbors to participate. More recently, the development of Web 2.0 applications has expanded the range of available informal social networks. Nowadays, extensive informal social networks exist online, and in the past years, we have seen several examples where organizers have used such virtual social networks to mobilize participants. These cases are typical examples of organizing without organizations (see Earl and Kimport 2011). There is no uniform actor and not necessarily one uniform message or tactic.

Between these two extremes, we find mobilizing structures that combine formal and informal networks. One common type of such a combined mobilizing structure is the *coordination structure* (see Box 2 in Figure 11.1): in such structures, a combination exists of movement organizations, groups and networks, and individuals and informal social networks. These structures act together for a common goal, but there is space for diversity and disagreement. This is used, for example, to coordinate (inter)national days of action, where initiators ask everyone to locally organize something (anything) in support of the common goal.

The roles of the organizers and their goals are different in the different types of mobilizing structures. Using formal structures may be advantageous because through organizations, many members may be recruited en bloc (Oberschall 1973); by engaging the leadership, other members are pulled in. Moreover, having a (large) organization on board may give credibility to the cause, signal the importance of the issue, and raise expectations about turnout and effectiveness of the event. In this respect, building a coalition may thus be more effective than building a coordination structure or using informal networks. However, especially young people are increasingly no longer members of formal organizations (see, e.g., Visser 2006; Scarrow and Gezgor 2010) and, consequently, often cannot be reached through such formal bonds. Informal and virtual networks may be more suited to reach these unorganized groups of people. In addition, cooperation between formal structures is often difficult, and sometimes impossible, owing to the formality and need for uniform agreement as the groups involved may be reluctant to give up on their own principles or identities. Generally, research shows that the more formal and enduring the desired cooperation (Staggenborg 1986), the more commitment and resources are asked for (Meyer and Corrigall-Brown 2005), and the greater is the pressure for ideological conformity (Gerhards and Rucht 1992), the more difficult it is to mobilize organizers to participate in the mobilizing structure and to maintain cooperation. Looser forms of cooperation that focus on a narrower goal and for a shorter amount of time

(Staggenborg 1986) are easier to achieve. Thus building a formal enduring coalition will be most difficult to achieve and maintain, building a coordination structure will be easier, and using informal social networks without any form of formalized cooperation, obligation, or commitment will be easiest.

Where organizers end up on the continuum, however, is not necessarily a conscious choice but rather depends on the bonds the organizers have and thus on who can be recruited to join the mobilizing structure (Boekkooi 2012). When the initiator is a representative of a large formal organization, he might be more inclined to form a coalition, whereas an Internet-savvy student might be more inclined to use informal virtual networks.

In what follows, illustrative evidence is provided from three cases representing three types of mobilizing structures: (1) a coalition, (2) a coordination structure, and (3) informal networks. These cases show how different initiators bring different network constellations into play, leading to different types of mobilizing structures and thus creating different dynamics of protest.

A Coalition: Quarreling and Protesting

On February 15, 2003, about twenty million people took to the streets in over sixty countries to protest the upcoming war in Iraq. In the Netherlands, around seventy thousand people marched in the streets of Amsterdam. (For a more elaborate discussion of this case, see Boekkooi, Klandermans, and Van Stekelenburg 2011.)

The Dutch demonstration was organized by the Coalition against the New War, which was set up a year earlier, in the week following 9/11. The initiators of the coalition came from a (submerged) network of longtime peace activists, some of whom were still active in small peace groups, while others had moved to other left-wing groups such as the Socialist Party (SP). The embeddedness in an existing network of peace activists greatly facilitated the startup of the coalition by providing trust among the participants. However, widening the circle proved considerably more problematic. The Green Party only joined after a year of persuasion but never actively mobilized, while the unions and other large nongovernmental organizations did not want to join at all. These organizations saw the coalition as either "a bunch of radicals" or "an umbrella organization of the SP"; either way, they did not identify with or trust the coalition.

The initiative to join the global call to demonstrate against the war in Iraq did not come from the initiators but from newcomers to the coalition: the International Socialists, a small Marxist–Leninist group. The initiators were skeptical about the possibility of organizing a large demonstration and instead proposed to make it a rally or a public meeting. When, after almost a month of fighting, it was decided that they would demonstrate, the division within the coalition had crystallized. They soon found themselves diametrically opposed again when they needed to decide on a slogan. Whereas the Marxist group wanted to protest under the banner "Stop the War," the initiators preferred "Stop the War *and* Stop Saddam." As a formal coalition needs to speak with one voice, there was no room for diversity. It took two weeks of bitter fighting to reach an agreement. As a result, the mobilization campaign could not start until one month before the demonstration was set, and media attention on antiwar protest in general, and the upcoming demonstration in particular, started equally late.

Consequently, the turnout of participants was comparatively low. Around 0.4 percent of the Dutch population took to the streets that day, which was at least ten times less than in Spain and Italy that same day and in the Dutch peace demonstration of 1983 (see Walgrave and Rucht 2010; Klandermans and Oegema 1987). Both the problems with forming the coalition and with forging agreement within the coalition hampered the mobilization of participants. The narrow coalition implied that only a relatively small amount of the mobilization potential could be mobilized through organizational channels. Owing to something as seemingly trivial as quarrels over tactics and slogans, the news about the upcoming demonstration appeared only one week in advance in the newspapers. This further explains the low turnout. The majority of angry Dutch heard only one week in advance that there would be a demonstration. During that week, they had to decide whether they were willing and able to participate.

This case shows not only the difficulties of forming and cooperating in a formal coalition but also the consequences of the organizers' relationships, actions, and decisions on the mobilization campaign and, eventually, on the turnout of the demonstration.

A Coordination Structure: Step It Up

Cooperation in a coordination structure proved much easier. On November 3, 2007, thousands of people participated in 481 different events all over the United States as part of a national climate action day. The day was organized by Step It Up (SIU), which was founded earlier that year by the well-known environmental writer Bill McKibben.

SIU was neither an organization nor a formal coalition: it consisted almost exclusively of a website designed to function as an online coordination structure. The SIU website included materials to help people organize events in their own communities, but more important, it tracked all of the local actions that were being organized around the country. An interested person could enter her postal code or state to find events planned near her place of residence. If an event was planned, people could sign up online to join the event or contact the organizer if they wanted to help with organizing. If there were no events planned yet—or people did not like the events that were planned—they could add their own initiatives to the website.

What stands out about the SIU campaign is how smoothly everything went in terms of cooperation. Many of the organizers of these events were interested individuals, while formal organizations played a relatively small role. They usually got together with the people they knew, sometimes with people with whom they had organized before to start things up. As goals and demands of the campaign were preset, organizational competition was absent, and as everyone was encouraged to start his own initiative, there were no difficult discussions necessary; whoever did not agree just did not join or staged their own events. Furthermore, the cooperation was always meant to be a one-off activity; organizers never tried to build anything lasting with its own platform or identity. Consequently, meetings were very informal, everyone was asked simply to contribute whatever she could, and after the events, participants went their own way again.

For most organizers, the main mobilization strategy was online. They made heavy use of e-mail lists but also tried to get their messages on different websites and blogs, started Facebook pages, posted calls for action on YouTube and MySpace, and used Meetup groups to mobilize participants for their event. Consequently, the Internet was the most important mobilization channel: it mobilized 37 percent of the participants (Fisher and Boekkooi 2010). One in four participants was mobilized through interpersonal networks, and because of the absence of organizations, "only" 18 percent of the participants were mobilized by an organization. They also mobilized quite different people compared to other demonstrations. On average, there were more passive and nonmembers at the events than in most other events; moreover, an astonishing 43% of participants came to the events on their own (compared to 25 percent on average in other demonstrations), a phenomenon that seems to be related to this online mobilization strategy.

Finally, mobilization via a coordination structure affected the protest events. While format, goals, and demands of the events were preset, what *type* of event to stage was left completely up to the participants. Participants were to organize small events around the country, demanding legislation on the environment and inviting (local) politicians to come to the event and declare their support. The events were to be open and accessible to enable regular people everywhere to show that they, too, want politicians to start acting. Consequently, events during the day ran the gamut from traditional demonstrations and marches to discussion meetings and performance art (for a more elaborate discussion of this case, see Boekkooi 2011; Fisher and Boekkooi 2010).

Informal and Virtual Networks: High School Uprisings

The third case represents an example on the informal end of the continuum: organizing via informal and virtual networks. In November 2007, twenty thousand Dutch secondary school pupils took to the streets to protest the deteriorating quality of their education. This protest took the shape of several protests of relatively small groups geographically scattered and diffused over longer periods of time that were impromptu organized and mobilized, improvised and short-lived. The protests were staged in the absence of clear leadership. They were initiated by a guy-next-door whose call for action virally spread via virtual personal networks (e.g., MSN instant messaging, Hyves—at that time the biggest social network site in the Netherlands), YouTube, mobile phones, and face-to-face.

As a message spreads virally, tens of thousands of people may be reached in a matter of days or even hours because people send the message to hundreds of "friends" at a time. Via mobile phones, pupils uploaded unrest films on YouTube, serving as vivid proof that pupils protest. These YouTube films facilitated a rapid process of frame alignment. In nearly real time, *potential* protesters come to share grievances, emotions, and efficacy with *actual* protesters. Uploaded unrest vividly shows angry, empowered protesters, which may enhance the collective efficaciousness of potential protesters and thus their motivation to take part in the protest. Moreover, questions related to expected participation of others are instantly answered by the uploaded films and instant messages. Social media and smart phones, but also YouTube, facilitated a process of virtual cognitive liberation.

This case shows that organizing without organizations via informal and virtual networks affects the dynamics of protest significantly. It affects who organizes (individuals vs. organizations); what mobilizing channels they employ (informal [virtual] networks vs. organizational channels); their mobilization potential (virtually embedded vs. organizationally embedded people); and finally, the form of the protests (rhizomatic vs. staged protests). The lack of coordination and the loosely coupled informal (virtual) social networks have led to so-called *rhizomatic mobilization* (see Van Stekelenburg and Klandermans 2013). Rhizomatic mobilization moves from one person to another—individually, as part of a larger carbon copy list, via a Listserv, or by a social network such as Facebook or MySpace. In a process that continues to reproduce itself, the message is copied and redistributed. An original sender cannot know where or when the message stops traveling, stops being copied and redistributed, or stops being translated. Messages with higher degrees of resonance will be dispersed in greater densities. The emerging and fluid networks of actions unfold with little planning, are coordinated by ICTs, and are unbounded and uncontrolled. The resulting actions often emerge as simultaneous street demonstrations at multiple locations.

Conclusion

Taking previous theoretical and empirical observations into consideration may help us understand the contemporary paradox of mobilization that contentious political participation is *increasing* while embeddedness in the traditionally most important building blocks for mobilizing structures is *decreasing*. Mobilization via traditional solid structures still plays a major role in contemporary mobilization, but organizers are increasingly using liquid (virtual) structures as well to mobilize participants for their events. Scholars examining mobilization solely via solid structures may therefore miss out on important mobilization processes.

Individualization and liquefying (virtual) structures have given the world a new look, and organizers for social change are faced with new uncertainties and challenges. Whether these changes made it harder or easier for organizers to stage an event is a difficult question to answer because, on one hand, light structures and light identities make it *harder* to reach and motivate people, whereas ICTs, on the other hand, make it *easier* to reach people. Given our empirical observations of the coordination structure SIU and the rhizomatic mobilization of the high school students, it seems at least safe to conclude that setting up a campaign is different these days. Protest is less and less staged by the usual suspects such as the unions, political parties, or large nongovernmental organizations. Instead, a plethora of social networks and structures develop both online and offline in complex and overlapping patterns. Although social networks have always existed, the rise of Web 2.0 has made them (much) more extensive and more visible (e.g., Facebook). Communication through them has taken the form of many to many, making it easier, cheaper, and—especially—much faster for organizers to reach a large group of potential participants through informal networks.

Formal coalitions still seem an important tool capable of turning out a large mass of people. Yet, despite the fact that we know quite a lot about formal coalitions and their mobilizations, our case study on formal coalitions shows that, in most cases, even structures specifically designed for protest on the issue may not join the mobilizing structure. Who joins and who does not join depends on the initiators: who are they? Who do they know? How do they try to recruit new organizers? All these issues are important because they eventually affect who participates in their protests (Boekkooi 2011).

We know much less about the newer mobilizing structures and the consequences of the shift from solid to liquid mobilizing structures. These newer mobilizing structures—the coordination structure and (virtual) networks—seem to fit especially well with the new liquid society. As they are more ad hoc, less constraining, and usually only exist for a limited amount of time, they fit well with many people's desire for individuality, autonomy, and a flexible, modern online–offline hybrid lifestyle. However, these loose structures may also have their drawbacks. Although they seem a suitable tool for organizers to draw youngsters onto the streets, they may be less effective at mobilizing older generations (Organisation for Economic Co-operation and Development 2007; Lera-Lopez, Billon, and Gil 2011; Jones and Fox 2009). And the fact that these loose structures leave so much room for individuality and personal initiative may make them more attractive for the resourceful—those with the time, money, and, most important, skill to take that initiative, that is, the higher educated and middle classes—and less effective in attracting the less individualized and less resourceful. Moreover, loose structures are by definition less long-lasting, less demanding, and more diverse. Are organizers therefore less able to draw people onto the streets for higher risks, higher costs, or more enduring action when using liquid structures rather than solid ones? The Green Revolution in Iran but also the Arab Spring seem to indicate that liquid online bonds can mobilize people for high-risk, high-cost, and more enduring action. How can these successful mobilizations be explained? We hold that focusing on the organizers of protest, the mobilizing structures they build, the campaigns they stage, and the demonstrators that populate their events may help us take a step forward toward studying and answering these questions.

References

Arquilla, John, and David Ronfeldt. 2001. *Networks and Netwars*. Santa Monica, Calif.: RAND.

Baldassarri, Delia, and Mario Diani. 2007. "The Integrative Power of Civic Networks." *American Journal of Sociology* 113:735–80.

Bauman, Zygmunt. 2000. *Liquid Modernity*. Cambridge: Blackwell.

Bekkers, V. J. J. M., A. R. Edwards, R. F. I. Moody, and H. J. G. Beunders. 2008. "New Media, Micro-mobilization, and Political Agenda-Setting: How Young People Have Used Web.2.0 to Change the Educational Agenda in the Nether-

lands." Paper presented at the Annual Conference European Group of Public Administration, Rotterdam, Netherlands.
Bennett, W. Lance. 2003. "Communicating Global Activism: Strengths and Vulnerabilities of Networked Politics." *Information, Communication, and Society* 6:143–68.
Bennett, W. Lance, Christian Breunig, and Terri Givens. 2008. "Communication and Political Mobilization: Digital Media and the Organization of Anti–Iraq War Demonstrations in the US." *Political Communication* 25:269–89.
Bimber, B. 1998. "The Internet and Political Transformation: Populism, Community, and Accelerated Pluralism." *Polity* 31:133–61.
———. 2001. *Information and American Democracy: Technology in the Evolution of Political Power.* Cambridge: Cambridge University Press.
Boekkooi, Marije E. 2012. "Mobilizing Protest: The Influence of Organizers on Who Participates and Why." PhD diss., VU-University.
Boekkooi, Marije, Bert Klandermans, and Jacquelien van Stekelenburg. 2011. "Quarreling and Protesting: How Organizers Shape a Demonstration." *Mobilization* 16, no. 2: 498–508.
Boulos, K. M. N., and S. Wheeler. 2007. "The Emerging Web 2.0 Social Software: An Enabling Suite of Sociable Technologies in Health and Healthcare Education." *Health Information and Libraries Journal* 24, no. 1: 2–23.
boyd, D. M., and N. B. Ellison. 2007. "Social Network Sites: Definition, History, and Scholarship." *Journal of Computer-Mediated Communication* 13, no. 1. http://jcmc.indiana.edu/vol13/issue1/boyd.ellison.html.
Brainard, L., and P. Siplon. 2000. "Cyberspace Challenges to Mainstream Advocacy Groups: The Case of Health Care Activism." Paper presented at the Annual Meeting of the American Political Science Association, Washington, D.C.
Castells, Manuel. 1996. *The Rise of the Network Society.* Cambridge: Blackwell.
Coser, Lewis A. 1967. "Greedy Organizations." *Archives Européennes de Sociologie* 8:196–215.
Diani, Mario. 2004. "Networks and Participation." In *The Blackwell Companion to Social Movements,* edited by David A. Snow, Sarah A. Soule, and Hanspeter Kriesi, 337–59. Oxford: Blackwell.
Earl, Jennifer, and Katrina Kimport. 2011. *Digitally Enabled Social Change: Activism in the Internet Age.* Cambridge, Mass.: MIT Press.
Earl, Jennifer, and Alan Schussman. 2003. "The New Site of Activism: On-line Organizations, Movement Entrepreneurs, and the Changing Location of Social Movement Decision-Making." *Research in Social Movements, Conflict, and Change* 24:155–87.
Fisher, Dana, and Marije Boekkooi. 2010. "Mobilizing Friends and Strangers: Understanding the Role of the Internet in the Step It Up Day of Action." *Information, Communication, and Society* 30:193–208.

Fisher, Dana, Kevin Stanley, David Berman, and Gina Neff. 2005. "How Do Organizations Matter? Mobilization and Support for Participants at Five Globalization Protests." *Social Problems* 52:102–21.

Gerhards, Jurgen, and Dieter Rucht. 1992. "Mesomobilization: Organizing and Framing in Two Protest Campaigns in West Germany." *American Journal of Sociology* 98:555–96.

Goodwin, Jeff, and James M. Jasper. 1999. "Caught in a Winding, Snarling Vine: The Structural Bias of Political Process Theory." *Sociological Forum* 14:27–54.

Gould, Roger V. 2003. "Why do networks matter? Rationalist and structuralist interpretations." In *Social Movements and Networks: Relational Approaches to Collective Action,* edited by M. Diani and D. McAdam, 233–57. Oxford: Oxford University Press.

Granovetter, Mark S. 1973. "The Strength of Weak Ties." *American Journal of Sociology* 78:1360–80.

Heaney, Michael T., and Fabio Rojas. 2008. "Coalition Dissolution, Mobilization, and Network Dynamics in the US Antiwar Movement." *Research in Social Movements, Conflicts, and Change* 28:39–82.

Jasper, James M. 2004. "A Strategic Approach to Collective Action: Looking for Agency in Social-Movement Choices." *Mobilization* 9, no. 1: 1–16.

Jones, Sydney, and Susannah Fox. 2009. "Generations Online in 2009." http://www.floridatechnet.org/Generations_Online_in_2009.pdf.

Kitts, James A. 2000. "Mobilizing in Black Boxes: Social Networks and Participation in Social Movement Organizations." *Mobilization* 5:241–57.

Klandermans, Bert. 2004. "The Demand and Supply of Participation: Social-Psychological Correlates of Participation in Social Movements." In *The Blackwell Companion to Social Movements,* edited by David A. Snow, Sarah A. Soule, and Hanspeter Kriesi, 360–79. Oxford: Blackwell.

Klandermans, Bert, and Dirk Oegema. 1987. "Potentials, Networks, Motivations, and Barriers: Steps towards Participation in Social Movements." *American Sociological Review* 52:519–31.

Klandermans, Bert, Jojanneke van der Toorn, and Jacquelien van Stekelenburg. 2008. "Embeddedness and Identity: How Immigrants Turn Grievances into Action." *American Sociological Review* 73:992–1012.

Lera-Lopez, Fernando, Margarita Billon, and Maria Gil. 2011. "Determinants of Internet Use in Spain." *Economics of Innovation and New Technology* 20:127–52.

Levi, Margaret, and Gillian H. Murphy. 2006. "Coalitions of Contention: The Case of the WTO Protests in Seattle." *Political Studies* 54:651–70.

Lichbach, Mark I. 1998. "Contending Theories of Contentious Politics and the Structure-Action Problem of Social Order." *Annual Review of Political Science* 1:401–24.

Lichterman, Paul. 1996. *The Search for Political Community: American Activists Reinventing Commitment.* Cambridge: Cambridge University Press.

McAdam, Doug, John D. McCarthy, and Mayer N. Zald, eds. 1996. *Comparative Perspectives on Social Movements: Political Opportunities, Mobilizing Structures, and Cultural Framings.* Cambridge: Cambridge University Press.

McAdam, Doug, and Ronnelle Paulsen. 1993. "Specifying the Relationship between Social Ties and Activism." *American Journal of Sociology* 99:640–67.

McPhail, Clark, and John D. McCarthy. 2005. "Protest Mobilization, Repression, and Their Interaction." In *Repression and Mobilization,* edited by C. Davenport, H. Johnston, and C. Mueller, 3–32. Minneapolis: University of Minnesota Press.

Meikle, G. 2002. *Future Active: Media Activism and the Internet.* New South Wales: Pluto Press.

Meyer, David S., and Catherine Corrigall-Brown. 2005. "Coalitions and Political Context: US Movements against Wars in Iraq." *Mobilization* 10, no. 3: 327–44.

Norris, P. 2001. *Digital Divide? Civic Engagement, Information Poverty, and the Internet Worldwide.* Cambridge: Cambridge University Press.

———. 2002. *Democratic Phoenix: Reinventing Political Activism.* Cambridge: Cambridge University Press.

Oberschall, Anthony. 1973. *Social Conflict and Social Movements.* Englewood Cliffs, N.J.: Prentice Hall.

Oliver, Pamela E., Gerald Marwell, and Ruy Teixeira. 1985. "A Theory of the Critical Mass. I. Interdependence, Group Heterogeneity, and the Production of Collective Action." *American Journal of Sociology* 91:522–56.

Organisation for Economic Co-operation and Development. 2007. "Broadband and ICT Access and Use by Households and Individuals." Report DSTI/ICCP/IE (2007)4/FINAL. Paris: Working Party on the Information Society.

Scarrow, Susan E., and Burcu Gezgor. 2010. "Declining Memberships, Changing Members? European Party Members in a New Era." *Party Politics* 16:823–43.

Snow, David A., Louis Zurcher Jr., and Sheldon Ekland-Olson. 1980. "Social Networks and Social Movements: A Microstructural Approach to Differential Recruitment." *American Sociological Review* 45:787–801.

Staggenborg, Suzanne. 1986. "Coalition Work in the Pro-Choice Movement: Organizational and Environmental Opportunities and Obstacles." *Social Problems* 33:374–90.

———. 1989. "Organizational and Environmental Influences on the Development of the Pro-Choice Movement." *Social Forces* 68:204–40.

Tarrow, Sidney. 1994. *Power in Movement: Social Movements, Collective Action, and Politics.* Cambridge: Cambridge University Press.

Van de Donk, W., B. D. Loader, P. J. Nixon, and D. Rucht. 2004. *Cyberprotest: New Media, Citizens, and Social Movements.* London: Routledge.

Van Dyke, Nella. 2003. "Crossing Movement Boundaries: Factors That Facilitate Coalition Protest by American College Students, 1930–1990." *Social Problems* 50:226–50.

Van Laer, Jeroen, and Peter Van Aelst. 2009. "Cyber-protest and Civil Society: The Internet and Action Repertoires in Social Movements." In *The Handbook of Internet Crime,* edited by Yvonne Jewkes and Majid Yar, 230–54. Cullompton: Willan.

Van Stekelenburg, Jacquelien, and Bert Klandermans. 2010a. "The Social Psychology of Protest." *Sociopedia.isa.* http://www.sagepub.net/isa/admin/viewPDF.aspx?&art=Protest.pdf.

———. 2010b. "Individuals in Movements: A Social Psychology of Contention." In *Handbook of Social Movements across Disciplines,* edited by Bert Klandermans and Conny Roggeband, 157–204. New York: Kluwer.

———. 2013. "Collective versus Connective Action: Mobilization and Participation of Two Campaigns Compared." Unpublished manuscript.

Visser, Jelle. 2006. "Union Membership Statistics in 24 Countries." *Monthly Labor Review,* January, 38–49.

Walgrave, Stefaan, and Dieter Rucht, eds. 2010. *Protest Politics: Anti-war Mobilisation in Western Democracies.* Minneapolis: University of Minnesota Press.

Wellman, Barry, Anabel Quan-Haase, Jeffrey Boase, Wenhong Chen, Keith Hampton, Isabel Isla De Diaz, and Kakuko Miyata. 2003. "The Social Affordances of the Internet for Networked Individualism." *Journal of Computer-Mediated Communication* 8. http://jcmc.indiana.edu/vol8/issue3/wellman.html.

12
Ethnicity, Repression, and Fields of Action in Movement Mobilization

Pamela E. Oliver

European and American studies of protest came into dialogue through the overt efforts of bridge builders, particularly Bert Klandermans. These studies focused on the dynamics of protest mobilization in the democratic contexts of North America and western Europe and developed cumulative research showing how mobilization actually happens in political and organizational contexts. Mobilization happens through social networks, and social networks are changed in the process of mobilization; identities shape mobilization, and mobilization changes identities; political and organizational structures constrain mobilization, and mobilization changes political and organizational structures. Focusing on the protesters has led to tremendous advances in understanding protest.

But this focus on overt intentional protest mobilization has come at a cost. First, it has led to a relative neglect of theorizing the other actors, forces, and types of action in the field. Second, it has led to a relative neglect of theorizing the differences between different social groups in their prospects for mobilization and the ways in which ethnic divisions affect mobilization. The issue of the mass incarceration of African Americans illustrates some of the gaps left by protest-centered research, the usefulness of a broader evolutionary perspective, and the importance of theorizing group differences within and between social movements.

The field of action, that is, the political opportunity structure, is never the same for every movement in the same field. Some groups have more influence; some groups are repressed more. In particular, the political opportunities available to members of majority ethnic groups are different from those available to isolated disadvantaged ethnic minorities. Opportunities for resourceful ethnic minorities are different from those for resourceful ethnic majorities. General social movement theory should incorporate these distinctions into its core. Otherwise, it risks marginalizing itself by claiming that a general theory is the theory of affluent majorities and relegating movements by oppressed minorities to the periphery of theoretical concern.

The Case of Racial Disparities in Criminal Justice

My thoughts on these issues have been influenced by the movement to reduce racial disparities in imprisonment in the United States. I have participated in this movement as a public sociologist and participant in advocacy and governmental organizations (for details, see Oliver 2009). My own research is focused on analyzing and presenting the disparities themselves and on theorizing the interplay between repression, ethnic conflict, and social control. This essay draws on both my sociological research and my informal observations as a participant in the movement.

African Americans have extraordinarily high incarceration rates. The gross black incarceration rate in 2006 was 2.5 percent. The Bureau of Justice Statistics estimated that in 2008, over 10 percent of black men aged twenty-five to forty were incarcerated. Black Americans are seven times more likely to be incarcerated than non-Hispanic white Americans.[1] However non-Hispanic whites also have very high incarceration rates by world standards: the 2006 rate of 0.4 percent was higher than the rate of all of the world's nations, except Russia and two other former Soviet republics, plus ten small island nations with high tourism (Walmsley 2007).[2]

Although the details of this case are peculiarly American, they point to principles relevant to Europe today as it faces increased immigration and cultural diversity. Some sort of ethnic, racial, religious, or nationality disparity in arrest and incarceration is the norm, not the exception (Tonry 1997). Blacks in the United States and the United Kingdom and indigenous people in Canada and Australia have comparable disparities in incarceration (Tonry 1994), as do the Maori in New Zealand (Marie 2010). The Roma are widely viewed as criminal in much of Europe, and disparate incarceration of Roma has been documented in Bulgaria (Gounev and Bezlov 2006). Muslim immigrants or their children are also viewed as dangerous in much of Europe and are disproportionately incarcerated. Quoting from Tonry's summary introduction to an edited volume of research about Europe,

> *In Every Country, Crime and Incarceration Rates for Members of Some Minority Groups Greatly Exceed Those for the Majority Population.* Perhaps most

important, comparable disparities exist both for racial and ethnic minorities and for national origin minorities who are not visible racial minorities. In England and Wales, and the United States, black residents are seven-to-eight times more likely than whites to be confined in prisons, and the black/white imprisonment disparities in the Canadian province of Ontario are greater (Roberts and Doob). In Australia and Canada, arrest and imprisonment disparities affecting Aborigines and natives are even greater than black/white disparities in the other English-speaking countries. In the Netherlands, however, the greatest disparities affect people from Morocco and Surinam (Junger-Tas). In Sweden, Finns have higher rates than Swedes, and the highest disproportions in arrests affect immigrants from Arab countries, South America (notably Chileans, of whom those in Sweden are mostly of European descent), and Eastern Europe (Martens). In the German state of North Rhine-Westphalia in 1993, Romanians experienced by far the highest arrest rates (nearly 740 per year per 1,000 people, 44 times the German arrest rate) and the most disproportionate imprisonment rate (1608 per 100,000 population, 21 times the German rate) (Albrecht). In France, the highest imprisonment rates characterize people from the Maghreb countries of Algeria, Morocco, and Tunisia (Tournier). (12; includes minor edits; citations in quotation are to chapters)

Tonry's introduction adds additional generalizations from research on criminal justice disparities: groups with high criminal justice disparities are always disadvantaged, but not all disadvantaged groups have high disparities; most (but not all) observed racial or ethnic disparity is due to differential offending; disparities are generated by the routine operation of seemingly ethnicity-blind routines and procedures; and subcultural differences in dress or mannerisms or language become treated as proxies for criminality by the majority public and by actors in the criminal justice system. Official rules against recording ethnic information do not eliminate it from consideration by officials. Culturally salient ethnic differences are generally readily identified through physical appearance, clothing, names, or accents, regardless of whether they are officially recorded. Albrecht (1997) describes how German police use euphemisms to identify "Gypsies" in their records, despite the ban on recording ethnicity. Junger-Tas (1997) considers the extremely disproportionate confinement of immigrants in the Netherlands and discusses the ways in which cultural stereotypes feed into the treatment of offenders. Although ethnicity is taboo, nationality is often recorded in European records, and there is frequently a high incarceration disparity for "aliens," as they are called in the *European Sourcebook of Crime and Criminal Justice Statistics* (Crutchfield and Pettinicchio 2011;

Killias et al. 2010). Officials' actions and perceptions can also be influenced by factors they choose not to record in their official records.

There is great resistance in many quarters, including among many social scientists, to viewing racial or ethnic disparities in arrest and incarceration as anything other than a simple response to criminality. However, criminologists have long studied the factors that lead to more or less punitive social control responses to any given amount of crime and have long recognized the importance of ethnic and class factors in differential treatment. My own calculations indicate that the ratio of prison sentences to crimes varies greatly between U.S. states, with the most punitive states having a ratio up to ten times higher than the least punitive states; the ratio of prison sentences to arrests is similarly variable across states and, in addition, varies across race, with substantially higher ratios for blacks than whites in most states.

In the United States, a history of overt racial discrimination against racial minorities and of movements of liberation by racial and ethnic minorities creates a meaningful context for movement mobilization around the idea that statistical disparities in criminal justice are unjust and discriminatory. Although most European nations lack a similar meaning-making context, they face similar problems of ethnic conflict and stigmatization of some ethnic or national groups as criminal. Beckett and Godoy (2008), among many others, argue that support among majorities for punitive policies is paradoxically a response to expansions of democracy as crime talk typically involves coded references to intergroup hostilities. Although European incarceration rates remain low relative to the U.S. rates, they did increase in the 1990s (Walmsley 2003) amid tensions around immigration and cultural conflict. Thus both the criminal justice disparity itself and the movements against such disparities point to theoretical issues of broader generality for scholars of social movements.

Cultural Integration and Inequality in Mobilization: A Typology of Movement Actors

Too little attention has been given in social movement theorizing to the significance of ethnic divisions. Globalization has led to greater ethnic diversity in most nations. One consequence of both the older globalization of European colonialism and the slave trade and the newer globalization of immigration and international labor markets is the mixing of and conflicts among people of different ethnicities. Social movements have a dual character. On one hand, they are defined by their goals or issues, by a set of preferences for change or a belief system (Marwell and Oliver 1984; McCarthy and Zald 1977). On the other hand, they are defined by the people who take part in actions or advance the goals. These people never represent a random sample of society but rather

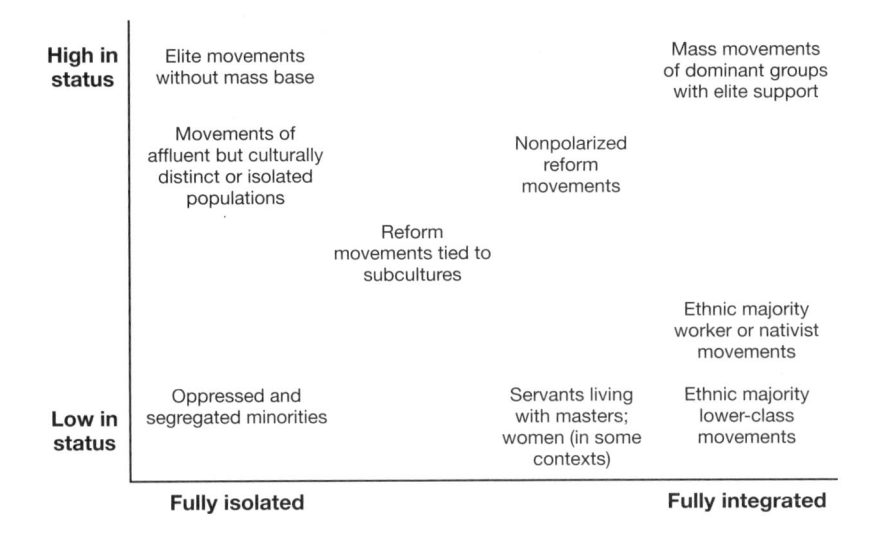

	Fully isolated		Fully integrated
High in status	Elite movements without mass base		Mass movements of dominant groups with elite support
	Movements of affluent but culturally distinct or isolated populations	Nonpolarized reform movements	
		Reform movements tied to subcultures	
			Ethnic majority worker or nativist movements
Low in status	Oppressed and segregated minorities	Servants living with masters; women (in some contexts)	Ethnic majority lower-class movements

Figure 12.1. Conceptual space for distinguishing movements by participant status and degree of integration with the dominant cultural or ethnic group in a society.

have a particular social location: they have a specific class, ethnic, and gender constellation. There has been relatively little attention paid to the importance of the social location of the people who make up a movement as affecting its mobilization. Morris and Braine (2001, 34) argue that the social position of the carriers of a movement matter and specifically that movements "whose carriers have a historically subordinate position within an ongoing system of social stratification" should be distinguished from movements whose carriers are not from historically subordinate or oppressed groups.

Figure 12.1 builds on Morris and Braine (2001) to typologize the social location of ethnic groups in a society and provides the basis for a more abstract typology of "types" of collective actors. The hierarchical or vertical dimension is the class position of a movement's carriers, its position in the overall stratification system. The horizontal dimension is the extent to which a group is socially and culturally integrated with—has network ties to—the wider society, reflecting both its relative size and the degree of its social and political integration with other fractions of society. In democratic societies, numerical dominance is typically tied to political dominance. Figure 12.1 includes examples of different parts of the space.

A group's location in this two-dimensional space has a large influence on the type of contentious politics it can pursue and on mobilization processes.

Social movements tend to arise from groups on the right-hand (socially integrated, majority) side of the space.

Groups in the upper right corner are both powerful and well integrated: they are affluent and part of the ethnic or cultural majority of a country. They have ready access to resources for mobilization, have network ties that reach to power holders, and are unlikely to encounter significant repression. Examples of such movements abound in most democratic countries across a wide range of issues both liberal and conservative, including pro- and antiabortion groups, pro- and antiwar groups, pro– and anti–health insurance reform groups, and so on. Affluent, well-integrated groups tend to be the carriers of "social responsibility movements" (Morris and Braine 2001) that address conditions affecting the general population. They also may be the "conscience constituents" (McCarthy and Zald 1977) for movements on behalf of other groups.

Groups in the lower right corner are economically disadvantaged ethnic majorities. This subdivides into two cases, depending on whether the economic elites are of the same or different ethnicity as the majority. Lower-class members of a dominant ethnic group have historically often organized around class politics versus the upper classes of their own group, but historically, they have also often organized around hostile antiminority or anti-immigrant or nativist movements; it is not uncommon for the same people to do both. This cell would include Europe and countries with European-descent majorities, India, and China. In these countries, especially if they are democratic, disadvantaged majorities typically have ties to affluent and powerful co-ethnics that foster mobilization.

The second subcase includes many Asian, African, and Latin American countries with a disadvantaged ethnic majority that has electoral political control while an ethnic minority has economic power, such as black South Africans, indigenous people in Central America, Javanese in Indonesia, or Malays in Malaysia. In some cases, the affluent minority keeps power through coercive control, although in many cases, a popular majority revolution has ultimately expelled the dominant minority. When the majority rules, ethnic violence against the wealthy minority has often occurred in such countries, frequently in a context of encouragement from majority-ethnic political elites.

Ethnic minorities on the left side are less likely to be able to support mass mobilizations. Groups in the upper left corner are powerful and economically dominant but not well integrated into the larger society such as white South Africans, Chinese Indonesians, Chinese Malaysians, or Euro-Americans in Central America. These groups either maintain dominance by coercion or reach some kind of political settlement with the majority. They are rarely the carriers of any kind of social movement and are often at risk of ethnic violence if they lack political control (as in Indonesia and Malaysia). They are unlikely to use mass mobilization as a strategy and are thus unlikely to show up in protest-centered research. Instead, they are more likely to use professionalized tactics that require resources and influence but not numbers such as quieter "insider" channels of influence or lobbying to accomplish their goals.

The lower left corner represents economically disadvantaged minorities like blacks or Hispanics in the United States, non-European immigrants in Europe, and illegal immigrants everywhere. These groups combine weak political influence with a disadvantaged economic position. They are likely to face repression when they protest. Immigrants are typically socially isolated by language and culture and are politically weakened by limits on citizenship. Illegal immigrants are particularly vulnerable. It is rare for immigrants to be able to sustain strong collective mobilizations. Insurgency or violence by immigrants, especially illegal immigrants, is typically met by severe repression. Historically oppressed minorities can also be disenfranchised through restrictions on voting. Their segregation may permit them to form an organizational infrastructure to support mobilization, but they are unlikely to succeed unless they can attract outside support. Scholarship about African Americans has stressed the importance of black-controlled spaces where blacks organize themselves and can be relatively free of white surveillance (McAdam 1982; Morris 1984) and electoral realignments that made blacks significant swing votes in key areas. This period of mass mobilization and success in the civil rights era should not obscure the long history of unsuccessful struggle by African Americans. As the political tides turned, the relative isolation and political weakness of African Americans is why the late 1980s drug war could be targeted to them. Other minority groups in the United States—indigenous people, Latinos, Asians, religious minorities—have had substantially less success in winning victories through protest mobilization.

Examples of intermediate positions are given in Figure 12.1 to indicate that the vertical dimension of hierarchy and the horizontal dimension of cultural and social integration are both continua. The dimension of cultural integration originates in the idea of ethnicity but could be understood more broadly to track any social boundary that tends to reduce connections and communication between groups of people. For example, white conservative Christians in the United States are socially, culturally, and spatially isolated from whites who are secular and liberal. They meet most academic definitions of subcultures, and there is a nontrivial sense in which they could be considered proto-ethnic groups. There is research evidence to suggest that there are similar political subcultures in some European nations as well. This essay cannot develop or defend this argument empirically, but I do believe this suggestion is worth further exploration as a way of tying important advances in understanding culture and identity in movements with studies of the network underpinnings of movements.

This typology elides some important distinctions. The visual display does not capture the number of network ties among groups. A better display would have at least three dimensions: a network ties map on the x axis, economic resources on the y axis, and coercive power on the z axis. But even my oversimplified display points to the dimensions of difference in movements' social locations. In particular, this typology illuminates some of the core concerns of this volume. It specifically addresses the impact of ethnic diversity on mobilization and provides some tools for theorizing the difference between movements by racial or ethnic minorities versus the nativist or xenophobic movements by working- or lower-class people who are members of ethnic majorities (as in the current wave of anti-immigrant movements that are discussed in other chapters in this volume) and for comparing these movements with new social movements, such as environmentalism, peace, and gay–lesbian rights, along with the older working-class movements.

Social Location and the Coevolution of Repression and Protest

A general coevolutionary approach to theorizing movements (Koopmans 2004, 2005; Oliver and Myers 2003) can accommodate social cleavages and locate protest within a broader field of action. This approach views continuity and change as arising from the same underlying processes of strategic action and mutual adaptation by multiple actors in multiactor fields. Specific protest forms are one part of a larger stream of actions by specific groups oriented to promoting or resisting social change. These actions are constrained by physical limits and by the actions of others. Outcomes are created by the ongoing interactions of multiple actors in a context of structural constraints and random external events. Actors choose actions for their expected outcomes, but no single actor can control outcomes. Movements and regimes mutually adapt to each other, with movements repeating tactics that succeed and regimes changing their policies in response to movements or finding new ways to repress (e.g., Koopmans 1997; Moore 1998; McAdam 1983).

Movements also evolve in interaction with other movements as they compete for resources, cooperate around shared goals, and learn from others' successes and failures (see, e.g., Meyer and Whittier 1994; Oliver and Myers 2003; Rucht 2004). Channels of communication, particularly the mass media, are often actors in their own right, pursuing agendas as they decide which information to pass on, sometimes speaking "for" movements, other times speaking "for" regimes, other times constructing themselves as the arena within which "significant" events are defined (e.g., McCarthy, McPhail, and Smith 1996; Oliver and Maney 2000; Oliver and Myers 1999; Rucht 2004).

Social Location and the Coevolution of Repression and Mobilization

Social movement dynamics can be understood only by viewing protest forms in a broader field of types of action and recognizing the importance of social location. Well-integrated groups with political and economic power usually pursue their goals through regular political channels with no need of protest. Aggrieved majorities often pursue exclusionary or hostile agendas without resort to protest because of their control of political or coercive systems. Police surveillance and arrest have long been used in the United States as an important tool for preserving racial segregation; all-white communities historically had overt practices of police stopping and harassing blacks who entered their areas, and these practices continue covertly today in many areas (Loewen 2005). The move in the United States toward gentrifying the central cities has been augmented by well-documented patterns of policing to keep poor, minority, mentally ill, and other "disruptive" persons out of areas frequented by the affluent (Beckett and Herbert 2010; Wilson 2007).

When dominant majorities do protest, they often do so as a demonstration of strength and suffer little repression. U.S. history is rife with instances in which the police supported or permitted violent white mob attacks on black, Mexican, and Chinese communities. One of Gamson's (1975) main findings in his quantitative study of U.S. social movements is that violence-using movements tend to be those of strong majorities, who typically gain benefits from their violence use.

By contrast, disadvantaged minorities are both less able to exert routine control over political or economic systems and more likely to be subject to repression that inhibits their capacity to mobilize. Protests by disadvantaged minorities are inhibited by repression, but protest-centric research has blinded researchers to the full range of repressive strategies. The mass incarceration of blacks in the United States calls attention to the overlap of ordinary policing and repression. Substantial historical evidence indicates that a major factor in the escalation of social control in the United States was the black riots of the late 1960s (Beckett 1997; Weaver 2007). Formal social control agencies have always been concerned with both ordinary crime and illegal dissent. Formal police departments in Europe developed to solve the dual problems of controlling urban riots by poor and working-class people and protecting the middle class from property crimes (Gurr 1976; Gurr, Grabosky, and Hula 1977). "Ordinary crime" and "illegal dissent" overlap in practice, especially for populations in rebellion, and police repression can work to control both at the same time (Oliver 2008).

Repression reduces the capacity for mobilizing dissent via incapacitation by killing, disabling, or incarcerating dissenters. Repression does not have to be justified in political terms to produce the effect of political repression: consequences matter more than intent. Police generally view their actions as controlling crime, not as suppressing dissent. Many black Americans support punitive policies in black areas. Regardless of intent, the repressive consequences of mass incarceration and intensive policing have a major impact on community mobilization.

Incapacitation indirectly affects the mobilization potential of whole communities as those who remain must take on the extra burdens of everyday life and have less time and fewer resources for political mobilization. The combination of mass incarceration of poor men and the removal of long-term income supplements from poor women has dramatically reduced the reservoir of discretionary free time among adults in low-income communities in the United States. African Americans who return from incarceration face poor job opportunities through the double burden of racial discrimination and criminal stigma: they frequently either add an unemployed burden to their families or return to crime as a source of income. Community institutions such as churches or voluntary associations are also inhibited from providing an organizational base for collective action as more of their efforts are spent in supporting the families and children stressed by economic decline, substance abuse, and the loss of young adults to incarceration and crime.

Repression also works indirectly through deterrence. The threat of sanctions such as incarceration, monetary fines, job loss, expulsion from school, and debarment from public housing or welfare works indirectly to deter people from undesired activities by raising the costs associated with defiance. People who live where many have suffered these sanctions are often fearful of challenging authorities and are convinced that taking the risk is unlikely to be effective.

Beyond this, extensive surveillance and monitoring of the so-called criminal population further reduces political capacity. The extensive undercover operations in and day-to-day intensive monitoring of low-income black communities in the name of the drug war and crime control tend to break up meetings and mobilizations before they happen. Bonds of social trust and neighborliness are weakened by policies that encourage offenders to fabricate charges against others to get their own otherwise draconian penalties reduced (Brown 2007). People who have been convicted of serious crimes are barred from voting for some period (in some cases permanently) in most states of the United States. People who are on community supervision (i.e., probation or parole[3]) are subject to a wide variety of rules about their behavior that are supposed to contribute to their rehabilitation and avoidance of further crime but also have the effect of incapacitating them from any kind of challenging collective action. People on probation or parole cannot risk arrest at a disruptive protest, and the terms of supervision frequently require the parole officer's permission to attend any kind of group meeting. People on supervision—and their families—justly fear incarceration as retaliation for any challenge to the political system.

These effects can be complex: removal of a small percentage of people who prey on their families and neighbors can improve life for others, but incapacitation of those whose victims are outside the community or whose crimes involve illegal market activities (e.g., drug sales) reduces community resources. Repression of certain kinds of crimes can simultaneously benefit people in one social location while hurting those in another (Oliver 2008). It is impossible to analyze adequately the impacts of repression on mobilization without considering social cleavages.

Grievance and the Mobilizing Effects of Repression

Even if the overall level of repression is low enough to avoid destabilizing and demobilizing communities, racial, ethnic, or national disparities in social control may still increase ethnic conflict. Political scientists have long emphasized the two-sided nature of repression. Groups that are themselves targets of repression almost inevitably reduce their support for the regime and almost always increase their sense of grievance and injustice. Unless the repression is strong enough to be truly incapacitating, the short-term (and sometimes long-term) consequence of repression is typically a reinvigoration of the will to resist among those repressed. For this reason, there has been extensive discussion and research on the issue of whether repression has positive or negative effects on mobilization (Earl 2003, 2004).

Recognizing that groups vary in their social location is one way to bring some order to this issue. Repression of dissident majorities or those socially tied to dissident majorities often fuels grievance and rebellion in the wider society. It is in repressing majorities that a regime going down a repressive path paves the way for its own destruction. Once on the coercive path, regimes that rely on repressing majorities have to maintain the coercive apparatus to survive, and the easing of coercion often opens the door to mass mobilization and rapid regime change.

But repression of stigmatized isolated minorities is often ignored or even celebrated by the majority. Stigmatized isolated minorities have often been expelled or exterminated by regimes with the support of the majority, precisely because the minority has been defined as dangerous and criminal by the majority.

If they are not killed or expelled, minorities that are subject to high levels of repression are likely to have a higher sense of grievance and injustice, as are the people tied to them by social networks. They are less likely to assimilate and more likely to develop or maintain oppositional subcultures. Thus extensive repression of minorities (whether for political dissent or for criminality) is quite likely produce a feedback loop like that in Figure 12.2.

When the object of grievance is itself excessive repression by police and the criminal justice system, the object of protest (the repression) itself inhibits overt protest against it but exacerbates rather than reduces grievance. Crime or dissent may be repressed by coercive incapacitation, but the repression itself fuels the isolation and disadvantage that contribute to crime.

Although repressed minorities can and do protest against repression, this protest is itself often ignored or repressed. Successful movements against repression of disadvantaged minorities typically have to have strong support from or be carried by outsiders who are not themselves repressed. This tends to lead to strong involvement of professional reformers and outside allies. The strategies and tactics people use in this context are tied both to whom they are and to their perceptions of what might work to affect change. Protest-centric research can miss much of this entire dynamic.

Coevolution and Mobilization in a Complex Multidimensional Field of Action

Social movements are embedded in a much larger field of actors (e.g., Klandermans 1990; Rucht 2004). The coevolutionary perspective emphasizes the importance of this whole field as all these different actors mobilize for action in interaction with all the others. Again, the racial disparity movement is instructive. Like many other ongoing social divisions, today's mass incarceration regime in the United States is a consequence of past movements and countermovements. Law enforcement institutions and extralegal violence by white people were overtly used to maintain white domination over black people within the memory of people still living today. The civil rights movement of the 1950s and 1960s and the riots of the 1960s led to profound political changes and partisan realignments. Control of crime and control of dissent were confounded in the rise of punitive social control after the 1960s. In short, the black idea that criminal justice institutions are agents of white domination and the white idea that blacks are a threatening group that needs to be controlled represent an ongoing social and political cleavage within which a debate about criminal justice policy is understood in the United States.

My analysis of data from the 1980s and 1990s distinguishing prison admissions by offense indicates that the rise in the racial disparity in imprisonment arose almost entirely from the late 1980s drug war, not from ordinary crime.

```
┌─────────────┐   ┌─────────┐   ┌──────────┐   ┌──────────────┐
│ Isolation and│──▶│Grievance│──▶│Dissent and│──▶│Repression and│
│ disadvantage │   │         │   │  crime   │   │discrimination│
└─────────────┘   └─────────┘   └──────────┘   └──────────────┘
       ▲                                               │
       └───────────────────────────────────────────────┘
```

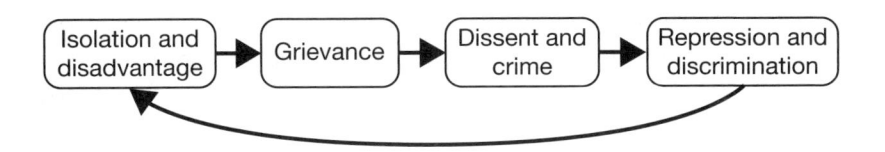

Figure 12.2. Repression feedbacks for disadvantaged, isolated minorities.

Between 1988 and 1992, the vast majority of people sent to prison on drug charges were black, even though the rate of illegal drug use was roughly comparable by race. Even for crack cocaine, which was disproportionately used by blacks, the majority of users were white. This war arose in partisan political jockeying for votes amid an actual problem of increased crack cocaine use and sensationalist media coverage that both overstated the pharmacological dangers of the drug and used only images of black drug addicts (Beckett and Sasson 2004) to illustrate it. Many blacks supported the punitive turn because their neighborhoods were disproportionately affected by crime and illegal drugs.

But the racial cleavage is not the only ongoing movement–countermovement dynamic in U.S. criminal justice policy. My own analysis of data from the 1970s finds no rise in the black–white disparity before the mid-1980s, although prison admissions overall rose steadily. Other sources of collective political turmoil in the United States in the 1960s fueled the rise in punitive social control. The student-centered and predominantly white antiwar movement became increasingly radical and also engaged in property riots and street battles with police, and repression escalated against all movements. Ordinary street crime was also at historically high levels. Gottschalk (2006) argues that the victim's rights movement, with ties to the women's movement, played another key role. Garland (2001) argues that the escalation in punitiveness was a worldwide phenomenon tied to global cultural shifts. The "nothing works" movement among criminologists provided intellectual justification for abandoning rehabilitative programs and substituting incarceration under the logic of incapacitation (Braithwaite 1993; Bushway and Paternoster 2009).

The pan-racial movement toward greater punitiveness always had opposition among professionals and academics, who favored rehabilitative strategies for crime control or social and redistributive programs to address the underlying problems of job loss in economic restructuring, family instability, and drug addiction. The movements for criminal justice reform in a more rehabilitative direction and against racial disparities in criminal justice were never absent as the tide ran the other way between 1970 and the late 1990s, but they were waging a largely losing battle.

Picking up the situation in the late 2000s, we find a field dominated by three main movement–countermovement oppositions. The first axis is racial. Institutionalized black movement organizations advocate for a broad range of policies against racial discrimination and in favor of programs to benefit blacks and other racial and ethnic minorities, and they locate racial disparities in criminal justice within this frame. Opponents along this axis deny that racial discrimination exists, resist collecting or analyzing data on racial patterns, and claim that racial patterns that do exist simply track black criminality. Although overt white racist groups continue to exist, they are politically marginalized. Whites rarely advocate for racial discrimination in criminal justice or any other field. Instead, the politics of the white majority is dominated by an ideology, referred to as "color-blind racism" by its critics, that declares that any political action that seeks to better the conditions of racial minorities is itself inherently racist.

The second polarity is between the anticrime movement (and the associated antidrug, anti–drunk driving, and victim's rights movements) and those who advocate less punitive policies. This is a very different kind of countermovement pair. Much of the polarity is carried by professional reformers and academics with dueling theories of social control and careers to be made in advocating particular policies. Private businesses (both for profit and nonprofit) also lobby for policies that will create a need and funding for their services in the criminal justice system, ranging from private prisons at the punitive end of the spectrum to treatment and restoration projects at the nonpunitive end. Nonprofessional mobilization tends to be reactive. The anticrime pro-punitive side tends to mobilize around specific incidents or problems, especially violent crimes, drug dealers, and drunk drivers. Popular mobilization for less punitive policies is often carried by families of people incarcerated on drug charges. Other mobilization comes from groups with a broader ideology who add criminal justice issues to their menu of issues, including leftists concerned with the prison–industrial complex, human rights activists concerned with the inhumane treatment of prisoners in U.S. prisons, and religious activists concerned with social justice.

The third axis of conflict is the partisan battle between Democrats and Republicans for political control. Both parties make tough-on-crime statements to gain votes, and much of the escalation in punitiveness can be traced to partisan jockeying, as Republicans (who do not try to win black votes) sought to gain white votes through racially coded messages, while Democrats (who rely on both black and white votes) sought ways to appear equally tough on crime without alienating voters of either race. Politicians are typically more attentive to claims of racial discrimination in jurisdictions where blacks compose a significant fraction of the electorate but are not necessarily any less punitive.

These three polarities overlap, but the lines are not simple. Activists specifically concerned about racial disparities in criminal justice typically advocate less punitive policies overall, but not always: some advocate more aggressive and punitive policies toward whites to even the balance. Racial politics were central to the party realignment after the 1960s, and discussions of crime and drugs are deeply racialized, often at a nonverbal emotional level. But imprisoned drunk drivers are overwhelmingly white, as was the anti–drunk driving movement. Many black Americans have punitive attitudes toward crime and drugs and strongly backed punitive approaches to drug dealing and urban crime, even as they simultaneously believed that the police unfairly targeted black people and that policing was a tool of white dominance.

Through the 2000s, there was relatively little sustained popular mobilization or protest in any of the camps, although there are strong sentiment pools of public opinion backing the different parts of the field. Instead, the field of contention is heavily dominated by professional politicians, reformers, and service providers, who are simultaneously pursuing social change goals and their own professional advancement or organizational survival. The field also includes ongoing white-dominated leftist political groups and ongoing multi-issue black (and occasionally Hispanic) social movement organizations, which pick up the "prison issue" as one of many, and local ad hoc grassroots organizations and individual activists who have no professional agenda. These sometimes adopt traditional protest forms, but protests are typically targeted toward very specific incidents or policies and are typically short-lived and ineffective. One advocacy group with which I am involved is dominated by longtime activists who have a history of protesting around many issues. When I first became involved with it, the group regularly recruited people for protests at the super-max prison or at the state capitol. The group rarely protests now, not because its members have any aversion to protest tactics, but because protest had no impact. Instead, the group has put on informational conferences, worked to influence public officials, and participated in providing services to returning offenders.

Adding to movement complexity is the complex structure of governance in the United States and, thus, of the targets of movement action. Crime control in the United States is generally a "state" (i.e., nonfederal) or local (municipal or county) function. City mayors appoint and control police chiefs. Local county sheriffs, district attorneys, and judges are frequently elected and thus have independent power bases and autonomy to set their own policies. Government actors who affect imprisonment rates include legislators, who set penalties; police, who determine where and how they will patrol and what crimes they will react to with arrest; district attorneys, who make charging decisions and make the plea bargains that account for more than 95 percent of the adjudications in the United States; defense attorneys, and especially the public defenders, whose job is to represent indigent defendants while carrying high caseloads for relatively little remuneration; judges, who ratify plea bargains and make the final sentence determinations (within the bounds set by legislation); sheriffs, who act as police outside cities and control conditions in jails (local confinement facilities in the United States); and departments of correction, who supervise prison and conditions of confinement and make decisions about release to and revocation from probation and parole. At the same time, federal government policies have also had a large impact. Drugs became the political issue of choice for Republican presidents because it could claim jurisdiction over an illegal trade that crosses state boundaries. Federal legislation and regulations have provided substantial financial incentives to states to bring local practices into line with federal policies both by tying the receipt of federal funds to the adoption of particular programs and, in the drug war, by encouraging forfeiture laws that permit police departments to confiscate for their own use automobiles and other valuable goods that are deemed to have been used in the drug trade.

All this complexity means that activists seeking to influence policy have both many points of entry and many different types of targets. On the movement side, the field of actors is similarly diverse, both in terms of the kind of actor and the level at which it acts (federal, state, local). Anticrime pressures often have a local grassroots base as citizens generate ad hoc mobilizations in response to crime waves, while the public discourses that fueled punitive rhetoric and national policy typically originated with federal- or state-level politicians and national-or state-level media outlets. The pro-drug legalization movement has conducted civil disobedience protests, such as smoke-ins, but these have been overwhelmingly dominated by young white—and frequently affluent—participants who felt relatively immune from the possible consequences of arrest. It is exceedingly rare to have any sustained grassroots protest against crime control or unfair policing in general, although ad hoc protests do sometimes emerge around particular cases in which the behavior of authorities is especially egregious. Most of the nonpunitive grassroots activism is focused on efforts to rehabilitate offenders or provide services to and support for their families. There is generally more popular support for rehabilitative efforts for young offenders.

The ideological work of articulating and advocating policies has been done within government agencies (especially the federal Department of Justice and its state counterparts), with academics and independent think tanks playing major roles in generating research studies that support various punitive and nonpunitive approaches. Black civil rights organizations, such as the NAACP and the Urban League, as well as local black organizations, frequently raise issues about policing or incarceration as part of their broader agendas. Many nongovernmental organizations concerned about criminal justice reform more generally have picked up on the racial disparities of the system as a way of gaining purchase for a broader critique. People with official roles in the criminal justice system, such as police, judges, public defenders, or district attorneys, may play a significant role in some sort of reform movement in their locales. Many—but not all—of the reformers inside the system are black or members of other ethnic or racial minorities. These reformers take a lead in trying to combat racial disparities in their departments or trying to pull in outside resources and often end up on special commissions or task forces to address the issue. There are also a wide variety of black and liberal white religious organizations that provide services to released inmates and (sometimes) seek to educate their members about the issues, social service groups advocating less punitive policies and greater funding for social services, anticapitalist and radical groups that link the issues to their broader ideological agendas, families of prisoners (frequently the more affluent families who have more time to work on the issues), human rights groups concerned about conditions of confinement, groups advocating liberalization of drug laws, and an assortment special-purpose groups advocating particular policies.

Nonprofit think tanks often employ social scientists to generate studies and reports. Websites make it possible to disseminate this information more widely than was possible with paper reports. One tactic that has proved useful is generating rankings of U.S. states by some new target criterion. This increases the political pressure on an issue within states that score badly. For example, the political pressure to "do something" about the racial disparity in imprisonment in Wisconsin followed Wisconsin's number one ranking in black incarceration in 2004 and the ensuing publicity when an article in an online magazine called Wisconsin the worst state in America to be black (Dixon 2005). Professional reformers publicize phrases like "driving while black" and engage in campaigns to require that data be collected by police and other agencies on the race of people arrested, charged, or sentenced so that other professional reformers can analyze the data and use them as a tool for pressuring for change. One reform group, the Vera Institute, promotes change by persuading district attorneys' offices to hire the group to analyze prosecution data: the selling point is that the district attorney will simultaneously have an improved data system for managing caseloads, while also identifying sources of racial disparity in the prosecution process. A variety of foundations and federal agencies have prepared guidelines and provided funding for local agencies to study their own racial disparity patterns and develop programs to remedy them.

As these examples indicate, professionalized movements, like all movements, are continually coevolving with the other actors in their environments, looking for successful tactical innovations and responding to the success or failure of past actions. The absence of sustained mass protest around racial disparities in criminal justice does not mean that there is no aggrieved group, nor that there is no mobilization. Rather, the repression itself has suppressed mobilization within the most aggrieved groups, and political conditions have been such that protest has been ineffective as a tactic for promoting movement goals.

Intramovement Conflicts

As many of the contributions to this volume attest, increased immigration has highlighted the problems of organizing in ethnically diverse contexts. Recognition of the difficult and tense dynamics between what McCarthy and Zald (1977) called "beneficiary constituents" and "conscience constituents" was a major topic of concern arising from the 1960s experiences of whites working in the black civil rights movement (e.g., McAdam 1988) and of white middle-class radicals working in black, Latino, and white poor neighborhoods. These dynamics have received less attention in the literature since 1980, but they remain a major problem for social movements seeking to cross the boundaries of social cleavages. As McCarthy and Zald hypothesized, tensions and conflicts abound between oppressed beneficiary constituents and their relatively privileged conscience allies. Tensions also arise among beneficiary constituents who differ along a major social cleavage. For example, there is significant discussion of the problems of racism and classism within the gay rights movement and of antigay attitudes among blacks.

Race and class divides permeate work on criminal justice issues in the United States. The targets of punitive policies are disproportionately ill-educated racial minorities; the reformers are disproportionately professionals. Ethnic and class differences and antagonisms can hinder common action among people who are nominally on the same side of an issue. Cultural differences in customs of organizing meetings, exerting leadership, and speaking publicly can lead to irritation and offense. Patterns of domination and subordination in the larger society tend to be replicated even among people who are trying to treat each other as equals: members of dominant groups tend to make tacit assumptions that their ideas and ways of doing things are right and that they should take the lead. The antagonism is typically mutual. Members of ethnic majorities often blame the problems on the minorities who are "different" and wonder why minorities do not participate more. Members of ethnic minorities typically view majority people as being domineering and culturally insensitive.

Differences in class and privilege also affect intragroup relations. More educated group members find it easier to do research and write reports and to speak and write in ways that signal competence to officials or politicians. Coordinating meetings or circulating draft documents via e-mail shuts out members who do not own personal computers. People who are the frequent targets of abrupt or aggressive or even insulting behavior by police or officials tend to believe that discrimination and oppression are common and the products of racism or classism. People from higher class positions, especially those occupying professional roles, are more likely to sympathize with the external pressures on police or officials that contribute to their behavior and are likely to question the standing of a convicted criminal to offer testimony in public debate.

There are also divisions and conflicts of interest among people who have basically the same agenda. Among professional reformers whose agenda is increasing social services for crime prevention, there are deep divisions about the allocation of public money among reform agencies. A long-standing grievance in my community is that the majority of at-risk youth in the community are people of color, but the nonprofit organizations that receive the bulk of local funding for social service provision are large and white dominated such as Lutheran Social Services. Social workers and teachers of color feel that white-dominated social service agencies tend to prefer white employees and that organizations controlled by people of color are discriminated against in local funding for social services. Professionals of color often complain that minority communities are effectively providing job opportunities for white social service providers and complain that white service providers do a poor job of providing intervention and rehabilitative programs for minority clients. White service providers find these accusations hurtful and are convinced that the ability to provide therapy and services does not depend on cultural matching between providers and clients but rather on professional qualifications and credentials.

Social hierarchies from the larger society find their way into every interstice of a movement. The racial hierarchy itself means that whites are treated as unbiased, neutral observers on racial issues, whereas blacks and other minorities lack standing because they are seen as pursuing an agenda. Similarly, convicted criminals are often ignored when they speak about punishment. And of course, illegal immigrants have to maintain silence or risk deportation.

People in different social locations may react personally to things said by people in other social locations even when the issue is not about them. For example, one Latino community member testified at a public hearing that he had recently experienced a flurry of unwarranted traffic stops in the months after a pro-immigration rally. A police representative took offense at this accusation against the police and tried to get the testimony excised from the report, even though an internal police department analysis supported the claim: their data had identified a "rogue" police officer who was harassing Latinos and had personally accounted for one-third of the suspicious traffic stops by the department. The white police representative genuinely advocated reducing racial disparities (and was backed by the black police chief, who was outspoken on the issue) but still was unhappy with anything that made the police department look bad. In another incident, several white members of a task force took offense and complained when a black member who worked with returning prisoners complained that the all-white construction crews on government projects were racist. It is possible that the offended people thought the black speaker was accusing the white workers of being racist, although this would entail a rather high level of racial cluelessness, as the topic of conversation was the problem of job opportunities for returning prisoners and the speaker's intent clearly referenced the problem of racial discrimination in the labor market, especially in the construction trades. It appeared that it was the word *racist* itself that offended them. This kind of interaction makes it almost impossible for people to work together along racial lines, and the only reason this particular meeting did not explode was that the black speaker was patient and polite and had a great deal of experience dealing with whites.

Conclusion

I wrote this essay in 2009, amid concerns about the right-wing Tea Party movement in the United States and nativist anti-immigrant movements in Europe and before the new wave of insurgency in the United States and the Middle East. I know too little about the Middle East to suggest how attention to social location and looking beyond protest events would inform those revolts, but paying attention to the social location of movement carriers is essential to understanding both the Tea Party mobilization of 2009–10 and the Wisconsin Uprising and Occupy movement of 2011 in the United States.

A typology of the ethnic integration and economic–political standing of carriers of movements helps to identify the contexts in which different kinds of actions are likely to arise. Mass actions are generally the tools of groups that are large enough or connected enough to expect to avoid or overcome repression. Ethnic majorities are the most common carriers of popular mobilizations. Disadvantaged ethnic majorities often support exclusionary class movements that advocate for worker issues while also seeking to attack or exclude ethnic minorities. Disadvantaged majorities can be extremely dangerous for minorities in times of social turmoil. Their nativism and nationalism are typically fanned by politicians seeking to gain political power through their votes.

Both European anti-immigrant movements and the U.S. Tea Party are movements of ethnic majorities that overtly and covertly express hostility to immigrants and ethnic minorities, attract significant support from the economically disadvantaged sectors of the ethnic majority, have significant ties to elites, and are intertwined with partisan political maneuvering. There are disputes in U.S. empirical research about the mix of economic advantage and disadvantage among Tea Party activists and supporters, and about complex patterns of relationships between Tea Party activists and the Republican Party, but it is clear that protest mobilization and partisan electoral politics are closely intertwined in the movement. Nativist anti-immigrant and antiminority discourse is a prominent part of the movement, and overt white racist organizations are known to have attempted to influence Tea Party actions and recruit new members at Tea Party events. Ethnic majority movements that target minorities as part of their agendas are a long-standing part of the political scene in many countries and have often been the source of violence, although there has been relatively little mass collective violence in the United States so far.

Disadvantaged ethnic minorities may have the internal solidary capacity for collective action but have little social influence and face substantial risk of repression if they seem to threaten the majority. Repression inhibits mobilization and especially inhibits mobilization against repression, but a protest-centric approach can ignore both the repression and the movements against it. Protest-centric research in the United States and Europe in the current era is all too often focused on the agendas and issues of the white ethnic majority, who are most likely to support and sustain protest movements in the current political environment. The only way to avoid the problems of protest-centric research is to identify the full range of groups in society, ask what their grievances or disadvantages are, and then look to see whether and how they are acting to address those grievances.

The bulk of this essay focused on the movement to address racial disparities in the wake of extreme repression in black communities and emphasized why the repression itself makes mobilization against the repression extremely difficult. In this repressive context, professional reformers play an important role. I emphasized the complexity of the movement field and the interplay of different kinds of actors with different kinds of agendas as well as the racial–ethnic and class tensions within the movement. I stressed that an emphasis on protest alone would miss and has missed most of the important action in this arena. I also revisited the problem of conscience constituents and the intramovement conflicts that arise as more advantaged outsiders dominate the field of reform on behalf of a repressed and disadvantaged minority. I also stressed how hard it is for disadvantaged minorities to bring their issues center stage in the absence of elite allies.

In the wake of the Tea Party movement, Republicans won many elections in 2010, including in Wisconsin, where the newly elected Republican governor announced draconian policies—including huge compensation cuts and an end to collective bargaining for all public employees—that led to a sustained protest in the state capital of Madison early in 2011. This protest, coupled with similar initiatives by Republican governors in many states, sparked a wave of pro-union protests all over the country. Later in the year, the Occupy Wall Street movement began in New York, and the Occupy movement spread throughout the United States. These movements serve to illustrate the importance of the social locations of the carriers of movements.

The Wisconsin protest was primarily carried by ethnic majority white, middle-class public workers and their friends, families, and neighbors. The protest had no central organization but was a genuine upsurge of reaction centered in unionized public workers (especially teachers), with deep involvement of unions and people who vote Democratic. Young people and racial and ethnic minorities were underrepresented at the protests. The protest was deeply partisan, with core protesters having daily strategy discussion with Democratic representatives. As is typical, national news coverage tended to stress the national implications of the protest and to ignore or misunderstand many of the state-level issues and actors. The protests and news coverage stressed the grievances of public workers, although the governor's bill also contained many direct threats to programs for low-income people.

Except for particular times when busloads of African Americans from Milwaukee arrived to protest cuts to social programs, African Americans and Latinos were generally seen as underrepresented at the rallies, even though a higher percentage of African Americans than whites are public workers, and they would be disproportionately affected by the cuts to Medicaid and other elements of the bill. There was discussion about why more minorities were not generally at the rallies, with little certainty about the answers in the face of the complexity of unfolding events. The state is 92 percent non-Hispanic white, and most of the state's African Americans live in Milwaukee, eighty miles from Madison, so some argued that the composition of the rallies essentially reflected the composition of the pool of people available to come to the rallies, adjusting for distance. However, many of the white protesters came on buses from much farther away. Many black and Latino people commented that they felt less safe at a protest and feared arrest or police harassment. People on probation or parole could not safely attend rallies, as this would violate the terms of their supervision. Many perceived that this was a protest by whites about their own issues. One black man, an ex-prisoner, speaking during the first week of protests at a previously planned event about racial disparities held at a white church, said to the predominantly white audience, "I know you people let him be elected. You didn't think they would come after *you*. You just thought they would come after black and brown and poor people."

The Occupy protests have similarly been disproportionately white. There have been critics of the white-centric character of the protests and some development of Occupy the Hood and other minority-centered spin-off movements. Overall, the Madison and Occupy protests demonstrate the point that a group's social location affects mobilization potential and that members of ethnic majorities have the resources and political ties that make mobilization easier as well as a dramatically lower fear of repression for their actions and a lower fear of the long-term consequences of being arrested or repressed. The Madison uprising had close ties to partisan politics and turned itself into an electoral movement to recall the governor. The Occupy movement is both critical of Democratic politicians and playing to partisan politics in seeking different economic policies.

The ongoing evolution of social movements and their opponents in the twenty-first century reveals the new outcomes of old principles. The specific types of actions that came to be recognized as "protest" by movement scholars never stood apart from other action forms but were always embedded in fields of routine political action and the communication of ideas. This is still so. There is much that is new, but the ways in which the new is created from the old—the principles of coevolution—seem ongoing. Agentic actors seek ways to pursue social change goals within particular contexts created by the prior actions of themselves and others. New issues are defined and new forms of action evolve as people modify old forms in new contexts. Successful forms of action spread, unsuccessful forms are abandoned. Groups with more favorable social locations carry most movements, and disadvantaged minorities are more easily repressed and find mobilization more difficult.

Notes

1. Hispanics are also a disadvantaged minority who are often classified as white, so the baseline for all comparisons is non-Hispanic whites; this is the usual convention in the United States.

2. The U.S. rates of incarceration for Hispanics–Latinos and American Indians are generally substantially higher than for non-Hispanic whites but substantially lower than for blacks. Hispanics–Latinos and American Indians also frequently perceive the criminal justice system as discriminatory and oppressive and sometimes mobilize around the issue, even as they only infrequently form tight alliances with black groups around criminal justice issues. These groups are much more difficult to provide statistics for owing to great between-place and between-ethnicity variability as well as complex classification issues in public data that would require an extended tangent to explain.

3. *Probation* is a term of community supervision in lieu of a prison term; a person on probation can be sent to prison for violating the terms of that probation. Parole and related statuses that go by other names, such as *extended supervision,* refer to a period of community supervision after imprisonment; again, violating the terms of this supervision can result in a return to prison and, often, resetting the clock so that a new period of supervision will ensue the next time the person is released from prison.

References

Albrecht, Hans-Jörg. 1997. "Ethnic Minorities, Crime, and Criminal Justice in Germany." *Crime and Justice* 21:31–99.

Beckett, Katherine. 1997. *Making Crime Pay: Law and Order in Contemporary American Politics.* New York: Oxford University Press.

Beckett, Katherine, and Angelina Godoy. 2008. "Power, Politics, and Penality: Punitiveness as Backlash in American Democracies." *Studies in Law, Politics, and Society* 45:139–73.

Beckett, Katherine, and Steven Kelly Herbert. 2010. *Banished: The New Social Control in Urban America.* Oxford: Oxford University Press.

Beckett, Katherine, and Theodore Sasson. 2004. *The Politics of Injustice: Crime and Punishment in America.* Thousand Oaks, Calif.: Sage.

Braithwaite, John. 1993. "Beyond Positivism: Learning from Contextual Integrated Strategies." *Journal of Research in Crime and Delinquency* 30:383–99.

Brown, Ethan. 2007. *Snitch: Informants, Cooperators, and the Corruption of Justice.* New York: PublicAffairs.

Bushway, Shawn D., and Raymond Paternoster. 2009. "The Impact of Prison on

Crime." In *Do Prisons Make Us Safer? The Benefits and Costs of the Prison Boom,* edited by Steven Raphael and Michael A. Stoll, 119–50. New York: Russel Sage Foundation.

Crutchfield, Robert D., and David Pettinicchio. 2011. "'Cultures of Inequality': Ethnicity, Immigration, Social Welfare, and Imprisonment." *Annals of the American Academy of Political and Social Science* 633:134–47.

Dixon, Bruce. 2005. "Ten Worst Places to Be Black." *Black Commentator,* July 14. http://www.blackcommentator.com/146/146_cover_dixon_ten_worst.html.

Earl, Jennifer. 2003. "Tanks, Tear Gas, and Taxes: Toward a Theory of Movement Repression." *Sociological Theory* 21:44–68.

———. 2004. "Controlling Protest: New Directions for Research on the Social Control of Protest." *Research in Social Movements, Conflicts, and Change* 25:55–83.

Gamson, William A. 1975. *The Strategy of Social Protest.* Homewood, Ill.: Dorsey Press.

Garland, David. 2001. *The Culture of Control: Crime and Social Order in Contemporary Society.* Chicago: University of Chicago Press.

Gottschalk, Marie. 2006. *The Prison and the Gallows: The Politics of Mass Incarceration in America.* Cambridge: Cambridge University Press.

Gounev, Philip, and Tihomir Bezlov. 2006. "The Roma in Bulgaria's Criminal Justice System: From Ethnic Profiling to Imprisonment." *Critical Criminology* 14:313–38.

Gurr, Ted Robert. 1976. *Rogues, Rebels, and Reformers: A Political History of Urban Crime and Conflict.* Beverly Hills, Calif.: Sage.

Gurr, Ted Robert, Peter N. Grabosky, and Richard C. Hula. 1977. *The Politics of Crime and Conflict: A Comparative History of Four Cities.* Beverly Hills, Calif.: Sage.

Junger-Tas, Josine. 1997. "Ethnic Minorities and Criminal Justice in the Netherlands." *Crime and Justice* 21:257–310.

Killias, Martin, Marcelo F. Aebi, Bruno Aubusson de Cavarlay, Gordon Barclay, Beata Gruszczyńska, Stefan Harrendorf, Markku Heiskanen, Vasilika Hysi, Véronique Jaquier, Jörg-Martin Jehle, Olena Shostko, Paul Smit, and Rannveig Þórisdóttir. 2010. *European Sourcebook of Crime and Criminal Justice Statistics.* 4th ed. The Hague: Ministry of Justice, Research, and Documentation Center.

Klandermans, P. Bert. 1990. "Linking the 'Old' and the 'New' Movement Networks in the Netherlands." In *Challenging the Political Order,* edited by Russell J. Dalton and Manfred Kuechler, 122–36. New York: Oxford University Press.

Koopmans, Ruud. 1997. "Dynamics of Repression and Mobilization: The German Extreme Right in the 1990s." *Mobilization* 2, no. 2: 149–64.

———. 2004. "Protest in Time and Space: The Evolution of Waves of Contention." In *The Blackwell Companion to Social Movements,* edited by David A. Snow, Sarah A. Soule, and Hanspeter Kriesi, 19–46. Oxford: Blackwell.

———. 2005. "The Missing Link between Structure and Agency: Outline of an Evolutionary Approach to Social Movements." *Mobilization* 10, no. 1: 19–35.

Loewen, James W. 2005. *Sundown Towns: A Hidden Dimension of American Racism.* New York: New Press.

Marie, Dannette. 2010. "Maori and Criminal Offending: A Critical Appraisal." *Australian and New Zealand Journal of Criminology* 43:282–300.

Marwell, Gerald, and Pamela Oliver. 1984. "Collective Action Theory and Social Movements Research." *Research in Social Movements, Conflicts, and Change* 7:1–27.

McAdam, Doug. 1982. *Political Process and the Development of Black Insurgency, 1930–1970.* Chicago: University of Chicago Press.

———. 1983. "Tactical Innovation and the Pace of Insurgency." *American Sociological Review* 48:735–54.

———. 1988. *Freedom Summer.* New York: Oxford University Press.

McCarthy, John D., Clark McPhail, and Jackie Smith. 1996. "Images of Protest: Dimensions of Selection Bias in Media Coverage of Washington Demonstrations, 1982 and 1991." *American Sociological Review* 61:478–99.

McCarthy, John D., and Mayer N. Zald. 1977. "Resource Mobilization and Social Movements: A Partial Theory." *American Journal of Sociology* 82:1212–41.

Meyer, David S., and Nancy Whittier. 1994. "Social Movement Spillover." *Social Problems* 41:277–98.

Moore, Will H. 1998. "Repression and Dissent: Substitution, Context, and Timing." *American Journal of Political Science* 42:851–73.

Morris, Aldon. 1984. *The Origins of the Civil Rights Movement: Black Communities Organizing for Change.* New York: Free Press.

Morris, Aldon, and Naomi Braine. 2001. "Social Movements and Oppositional Consciousness." In *Oppositional Consciousness: The Subjective Roots of Social Protest,* edited by Jane Mansbridge and Aldon Morris, 20–37. Chicago: University of Chicago Press.

Oliver, Pamela. 2008. "Repression and Crime Control: Why Social Movement Scholars Should Pay Attention to Mass Incarceration as a Form of Repression." *Mobilization* 13, no. 1: 1–24.

———. 2009. "Talking about Racial Disparities in Imprisonment: A Reflection on Experiences in Wisconsin 2009." In *Handbook of Public Sociology,* edited by Vincent Jeffries, 281–98. Lanham, Md.: Rowman and Littlefield.

Oliver, Pamela E., and Gregory M. Maney. 2000. "Political Processes and Local Newspaper Coverage of Protest Events: From Selection Bias to Triadic Interactions." *American Journal of Sociology* 106:463–505.

Oliver, Pamela E., and Daniel J. Myers. 1999. "How Events Enter the Public Sphere: Conflict, Location, and Sponsorship in Local Newspaper Coverage of Public Events." *American Journal of Sociology* 105:38–87.

———. 2003. "The Coevolution of Social Movements." *Mobilization* 8, no. 1: 1–24.

Rucht, Dieter. 2004. "Movement Allies, Adversaries and Third Parties." In *The Blackwell*

Companion to Social Movements, edited by David A. Snow, Sarah A. Soule, and Hanspeter Kriesi, 197–216 . Oxford: Blackwell.

Tonry, Michael. 1994. "Racial Disproportion in US Prisons." *British Journal of Criminology, Delinquency, and Deviant Social Behaviour* 34:97–115.

———. 1997. "Ethnicity, Crime, and Immigration." *Crime and Justice* 21:1–29.

Walmsley, Roy. 2003. "Global Incarceration and Prison Trends." *Forum on Crime and Society* 3:65–78.

———. 2007. *World Prison Population List.* 7th ed. Edited by Kings College London School of Law. London: International Center for Prison Studies.

Weaver, Vesla M. 2007. "Frontlash: Race and the Development of Punitive Crime Policy." *Studies in American Political Development* 21:230–65.

Wilson, David. 2007. *Cities and Race: America's New Black Ghetto.* New York: Routledge.

13

Identity Dilemmas, Discursive Fields, Identity Work, and Mobilization: Clarifying the Identity–Movement Nexus

David A. Snow

In this chapter, I elaborate a number of dilemmas that are pertinent to understanding the relationship between identity and the mobilization of potential and actual movement adherents. I use the term *dilemmas* to encompass both identity-related issues that confront scholars examining the identity–movement nexus and activists tussling with the strategic use of identity, although in this chapter, I focus on the former. That is, I examine a set of identity dilemmas that encumber our understanding of the identity–movement nexus because they are either glossed over or insufficiently examined among social movement scholars. The identity dilemmas I elaborate include the dilemma of multiple identities, the dilemma of identity salience, the dilemma of pervasive identities, and the dilemma of discursive fields and identity work. In discussing these identity dilemmas and related topics, I do not pretend to cover the vast literature on identity in the fields of psychology, social psychology, and sociology; rather, I draw most heavily on the literature within sociology and sociological social psychology that bears most directly on participant mobilization within the study of social movements. Before elaborating each of the listed dilemmas, I contextualize the movement field's current interest in the relevance of matters of identity and collective identity for understanding participant mobilization.

Contextualizing the Importance of Identity and Collective Identity

Interest among social movement scholars in the relationship between identity, particularly collective identity, and participant mobilization crystallized during the latter fifth of the past century, largely owing to the intersection of three sets of factors. The first set encompasses broad contextual factors that make matters of identity and collective identity pressing issues for increasing numbers of individuals and social categories. A core tenet of the symbolic interactionist perspective in sociology is that interaction between two or more sets of actors minimally requires that they be situated as social actors (Stone 1962), which entails the announcement or attribution of identities. Inasmuch as this is true, it is arguable that the reciprocal avowal and imputation of identities has always been a necessary condition for interaction among humankind. Yet it is also a sociological truism that matters of identity become more problematic and unsettled as societies become more structurally differentiated, fragmented, and culturally pluralistic, loosening in some instances and shattering in others the cultural and structural moorings to which identities were once anchored, thus giving rise to the construction, extension, negotiation, and challenge of various combinations and permutations of identities. The latter part of the twentieth century has generally been regarded as one such period of identity and collective identity effervescence and clustering, with a number of scholars characterizing this period in terms of identity crises and collective searches for identity (Castells 1997; Gergen 1991; Giddens 1991; Klapp 1969; Turner 1969).

Embedded within this context is the second factor associated with the crystallization of scholarly interest in identity and collective identity in relation to politics and social movements: the rise of identity politics and identity movements in the 1970s (Bernstein 2005). The politics and movements that cluster under the identity canopy include those associated with marginalized status groups tied mainly to racial, gender, and ethnic divisions, sexual orientation, disabilities, and religious orientation. Concrete examples of movements emanating from these groupings and for which identity is accented include the feminist movement, lesbian–gay–bisexual–transgender movements, the Black Power movement, the disability rights movement, and, most recently, the fat acceptance movement. For these movements—often clustered along with less identity-oriented movements, such as the environmental movement, under the new social movements umbrella (Kriesi et al. 1995; Laraña, Johnston, and Gusfield 1994; Melucci 1989)—concern with distributional inequities and injustices tends to take a backseat to procedural issues and injustices bearing on rights and associated matters of inclusion and exclusion and to group reputational issues. Central to each movement's objectives is reframing dominant, stereotypic characterizations and public understandings, as reflected in such slogans as "Black Is Beautiful," with the goal of greater self-determination and, in some cases, self-understanding.

The emergence and clustering of these movements over the past quarter of a century no doubt stimulated interest among movement scholars in the identity–movement nexus. Among the scholars who made this nexus a focus of their work, none was more influential than the late Alberto Melucci (see Melucci 1988, 1989, 1995). Following on Melucci's theorizing, along with others', the concepts of identity and collective identity came to figure prominently in subsequent theorizing and research on movement mobilization and participation (see Hunt and Benford 2004; Jasper and Polletta 2001; Stryker, Owens, and Whyte 2000). And now, what can be regarded as the base, orienting identity proposition—that identification with a collectivity enhances the probability of movement participation on behalf of that collectively—appears to be widely confirmed, as evidenced by research on shared identification among gay men (Simon et al. 1998), Dutch farmers (Klandermans and De Weerd 2000), young women engaging in feminist activism (Liss, Crawford, and Popp 2004), striking workers (Dixon and Roscigno 2003), participants in an antiroad protest in London (Drury, Reicher, and Scott 2003), homeless movement participants (Corrigall-Brown et al. 2009), and even Jewish resistance fighters in the Nazi-occupied Warsaw ghetto (Einwohner 2006).

Yet this mounting spate of corroborating research notwithstanding, there are still a number of insufficiently theorized and examined issues regarding the intersection of identity and collective identity and participant mobilization. For example, in examining the impact of globalization processes and transnational mobilization, some work suggests that transnational mobilization is more difficult than national mobilization and that perhaps this greater difficulty is partly due to the challenge of generating overarching collective identities. In his book *The New Transnational Activism,* for example, Tarrow (2005) reports data from the Eurobarometer, from between 1995 and 2003, that show that close to 90 percent of European Union (EU) citizens claimed local or national attachments, which was a significantly higher percentage than those who claimed attachment to the EU. In light of these findings and those of parallel studies, Tarrow concluded that "among both elites and ordinary citizens territorial identities are narrowly diffused, nationally contingent, and remain rooted in national and regional contexts" (72). Similarly, in a study of 168 Dutch farmers, between fall 1993 and fall 1995, Klandermans and De Weerd (2000) found that their respondents identified at much higher rates with regional and national farmers (over 92 percent and 85 percent, respectively) than with EU farmers (between 45 percent and 58 percent). Taken together, such research findings beg the question of why the generation and maintenance of large-scale, transnational collective identities may be particularly challenging for transnational activists and movements. This question also hints at another similar one: might we expect locality-based identities to be more potent than, and override, national movement identities? But whether national identities override transnational ones, or local identities override national ones, would seem to be dependent on a number of moderating factors such as the relative strength of the national or local identities and whether the broader, translocal or transnational movement addresses issues that are experienced on the local or national levels but not addressed at those levels. Additionally, it may be the case that more identity-based movements are more likely to transcend residential community and national boundaries because of the pervasiveness of those identities. These and related issues raise important questions for which we do not have clear-cut answers. In what follows, I address a number of these questions by elaborating what I take to be important identity-related dilemmas or challenges associated with participant mobilization.

The Dilemma of Multiple Identities

An ongoing challenge to social movement organizers is the simple sociological and social psychological fact that citizens everywhere are carriers of multiple identities, of which there are at least three distinct types: social, personal, and collective. Although they often overlap, one cannot be inferred from the other, hence the necessity of distinguishing among them.

The primary sources of our various identities are the roles we assume or play, such as police officer, physician, or community organizer, and the groups and broader social categories to which we belong, such as gender, racial, ethnic, and national categories. The former are referred to as *role identities* (Stryker 1980) and the latter as *categorical identities* (Calhoun 1997); together they constitute what are commonly called *social identities* (Tajfel and Turner 1986). Whatever their specific sociocultural base, social identities are fundamental to social interaction in that they provide points of orientation to "alter" or "other" as a social object.

However, social identities do not always predict or evoke congruent personal identities, which are the attributes and meanings attributed to oneself by the actor. Personal identities include aspects of one's biography and life experiences that congeal into relatively distinctive personal attributes that function as pegs on which social identities can be hung (Goffman 1963). The importance of distinguishing between social and personal identities is twofold. First, the distinction rests in part on the fact that personal identities are self-designations rather than purely role or category based or other-attributions. And second, individuals oftentimes reject other-imputed or structurally based social identities, especially when they are insulting and demeaning, as when homeless individuals are called "lazy bums," student protestors "commie, pinko fags," and the police "fascist pigs" (Snow and Anderson 1987). Such observations suggest that personal identities may sometimes be grounded in social identities that derive from role incumbency or category-based memberships, but without necessarily being determined by those social identities.

Just as social and personal identities are different yet typically interacting constructs, so, too, is the relationship between collective and social and personal identities. Although there is no consensual definition of *collective identity*, discussions of the concept invariably suggest that its essence resides in a shared sense of "one-ness" or "we-ness" anchored in real or imagined shared attributes and experiences among those who comprise the collectivity and in relation or contrast to one or more actual or imagined sets of "others" (Hunt and Benford 2004; Polletta and Jasper 2001; Taylor and Whittier 1992). Identifying with a collectivity is often based on an individual's social identity, such as identifying as an ethnic minority or a citizen of a particular country, but such category-based associations do not automatically give rise to collective identity. Instead, the development and expression of collective identity are often triggered by contentious encounters among conflicting groups, as between demonstrating protestors and counterprotestors or social control agents, by unanticipated events, such as the World Trade Center terrorist attacks of September 11, 2001, or by threats to group or community integrity or viability, as in the case of much social movement activity. A significant part of the power of collective identity comes from the collective solidarity, efficacy, and agency it provides, which individuals are not as likely to experience via their personal or social identities.

Considered together, these three sets of identities point to a challenge confronting movement mobilization efforts: engagement in some form of collective action is partly contingent on whether one or more of these identities is aligned with the collectivity, and its animating grievances, carrying the challenge. Identity alignment or correspondence, conceptualized simply as "the alignment or linkage of individual (personal) and collective identities and action" (Snow and McAdam 2000, 42), would not be much of an issue if we were carriers of only a couple of identities. But the fact that most people play various roles and are associated with various social categories, coupled with the fact that sometimes people have contrary or loosely coupled personal identities, in the sense that they are not tightly integrated, means not only that we all have multiple and often intersecting social identities but that some form of identity alignment work is probably most often necessary to affect mobilization. Apropos this point, recall that in the research cited earlier, some EU citizens and Dutch farmers carried multiple category-based identities, as they expressed local, national, and EU identities, but the local or national were more broad based and prominent. This raises the question of why and when some identities are activated or mobilized over others. In the case of global movements and transnational mobilization, for example, identification with a global issue and the associated movement hardly guarantees personal mobilization in support of that movement. This should not be surprising in light of the series of studies, conducted by Klandermans and Oegema (Klandermans and Oegema 1987; Oegema and Klandermans 1994), on the efforts of the Dutch peace movement to mobilize citizens against the deployment of the cruise missile in the mid-1980s. Most relevant to this chapter, they found that sympathy or identification with the movement and its goals, even when targeted or recruited for participation in a protest event, did not assure participation. Or as Klandermans (1984) emphasized with his distinction between *consensus mobilization* (shared grievances and goals) and *action mobilization* (actual participation), the former does not necessarily guarantee the latter. In other words, identifying with a collectivity and its cause indicates mobilization potential but does not ensure participation. To fully understand this dilemma takes us to the dilemma of identical salience.

The Dilemma of Identity Salience

Identity salience refers to the relative prominence of any single identity (e.g., woman, student, movement activist) in relation to other identities that have been conceptualized as being ordered in a salience hierarchy (Stryker 1980). The higher the placement of the identity within the hierarchy, the greater its prominence and the more likely it is that it will be invoked. The relative salience or prominence of an identity is the result of a number of interacting factors. These factors include the extent to which the individual's own view of self is congruent or incongruent with the identity, the relevance of the identity to the situation, how much the individual's view is supported by relevant others, and the degree to which the individual has committed herself to the particular content of the identity.

The observation that individuals have differing levels of commitment to various identities suggests the variable concept of identity commitment. *Identity commitment* is related to identity salience in a cause–effect manner: those identities to which an individual's significant relational others are most highly committed are most likely to be salient in the individual's identity hierarchy. According to Stryker's (1980) role-identity theory, one is committed to an identity to the extent to which one's relationships with others are based on that particular identity. For example, a movement activist shows commitment to his activist role identity inasmuch as other movement activists and participants interact with him in terms of that activist role identity. Therefore the activist identity becomes more salient within his identity hierarchy the more he interacts with others who are oriented in terms of the activist role identity rather than some other identity within his hierarchy. To the extent that relational commitment to that role falters, so will the relative salience of the corresponding identity.

Commitment to a particular identity can also be affected by instrumental and moral factors, in addition to relational factors, with almost unyielding commitment in play when all three sets of factors are activated.

Because our multiple identities are typically arrayed in an identity hierarchy, and because the relative salience of an identity in that hierarchy can be affected by various concatenations of situational, instrumental, relational, and moral factors, scholars of collective action often misconstrue how a particular identity may or may not be linked to collective action. For example, one reason Marx's prophesied proletariat revolution never materialized in advanced capitalist societies was that the development of strident working-class consciousness has been neutralized or counteracted by multiple, cross-cutting identities rooted in ethnicity, race, religion, and gender and by the nonclass character of many competing sides of many public issues, such as crime control (see Oliver, chapter 12) and the debate over abortion. Similarly, one of the reasons working-class folks in the United States and elsewhere often do not act in accordance with their observed material interests, and their presumed class identity, may be due to the greater salience of moral and lifestyle considerations and their associated identities. All these factors can be construed as *cross-pressures,* or countervailing forces that work against the activation of some presumed identities over others (see Van Doorn, Prins, and Welschen, chapter 4, for further discussion of cross pressures), and thus highlight further the challenge of the dilemma of identity salience.

The Dilemma of Identity Pervasiveness

The relative salience of many identities within one's identity hierarchy is often situationally based such that the situation calls forth the role identity in play. In the classroom, for example, the roles of professor and student are called forth, not those of parent or son or daughter. Yet some identities transcend situation such that they are more *pervasive* than other identities. *Pervasiveness* and what Cornell and Hartmann (1998) call *comprehensiveness* are parallel terms for the observation that any particular identity may vary considerably in terms of its situational reach and the corresponding degree to which it is central to the character and flow of interaction in various domains of social life. Metaphorically, a relatively pervasive or comprehensive identity can be thought of as a "thick" identity in that its band of influence is quite broad (Cornell and Hartmann 1998).

That some identities may be more pervasive, and thus generalized rather than compartmentalized, is not a particularly novel observation theoretically. Role compartmentalization has long been regarded as part and parcel of modernity (Durkheim [1893] 1964) and bureaucratization (Weber 1947). Nevertheless, not all roles are compartmentalized. Hughes's (1945) important distinction between master and subordinate statuses suggests that some of our statuses—such as gender, race, religion, and profession—are more central than others both to our behavior and to the way we view ourselves and the way others view us and may thus function as master statuses. And Banton's (1965) threefold classification of roles based on their differentiation and generality similarly suggests that basic or ascribed roles, such as gender and race, determine the allocation and performance of other roles in a wide range of situations and thus are relatively pervasive.

Given that some movements are particularly greedy in terms of the time, resources, and energy commanded from participants, it follows that some movement role identities can be quite pervasive in that they are generalized to a broad array of situations. It is not that the situation calls forth the movement identity; rather, it is the generalized salience of that identity that makes it pervasive because of strong commitment to the movement, most likely fostered by the intersection of relational, affective, and moral commitments.

Movements most likely to be greedy and in which members' movement identities are pervasive include those that are religiously deviant or fundamentalist (e.g., Taliban movement) or utopian (e.g., Communist movements) in terms of goals and participation expectations, communal organizationally (e.g., Hare Krishna), and/or threatening or indirectly challenging via succession (exiting) or terrorism and/or driven underground (e.g., al-Qaeda, Baader Meinhof Gang, Jim Jones movement).

Although not all pervasive movement identities involve conversion, convert identities are typically pervasive (Snow and Machalek 1983; Travisano 1970); as such, they can be used as a kind of ideal type that illustrates more clearly the characteristics of a pervasive identity. Unlike basic role identities or master statuses, which are typically a function of ascription or labeling, the convert role identity is typically volitional and achieved. A second and perhaps more significant difference is that the convert role, unlike most master statuses or basic roles, comprises a kind of representative role. Although Parsons (1951, 100), who coined the term *representative role,* restricted its usage to leadership roles having to do with affairs external to the collectivity, any group or movement role that leads one to act as a functionary in extragroup activities and relations constitutes a representative role. Drawing on this concept in his discussion of ideology and conflict, Coser (1956, 113–14) noted that "in the Marxian labor movement... any active member, whether or not he had a leadership role in the organization, was expected 'to represent' the movement to the outside world." In a similar vein, all members of the Nichiren Shoshu

Buddhist movement that I studied in the 1970s (now called Sokagakkai International) were expected to act at all times, in the words of one member, as "representatives of the movement, as ambassadors of 'the Master.'" They were constantly instructed by their leaders and the movement's newspaper that whatever they did, collectively or individually, whether in the context of family, work, school, or leisure, was to be done with the interests of the movement in mind. As a major leader explained before a gathering of more than five thousand members,

> the relationship of (the movement) to the other people in society with whom we work, live, and meet every day is very important. We should keep in mind that how we live our daily life is an exact image of the entire movement.... Therefore, in every action you make and in every activity you participate, you can be carrying out the movement's mission.

To be sure, not all religions, causes, or movements are as greedy (Coser, 1967) as Nichiren Shoshu–Sokagakkai, nor do all members act in accordance with such demanding expectations. But some movement members appear to consider their groups' interests and expectations in the construction of their lines of action in nearly all extragroup activities and domains of life. But unlike many incumbents of traditional representative roles, converts do not view themselves as mere functionaries whose commitment is based primarily on instrumental or extraneous considerations (Becker 1960). Instead, the convert embraces the convert role identity. Not only are converts likely to introject and see themselves in terms of the convert role but the convert role governs their orientation in most situations. Daily activities and routines that were formerly taken for granted or interpreted from the standpoint of various situationally specific roles are now interpreted from the standpoint of the convert role identity, which is seen as the embodiment of the movement's interests and mission. Hence the convert does not act merely in terms of self-interest but in the interest of the cause or mission. Daily routines are infused with new meaning and added significance. As a Nichiren Shoshu convert, who aspired to be a nationally ranked tennis player, explained, "Before I started to chant, I had no concrete purpose in playing tennis. I used to think of all the troubles other people had and tennis seemed like a joke. But at those last two tennis tournaments I felt like I was playing for world peace."

A third distinction between the convert role as a pervasive identity and traditional master statuses, such as race and sex, is that converts are more likely to enthusiastically announce their identity in nearly all situations. In fact, the pervasive role identity seldom lets others forget this role identity during the course of interaction in public contexts. It is worn like a uniform and is regularly on display, sometimes literally, as in the case of Hare Krishna devotees, with their saffron-colored robes, and Taliban adherents, with the burkas worn by women and the measured beards, cropped hair, and head coverings of the men. Perhaps this is another reason why conversation with movement members with pervasive identities is often a halting and exasperating affair. The parents of a Nichiren Shoshu convert lamented when discussing interaction with their son, "In many ways [our son] is more pleasant to be around since he joined Nichiren Shoshu. He smiles more and he is not so argumentative. But he has this irritating habit of relating just about everything we say or do to karma or chanting."

Finally, embracement of the convert role gives rise to "the ubiquitous utilization" of the identity associated with the convert role (Travisano 1970, 605). Metaphorically, it is not merely a mask that is taken off or put on according to the situation; rather, it is salient in nearly all situations. For the movement convert or member for whom the corresponding role identity is pervasive, other, more mundane role identities, such as parent, sibling, and student, take a backseat to the pervasive role identity of movement member or convert.

The foregoing elaboration of the convert role identity should be construed as an ideal typical rendering of the characteristic features of a pervasive movement identity. Obviously, the pervasiveness of any set of movement role identities will vary with the greediness or role demands of the movement and with how it varies in terms of membership inclusiveness and exclusiveness. Hypothetically, the identities of members of movements that are greedier and more exclusive are likely to be more pervasive. But such questions have not occasioned much empirical investigation, nor do we know much about variation in identity pervasiveness among participants or members within the same movement other than to note that some members are career activists and that the career activist identity sometimes jumps or transcends any particular movement within a movement family or genre. Such questions underscore the dilemma of pervasive identities, both from a scholar-analytic and an actor-strategic standpoint. But these dilemmas, as well as the dilemma of multiple identities and identity salience, are also complicated by the dilemmas of discursive fields and identity work.

The Dilemmas of Discursive Fields and Identity Work

At the outset, I suggested that interaction with another social object, be it an individual, collectivity, or material symbolic representation thereof, requires that that object be identified in some fashion or another. The identity may be avowed or claimed, verbally or nonverbally; it may be imputed or assigned; or it may be negotiated. But however the identity of a social object is established, it must be established before action toward it is possible. In other words, it must be named in the sense of classifying or situating the object as a member of a particular category (e.g., a soldier, a woman, an environmentalist, a Muslim). This implies that the establishment of identities occurs within a relational context or field of actors. That field is typically quite small in the course of most face-to-face encounters, and the identities invoked or projected are typically accepted at face value in the course of most everyday routines, but when contested public interests are in play, that field can become quite large in terms of the sets of actors involved and the various identities they claim or impute. Elsewhere, I have referred to the field in which the contested issues are debated and discussed, via such meaning-making processes as framing and narration, among various sets of interested actors as *discursive fields* (Snow 2004, 2008).

Discursive fields evolve during the course of discussion and debate, sometimes but not always contested, about relevant events and issues and encompass cultural materials (e.g., beliefs, values, ideologies, myths) of potential relevance and various sets of actors (e.g., social movements, targeted authorities, social control agents, countermovements, media) whose interests are aligned, albeit differently, with the issues or events in question, and who thus have a stake in how those events and issues are framed and/or narrated.[1] Examples of contentious discursive fields abound, encompassing alternative contested framings among actors debating the causes of and solutions to specific events, such as the Paris–French riots of 2005, the 2005 Hurricane Katrina disaster, and the 2010 mid-term elections in the United States featuring the Tea Party movement, and more general, transnational issues, such as the Iraq War, global warming, and terrorism. In each case, alternative identities were or are being avowed and imputed by the contesting collectivities involved.

Thus I expand this conception of discursive fields to include the range of identity work involved in the imputation, avowal, and negotiation of collective identities. Identity work encompasses the range of activities in which individuals and groups engage to give meaning to themselves and others by selectively presenting or attributing and sustaining identities congruent with their interests (Schwalbe and Mason-Schrock 1996; Snow and Anderson 1987; Snow and McAdam 2000). Included among these activities are the construction and display of physical settings and props, as in the case of designing and displaying protest placards avowing and attributing contrasting identities; the arrangement of appearance, as exemplified by stylized clothing and bodily markings associated with a particular cause; selective association with other individuals and groups, as occurs in most movements but especially those skewed toward the ends of the left–right continuum; and verbal constructions and assertions, as when collectively vocalizing adversarial epithets during protest events. Referred to as *identity talk,* this fourth type of identity work has been found to be widely practiced, even among the downtrodden and stigmatized, as in the case of movements and associated protests among the homeless. Each of these types of identity work can facilitate individual or group embracement of, or distancing from, imputed or avowed social identities.

For the purposes of this chapter, I focus on the verbal or discursive variety of identity work (see also Van Doorn et al., Prins, and Welschen, chapter 4). This involves, in relation to social movement mobilization, principally framing processes entailing the avowal and imputation of characteristics relevant to at least three generic sets of actors within a movement's discursive field that Hunt, Benford, and Snow (1994) have discussed in terms of three separate *identity fields*: protagonists, antagonists, and audiences. Protagonist identity fields encompass movement activists, leaders, other rank-and-file adherents and constituents, and various supportive movement allies. The associated identity talk includes identity attributions about individuals and groups construed as capable of overcoming injustice or solving the problem the movement has identified. They include collective identity claims about the movement and its allies and typically involve positive identity avowals and attributions such as "heroes" and "heroines," "innocent victims," "aggrieved populations," and "future generations."

Antagonist identity fields encompass constellations of identity attributions about individuals and groups identified as the movement's opponents or enemies. From the standpoint of diagnostic framing, these individuals or groups are designated as the responsible agents for the problem or issue the movement seeks to overcome or as obstructionists standing in the way of the changes the movement seeks. Movement protagonists often vilify their opponents, referring to them by caustic labels such as "baby killers," "fascists," and "capitalist pigs" (Benford and Hunt 1992). Such vilifying framing of the collective character of an antagonist–opponent functions to demarcate boundaries between "us" and "them," good and evil, and right and wrong as well as aiming to discredit a movement's opponents.

Audience identity fields include clusters of individuals and groups assumed to be neutral or uncommitted observers who are in a position to react to, report on, and perhaps eventually oppose or support the movement's goals and campaigns. Allied and potential allied social movement organizations, the media, elites, marginal supporters, sympathizers, and bystander publics all make up a movement's audience identity field. The audience field in general, and bystander publics in particular, are presumed to be persuadable and thus constitute the target of a movement's "consensus mobilization" (Klandermans 1984) efforts to align themselves with the movement and perhaps even contribute significant resources to it. For this reason, a great deal of social movement framing activity is directed toward the audience field. This makes the protagonists' framing of their own identities and those of their opponents all the more critical. By the same token, movement protagonists attend to how they frame the targeted audience's identity, frequently casting them in the role of those who are fair, just, and humane and whose values, beliefs, and interests are aligned with those of the protagonists (Snow et al. 1986).

These identity fields are constituted and reconfigured throughout a movement's life course as its participants identify a problem and attribute blame or causality to antagonist "others" (Snow and Benford 1988), as they seek to mobilize support for their cause by employing various frame alignment strategies (Snow et al. 1986), as they respond to criticisms and other attacks from designated antagonists (e.g., countermovements, targets of change, and unfriendly media) (Benford and Hunt 2003), and as they talk with one another to reflect on and redefine movement tactics and successes and failures (Hunt and Benford 1994). In each of these processes, identities are being affirmed or attributed, refined or elaborated, and parried or rejected in relation to and/or in response to other actors within the field, many of whom are also engaged in the business of identity work. Furthermore, this variant of identity work, as noted earlier, occurs primarily through discourse, that is, through talk and its textual application; hence it is essentially discursive. Additionally, the three identity fields—protagonist, antagonist, and audience—are not independent fields but are part and parcel of the enveloping discursive field. And because the identity work that occurs within each field is interdependent and thus relational, I suggest that identity fields be considered as elements of the broader discursive field in which each movement is embedded.

But the more important question for this chapter is not whether identity fields are best conceived as discursive fields; rather, it is the recognition that both individual and collective identities within the social movement arena are a product of intergroup interaction within the field and thus are dynamic entities that are subject to varying degrees of change as the interactants that constitute the field change or the patterns of interaction change among the various sets of actors within the field. The dilemma confronting social movement scholars, then, is the danger of glossing over or ignoring the way in which collective identities are embedded within these dynamic, interactional, discursive fields.

Conclusion

Too often, social movement scholars write as if the identity–movement nexus is a relatively simple one: identification with a movement (i.e., its goals–objectives and/or its tactics) is strongly predictive of participation, all other things being equal. Of course, all other things are never equal, and the correspondence or alignment of individual and collective identities is more complicated than often assumed. Just as we know from the work of Klandermans and others that "consensus mobilization" does not guarantee participation, so we know that identity correspondence ensures neither initial nor sustained participation. This is due in no small part to the various identity dilemmas elaborated in this chapter. Because we have multiple identities, a salient movement identity may be no more salient than other identities; thus its salience must be accented or amplified in relation to other identities, and for sustained participation, especially when the risks and costs of association and participation are relatively high, that salient identity may need to be transformed into a pervasive identity in the sense of overriding and taking precedence over other role identities and their attendant obligations. This certainly appears to be part of the dynamic of participation in movements that are viewed publicly and politically as threatening and/or revolutionary, as, for example, with the Black Panthers, the Weather Underground, the Bader Meinhof Gang, and terrorist movements. But the concept of pervasive identities is also relevant to understanding career activism—whether with the same movement, such as Catholic Workers, within movement families or sectors, such as peace and environmental movements, or across a temporally bound movement industry. As well, pervasive identities appear to be a requisite condition for participation in communal movements, such as the Bruderhoff, the Shakers, and the Oneida (Kanter 1972; Zablocki 1971), and in offbeat, culturally idiosyncratic religious movements, such as the movement for Krishna consciousness (Rochford 1985). And what complicates these movement identity dilemmas or challenges even more is that all are contingent on the occurrence of various forms of identity work, which in turn are complicated by the discursive fields in which movement identity work processes are embedded.

Taking these observations into consideration helps to better understand the challenge, posed at the chapter's outset, of generating and maintaining transnational, collective identities. More concretely, we can hypothesize that one of the following conditions must occur for transnational identities to be generated and maintained: either other role- or category-based identities, or personal identities, have to be salient and aligned with the broader collective identities, or identity correspondence has to be constructed through various forms of identity work or, perhaps, through the occurrence of various disrupting life course events or trends that highlight and sharpen the connection between one or more role- or category-based identities, or personal identities, and the broader cause or transnational movement. How these identity alignment or correspondence processes occur through movement identity work within the enveloping contexts of discursive fields is a topic for ongoing discussion and research, likely to yield a more thorough and dynamic understanding of the identity–movement nexus in relation to participant mobilization.

Note

1. For an elaborated discussion of discursive fields and their conceptualization, see Snow (2004, 2008), Spillman (1995), Steinberg (1999), and Wuthnow (1989).

References

Banton, Michael. 1965. *Roles: An Introduction to the Study of Social Relations.* New York: Basic Books.

Becker, Howard S. 1960. "Notes on the Concept of Commitment." *American Journal of Sociology* 66:32–40.

Benford, Robert D., and Scott A. Hunt. 1992. "Dramaturgy and Social Movements: The Social Construction and Communication of Power." *Sociological Inquiry* 62:36–55.

———. 2003. "Interactional Dynamics in Public Problems Marketplace: Movements and the Counterframing and Reframing of Public Problems." In *Challenges and Choices: Constructionist Perspectives on Social Problems,* edited by J. A. Holstein and G. Miller, 153–86. New York: Aldine de Gruyter.

Bernstein, Mary. 2005. "Identity Politics." *Annual Review of Sociology* 31:47–74.

Calhoun, Craig. 1997. *Nationalism.* Minneapolis: University of Minnesota Press.

Castells, Manuel. 1997. *The Power of Identity.* Oxford: Blackwell.

Cornell, Stephen, and Douglas Hartmann. 1998. *Ethnicity and Race: Making Identities in a Changing World.* Thousand Oaks, Calif.: Pine Forge Press.

Corrigall-Brown, Catherine, David A. Snow, Theron Quist, and Kelly Smith. 2009. "Explaining the Puzzle of Homeless Mobilization: An Examination of Differential Participation." *Sociological Perspectives* 52:309–35.

Coser, Lewis A. 1956. *The Functions of Social Conflict.* New York: Free Press.

———. 1967. "Greedy Organizations." *Archives Européennes de Sociologie* 8:196–215.

Dixon, Marc, and Vincent J. Roscigno. 2003. "Status, Networks, and Social

Movement Participation: The Case of Striking Workers." *American Journal of Sociology* 108:1292–1327.

Drury, John, Steve Reicher, and Clifford Scott. 2003. "Transforming the Boundaries of Collective Identity: From the 'Local' Anti-road Campaign to 'Global' Resistance?" *Social Movement Studies* 2:191–212.

Durkheim, Emile. (1893) 1964. *The Division of Labor in Society.* New York: Free Press.

Einwohner, Rachel L. 2006. "Identity Work and Collective Action in a Repressive Context: Jewish Resistance on the 'Aryan Side' of the Warsaw Ghetto." *Social Problems* 53:38–56.

Gergen, Kenneth. 1991. *The Saturated Self: Dilemmas of Identity in Contemporary Life.* New York: Basic Books.

Giddens, Anthony. 1991. *Modernity and Self-Identity: Self and Society in the Late Modern Age.* Stanford, Calif.: Stanford University Press.

Goffman, Erving. 1963. *Stigma: Notes on the Management of Spoiled Identity.* Englewood Cliffs, N.J.: Prentice Hall.

Hughes, Everett C. 1945. "Dilemmas and Contradictions of Status." *American Journal of Sociology* 50:353–59.

Hunt, Scott A., and Robert D. Benford. 1994. "Identity Talk in the Peace and Justice Movement." *Journal of Contemporary Ethnography* 22:488–517.

———. 2004. "Collective Identity, Solidarity, and Commitment." In *The Blackwell Companion to Social Movements*, edited by David A. Snow, Sarah A. Soule, and Hanspeter Kriesi, 433–57. Oxford: Blackwell.

Hunt, Scott A., Robert D. Benford, and David A. Snow. 1994. "Identity Fields: Framing Processes and the Social Construction of Movement Identities." In *New Social Movements: From Ideology to Identity*, edited by E. Laraña, H. Johnston, and J. R. Gusfield, 185–208. Philadelphia: Temple University Press.

Jasper, James, and Francesca J. Polletta. 2001. "Collective Identity and Social Movements." *Annual Review of Sociology* 27:283–305.

Kanter, Rosabeth. 1972. *Commitment and Community: Communes and Utopias in Sociological Perspective.* Cambridge, Mass.: Harvard University Press.

Klandermans, Bert. 1984. "Mobilization and Participation: Social Psychological Expansions of Resource Mobilization Theory." *American Sociological Review* 49:583–600.

Klandermans, Bert, and Marga de Weerd. 2000. "Group Identification and Political Protest." In *Self, Identity, and Social Movements*, edited by Sheldon Stryker, Timothy J. Owens, and Robert W. White, 68–90. Minneapolis: University of Minnesota Press.

Klandermans, Bert, and Dirk Oegema. 1987. "Potentials, Networks, Motivation, and Barriers: Steps toward Participation in Social Movements." *American Sociological Review* 52:519–31.

Klapp, Orrin. 1969. *Collective Search for Identity.* New York: Holt, Rinehart, and Winston.

Kriesi, Hanspeter, Ruud Koopmans, Jan Willem Duyvendak, and Marco Giugni. 1995. *New Social Movements in Western Europe: A Comparative Analysis.* Minneapolis: University of Minnesota Press.

Laraña, Enrique, Hank Johnston, and Joseph R. Gusfield, eds. 1994. *New Social Movements: From Ideology to Identity.* Philadelphia: Temple University Press.

Liss, Miriam, Mary Crawford, and Danielle Popp. 2004. "Predictors and Correlates of Collective Action." *Sex Roles* 50:771–79.

Melucci, A. 1988. "Getting Involved: Identity and Mobilization in Social Movements." *International Social Movements Research* 1:329–48.

———. 1989. *Nomads of the Present: Social Movements and Individual Needs in Contemporary Society.* Edited by John Keane and Paul Mier. Philadelphia: Temple University Press.

———. 1995. "The Process of Collective Identity." In *Social Movements and Culture,* edited by Hank Johnston and Bert Klandermans, 41–63. Minneapolis: University of Minnesota Press.

Oegema, Dirk, and Bert Klandermans. 1994. "Why Social Movement Sympathizers Don't Participate: Erosion and Nonconversion of Support." *American Sociological Review* 59:703–22.

Parsons, Talcott. 1951. *The Social System.* New York: Free Press.

Polletta, Francesca, and James M. Jasper. 2001. "Collective Identity and Social Movements." *Annual Review of Sociology* 27:283–305.

Rochford, E. Burke., Jr. 1985. *Hare Krishna in America.* New Brunswick, N.J.: Rutgers University Press.

Schwalbe, M. L., and D. Mason-Schrock. 1996. "Identity Work as Group Process." *Advances in Group Processes* 13:113–47.

Simon, Bernd, Michael Loewy, Stefan Sturmer, Ulrike Weber, Peter Freytag, Corinna Habig, Claudia Kampmeier, and Peter Spahlinger. 1998. "Collective Identification and Social Movement Participation." *Journal of Personality and Social Psychology* 74:646–58.

Snow, David A. 2004. "Framing Processes, Ideology, and Discursive Fields." In *The Blackwell Companion to Social Movements,* edited by David A. Snow, Sarah A. Soule, and Hanspeter Kriesi, 380–412. Oxford: Blackwell.

———. 2008. "Elaborating the Discursive Contexts of Framing: Discursive Fields and Spaces." *Studies in Symbolic Interaction* 30:3–28.

Snow, David A., and Leon Anderson. 1987. "Identity Work among the Homeless: The Verbal Construction and Avowal of Personal Identities." *American Journal of Sociology* 92:1336–71.

Snow, David A., and Robert D. Benford. 1988. "Ideology, Frame Resonance, and Participant Mobilization." *International Social Movement Research* 1:197–217.

Snow, David A., and Richard Machalek. 1983. "The Convert as a Social Type." *Sociological Theory* 1:229–89.

Snow, David A., and Doug McAdam. 2000. "Identity Work Processes in the Context of Social Movements: Clarifying the Identity/Movement Nexus." In *Self, Identity, and Social Movements,* edited by Sheldon Stryker, Timothy Owens, and Robert White, 41–67. Minneapolis: University of Minnesota Press.

Snow, David A., Burke Rochford Jr., Steven K. Worden, and Robert D. Benford. 1986. "Frame Alignment Processes, Micromobilization, and Movement Participation." *American Sociological Review* 51:464–81.

Spillman, Lyn. 1995. "Culture, Social Structures, and Discursive Fields." *Current Perspectives in Social Theory* 15:129–54.

Steinberg, Marc W. 1999. "The Talk and Back Talk of Collective Action: A Dialogic Analysis of Repertoires of Discourse among Nineteenth-century English Cotton-Spinners." *American Journal of Sociology* 105:736–80.

Stone, Gregory P. 1962. "Appearance and the Self." In *Human Behavior and Social Processes,* 86–118. Boston: Houghton Mifflin.

Stryker, Sheldon. 1980. *Symbolic Interactionism: A Social Structural Version.* Menlo Park, Calif.: Benjamin-Cummings.

Stryker, Sheldon, Timothy J. Owens, and Robert W. White. 2000. *Self, Identity, and Social Movements.* Minneapolis: University of Minnesota Press.

Tajfel, Henri, and John C. Turner. 1986. "The Social Identity Theory of Intergroup Behavior." In *The Social Psychology of Intergroup Relations,* edited by S. Worchel and W. G. Austin, 7–24. Monterey, Calif.: Brooks/Cole.

Tarrow, Sidney. 2005. *The New Transnational Activism.* New York: Cambridge University Press.

Taylor, Verta, and Nancy Whittier. 1992. "Collective Identity in Social Movement Communities: Lesbian Feminist Mobilization." In *Frontiers in Social Movement Theory,* edited by Aldon D. Morris and Carol McClurg Mueller, 104–29. New Haven, Conn.: Yale University Press.

Travisano, Richard V. 1970. "Alternation and Conversion as Qualitatively Different Transformations." In *Social Psychology through Symbolic Interaction,* edited by G. P. Stone and H. A. Faberman, 594–606. Waltham, Mass.: Ginn-Blaisdell.

Turner, Ralph H. 1969. "The Theme of Contemporary Social Movements." *British Journal of Sociology* 20:390–405.

Weber, Max. 1947. *The Theory of Social and Economic Organization.* Translated by A. M. Henderson and T. Parsons. New York: Oxford University Press.

Wuthnow, R. 1989. *Communities of Discourse.* Cambridge, Mass.: Harvard University Press.

Zablocki, Benjamin. 1971. *The Joyful Community.* Baltimore: Penguin Books.

14

Movements of the Left, Movements of the Right Reconsidered

Swen Hutter and Hanspeter Kriesi

Social movement scholars tend to neglect the existence of different channels of mobilization, which leads them to misconstruct the changing dynamics of mobilization in a global age (McAdam and Tarrow, chapter 16). Usually, social movement scholars focus on the protest arena and do not pay much attention to the electoral channel (where parties link citizens to the decision-making arenas in parliament and government) or the channel of interest intermediation (where established interest groups link citizens to the decision-making arenas in public administration and government). More specifically, by neglecting the electoral channel, social movement research tends to overlook the most important contemporary collective actors mobilizing against the consequences of globalization—the populist radical right, which effectively mobilizes the cultural anxieties of the losers of globalization (Mudde 2007, 184; Kriesi et al. 2008). Note that we define *globalization* very broadly as processes that lead to the lowering and unbundling of national (economic, cultural, and political) boundaries (e.g., Held et al. 1999; Zolo 2007).

Although the populist radical right is very critical of the representative politics in the electoral channel and pleads for a more direct linkage of masses to elites (Taggart 2002, 67), ironically, the populist radical right tends to choose the electoral channel to mobilize the people in the name of the redemptive face of democracy (see Canovan 1999). As Mény and Surel (2002, 11) observe, the common denominator of populist movements puts an emphasis on the fundamental role of the people; it claims that the people have been betrayed by those in charge, that is, that the elites are accused of abusing their position of power, and that the primacy of the people has to be restored. However, populism expresses itself in the electoral channel of representative politics, and in the way they mobilize, populists often rely on charismatic leadership or at least centralized political organizations. In this chapter, we argue that this paradox is linked to the basic value orientations characterizing the left and the right, which ultimately lead to a different relationship of the mobilization in the electoral and protest arenas, depending on whether we look at movements of the left or movements of the right.

By focusing on the mobilization of public protest, social movement scholars privilege social movements of the left. Whereas movements of the right tend to mobilize in the electoral channel, the mobilization of public protest has been dominated by the left since the rise of the new social movements. For instance, the limits of this focus on public protest are reflected in della Porta and Tarrow's (2005, xiv) programmatic statement that transnationalization is "the most important challenge" currently faced by movement scholars, activists, and their opponents. Thus social movements are expected to partly react to globalization by globalizing themselves. This may be the case, as far as the global justice movement is concerned (della Porta 2007). But this movement has been a rather marginal phenomenon in contemporary mobilization in Western European countries, and the transnationalization of social movements has generally remained very limited indeed (Hutter 2012). Once we open our perspective to the electoral channel, we are able to grasp the key implications of globalization processes for politics, which, unexpectedly, have little to do with transnationalization and very much to do with a renaissance of nationalism.

This chapter is divided into three parts. First, we focus on conflicts over globalization issues (i.e., immigration, European integration, and neoliberal globalization) in protest politics. By tracing the salience of and the average positions taken relative to these key issues linked to the opening up of cultural, political, and economic boundaries, we can say more about the transformative power of globalization in the protest arena. At the same time, we see what social movement scholars miss when sticking to this channel of mobilization. Second, we argue that basic value orientations might explain why the populist radical right prefers the electoral channel over the protest arena. Third, we suggest that the contrasting arena preferences of the left and of the right result in different relationships between electoral and protest politics: the left waxes and wanes at the same time in both arenas, while for the right, when its actors and issue positions become more salient in one arena, their salience decreases in the other one. We rely on protest event and survey data to illustrate our points.

Conflicts over Globalization Issues

As Stefaan Walgrave (chapter 10) suggests, mobilization dynamics depend on the issues at stake, and the issue that has risen to great prominence in Western European protest politics in the age of globalization is the issue of immigration. In the 1970s and 1980s, under the impact of the new social movements, protest politics in Western Europe was dominated by cultural issues, above all by issues linked to cultural liberalism. In the course of the 1990s and 2000s, the protest arena was still dominated by cultural issues, but now immigration emerged as a new dominant theme. Figure 14.1 illustrates this trend based on protest event data (which extend the data collected by Kriesi et al. [1995] up to 2005 and add the United Kingdom and Austria to the original four countries, i.e., to France, Germany, the Netherlands, and Switzerland).[1]

The figure indicates that protest politics is affected by globalization processes. By and large, cultural liberalism lost ground after the 1980s, as one can see by the precipitous drop in the number of participants. However, the issue does not fade away. Indeed, cultural liberalism is once again on the rise during the early 2000s, that is, after a period when most scholars observed the institutionalization of its main promoters (e.g., Giugni and Passy 1999).

If one looks at the number of protest events, immigration became even more salient than cultural liberalism by the 1990s. So our results forcefully underline Koopmans and colleagues' (2005, 3) claim that "immigration and ethnic relations . . . constitute since the early 1990s the most prominent and controversial fields of political contention in West European polities." At the same time, the number of participants puts this into perspective. While the number of participants focused on immigration has increased since the 1970s, the mobilization levels never reached the high values of cultural liberalism. Moreover, the mobilization level has even declined since its peak in the 1990s.

Though immigration is on the rise in all of our countries, the trend is most pronounced in West Germany. Protest by, on behalf of, and against migrants has dominated the German protest landscape since the early 1990s, especially in terms of the share of events (Rucht 2003; Koopmans and Olzak 2004; Karapin 2007). In terms of the ratio of anti- to pro-immigration events, British and German protest politics are the most polarized, tending to support our initial thesis that there is an inverse relationship between electoral and protest politics. Thus voices against immigration are relatively more prominent in countries where the populist radical right could not establish itself in the electoral arena (Dolezal 2008; Kriesi and Frey 2008).

Other issues linked to globalization, such as European integration or neoliberal globalization, are far less salient in the protest arena (Figure 14.1).

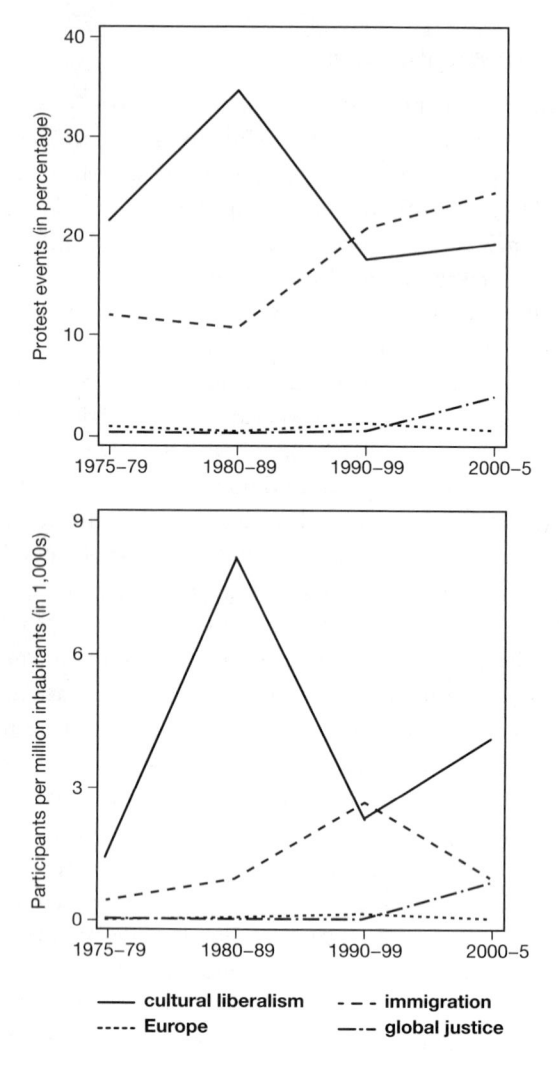

Figure 14.1. Salience of cultural liberalism, immigration, Europe, and global justice by decade.

Note. Cultural liberalism includes all events focused on the rights of women and homosexuals, international peace, solidarity expressed with developing countries, and "free spaces for alternative lifestyles." *Immigration* includes protests by, against, or on behalf of migrants that focus on the situation of migrants in the country of residence in Western Europe. *Europe* includes all events focused on issues of "membership," "competences," and "decision-making rules" as regards the European integration process. *Global justice* includes all events making claims for or against neoliberal globalization and its supposed main promoters, including the G8, WEF, World Bank, or WTO. Share of events that focus on an issue as a percentage of all coded events in that period (N = 17,315 protest); percentages do not add to 100 owing to other issue categories; number of participants per million inhabitants who take part in protest events (yearly average). The values indicate the average salience in six West European countries (Austria, France, Great Britain, the Netherlands, Switzerland, and West Germany).

From 1975 until 2005, only 0.4 percent of events have European integration (major reforms, enlargement processes) as the central focus, and the share of participants is minimal. In addition, we witness only a very limited increase over time. "Europe" has yet to become an issue in national protest politics (Imig and Tarrow 2001; Balme and Chabanet 2008, 82; della Porta and Caiani 2009, 42). We observe a more pronounced increase as regards global justice. After its international take-off in Seattle 1999, the issue has entered the arenas of Western European protest politics. There certainly were protest events before Seattle that focused on neoliberal globalization (Holzapfel and König 2001; Pianta and Marchetti 2007, 32), but their salience measured by event share and participants remained very low. Yet our findings highlight that global justice remains relatively insignificant, with only 3.7 percent of all reported events and 3.6 percent of all participants (2000–5) addressing neoliberal globalization.[2]

What might account for the different saliences of the three globalization issues in the protest politics arena? We suggest, in line with the political process approach, that differing institutional contexts are a main explanatory factor (see Kriesi 2004; Meyer 2004).[3] Issues of economic globalization and European integration are far more often the object of political negotiations beyond the national level. They follow a logic of highly visible but rare international events staged by governmental actors. Though these events provide windows of opportunity for highly publicized protest events, their scope is far more restricted and short-lived than the more continuous, localized struggles over migration-related issues.

This can also be seen when comparing the share of protest events that target a *transnational addressee* across issues. Overall, this share increased more or less linearly from 14.0 percent (1970s) to 21.0 percent (early 2000s), which indicates a certain transnationalization of protest politics. Relying on logistic regressions and using single protest events as our cases, we found that both global justice and Europe have a positive impact on transnationalization (results not shown). This is in sharp contrast to the most salient new issue, immigration. Protests focusing on immigration—above all those opposing it—are far more likely to focus on the national or even subnational level. Though it constitutes one of the main issues linked to globalization processes, the political mobilization of migration-related questions is firmly linked to the national container (Koopmans et al. 2005, 74).

Finally, it is important to take into account both the salience of new issues and the average *positions* taken relative to these issues in the protest arena. Overall, protest politics constitutes the domain of the left, as issue positions that are nowadays most closely associated with the political left (defensive on the economic dimension and integrationist on the cultural dimension) dominate in this channel (Hutter 2012). For example, virtually no protests favor economic liberalism, reducing the welfare state or enforcing budgetary rigor. This runs against the thesis of a "normalization" of protest—if the thesis implies not just the spread of protest politics but its use to advance almost any political position (McCarthy, Rafail, and Gromis, chapter 18; Meyer and Tarrow 1998; Van Aelst and Walgrave 2001; Walgrave, chapter 10). One finds such a left-wing accent of protest politics from the mid-1970s onward.

It is significant to note that the dominance of left-wing positions holds with respect to both issues related to cultural liberalism and issues related to immigration. Protests by and on behalf of migrants heavily outweigh protests against them, although, in contrast to cultural liberalism, the rise of the immigration issue is linked to a certain return of the right to the protest arena. Coding all events in favor of immigration as 1 and all events against it as –1, the average position became less immigration friendly from the 1980s (0.52) to the early 2000s (0.22). This trend toward tougher stances on immigration is less pronounced when one looks at the number of participants rather than the number of events, however.

The continued predominance of the left in the protest arena should, however, not lead us to believe that the political reaction to globalization is primarily dominated by cosmopolitan forces. It is true that the left's mobilization of protest has been characterized by the cosmopolitanism of the globalization winners. But articulating the cosmopolitanism of the globalization winners in the protest arena, the left has missed the grievances of the globalization losers who are now mobilized by the new populist radical right. Taking the electoral arena into account, the nationalist-defensive mobilization of the globalization losers by the new populist radical right has arguably been by far the most impressive mobilization process linked to globalization.[4] As Mudde (2007, 196) frames it, "populist radical right parties are the most ideologically pure and electorally successful opponents of globalization."

The Political Paradox of the Populist Radical Right

In the introduction, we argued that though the populist radical right fights for "the common man" and is highly critical of the political classes and of representative democracy, it mostly uses the channels of electoral politics and (if available) more institutionalized direct democratic instruments to advance its claims. In this section, we put forward some speculative arguments for this "political paradox of the populist right." On one hand, we think it is part of a *strategy* of double differentiation. Populist radical right leaders and followers try to set themselves apart from their adversaries on the left, who are viewed as "chaotic" protesters (Haider 1993, 19–20; Le Pen 1984, 54, 69).[5] At the same time, populists try to set themselves apart from the extreme and neofascist right—not only for historical but also for more practical reasons. If those who openly advocate the most right-wing and racist ideologies take part in protest events organized or supported by populist radical right parties, then the populists run the risk of being equated with them.

On the other hand, we think that this strategy is linked to the basic *value orientations* characterizing the left and the right, respectively. Rebels on the right tend to have authoritarian and materialist values and prefer (orderly) conventional political action over (disorderly) protest politics, whereas rebels on the left tend to share libertarian and postmaterialist values, which predispose them for unconventional protest politics. For challengers on both the left and the right, the "medium is the message"; that is, the choice of the channel in which they express themselves is at the same time an expression of their underlying message.

Thus Flanagan and Lee (2003, 260), in their comparative analysis of authoritarian–libertarian value change in the twelve largest and most affluent Western nations, find differing orientations toward political involvement between authoritarians (who tend to be closer to the right) and libertarians (who tend to be closer to the left). Authoritarians are joiners of conventional groups, such as political parties or professional associations, in essentially equal proportions with libertarians. However, they are not as likely to join political action–oriented groups. Authoritarians have a more parochial and less cosmopolitan outlook on politics, and above all, they have a much lower protest potential than libertarians. Similarly, Gundelach (1998) explains the individuals' involvement in four types of protest activities mainly with value orientations characteristic of the left. In the twelve Western European countries he analyzed, he found that social or political libertarianism and postmaterialism were associated with grassroots activity, and postmaterialism turned out to be most important in stimulating such activity. Kriesi's (1993, 249) more detailed results for the Netherlands in particular showed that the adherents of the left in general, and of the New Left in particular, shared the antiauthoritarian and emancipatory values of the new social movements.

There are two more relevant results from Flanagan and Lee (2003): they show that libertarians exhibit higher levels of organizational membership but are no more likely to do unpaid voluntary work in the organizations to which they belong than are authoritarians. Moreover, authoritarians are vastly more likely to do voluntary work out of a desire to be of service to others, whereas motivations of libertarians seem to be more self-serving. Libertarians seem to prefer less continuous, more task-specific, more individualistic forms of political involvement—such as those provided by public protesting—whereas the more traditional forms of political involvement provided by party politics seem to correspond more to the worldviews of the authoritarians (see also Inglehart 2008).

On the basis of more recent data, Van der Meer et al. (2009, 15) once again show that left-wing citizens are more likely to turn to protest activities than their counterparts on the right in all twenty Western democracies that they studied during the early 2000s.[6] Dalton, Van Sickle, and Weldon (2010) find also a significant effect of postmaterialism and left ideology on protest behavior in their eighty-seven-nation study based on the World Values Survey (WVS; wave 1999–2002). Using multilevel models, the authors show that the effects of both left–right self-placement and postmaterialist attitudes are magnified by the democratic and economic development of a country. More specifically, the effects are most pronounced in established and affluent democracies—that is, the countries on which we focus here.

In the following, we contribute to this literature by presenting additional findings based on the WVS (waves 1999–2002 and 2005–7) for the six Western European countries covered by our protest event data. In contrast to other recent survey analyses, we replace the general left–right orientation with more specific issue and party preferences. This allows us to get closer to the factors that underlie the political paradox of the populist radical right.

Our dependent variable is an additive protest potential index (ranging from 0 to 3) (for similar measures, see Jenkins, Wallace, and Fullerton 2008; Dalton, Van Sickle, and Weldon 2010). The index indicates whether a respondent has signed petitions, joined in boycotts, and attended peaceful demonstrations, or might do so. We use ordered logit analyses to test the effect of party and issue preferences on protest potential. We group the different parties into four party groups: radical left, moderate left, moderate right, and radical right. The radical left includes the old communist as well as the new libertarian left (e.g., green parties), and the moderate left corresponds to the social democrats. The moderate right is composed of liberals, conservatives and Christian democrats, whereas the radical right includes populist radical right parties (new and transformed) and other small radical right parties. We use vote intention as our measure ("If there were a national election tomorrow, for which party would you vote?"). We look at preferences on the two main cultural issues in the protest arena, that is, cultural liberalism and immigration.[7] In addition, we control for some of the most important explanatory variables of protest participation: biographical availability (sex, age, educational level, and children), political engagement (interest in politics), and structural availability (number of organizational affiliations) (see Schussman and Soule 2005).[8]

The first model in Table 14.1 includes only the control variables as regards biographical availability, engagement, and structural availability. All significant effects are in line with previous research (Schussman and Soule 2005, 1090). Highly educated, young men who are interested in politics and belong to many associations are most likely to participate in protest activities. Model 2 shows that respondents who would vote for radical and moderate left parties are more likely to protest than adherents to the moderate and radical right, respectively. In addition, the more a respondent favors immigration and cultural liberalism, the higher is her protest potential (model 3). If we include these issue preferences in our model, the effect of party preferences becomes insignificant (moderate left) or is substantially reduced (radical right). This suggests that the different protest potentials of adherents of the right and of the left, respectively, are mainly due to different issue preferences or value orientations.

Different Logics on the Left and on the Right

In this final section, we show that the differences we highlighted with respect to the preferred channel of mobilization ultimately led to different relationships of the mobilization in the electoral and protest arenas, depending on whether we look at movements of the left or movements of the right. More specifically, we suggest that the relationship between the two arenas differs depending on the political orientation of the actors involved. For the political left, we expect that it promotes its claims in both arenas at one and the same time. For the political right, by contrast, we expect a substitutive relationship between the two arenas: it uses the one or the other. In adopting such contrasting expectations, we follow Meyer and Minkoff's (2004, 1484) call to move beyond assuming a simple, positive relationship between protest mobilization and its political context (mobilization in the electoral arena, in our case) (see McAdam and Tarrow 2010; see also their chapter 16).

As far as the populist radical right is concerned, our previous cross-national findings have already hinted at an inverse relationship between right-wing success in the electoral arena and protest politics. Thus, as already discussed, it is precisely in Germany and the United Kingdom where the mobilization against immigration in the protest arena is more salient than in the other four countries covered by our protest data; that is, right-wing protest is most salient in those two countries where, for different reasons, no populist challenger on the right has so far been able to establish itself as a significant structuring force in national party competition. This suggests that it is only when they cannot get a foot on the ground in the electoral arena that the new populist radical right challengers radicalize and mobilize in the protest arena.

Table 14.1. Impact of party and issue preferences on protest potential (range 0 to 3)

	Model 1			Model 2			Model 3		
	Coeff.	SE	P > t	Coeff.	SE	P > t	Coeff.	SE	P > t
Biographical availability									
Male	0.22	0.13	*	0.26	0.13	**	0.35	0.13	***
Age (log)	−1.32	0.20	***	−1.25	0.21	***	−1.05	0.21	***
Education	0.51	0.05	***	0.50	0.06	***	0.37	0.04	***
Children	0.06	0.10	n.s.	0.05	0.10	n.s.	0.09	0.11	n.s.
Political engagement									
Interest in politics	0.69	0.09	***	0.70	0.08	***	0.65	0.07	***
Structural availability									
No. of organizational affiliations	0.16	0.03	***	0.16	0.03	***	0.16	0.03	***
Party preferences[a]									
Radical left				1.01	0.26	***	0.73	0.27	***
Moderate left				0.48	0.23	**	0.27	0.21	n.s.
Moderate right				−0.09	0.14	n.s.	−0.19	0.14	n.s.
Issue preferences									
Immigration							0.16	0.02	***
Cultural liberalism							0.36	0.03	***
Country dummies		yes			yes			yes	
Countries		6			6			6	
(N)		(4,923)			(4,923)			(4,923)	
Pseudo-R^2		0.08			0.10			0.11	

Note. Cutoff points and estimates for country dummies are not reported. Unfortunately, the last World Values Survey wave does not include information on party preferences in France, Great Britain, and the Netherlands. Austria is not covered at all. Thus we rely on the wave 1999–2002 for Austria, France, Great Britain, and the Netherlands. The Swiss and German data come from wave 2005–7. Since respondents from the same country share a common context, observations within the same country are not independent. To account for this context dependence, we include country dummies and additionally cluster the standard errors on the country level to address the related problem of within-country correlation of errors. The data are weighted by the sampling weight.

[a]Radical right as reference category.

***$p < 0.01$. **$p < 0.05$. *$p < 0.1$; ordered logit regression, unstandardized coefficients, and robust standard errors (clustered on country).

Table 14.2. Impact of party group and electoral strength on presence in protest politics

	Model 1			Model 2		
	Coeff.	SE	$P > t$	Coeff.	SE	$P > t$
Party group						
Radical left	2.16	1.26	*	1.95	0.68	***
Moderate left	1.37	0.69	**	1.64	0.53	***
Radical right	0.25	1.26	ns	1.91	0.63	***
Moderate right (ref.)						
Presence in electoral politics						
Share of votes	−0.02	0.03	ns	−0.00	0.04	ns
Share of votes × Radical left				0.16	0.07	**
Share of votes × Radical right				−0.15	0.06	**
Dummies for country and decade included						
Constant	2.86	1.44	*	1.68	0.66	**
(N)		(92)			(92)	
Adj. R^2		0.24			0.34	

Note. The dependent variable is the share of protest events that are supported by a party group as a percentage of *all* coded protest events. The number of cases equals four party groups multiplied by four decades multiplied by six countries; missing values for Switzerland during the 1990s.
***$p < 0.01$. **$p < 0.05$. *$p < 0.1$; ordinary least squares regressions, unstandardized coefficients.

To test this hypothesis more systematically, we turn back to our protest event data and take a closer look at the presence of different party groups in protest and electoral politics. Political parties are the most important players in the electoral arena, but political parties are also more directly involved in protest events as they both stage their own and co-organize or support events by other actors. Overall, parties were involved in 7.8 percent of all protest events we coded, and around 15 percent of all protest participants are involved in party-supported events. More specifically, we propose to analyze the parties' protest activities as a function of their electoral strength. For this analysis, we again classify the parties into four groups: radical left, moderate left, moderate right, and radical right. We measure the presence (or success) in the electoral arena by the share of votes in national parliamentary elections. For the protest arena, we focus on a party group's share of all coded events. We aggregate across decades and include dummy variables to control for country and decade effects (Table 14.2).

The first model in Table 14.2 shows that the two party groups on the left are more likely to turn to protest activities to voice their claims than the parties on the right. The radical right is not significantly more salient than the moderate right (reference category). Furthermore, if we control for party groups, electoral strength does not have an added impact on how forcefully different parties enter the protest arena. The second model, which includes all significant interactions between party groups and vote shares, shows that the impact of electoral strength on protest activities varies from one party group to the other. In general, the radical left, moderate left, and radical right parties are all more likely to enter the protest arena than is the moderate right. The interaction terms, however, highlight that different logics are at work with respect to the radical left and the radical right. Whereas electoral success leads the radical right to abstain from protest activities, it incites the radical left to engage more in protest politics.

Conclusion

Our main point is that social movement scholars tend to neglect the existence of different channels of mobilization, which leads them to misconstruct the changing dynamics of mobilization in a global age. Thus we again urge movement scholars to get past disciplinary proclivities, to recognize that public protest is only one potential route to influence, and to recall that social movements are integrally related to mainstream politics. To be fair, movement scholars (especially the proponents of the political process approach) have always put movement activities in their broader political context, but we side with McAdam and Tarrow (2010) and Walder (2009), who noted in recent reviews that the field has become more movement-centric during the last years.

On the basis of this general impression, we highlighted what kinds of issues, positions, and degrees of transnationalization movement scholars observe when sticking to the protest arena. Overall, the left in general, and positions favoring the opening up of cultural boundaries more specifically, have prevailed in the protest arena over the last thirty years. In line with a twofold transformation, cultural liberalism peaked during the 1970s and early 1980s. Since the 1990s, immigration has emerged as a new, highly contested cultural issue, lending support to the argument that globalization has transformed Western European protest arenas. The other two globalization issues, global justice and Europe, are far less important in the protest arena, by contrast. In addition, there is an inverse relation between the relevance of a globalization issue and the transnationalization of protest. The most salient globalization issue, immigration, is articulated in particular on the (sub-)national level.

On one hand, this left-wing accent of the protest arena should lead movement scholars to reconsider parts of the "movement society thesis" (McCarthy, Rafail, and Gromis, chapter 18; Meyer and Tarrow 1998; Soule and Earl 2005). On the other hand, the accent of the protest arena should, however, not lead us to believe that the political reaction to globalization is primarily dominated by cosmopolitan forces. Taking the electoral arena into account, the nationalist-defensive mobilization of the globalization losers by the new populist radical right has arguably been by far the most impressive mobilization process linked to globalization (Mudde 2007; Kriesi et al. 2008). Populist radical right parties, as the main driving forces of this change, are characterized by a *political paradox,* however. Though very critical of representative politics in the electoral channel, and pleading for a more direct linkage of masses to elites, the populist radical right tends to choose the electoral channel, and not the protest arena, to mobilize the people.

This paradox is linked to what we call a strategy of double differentiation, which is rooted in core value orientations of populist radical right leaders and adherents. For the challengers on both the left and the right, the "medium is the message"; that is, the choice of the channel in which they express themselves is at the same time an expression of their underlying message. Whereas the rebels on the right have authoritarian and materialist values, and prefer (orderly) conventional political action over (disorderly) protest politics, rebels on the left share libertarian and postmaterialist values, which predispose them for unconventional protest politics. We looked at the writing of main protagonists of the populist radical right in Western Europe and cited survey research to support our claim, but more research is needed here to search for possible explanations why the populist radical right differs so much from the libertarian left when it comes to the preferred channel of mobilization.

In addition, the differences with respect to the preferred channel of mobilization lead to different relationships of mobilization in the electoral and protest arenas, depending on whether we look at movements of the left or movements of the right, respectively. In doing so, we urge movement scholars to move both beyond a restricted focus on protest politics and beyond a "simple, positive relationship" (Meyer and Minkoff 2004, 148) between protest mobilization and its broader political context (electoral mobilization, in our case). Although our results are provisional, we suggest that with respect to the interplay of the arenas, different logics are at work on the left and right. Issue positions and actors on the right tend to follow an either–or logic, whereas those on the left tend to be more congruent: protest and electoral politics tend to rise and fall in tandem. However, our findings are in need of further exploration—especially beyond the Western European context.

Notes

1. A more detailed discussion of the data and a presentation of empirical results can be found in Kriesi et al. (2012).

2. While this may be a too restrictive coding of global justice, it does raise the question of just how relevant a force the contemporary global justice movement is in Western Europe. The results highlight the small number of protest events whose primary focus is neoliberal globalization, though this does not mean the frames and organizations emerging out of the global justice movements are unimportant in Western European protest arenas (e.g., Ancelovici 2002).

3. There are other reasons for the differences in salience, including characteristics of the issue itself (e.g., complexity, obtrusiveness, emotionality) or movement–countermovement dynamics (Meyer and Staggenborg 1996). The latter are clearest in the case of migration-related mobilization.

4. Even though "the electorates of populist radical right parties in Europe are heterogeneous, just like those of other political parties" (Mudde 2007, 225), the literature on its social and attitudinal characteristics underscores that the social groups of "globalization losers" have been mainly mobilized by new entrants or by transformed mainstream parties on the right and that cultural issues related to globalization have become central for explaining the vote for populist radical right parties (e.g., Lachat 2008; Arzheimer 2009).

5. Studies on the populist radical right focus on its general relation to (representative) democracy (Mudde 2007). Relations to protest politics are often not addressed. On the basis of biographies of its most prominent representatives in our countries (Christoph Blocher, Jörg Haider, and Jean-Marie Le Pen) and newspaper articles, we find evidence of strong opposition to the ideas and legacy of the protests associated with 1968. Haider rejected such activities most forcefully, and Blocher, too, takes a rather critical stance. Interestingly, protest events (co-)organized by the Swiss People's Party (SVP) are labeled as "marches" or "manifestations" to explicitly avoid the term *demonstration*, which is used to characterize their opponents' actions (NZZ 1995; Skenderovic 2009). Jean-Marie Le Pen's critique of protest politics is less forceful, perhaps due to the French political context or Le Pen's own "student activism" (Marcus 1995, 30).

6. They use the data from the Comparative Studies of Electoral Systems. As they

focus on a single left–right scale, left means not only left in the classical economic sense but that the "'old'—that is, proletarian—connotations of the left side of the ideological spectrum have gradually been replaced by the 'new' meanings," i.e., postmaterialist concerns. Their results are in line with the ones based on the International Social Survey Program (Anderson and Mendes 2006) or on the data set from the project on Citizenship, Democracy, Involvement (Teorell, Sum, and Tobiasen 2007).

7. Both variables are measured by factor scores. For cultural liberalism, we rely on issue positions about homosexuality, abortion, and divorce ("Please tell me for each of the following actions [i.e., homosexuality, abortion, divorce] whether you think it can always be justified, never be justified, or something in between," ten answer categories). For immigration, we use the following two questions: "When jobs are scarce, employers should give priority to *British* people over immigrants" (three answer categories) and "How about people from other countries coming here to work. Which one of the following do you think the government should do? (1) Let anyone come who wants to?, (2) Let people come as long as there are jobs available?, (3) Place strict limits on the number of foreigners who can come here?, (4) Prohibit people coming here from other countries?" All principal component analyses result in one-dimensional solutions (one factor per issue and country).

8. We take the natural logarithm of age. Educational level is categorized into three levels (completed primary or lower, completed secondary, completed tertiary). Sex (male = 1), children (having children = 1), and political interest (very or somewhat interested = 1) are dummy variables. The number of organizational affiliations is measured by an additive index of belonging to a maximum of fifteen different types of organizations (e.g., sports or recreational associations, labor unions, political parties, or environmental groups).

References

Ancelovici, Marcos. 2002. "Organizing against Globalization: The Case of ATTAC in France." *Politics and Society* 30:427–63.

Anderson, Christopher J., and Silvia M. Mendes. 2006. "Learning to Lose: Election Outcomes, Democratic Experience, and Political Protest Potential." *British Journal of Political Science* 36:91–111.

Arzheimer, Kai. 2009. "Contextual Factors and the Extreme Right Vote in Western Europe, 1980–2002." *American Journal of Political Science* 53:259–75.

Balme, Richard, and Didier Chabanet. 2008. *European Governance and Democracy: Power and Protest in the EU*. Lanham, Md.: Rowman and Littlefield.

Canovan, Margaret. 1999. "Trust the People! Populism and the Two Faces of Democracy." *Political Studies* 47:2–16.

Dalton, Russell, Alix Van Sickle, and Steven Weldon. 2010. "The Individual-Institutional

Nexus of Protest Behaviour." *British Journal of Political Science* 40:51–73.
della Porta, Donatella, ed. 2007. *The Global Justice Movement: Cross-National and Transnational Perspectives.* Boulder, Colo.: Paradigm.
della Porta, Donatella, and Manuela Caiani. 2009. *Social Movements and Europeanization.* Oxford: Oxford University Press.
della Porta, Donatella, and Sidney Tarrow, eds. 2005. Preface to *Transnational Protest and Global Activism,* xiii–xv. Lanham, Md.: Rowman and Littlefield.
Dolezal, Martin. 2008. "Germany: The Dog That Didn't Bark." In *West European Politics in the Age of Globalization,* edited by Hanspeter Kriesi, Edgar Grande, Romain Lachat, Martin Dolezal, Simon Bornschier, and Timotheos Frey, 208–33. Cambridge: Cambridge University Press.
Flanagan, Scott C., and Aie-Rie Lee. 2003. "The New Politics, Cultural Wars, and the Authoritarian-Libertarian Value Change in Advanced Industrial Democracies." *Comparative Political Studies* 36:235–70.
Giugni, Marco, and Florence Passy. 1999. *Zwischen Konflikt und Kooperation: die Integration der sozialen Bewegungen in der Schweiz.* Chur, Switzerland: Rüegger.
Gundelach, Peter. 1998. "Grass-Roots Activity." In *The Impact of Values,* edited by Jan W. Van Deth and Elinor Scarbrough, 412–40. Oxford: Oxford University Press.
Haider, Jörg. 1993. *Freiheit, die ich meine.* Frankfurt am Main, Germany: Ullstein.
Held, David, Anthony McGrew, David Goldblatt, and Jonathan Perraton. 1999. *Global Transformations.* Cambridge: Polity Press.
Holzapfel, Miriam, and Karin König. 2001. "Chronik der Anti-Globalisierungsproteste." *Mittelweg* 36:24–34.
Hutter, Swen. 2012. "Restructuring Protest Politics: The Terrain of Cultural Winners." In *Political Conflict in Western Europe,* edited by Hanspeter Kriesi, Edgar Grande, Martin Dolezal, Marc Helbling, Swen Hutter, Dominic Hoeglinger, and Bruno Wüest, 151–81. Cambridge: Cambridge University Press.
Imig, Doug, and Sidney Tarrow. 2001. "Mapping the Europeanization of Contention: Evidence from a Quantitative Data Analysis." In *Contentious Europeans: Protest and Politics in an Emerging Polity,* edited by Doug Imig and Sidney Tarrow, 27–49. Lanham, Md.: Rowman and Littlefield.
Inglehart, Ronald. 2008. "Changing Values among Western Publics from 1970 to 2006." *West European Politics* 31:130–46.
Jenkins, J. Craig, Michael Wallace, and Andrew S. Fullerton. 2008. "A Social Movement Society? A Cross-National Analysis of Protest Potential." *International Journal of Sociology* 38:12–35.
Karapin, Roger. 2007. *Protest Politics in Germany: Movements on the Left and Right since the 1960s.* University Park: Pennsylvania State University Press.
Koopmans, Ruud, and Susan Olzak. 2004. "Discursive Opportunities and the Evolution of Right-Wing Violence in Germany." *American Journal of Sociology* 110:198–230.

Koopmans, Ruud, Paul Statham, Marco Giugni, and Florence Passy. 2005. *Contested Citizenship: Immigration and Cultural Diversity in Europe.* Minneapolis: University of Minnesota Press.

Kriesi, Hanspeter. 1993. *Political Mobilization and Social Change: The Dutch Case in Comparative Perspective.* Aldershot, U.K.: Avebury.

———. 2004. "Political Context and Opportunity." In *The Blackwell Companion to Social Movements,* edited by David A. Snow, Sarah A. Soule, and Hanspeter Kriesi, 67–90. Oxford: Blackwell.

Kriesi, Hanspeter, and Timotheos Frey. 2008. "The United Kingdom: Moving Parties in a Stable Configuration." In *West European Politics in the Age of Globalization,* edited by Hanspeter Kriesi, Edgar Grande, Romain Lachat, Martin Dolezal, Simon Bornschier, and Timotheos Frey, 183–207. Cambridge: Cambridge University Press.

Kriesi, Hanspeter, Edgar Grande, Martin Dolezal, Marc Helbling, Dominic Hoeglinger, Swen Hutter, and Bruno Wüest. 2012. *Political Conflict in Western Europe.* Cambridge: Cambridge University Press.

Kriesi, Hanspeter, Edgar Grande, Romain Lachat, Martin Dolezal, Simon Bornschier, and Timotheos Frey. 2008. *West European Politics in the Age of Globalization.* Cambridge: Cambridge University Press.

Kriesi, Hanspeter, Ruud Koopmans, Jan Willem Duyvendak, and Marco Giugni. 1995. *New Social Movements in Western Europe: A Comparative Analysis.* Minneapolis: University of Minnesota Press.

Lachat, Romain. 2008. "The Electoral Consequences of the Integration–Demarcation Cleavage." In *West European Politics in the Age of Globalization,* edited by Hanspeter Kriesi, Edgar Grande, Romain Lachat, Martin Dolezal, Simon Bornschier, and Timotheos Frey, 296–319. Cambridge: Cambridge University Press.

Le Pen, Jean-Marie. 1984. *Les Français d'abord.* Paris: Éditions Carrere–Michel Lafon.

Marcus, Jonathan. 1995. *The National Front and French Politics: The Resistible Rise of Jean-Marie Le Pen.* New York: New York University Press.

McAdam, Doug, and Sidney Tarrow. 2010. "Ballots and Barricades: On the Reciprocal Relationship between Elections and Social Movements." *Perspectives on Politics* 8:529–42.

Mény, Yves, and Yves Surel. 2002. "The Constitutive Ambiguity of Populism." In *Democracies and the Populist Challenge,* edited by Yves Mény and Yves Surel, 1–21. Basingstoke, U.K.: Palgrave Macmillan.

Meyer, David S. 2004. "Protest and Political Opportunities." *Annual Review of Sociology* 30:125–45.

Meyer, David S., and Debra C. Minkoff. 2004. "Conceptualizing Political Opportunity." *Social Forces* 82:1457–92.

Meyer, David S., and Suzanne Staggenborg. 1996. "Movements, Countermovements, and the Structure of Political Opportunity." *American Journal of Sociology* 101:1628–60.

Meyer, David S., and Sidney Tarrow, eds. 1998. *The Social Movement Society.* Lanham, Md.: Rowman and Littlefield.

Mudde, Cas. 2007. *Populist Radical Right Parties in Europe.* Cambridge: Cambridge University Press.

NZZ. 1995. "Blochers Kundgebung vom 23. September." *Neue Zürcher Zeitung* 14:55.

Pianta, Mario, and Raffaele Marchetti. 2007. "The Global Justice Movements: The Transnational Dimension." In *The Global Justice Movement: Cross-National and Transnational Perspectives,* edited by Donatella della Porta, 29–51. Boulder, Colo.: Paradigm.

Rucht, Dieter. 2003. "The Changing Role of Political Protest Movements." *West European Politics* 26:153–76.

Schussman, Alan, and Sarah A. Soule. 2005. "Process and Protest: Accounting for Individual Protest Participation." *Social Forces* 84:1083–1108.

Skenderovic, Damir. 2009. *The Radical Right in Switzerland: Continuity and Change, 1945–2000.* Oxford: Berhahn Books.

Soule, Sarah A., and Jennifer Earl. 2005. "A Movement Society Evaluated: Collective Protest in the United States, 1960–1986." *Mobilization* 10, no. 3: 345–64.

Taggart, Paul. 2002. "Populism and the Pathology of Representative Politics." In *Democracies and the Populist Challenge,* edited by Yves Mény and Yves Surel, 81–98. Basingstoke, U.K.: Palgrave Macmillan.

Teorell, Jan, Paul Sum, and Mette Tobiasen. 2007. "Participation and Political Equality: An Assessment of Large-Scale Democracy." In *Citizenship and Involvement in European Democracies: A Comparative Analysis,* edited by Jan Van Deth, José Ramón Montero, and Anders Westholm, 384–414. London: Routledge.

Van Aelst, Peter, and Stefaan Walgrave. 2001. "Who is that (wo)man in the street? From the normalisation of protest to the normalisation of the protester." *European Journal of Political Research* 39:461–86.

Van der Meer, Tom W. G., Jan van Deth, and Peer L. H. Scheepers. 2009. "The Politicized Participant: Ideology and Political Action in 20 Democracies." *Comparative Political Studies* 42:1426–57.

Walder, Andrew G. 2009. "Political Sociology and Social Movements." *Annual Review of Sociology* 35:393–412.

Zolo, Danilo. 2007. *Globalisation: An Overview.* Colchester, U.K.: ECPR Press.

Discussion: Mobilization and the Changing and Persistent Dynamics of Political Participation

Christopher Rootes

We live in interesting times. Even in established liberal democracies, societies and politics are changing. As the institutions, economic conditions, and social strictures of the mid-twentieth century receded into history, these more affluent societies are said to have become more fluid and more participatory. Certainly it appears that participation in various forms of hitherto unconventional political action has increased, even as participation in electoral politics has tended to decline. However, as we will see, obdurate realities persist.

Globalization has seized the imaginations of social scientists, but globalization is not responsible for all the disconcerting changes in affluent societies. Rather, it is, as Walgrave intimates in his introduction (chapter 10), a more fundamental and pervasive modernization of these societies that has transformed the who, the how, and the why of collective mobilization. Who is mobilized into collective action? How are they mobilized? Why? Why have some been mobilized, but not others? Why does their collective mobilization take the forms it does? Modernization creates new actors and the possibilities of new forms of action, and because it generates new concerns and discontents, it brings new reasons for acting collectively.

But if modernization is the more general process, globalization—economic, cultural, and political—provides one particularly powerful lens through which the processes and discontents of late modernity have been viewed. Hutter and Kriesi (chapter 14) address some of the more prominent collective responses to it. Yet, although globalization has raised new issues, these have more often been channeled by the older forms of parties and interest groups than by new forms of protest. By contrast, it is most conspicuously the new information and communication technologies (ICTs), the key technologies of this phase of modernization, whose impacts Van Stekelenburg and Boekkooi (chapter 11) discuss and that have facilitated new forms of mobilization. Snow (chapter 13) discusses the implications of the ICT revolution for the role of identity in collective action. Where identities have, under the impact of social and technological change, become unprecedentedly multiple, fluid, and/or fragmented, it may be doubted whether identity is still a glue capable of holding social movements together. More generally, in explanations of differential patterns of participation in collective action, the role of shared identity is easily exaggerated. The lack of an adequately developed shared identity is by no means the most potent factor impeding the collective mobilization of the disadvantaged. As Oliver (chapter 12) reminds us, those who are chronically marginalized and disadvantaged, socially and economically, are effectively excluded politically, even from the relatively uninstitutionalized forms of nonviolent collective action. In a rapidly changing world, not everything changes. Class inequality and racial exclusion have persistent effects on the dynamics of mobilization.

Modernization and Its Discontents

One leading candidate for principal cause of the recent rise of unconventional participation is the dramatic extension, during the past fifty years, of higher education. No longer the preserve of preponderantly male social and intellectual elites, universities now provide rites of passage for around half of young adults. Higher education bestows on many of its graduates enhanced cognitive skills, increased self-confidence, and expanded social networks, all of which stimulate political efficacy and so are facilitative of political participation. The increased numbers and salience of the highly educated stimulated increased membership in civil society organizations of all kinds, and this increase in numbers of people well resourced for participation also stimulated discontent with the constraints of minimally participatory political institutions. One consequence was that the expansion of repertoires of political participation as forms of collective action hitherto associated with the socially disadvantaged became more common among the highly educated (Barnes et al. 1979; Mayer, chapter 19). New social movements arose around new issues that appealed disproportionately to an emergent "new (middle) class" whose members identified closely neither with established elites nor with the (now shrinking) industrial working class, nor yet with a labor movement that was almost everywhere in decline (Ehrenreich and Ehrenreich 1979; Gouldner 1979).

If social changes have transformed the demographics of participation in social movements, they have also changed the forms of collective action and the means by which people are recruited to such action. Organizational membership has long been the best single predictor of political participation, and in old social movements, such as the labor movement, organizations themselves mounted protests and mobilized people into the streets, and frequently into electoral campaigns as well. By comparison with such relatively institutionalized forms of action, the wave of collective action that began in the 1960s was anarchic, was not generally mobilized by organizations, and did not stimulate the development of organizations analogous to trade unions and socialist parties. Even the new political parties that it did foster—notably the greens—pitched themselves as antiparty or movement parties and, especially in their early years, were remarkable for their disregard for the conventions of political organization.

These developments reflected the social characteristics of the new wave of protesters: young, highly educated, but often still students, and so both relatively unconstrained by obligations of employment and family and relatively isolated from the specific mobilizing potential of shared conditions of work. They also reflected the libertarian spirit of an epoch in which the austerities of postwar reconstruction were abandoned on a wave of unprecedented affluence and utopian aspirations. Thus block recruitment to collective action was increasingly replaced by the mobilization of individuals, many of whom admitted to no organizational allegiance at all.

If the challenge of social movement mobilization is the getting and maintaining of commitment, in the absence of stable organizations, new problems of maintaining commitment arise. Thus student movements, recruited from people whose status was temporary, whose availability for action was fragmented by the academic calendar, and whose generational replacement was annual, proved especially ephemeral. The identity movements of sexual and ethnic minorities, reflecting the more enduring shared conditions of their participants, proved more durable. Peace movements survived the ebb and flow of mobilizing triggers because, atypically, they cohered around long-standing formal organizations. Environmental movements spawned new organizations, and breathed new life into old ones, but persist as complex and diverse networks of organizations and individuals variably committed to diverse conceptions of the common cause. Organizations undoubtedly play a part in the creation of opportunities for environmental and antiwar mobilizations, but many such mobilizations are ad hoc, and many who are mobilized have no strong links to any of the organizations involved. Identity may help explain such relatively unorganized mobilization, but less demanding and less defining "shared concern" is more general.

If participation in collective action is increasingly individual, the generally increased aggregate levels of participation, in the absence of strong organizational stimuli, reflect the disinhibition of citizens about participation in forms of political participation more public and more demanding than the simple act of voting. The recruitment of individuals to protest is increasingly via personal networks that are loose and fluid and often as a result of exposure to mass media reports of previous or impending protests.

Globalization: New Actors, Old Forms of Action

Because public protest is the most spectacular and readily visible form of collective action associated with social movements, scholars have been prone to highlight its role in social movements and have neglected other, less public or more institutionalized means by which collective goals may be pursued. However, if we conceive of a social movement as a loose, noninstitutionalized network of informal interactions among individuals and groups engaged in collective action (Diani 1992), social movements are not coterminous with protest, and it is not fruitful to conceive of protest as an essential constitutive element of social movements so much as one possible means of collective action—which *is* essential to a social movement. Indeed, just as it is possible to have many protests without a social movement (where protests are not networked or based on shared identity or concern), so social movements may persist even where protest is absent or is conducted mainly through institutionalized channels.

The salience and novelty of protests associated with the new social movements have, as Hutter and Kriesi suggest, led social movement scholars to focus disproportionately on protests at the expense of proper examination of larger and more consequential mobilizations through electoral channels or interest groups. Nowhere is this imbalance of attention more stark than in the case of mobilizations around globalization.

Social movement scholars were quick to see potential in protests against neoliberal globalization, to identify them as constitutive of a movement, variously labeled the antiglobalization, alterglobalization, or global justice movement, and to undertake research on them. They mostly left to political scientists a much more politically significant phenomenon—the mobilization, as resurgent right-wing populism and ethnonationalism, of those who have lost rather than gained from globalization and modernization. This is odd because even though right-wing populist parties command only minority electoral support, as a proportion of all protests and of protesters mobilized, protests against neoliberal globalization are marginal even within the universe of protest.

Hutter and Kriesi conclude that the new populist right is therefore the most impressive mobilization around globalization. This, however, is to overlook those other mobilizations around globalization that are less clearly differentiated from and more integrated with the mainstream political life of parties and interest groups. Representing vastly larger numbers of members and supporters than the participants in protests against neoliberal globalization or the members of neopopulist parties, nongovernmental organizations (NGOs) whose primary concerns are with aid, trade, and development in the global South, together with humanitarian and environmental NGOs and sometimes trade unions, also campaign against neoliberal globalization, often in concert with one another and sometimes in tandem with activists who orchestrate more demonstrative forms of collective action. Certainly their concerns are overlapping rather than identical, and their primary identities may be quite other (e.g., religious, in the case of many aid, trade, and development NGOs), but they constitute a global justice movement that might reasonably be claimed to be "the most impressive mobilization around globalization" but that has also been neglected by social movement scholars fixated on street protests (Rootes and Saunders 2007).

It is a mistake to counterpose social movements, on one hand, to political parties and pressure groups, on the other; both are means by which grievances and aspirations may be mobilized. Historically, the mobilizations of the extreme right, as well as those of the left, combined the forms of movement and party; the postwar fascist party in Italy even called itself the Movimento Sociale Italiano. Moreover, as the case of green parties and environmental movements demonstrates even more clearly than does the resurgence of the populist right, parties, pressure groups, and NGOs may be alternative strategies of mobilization under the broad umbrella of the same movement (Rootes 2004). Whether one strategy rather than another is chosen, or which predominates in a particular place or at a particular time, will be shaped by the prevailing structure of political opportunities as well as the values and beliefs of the actors concerned. Whereas the expansive, even utopian politics of the highly educated young has favored protest mobilizations, the defensive politics of those who feel threatened by the social, economic, and political effects of globalization has more often been channeled by populist parties.

Moreover, globalization has generated new issues for national politics faster than it has led to the transnationalization of political mobilization. Thus, despite occasional protests around international economic summits, most collective action remains mobilized at the national level and addresses national targets. Though this is especially true of the issues of greatest concern to the populist right—notably immigration and multiculturalism—it is also true of those issues raised by the libertarian left. The long shadows of national political opportunity structures lie dark on aspirations to a transnational, even global politics.

New Technologies, New Forms of Mobilization

If globalization has not produced the anticipated transnationalization of collective action, technological innovation has transformed the means of mobilization within nations. As Van Stekelenburg and Boekkooi demonstrate, ICTs have made informal, bottom-up, grassroots mobilizations easier to achieve and more frequent, even without formal organizations such as were associated with mobilizations in the past (Aitchison and Peters 2011, 47–48; Polletta et al., chapter 2). Flash mobs can be summoned via Facebook and Twitter with a rapidity that often defeats police surveillance and intelligence-gathering capacities and, as in London in winter 2010–11, can produce highly mobile and flexible protests that defy attempts to contain them. There is, in London, even an iPhone app that maps the disposition of police forces in real time and so facilitates the rerouting of protests to avoid their containment by the police. Now ubiquitous digital cameras and camera phones, often enabled to upload instantly to YouTube or Flickr, are both a tool for the rapid and wide publicizing of protest and a defensive weapon against illegal policing.

Mass media may still be an important vehicle for raising awareness of issues and campaigns, especially among the uninitiated, but alternative media, web-based bulletin boards, and electronic social networks distribute more information from a wider diversity of authors to potential audiences that have in common little more than their access to the Internet, whether via computer, smart phone, or iPad. Thus communication antecedent to collective action has become increasingly unmediated, and this relative absence of mediation increases activists' margin of autonomy. It is, however, communication that is also relatively promiscuously distributed, and this has more uncertain implications for activists and would-be organizers, rather as indiscriminately distributing invitations to a house party may lead to a surfeit of unwelcome and troublesome guests. Organizations not only served as bases for block recruitment to mobilization and channels for communication but also as mechanisms for maintaining order and discipline—recall, for example, the famously disciplined, self-policed demonstrations of trade unions and communist parties. Now, however, such organizations, weakened by declining numbers and obliged to attempt to mobilize people from beyond their core membership, have often lost the capacity to impose discipline and to exclude unwelcome outsiders.

Face-to-face personal networks remain powerful vehicles of mobilization, but communication via vastly more extensive electronic virtual networks is rapid, sometimes almost instant, and so may sustain new forms of rapid mobilization. Loose physical networks are vulnerable to infiltration by opponents or police, and web pages, e-mails, and social networks are monitored by intelligence officers, but even though they may be monitored, such is the speed of communication by Twitter and SMS that police are often unable to keep up, with the result that protest preserves its autonomous capacity to surprise.

Nevertheless, the euphoria over the mobilizing potential of ICTs may be premature. Although they are not mediated in the highly institutionalized manner of the mainstream mass media, these new media are not, for the most part, controlled by activists but by monopolistic corporations. Indeed, as the purging of U.K. activist pages from Facebook in April 2011 demonstrated, the flow of information to the potentially mobilizable may easily be interrupted by the host organization, with or without urging from police or security authorities, and it may, as in China, Iran, and the Middle East, be directly blocked by censorious governments (Peters 2011). Although it is possible for activists to use open source and peer-to-peer alternatives such as Thimbl, Diaspora, and Quora, these do not have—and are unlikely to achieve—the extensive reach of Facebook and Twitter. Thus the former are likely to stand in the same relationship to the latter as Indymedia does to mainstream mass media—a useful medium for insiders but an esoteric niche too far removed for the uninitiated.

Nor does an abundance of easily accessed information necessarily enable individuals to "organise without organisations." UK Uncut, the campaign of store occupations designed to draw attention to corporate tax avoidance, "organised almost exclusively via Twitter and Facebook," is cited as evidence contradicting Gladwell's (2010) claim that only strong "offline ties create the necessary relationships of trust and support that lead people to engage in direct action together. Through the UK Uncut networks, groups of strangers come together to carry out actions, often at personal risk to themselves. By taking part in these actions together, they strike up the 'strong bonds' of friendship and trust on which they can build a more concerted campaigning effort. In this way, online and offline activism are interlaced and reinforce each other" (Aitchison and Peters 2011, 53). This may be true, but because such actions and networks are highly vulnerable to infiltration by police, agents provocateurs, and agents of their targets, the trust that these activists invest may be misplaced, and trust betrayed may be demobilizing.

Protests are, in any case, typically mere moments in a campaign. Can protests summoned by ICTs be sufficiently sustained to give leverage to effective campaigns, let alone to cohere into social movements? Does mobilization need to be organized to be effective? Much depends on the resolve and responsiveness of governing elites and their susceptibility to mobilized opinion, and it is unlikely that they will be swayed by the numbers or noise of protesters alone. How does mobilized opinion as represented by public protest relate to public opinion more generally? The former may be much less impressive, whereas, as in most liberal democracies, the latter is regularly monitored. Under irresolute autocracies, conversely, in the absence of reliable opinion polling, large numbers of feet in the street may have more effect. But the general point remains: in the absence of organization, spontaneous, grassroots mobilizations may challenge the powerful but are unlikely to secure their objectives, raising the specter of repeated but doomed waves of mobilization.

So far, the new virtual networks have supplemented physical networks. But is it possible that virtual networks are *displacing* physical networks and making social movement organization more rather than less difficult to maintain? There is a risk that more messages merely means more noise and, in the absence of organization, less constraint on the members of networks actually to act rather than to message, tweet, or sign online petitions. Networking is not a novelty of the age of Facebook, and it is not confined to linkages among individuals. Indeed, the most persuasive definition of a social movement is as a network of organizations as well as individuals, and although online tools *can* be used to facilitate leaderless, network-based collective action, "they are far more commonly used to extend the reach of a more traditional hierarchical model" (Brandzel 2010).

ICTs may instantiate personal networks that facilitate protest in the absence of organization, but it seems unlikely that they can perform the functions of sustaining mobilization and strategically articulating pressure that have been the rationale for organizations. What, in the absence of organization, might personal networks employ to maintain mobilization? Personal networks may be akin to affinity groups rather than solidaristic communities, and to that extent, they may be held together by shared concern rather than identity. An individual may, after all, have a variety of concerns that are shared with members of different networks but do not overlap, let alone cohere into a single identity.

Identity: Multiple, Fluid, Fragmented

This raises large questions for those who insist on the role of identity in the mobilization of collective action. Shared identity facilitates solidarity, though it is unclear to what extent it is either sufficient or necessary. Does the new ICT foster or fragment identity? If fragmentary identities are sufficient to sustain flash mobilizations, might they be sufficient to sustain a social movement? Is the *use* of social media itself reflective, or perhaps constitutive, of a (very loose) identity sufficient to sustain a *form* of mobilization with no specific thematic or ideological content? How is identity to be constituted among people who have no, few, or only very loose primary ties to organizations or physical networks? If identity is important to mobilization, is it cause? Or effect? How *much* identity is necessary? Is organization possible or sufficient even without identity?

The role of identity in social movements is problematic. The new social movements of the 1970s and 1980s were not, as Snow suggests, all or only concerned with matters of identity. The sexual minority movements may indeed have been concerned primarily with procedural and group reputational issues, but the women's and ethnic minority movements, arguably the most momentous, if not the most durable, of the movements that emerged from the ferment of the 1960s, were at least as much concerned with distributional inequalities. The great survivor among the new movements—the environmental movement—has, like the repeatedly resurrected peace movement, been much more focused on the achievement of principled but practical action to address universal problems than on matters of identity and has latterly become more concerned with distributional inequalities on a global scale (Rootes 2006). That is not to say that processes of identity formation have not been important in peace and environmental movements but merely to observe that questions of identity have not loomed so large in all the movements bundled together as the new social movements.

Shared identification with a collectivity does indeed make participation in collective action more likely, but far from being essential to the constitution of a movement, it may actually be a source of fragmentation and ineffectiveness; the more clearly defined the identities of organizations and individuals within a movement, the sharper the conflicts within it (Saunders 2008). Conversely, groups and individuals whose identities are relatively diffuse or fluid are better placed to play the brokerage roles by which movements may be held together and by which effective collective action may be achieved.

Identification with an issue or a movement may be an indicator of mobilization potential, but it is by no means a perfect predictor of participation in collective action; as Klandermans and Oegema (1987) so ably demonstrated, there are many slips between the brimming cup of mobilization potential and the thin lip of action. Snow argues that as individuals have multiple identities, of which the activist identity is but one, an individual's activist identity will be more salient the more that individual interacts with people relevant to the activist identity as opposed to others who are not. Now, in an age in which many interactions are virtual rather than physical, the opportunities to develop and maintain a diversity of networks without extensive—or any—physical interaction are greatly enlarged. This suggests that an individual's identities might, in consequence, be multiplied even as opportunities for the physical interaction helpful to building solidaristic commitment are reduced. Thus identity may become less important as an antecedent of mobilization simply because, identities having become more multiple, the *sustained* salience of any one identity becomes less likely. Moreover, insofar as opportunities for physical interaction in the course of mobilization or its aftermath are reduced by the intermittency of mobilization and the relative absence of solidaristic organizations, activist identities are less likely to be developed or reinforced as a consequence of participation. It is noteworthy that the "pervasive identities" to which Snow refers are all associated with extreme political or religious movements quite unlike the social movements that predominate in liberal democratic states.

Snow is surely right when he insists that collective identities are embedded in dynamic, interactional discursive fields. But what happens when those fields are especially and increasingly fluid? Surely, then, identities themselves will tend to be fluid and will require rather less negotiation to permit or encourage action than they might have done when identities and the interactional contexts that shaped them were more stable. Thus a tendency already apparent in the new social movements, where multiple identities and weak organizations made solidaristic commitment less common than it had been in the labor movement, may be exacerbated by the ubiquity of ICTs and the pattern of flash mobilization that they make possible and encourage.

That is not, of course, to suggest that all is fluid. As Snow suggests, the failure of transnational movements to flourish even under the propitious conditions provided by the European Union is testimony to the persistent pull of primordial national or subnational identities, but it also testifies to the divisive power of languages and of political opportunities still primarily structured by national states. National identities may be challenged by globalization and transnationalization, but the practical constraints of language and national political systems remain more compelling than the pull of universalizing processes.

Identity and identification are not inconsequential, but the focus on identity diverts attention from the impact of material conditions on the patterning of collective action. Thus, pace Snow, the failure of the proletariat to perform according to Marx's revolutionary script may owe less to the impacts of competing identities than it does to the dull compulsion of economic life under capitalism.

Class, Ethnicity, and Political Exclusion

One conspicuous accompaniment of globalization is mass migration from the less prosperous South and the creation in the more affluent North of new ethnic minorities and new dynamics of inclusion and exclusion that impact patterns of political participation and exist alongside those that afflicted old ethnic minorities. Ethnicity and class interact, and stereotyping and fear of the "dangerous other" extend from the elites who benefit from the labor of immigrants to the mass of the host population who fear the competition of new arrivals for jobs and housing and who experience, not the excitement of a new cosmopolitanism, but the unwelcome transformation of their neighborhoods. The extreme right mobilizations of which Hutter and Kriesi write are not, despite the charismatic roles of a few maverick populist politicians of elite origin, stimulated by elites so much as they are expressions of resentment and despair by losers from globalization who, near the bottom of the domestic social pile, compete directly with economically disadvantaged ethnic minorities for space and resources and fear the loss of their cultural identity. Class and ethnicity intersect, but at least in the initial encounters—and more enduringly in the United States—the shared interests that derive from a common class condition fail to subsume the obvious differences of ethnicity.

Oliver highlights the difficulties that confront the socially unintegrated poor. Not only do they have fewer resources for political participation but they have fewer structural opportunities and fewer informal opportunities to secure effective access to and influence over political processes, and so they are more likely to be misunderstood, misrepresented, and repressed. It is a major flaw of liberal democracies that those who have most need of political action to redress their grievances have fewest resources to participate effectively within the formal institutions and processes of the democratic system (Piven and Cloward 1977). Thus excluded from, or at best marginal to, the constitutional political system, their politics, aside from generally low levels of routine and ritualized electoral participation, has been marked by sporadic outbursts of violent protest. Sometimes this has yielded results: in the 1960s and early 1970s in the United States and in the 1980s in Britain, "bargaining by riot" produced welfare gains and temporary relief from repressive policing. But, by exciting fears of disorder among the majority population, a more enduring result has been that the specter of the unruly ethnic minority poor has justified increased surveillance and repression rather than encouraging systematic and sustained attention to their grievances.

Such repression depresses the capacities of the disadvantaged to mobilize politically, and so many of the protests that draw attention to their grievances are protests mounted by others on their behalf; these, however, are rarely effective and so are less common than advocacy through more institutionalized channels. Yet so fascinated are we by the protest that *does* occur that we neglect to explore the reasons for the relative absence of collective mobilization among those who have greatest reason to protest (Gamson 1975). It is not the manifest repression of the protests of the disadvantaged that most demands our attention but the systematic conditions of marginalization that ensure that their protests are rare. Poverty ensures the diversion to support the destitute and the vulnerable of resources that might otherwise have been available to sustain political mobilization. Social exclusion, deliberate or unintended, suppresses possibilities for the articulation and communication of grievances and so produces an unpolitics of nonissues (Lukes 1986).

As Oliver observes, despite the best intentions of advocacy groups that take up the grievances of the politically disadvantaged poor and ethnic minorities, differences in perspectives, education, and culture mean that the patterns of domination and subordination inscribed in the structures of the dominant society are reproduced in interactions between the disadvantaged and those who seek to advocate on their behalf. The best efforts of well-intentioned advocates for the disadvantaged are a poor substitute for the collective mobilization on their own behalf of the disadvantaged themselves because only thus can their effective inclusion be assured. The principal obstacle to that is the persistence of the not-so-hidden injuries of class and the patterns of social exclusion that sustain the dominance of social and economic elites that have no interest in undermining the foundations of their own privilege.

Conclusion

In the liberal democratic states of the affluent North, inequalities of wealth and income are now wider than at any other time in more than a hundred years. Despite the constitutional formalities of democracy, inequalities of power are stark. It is improbable that such gross inequalities will continue to increase indefinitely. It is also difficult to imagine that they will be reduced without a political mobilization that, using all the resources of new communications technologies as well as old-fashioned organization, strives to transcend the new social divisions introduced by globalization as well as the old, institutionalized ones. The dynamics of mobilization are likely to remain a compelling object of study.

References

Aitchison, Guy, and Aaron Peters. 2011. "The Open-Sourcing of Political Activism: How the Internet and Networks Help Build Resistance." In *Fight Back! A Reader on the Winter of Protest,* edited by Dan Hancox, 44–60. London: openDemocracy/ ourKingdom. http://www.opendemocracy.net/ourkingdom/guy-aitchison-aaron-peters/open-sourcing-of-political-activism-how-internet-and-networks-.

Barnes, Samuel H., Max Kaase, et al. 1979. *Political Action: Mass Participation in Five Western Democracies.* London: Sage.

Brandzel, Ben. 2010. "What Malcolm Gladwell Missed about Online Organizing and Creating Big Change." *The Nation,* November 15. http://www.thenation.com/article/156447/what-malcolm-gladwell-missed-about-online-organizing-and-creating-big-change#comment.

Diani, Mario. 1992. "The Concept of Social Movement." *Sociological Review* 40:1–25.

Ehrenreich, Barbara, and John Ehrenreich. 1979. "The Professional-Managerial Class." In *Between Labor and Capital,* edited by P. Walker, 5–45. Brighton, U.K.: Harvester.

Gamson, William A. 1975. *The Strategy of Social Protest.* Homewood, Ill.: Dorsey.

Gladwell, Malcolm. 2010. "Small Change: Why the Revolution Will Not Be Tweeted." *The New Yorker,* October 4. http://www.newyorker.com/reporting/2010/10/04/101004fa_fact_gladwell?printable=true#ixzz12Alw6lIq.

Gouldner, Alvin W. 1979. *The Future of Intellectuals and the Rise of the New Class.* London: Macmillan.

Klandermans, Bert, and Dirk Oegema. 1987. "Potentials, Networks, Motivations, and Barriers: Steps towards Participation in Social Movements." *American Sociological Review* 52:519–31.

Lukes, Steven. 1986. *Power: A Radical View.* 2nd ed. Oxford: Blackwell.

Peters, Aaron. 2011. "The Facebook Purge: Corporate Power, Political Influence, and the Need for Independent, Powerfully Popular Social Media Networks." *openDemocracy,* April 30. http://www.opendemocracy.net/ourkingdom/aaron-peters/facebook-purge-corporate-power-political-influence-and-need-for-independent-.

Piven, Frances F., and Richard A. Cloward. 1977. *Poor People's Movements: Why They Succeed, How They Fail.* New York: Pantheon.

Rootes, Christopher. 2004. "Environmental Movements." In *The Blackwell Companion to Social Movements,* edited by David A. Snow, Sarah A. Soule, and Hanspeter Kriesi, 608–40. Oxford: Blackwell.

———. 2006. "Facing South? British Environmental Movement Organisations and the Challenge of Globalisation." *Environmental Politics* 15:768–86.

Rootes, Christopher, and Clare Saunders. 2007. "The Global Justice Movement in Great Britain." In *The Global Justice Movement: Cross-National and Transnational Perspectives,* edited by Donatella della Porta, 128–56. Boulder, Colo.: Paradigm.

Saunders, Clare. 2008. "Double-Edged Swords? Collective Identity and Solidarity in the Environment Movement." *British Journal of Sociology* 59:227–53.

IV
The Changing Context of Contention

15

The End of the Social Movement as We Know It? Adaptive Challenges in Changed Contexts

Ruud Koopmans

The character of the nation-state has undergone important changes. Banaszak, Beckwith, and Rucht (2003) note that formal state authority has been relocated or transferred from one governmental level or branch to another. There has been *uploading* of responsibilities to supranational organizations such as the European Union (EU), the United Nations, or the World Trade Organization. Authority and responsibilities have also been *downloaded* to substate, regional, or local governments. Parallel to these vertical changes, *lateral loading* of power occurs, particularly from the legislative to the executive arena. Finally, states also *offload* responsibilities to nonstate actors or to the impersonal forces of the market.[1] These trends—some of them more than others—pose important challenges to social movements as we have known them during the nineteenth and twentieth centuries. One of the lasting lessons of Charles Tilly's work (e.g., Tilly 1995, 2004) has been that the rise of the social movement and the repertoires of protest that have been historically linked to it were intimately tied to the rise of democratic nation-states, parliaments, and political parties, on one hand, and the long-term trend of increased state intervention in markets and income redistribution, on the other. With the profound recent changes in these contextual conditions that gave rise to the birth of the social movement, the question is raised whether social movements can successfully adapt to these changed circumstances and maintain the salience and influence that they have had over the last two hundred years. Of course, it is highly unlikely that social movements and protest politics will entirely disappear, but it is not so sure, in my view, whether they will be able to avoid the fate of other children of the democratic, national, redistributive welfare state such as political parties and labor unions, of which the formal–institutional skeletons still stand but which have lost much of their former mobilizing power and, with it, arguably also their influence on decision-making processes and public opinion formation.

The interconnection between parliamentary and social movement politics is at the heart of McAdam and Tarrow's contribution to part IV of this volume (chapter 16), which stands very much in the Tillian tradition. By emphasizing how important linkages between elections and social movements are, they implicitly also raise the question what the erosion of the central position of national parliaments and parties means for social movements. In very much the same vein, della Porta (chapter 17) describes the challenges for social movement activists and scholars of a shift of power from the nation-state to international governmental organizations, from parties and legislatures to executives, and from states to markets. McCarthy, Rafail, and Gromis's (chapter 18) claim about national-level demobilization and local-level mobilization in the United States also fits in this framework, as does Mayer's (chapter 19) analysis of the "relative autonomization" of the social movement sector from the partisan and political field and its incumbents.

In this chapter, I first make some remarks on the strength and uniformity of the transfers of authority identified by Banaszak, Beckwith, and Rucht (2003) and present some evidence on their consequences for social movements. Second, I raise some empirical questions about recent trends in mobilization that might indicate how social movements have adapted to new contextual challenges. Partial answers to these questions are presented in the four other contributions to this section.

Let us begin by examining the degree to which various forms of "loading away" of authority from the nation-state have actually occurred. In two fields in which I have actively researched over the last decade, original claims of "denationalization" have turned out to be premature and exaggerated. In the field of immigration, 1990s theories of "postnational" rights and "transnational communities" (e.g., Soysal 1994; Sassen 1996) saw the nation-state no longer as a very relevant point of reference for claim making on immigration and cultural diversity, which were said to thrive on global human rights discourses, transnational linkages of immigrants, and support for immigrant rights against restrictive nation-states by supposedly more inclusive supranational spheres of governance such as the EU. In a five-country comparative study (Koopmans et al. 2005), we found, however, only limited references in claim making, whether by migrants or by other actors, to supranational institutions or treaties or, transnationally, to other countries. Instead, we found that immigrant claim making, but also mobilization by right-wing anti-immigrant groups and by left-wing antiracist movements, strongly diverged across countries and reflected national institutional and discursive opportunity structures. More recently, this national orientation of immigration and immigrant integration politics only seems to have become stronger, with a renewed emphasis on national citizenship, a "return of assimilation," and a stagnation of once ambitious plans to turn immigration politics into a full-fledged supranational EU policy field.

More generally, the 1990s were a decade of widespread wishful thinking, among both European academics and the political elite, about a postnational EU polity that would soon make the nation-state a unit of implementation of decisions taken in supranational spheres—which were usually seen as a benign and friendly environment for nongovernmental organizations (NGOs), social movements, and civil society groups more generally, compared to a restrictive and repressive nation-state (e.g., Keck and Sikkink 1998; Hix and Goetz 2000).

Although one should not commit the opposite error of declaring the European integration process dead after the lost referenda on the European constitutional treaty, it has become clear that even within the EU, the nation-state remains the most important arena for political contention in most issue fields, including many that are at the core of the concerns of social movements such as redistributive issues, education, and immigration. In a study on political contention in six issue fields during the period 1990–2002 in seven European countries, we found that 91 percent of claims on education issues, 88 percent of claims on pensions and retirement, and 63 percent of claims on immigration had a purely national frame of reference, meaning that actors, addressees, and the framing of the issue remained confined to the context of the country of the reporting newspaper (Koopmans and Statham 2010, 77). In three other issue fields, we found high rates of denationalization of claim making: 51 percent of claims on military interventions, 59 percent of claims on agriculture and food safety, and as much as 83 percent of claims on monetary politics made at least some reference to actors in other countries, to supranational institutions, or to international norms and conventions.

All in all, though we can certainly discern denationalization trends in some issue fields, particularly and significantly those related to common-market making—monetary politics and agriculture—they are much more limited in others. Theories of post-, trans-, and other varieties of beyond-nationalism that were popular during the 1990s have grossly extrapolated the short-lived trend of global coziness that characterized the immediate aftermath of the collapse of world communism and the end of the Cold War. Contrary to Fukuyama's (1992) claim, history has not ended, and nation-states continue to be core actors in its making.

The supposed downloading of decision-making power to the local level has been a recurrent theme in political science already since the 1970s, but as far as I can see, the empirical evidence for this trend is not overwhelming. Certainly in some countries and some issue fields, decentralization has occurred, but it is also not difficult to think of contrary examples. At least for the two countries I know best—Germany and the Netherlands—I see no strong or consistent trend of empowerment of local and regional authorities compared to national governments. And in the issue field I know best—immigration—local differences within countries continue to be dwarfed by cross-national differences (Koopmans 2004).

There is stronger evidence for the two other types of transfer of authority as Banaszak, Beckwith, and Rucht (2003) sketched, and it is here that the emergence of multilevel systems of decision making, such as those in the EU, has its greatest impact. In many Western democracies, there is a growing dominance of the executive over parties and legislatives. Political parties' role as channels of mass participation in politics has dwindled continuously since the 1950s, with dramatic reductions in membership and the disappearance of previously important channels of mass mobilization such as youth and cultural party organizations and party newspapers. Recently rising populist parties often do not even bother any longer to mobilize a membership base and instead rely exclusively on the mobilization of mass media attention and a strong personalization around media-savvy leaders. The most important impact of the supranationalization of political governance has also been a strong strengthening of the hands of national executives. Transnational politics—including the lion's share of EU politics—mostly consists of negotiated settlements among national executives, who can strike deals with their counterparts in other countries in mostly nonpublic negotiations, relatively shielded from the scrutiny of national parliaments.

This can be illustrated with findings from the earlier cited study on political contention in seven European countries. Figure 15.1 shows the shares of different types of actors in claim making. It compares those claims that are Europeanized, in the sense that they involve European-level actors, addressees, or issue frames, to those claims that remain entirely within a domestic context. This comparison shows us how the Europeanization of issue fields affects the relative discursive influences of various actors. Figure 15.1 first illustrates the shift of influence from the legislative and political parties to the executive branches of—national and European—governance. Whereas among the domestic claims, executive actors outnumber legislative and party actors by a factor of about two to one, among the Europeanized claims, the executive appears four times as frequently as a claimant as legislatives and parties. More dramatic still is the erosion of the influence of civil society actors.

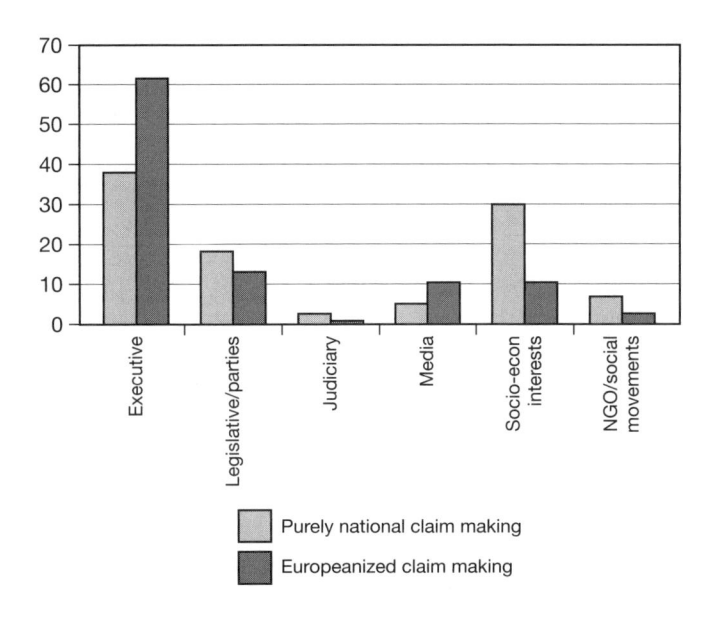

Figure 15.1. Share of different types of collective actors in claim making with a national or European frame of references across seven European countries, 1990–2002.

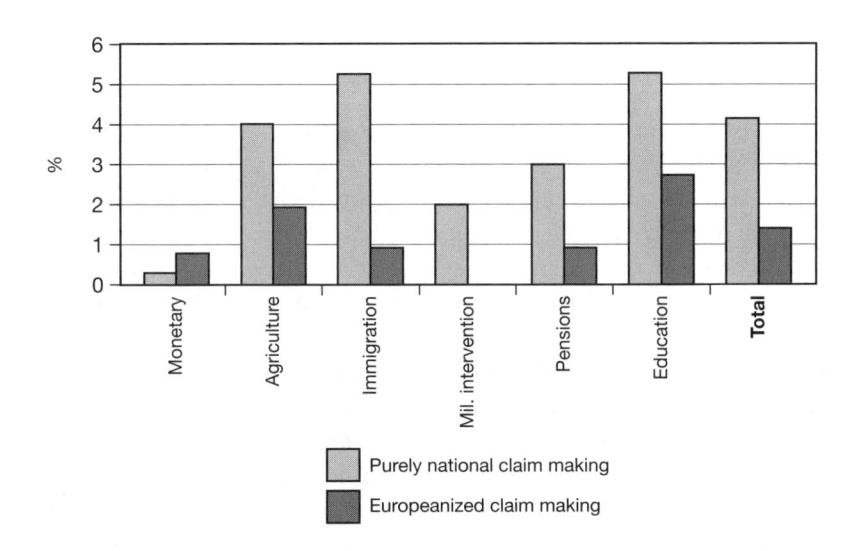

Figure 15.2. Share of protest in claim making by issue field and national or European frame of references across seven European countries, 1990–2002.

Socioeconomic interest groups such as employers, labor unions, consumers, farmers, and other professional groups command a respectable share of 29 percent of domestic claims but are responsible for only 11 percent of the Europeanized claims. NGOs and social movement groups, such as environmental and peace organizations, women's groups, and immigrant associations, are already quite marginal on the domestic level, with 7 percent of claims, but this share is further reduced to less than 3 percent among the Europeanized claims.

This trend is corroborated if we consider protest as a form of contention. Figure 15.2 compares the share of protests among all claims in domestic and Europeanized claim making in six issue fields. In all issue fields, protest is a relatively infrequent form of domestic claim making in immigration and education politics, accounting at most for about 5 percent of claims. In Europeanized contention, protest is, however, much less frequent still, accounting overall for only 1.4 percent of Europeanized claims, compared to 4 percent across all domestic claims. In sum, Europeanization goes along with a strongly reduced salience of both NGOs and social movement organizations as actors and of protest as a form of contention.

In part, these negative effects on social movement influence are related to the correlation of political supranationalization, with the fourth trend distinguished by Banaszak, Beckwith, and Rucht (2003): the offloading of responsibility from the state to other societal actors, most importantly, as della Porta emphasizes in her contribution, to market actors. Supranational cooperation and coordination consist mostly of so-called negative integration, that is, the eradication of national trade barriers and other forms of national regulation, which are only to a limited extent replaced by new forms of binding regulation on the supranational level. This may sometimes have good efficiency reasons, but in replacing national state regulation by transnational markets and diffuse forms of accountability, the opportunities for social movement intervention are tendentially undermined.

Summing up, the major challenge to social movements is not so much the declining relevance of the nation-state as the weakening of the institutions of representative democracy—parties and parliaments—and the more general decline in the role of political authorities compared to market forces, not just nationally but also globally and locally. This deparliamentarization of politics and the shift from state to market regulation cannot leave social movements and protest politics unaffected and might require fundamental adaptations in their repertoires or may even make the social movement as we know it historically redundant, just as it seems to be eroding the influence and mobilizing power of the political party and the labor union. Della Porta, in her chapter, asks us to rethink our conception of democracy, that is, the minimalist conception of democracy with its emphasis on representative power and majority voting, in favor of associative and deliberative forms of democracy. But if Tilly is correct that the social movement has arisen precisely thanks to the emergence of this "minimalist" form of democracy, her call might lead us and social movements to devalue precisely those democratic institutions to which social movements historically owe their diffusion and influence. Representative and accountable parliaments give social movements leverage and power because they put them in a position to affect public opinion and the outcomes of elections. Absent that, where should the power of social movements come from? I am skeptical that in deliberative democracy, good arguments alone are going to do the trick.

This brings me to a set of empirical questions, which I pose rather than answer. How have social movements and protest politics evolved in Europe and North America since the early 1990s? In the contributions to part IV, we find several, sometimes contradictory answers. McCarthy, Rafail, and Gromis see national-level demobilization but local-level mobilization. Mayer discerns a long-term trend of pacification and institutionalization of social movements as well as new forms of "post-it" activism: in ad hoc specialized structures on punctual issues, in sharp contrast to the old communist model of activism, global, long lasting, and with a political perspective. Della Porta, in her chapter, describes similar trends. But contrary to these more negative assessments, Rucht (2007) titled his contribution to the recent *Oxford Handbook of Political Behavior* "The Spread of Protest Politics" and claims that levels of protest have increased over the last decades and have spread out across countries and social categories.

The structural changes discussed in this essay would lead me to expect declining levels of social movement mobilization, as movements face the difficult process of adapting to a political environment in which their historic addressees—parliaments, parties, and regulatory welfare states—have lost much of their former relevance. With Mayer and della Porta, I also see a growing routinization of protest, and McCarthy, Rafail, and Gromis are likely correct that—partly, of course, as a result of the routinization and attendant increased predictability of their movement opponents—police and other control agencies have become more effective in taming and channeling protest.

We currently lack longitudinal data that would allow us to answer these empirical questions with sufficient accuracy. The Kriesi and colleagues (1995) data showed increases of mobilization levels from the 1960s through the end of the 1980s in three of the four countries—Germany, the Netherlands, and Switzerland—and fluctuation without a clear trend in France. Rucht's (2001) Prodat data show that the increase in Germany lasted at least into the mid-1990s, but there the data stop.

Theoretically, it is, of course, possible that both Mayer and della Porta, on one hand, and Rucht, on the other, are right. Rucht may be right that, by and large, levels of protest have further increased or at least not declined in most countries, but protest may at the same time have become so much part and parcel of the normal state of affairs that no one—mass media, politician, or citizen—is bothered with it anymore. When protests, even large ones, provoke no more than a shrug of shoulders, we may have identified another reason why the repertoire of tactics associated with the social movement has entered a period of crisis. In 2010, Berlin experienced the twenty-third repetition of the Kreuzberg May Day riots. I, and most Berliners with me, have long stopped being interested: the same routine every year—why should any one care?

One of the lasting impressions that Sidney Tarrow's (1989) *Democracy and Disorder* made on me as a PhD student was in his analogy, drawn from an Italo Calvino novel, in which a baron goes to live up in a tree and, by doing something so out of the ordinary, brings his family's routines into complete disarray. If disruption of routines through the creation of such "moments of madness" is indeed at the core of what makes social movements distinctive and influential—as has also been forcefully argued by Piven and Cloward (1977)—then social movements may currently phase an existential problem, despite perhaps continuing high protest frequencies. This leads to a final empirical question: do we see signs of a newly emerging repertoire of protest that not only has the potential to deal with shifted political configurations, as outlined earlier, but can also again provoke the kind of disruptive disarray among authorities, media, and publics that Calvino's baron caused among his family?

Note

1. The framing in terms of Banaszak, Beckwith, and Rucht's (2003) four transfers of authority I owe to Conny Roggeband's introduction to the symposium "Changing Dynamics of Contention" on the occasion of Bert Klandermans's retirement.

References

Banaszak, Lee Ann, Karen Beckwith, and Dieter Rucht. 2003. *Women's Movements Facing the Reconfigured State.* Cambridge: Cambridge University Press.
Fukuyama, Francis. 1992. *The End of History and the Last Man.* New York: Avon.
Hix, Simon, and Klaus H. Goetz. 2000. "Introduction: European Integration and National Political Systems." *West European Politics* 23:1–26.

Keck, Margaret E., and Kathryn Sikkink. 1998. *Activists beyond Borders: Advocacy Networks in International Politics.* Ithaca, N.Y.: Cornell University Press.

Koopmans, Ruud. 2004. "Migrant Mobilisation and Political Opportunities: Variation among German Cities and a Comparison with the United Kingdom and the Netherlands." *Journal of Ethnic and Migration Studies* 30:449–70.

Koopmans, Ruud, and Paul Statham, eds. 2010. *The Making of a European Public Sphere: Media Discourse and Political Contention.* Cambridge: Cambridge University Press.

Koopmans, Ruud, Paul Statham, Marco Giugni, and Florence Passy. 2005. *Contested Citizenship: Immigration and Cultural Diversity in Europe.* Minneapolis: University of Minnesota Press.

Kriesi, Hanspeter, Ruud Koopmans, Jan Willem Duyvendak, and Marco Giugni. 1995. *New Social Movements in Western Europe: A Comparative Analysis.* Minneapolis: University of Minnesota Press.

Piven, Frances Fox, and Richard Cloward. 1977. *Poor People's Movements: How They Succeed, Why They Fail.* New York: Free Press.

Rucht, Dieter. 2001. *Protest in der Bundesrepublik Deutschland: Strukturen und Entwicklungen.* Frankfurt, Germany: Campus.

———. 2007. "The Spread of Protest Politics." In *The Oxford Handbook of Political Behavior,* edited by Russell J. Dalton and Hans-Dieter Klingemann, 708–23. Oxford: Oxford University Press.

Sassen, Saskia. 1996. *Losing Control? Sovereignty in an Age of Globalization.* New York: Columbia University Press.

Soysal, Yasemin. 1994. *Limits of Citizenship: Migrants and Postnational Membership in Europe.* Chicago: University of Chicago Press.

Tarrow, Sidney. 1989. *Democracy and Disorder: Protest and Politics in Italy, 1965–1975.* Oxford: Clarendon Press.

Tilly, Charles. 1995. *Popular Contention in Great Britain, 1758–1834.* Cambridge, Mass.: Harvard University Press.

———. 2004. *Social Movements, 1768–2004.* Boulder, Colo.: Paradigm.

16

Social Movements and Elections: Toward a Broader Understanding of the Political Context of Contention

Doug McAdam and Sidney Tarrow

The study of politics has long been marked by a stark disciplinary divide. Forty years ago, the study of formal political institutions was seen as the proper province of political science, while research on social movements was left to psychologists or "social psychologists whose intellectual tools prepare him to better understand the irrational" (Gamson 1990, 133). All that changed with the turbulence of the 1960s. A new generation of scholars who were either involved in or sympathetic to the progressive movements of the period rejected collective behavior theory in favor of newer perspectives on movements that emphasized their political and organizational dimensions. The most explicitly political of these theories was the *political process* model in sociology (McAdam [1982] 1999; Tilly 1978) and the parallel study of protest in political science (Lipsky 1968; Piven and Cloward 1977; Tarrow 1983).

But the key figure whose work linked institutional and movement politics from the beginning was Charles Tilly. From his revised PhD thesis, *The Vendée* (Tilly 1964) to his major works on Britain (Tilly 1995) and France (Tilly 1986) to the culmination of his career in *Contentious Performances* (Tilly 2008), Tilly rejected the division of narrow academic specialties for a much broader concept he called *contentious politics*. In his last book, Tilly blended the narrative and statistical approaches he had used in earlier work and showed how he approached collective action, where he put the emphasis, and how he thought we should proceed to produce good research.

Central to his perspective was the claim that social movements and systems of institutional politics are mutually constitutive; that to understand the ebb and flow of movements, they need to be seen, at least in part, as a product of changes in systems of institutionalized politics; and that the reverse is true as well: changes in institutionalized politics often bear the imprint of movements, a point that—together with Tilly—we argued elsewhere (McAdam, Tarrow, and Tilly 2001) and that he extended in his *Regimes and Repertoires* (Tilly 2006).

Tilly has not been alone in rejecting the insulation of social movements from contentious politics in general. Europeans like Hanspeter Kriesi, writing with his students (Kriesi et al. 1995) and on his own (Kriesi 2004), have argued that the boundaries between transgressive and contained forms of popular mobilization are fluid and permeable. But as influential as Kriesi's work has been, it does not go as far as we would like to go. In most of the work that centers on social movements, the emphasis has been on *those who mobilize*. In short, the field has become decidedly movement-centric in its focus.

Viewing elections and movements as mutually constitutive forms of politics, we seek, in this chapter, to (1) demonstrate anew the analytic value of the dynamic, interactive perspective on politics that Tilly pioneered, while (2) going beyond Tilly to propose a new framework for analyzing *electoral contention*. We begin by briefly offering evidence of the sharp disciplinary division of labor that characterizes the study of social movements, on one hand, and elections, on the other. We then describe four ways in which social movements and elections may be linked and conclude by using a single extended example—political contention over race in the United States—to illustrate our perspective on electoral contention.

Movements without Elections/Elections without Movements

With some exceptions, largely centering in Western Europe (Kitschelt 1986; Koopmans 1995; della Porta 1995; Kriesi et al. 1995; Kriesi 2004; Hutter and Kriesi, chapter 14), we find strikingly little interest among social movement scholars in the connections between movements and electoral politics. The index to *The Blackwell Companion to Social Movements,* arguably the definitive contemporary resource on the subject, includes exactly two page listings for "elections." By contrast "religion" has twenty-one listings, "emotion" boasts thirty-two, and even "communism" has fifteen (Snow, Soule, and Kriesi 2004, 717–54). The most centrally political essay in the book, Hanspeter Kriesi's chapter on "political context and opportunity," mentions electoral systems only once (Kriesi 2004, 71).

To be fair, elections figure centrally in a number of empirical accounts of *specific* movements or episodes of contention. This is especially true of work on democratization. So, for example, in his work on both the collapse of the former Soviet Union (Beissinger 2002) and the so-called color revolutions of 2000–5 (Beissinger 2007), Mark Beissinger depicts elections and democratic opposition movements as inextricably linked. Nor are these the only instances in which we find a close connection between elections and movement mobilization during episodes of democratization. Elections figure prominently in analyses of any number of other cases, including the former Czechoslovakia in 1989 (Glenn 2001), Spain in 1976 (Pérez Díaz 1993), and the Philippines in 1986 (McAdam, Tarrow, and Tilly 2001; Boudreau 2002). The unrest in Iran following the disputed 2009 presidential election is only the most recent example of what has become a very common phenomenon.

But if the empirical literature on movements is replete with cases that bear the unmistakable causal imprint of elections and/or electoral politics, social movement scholars have been slow to recognize the general theoretical significance of elections qua elections in their work on movement dynamics. Few scholars have explicitly identified elections per se as a source of significant political opportunity (or threat) for movement groups (e.g., see Imig 1998; Boudreau 2002; Van Dyke 2003; Bunce and Wolchik 2006, 2010, 2011). Perhaps more tellingly, the initial formulations of the political process perspective fail to make any mention of elections as an important catalyst of movement activity (Tilly 1978; McAdam [1982] 1999; Tarrow 1983). This is an omission that needs to be remedied.

If elections are generally absent from the study of social movements, the converse is true as well. Few analysts of elections touch on the presence or absence of movements—or even interest groups—in elections. The index of the *Oxford Handbook of Comparative Politics* has subject headings for elections and electoral systems, but in neither of these headings do we find cross-references to social movements (Boix and Stokes 2008, 979–80). Not even the essay on "Voters and Parties" in that compendium has a reference to social movements (Wren and McElwain 2008, 555–81). The index of *A New Handbook of Political Science* shows a similar absence of cross-reference between elections and social movements (Goodin and Klingemann 1996, 808). Of the electoral scholars represented in that volume, only Russell Dalton mentions social movements (Dalton 1996, 336–71; also see Dalton 2005). Two other general reference volumes on politics, the *Handbook of Political Sociology,* edited by Janoski et al. (2005), and Leicht and Jenkins's (2010) *Handbook of Politics,* do a somewhat better job of acknowledging the link between movements and elections—each features at least one chapter that touches on the topic—but these exceptions only serve to highlight the general neglect of the topic. Despite mounting empirical evidence of connection, movements and elections remain largely separate areas of inquiry in sociology and political science, respectively.

Why such an absence of attention to social movements in electoral studies?

First, to reiterate a point made earlier, the focus of political science has always been squarely centered on political institutions and institutional politics, and this is no less true for the new as for the old institutionalism. Second, since the 1960s, students of elections have moved away from the close examination of the social networks in which electoral decisions are made and turned in depth to the cognitive dimensions of electoral choice (Pappi, Huckfeldt, and Ikeda 1998). Both developments dovetail with the growing influence of methodological individualism within political science, which leaves little room for the emphasis on collective dynamics and network-based influence processes in social movement theory.

Reciprocal Links between Movements and Elections

Thus far, we have documented a general reciprocal indifference among social movement scholars and those who study elections. Given the many consequential ways in which movements and elections influence each other, we find this remarkable. Although scholars tend to associate movements with noninstitutional forms of politics, the reality is quite at odds with this generalization. Although it is true that movements often employ nonroutine forms of action, the vast majority of movements in democratic societies rely more on institutionalized than on noninstitutionalized tactics, for example, devoting enormous effort to educational and propaganda activities, organizational work, elections, and lobbying. Think back to the example we examine in detail later: the American civil rights movement. It is generally remembered for the nonviolent street politics of the 1960s, but its modern origins can be found in the electoral and judicial politics of the previous decade (McAdam [1982] 1999).

In this section, we offer a systematic framework for analyzing what might be termed *electoral contention*. By electoral contention, we mean that set of recurring links between elections and movements that powerfully shapes movement dynamics and electoral outcomes. We distinguish five such processes: elections as a movement tactic, proactive and reactive electoral mobilization by movement groups, the longer-term impact of changes in electoral regimes on patterns of movement mobilization and demobilization, and what we have termed *movement-induced party polarization*.

Movement Tactics: Taking the Electoral Option

As previously noted, movements have come to be seen as synonymous with noninstitutionalized—and often disruptive—forms of action. In this view, movements are a noninstitutionalized alternative to elections and other forms of institutional politics. But the tactics and strategies employed by movement groups frequently include the "electoral option." At the extreme, we can even speak of *movement regimes,* that is, movements that came to power via elections. Of course, Nazi Germany and fascist Italy are not examples that movement scholars care to remember, yet each came to power through electoral and parliamentary means (Linz and Stepan 1978). Depending on how narrow or broad one's definition of a movement is, contemporary examples of democratically elected "movement states" would include the governments of South Korea, Taiwan, Iran, South Africa, Venezuela, and Bolivia, among others.

Short of full-blown movement states, political parties rooted in movements can exert considerable influence over domestic politics. This is especially true in political systems based on proportional representation. That is, in multiparty systems where no single party holds a majority of legislative seats, even small parties can wield considerable power as potential partners in a coalition government. In such a system, the electoral option can be very attractive for movement groups. The greens came to political prominence in Germany—and, by extension, in Europe—in exactly this way.

At first blush, the American winner-take-all system would not seem to be especially conducive to electoral mobilization by movement groups. However, at the same time, there has been no shortage of third-party movements in U.S. history, many of which have either played the role of spoilers in presidential elections (e.g., Ralph Nader's candidacy denied Al Gore the White House in 2000) or dramatically reshaped the contours and logic of electoral politics through what Burnham (1970) long ago termed *critical elections.* George Wallace's surprising showing in the 1968 presidential contest helped to make it an especially pivotal election, effectively ending thirty-six years of liberal democratic dominance and ushering in the extended period of Republican dominance that only came to an end with Obama's election in 2008. Still, movements in the United States have more opportunity to influence electoral outcomes below the national level. The U.S. system is so decentralized that it presents activists with far more electoral opportunities than might, at first, be apparent. In particular, movement groups can be expected to contest elections in which, by virtue of low voter turnout, a mobilized movement minority can exercise disproportionate influence.

Two specific categories of elections come to mind in this regard. The first category comprises primary, as opposed to general, elections. The second comprises electoral contests that are typically decided by small percentages of all eligible voters. These would include school board, city council, and other local elections. For many movements, these lesser offices are perfectly suited to their substantive goals. So, for instance, Binder (2002) highlights the successful use of local school board elections by creationist groups intent on reshaping science education in school.

Nor does seeking office exhaust the electoral options open to movement groups. Indeed, in the contemporary United States, activists probably rely as much on propositions, referenda, or other ballot measures to press their claims as they do on recruiting or actively backing candidates for office. So, for example, the countermovement against same-sex marriage has relied heavily on ballot propositions to overturn or preempt statutes legalizing such unions.

Proactive Electoral Mobilization

Proactive electoral mobilization occurs when movement groups become more active in the context of an electoral campaign. This is one of two general processes that Blee and Currier (2006) document in their innovative ethnographic study of the behavior of social movement groups (SMGs) in Pittsburgh in the run-up to the 2004 presidential election. Those SMGs who saw in the election either a "threat" to, or an "opportunity" to advance, group interests increased their activity levels. Conversely, those SMGs that perceived the election as largely irrelevant to their identity and mission as progressive grassroots groups remained inactive during the campaign. Sarah Sobieraj's (2011) study of the efforts of activists to use the 2000 Republican Convention to communicate their message to a broader audience affords another fascinating example of proactive mobilization in action.

Without a doubt, however, the best example of this particular electoral mechanism is the contemporary Tea Party movement in the United States. Backed by influential television and radio personalities as well as high-profile politicians (e.g., Sarah Palin), the movement was largely responsible for the stunning losses suffered by the Democratic Party in the 2010 midterm elections, nor does the movement show any signs of waning even after the Republican loss in the 2012 presidential election. Indeed, the movement may yet spawn its own third-party candidate in the election, opting to move from proactive electoral mobilization back to the more formal electoral option. The more recent Occupy movement was decidedly anti-institutional politics, yet its dramatic eruption on the urban and campus scenes in 2011 helped to move the centrist Democratic administration of Barack Obama toward a more populist line in the presidential campaign of 2012.

Reactive Electoral Mobilization

Reactive electoral mobilization involves escalating protest in the wake of a disputed election. Although not unknown in democracies—consider only the rash of protests in Florida in 2000 in the wake of the disputed election results in the presidential contest between Bush and Gore—this process, as we have seen, is far more common in nondemocratic countries, where voter intimidation and electoral fraud are more widespread. Indeed, disputed elections have become one of the most common catalysts of protest movements in nondemocratic states. It was massive protests in the wake of a disputed election in Serbia that finally proved Milošević's undoing in Serbia in 2000. In 2008, Zimbabwe was plunged into another short-term episode of violent contention when longtime dictator Robert Mugabe was accused of blocking the legitimate ascension to power of the opposition candidate.

We described three other instances of reactive mobilization earlier: the general strike and street protests that drove Marcos out of office in the Philippines in February 1987; the massive demonstrations triggered by the disputed 2009 presidential election in Iran; and the color revolutions that toppled authoritarian regimes in Ukraine, Georgia, and Kyrgyzstan. Indeed, so central were elections to the color revolutions that they came to be seen by opposition leaders as the strategic linchpin in the episodes of contention they hoped to orchestrate (Beissinger 2007). That is, democracy activists timed their efforts to synchronize with regularly scheduled elections. The important suggestion here is that successful reactive mobilization probably depends on at least some level of proactive mobilization.

Electoral Regimes and the Long-Term Fate of Movement Families

All the previous links involve a close temporal coupling of movement activity on either side of a scheduled election. But our fourth causal connection between elections and movement activity unfolds over a much longer time frame: the more gradual processes of mobilization and demobilization set in motion by enduring shifts in electoral fortune. What do we mean by "enduring shifts in electoral fortune"? Consider the history of presidential politics in the twentieth-century United States. We tend to think of the White House as the object of intense competition between the two parties every four years, and certainly the amount of time, energy, money, and verbiage spent on the campaigns reinforces this view. But seen through the prism of historical perspective, things are not as competitive as the popular view would have us believe. All the presidencies of the twentieth century can be grouped into three generally stable electoral regimes:

- 1900–32: Republicans dominate. Only Woodrow Wilson (1900–32) interrupts the string of six Republican presidents.
- 1932–68: Democrats dominate. Of the five presidents to serve during

this period, only one—Dwight Eisenhower (1952–60)—is a Republican.
- 1968–2008: Republicans again dominate, occupying the White House for twenty-eight of the forty years of the period.

What does this have to do with social movement activity? Everything. The onset and solidification of an enduring electoral regime powerfully condition the prospects for successful mobilization by all groups in society. This is true for both substantive and psychological reasons: substantively, those to whom the party in power owe electoral debts can be expected to enjoy more institutional access and responsiveness than opposition groups, encouraging them to mobilize; psychologically, being on the political margins tends to demoralize and eventually encourage demobilization.

Should we be surprised, then, that the period of Democratic dominance in the middle decades of the century was marked by the rise of the labor movement, considerable popular support for socialist and other leftist groups, the rise of the civil rights movement, and later, the full flowering of the New Left protest cycle? And is it a coincidence that the Reagan years saw the rise of the Christian right, the brief effervescence of the militia movement, a strong and sustained pro-life movement, and rising anti-immigration sentiment? This waxing and waning of movement fortunes in connection with electoral alignments is exactly what the political process perspective would predict.[1] Progressive left movements can be expected to flourish during periods of liberal institutional politics, whereas the right should be ascendant when conservatives hold institutional power. Elections as the symbol and vehicle of these institutional transitions shape this longer-term oscillation of popular mobilization.

Movement-Induced Party Polarization

The final link between movements and electoral politics comes via movement influence on the ideological character and unity of political parties. For example, we see an increasing influence of social movements on the American party system over the past forty years, making it far less pragmatic than the system our predecessors described and praised and far more like the ideological systems that they abhorred in Europe. In a related paper (McAdam and Tarrow 2010), and drawing on the work of a number of American colleagues (Woehrle, Coy, and Maney 2009; Heaney and Rojas 2007), we described this dynamic with respect to the influence of the antiwar movement on the American party system in the years following September 11, 2001. In this essay, we illustrate it by calling attention to a recurring dynamic evident in the United States over the past forty years.

The dynamic can be described fairly easily. In the last section, we noted that besides their shorter-term effects on movements, elections encourage longer-term oscillations in mobilization and demobilization by granting institutional access and ideological standing to some movements, while denying it to others. In short, the movement allies of those who have newly come to institutional power can be expected to mobilize to take advantage of this access or standing, while the "losers"—generally after a period or reactive mobilization—get discouraged and gradually demobilize.

At first blush, the reactive mobilization of the movement wing of a victorious party would seem to be wholly positive for those newly in power, and properly managed, the presence of mobilized movement supporters can indeed aid and abet a party in power. But there is an inherent tension between the logics of movement and electoral politics that, at times, has compromised the ability of incumbent parties to retain power. Electoral politics turns on a centrist, coalitional logic. As Downs (1957) argued persuasively more than a century ago, parties in the United States succeed by hewing to the middle and appealing to an imagined median voter. Extreme views and preoccupation with single issues are antithetical, in this view, to electoral success. Movements, conversely, tend toward narrow—sometimes extremist—views and an uncompromising commitment to single issues. The threat here is as obvious as it is ironic. As a party attains power and encourages reactive mobilization by its movement wing, it runs the risk of setting in motion internal party competition corrosive of the centrist stance so key to victory in the first place. Seeing in the party the vehicle for achieving movement aims, activists begin to challenge pragmatic party regulars for control of the organization. Success in this effort, however, has the potential to move the party off center, encouraging wholesale electoral defections by moderate voters who now regard the party as too extreme in its views.

This appears to be what happened in the United States to the Democratic Party in 1972 and to the Republicans twenty years later. In the first case, the so-called McGovern Revolution and its associated procedural reforms allowed the mobilized remnants of the New Left to exercise considerable control over the 1972 Democratic Convention and campaign. The U.S. electorate reacted predictably, reelecting Richard Nixon by one of the most lopsided margins in American presidential history; in the second, the mobilization of the right following Reagan's victory in 1980 initially redounded to the benefit of the Republican Party. By the time of its convention in Houston in 1992, however, the power and influence of the Christian Right and pro-life forces had grown so great within the Republican Party that moderate voters rejected the incumbent, George H. W. Bush, in favor of the more centrist candidacy of Bill Clinton. The tension between the logic of a centrist electoral strategy and the typically more extreme, ideologically inflected views of movement groups is once again on display in the United States courtesy of the Tea Party movement. It will be fascinating to see how the Republican Party seeks to manage these tensions during the 2012 presidential campaign.

Elections, Movements, and the Politics of Racial Contention

To this point, we have treated the literatures on elections and movements separately, documenting their mutual indifference to each other and then arguing for how, in fact, movements shape elections, and vice versa. We now turn to an extended empirical example, designed to better integrate and illustrate the perspective on electoral contention we have sought to develop. The example concerns racial contention in the United States as told through six pivotal moments in the history of the ongoing conflict.

From Abolitionism to the Republican Party: Taking the Electoral Option

In the United States, the Republican Party—the party of Ronald Reagan and George W. Bush—is now thought of as a bastion of political and social conservatism, but it is worth remembering that it was born as one of only two movement regimes in the nation's history. And the movement that gave birth to the party—abolitionism—was among the most radical in U.S. history. Indeed, there were plenty in the antislavery ranks who rejected the *electoral option* as insufficiently radical when the movement's more moderate wing helped to found the party in 1854. At the same time, nearly everyone else—especially southern Democrats—saw the Republicans as a collection of wild-eyed, moral zealots, intent on imposing their values on the rest of the country (Klinkner 1999).

Given this view, we should not be surprised that Abraham Lincoln's election in 1860 triggered the most consequential instance of reactive mobilization in U.S. history. We refer, of course, to the mobilization by Southern secessionists that led to the founding of yet another movement regime in the form of the Confederate States of America. In short, this first moment bears the imprint of two of our four linkages described earlier. The choice of the electoral option by moderate abolitionists led to the creation of a Republican movement regime, which in turn triggered reactive mobilization by Southern secessionists, leading to the founding of a rival movement regime. Could elections and movements—to say nothing of the prospects for racial justice in the United States—have been more closely intertwined than in this example?[2]

The Year 1876 and the End of the Movement Regime

With the end of the Civil War, abolitionist Republicans were in firm control of the federal government and free to impose a radical Reconstruction on the vanquished Confederate states. Federal troops were stationed throughout the South to safeguard the new social, economic, and political rights granted to the former slaves. But Reconstruction and the civil rights that went with it lasted just eleven years. And once again, history pivoted on a critical election—the contested election of 1876 (Klinkner 1999)—bringing to a close the Republican movement regime and putting in place an electoral regime that lasted until the New Deal.

The Year 1932 and the Onset of the New Deal Electoral Regime

If the agreement of 1876 effectively organized race out of federal politics, Franklin Delano Roosevelt's ascension to the White House in 1932 marked the beginning of a process that would gradually restore the issue to national prominence. The consequential changes that followed from FDR's election included the following (Shesol 2009):

- *The transformation of the Democratic Party.* By embracing pro-labor policies and granting labor leaders considerable voice in party as well as policy circles, Roosevelt dramatically expanded the party's northern, liberal labor wing, undercutting the power of the Dixiecrats (e.g., southern segregationist Democrats) in the process.
- *The shift of black voters from the Republican Party to the Democratic Party.* In the United States, African American voters are now thought of as the most loyal of Democrats, but the so-called black vote was once the most reliable component of the Republican coalition. The reason: loyalty to the party of Lincoln and opposition to a southern-dominated Democratic Party. Even in 1932, blacks favored the despised Republican incumbent, Herbert Hoover, over Roosevelt by a wide margin. Roosevelt's New Deal policies changed all of that, with black voters turning overwhelmingly to Roosevelt in 1936. The addition of African Americans to the Democratic column strengthened the northern, liberal labor wing of the party even more, further undermining the power of the Dixiecrats.
- *The realignment of the Supreme Court.* Roosevelt spent much of his first term and part of his second battling a court that rejected key New Deal programs. In the end, however, the president simply outlasted the Court's aging conservatives and transformed the Court by posting liberal jurists to the vacancies.

Consistent with the preceding argument, the specific changes documented here helped both to solidify the New Deal electoral regime and encourage the longer-term mobilization of civil rights forces and demobilization of segregationists. For example, encouraged by the increasing liberalism of the Supreme

Court, the era's leading civil rights organization—the National Association for the Advancement of Colored People (NAACP)—launched its long-term legal campaign to overturn "separate but equal." The period also saw a sharp rise in membership in the NAACP and other civil rights organizations (Anglin 1949; McAdam [1982] 1999, 103–4).

The Year 1948: The Revolt of the Dixiecrats

For all the significance of Roosevelt's years in office, it is important to note that he himself remained fundamentally silent on racial matters throughout his four-term presidency, refusing even to endorse antilynching legislation on the many occasions such bills were brought before Congress. In sharp contrast, almost immediately upon taking office, FDR's successor, Harry Truman, became the first president since Reconstruction to publicly embrace the need for civil rights reform. He did so first in 1946 when he created a national Committee on Civil Rights and charged it with investigating the state of civil rights in the country and recommending "remedies for deficiencies uncovered." Two years later, Truman issued two landmark executive orders, the first establishing a fair employment board within the Civil Service Commission and the second calling for gradual desegregation of the armed forces.

What prompted Truman to act when Roosevelt had not? The key to the mystery lies not in domestic politics but in the new pressures thrust on the United States by the onset of the Cold War. Locked into an intense political–ideological struggle with the Soviet Union for influence around the globe, the United States quickly realized what a significant liability American-style racism was to its critical foreign policy aims. This prompted calls—initially from the diplomatic corps and State Department—for civil rights reforms to counter Soviet efforts to exploit American racism for its obvious propaganda value (McAdam 1999; Dudziak 2000; Layton 2001). In short, the Cold War made federal complicity in the southern system of racial segregation untenable, forcing Truman to act.

Domestic political considerations would appear to have played little or no role in Truman's violation of the long-standing federal hands-off policy with respect to race. Indeed, Truman's status as a nonincumbent made him uniquely vulnerable to challenge as he headed into the 1948 election. Moreover, with black voters now returning solid Democratic majorities, Truman seemingly had little to gain and everything to lose by alienating the segregationist-dominated southern wing of his party. And that, of course, is precisely what his advocacy of civil rights did. Angered by Truman's proactive support for civil rights, segregationists chose the electoral option and ran their own candidate, Strom Thurmond, for president. In the end, Truman confounded the pollsters and survived the Dixiecrat revolt, but his actions had the effect of putting two key components of the Democratic coalition—the civil rights movement and white supremacists—on a collision course with each other, the Democratic Party, and the American state.

The Year 1964: Freedom Summer as an Example of Proactive Mobilization

The heyday of the civil rights movement came in the early 1960s when two liberal Democrats, John F. Kennedy and Lyndon Johnson, occupied the White House. Survey data from the period show that optimism regarding the prospects for significant racial change was higher within the black community than at any time before or since (McAdam [1982] 1999, 161–63). All this fueled a dramatic expansion in black activism, as the ranks of civil rights organizations swelled and rates of collective action jumped sharply (McAdam [1982] 1999).

The perception of Kennedy and Johnson as sympathetic to the movement keyed the central strategic dynamic that fueled the major civil rights campaigns of the period. "Lacking sufficient power to defeat the supremacists in a local confrontation, [civil rights] insurgents sought to broaden the conflict by inducing their opponents to disrupt public order to the point where supportive federal intervention was required" (McAdam [1982] 1999, 174). But as functional as the dynamic was for civil rights forces, it was a strategic nightmare for Democratic presidents, intent as they were on mollifying the Dixiecrats, even as they sought to accommodate the movement. Sensitive to this strategic dilemma, mainstream civil rights leaders agreed to a moratorium on direct action in the run-up to the 1964 presidential election. The goal was to avoid alienating the white South on the eve of the election. But the most radical of the civil rights organizations, the Student Nonviolent Coordinating Committee (SNCC), saw the election as an opportunity to dramatize the continued denial of black voting rights in the South. Rejecting the informal agreement, the SNCC instead engaged in a highly innovative form of proactive electoral mobilization: in the hope of registering black voters in advance of the election, the SNCC brought one thousand primarily white, northern college students to Mississippi in summer 1964.

Very quickly, however, southern white voter registrars made it clear that they were not about to let this happen, prompting the SNCC to change tactics. If Mississippi would not allow blacks to participate in the regular electoral process, the SNCC would create a parallel system. They created the Mississippi Freedom Democratic Party (MFDP), "freedom registered" thousands of black Mississippians, and, as the summer wore on, assembled an MFDP delegation that would go to Atlantic City and challenge the seating of the state's regular, lily-white delegation. For a time, it appeared as if the challenge would succeed. On the eve of the November general election, however, Johnson, determined to avoid antagonizing the southern wing of his party, managed to repel the challenge and offered the seats to the regular Mississippi delegation. Johnson succeeded in staving off the challenge but not the anger and alienation of white southern voters.

In one of the great ironies of American history, perhaps the proudest accomplishment of the civil rights struggle—the restoration of black voting rights in the South—set the stage for the resurrection of the Republican Party and the remarginalization of race as an issue in U.S. politics.

The Year 1968: The South (and the Republicans) Rise Again

In popular narrative accounts of the 1960s in the United States, the 1968 election is typically represented as a referendum on the War in Vietnam. Without denying the salience of the issue, this account is nonetheless misleading. The election, and the dramatic turn it signaled in American politics, was fundamentally about race. Southern white discontent on the issue had grown exponentially since 1964, as waves of newly registered black voters poured into the Democratic Party in the South. As they did, southern whites left the party in droves, gravitating toward newly minted Republican Party organizations. But white discontent over the civil rights issue was not confined to the South. Alarmed by the riots of the late 1960s, the specter of "black power," and imagined threats to their neighborhoods, schools, and jobs, northern whites—especially from the lower middle and working classes—were restive on the issue as well. Running as a Republican in 1968, Richard Nixon sought to exploit this growing white discontent by devising a strategy designed to play on both the country's deepening racial divide and the association of blacks with the Democratic Party. Election statistics reveal just how successful the Republican strategy was.

The negative political consequences of the 1968 election for African Americans were not confined to the substantive policy outcomes that followed from Nixon's ascension to office. As least as damaging was the effect the election had on the political perceptions and evolving strategies of the two major parties. In this, the remarkable success enjoyed by George Wallace's third-party candidacy in 1968 proved decisive. Wallace's candidacy, as we noted earlier, was among the most consequential examples of a movement-based third party challenge in U.S. history. As governor of the southern state of Alabama during the early 1960s, Wallace had become the darling of white supremacists when he literally blocked the entrance to the University of Alabama to deny the court-ordered admission of its first black student. Wallace's presidential candidacy should thus be viewed as a case of the white supremacist countermovement exercising the electoral option.

The impact of Wallace's third-party challenge far exceeded the 14 percent of the overall vote that he garnered in the election. With the two major parties evenly dividing roughly 86 percent of the popular vote, the remaining 14 percent who cast their votes for Wallace clearly emerged as a potential balance of power in future elections. For the Republicans, Nixon's narrow victory suggested that the party's future lay not in the 43 percent of the popular vote he achieved but in the 57 percent he shared with Wallace. Republican strategists believed this total represented a potentially dominant conservative majority that, if successfully tapped, could well ensure the success of the party for years to come.

This prediction proved remarkably prescient. With his resounding win over the liberal Democratic candidate George McGovern in 1972, Nixon was well on his way to solidifying this "white center" coalition before Watergate intervened and muddied the waters for the Republicans in 1976. It took Ronald Reagan's victory in 1980 to seal the deal, set the stage for another twenty-eight years of Republican dominance of the presidency, and effectively organize civil rights forces out of any meaningful role in American politics.

Summary

Throughout this brief narrative, we have tried to highlight the various electoral–movement linkages evident in these six moments. It might be helpful, however, to close with an aggregate summary. A full accounting of the linkages we have specified would include the following:

- *Use of the electoral option by movement (or countermovement) forces in 1860, 1948, and 1968.* Indeed, the success of the Republicans in 1860 led to the constitution of not one but two movement regimes: the Lincoln administration, on one hand, and the Confederate States of America, on the other.
- *Proactive mobilization by movement groups.* This is a feature of most presidential elections, but with respect to race, the process was especially evident in the Dixiecrat (white) Revolt of 1948 and in the (black-led) Freedom Summer campaign of 1964.
- *Two highly consequential instances of reactive mobilization.* The first was the secessionist movement triggered by Lincoln's election in 1860; the second was the historic rejection of the Democratic Party by white southerners in reaction to the MFDP challenge at the 1964 convention.
- *The longer-term impact of shifts in electoral regimes.* Just as the dominance of liberal Democrats between 1932 and 1968 set the stage for the

rise and success of the modern civil rights movement, the collapse of the coalition on which that ascendancy was based ushered in a period of sustained conservatism that encouraged gradual demobilization on the left and increased activism on the right.

- *Finally, several instances of movement-influenced party polarization.* None had longer-term consequences than the instance that took place at the 1964 Democratic National Convention in Atlantic City. The MFDP challenge to the seating of the regular, all-white Mississippi delegation made headlines and roiled the convention that summer, but in the end, as we noted previously, the Democratic candidate, Lyndon Johnson, was able to rebuff the challenge and soundly defeat the Republican challenger in the November election. But the memories of Atlantic City lived on, as did the divisions within the party opened up by the convention challenge. These divisions were fully evident four years later, when virtually the entire white South abandoned the Democratic standard-bearer, Hubert Humphrey, for either Richard Nixon or third-party candidate George Wallace. The period of Democratic dominance in presidential politics—and the access and opportunities it afforded civil rights forces—was at an end.

Conclusions

Using only one sector of movement activity, racial contention, in only one country, the United States, we have illustrated a variety of ways in which social movements and elections interact. It would take an entire book—perhaps a library of books—to demonstrate the same connections for other American movements or across the globe. Our goals have been more modest. First, we tried to highlight the persistent disciplinary divide within the United States that relegates the study of movements to sociology and elections to political science. Second, we sought to demonstrate how critically a full understanding of racial contention in the United States depends on a more integrated perspective that focuses on the reciprocal relationship between movements and elections.

Of course, the use of a single case to illustrate a conceptual framework, however extended, raises the "*N* of 1" problem. Is the single case representative of some broader population of cases to which the framework could be applied? And do we see this same kind of tight, reciprocal connection between movements, parties, and elections (1) over time in the United States and (2) within other political systems, most notably the countries of contemporary Europe? A full answer to these questions is, of course, well beyond the scope of this chapter. In the hope of stimulating ongoing conversation, however, we close with some brief thoughts on the two issues.

1. *The coupling of movements and elections in the United States.* If anything, we see movements, parties, and elections as more tightly coupled in the United States now than they were during the periods we dealt with in most of this chapter. During the middle decades of the twentieth century, the two major American parties were substantial organizations that functioned as the main vehicles by which individuals were socialized into American politics. Large segments of the voting public identified with these two parties and felt a strong allegiance to their candidates and substantive platforms. Internally, the parties were ideologically heterogeneous, and their links with major voting and interest groups were loose and shifting, but they had strong local and state-level organizations for candidate selection and for getting out the vote.

But these factors have undergone profound changes. First, the proportion of the U.S. public who feel a close identification with one or the other major party today has declined dramatically. Second, the parties have lost the local linkages to their base that they had during their classical period. This has often been seen to produce apathy and privatization, but as the parties have atrophied, movement and other single-issue groups have mushroomed. We would argue that movements are now the central socializing force in U.S. politics; that is, the majority of Americans who are politically involved tend to hew to a polarized ideological conception of politics rather than the kind of centrist, electoral politics characteristic of earlier periods. In both Obama's 2008 electoral victory and the contemporary Tea Party movement, we see the clear imprint of the perspective sketched earlier.

2. *The decoupling of movements and elections in Europe.* What happens when we seek to apply our general perspective elsewhere? For instance, how would it apply to contemporary European politics? Our provisional answer is that it does. For while the mainstream political parties have declined in both the United States and in most European countries, they have done so for different reasons and with very different affects. In the United States, the rise of a divisive, partisan movement politics following the 1960s has undermined the appeal of the traditionally more centrist, pragmatic parties, strengthening the former and weakening the latter. Movement groups have sought to exploit popular disillusionment with the parties by taking over many political functions once reserved for the parties: designating candidates for office, orchestrating electoral campaigns, targeting incumbents for removal from office, and so on. The recent episode of the Tea Party movement is but the latest manifestation of this dynamic.

The situation in Europe seems to us to be very different. Traditional parties have declined, not so much because of growing popular support for movements as because of changes in the parties' organizational models and institutional trends in policy making both at the national and European Union levels. With respect to the first set of changes, the late Peter Mair's (1997) work on party system change does a far better job than we could do in laying out the lineaments of a party system that has left behind both the class-mass parties of the interwar period and the catch-all parties of the 1950s and 1960s. Mair has shown that European parties are now best understood as cadres of professional politicians loosely linked to a base that is both ambiguous and shifting. In his recent work with Petr Kopecký, Mair investigated the extent to which European parties engage in more or less systematic patronage practices.[3] To us, this sounds very much like the traditional American party system that we think has declined in the United States.

Of course, the professionalization and decoupling of parties from their traditional base have had reactive effects: on the left, an extraparliamentary global justice movement has developed in implicit criticism of the old center-left parties (della Porta 2005); on the right, populist movements have sprung up all over Europe (Meny and Surel 2002). We see these trends as part of what we earlier called a process of reactive mobilization. It can be traced not only to the professionalization of the traditional parties but to the evolution of the European community and to changes in administrative politics at the national level. This has produced both the transfer, or uploading, of decisions over some policy issues to Brussels and Luxembourg and the insulation of major policy areas from party competition.

Comparative scholars have observed both a "lateral loading" (Banaszak, Beckwith, and Rucht 2003) of policy discretion to a number of independent commissions and new forms of regulation (Hayward and Menon 2003; Kriesi et al. 2008). In combination, these trends have had the effect of hollowing out the domestic political sphere and reducing the overall influence and salience of national parties, unions, and other traditional political actors, leaving space for nonparty and semiparty movements on the extremes.

What of the so-called Arab Spring, which, at this writing, has stretched into a hot summer and a possibly very long winter of discontent? Here the surprises were great but dovetail with the perspective taken in this chapter. First, apparently out of nowhere, movements for liberation from the heavy hand of authoritarian regimes sprang up in sequence all over the region using the new tools of movement mobilization recently seen in the North; second, these movements induced several regimes to reform their policies and others to organize elections, which forced these movements to engage in electoral competition; third, in both Tunisia and Egypt, it was not the movements of

2011 that profited from these elections but older, long-suppressed Islamic movements that were better positioned to turn themselves into electorally oriented parties. It is too soon to tell whether this process of movement mobilization will lead to greater or lesser polarization.

These concluding remarks obviously simplify much more complex dynamics in both the United States and Europe, to say nothing of the rest of the world. We offer them in the same spirit of open dialogue and exchange that has characterized the sustained and productive conversation between European and U.S. social movement scholars for the past quarter century. It is only fitting that this chapter appear in a volume in honor of one of the principal architects of that transatlantic conversation. In the searching, critical spirit that has informed all of Bert Klandermans's work, we invite scholars, in their own countries, to systematically examine the dynamic relationship between movements, parties, and elections. Let the conversation continue.

Notes

We would like to thank Craig Jenkins and the editors of this volume for their extremely useful comments and suggestions on an earlier version of the chapter.

1. There are, of course, exceptions to these general trends. McCarthyism occurred during the period of liberal Democratic dominance, and as Gould (2009) notes, ACT-UP flourished at the height of the Reagan years. European scholars have generally found an inverse relationship between the election of left-leaning governments and the fate of progressive movements. See, for example, Kriesi et al. (1995).

2. We have given more sustained attention to the movement–electoral intersection of the coming of the Civil War in McAdam, Tarrow, and Tilly (2001, chapter 6).

3. Go to http://www.eui.eu/DepartmentsAndCentres/PoliticalAndSocialSciences/People/Professors/Profiles/PeterMair.aspx for a summary of this recent research.

References

Anglin, Robert A. 1949. "A Sociological Analysis of a Pressure Group." PhD diss., University of Indiana.

Banaszak, Lee Ann, Karen Beckwith, and Dieter Rucht. 2003. *Women's Movements Facing the Reconfigured State.* Cambridge: Cambridge University Press.

Beissinger, Mark R. 2002. *Nationalist Mobilization and the Collapse of the Soviet State.* Cambridge: Cambridge University Press.

———. 2007. "Structure and Example in Modular Political Phenomena: The Diffusion of Bulldozer/Rose/Orange/Tulip Revolutions." Unpublished manuscript.

Binder, Amy. 2002. *Contentious Curricula*. Princeton, N.J.: Princeton University Press.
Blee, Kathleen M., and Ashley Currier. 2006. "How Local Social Movement Groups Handle a Presidential Election." *Qualitative Sociology* 29:261–80.
Boix, Carles, and Susan Stokes, eds. 2008. *Oxford Handbook of Comparative Politics*. Oxford: Oxford University Press.
Boudreau, Vincent. 2002. "State Repression and Democracy Protest in Three Southeast Asian Countries." In *Social Movements: Identity, Culture, and the State*, edited by David Meyer, Nancy Whittier, and Belinda Robnett, 28–46. New York: Oxford University Press.
Bunce, Valerie, and Sharon Wolchik. 2006. "Diffusion and Postcommunist Electoral Revolutions." *Communist and Postcommunist Studies* 39:283–304.
———. 2010. "Transnational Networks, Diffusion Dynamics, and Electoral Change in the Postcommunist World." In *The Diffusion of Social Movements*, edited by R. Givens, K. Roberts, and S. Soule, 140–62. New York: Cambridge University Press.
———. 2011. *Defeating Authoritarian Leaders in Mixed Regimes: Electoral Struggles, U.S. Democracy Assistance, and International Diffusion in Post-communist Europe and Eurasia*. New York: Cambridge University Press.
Burnham, Walter Dean. 1970. *Critical Elections and the Mainsprings of American Politics*. New York: W. W. Norton.
Dalton, Russell J. 1996. "Comparative Politics: Micro-behavioral Perspectives." In *A New Handbook of Political Science*, edited by Robert E. Goodin and Hans-Dieter Klingemann, 336–52. Oxford: Oxford University Press.
———. 2005. *Citizen Politics: Public Opinion and Political Parties in Advanced Industrial Democracies*. 4th ed. Washington, D.C.: Congressional Quarterly Press.
della Porta, Donatella. 1995. *Social Movements, Political Violence, and the State: A Comparative Analysis of Italy and Germany*. Cambridge: Cambridge University Press.
———. 2005. "Making the Polis: Social Forums and Democracy in the Global Justice Movement." *Mobilization* 10, no. 1: 73–94.
Downs, Anthony. 1957. *An Economic Theory of Democracy*. New York: Harper and Row.
Dudziak, Mary L. 2000. *Cold War Civil Rights*. Princeton, N.J.: Princeton University Press.
Gamson, William A. 1990. *The Strategy of Social Protest*. 2nd ed. Belmont, Calif.: Wadsworth.
Glenn, John K., III. 2001. *Framing Democracy: Civil Society and Civic Movements in Eastern Europe*. Stanford, Calif.: Stanford University Press.
Goodin, Robert E., and Hans-Dieter Klingemann, eds. 1996. *A New Handbook of Political Science*. Oxford: Oxford University Press.
Gould, Deborah B. 2009. *Moving Politics: Emotion and ACT UP's Fight against AIDS*. Chicago: University of Chicago Press.
Hayward, Jack, and Anand Menon, eds. 2003. *Governing Europe*. Oxford: Oxford University Press.

Heaney, Michael, and Fabio Rojas. 2007. "Partisans, Nonpartisans, and the Antiwar Movement in the United States." *American Politics Research* 35:431–64.

Imig, Douglas. 1998. "American Social Movements and Presidential Administrations." In *Social Movements and American Political Institutions,* edited by Ann Costain and Andrew McFarland, 159–70. Lanham, Md.: Rowman and Littlefield.

Janoski, Thomas, Robert Alford, Alexander Hicks, and Mildred A. Schwartz, eds. 2005. *The Handbook of Political Sociology.* Cambridge: Cambridge University Press.

Kitschelt, Herbert. 1986. "Political Opportunity Structures and Political Protest: Anti-nuclear Movements in Four Democracies." *British Journal of Political Science* 18:57–85.

Klinkner, Philip A., with Rogers M. Smith. 1999. *The Unsteady March: The Rise and Decline of Racial Equality in the United States.* Chicago: University of Chicago Press.

Koopmans, Ruud. 1995. *Democracy from Below: New Social Movements and the Political System in West Germany.* Boulder, Colo.: Westview Press.

Kriesi, Hanspeter. 2004. "Political Context and Opportunity." In *The Blackwell Companion to Social Movements,* edited by David A. Snow, Sarah A. Soule, and Hanspeter Kriesi, 67–90. Oxford: Blackwell.

Kriesi, Hanspeter, Edgar Grande, Romain Lachat, Martin Dolezal, Simon Bornshier, and Timotheos Frey. 2008. *West European Politics in the Age of Globalization.* Cambridge: Cambridge University Press.

Kriesi, Hanspeter, Ruud Koopmans, Jan Willem Duyvendak, and Marco G. Giugni. 1995. *The Politics of New Social Movements in Western Europe.* Minneapolis: University of Minnesota Press.

Layton, Azza Salama. 2001. *International Politics and Civil Rights Policies in the United States, 1941–1960.* Cambridge: Cambridge University Press.

Leicht, Kevin T., and J. Craig Jenkins. 2010. *Handbook of Politics: State and Society in Global Perspective.* New York: Springer.

Linz, Juan, and Alfred Stepan. 1978. *The Breakdown of Democratic Regimes.* Baltimore: Johns Hopkins University Press.

Lipsky, Michael. 1968. "Protest as a Resource." *American Political Science Review* 62:1144–58.

Mair, Peter. 1997. *Party System Change: Approaches and Interpretations.* Oxford: Oxford University Press.

McAdam, Doug. (1982) 1999. *Political Process and the Development of Black Insurgency, 1930–1970.* Chicago: University of Chicago Press.

McAdam, Doug, and Sidney Tarrow. 2010. "Ballots and Barricades: On the Reciprocal Relations between Elections and Social Movements." *Perspectives on Politics* 8:529–42.

McAdam, Doug, Sidney Tarrow, and Charles Tilly. 2001. *Dynamics of Contention.* Cambridge: Cambridge University Press.

Meny, Yves, and Yves Surel, eds. 2002. *Democracies and the Populist Challenge*. London: Palgrave Macmillan.

Pappi, Franz U., Robert Huckfeldt, and Ken'chi Ikeda. 1998. "Social Networks, Political Discussion and the Social Embeddedness of Citizenship." Paper presented at the annual meeting of the Midwest Political Science Association, Chicago.

Pérez Díaz, Victor. 1993. *The Return of Civil Society: The Emergence of Democratic Spain*. Cambridge, Mass.: Harvard University Press.

Piven, Frances Fox, and Richard Cloward. 1977. *Poor People's Movements: Why They Succeed, How They Fail*. New York: Vintage.

Shesol, Jeff. 2009. *Supreme Power: Franklin Roosevelt vs. the Supreme Court*. New York: W. W. Norton.

Snow, David A., Sarah A. Soule, and Hanspeter Kriesi, eds. 2004. *The Blackwell Companion to Social Movements*. Oxford: Blackwell.

Sobieraj, Sarah. 2011. *Soundbitten: The Perils of Media-Centered Political Activism*. New York: New York University Press.

Tarrow, Sidney. 1983. *Struggling to Reform: Social Movements and Policy Change*. Western Societies 15. Ithaca, N.Y.: Cornell University.

Tilly, Charles. 1964. *The Vendée*. Cambridge, Mass.: Harvard University Press.

———. 1978. *From Mobilization to Revolution*. Reading, Mass.: Addison-Wesley.

———. 1986. *The Contentious French*. Cambridge, Mass.: Harvard University Press.

———. 1995. *Popular Contention in Great Britain, 1758–1834*. Cambridge. Mass.: Harvard University Press.

———. 2006. *Regimes and Repertoires*. Chicago: University of Chicago Press.

———. 2008. *Contentious Performances*. New York: Cambridge University Press.

Van Dyke, Nella. 2003. "Protest Cycles and Party Politics: The Effects of Elite Allies and Antagonists on Student Protest in the United States, 1930–1990." In *States, Parties, and Movements,* edited by Jack Goldstone, 226–45. Cambridge: Cambridge University Press.

Woehrle, Lynne M., Patrick G. Coy, and Gregory M. Maney. 2009. *Contesting Patriotism: Culture, Power, and Strategy in the Peace Movement*. Lanham, Md.: Rowman and Littlefield.

Wren, Anne, and Kenneth M. McElwain. 2008. "Voters and Parties." In *Oxford Handbook of Comparative Politics,* edited by Carles Boix and Susan Stokes, 555–81. Oxford: Oxford University Press.

17

Social Movements, Power, and Democracy: New Challenges, New Challengers, New Theories?

Donatella della Porta

Democracy and Power in Social Movement Studies

Neoliberal globalization is changing the nature of the state, so also altering the contexts in which social movements operate, thereby forcing us to rethink our concepts and theories. In this process, if there are emerging challenges to social movements, there are, however, also opportunities they can exploit. This implies not only minor strategic adjustments but also major changes in the conceptions and practices of democracy. These changes affect not only the opportunities for success but also the ways in which collective identities develop.

Even though there is a broad understanding that democracy is important for movements, and vice versa, social movements have often been important for democracy, and reflections on democracy as such have been rare in social movement studies, which have rarely been concerned with their democratic functions as well as (democratic) functioning. This is true, with few valuable exceptions, for analyses concerning all the different steps in the process of democratization. On their side, political scientists have focused their attention on more institutionally recognized actors and processes such as political parties and elections.

A concern with the ways in which democratic regimes influence the conditions and forms for protest has entered social movement studies through the political process approach, which has had the merit of firmly linking social movements to the normal political process. However, given the (geographical, historical, and disciplinary) context in which this approach developed, it linked social movements to a geographically, historically, and disciplinarily specific set of political opportunities that were conceptualized as being rooted within (1) the nation-state, (2) party democracies, and (3) mature welfare states.

Through the seminal work of Charles Tilly (1978) and Michael Lipsky (1965), a modified version of Easton's political system model has spread into social movement studies. Though stressing the presence of interests in conflicts (as in Bachrach and Baratz 1970), research in social movements has located them at the border of the black box where decisions are made and stressed their need for alliance with powerful gatekeepers (as political parties or elites) to make their voice audible.

In Europe, where cross-national comparative analyses addressed the effects of political opportunities on protest and social movements (Kriesi et al. 1995; della Porta 1995), the traditional conceptualizations in political science entered social movement studies via an updated version of Lijphart's influential classification of majoritarian versus consensual democracies. Majoritarian—or exclusive—democracies were expected to produce a more limited number of more radical protests; consensual—or inclusive—democracies were expected to produce more protests, but of a less radical nature.

Additionally, especially in Europe, the first reflections on social movements tended to point at the differences of new social movements when compared with their ancestor, the labor movement. Not only did research in the field stress such aspects as the reticular organizational structures and the focus on issues outside the realm of production (Touraine 1977; Melucci 1989) but it also assumed the pacification of the old class cleavage and the development of new conflicts. Even though democracy was not central to this approach, it assumed a developed welfare state.

With few exceptions (see Polletta 2002; della Porta 2009a, 2009b, 2009c; Epstein 1991; Leach 2006), what remains a large gap in social movement research is the way in which democracy plays inside social movements. This is all the more surprising because many social movement organizations are reflexive actors that often explicitly address the issue of democracy. In particular, the progressive movements, including global justice movements, not only criticize representative democracies and advocate participatory and direct democratic visions but also prefigure different models of democracy in their own organizations.

In what follows, I first discuss how broad trends of transformations in democracies challenge some of the mentioned assumptions of the political opportunities for social movement development. However serious the challenges in terms of democratic openness to oppositional movements, I observe that some recent transformations might also open up some new opportunities. To capture them, we need to reflect on the very conceptions of democracy that subtend our theorizations on the political context for social movements, distinguishing the dominant, liberal vision of democracy from liberal–

deliberative, radical–participatory, and participatory–deliberative ones. Reflections on different conceptions of democracy seem relevant to understand how social movements are adapting to perceived transformations in their contexts.

Transformations in Democracies as Challenges

The so-called political process approach—used especially to analyze Western democracies—assumed three characteristics: the full sovereignty of the nation-state, party democracies, and well-established welfare states. These characteristics have been transformed, however, in the recent evolution of the political and societal fabric at the turn of the millennium. In particular, neoliberal globalization as well as other general evolutions in contemporary democracies have produced the following:

- a shift of power from the nation-state to international governmental organizations (IGOs)
- a shift of power from the state to the market, with some developments from welfare states into warfare states
- a shift of power from parties (and representative institutions) to the executive

Talking of shifts, I do not want to state that these are either complete, natural, or irreversible trends. They are, however, for sure challenges to the established visions of the political context considered as more relevant for social movements.

As far as the shift from the national to the international is concerned, there is first of all an increase in the number of IGOs as well as an increase in the power of international financial institutions—the World Bank, the International Monetary Fund, and the World Trade Organization (WTO)—through an acquired capacity to make economic help conditional on national governments accepting some specific policies. Along with international financial institutions, macroregional institutions (e.g., the European Union [EU]) have also increased their sanction capacity. Furthermore, while the majority of IGOs function mainly as meeting places and discussion forums where decisions are made unanimously and then ratified by national organs, there is a growing number of supranational organizations within which decisions binding for all member states are made on a majority basis (Zuern and Ecker-Ehrhardt 2011). Vis-à-vis its predecessor, the General Agreement on Tariffs and Trade, in the WTO dispute, settlement procedures moved from a system of negotiation to one of adjudication (O'Brian et al. 2000, 71). EU institutional design developed in a similar direction.

This does not mean, of course, that the states have no power left. First, the growing political globalization is not so much related to technological challenges and opportunities or to market dynamics as it is the product of political decisions in which the states participated. The liberalization of trade and particularly of financial markets is driven by political actors within single states (and in particular within the most powerful one, the United States) as well as by international actors, first and foremost the mentioned international financial institutions. Market deregulation and the privatization of public services are not natural effects of technological development but rather a strategy adopted and defended by international financial institutions and by the governments of the most powerful nations (in particular, through the G7 and the G8), to the advantage of multinational corporations. As Crouch (2003, 95) has observed, the establishment of the ideology of a free market has clearly been facilitated by the WTO, whose postdemocratic aim is the liberalization of international exchanges of goods and services. Neoliberal globalization, therefore, is a matter not only of new technologies and modes of production but also of the *political* tools set in place to regulate and reproduce this social structure through, among other means, the proliferation of IGOs (Boli and Thomas 1999). Moreover, as in the past, sovereignty is formally equal but substantially unequally distributed. Some states have more power over their own territories, others much less. Also, as research on the EU clearly indicates, states keep a (differential) capacity to influence IGOs and especially keep an important role in the implementation of international treaties.

As for the shift from the state to the market, research on the welfare state has pointed at its retrenchment. In the last two decades, deregulation of financial markets, reduction of taxes, and privatization of public services have indeed been common trends in advanced democracies, although with some differences between European countries and the United States (Crouch 2003). Lacking a conception of positive international integration, "national governments, terrified of the implicit threat of capital flight, have let themselves be dragged into a cost-cutting deregulatory frenzy, generating obscene profits and drastic income disparities, rising unemployment, and the social marginalization of a growing population of the poor" (Habermas 2001, 79). Additionally, thanks to the opening of borders for goods, services, and finance, multinational corporations grew in size and power of influence on (weaker) states, while labor has not been given such freedom.

Here as well, some caveats require mention. First, the welfare state retrenchment took on different characteristics in different welfare models. Second, in the face of the recent financial crisis, the hegemonic capacity of neoliberal ideology has been challenged, even if it is far from being defeated. Also, the hypothesis of an unavoidable adaptation to a global economy and free market is nowadays broadly recognized as misleading.

Finally, as for the shift from representative institutions to the executive, recent research has observed a rapid decline in the capacity of political parties to function as mediators between the civil society and political institutions (della Porta 2008a). In particular, they seem to have lost much of their power of identification, that is, their capacity to function as powerful identifiers, helping to define long-term collective identities (Pizzorno 1981). The decline in the number of party members and, especially, activists (with the related spread of memberless and personalized parties) and the weakening of party loyalties (with the increase in electoral volatility and opinion voting) are tangible signs of these transformations (della Porta 2008a).

Here, as well, some caveats are in order. Empirical research in Western democracies has stressed that the extent of some declining trends in conventional forms of political participation (such as party memberships and voting) varies cross-nationally (Dalton 2008). Especially in the global South, political parties seem sometimes even to increase their societal roots. Moreover, even where political parties have lost rootedness in society, they have not reduced their weight in government (della Porta 2008a). Also, notwithstanding increasing reciprocal mistrust, political parties of the left remain important allies in protest campaigns (della Porta 2009c).

Even with all these caveats, if we read these changes in terms of the hypotheses that have been widespread in the social science literature, there is no doubt that they imply a closing down of traditional political opportunities for social movements. A basic assumption in the political process approach is in fact that institutions tend to be more responsive to movement claims the more democratically accountable they are: as Eisinger (1973) had noted comparing U.S. local governments, social movement claims have more chance to be heard by governments led by elected administrators (vs. by reformed, "technical" governments). Additionally, territorial decentralization of power has been considered an opportunity for movements (Kriesi et al. 1995); the nation-state as the arena for the development of proper social movements (Tilly 1984); and political parties as the most important allies for social movements (Tarrow 1989; della Porta 1996). The pacification of the class cleavage in advanced democracies has been seen as a condition for the institutionalization of the labor movement and the development of new movements (Kriesi et al. 1995).

In sum, whereas social movement flourished with democracy (Tilly 2007), recent transformations have been seen to reduce democratic quality. Political sociologists and political scientists alike have pointed to several indicators of a general malaise in democratic countries, to challenges both within and without the nation-state, and to both (traditional) conceptions of legitimization from the input side as well as (more recent) conceptions of legitimization from the output side of the democratic process.

At the national level, procedural legitimization of democracy as a regime based on electoral accountability is limited by the decline of electoral participation (visible at all territorial levels) but also the mentioned transformation in the political parties as the main actors that, giving continuity in time to preelectoral promises and judgment of postelectoral performances, have been allowed to implement it.

At the transnational level, challenges to democracy on the input side arise from the necessity to adapt conceptions and practices of democratic decision making developed at the national level to a reality in which transnational actors and global events have increasingly greater influence. As John Markoff (1999, 283) observed, globalization changes the ways in which democratization is addressed in a world of transnational connections: democratization of the states is no longer the central issue. The normative conceptions and empirical implementations of democracy developed in and about the nation-state are very difficult to apply at the supranational level. Indeed, "democracy as we know it within countries does not exist in a Globalized Space. More accurately, to the extent that Globalized Space is marked by conventional democratic procedures, these are ad-hoc, non systematic, irregular and fragile" (Rosenau 1998, 39). Not only do IGOs usually have no electoral accountability, but a transnational conception of citizenship and citizenship rights is hard to develop (Archibugi 2003, 7). At the same time, however, democratic accountability, transparency, and participation are increasingly needed in the face of processes of politicization of international politics (Zuern and Ecker-Ehrhardt 2011).

From the output side, an additional challenge comes (at both national and transnational levels) from the transformation in economic politics and its effect on the capacity of democracies to produce public goods. Economic globalization as a "return to the market" has certainly reduced the potential for state intervention into economic inequalities, challenging the assumption (previously dominant in Europe but also in Keynesian political economy) about its role in ensuring economic development but also social justice. In turn, the reduced effectiveness of public administration also affects the legitimacy of state institutions. In fact, "as markets drive out politics, the nation-state increasingly loses its capacities to raise taxes and stimulate growth, and with them the ability to secure the essential foundations of its own legitimacy" (Habermas 2001, 79).

Transformations in Democracies as Opportunities

If a narrative in terms of crisis of democracy, or at least of reduction of democratic qualities even in advanced democracies, has been long widespread, a sort

Challenges	Opportunities
Less democracy in democratic countries	More countries with at least minimal level of democracy
Less conventional forms of participation	More innovative forms of participation
Less media freedom	More partial public spheres
Less electoral accountability	More capacity of scrutiny on institutions
Less state intervention against social inequalities	More recognition to other-than-social rights (e.g., gender, environmental, human)

Figure 17.1. Challenges and opportunities for democracy.

of counternarrative started to develop, stressing the opportunities that some recent transformations have brought about for democracy. Some empirical research has singled out potential opportunities for improvement in (some) democratic qualities that have arisen owing to recent transformations (see Figure 17.1).

Not only has there been growth in the number of democratic countries after the third wave of democratization, but there has also been growth in the use of nonconventional forms of protest as well as in interest in politics and in political competences. While some more conventional forms of participation (such as voting or party-linked activities) are declining, protest forms are being increasingly used (Dalton 2008). Citizens vote less but are not less interested in and knowledgeable about politics. And if some traditional types of associations are less and less popular, others (among which are social movement organizations) are growing in resources, legitimacy, and membership. Media studies have discussed the increasing participatory opportunities linked to the new technologies, which also, to a certain extent, allow bypassing the shortcomings linked to a growing commercialization of traditional media. Both trends increase the capacity of oversight of elected representatives, even if their electoral accountability is declining. Moreover, if the capacity of state intervention into market inequalities is reduced, civil rights issues have increasingly entered the political debate.

This goes along with a growing attention to the need to balance the perceived crisis of the representative (electoral) conception of democracy with a sort of revival of other conceptions that, even though not hegemonic, belong to deep-rooted traditions in both democratic thinking and the development of democratic institutions that go beyond electoral accountability.

Some opportunities have, in fact, also been singled out in broader assessments of transformations in conceptions and practices of democracy. As Pierre Rosanvallon (2006, 12) has suggested, "the idea of popular sovereignty found historical expression in two different ways. The first was the right to vote, the right of citizens to choose their own leaders. This was the most direct expression of the democratic principle. But the power to vote periodically and thus bestow legitimacy to an elected government is almost always accompanied by a wish to exercise a more permanent form of control over the government thus elected." In the historical evolution of democracy, near to the growth of institutions of electoral accountability, there has been the consolidation of a circuit of oversight anchored outside state institutions. This second conception of sovereignty found its incarnation in growing societal powers of sanction and prevention. In fact, the understanding of democratic experiences requires the consideration, at the same time, of the "functions and dysfunctions" of electoral representative institutions but also of the organization of distrust (Rosanvallon 2006).

Thinking in terms of other conceptions of democracy paves the way to addressing contemporary transformations as not only challenges to but also opportunities for democracy. The different elements of what Rosanvallon (2006, 8) defined as counterdemocracy do not represent, in fact, "the opposite of democracy, but rather a form of democracy that reinforces the usual electoral democracy, a democracy of indirect powers disseminated through society." If mistrust is the disease, it might be part of the cure; "a complex assortment of practical measures, checks and balances, and informal as well as institutional social counter-powers has evolved in order to *compensate for the erosion of confidence, and to do so by organizing distrust*" (4).

In the same vein as Rosanvallon (2006), other scholars have stressed at the same time the crisis of the traditional, liberal (representative) conceptions of democracy and the revival of democratic qualities usually considered under the formula of a "democracy of the ancients." To take a few examples, Bernard Manin (1995, 295) has described the contemporary evolution from a "democracy of the parties," in which the public sphere was mainly occupied by the political parties (which were able to structure public opinion but also provided arenas in which discussion of public decisions developed), to a "democracy of the public," in which, freed from the ideological control of the parties, the channels of formation of public opinion developed outside them. This also means that the cleavages within public opinion no longer reflect electoral preferences, developing instead from individual preferences formed outside of the political parties.

In his *Postdemocrazia (Postdemocracy)*, Crouch (2003, 9) observes that politics and governments lose ground or are conquered by privileged elites, and the welfare state—the product of the mid-century compromise between capital and workers—falls victim to a new, antiegalitarian conception. Additionally, the dominant neoliberal model is based on an elitist conception of electoral participation for the mass of the citizens and free lobbying for stronger interests, along with low levels of state intervention. Even in this more pessimistic account, however, not only is the perception of a growing mistrust seen as an incentive for the political elites to encourage "a maximal level of minimal participation" (126) but also the continuous creation of new social identities, as well as their pressures to have their claims recognized, is perceived as a dynamic challenge to the "world of official politics" (131).

In this debate on transformations in democracies, social movements appear to play a potentially crucial role. Recognizing the democratic potential of mistrust means, in fact, to push forward reflections on the democratic role played by social movements as actors of the political system. They are considered as most relevant for conceptions of democracy in which society has a voice, collective sentiments can be articulated, judgments on government and its actions are formulated, and claims are raised (Rosanvallon 2006, 20).

Also, some studies focusing on conceptions and visions of democracy in social movements (della Porta 2009a, 2009b; Smith et al. 2007) confirm their growing concern with the development of proposals for reform of real democracies, which go in directions that are resonant with the growing legitimacy of different conceptions of democracy, so transforming challenges into opportunities. Additionally, they point at the experimentation, within social movements, of democratic conceptions that openly challenge the liberal vision of democracy as a representative system based on majoritarian decision making.

Four Conceptions of Democracy

To understand this evolution, we have to reflect on which conception of democracy is challenged and which one instead finds emerging opportunities. With this aim in mind, I have constructed a typology of conceptions of democracy that I think well captures recent debates on democracy as well as democratic innovations.

In the intense debate in normative theory, we can single out two dimensions of democratic conceptions that are relevant for our reflections on social movements. The first dimension refers to the recognition of conflict as an integral part of democracy; a second one looks at the construction of political identities as exogenous versus endogenous to the democratic process (which I do not consider as limited to state institutions but as enlarged to include interactions within civil society). Crossing the two dimensions, we can single out four different models of democracy (Figure 17.2).

Liberal democracy assumes identities that are built outside of the democratic process that channels them inside the political system. The distinctive institutions of Dahl's polyarchal democracy include the presence of officials elected in free, fair, and frequent elections as well as freedom of expression and association and alternative sources of information (Dahl 1998). Though, of course, interests differ, a broad consensus is assumed among compatible interests, and conflicts tend to be considered as negative, as they risk overloading the system (Crozier, Huntington, and Watakuni 1975). The actors carrying fundamental conflicts are seen as antisystemic (Sartori 1976).

This liberal conception of democracy has been challenged, among others, by a *participatory* conception. Theories of participatory democracy have stressed the importance of involving citizens beyond elections (Arnstein 1969; Pateman 1970; Barber 1984). Citizens should be provided with as many opportunities to participate as there are spheres of decision (Pateman 1970). A "strong democracy" is a government in which citizens participate at least some of the time in the decisions that affect their lives (Barber 1984). For Arnstein (1969, 216), "citizen participation is a categorical term for citizen power." This means that "there is a critical difference between going through the empty ritual of participation and having the real power needed to affect the outcome of the process" (216). Going beyond electoral accountability, this conception singles out the educative virtue of participation: the more citizens participate in decision-making processes, the more they are enlightened and informed, and the more they will vote at the national level (Pateman 1970). In Pateman's participatory theory, participation refers to (equal) participation in the making of decisions, implying equality of power in determining the outcomes of decisions.

Participatory visions are especially widespread among social movement scholars, who consider conflict as a fundamental and dynamic element of our societies. The European tradition in social movement studies has looked at new social movements as potential carriers of a new central conflict in our postindustrial societies, or at least of an emerging constellation of conflicts. In the American tradition, the resource mobilization approach reacted to a then-dominant conception of conflicts as pathologies. In his influential book *Social Conflict and Social Movements,* Anthony Oberschall (1973) defined social movements as the main carriers of societal conflicts. In *Democracy and Disorder,* Sidney Tarrow (1989) pointed at the relevant and positive role of unconventional forms of political participation in democratic processes. From

	Identities: exogenous to the democratic process	Identities: endogenous to the democratic process
Consensus	Liberal democracy	Liberal deliberative democracy
Conflict	Radical, participatory democracy	Participatory deliberative democracy

Figure 17.2. Conceptions of democracy.

Michael Lipsky (1965) to Charles Tilly (1978), the first systematic works on social movements developed from traditions of research that stressed conflicts of power, both in society and in politics. In fact, a widely accepted definition of social movements introduced conflicts as a central element for their conceptualization: "social movement actors are engaged in political and/or cultural conflicts, meant to promote or oppose social change. By conflict we mean an oppositional relationship between actors who seek control of the same stake—be it political, economic, or cultural power—and in the process make negative claims on each other—i.e., demands which, if realized, would damage the interests of the other actors" (della Porta and Diani 2006, 21).

Visions of participatory democracy tend, however, to consider the formation of collective identities as exogenous to the democratic process. This is the case, in particular, of the theorization of radical democracy, where the formation of interests and identities is left outside of the (conflictual) political sphere. The interest in "articulation" as practices that establish a relation among elements, so that identities are modified (Laclau and Mouffe 2001, 105), does not bring about a definition of the (democratic) conditions under which this articulation might happen. Additionally, it stresses a separation between political institutions and society. Radical democracy is plural also in the sense that it includes the "struggle for a maximum of autonomization of spheres on the basis of generalization of the equivalent-egalitarian logic" (Laclau and Mouffe 2001, 147). So, for Chantal Mouffe (2005, 360), the political is "the dimension of antagonisms that I take to be constitutive of human society," while politics is the "set of practices and institutions through which an order is created, organizing human coexistence in the context of conflictuality provided by the political." Identities are not constructed through democratic processes, and the function of democracy is "to provide institutions that will allow them to take an agonistic form, in which opponents will treat each other not as enemies to be destroyed, but as adversaries who will fight for the victory of their position while recognizing the right of their opponents to fight for theirs" (Mouffe 2009, 53). In this sense, agonism recognizes the conflicting relation but also the legitimacy of the others: "while antagonism is a we/they relation in which the two sides are enemies who do not share any common ground, agonism is a we/them relation where the conflicting parties, although acknowledging that there is no rational solution to their conflict, nevertheless recognize the legitimacy of their opponents.... This means that, while in conflict, they see themselves as belonging to the same political association, as sharing a common symbolic space within which the conflict takes place" (Mouffe 2005, 20). What is shared in this vision is the "adhesion to the ethical-political principles of liberal democracy: liberty and equality. But we disagree concerning the meaning and implementation of those principles, and such a disagreement is not one that could be solved through deliberation and rational discussion" (Mouffe 2000, 245).

There is a second alternative to liberal conceptions of democracy that has stressed consensus as a basis for the formation of collective identities. Whereas the liberal conception of democracy is based on the aggregation of exogenously generated, individual preferences (through vote or negotiation), *deliberative* democratic theory has stressed "the transformation of preferences in interaction" (Dryzek 2000, 79). In this model of democracy, "the political debate is organized around alternative conceptions of the public good" (Cohen 1989, 19). This is achieved through *rational argumentations,* as people are convinced by the force of the best argument. In particular, deliberation develops with horizontal flows of communication, multiple contributors to discussion, wide opportunities for interactivity, confrontation on the basis of rational argumentation, and attitude to reciprocal listening (Habermas 1981, 1996). Deliberative arenas are legitimated by three main characteristics. The first is *equality*: deliberation must exclude power deriving from coercion but also avoid an unequal weighting of the participants as representatives of organizations of different size or influence. A second characteristic is *inclusiveness*: all citizens with a stake in the decisions to be made must be included in the process and able to express their opinions. This requires the deliberative process to take place under conditions of plurality of values, where people have different perspectives but face common problems. Finally, democratic arenas have to be *transparent,* as public deliberation can "replace the language of interest with the language of reason" (Elster 1998, 111).

Some limits have been noted in these (normative) positions, and a fourth model of democracy as *deliberative and participatory* has so developed. First, critics have observed the exclusionary nature of the public sphere, especially as it is conceived in the Habermasian proposal. As Nancy Fraser (1997, 75) noted, "not only was there always a plurality of competing publics, but the relations between bourgeois publics and other publics were always conflictual. Virtually from the beginning, counterpublics contested the exclusionary norms of the bourgeois public, elaborating alternative styles of political behavior and alternative norms of public speech. Bourgeois publics, in turn, excoriated these alternatives and deliberately sought to block broader participation." Subaltern counterpublics (including workers, women, ethnic minorities, etc.) formed, in fact, parallel discursive arenas, where counterdiscourses developed, allowing for the formation and redefinition of identities, interests, and needs (Fraser 1997).

Second, and linked to this, deliberative theories tend toward an institutional bias denying that democracy develops (also or mainly) outside of public institutions. Instead, social movements are better positioned to build deliberative spaces because they keep a critical eye on institutions (Dryzek 2000). Additionally, deliberation requires enclaves, free from institutional power—social movements being among these free spaces (Mansbridge 1996).

Third, public spheres have different grammars (Talpin 2011; Haug 2010). Not only does the historical account of the bourgeois public sphere leave aside the proletarian account (see also della Porta 2011) but the very communicative style normatively stressed by Habermas has been considered as reflecting elitarian norms. The emphasis on reason belittles storytelling, and politeness tends to exclude passions. What is more, social inequalities reduce the capacity of oppressed groups to learn the rules of the game as oppression "consists in systematic institutional processes which prevent some people from learning and using satisfying or expansive skills in socially recognized settings, or which inhibit people's ability to play and communicate with others or to express their feelings and perspective on social life in contexts where others can listen" (Young 2000, 156). The emphasis on discourse is therefore linked with a positive appreciation of protest: "processes of engaged and responsible democratic participation include street demonstrations and sit-ins, musical works and cartoons, as much as parliamentary speeches and letters to the editor" (Young 2003, 119).

Fourth, and most fundamentally, deliberative liberal democracy assumes the possibility to reach consensus through dialogue, thus excluding fundamental conflicts, which are instead part and parcel of democratic development. As Flyvbjerg (1998, 229) observed, "with the plurality that a contemporary concept for civil society must contain, conflict becomes an inevitable part of this concept. Thus civil society does not mean 'civilized' in the sense of well-mannered behavior. In strong civil societies, distrusts and criticism of authoritative action are omnipresent as is resulting political conflict." Public spheres are conflictual, as they are selective: "If some of the interests, opinions, and perspectives are suppressed..., or if some groups have difficulties getting heard for reasons of structural inequality, cultural misunderstanding, or social prejudice, then the agenda or the results of public policy are likely to be biased or unfair. For these reasons, the public sphere will properly be a site of struggle—often contentious struggles" (Young 2000, 178). This element is taken seriously, especially in conceptualizations of radical democracy as based on agonistic interactions. As Mouffe (2000, 98) wrote, "taking pluralism seriously requires that we give up the dream of rational consensus which entails the fantasy that we could escape from our human form of life." The need for a deliberation inside counterpublics, or enclaves of resistance, is instead recognized by the theoreticians of participatory forms of deliberation. Among them, Jane Mansbridge (1996, 46–47) stresses that "democracies also need to foster and value informal deliberative enclaves of resistance in which those who lose in each coercive move can rework their ideas and their strategies, gathering their forces and deciding in a more protected space in what way or whether to continue the struggle." All these aspects became central in the elaboration of proposals to democratize international governmental institutions and, more broadly, the world system (Smith 2008).

Social movements have contributed to the development of these alternative conceptions of democracy. If liberal democracy is mainly based on a principle of delegation and majority votes, social movements have long since been considered as the carriers of *participatory* visions and practices of democracy, with criticism of delegation and positive emphasis on the importance of directly involving citizens in decision making. In some recent social movements, such as those active on issues of global justice, the development of movement-controlled arenas—such as the social forums—of reflection and exchange of ideas among a plurality of different social and political actors testifies to the growing democratic importance recognized in the construction of multiple and critical public spheres. Their visions and practices resonate, in fact, with participatory and deliberative democracy, referring to decisional processes in which, under conditions of equality, inclusiveness and transparency, a communicative process based on reason (the strength of a good argument) is able to transform individual preferences, leading to decisions oriented to the public good (della Porta 2005). Their normative position could be read as constructing an alternative not only to the traditional conceptions of liberal democracy but also to liberal deliberative conceptions.

These alternative conceptions also found resonance in social movement studies. As mentioned in the introduction, a critique of the liberal understanding of democracy has indeed been at the basis of the political process approach to social movements. To capture challenges and opportunities for social movements in our democracy in transformation, however, we must also reflect on visions and practices that not only are dominant in social movements but have also penetrated the democratic state (della Porta 2011).

Social Movements and Democracy: Responding to Challenges and Opportunities

Recognizing the presence of different conceptions of democracy, in permanent tension but also reciprocal adaptation, can help us understand the interactions between political–social transformations and social movements, addressing the challenges to contentious politics linked to the transformations away from nation-state-bounded, party-dominated welfare democracies. Reflections on other conceptions of democracy allow a better grasp of the multiple ways in which social movements can interact with other actors and produce effects. The political process approach tended to locate social movements at the input of the political process. Understanding contemporary social movements requires a critical view of the liberal definition of democracy as not only normatively contested but also heuristically weak. First, this conception of democracy, with its emphasis on representative power and majority voting, is a specific normative vision of democracy. Other conceptions have been kept alive (among other means, by social movements). Additionally, the existing democratic regimes have indeed always mixed the majoritarian and representative elements of democracy with others—again, participatory and deliberative ones. Political institutions mainly reflect the liberal model of democracy—but not only that. What Dahl defined as "real existing democracy" grew by mixing participatory elements with representative ones and deliberation with voting.

This means that the liberal conception has *not* been historically either unchallenged or immutable. The labor movement has (often successfully) challenged the liberal, individualistic conception of rights, bringing about the recognition of collective civil and political rights as well as social rights as part and parcel of democratic citizenship (della Porta 2011). So-called new social movements asked, a few decades ago, for broader spaces of participation, producing some relevant institutional changes. And visions and practices of democracy centered around the development of public spaces are relevant for present-day movements, even finding some resonance in institutional reforms. As Tilly (2007) noticed, if there is no doubt that democracy was essential for social movements, social movements, with their challenging visions and practices, have been essential for the development of institutional democracy well *beyond* its liberal definition.

Notwithstanding the challenges to liberal democracies, social movements and protest behavior seem to be alive and widespread. Their very existence pushes toward some conceptual innovations in social movement studies, with a (theoretical) recognition of the power of agency over structures as well as of the (methodological) need for more dynamic, processual understandings of contentious processes.

Let's return to the three shifts I mentioned at the beginning of this essay and see how contemporary social movements adapted to them. First, social movements have addressed, and even contributed to, processes of *transnationalization*. They have reacted to the shift of power from the nation-state to IGOs by developing multilevel protests, targeting multilevel governance. They have mobilized in transnational campaigns and global social forums, taking global politics to the street, with continuous processes of upward and downward shifting. But they also combined protest in the street with other repertoires of action, infiltrating national delegations at international meetings and also penetrating the bureaucracy of IGOs as well as constructing alternatives in the field. Even if not many in absolute terms, the growing number of transnational protests were particularly eventful in their capacity to contribute to the development of cosmopolitan and tolerant identities (della Porta 2005, 2008b; della Porta and Tarrow 2005). Over the last decades, transnational protest campaigns have multiplied, in particular on issues such as environmental protection, gender discrimination, and human rights, targeting international financial organizations as well as other IGOs. During these campaigns, common frames developed around global justice and global democracy, and transnational networks consolidated. The organizations of the global justice movement as well as the cosmopolitan activists we have studied in the Demos project have, indeed, some emerging characteristics such as the construction of global and cross-issue framing; transnationally networked organizational structures with an emphasis on consensual, deliberative conceptions and practices of democracy; and intense participation in various protests beyond borders (della Porta 2009a, 2009b; della Porta and Rucht 2012). The limited electoral accountability of IGOs notwithstanding, transnational protests have been possible (and even, sometimes, successful) thanks to some liberal–deliberative quality of decision making in international institutions. Given a limited coercive power, consensual decision making (even if mainly through bargaining) opens some channels of influence to social movements of different types.

Second, in the face of the shift from the state (public) to the market (private), we have an ongoing process of the *resocialization* of social movements. As Mayer (chapter 19) and McCarthy, Rafail, and Gromis (chapter 18) noted in their contributions to this volume, recent mobilizations testify to a "return of the social," in terms of concerns with social justice as well as the mobilization of the labor movement (in alliance with broad coalitions at community and global levels). Here protests have addressed processes of privatization as well as the growing power of big corporations by developing collective action strategies that directly tackle private actors, through, among other means, communication campaigns and political consumerism (boycott and buycott). This adjustment has been resonant with participatory and deliberative conceptions of democracy, which have not only legitimated conflicts but also called for an extension of democratic practices beyond the states into working places and leaving spaces.

Finally, processes of *autonomization* have followed the declining trust in and competences of political parties. The weakening of political parties as political allies for social movements has brought about a repoliticization of social movements that can no longer delegate the political representation of movements' collective interests and identities to other actors. A recognition of the complex and ever-changing conceptualizations of democracy helps in understanding internal changes in social movements as promoters of conceptions that challenge liberal democracy. Linked to this, a participatory deliberative framing of democracy developed within recent social movements as a way to construct common mobilization among different actors.

In sum, conceptualizing the social movement context in democracies in transformation requires a recognition of the different conceptions and practices of democracy, which goes well beyond the liberal conception that has been at the basis of much political science but also the participatory vision that has being dominant in social movement studies. From the empirical point of view, much research is needed to single out the effects of democratic transformations on social movements, but also, vice versa, the effects of social movements on those transformations. From the theoretical point of view, we need to dare to go beyond the established models, rethinking the development of democratic institutions during a long history of contestation and adaptation (della Porta and Tarrow 2005).

In this, we might be helped by some trends toward cross-fertilization, which might answer Tarrow's (and others') concerns to go beyond social movements into contentious politics. In the beginning, social movement studies struggled in going beyond case studies of specific social movement organizations or events (carried out by sympathetic scholars) to build a tool kit of concepts and theory. Bert Klandermans has done much to bridge, not only different countries' traditions, but also different disciplinary fields and approaches, from the political opportunities of comparative politics to the resource mobilization in organizational theory, from the framing in symbolic interactionism to the collective identities in the sociology of conflicts. These positive exchanges, however, need some opportunities, frames, and resources. As Klandermans notes, the interactions between scholars on the two sides of the Atlantic do not come naturally but need entrepreneurial effort that might be more difficult in times of geopolitical isolationism or disciplinary war (methodological or otherwise). Also, in a typical process of institutionalization, success might bring about a sclerosis around (now mainstream) concepts and theory.

The positive sign I see counteracting these potential risks is, however, the increasing attention to social movement studies within other, dynamic fields of research: critical terrorism studies or the so-called third wave of research into the politics of religion testify to this attention to concepts and theories developed in our fields of study. The recent global protests have attracted the attention not only of sociologists, political psychologists, and (narrowly understood) political scientists but also of those working in the disciplinary fields of anthropology, geography, international relations, and normative theory, to name just a few. In this chapter, I aimed at bridging social movement studies with debates in normative theory. I am confident that this and other encounters can enrich the field of social movement studies, in the spirit of Bert Klandermans's tolerant identity and fervent networking.

Note

I wish to thank Marco Giugni, Jackie Smith, and the editors of this volume for very useful and constructive comments.

References

Archibugi, D. 2003. "Cosmopolitical Democracy." In *Debating Cosmopolitics*, edited by D. Archibugi, 1–15. London: Verso.
Arnstein, Sherry R. 1969. "A Ladder of Citizen Participation." *Journal of the American Institute of Planners* 35:216–24.
Bachrach, P., and M. S. Baratz. 1970. *Power and Poverty.* New York: Oxford University Press.
Barber, Benjamin. 1984. *Strong Democracy: Participatory Politics for a New Age.* Berkeley: University of California Press.
Boli, John, and George M. Thomas. 1999. *Constructing the World Culture: International Nongovernmental Organizations since 1875.* Stanford, Calif.: Stanford University Press.
Cohen, Joshua. 1989. "Deliberation and Democratic Legitimacy." In *The Good Polity,* edited by A. Hamlin and P. Pettit, 17–34. Oxford: Blackwell.
Crouch, C. 2003. *Postdemocrazia.* Rome: Laterza.

Crozier, Michel, Samuel Huntington, and J. Watakuni. 1975. *The Crisis of Democracy.* New York: New York University Press.

Dahl, Robert A. 1998. *On Democracy.* New Haven, Conn.: Yale University Press.

Dalton, Russell. 2008. *Citizen Politics: Public Opinion and Political Parties in Advanced Industrial Democracies.* 5th ed. Washington, D.C.: Congressional Quarterly Press.

della Porta, Donatella. 1995. *Social Movements, Political Violence, and the State.* Cambridge: Cambridge University Press.

———. 1996. *Movimenti Collettivi e Sistema Politico in Italia, 1960–1995.* Bari, Italy: Laterza.

———. 2005. "Making the Polis: Social Forums and Democracy in the Global Justice Movements." *Mobilization* 10, no. 1: 73–94.

———. 2008a. *I partiti politici.* 3rd ed. Bologna, Italy: Il Mulino.

———. 2008b. "Eventful Protest, Global Conflict." *Distinktion: Scandinavian Journal of Social Theory* 17:27–56.

———. 2009a. "Consensus in Movement." In *Democracy in Social Movements,* edited by Donatella della Porta, 73–99. London: Palgrave.

———, ed. 2009b. *Another Europe.* London: Routledge.

———, ed. 2009c. *Democracy in Social Movements.* London: Palgrave.

———. 2011. "I movimenti sociali e la democrazia." In *Lo Stato Democratico,* edited by A. Pizzorno, 193–332. Milan, Italy: Feltrinelli.

della Porta, Donatella, and Mario Diani. 2006. *Social Movements: An Introduction.* Oxford: Blackwell.

della Porta, Donatella, and Dieter Rucht, eds. 2012. *Meeting Democracy.* Cambridge: Cambridge University Press.

della Porta, D., and S. Tarrow, eds. 2005. *Transnational Protest and Global Activism.* New York: Rowman and Littlefield.

Dryzek, John S. 2000. *Deliberative Democracy and Beyond.* New York: Oxford University Press.

Eisinger, Peter K. 1973. "The Conditions of Protest Behavior in American Cities." *American Political Science Review* 67:11–28.

Elster, Jon. 1998. "Deliberation and Constitution Making." In *Deliberative Democracy,* edited by Jon Elster, 97–122. Cambridge: Cambridge University Press.

Epstein, Barbara. 1991. *Political Protest and Cultural Revolution.* Berkeley: University of California Press.

Flyvbjerg, B. 1998. "Habermas and Foucault: Thinkers for Civil Society?" *British Journal of Sociology* 49:211–33.

Fraser, Nancy. 1997. *Justice Interruptus.* London: Routledge.

Habermas, Juergen. 1981. *Theorie des kommunikativen Handeln.* Frankfurt am Main, Germany: Suhrkamp.

———. 1996. *Between Facts and Norms: Contribution to a Discursive Theory of Law and Democracy.* Cambridge, Mass.: MIT Press.

———. 2001. *The Postnational Constellation*. Cambridge: Polity.
Haug, Christoph. 2010. "Discursive Decision-Making in Meetings of the Global Justice Movements: Culture and Practice." PhD diss., Freie Universität Berlin.
Kriesi, Hanspeter, Ruud Koopmans, Jan-Willem Duyvendak, and Marco Giugni. 1995. *New Social Movements in Western Europe*. Minneapolis: University of Minnesota Press.
Laclau, E., and Chantal Mouffe. 2001. *Hegemony and Socialist Strategy*. London: Verso.
Leach, Darcy K. 2006. "The Way Is the Goal: Ideology and the Practice of Collectivist Democracy in German New Social Movements." PhD diss., University of Michigan, Ann Arbor.
Lipsky, Michael. 1965. *Protest and City Politics*. Chicago: Rand McNally.
Manin, Bernard. 1995. *Principes du gouvernement représentatif*. Paris: Flammarion.
Mansbridge, Jane. 1996. "Using Power/Fighting Power: The Polity." In *Democracy and Difference: Contesting the Boundaries of the Political*, edited by Seyla Benhabib, 46–66. Princeton, N.J.: Princeton University Press.
Markoff, John. 1999. "Globalization and the Future of Democracy." *Journal of World-System Research* 2:277–309.
Melucci, Alberto. 1989. *Nomads of the Present*. London: Hutchinson Radius.
Mouffe, Chantal. 2000. *The Democratic Paradox*. London: Verso.
———. 2005. *On the Political*. London: Routledge.
———. 2009. *The Democratic Paradox*. London: Verso.
Oberschall, Anthony. 1973. *Social Conflict and Social Movements*. Englewood Cliffs, N.J.: Prentice Hall.
O'Brian, R., A. M. Goetz, J. A. Scholte, and M. Williams. 2000. *Contesting Global Governance*. New York: Cambridge University Press.
Pateman, Carole. 1970. *Participation and Democratic Theory*. Cambridge: Cambridge University Press.
Pizzorno, Alessandro. 1981. "Interests and Parties in Pluralism." In *Organizing Interests in Western Europe*, edited by S. Berger, 232–82. Cambridge: Cambridge University Press.
Polletta, Francesca. 2002. *Democracy Is an Endless Meeting: Democracy in American Social Movements*. Chicago: University of Chicago Press.
Rosanvallon, Pierre. 2006. *La contre-démocratie: La politique a l'age de la defiance*. Paris: Seuil.
Rosenau, J. 1998. "Governance and Democracy in a Globalizing World." In *Re-imagining Political Community: Studies in Cosmopolitan Democracy*, edited by D. Archibugi, D. Held, and M. Kohler, 28–57. Cambridge: Polity Press.
Sartori, Giovanni. 1976. *Parties and Party Systems*. Cambridge: Cambridge University Press.
Smith, Jackie. 2008. *Social Movements for Global Democracy*. Baltimore: Johns Hopkins University Press.

Smith, Jackie, Marina Karides, Marc Becker, Dorval Brunelle, Christopher Chase-Dunn, Donatella della Porta, Rosalba Icaza Garza, et al. 2007. *Global Democracy and the World Social Forum.* Boulder, Colo.: Paradigm.

Talpin, Julien. 2011. *Schools of Democracy: How Ordinary Citizens Become Competent in Participatory Budgeting Institutions.* Essex, U.K.: ECPR Press.

Tarrow, Sidney. 1989. *Democracy and Disorder: Protest and Politics in Italy, 1965–1975.* Oxford: Oxford University Press.

Tilly, Charles. 1978. *From Mobilization to Revolution.* Reading, Mass.: Addison-Wesley.

———. 1984. "Social Movements and National Politics." In *State-Making and Social Movements: Essays in History and Theory,* edited by C. Bright and S. Harding, 297–317. Ann Arbor: University of Michigan Press.

———. 2007. *Democracy.* New York: Cambridge University Press.

Touraine, Alain. 1977. *The Self-Production of Society.* Chicago: University of Chicago Press.

Young, Iris Marion. 2003. "Activist Challenges to Deliberative Democracy." In *Debating Deliberative Democracy,* edited by James S. Fishkin and Peter Laslett, 102–20. Malden, Mass.: Blackwell.

Young, Marion. 2000. *Inclusion and Democracy.* Oxford: Oxford University Press.

Zuern, Michael, and Matthias Ecker-Ehrhardt. 2011. *Gesellschaftliche Politisierung und internationale Institutionen.* Frankfurt am Main, Germany: Surkamp.

18

Recent Trends in Public Protest in the United States: The Social Movement Society Thesis Revisited

John D. McCarthy, Patrick Rafail, and Ashley Gromis

In stark contrast with trends in many Western European nations, evidence suggests that public protest participation in the United States during recent decades has been far less common than earlier, suggesting caution in concluding that the United States has become a social movement society. The strong thesis that the United States has become a social movement society rests on four empirical claims: (1) that protests have become more widespread over time, (2) that participation in protests has diffused to a wider array of social groups over time, (3) that protests have become more institutionalized over time, and (4) that protest is subject to less repressive and more institutionalized state response over time (Meyer and Tarrow 1998; Soule and Earl 2005).

Much anecdotal evidence suggests that mass protest in the United States has become rarer up until the turn of the twenty-first century. Evidence from several sources is assembled here, aimed at providing several glimpses at recent U.S. protest trends during the twentieth and early twenty-first centuries, including national survey evidence, protest event evidence from the *New York Times*, and newspaper reports of university campus protests during the last decade. We then discuss the sudden spurt of protest activity, starting with the emergence of the conservative Tea Party in 2009 and the progressive Occupy Wall Street movement in 2011, drawing on newspaper reports of both movements. Together this evidence allows a tentative assessment of the extent to which the United States has become a movement society.

We consider a number of factors as having potentially central roles in the trends of public protest we describe, including movement actor agency embedded in longer-term trends of social movement organization (SMO) formation and evolution, institutionalized processes of channeling and repression of public protest, and the emergence of new forms of civic engagement that compete with more traditional social movement mobilization in general and with protest in particular. We will argue that a broader conceptualization of the elements of a social movement society, consistent with our focus on supply-side processes, can better illuminate trends in public protest in the United States.

The U.S.–European Contrast

Evidence that protest participation remained quite a bit more vigorous during the last decades of the twentieth century in a number of European nations than in the United States comes from the World Values Survey (Van Aelst and Walgrave 2001; Norris 2002; Norris, Walgrave, and Van Aelst 2005). Despite the well-known difficulties in interpreting the meaning of the protest participation item used in those surveys,[1] comparisons of protest trends in European nations with those in the United States show only moderate increases in U.S. participation. Specifically, between 1981 and 2000, the United States only witnessed an 8 percent increase in reported protest participation relative to larger increases in Belgium (26 percent), the Netherlands (20 percent), Sweden (20 percent), and France (12 percent). The percentage of respondents at the turn of the century reporting to have ever protested shows similar patterns, at 20 percent in the United States and 39 percent in Belgium, 32 percent in the Netherlands, 35 percent in Sweden, and 38 percent in France (Norris, Walgrave, and Van Aelst 2005, 199). Norris (2002, 200) shows that the United States (2.9 percent) is well below the mean in increase in demonstration participation (5.5 percent) between the early 1980s and the early 1990s internationally.

The foregoing analyses have shown how normal protest has become in recent decades in many Western democracies, and that has clearly become truer in European nations than in the United States. This trend evidence has buttressed the broader generalization that many European nations have become *social movement societies,* where protest has increasingly become a normal part of the political process. Indeed, Mayer's analysis (chapter 19), although not phrased in terms of the movement society thesis, makes a strong case that France has become the quintessence of a social movement society.

We do not aim to account for the stark differences between these several European nations and the United States here, although we will speculate on their origins in our conclusion. We point to these differences mainly to make the contrast the starting point of our inquiry into whether protest has atrophied in the United States in the late twentieth century, following its flourishing in the late 1960s and early 1970s, and, as we show, has also languished, especially among youths, into the first decade of the twenty-first century.

A Substantive Post-Twentieth-Century Narrative of U.S. Protest Trends

For the first eight years since the turn of the twenty-first century, the U.S. state, controlled by the Bush administration, was almost totally closed to pressure by the new social movements (peace, gay and lesbian, environmental, and women's). During that time, the *level of channeling and repression of protest increased,* both at the federal and state and local levels (including even on university campuses). In the midst of probably the two most unpopular U.S. wars in the modern era, the level of protest against the war in Iraq was anemic and against the war in Afghanistan almost nonexistent. Is this a fair characterization of recent protest mobilization? If so, has the lack of protest mobilization resulted primarily from the closing of political opportunity (openness to influence and the effective action of consequential elite allies) and changing dynamics of repression, or are movement-related factors as well as broader societal-level processes also responsible? We cannot definitively answer these questions here, but much like archeologists, we will assemble bits and pieces of evidence in an attempt to evaluate their degree of plausibility.

The few mass demonstrations against the war in Iraq that have been fielded since its start have been modest in size. Maybe the most widely noticed protest events against the Iraq War were a series of simultaneous vigils held in 2005 in more than sixteen hundred communities across the United States by MoveOn, in support of Cindy Sheehan's vigil at President Bush's Texas ranch. There has been little sustained mobilization on college and university campuses surrounding issues of peace and war, and by some indications, repression against movement mobilization has increased on campuses. For instance, a modest sit-in in 2008 by students who aimed to have Penn State University become more vigilant about labor standards for workers in offshore clothing manufacturing (who create clothing with Penn State logos) resulted in thirty-one arrests. In contrast, when hundreds of students occupied the Penn State student union seven years earlier, they faced no subsequent punishment for their behavior. This pattern, however, is not so widespread in the more systematic evidence we will present later.

Repression of social movement activities, both public protest and organizational, appears to have increased at the local level as well as the national level. Two developments provide evidence here: first, there has been the proliferation of what were formerly called "red squads" in U.S. cities, facilitated by funding associated with the War on Terror. Exposés in a number of U.S. cities have revealed that after 9/11, local police departments created new surveillance units aimed at penetrating terrorist cells, but they, probably inevitably, expanded their scope to the infiltration of mainstream social movement groups such as Amnesty International or groups opposing the Iraq War (for an example of these police activities in Baltimore, Maryland, see Rein 2008; Rein and White 2009). We expect that these undercover activities were quite common across cities in the United States, but most of them have yet to be exposed.[2]

At the same time, local policing of protest in U.S. cities has been evolving, although there is some debate about its general outlines—certainly there is much variation across cities. Nevertheless, Vitale's (2005, 2008) description of the practices of New York City's police in escalating their enforcement of minor law violations during protests suggests a major reversal of the tolerance of minor infractions of protesters during the "negotiated management" era and an escalation of the costs of protest. The evidence we provide for New York City largely corroborates Vitale's analyses.

Finally, the trajectory of the U.S. global justice movement suggests an atrophying of public protest in the face of closed political opportunities and increased repression. That movement seemed on a steep upward trajectory after the "battle in Seattle," which was followed by some major protest demonstrations, but has since declined by all indications. In their analysis of the national-level demobilization of global justice protest, Edwards and Gillham (2008) show how the Washington, D.C., mass demonstration that was planned before 9/11 saw a large number of coalition members withdraw as sponsors and participants following the 9/11 attacks. The sponsors that withdrew tended to be the more mainstream social movement groups, including many new social movements groups. Wood's (2007) analysis suggests, as well, that increasing police repression was responsible for limiting the diffusion of the creative tactics used by protesters in the "battle in Seattle" even before the events of 9/11. Some scholars, notably Hadden and Tarrow (2007), have suggested that the decline in the global justice movement is linked to heightened domestic mobilization after the 9/11 attacks. However, our results suggest that the decrease in global justice protest is likely symptomatic of a broader decline in social movement activism on the whole.

More Systematic Glimpses of Protest Trends in the United States

The most systematic effort thus far to assess the four major claims of the social movement society thesis empirically was accomplished by Soule and Earl (2005) for the 1960–86 period, and they found, using an early version of the Dynamics of Collective Action (DCA) data set, that while U.S. protests reported in the *New York Times* had become larger during that time, the number of protests had declined. We extend their analysis through 2006, which allows us to assess more contemporary trends in U.S. protest.

Proponents of the social movement society thesis have focused their attention almost exclusively on protest and demonstrations, ignoring for the most part associated trends in the expansion of more or less formally organized groups in the "advocacy sector" (Andrews and Edwards 2004). Yet the activities pursued by SMOs, which by all accounts became far more numerous during the 1980s in the United States, are quite diverse, typically including the sponsorship of protest events as just one among many other tactics aimed at generating social change (McCarthy, Smith, and Zald 1996). The size of this social movement sector (McCarthy and Zald 1977; Larson and Soule 2009) and the decisions of constituent SMO leaders in the sector are central to understanding trends in both the number and size of protest events.

Our focus in this essay is primarily on trends in protest events, as we have said, because trend data on individual protest participation in the United States, as elsewhere, are rather scarce and almost always depend on responses to some variation of a question about "ever having participated in a protest." As a consequence, responses include for older cohorts reports of participation in protests that could have occurred decades previously. A recent analysis by Caren, Ghoshal, and Ribas (2012) raises the possibility that such considerations are extremely important factors in understanding historical trends in protest participation. Caren and colleagues aggregate several cross-sectional surveys with measures of U.S. protest participation to estimate period and cohort effects in protest participation rates. Their conclusions raise strong doubts about several key claims of the movement society thesis. In particular, they note that the modest increase in protest participation in the United States (e.g., the 8 percent figure from the World Values Survey we mentioned earlier) is largely explained by above-average participation rates by those in their teens or twenties during the protest wave of the 1960s. In contrast, there is little evidence that protest participation has become more common in younger generations, as the social movement society thesis predicts.

In what follows, we draw on multiple different sources of evidence aimed at describing protest event trends in general and student protest trends, focusing our attention particularly on the most recent period. Establishing historical trends in the rate of protest participation and the number and size of protest events in a nation is akin to establishing the outlines of the features of an elephant hindered by a blindfold. The tools that social scientists have for doing so are quite blunt instruments since more precise ones would be prohibitively expensive. As a result, we will try to be appropriately cautious as we interpret the evidence we present later. After we have described our trend evidence, we will return to a discussion of factors that might be implicated in producing them.

Protest Events in New York City, 1960–2006

By combining two independent protest event data sets, we are able to generate a glimpse of the number of protest events and several of their important features for a forty-seven-year period in New York City, starting in 1960 and ending in 2006. New York represents a conservative test of our expectations about the atrophying of U.S. protest because we would expect protest there to be more vigorous than in many other U.S. communities.

Data Sources

Our analyses of protest events in New York City are based on media reports in the *New York Times* between 1960 and 2006. We focus on any protest event taking place in the five boroughs that collectively compose the city of New York. Several studies (e.g., Earl et al. 2004; Myers and Caniglia 2004; Ortiz et al. 2005) suggest that events occurring in close proximity to New York have a much higher likelihood of coverage by the *New York Times*; however, our decision to focus on New York exclusively minimizes such regional bias. Our data are a composite of two major sources, which contain a combined 6,831 protest events. First, we use the DCA data set collected by Doug McAdam, John McCarthy, Susan Olzak, and Sarah Soule.[3] The DCA contains a record of all of the protest events reported in the *New York Times* between 1960 and 1995. Earl, Soule, and McCarthy (2003), Walker, Martin, and McCarthy (2008), and Rafail, Soule, and McCarthy (2012) provide more exhaustive discussions of the data collection procedures. Second, to pick up event coverage for the period between 1996 and 2006, we use Rafail's (2012) data on social movement mobilization in major U.S. cities. This data source draws on local newspaper coverage of protests and contains information on over eleven thousand demonstrations and other collective action events reported by local newspapers in twenty U.S. cities. For the purposes of this essay, we limited Rafail's data to the New York subsample, which also relies on coverage in the *New York Times* and is based on a similar sampling frame as the DCA.

Results

Analyses of trends in the volume of protest typically examine both the number of protests as well as the size of protests, and we display the first of these trends in Figure 18.1. In New York City, the period after Soule and Earl's (2005) time series, which ended in 1986, shows some increases in the annual number of

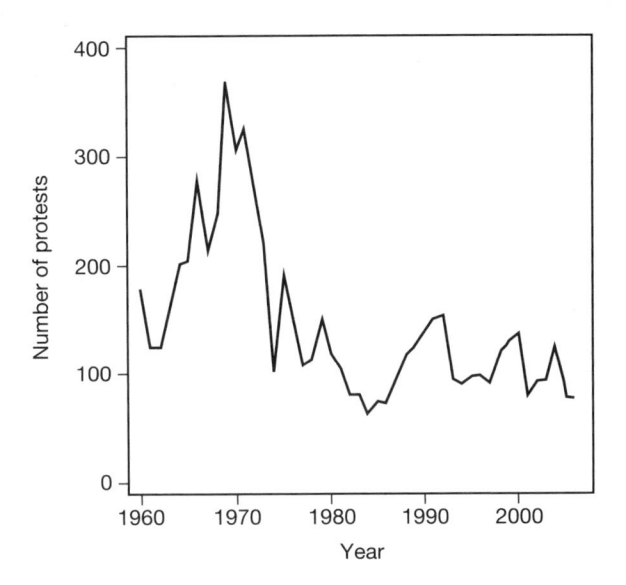

RECENT TRENDS IN PUBLIC PROTEST IN THE UNITED STATES 375

Figure 18.1. Number of reported protests in New York City, 1960–2006.

protests but nothing approaching the peak numbers seen in the late 1960s and early 1970s. If protest were becoming an important part of normal political processes, we would expect more steady increases here.

A common proxy that protest demonstrations are more thoroughly planned and staged is the presence of an identified SMO. Soule and Earl (2005) found that for all U.S. protests reported in the *New York Times,* not just those in New York City, the likelihood that an SMO was present increased between 1960 and 1986. In contrast, when we look only at New York City during the same period, there was a steady decline in SMO presence, which is inconsistent with the social movement society thesis. Note, however, that since the mid-1990s, there has been a moderate increase in reported SMO presence at demonstrations in New York City, as seen in Figure 18.2, consistent with the thesis.

Finally, consistent with the social movement society thesis, we would expect both demonstration participants and police to be decreasingly violent and aggressive over time. Figure 18.3 shows trends in three measures of the presence of civil disobedience, property damage, and the use of interpersonal violence by demonstrators. There was one spike in property damage in 2000, associated with a strike by Verizon workers with high levels of vandalism, particularly contentious protests due to the acquittal of the police officers involved in the Amadou Diallo shooting,[4] and mobilization surrounding the United Nations Millennium Summit. Despite these isolated set events, the

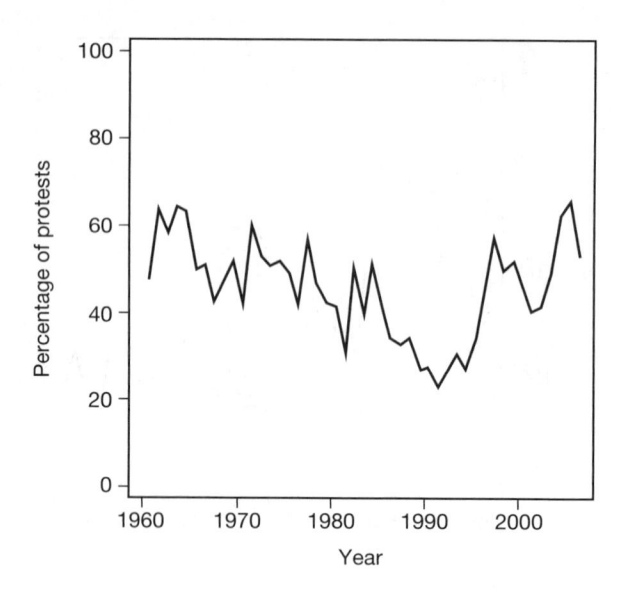

Figure 18.2. Social movement organization presence at protests in New York City, 1960–2006.

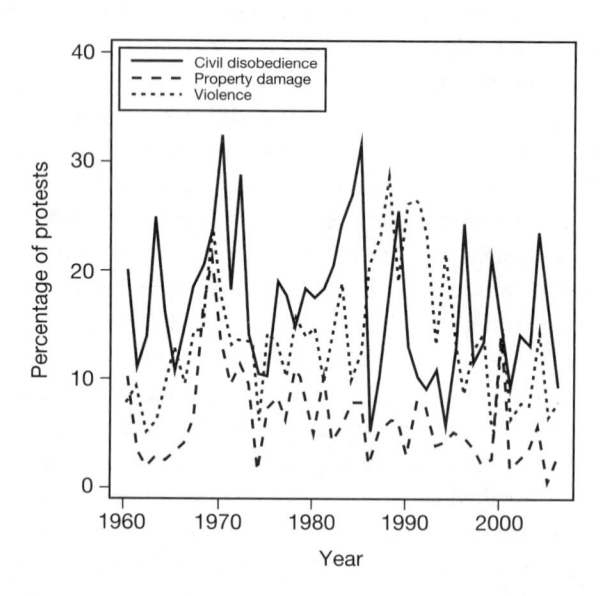

Figure 18.3. Protestor tactics in New York City, 1960–2006.

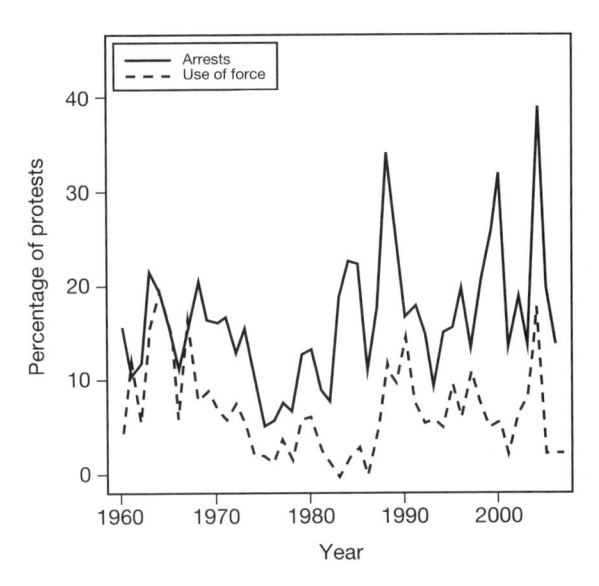

Figure 18.4. Police tactics at protests in New York City, 1960–2006.

trend appears to be a general, albeit highly variable, decline in recent decades. Again, with quite a bit of annual fluctuation, the trend in the use of violence by protesters appears to show a decline in recent decades. Conversely, the presence of civil disobedience by protesters during the last decade appears to be quite high, even by the standards of the protest peak of the late 1960s and early 1970s.

In contrast, as seen in Figure 18.4, police response in New York City does not reflect the expectations of the social movement society thesis—the use of force is elevated, on average, after the mid-1990s, and though the use of arrest by police has high levels of annual fluctuation, it is on average higher than during the peak of the 1960s cycle of protest. In sum, then, protesters in recent decades in New York City appear to be less violent, if more civilly disobedient, but police have been far more aggressive. Preliminary evidence suggests that this pattern of police response may be peculiar to New York City owing to the adoption of "broken windows" (see Kelling and Coles 1996; Vitale 2008) philosophies in dealing with perceived public disorder (Rafail 2012).

Finally, we also compared antiwar mobilization in New York City relating to the Vietnam War and the war in Iraq, and our evidence suggests that there has been a modest decline in antiwar protest as a proportion of all protest events. Of a total of 462 events reported by the *New York Times* in 1970–71, just over 14 percent were in support of the peace movement, opposed to the Vietnam War, or opposed to the draft. We also examined the primary claim for reported New York City events taking place between 2003 and 2006 and found that of the 378 reported protest events, only 11 percent were in support of the peace movement, against the wars in Afghanistan or Iraq, or against the War on Terror more generally. Though this represents only a 3 percent decline in protest activity, if a social movement society had taken root, one would expect considerably higher levels of resistance to the war and that such protests would increase after the Iraq War became increasingly unpopular. Instead, we find that by 2006, less than 8 percent of reported New York City protests made specific reference to the peace movement as their primary claim.

Overall, the evidence we have presented for New York City does not suggest a steady expansion of protest in recent decades, especially during the last decade for which we have indicators, nor does it portray a dramatic atrophying of protest. During the same period, demonstrators became less aggressive, while New York City police became more so.

Student Protest

We now turn to trends in protest by students in the United States, first examining an extended time series of survey evidence gathered from successive cohorts of graduating high school students and then presenting protest event data gathered for eighty college and university campuses for the previous decade.

Reported Protest Participation and Intention to Protest for High School Seniors, 1976–2008

Monitoring the Future is an annual survey of eighth-, tenth-, and twelfth-grade students (Johnston et al. 2008). Each year, students are selected for participation from a nationally representative sample of schools. The survey asks students a variety of questions and includes a small subset of questions pertaining to political participation. The data presented here were taken from the annual survey of twelfth-grade students from 1976–2008. Students were asked, "Have you ever done, or do you plan to do, the following things? Participate in a lawful demonstration." They could answer, "I already have," "I probably will," or "I probably won't." The results for the time series are presented in Figure 18.5.

First, it is clear that protest participation is a rare phenomenon for high school seniors in the United States during the entire period, never rising above 10 percent in any year. Consistent with the idea that protest was becoming increasingly legitimate, there was a gradual rise of about 10 percent in willingness to protest between the mid-1980s and the early 1990s. What, however,

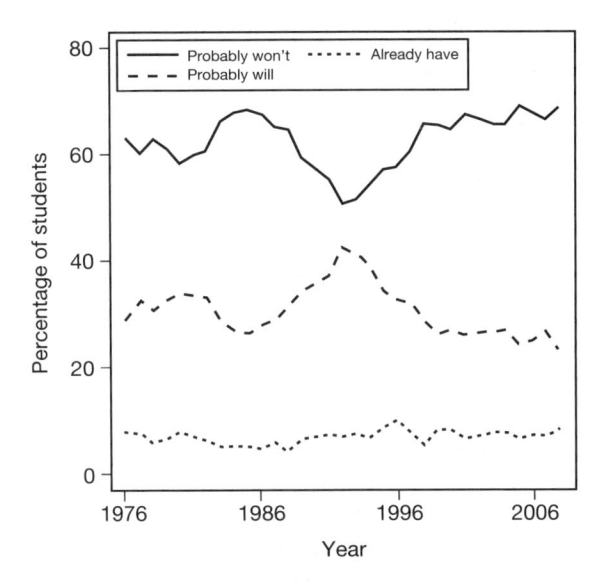

Figure 18.5. High school protest demonstration participation, 1976–2008.

is most striking about these trends is the steady decrease in stated willingness to protest after the early 1990s and the accompanying steady increase in the stated unwillingness to protest, reaching about 70 percent of high school respondents by 2008. If the United States were becoming increasingly like a social movement society, one would certainly expect an increasing proportion of high school graduating seniors to at least express a willingness to participate in protests, even if they have not yet had the opportunity to do so. As is seen later, however, the evidence presented on the prevalence of protest demonstrations on college and university campuses during the last decade is entirely consistent with the trends pointing to a decline in youth protest.

University Campus Protest during the First Decade of the Twenty-First Century

If the New York City evidence is a story more of stability than of increase or precipitous decline in U.S. protest, the evidence we have assembled on campus protest is more straightforward. We will summarize it and then try to place it in context by comparing it to evidence about campus protest in the 1970–71 academic year, during the height of the campus student movement.

The data presented here on contemporary student protest were gathered from a sample of eighty four-year colleges and universities located across the United States (Gromis 2010). The institutions were randomly sampled from a larger data set containing all four-year institutions of higher education located in the United States (Van Dyke, Dixon, and Carlon 2007). Local newspapers from the surrounding communities were used to gather reports on protest events that occurred at institutions from 1998 to 2008. For an event to be included in the final sample, it had to be a collective action that occurred in the public forum on or very near campus, and the participants had to articulate a specific claim—similar criteria to those used for inclusion of *New York Times* protest events reported previously.

All campuses were stratified on the basis of their prior history of student activism: (1) those with activism in both the 1960s and the 1990s, (2) those with activism in the 1960s but not in the 1990s, (3) those with activism in the 1990s but not in the 1960s, and (4) those with no history of activism in either era. Twenty campuses were randomly chosen from each stratum. This method of stratification was derived from Van Dyke's (1998) proposal of the existence of campus-based activist subcultures that affect the likelihood of subsequent student activism. Whereas the original research established a link between student activism in the 1930s and 1960s, the strata presented here were chosen to investigate the relationship between student activism in the 1960s and 1990s and contemporary student protest. The results show no differences in the prevalence of protest among the three strata of activist campuses, so Figure 18.6 presents the average number of reported protest events per campus for the activist campuses versus the protest-dormant campuses.

A total of 750 protest events were identified for the eighty campuses for the eleven-year study period. The average number of protests per year for campuses with no history of activism hovers around zero. On the activist campuses, the average number of protest events never reaches two per year. None of the reports for the 750 protest events identified mentioned the use of violence by protesters, nor was there any report of property damage taking place. In only 2.5 percent of the events were there reports of any arrests of participants, and in less than 1 percent of the events was there any report of the use of force by police. The portrait of protest on campuses during the recent decade is one of protest being quite rare and protest participants being extraordinarily ruly, and only rarely encountering heavy-handed police responses to their protests—and this is a sample of campuses heavily skewed toward those with a prior record of student activism (see also McCarthy, Martin, and McPhail 2007).

We have no directly comparable evidence from earlier periods on U.S. campuses, but the results of a survey of campuses where campus administrators reported on protest events for the 1970–71 academic year stand in vivid contrast to the evidence we have just summarized (Bayer and Astin 1971). The researchers sampled eight strata of institutions of higher education, including

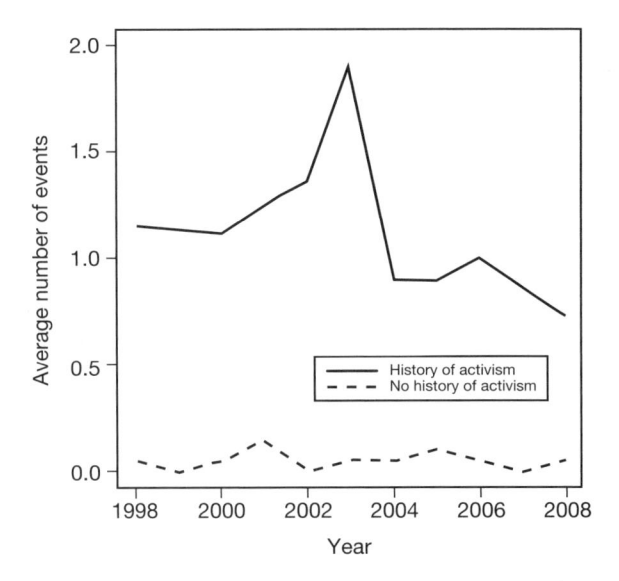

Figure 18.6. Average annual number of campus protests per institution, 1998–2008.

two-year schools. This resulted in a total of 369 campuses from a population of 2,362 campuses. They found an average of five protests per institution that year, and almost 20 percent of the campuses experienced a "severe" protest, defined as one "that involved one or more of the following acts: (1) burning a building, (2) bombing a building, (3) breaking into or wrecking a building or its furnishings, (4) destroying records, files, or papers, (5) any campus march, picketing, or rally accompanied by physical violence, (6) occupying a building or a section of a building, (7) obstructing a building entrance, (8) holding officials captive, (9) blocking vehicular traffic or streets, (10) interrupting a school function (e.g. classes, speeches or meetings), (11) a general campus strike or boycotting classes or a school function, (12) any other incidents that result in persons being injured or killed" (303). Admittedly, we are comparing a quiescent period on campuses with the one of the peak years of the student movement, but the difference in the extent and nature of protests between the two periods appears to be far greater than that between what we see for New York City protests. It is hard to avoid the conclusion, based on this evidence, along with evidence drawn from Monitoring the Future, that campus protest was almost dormant during the recent decade, which is certainly completely inconsistent with any expectations that could be derived from the social movement society thesis.

Toward a Supply-Side Understanding of Recent U.S. Protest Trends

Having established that protest mobilization in the United States has at best remained stagnant, and more than likely is in decline, we use this section to explicate our findings and situate them in broader trends taking place across the United States. Specifically, we explore several examples of fundamental mobilization processes that we believe have altered the landscape of organized dissent; that is, we look at organizational mobilization structures that affect the supply of opportunities for citizens to participate in collective action in general and protest in particular. Trends in the development of these structures are, we suggest, important in making sense of recent trends in protest in the United States.

Bert Klandermans's basic insight about *action mobilization* (Klandermans 1997) is that sympathetic potential participants must be made aware of participation opportunities, and in addition, they are most likely to participate if they are asked to do so, especially by people they know and trust. And it is organized social movement actors whose representatives and participants do most of the asking. Consequently, if one is to make sense of longer trends in movement mobilization and protest, an important place to look beyond the motivations of potential participants is the full landscape of social actors that constitute the universe of groups that attempt to mobilize citizens, both movement actors and the other actors with whom they compete for citizen attention and participation (see also Schussman and Soule 2005). The founding of SMOs and the evolution of fields of movement organizations are importantly governed by institutional processes that, once in motion, tend to be highly path dependent, even if they may have been strongly influenced by political structures and processes at their inception. We refer to these as *fundamental mobilization processes*.

Of course, we cannot easily account the entire landscape of social actors that seek citizen involvement (the full volume of asks), so we ground our findings in the emergence of what we see as two key, historically specific clusters of SMOs that have shaped the current level of movement mobilization in the United States as well as two other clusters of civic infrastructures that may draw potential participants away from movement mobilization of the type witnessed in the 1960s wave of protest. We briefly describe the evolution of four important institutional–organizational domains that has each had, and continues to have, an important impact on shaping the extent and form of social movement and protest mobilization, mostly at the local level. We then draw some general conclusions about the cases in an attempt to provide a partial answer to the question of what factors are affecting trends in protest.

Contemporary Labor Mobilization

After years of deep decline in membership and political influence, segments of organized labor in the United States have vigorously adopted social movement tactics, including various forms of protest, which is now beginning to reverse its fortunes. The labor movement has waged a series of successful organizing campaigns over the last several decades (Martin 2008a). Activists in the 1960s pioneered the tactic of the "corporate campaign," which brings a variety of pressures to bear on firms to bring them to the bargaining table, and it has now been widely adopted by a number of large labor unions. These unions have invested increasingly large amounts of resources into organizing and have also mobilized their memberships for local, state, and national elections.

The new labor repertoire includes public protest, but this tactic is used very strategically in concert with other strategies, and sustained protest campaigns are relatively rare. These unions also organized "Union Summer" (an internship program for college students to get a taste of labor organizing work) a decade ago, which, it has been shown, sowed the seeds for the student movement aimed at support of third world sweatshop workers through their own universities' purchase of branded apparel. The student movement against sweatshops has been the most active movement on college and university campuses in recent years, waging extended campaigns of protest and confrontation on many of them. The recent momentum of labor organizing continued to remain strong during the 1990s (Van Dyke, Dixon, and Carlon 2007; Martin 2008a, 2008b). The expected support for progressive labor groups from President Obama, however, has not subsequently materialized.

Community-Based Organizing

Beginning in the 1960s, two small tributaries of local community organizing began to expand, one by co-opting the structure of local church congregations (e.g., Industrial Areas Foundation) and the other by recruiting individual memberships (e.g., ACORN). These groups share a commitment to building power by organizing the members of less advantaged communities and disdain what they call "social movement activism," which is considered to be *issue* rather than *power* based. The leaders of these groups choose issues strategically rather than as the result of a preexisting preference. The first tributary has proliferated most dramatically in recent decades, with several networks of such groups becoming dense enough in some states to allow successful state-level efforts at influence. The second tributary depends more on external resources, because individual members have few resources, but have had notable successes that have helped their mobilization efforts. Community-based organizations

(CBOs) employ a wide variety of tactics, especially including confrontation protest, but they do so quite strategically (Walker and McCarthy 2004; Swarts 2008). There may be more than five thousand of these organizations in communities across the United States, and they are capable of mobilizing tens of thousands of supporters. The groups in the first tributary typically maintain a nonpartisan stance and have mostly stayed out of electoral politics beyond endorsing candidates. The organizations of the second tributary tend to be more partisan, having been quite active in political campaigns. For example, ACORN fielded extensive voter registration activities and turn-out-the-vote activities during the 2008 U.S. presidential campaign. Noteworthy is the fact that both leading Democratic Party presidential candidates in 2008 had, early in their careers, been involved in one of these CBOs, with President Obama having gone through the systematic training offered by one of the major CBO networks, Gamaliel. President Obama's election heartened the activists in the CBO community, who anticipated federal facilitation of their ongoing grassroots organizing projects. They were sorely disappointed, however, when a subsequent Republican-led attack on ACORN succeeded in discrediting the organization (Dreier and Martin 2010), its federal financial support was withdrawn, and its bankrupt central office was forced to spin off local affiliates to nonprofit independent status. This all occurred without any word of support from the new president or members of his administration.

Grassroots Lobbying

Beginning in the 1970s, movement organizations of both the right and the left began to develop new technologies for mobilizing the support of sympathizers (both their labor and their contributions), including direct mail, telephone solicitation, and, with the advent of the Internet, a variety of new mechanisms. This basic mobilization technology depends on what we call *thin social infrastructures* (McCarthy 1987; see also Roggeband and Duyvendak, chapter 5), which target masses of sympathizers and provide them with messages and targets of influence, ultimately facilitating their communication with those targets. The technology has come to be known as *grassroots lobbying*. Pioneered by movement groups and their technical facilitators, grassroots lobbying was quickly adopted by corporate groups as well as agencies of the state. The demand for these services quickly spawned an expanding industry of grassroots lobbying firms that offered their services to any groups willing to pay for them. Grassroots lobbying created a vast industry of operatives asking citizens to become active in a variety of ways: contacting politicians, writing letters to newspapers, and donating to groups of many kinds. This form of activism has expanded dramatically and provides citizens the feeling of participating in the support of causes. However, it does not constitute movement activism nor draw from the standard tactical repertoires that we traditionally consider protest, even when sponsored by progressive movements and especially when sponsored by corporate and nonprofit groups. Analysts of grassroots lobbying term the latter "astroturf" (Walker 2009).

Regressive Progressivism

During the last two decades, a massive (but so far not enumerated) number of public participation projects have been established in local communities across the United States (Lee 2007). Citizens have been incorporated into decision making in deliberative forums in governments, workplaces, and organizations as well as in many types of community-wide coalitions such as antidrug coalitions. Against the backdrop of a widespread discourse on the "decline of civic engagement" in the United States, motivated to a great extent by the work of Skocpol (1999) and Putnam (2000), the spread of these forms of citizen participation elicited enthusiasm. But what appears to have been a salutary growth in forums of deliberative democracy is now being more critically evaluated because the forums are mostly facilitated by elites, are heavily managed by professional facilitators, and deliberate over narrowly defined issue agendas, leading some critics to characterize the phenomenon as "regressive progressivism" (Lee, McQuarrie, and Walker 2009). A chronicle of the rapidly expanding number of antidrug coalitions during this period suggests that they, too, provide opportunities for very extensive participation, thereby both channeling the focus of community participants toward a small set of, usually noncontroversial, issues and absorbing large amounts of time, energy, and resources of those who become participants (McCarthy 2005). Most of these forums are intentionally nonpartisan and consensus seeking, eschewing either individual or collective confrontation of any kind.

Patterns seen in the first two domains, labor mobilization and community-based organizing, are consistent with our impressions about a surge of, or at least less stagnation in, local movement mobilization in recent decades. These patterns are also consistent with evidence showing the predominance of state and locally sponsored and focused protest events in Chicago, Illinois, since 1970, more marked in 2000 (McAdam et al. 2005). Furthermore, the patterns are also reflected in the extensive mobilization documented by Ingram, Yue, and Rao (2010) against the opening of new Wal-Mart stores in local communities across the United States. Between 1998 and 2005, Wal-Mart made proposals to open 1,599 new stores in U.S. communities, and in more than 35 percent of instances, local protests occurred opposing the openings. However, only about 17 percent of those protests appeared to have been organized by existing or newly formed local SMOs, suggesting that the majority of them were actually spontaneous, locally based, grassroots affairs.

The other two domains of local mobilization, grassroots lobbying and regressive progressivism, show the dramatic expansion of organizational fields that create many opportunities for citizen participation but not in SMOs or protests and demonstrations. To the extent that these opportunities, and ones like them, successfully compete with efforts by movement groups to mobilize, they may contribute what look like trends in movement demobilization. Together, they absorb the activist impulses of individuals with the potential for being mobilized for more traditional forms of national movement participation and protest. Each of the cases depends on the emergence and development of populations of organizations created by organizational entrepreneurs that have institutionalized particular organizational forms and sets of tactics for asking people to participate in collective action. It is this feature of these four cases that leads us to believe that the evolution of such institutionalized organizational arenas of mobilization is likely to be quite highly path dependent; that is, once these vehicles have been formed and are successful, they are quite unlikely to change their tactical or substantive approaches. Had similar clusters of movement organizations, or social movement industries, dedicated to more national-level protest mobilization emerged during recent decades, the trends we have described might have looked quite different. The clusters that did emerge focused more on local-level mobilization or on mobilization of other forms of civic engagement than on protest.

The Tea Party and Occupy Surprises

Intruding on the core theme of our narrative highlighting the languishing of protest in the United States was the emergence of the Tea Party movement in 2009 and the Occupy Wall Street movement, which burst on the scene in New York City in September 2011.

Over one thousand Tea Party events were held on April 15, 2009, with subsequent waves occurring in 2010 and 2011, and we expect them to continue for the next several years. Though the Tea Parties were generally portrayed as quintessential of populist anger resulting in grassroots mobilization, the Tea Parties had considerable backing from several grassroots lobbying organizations, including the American Family Association and Freedomworks, a group directed by one-time House of Representative speaker Dick Armey. In addition, several Fox News personalities devoted a considerable amount of airtime to the protests, and some covered the protests during their nightly programs.[5] We have collected a sample of over five thousand media reports drawn from 453 local newspapers coupled with the Internet listings of the

Tea Party locations.[6] Our preliminary results suggest that the Tea Parties were generally quite large: more than 26 percent had between 1,000 and 9,999 participants. Our preliminary results for the April 15, 2010, and 2011 Tea Party rallies suggest that there were fewer of them and that they were somewhat smaller each subsequent year, although, as we show, newspaper coverage of the Tea Party movement remained very intense. Nevertheless, those three waves of rallies together quickly alter our portrayal of the trend of protest in the United States since the turn of the twenty-first century but, we believe, reinforce the importance of the fundamental mobilization processes and structures we have emphasized in accounting for protest trends in general.

The simultaneous mobilization of these local protest demonstrations reflects the fundamental supply-side mobilization processes we have discussed. A number of national grassroots lobbying groups facilitated the first round of simultaneous local Tea Party protests in 2009 and again in April 2010 and 2011, and a coalition of local groups that formed during that period are now linked to a federation, known as the Tea Party Patriots, that was formed in late February 2009. But a survey conducted by the *Washington Post* in 2010 indicated that close to half the local groups were not affiliated with any national group (Gardner 2010).

It seems clear that the Tea Party movement marks the onset of a more active and vocal conservative movement that is vigorously embracing the traditionally progressive tactic of public protest. Its vigor is clearly partially the result of grassroots lobbying efforts, where national political operatives are instrumental in creating new opportunities for dissatisfied citizens to protest. As well, over 20 percent of Tea Parties in April 2009 had at least one speaker or participant who was a political figure, and of these, 95 percent were members of the Republican Party, suggesting the existence of strong associations between these events and local political party structures, creating an additional mobilization structure encouraging individual participation. The Tea Party movement appears to have maintained its muster, with a handful of well-funded candidates securing Republican nominations in the 2010 midterm elections as well as having fielded a large unified protest in Washington, D.C., on August 28, 2010, where several estimates indicated that at least one hundred thousand people were present, making it one of the largest protest events to occur in Washington, D.C., in over a decade.

Occupy Wall Street, in contrast to the Tea Party, is without question a fully grassroots phenomenon with roots in the Canadian activist group Adbusters. Following the first encampment in Zuccotti Park in New York City beginning September 17, 2011, there was a rapid diffusion of similar encampments in hundreds of other U.S. cities, in other cities around the world, and on many university campuses. Courting police orders to disperse by occupying public space twenty-four hours a day, the movement focused its attacks on Wall Street greed with the slogan "We Are the 99 Percent." During the first several months of 2012, police in many occupied cities forcibly dispersed Occupy campers, with one of the most confrontational dispersions occurring in Oakland, California.

Adopting a firm commitment to participatory democratic decision-making processes within their encampments, these local protest communities quickly drew national attention to the issue of growing U.S. income inequality. The decentralized nature of the movement, along with its deep commitment to local prefigurative political process, meant that little national coherence in specific policy views and/or recommendations emerged.[7] And unlike the Tea Party movement, the Occupy movement has thus far eschewed involvement in party politics. Thus its message, tactics, and organizational form have led astute critics to conclude that its impact is not likely to be through politics and public policy (Amenta 2012); rather, many argue (e.g., Gamson 2012) that Occupy's impact will be primarily cultural, bringing the discussion of inequality into the mainstream conversation during and following the 2012 presidential election.

Figure 18.7 shows very dramatically how the Occupy movement has captured the attention of newspapers in the United States during approximately the first five months of its efforts, contrasting its coverage with the ongoing coverage of the Tea Party movement. To create monthly estimates of the frequency of media coverage for both movements, we used full-text searches of 2,233 U.S.-based newspapers between January 1, 2011, and January 31, 2012.[8] It is clear from Figure 18.7 that coverage of the Occupy movement peaked in October 2011, and this continued through November, eclipsing even the coverage of the Tea Party. This is quite is remarkable, given the ongoing role of Fox News as an echo chamber for Tea Party activities and influence, widely understood to magnify its prominence in the news. As the occupations ended—either voluntarily or by force—media attention to the movement declined considerably, with a 50 percent decrease in coverage between November and December, followed by another significant drop between December and January 2012.

Even in the face of waning media attention to the Occupy movement itself, Figure 18.8 suggests that the Occupy movement may have altered public discourse. To construct Figure 18.8, we used monthly counts of the string "income inequality" from January 2011 to January 2012, using the same set of 2,233 newspapers used in Figure 18.7. The pattern shows overwhelmingly that, indeed, the rapidly expanding Occupy Wall Street movement had shifted

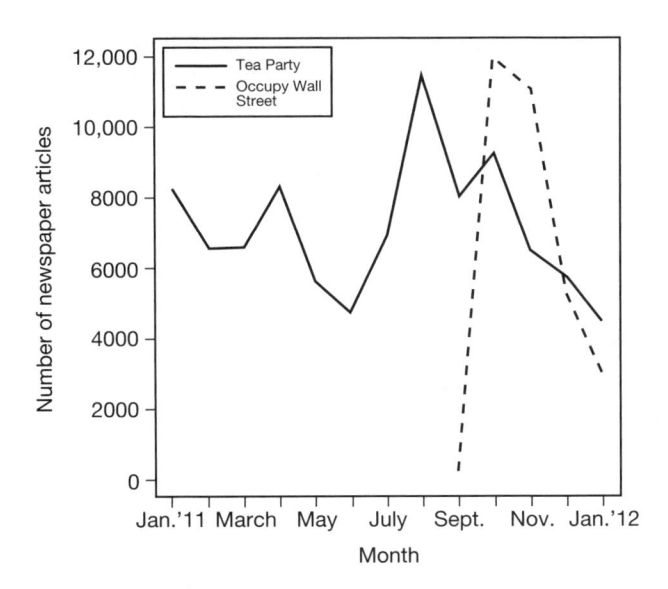

Figure 18.7. Newspaper coverage of the Tea Party and Occupy Wall Street movements in 2,233 newspapers, January 1, 2011, to January 31, 2012.

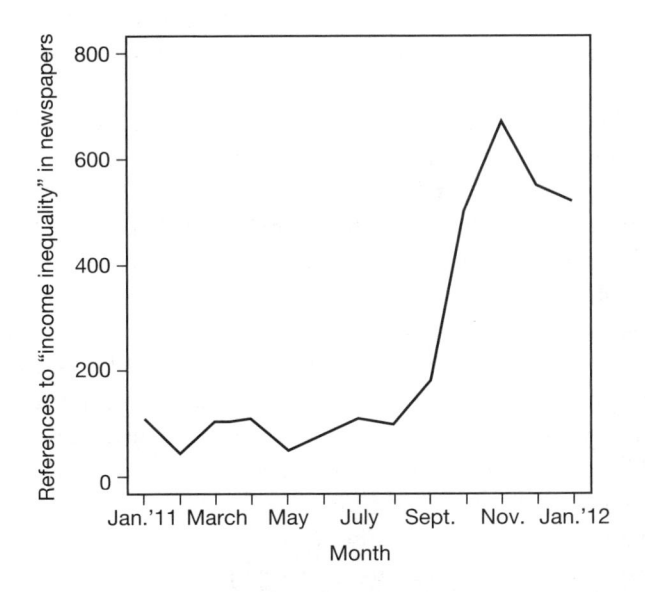

Figure 18.8. References to "income inequality" in 2,233 newspapers, January 1, 2011, to January 31, 2012.

media attention to the issues of income inequality, although some suggest that such attention rarely penetrates very deeply into the basic processes generating that inequality (see Goodwin 2012). Nonetheless, it is striking that even though attention to the Occupy movement itself declined relatively rapidly, discussions mentioning income inequality remained relatively high. From this we may cautiously conclude that the Occupy movement has shifted the political discourse in the United States, even if the occupations did not result in direct policy changes.

Summary and Conclusion

We began by questioning the notion that protest has become an increasingly common and largely a normalized facet of American political life, at least relative to other Western democracies. Our observations have largely been based on anecdotal evidence, and when more systematic analyses have been undertaken (e.g., Soule and Earl 2005), the social movement society thesis has received mixed support. Drawing from a more comprehensive number of sources examining protest trends over time, youth participation in activism, and campus mobilization, our analyses paint a somewhat more complicated picture. At best, they suggest that protest activity in the United States had stagnated through the first several years of the twenty-first century. For example, we provide strong evidence that protest rates in New York City have remained at a consistently lower rate relative to the 1960s wave of mobilization. That said, there is a definite ebb and flow to the trends we have examined, and there have been occasional increases in mean protest size or the frequency of civil disobedience. However, these are trends that appear far from stable and are likely related to specific events (e.g., the 2004 Republican National Convention in New York City) rather than a steady increase in heightened periods of contentious activism. This claim is further buttressed by the relative decline in antiwar mobilization despite the wide and rising unpopularity of the Iraq War. Again, it is important to emphasize that it appears as though more coercive protest control may be on the rise in New York City, rather than a tendency toward the increasingly institutionalized police response that social movement society advocates have hypothesized. The evidence we presented for high school student mobilization and campus activism points to largely complementary trends: high school seniors are increasingly *less* likely to participate in demonstrations, and even college campuses with an activist history average less than two reported protests per year. Finally, the analysis by Caren, Ghoshal, and Ribas (2012) suggests that individual protest participation has declined in recent decades. Overall, then, on the basis of the totality of the data we present, we do not find any compelling evidence that the United States has evolved into a social movement society based on trends in public protest in recent years, even if protest is now a more central and important component of the political process in other Western countries.

To explain these striking findings, we have invoked the central importance of supply-side factors that have altered the fundamental mobilization processes in the United States. More specifically, we argue that the labor movement has come to rely on street-level protests much more strategically rather than as a staple component of their tactical repertoire. As well, the increasing salience of CBOs such as ACORN has also funneled activism away from more traditional avenues of 1960s social movement participation. At the same time, the increasing frequency of grassroots lobbying, coupled with an increase in organizations espousing values of regressive progressivism, further dilutes the pool of would-be participants, ultimately decreasing participation across the entire social movement sector.

The sudden appearance of the Tea Party movement on the U.S. protest scene is quite consistent with our accounts of recent protest trends, though our very sketchy preliminary analysis clearly requires a more comprehensive evaluation. The emergence and rapid expansion of the Occupy movement, however, might pose a challenge to our central claims, especially with its highly confrontational tactics, grassroots spontaneity, and commitment to nonbureaucratic forms. The Occupy movement remains in its infancy, making it difficult to make definitive statements evaluating the movement; however, we provide two speculative comments about the movement. First, despite its rapid diffusion in fall 2011, the Occupy movement appeared to decline in activity just as quickly. It remains to be seen whether the Occupy movement will be able to maintain the momentum it gathered toward the end of 2011, particularly as media interest in the movement declines. If there is a resurgence of activity, then the Occupy movement does provide a striking counterexample to our central claims, but if the movement continues to decline in activity, we may conclude that it has been in many ways a temporary aberration in the overall pattern we have described. Second, much like the Tea Party movement, decentralized Occupy chapters have taken root in cities across the United States and beyond. This is quite consistent with our supply-side explanation and suggests that the Occupy movement's organization is at least somewhat compatible with our arguments.

Let us conclude by returning again to the concept of the social movement society. If, as we have argued, trends in protest can only be fully understood in relation to the size and shape of a society's social movement sector, then the local and national SMOs that make up the sector must also be conceived as important dimensions along with the extent, social composition, institutionalization, and tolerance by authorities of public protest. Observers suggested at the end of the cycle of mass protest during the 1960s and 1970s that it was importantly the result of the rapid expansion of SMOs accompanying it (McCarthy and Zald 1973). And although doing so is not our purpose here, in explaining the contrast between trends in protest in the United States and the same trends in several European nations that appear to more closely resemble the profile of social movement societies, we are inclined to invoke the centrality of political parties and labor movements. Both institutions remain substantially stronger in European nations than in the United States, despite Ruud Koopmans's (chapter 15) willingness to write their epitaph.

Notes

1. The standard item used to make the comparisons asks the respondent if she has "ever attended a lawful demonstration." Response options include "have done," "would do," and "would never do." Asked in this way, the results do not reflect rates of protest in any specified time period but over the lifetime of respondents and, therefore, over several decades, new cohorts of respondents as well as exiting cohorts. As a result, the analyst should be quite cautious in interpreting trends on the basis of responses.

2. In what appears to be the most comprehensive source to date, the American Civil Liberties Union has maintained a listing of spying and infiltration by U.S. states. Their findings suggest that law enforcement agencies have implemented such programs in a strong majority of states. This is available on the World Wide Web at http://www.aclu.org/spy-files/spying-first-amendment-activity-state-state.

3. This data set and all the accompanying documentation is available for download at http://www.dynamicsofcollectiveaction.com/.

4. Amadou Diallo was an unarmed Guinean immigrant who was shot and killed by four New York Police Department officers in 1999. The shooting and its aftermath led to a sustained and highly contentious campaign against police brutality and racial profiling.

5. Despite this, note that only approximately 10 percent of the five thousand newspaper articles we examine mention these sponsoring organizations or Fox News in particular.

6. Our research team includes the three authors and Edward T. Walker.

7. Attempts to construct a list of demands, such as the "99 Percent Declaration," were not universally adopted by all groups participating in the occupations.

8. For the Tea Party, our search string was "Tea Party" or "Tea Parties." For Occupy Wall Street, we used Occupy and Protest*. In the latter search string, the asterisk is a wildcard operator.

References

Amenta, Edwin. 2012. "The Potential Political Consequences of Occupy Wall Street." *Mobilizing Ideas,* January 2. http://mobilizingideas.wordpress.com/2012/01/02/the-potential-political-consequences-of-occupy-wall-street/.

Andrews, Kenneth, and Bob Edwards. 2004. "Advocacy Organizations in the US Political Process." *Annual Review of Sociology* 30:479–506.

Bayer, Alen E., and Alexander W. Astin. 1971. "Campus Unrest, 1970–71: Was It Really All That Quiet?" *Educational Record,* Fall, 301–13.

Caren, Neal, Raj Andrew Ghoshal, and Vanesa Ribas. 2012. "A Social Movement Generation: Cohort and Period Trends in Protest Attendance and Petition Signing." *American Sociological Review* 76:125–51.

Dreier, Peter, and Christopher R. Martin. 2010. "How ACORN Was Framed: Political Controversey and Media Agenda Setting." *Perspective on Politics* 8:761–92.

Earl, Jennifer, Andrew Martin, John D. McCarthy, and Sarah A. Soule. 2004. "Newspapers and Protest Event Analysis." *Annual Review of Sociology* 30:65–80.

Earl, Jennifer, Sarah A. Soule, and John D. McCarthy. 2003. "Protest under Fire? Explaining the Policing of Protest." *American Sociological Review* 68:581–606.

Edwards, Bob, and Patrick Gillham. 2008. "Legitimacy Preservation and Coalition Fragmentation: The Demise of the Mobilization for Global Justice in the Aftermath of the September 11th 2001 Terrorist Attacks." Unpublished manuscript.

Gamson, William. 2012. "Cultural Outcomes of the Occupy Movement." *Mobilizing Ideas,* January 2. http://mobilizingideas.wordpress.com/2012/01/02/cultural-outcomes-of-the-occupy-movement/.

Gardner, Amy. 2010. "Gauging the Scope of the Tea Party Movement in America." *Washington Post,* October 24.

Goodwin, Jeff. 2012. "Occupy the Media." *Mobilizing Ideas,* January 16. http://mobilizingideas.wordpress.com/2012/01/16/occupy-the-media/.

Gromis, Ashley. 2010. "'Is There Still Something Happening Here?' The Impact of Historical Activist Campus Sub-cultures on Contemporary Student Protest, 1998–2008." Undergraduate honors thesis, Pennsylvania State University, University Park.

Hadden, Jennifer, and Sydney Tarrow. 2007. "Spillover or Spillout? The Global Justice Movement in the United States after 9/11." *Mobilization* 12, no. 4: 359–76.

Ingram, Paul, Lori Qingyuan Yue, and Hayagreeva Rao. 2010. "Trouble in Store: Probes, Protests, and Store Openings by Wal-Mart, 1998–2007." *American Journal of Sociology* 116:53–92.

Johnston, Lloyd D., Jerald G. Bachman, Patrick M. O'Malley, and John E. Schulenberg. 2008. "Monitoring the Future: A Continuing Study of the Lifestyles and

Values of Youth, 1976–2008." Ann Arbor, Mich.: Inter-university Consortium for Political and Social Research.

Kelling, George L., and Catherine Coles. 1996. *Fixing Broken Windows: Restoring Order and Reducing Crime in Our Communities.* New York: Free Press.

Klandermans, Bert. 1997. *The Social Psychology of Protest.* Oxford: Blackwell.

Larson, Jeff A., and Sarah A. Soule. 2009. "Sector-Level Dynamics and Collective Action in the United States, 1965–1975." *Mobilization* 14, no. 3: 293–314.

Lee, Caroline W. 2007. "Is There a Place for Private Conversation in Public Dialogue? Comparing Stakeholder Assessments of Informed Communication in Collaborative Regional Planning." *American Journal of Sociology* 113:41–96.

Lee, Caroline W., Michael McQuarrie, and Edward T. Walker. 2009. "Democratizing Inequalities: Participation without Parity." Working project statement to the National Research Council.

Martin, Andrew W. 2008a. "The Institutional Logic of Union Organizing and the Effectiveness of Social Movement Repertoires." *American Journal of Sociology* 113:1067–1103.

———. 2008b. "Resources for Success: Social Movements, Strategic Resource Allocation, and Union Organizing Outcomes." *Social Problems* 55:501–24.

McAdam, Doug, Robert J. Sampson, Simon Weffer, and Heather MacIndoe. 2005. "'There Will Be Fighting in the Streets': The Distorting Lens of Social Movement Theory." *Mobilization* 10, no. 1: 1–18.

McCarthy, John D. 1987. "Pro-Life and Pro-Choice Mobilization: Infrastructure Deficits and New Technologies." In *Social Movements in an Organizational Society,* edited by Mayer N. Zald and John D. McCarthy, 49–66. New Brunswick, N.J.: Transaction.

———. 2005. "Velcro Triangles: Elite Mobilization of Local Anti-drug Coalitions." In *Routing the Opposition: Social Movements, Public Policy, and Democracy,* edited by David S. Meyer, Valarie Jenness, and Helen Ingram, 87–116. Minneapolis: University of Minnesota Press.

McCarthy, John D., Andrew W. Martin, and Clark McPhail. 2007. "Policing Disorderly Campus Protests and Convivial Gatherings: The Interaction of Threat, Social Organization, and First Amendment Guarantees." *Social Problems* 54:274–96.

McCarthy, John D., Jackie Smith, and Mayer N. Zald. 1996. "Accessing Public, Media, Electoral, and Governmental Agendas." In *Comparative Perspectives on Social Movements: Political Opportunities, Mobilizing Structures, and Cultural Framings,* edited by Doug McAdam, John D. McCarthy, and Mayer N. Zald, 291–311. New York: Cambridge University Press.

McCarthy, John D., and Mayer N. Zald. 1973. *The Trend of Social Movements in America: Professionalization and Resource Mobilization.* Morristown, N.J.: General Learning Press.

———. 1977. "Resource Mobilization and Social Movements: A Partial Theory." *American Journal of Sociology* 82:1212–41.

Meyer, David S., and Sidney R. Tarrow. 1998. *The Social Movement Society: Contentious Politics for a New Century.* Lanham, Md.: Rowman and Littlefield.

Myers, Daniel J., and Beth Schaefer Caniglia. 2004. "All the Rioting That's Fit to Print: Selection Effects in National Newspaper Coverage of Civil Disorders, 1968–1969." *American Sociological Review* 69:519–43.

Norris, Pippa. 2002. *Democratic Phoenix.* Cambridge: Cambridge University Press.

Norris, Pippa, Stefaan Walgrave, and Peter van Aelst. 2005. "Who Demonstrates? Anti-state Rebels or Conventional Participants? Or Everyone?" *Comparative Politics* 2:251–75.

Ortiz, David G., Daniel J. Myers, Eugene Walls, and Maria-Elena D. Diaz. 2005. "Where Do We Stand with Newspaper Data?" *Mobilization* 10, no. 3: 397–419.

Putnam, Robert D. 2000. *Bowling Alone: The Collapse and Revival of American Community.* New York: Simon and Schuster.

Rafail, Patrick. 2012. "Structural Contingencies and the Social Control of Protest." PhD diss., Pennsylvania State University, University Park.

Rafail, Patrick, Sarah A. Soule, and John D. McCarthy. 2012. "Describing and Accounting for the Trends in U.S. Protest Policing, 1960–1995." *Journal of Conflict Resolution* 56:736–65.

Rein, Lisa. 2008. "Md. Police Put Activists Names on Their Terror Lists." *Washington Post,* October 8, A1.

Rein, Lisa, and Josh White. 2009. "More Groups Than Thought Monitored in Police Spying." *Washington Post,* January 4, A1.

Schussman, Alan, and Sarah A. Soule. 2005. "Process and Protest: Accounting for Individual Protest Participation." *Social Forces* 84:1083–1108.

Skocpol, T. 1999. "Advocates without Members: The Recent Transformation of American Civic Life." In *Civic Engagement in American Democracy,* edited by Theda Skocpol and Morris P. Fiorina, 461–509. Washington, D.C.: Brookings Institution Press.

Soule, Sarah, and Jennifer Earl. 2005. "A Movement Society Evaluated: Collective Protest in the United States, 1960–1986." *Mobilization* 10, no. 3: 345–64.

Swarts, Heidi J. 2008. *Organizing Urban America: Secular and Faith-Based Progressive Movements.* Minneapolis: University of Minnesota Press.

Van Aelst, Peter, and Stefaan Walgrave. 2001. "Who Is That (Wo)man in the Street? From the Normalisation of Protest to the Normalisation of the Protester." *European Journal of Political Research* 39:461–86.

Van Dyke, Nella. 1998. "Hotbeds of Activism: Locations of Student Protest." *Social Problems* 45:205–20.

Van Dyke, Nella, Marc Dixon, and Helen Carlon. 2007. "Manufacturing Dissent: Labor Revitalization, Union Summer, and Student Protest." *Social Forces* 86:193–214.

Vitale, Alex S. 2005. "From Negotiated Management to Command and Control: How the New York Police Department Polices Protests." *Policing and Society* 15:283–304.

———. 2008. *City of Disorder: How the Quality of Life Campaign Transformed New York Politics.* New York: New York University Press.

Walker, Edward T. 2009. "Privatizing Participation: Civic Change and the Organizational Dynamics of Grassroots Lobbying Firms." *American Sociological Review* 74:83–105.

Walker, Edward T., Andrew W. Martin, and John D. McCarthy. 2008. "Confronting the State, the Corporation, and the Academy: The Influence of Institutional Targets on Social Movement Repertoire." *American Journal of Sociology* 114:35–76.

Walker, Edward T., and John D. McCarthy. 2004. "Alternative Organizational Repertoires of Poor People's Social Movement Organizations." *Nonprofit and Voluntary Sector Quarterly* 33:97S–119S.

Wood, Lesley J. 2007. "Breaking the Wave: Repression, Identity, and the Seattle Tactics." *Mobilization* 12, no. 4: 195–207.

19
The "Contentious French" Revisited

Nonna Mayer

Comparing declared levels of protest activity in the 1999 European and World Values surveys, Russell J. Dalton (2008, 50) describes the above-average propensity of the French to engage in challenging actions: "In just the single year following the 1999 French survey, truckers opposed to fuel increases blockaded gas stations, citizens demonstrated in support of a sheep farmer [José Bové, one of the main leaders of the French global justice movement] who had ransacked a McDonald's restaurant, bus and subway workers disrupted transportation systems in a dispute over shorter workweeks, scientists staged mass resignations in opposition to cuts in government funding, farmers protested the potential introduction of genetically modified crops, non-Christian religious groups demanded greater tolerance of minorities, and prostitutes demonstrated before government offices against unfair competition from immigrants. French protest knows few social bounds." Ten years later, as we will see, the level of protest is still higher in France than in other Western democracies. The aim of this chapter is to understand why this is so and to determine what is part of a general trend of protest normalization and what is specific to the French context. The French case is also interesting because the large and growing body of research devoted to social movements in France, which often goes unnoticed abroad, is critical of the dominant models and methodologies in the field (see Neveu 2002). We will draw on this literature to assess not only the trends in the social movement sector in the country but also the specific contribution of French scholars to social movement analysis. A short introductory section provides an overview of French research in this field. The second section shows the dynamics of the social movement sector in France, with a specific focus on demonstrations and strikes, the two basic means of collective action in Western liberal democracies. The third section places these developments in their cultural and political contexts. The last section builds on the French case to suggest new lines of research.

French Research on Social Movements

French research on protest and social movements took a new turn with the new social movements (NSMs) of the 1960s, to which Alain Touraine and his colleagues (*La société post-industrielle* [Touraine 1969] and *La voix et le regard* [Touraine 1978]) applied "sociological intervention" methods based on the active involvement of the researcher in the movement. After successively exploring the students' movement of 1968 (*Le Mouvement de Mai ou le Communisme utopique* [Touraine 1968]), the antinuclear movement (*La Prophétie antinucléaire* [Touraine 1980]), the Polish union Solidarnosc (*Solidarité* [Touraine 1982]), and the Occitan movement (*Le Pays contre l'État* [Touraine and Dubet 1981]), they concluded that none of these movements could compare with that of the working class and the historical part it once played (*Le mouvement ouvrier* [Touraine, Dubet, and Wieviorka 1984]). A second generation of studies appeared in the 1990s as new actors emerged in the social movement sector, bringing together materialist and postmaterialist claims: "coordinators" rejecting existing unions and associations; radical anti-AIDS networks such as ACT UP; myriad networks focused on social justice issues such as AC! (Acting against Unemployment), Droits Devant!! (Rights First), and DAL (The Right to Housing); defenders of the rights of *les sans* or the "have-nots," without papers, without a job, or without a roof; and global justice protesters led by Attac (Sommier 2003; Crettiez and Sommier 2006). This literature draws on Marx, Touraine, and Bourdieu as well as on the successive reformulations of "resource mobilization" and "political process" models (McCarthy and Zald 1973, 1977; McAdam 1982; McAdam, Tarrow, and Tilly 2001; Tilly and Tarrow 2007).

Yet, since the beginning, French scholars have distanced themselves from North American research. Summing up two decades of research, the reader for *Thinking Social Movements,* edited by Olivier Fillieule, Eric Agrikoliansky, and Isabelle Sommier (2010), begins by stating that "without going as far as speaking of a French school of sociology of social movements, one can easily see the original features of the research that make it different from the vast literature produced on the other side of the Atlantic: usage of the instruments of critical sociology; distrust in the positivists' modes of proof and of argumentation building; revival of the sociology of activism and individual commitment; de-partitioning of the canonical fields and development of researches on non-Western worlds; proliferation of studies on the movements of the 'have not,' but also more recently on work conflicts and unions action; dialogue with researches about interest groups, the construction of public issues and contentious uses of institutional channels of expression (such as law)" (Fillieule, Agrikoliansky, and Sommier 2010, 9; also Fillieule, Mathieu, and Péchu 2009).

For these French authors, the contentious politics paradigm has overstretched its main concepts (mobilizing structures, political opportunity structure, framework analysis, repertoire) and is losing its explanatory power. They plead for a historicization and a recontextualization of social movements that would take a long-term processual perspective and compare them with forms of protest outside the Western world such as in authoritarian regimes (Fillieule and Bennani-Chraibi 2003; Dorronsoro 2005). They criticize an approach seen as state centered, as focusing on large-scale public protests, and as placing excessive emphasis on organizations, structures, and the political arena. They extend the boundaries of social movements to include acts of resistance or self-help, protest against other movements, and other institutions (churches, courts, the medical profession, etc.). Their perspective is clearly actor centered and qualitative, seeking the meaning that individuals give to their actions, their emotions and affects, and their acceptance or modification of frameworks (Cefai and Trom 2001) at the microlevel. Indeed, their criticisms are very much in line with those expressed by authors such as Gamson and Meyer (1996) about the public opportunities structure; by Taylor (1989) about the "myth of the immaculate conception" of social movements; by Goodwin and Jasper (1999) about the structural bias of political process theory; and more recently by Armstrong and Bernstein (2008), who plead for a "multi-institutional politics approach" to social movements. They also readily embrace the cultural turn taken by social movement studies in the United States. The difference lies in the respective balance of these approaches in each country. As Neveu (2002, 7) reminds us, "indeed rational choice theories never gained serious influence in French political science, and the very small number of French social scientists with international recognition in quantitative data analysis has been both a national weakness and a real shield against number-crunching objectivism" (see also Billordo 2005a, 2005b; Mayer 2010, 51–60). The result is a rich collection of case studies on "unlikely" mobilizations (Boumaza and Hamman 2007) by prostitutes (Mathieu 2001), illegal immigrants (Siméant 1998; Mouchard 2001), and precarious performing artists (Sinigaglia 2009) as well as a detailed analysis of their tactical repertoires, ranging from hunger strikes (Siméant 2009) and squatting (Péchu 2010) to political consumerism (Dubuisson-Quellier 2009) and militant music (Traïni 2008).[1] But there is

Table 19.1. Protest potential in France (%)

"Here is a selection of means people sometimes use to express their opinions or their claims. For each of them, could you tell me if you would approve of the action or not, at least in certain circumstances?"

	1988	1995	2002	2007
Inflict material damage	1	2	2	–
Paint slogans on walls	6	6	5	–
Refuse to pay taxes	23	37	32	–
Occupy public buildings	28	42	43	42
Take part in street demonstrations	49	62	77	72
Go on strike	66	74	79	80
	(3,847)	(4,078)	(4,107)	(4,006)

Note. Cevipof electoral surveys 1988–95, French Electoral Panel 2002 (wave 1) and 2007 (wave 2), representative samples of registered voters. In 2007, the indicator dropped the three first modes and added petitions (accepted by 93% of the sample).

far less quantitative research, with the exception of the pioneer studies of demonstrations by Tartakowsky and Fillieule (Fillieule 1997; Tartakowsky 1997, 1998, 2004; Fillieule and Tartakowsky 2008), survey data on "protest potential" (Mayer 2010, 220–24), and several Individual Surveys in Rallies, a tool developed in France as early as 1994 (Favre, Fillieule, and Mayer 1997; Fillieule and Blanchard 2008) and applied to several alterglobalization protests in France and Europe (Agrikoliansky and Sommier 2005; also Sommier, Fillieule, and Agrikoliansky 2008).

The Vitality of the French Social Movement Sector

Three indicators are examined here: protest potential (survey data), declared participation in social movements (survey data), and effective participation (protest events and demonstration surveys).

A Rising Protest Potential

For lack of funds, France could not participate in Samuel Barnes and Max Kaase's (1979) pioneer study in *Political Action,* which showed the gradual acceptance of protest by Western publics. However, since 1988, Centre for Political Research of SciencesPo (Cevipof) surveys have included a similar battery of questions that measure the acceptance of modes of action challenging

Table 19.2. Approval of street demonstrations by cohorts (%)

Year of birth	Age 1988	1988	1995	2002	Age 2002	Evolution 1988/2002
1978–84		–	–	88	18–24	–
1971–77		–	83	89	25–31	+6
1964–70	18–24	68	74	87	32–38	+19
1957–63	25–31	65	73	85	39–45	+20
1950–56	32–38	62	71	79	46–52	+17
1943–49	39–45	51	61	71	53–59	+20
1936–42	46–52	44	51	70	60–66	+26
1929–35	53–59	36	47	62	67–73	+26
1922–28	60–66	32	40	48	74 +	+16
1915–21	67–73	30	32	–		
1908–14	74 +	23	–	–		
	Total	49 (3,847)	62 (4,078)	77 (4,107)		

Note. Cevipof surveys 1988/1995, French Electoral Panel 2002, wave 1.

authorities such as marching in the streets, going on strike, or occupying buildings (Table 19.1).

This indicator shows the growing legitimacy of these modes of action, long deemed unconventional. Though only a tiny minority accepts the idea of inflicting material damage, even just on walls, all the other means of action have gradually gained acceptance, with street demonstrations registering a record 28 percentage point increase between the first and third surveys. Half the sample approved of this mode of action in 1988, two-thirds did so in 1995, and over three-quarters approved in 2002—almost as many as those approving of strikes. In 2007, the share fell slightly but remained 23 points above its level in 1988. Each new cohort has become more supportive of street demonstrations than the previous cohort (Table 19.2). Furthermore, this contentious repertoire has gradually diffused throughout French society. A logistic regression controlling for age, gender, income, education, and political orientation shows that all variables have statistically significant effects, except for income. The probability of approving of demonstrations in 2007 is much higher among male, young, educated respondents and left wingers, but it remains above 50 percent in all categories, except for the elderly (aged sixty-five years or older).

Strong Support for Social Movements

The Social Movements Barometer run by the Conseils Sondages Analyses (CSA) polling institute on national samples representative of the French adult population provides a more precise measure of the support for current mobilizations. It starts in October 1995, on the eve of the largest wave of demonstrations France had known since 1968, triggered by the Juppé Plan to reform Social Security (November 15, 1995), and ends in January 2005. During these ten years, CSA selected the main social movements, which involved many different groups (pilots, laid-off workers, police, students, teachers, railway drivers, performing artists, antiglobalization protesters, tobacconists, etc.), and asked the same question: "What is your attitude toward this social movement: you support it, you have sympathy, you don't care, you are opposed, you are hostile?" Combining the first two options (support and sympathy) yields an average approval rate of 66.5 percent. The most popular movements are those of hospital staff, laid-off workers (Air Lib, Metal Europ, Daewoo), and the police; they are approved by over 90 percent of respondents. Only five movements (railway workers, professors in secondary schools, Air France pilots) garner less than 50 percent support. Social movements obviously enjoy widespread support in France, even when their consequences can be hard on users, such as when public transportation is blocked.

A Higher Level of Declared Protest Activities

Not only does a growing proportion of the population support these modes of action but, moreover, a rising number claim to have already practiced them. According to the European Values Survey, between 1981 and 2008, the proportion of the French population declaring they had at some time or another actually signed a petition climbed from 43 percent to 64 percent, as did participation in a lawful demonstration (25 percent to 42 percent) or a boycott (10 percent to 16 percent). Only the more radical means, such as going on a wildcat strike (10 percent to 12 percent) or occupying a building or a factory (7 percent to 9 percent), are not increasingly used. Compared to other Western democracies (World Values Survey), France stands out for its greater resort to acts of protest, especially the most challenging ones. Although it ranks seventh in the use of petitions, far behind New Zealand, Sweden, the United States, or Great Britain, it leads in demonstrations, wildcat strikes, and building occupations (Dalton 2008, 51).

The European Social Survey tells the same story, but with a different question limited to activities within the past year, thus making the answer dependent on the activity of protest movements at the time: "There are different ways of trying to improve things in France or help prevent things from going wrong. During the last 12 months, have you done any of the following?" Compared to other European Union members, the French stand out in 2002 for their greater propensity to engage in all protest actions, including petitions (only surpassed by Sweden and the United Kingdom) and illegal acts. These figures reflect a year marked by the high protest activity that occurred between the two rounds of the French presidential elections of 2002, when over one million demonstrators all over France took to the streets after Le Pen qualified for the second round. Yet the French distinction also held in the next three European Social Survey waves.[2]

A Rising Number of Demonstrations

Survey data have their limitations, and there can be large discrepancies between declared and actual protest behavior. Action depends on the time and place and on the networks' capacity to mobilize (Klandermans and Oegema 1987). In this respect, protest event analysis is more useful than surveys, but it, too, has limitations. Comparative studies based on press data have concluded that social movements in France declined after 1981, as they were demobilized by the victory of the socialist left; this was especially true for the NSMs on postmaterialist issues (Duyvendak 1995). Fillieule's (1997) study on street demonstrations in the three cities of Paris (933 events in 1991), Nantes (1,353 events between 1979 and 1991), and Marseille (2,080 events between 1980 and 1989), based on police records, reaches the opposite conclusion. The post-1981 drop was short-lived. In fact, the number of demonstrations has been steadily rising in the three cities, yielding a total estimate of 10,050 demonstrations per year in French cities with over two hundred thousand inhabitants, including one thousand demonstrations in Paris alone. Fillieule (1997, 385) shows that the number of demonstrations reported by *Le Monde* and *Libération* between January and June 1989 amounts to less than 10 percent of the total registered during the same period in police records. Another of his studies, on the coverage of environmental mobilizations by *Le Monde*, the global news agency Agence France-Presse, and the police, supplemented by interviews with journalists who specialize in this area, confirms and explains the magnitude of the discrepancies between press and police sources (Fillieule 2007). The newspapers only take into account the largest, most colorful, and politically oriented demonstrations, and their attention to social movements varies greatly, depending on other news and on the paper's focus. It is true, though, that the size of demonstrations has decreased and that micro- or medium-sized mobilizations are less noticed by the press.

The police data also belie Inglehart's theories about the rise of postmaterialist values and claims since the majority of these demonstrations still have to do with materialist claims about jobs, wages, and income. All social groups now take to the streets, but the working class still comes first by number of demonstrations and by weight among the demonstrators, followed by teachers. It is the unions, especially the working-class General Confederation of Labour, not the NSM entrepreneurs, that still form the bulk of mobilizing organizations (over 70 percent of calls for demonstrations). Finally, police data greatly temper the radical image of French movements that press data convey[3] by focusing on the most violent and spectacular events. Only a very small minority (5 percent) of the 4,366 French demonstrations studied by Fillieule (1997, 146–62, 305–64) gave rise to violence such as damaging property or injuring people, with the most radical groups being farmers (Duclos 1998), small shopkeepers and artisans in business decline, and workers in plants threatened by closure. The gradual moderation of demonstrations reflects both the professionalization of the police forces (della Porta and Fillieule 2006) and a larger process of pacification in Western democracies (Sommier 1998; Braud 2004).

A Growing Number of Workplace Conflicts

In large-scale social movements, street demonstrations and labor strikes often go hand in hand.[4] However, the two do not follow exactly the same trend. According to official statistics, the number of strikes in France seems to have steadily declined since the massive May 1968 social movement, when France was paralyzed as factories were occupied for almost two months. This holds if strikes are measured in terms of individual working days lost (JINT), that is, strikes of at least twenty-four hours in the corporate sector. On a JINT basis, France is close to the European median, with 40.5 JINT for one thousand wage earners in 2004 (versus 44.9 in the European Union), far behind Italy (134.7) and Spain (219.7) (Groux and Pernot 2008, 119). But if the public sector is included, several strike peaks become apparent since 1968, the two main ones being the 1995 mobilization against the Juppé Plan to reform the Social Security system, which led to a record six million JINT, and the spring 2003 mobilization on pensions, with almost five million JINT (Groux and Pernot 2008, 87). The public sector alone, which represents some 2.5 million workers, who are more protected than their corporate counterparts, accounts for more than 60 percent of JINT since 1995 (Groux and Pernot 2008, 93). The periodic administrative Survey on Professional Relations and Firm Negotiations, conducted by the Ministry of Labour every six years since

1992–93 on a sample of three thousand companies with twenty employees or more (Penissat 2009), shows that long conventional strikes did indeed decline between 1996–98 and 2002–4, during a period of recession and redundancies. However, at the same time, short cessations of work increased (+2.5 percent), as did diffuse forms of striking (slowdowns, work-to-rule) and the refusal of extra working hours (+6.4 percent), hand in hand with increases in other forms of conflict and resistance such as petitions (+2 percent) and demonstrations (+1.8 percent). Far from declining, French worker conflicts have been rising. While in 1996–98, 20 percent of firms with fewer than twenty employees experienced at least one collective conflict, 30 percent did in 2002–4 (Carlier and Tenret 2007; Giraud 2009).

This propensity to protest is confirmed by recent press and survey data. Since 1995 and the anti-Juppé demonstrations, several large-scale cycles of mobilization have occurred, regularly driving millions of people to the streets on the following issues: the reform of retirement pensions (spring 2003), the "CPE" or First Hire Contract for youth (2006), the defense of purchasing power (January and March 2009), and the defense of retirement at the age of sixty (September 7 to November 6, 2010). The latter led to eight waves of mobilization, which peaked on October 12, with 3.5 million demonstrators according to the unions and 1.2 million according to the police.[5] In fact, most of the reforms implemented under the presidency of Nicolas Sarkozy since his election in 2007 (university and public hospital reforms, the privatization of public services such as the postal service and gas and power, and stricter legislation against illegal immigrants and their children) have aroused massive protest. And the current economic recession, far from curbing mobilizations, appears to have further encouraged them. Action against plant closures or relocations is growing. According to police data from the Department for Public Order and Traffic, social tensions are increasing. In Paris alone, during the first six months of 2009, the number of street demonstrations increased by 31.8 percent compared to the same period in the previous year, rising from 1,116 to 1,471 and amounting to an average of eight per day, compared to three to four during the period studied by Fillieule (see also Tartakowsky 2004, 1–23). All these movements enjoy widespread public support that is hardly lower than in the previous period.[6] Average support for the first six waves of the anti–pension reform mobilizations of September–October 2010 rose above 68 percent.

Changing Contexts, Changing Protests

The rise in protests is not specific to France. Most Western democracies have experienced a routinization of the collective means of action first initiated by the working-class movement and then adopted by the middle classes. A growing proportion of citizens now view striking, demonstrating, and blocking streets as legitimate behavior. Global trends likely explain the shift. Over thirty years ago, Inglehart predicted this "elite challenging" attitude as a by-product of the postindustrial society and intergenerational value change (Inglehart 1977; Inglehart and Catterberg 2002). The rising levels of education and information, and the progression of postmaterialist values fostering autonomy and self-expression, have made citizens more "critical" (Norris 1999) and more likely to directly challenge the political elites and to bypass their elected representatives. Yet from one country to the next, the level, rhythm, and repertoire of protest have varied according to the cultural and political contexts.

From Protest to Social Movement

The French have a long history of revolutions (1789, 1830, 1848, the Parisian Commune of 1871), barricades, and episodes of social unrest (Shorter and Tilly 1974; Tilly 1986) that have been preciously preserved and kept alive in the collective memory. Every year, left-wing parties place flowers on the Mur des Fédérés (Wall of the Federals) in the Père Lachaise cemetery to commemorate the May 28, 1871, shooting of 147 Commune insurgents by the Versaillais (the regular troops). Every large episode of contention (May 68, the "Other Summit" of 1989, the anti-Juppé mobilization of December 1995) revives the symbols of the 1789 Revolution (Etats généraux, Tiers Etat, Sans culottes, Cahiers de doléances, i.e., the States General, the Commons, the Without Breeches, and grievance registers) (Tartakowsky 2004, 65–80; Agrikoliansky 2005, 51–52). French unions are still imbued in the culture of "revolutionary unionism," which carries the myth of the "general strike," favors direct action, and claims independence from the political and partisan spheres, as stipulated in the Charter of Amiens (1906). Meanwhile, French institutions perpetuate this culture of conflict (Hoffmann et al. 1963; Crozier 1970). Effective processes of conflict resolution and negotiation are still lacking, even though important labor law reforms have been passed, from the Auroux laws in 1982 to the modernization of the social dialogue in 2007.

However, a fraught relationship with authority and propensity to protest are not necessarily conducive to sustained social movements. These depend on the political opportunity structure, the prevailing strategies vis-à-vis challengers, and the configuration of alliances. Comparative studies on the emergence of NSMs in Europe present France as a paradigmatic case of a closed polity, which combines all the obstacles to the influence of social movements (Kriesi 2004). Using press data collected between 1975 and 1989, Duyvendak shows that in comparison to the Netherlands, West Germany, and Switzerland, France has the lowest number of protest events, especially in the NSM sector (Kriesi 1995; Duyvendak 1995; Kriesi et al. 1995). Its political opportunity structure comprises a strong and centralized state, an electoral system based on majority rule that is unkind to small parties and newcomers, a fragmented and undisciplined party system, and a lack of inclusive strategies vis-à-vis challengers (Kriesi 1995; Kriesi et al. 1995). The socialist left's rise to power in 1981, as well as the weight of the Communist Party, narrowed the political space for the NSM, whose claims were either preempted by the socialists (feminist and antiracist issues) or rejected (denuclearization). On the whole, for Kriesi (1995, 178), "the French context of full exclusion invites disruptive strategies on the part of the challengers. As Wilson (1987, 283) observes, the strength of the French state gives rise to its greatest weakness: unable to allow challengers to articulate their concerns through formal or informal channels of access, it is periodically confronted by large-scale explosions of discontent. In such moments of great discontent, the French state may be forced to make substantive proactive concessions or to abandon a project." Indeed, street demonstrations in France have become a normal way to express claims or opposition to the government between two elections, thus bypassing elected representatives. They are commonly referred to as the "third round of elections," that is, the "social" round. And there are numerous examples of the government yielding to the pressure of the street (Tartakowsky 2004), from the withdrawal of the Savary law to reform private school funding in 1984, after a protest march of over a million people, to the abrogation of the First Hire Contract (setting a minimum wage and a two-year conditional period of hire for young workers entering the job market) in 2006, after two months of unrest in universities and high schools.

However, political contexts, opportunities, and alliances can change and become favorable to full-fledged social movements. Duyvendak's study is biased because it relies on press data and because it ends at the very moment when the revival of the social movement sector began, after the reelection of Mitterrand in 1988. The socialists' turn to the right and the decline of the Communist Party opened a political space to "the left of the left," bringing together groups that traditionally opposed one another such as Marxists, Third World Christians, communists, and Trotskyists disillusioned by the socialist experiment (see Waters 2003). The largely unnoticed prelude to the gathering of these groups was the countersummit held in Paris in 1989, targeting the G7 and the French government and calling for the cancellation of Third World debt. The second step was the two-month-long mobilization against the Juppé Plan in fall 1995 that portrayed itself as *the* Social Movement (Béroud, Mouriaux, and Vakaloulis 1998). The third step was the victorious "No" campaign during the referendum on the European Union draft constitution (on May 9, 2005, 55 percent voted no). The vote was not directed against the European Union so much as it was against the neoliberal and undemocratic character of the text and the Europe of big business. One by one, these mobilizations brought together what began as a heterogeneous coalition of movements defending the withouts and the have-nots, coordinators and dissident unions like Sud or the Confédération Paysanne (Peasant's Confederation), antiglobalization networks like Attac, radical intellectuals led by sociologist Pierre Bourdieu, anti-AIDS movements like ACT UP, and so on. Their opposition to neoliberal globalization served as a common framework.

Two more recent factors that helped strengthen the movement were the election of Nicolas Sarkozy in the 2007 presidential elections and the global recession that started the very same year, with the financial crisis linked to the U.S. subprime mortgage crisis. The French president has implemented a series of reforms deemed unfair that have fueled protest (harsher laws on immigration, tax breaks and fiscal shields for the highest income earners, changes in governance and funding rules for universities and research centers, postponement of the age of retirement, etc.). The rise in unemployment and the public spending cuts and austerity measures accompanying the recession added to the general feeling of discontent, causing President Sarkozy's popularity to plummet to its lowest level in December 2010 (24 percent positive). The global recession has appeared to confirm the dangers of neoliberal economics.

New Levels of Governance

The political opportunity structure is not written in stone, and even core institutions such as the nation-state can change when confronted with new levels of governance, both subnational and supranational (Koopmans, chapter 15), that open new opportunities to social movements. France is a centralized country, and from the time of the monarchy, Paris has held the bulk of the power. However, laws enacted in 1980 started a decentralization process granting more power to the regions. Greater power was granted to regionally elected representatives in 1986 as well as to the mayors of large cities. Consequently, mobilization in the regions is catching up with that in the capital, as illustrated by the maps that the national press has systematically displayed since 1995, showing the number of demonstrators in all cities, and not just in Paris, as had previously been the case. A new geography of French demonstrations is appearing along the lines of the "no" to the Treaty of Maastricht in 1989 (Tartakowsky 2004). Other towns have been taking the lead before Paris, as they did, for instance, during the youth mobilization against the

Professional Insertion Contract of 1994 or the movement of parents, teachers, and high school students asking for more means for the Seine Saint Denis school district in 1998.

In the same vein, a process of decentralization of the French public higher education system began with the Liberty and Responsibility of the Universities law of 2007. The main universities used to be highly concentrated in Paris. The May 1968 movement, for instance, was mostly Parisian. Since then, the student population outside Paris has grown. Today, France has eighty-three public universities, its student population numbers around 2.2 million, thirty-seven towns have over ten thousand students, and cities like Lyon, Marseille, Lille, Toulouse, Nantes, and Rennes have over five thousand students each. These young populations are potentially available to participate in social movements.

Protest is becoming more local, but it is simultaneously becoming more global. The number of demonstrations targeting European Union institutions or asserting worker solidarity across countries is slowly rising in France, as it is throughout Europe (Balme and Chabanet 2008). The World Social Forums, the antiglobalization protests (Agrikoliansky and Sommier 2005; Fillieule and Blanchard 2009), the anti–Iraq War mobilizations of February 2003 (Reynié 2004), and the recent mobilizations against austerity plans in Europe point to the emergence of transnational protest.

Changing Forms of Participation in Social Movements

A More Distant and Individualized Commitment

At the same time, political behavior is changing. Jacques Ion (1997) coined the term *post-it activism* to describe a spreading form of engagement that is distinct from the type of activism that was characteristic of the Communist Party or Roman Catholic Church organizations. It is a short-term engagement that is less involving and is based on loose horizontal relations in ad hoc structures seeking concrete solutions to specific issues. This contrasts sharply with the former model of activism, which was lifelong, global, hierarchically and vertically structured, and politically oriented. The new activist is always available for a new cause and will easily drop out and turn to another one, hence the post-it image. Ion's analysis has been criticized (Collovald 2002) for oversimplifying the communist model, forgetting the high turnover among the Communist Party's followers, idealizing middle-class activism in comparison to the former working-class model, and exaggerating the opposition between old parties and unions and new social networks. Yet this "distanciated" activism is congruent with a more general tendency toward "individuation," reflecting the influence of postmaterialist values based on self-expression and autonomy (Van Stekelenburg and Boekkooi, chapter 11). It can explain the vitality of the social movement sector in France but also its fragmentation into myriad causes and its difficult relations with the partisan and political spheres.

A Disconnection from Party Politics

In her book *Democratic Phoenix,* Norris (2002) describes a growing disconnect between conventional politics and movements, which are more oriented toward cultural change than toward electoral or lobbying activities: "The primary goals of new social movements often focus upon achieving social change through direct action strategies and community-building, as well as by altering lifestyles and social identities, as much as through shaping formal policy making processes and laws in government" (9–10). The idea that social movements form a sector grouping all the social movement industries (McCarthy and Zald 1977), or a "multiorganizational field" (Curtis and Zurcher 1973), is not new. But Mathieu (2007) goes further, theorizing, in the case of France, the autonomization of what he calls the "social movement space." This space is distinct from that of the unions or parties because it calls for specific skills ("activist capital"; see Matonti and Poupeau 2004) and creates an environment in which interdependent actors are in competition. The distrust in party politics developed in the aftermath of May 1968 and increased during the socialist era, after the neoliberal turn in the left's economic policies (1983) and several experiences of "cohabitation" with the right. The social movement of 1995 strengthened the mobilization of the left of the left. A symptom of the social movement sector's dissociation from the parties of the left was its "We Are the Left" rallying call, which was launched during the parliamentary elections of 1997. The slogan underscored the belief that the socialists and government parties no longer represented them because they were neglecting the issue of social and economic justice. A second symptom was the call "for an autonomy of the social movement," after the Communist Party had tried to enroll the leaders of some of these networks as candidates for the 1999 European elections (Mathieu 2007). In the long run, this disconnection from electoral and party politics could lead to a dead end, depriving the movement of a political outlet and developing what Rosanvallon (2006) has called the "democracy of distrust."

The Return of Violence?

Over the past thirty years, the global trend in established democracies has been a pacification of protest on the part of both the demonstrators and the police. However, this might be changing.

Violent incidents regularly erupt during alterglobalization meetings and countersummits. In the past three years, episodes of violence similar to those of the 1970s have occurred during several demonstrations by students, who are anxious for their future in a context of accelerated reform and high unemployment. Ethnic violence has increased, as exemplified by the 2005 antiwhite scuffles that occurred during the 2005 high school student demonstrations in Paris. That same year, on October 27, the death of two young boys in Clichy-sous-Bois after they were electrocuted while running away from the police sparked three weeks of violent riots in the disadvantaged suburbs around the capital: 274 communes were affected, more than nine thousand cars were burned, damages were estimated at 250 million euros, 4,770 suspects were arrested, and a general curfew was proclaimed (*Le Monde*, December 2, 2005). The riots crudely revealed the malaise of immigrant-born youth who have French citizenship and school degrees but are excluded from the job market. They would like for their identity to be recognized and do not feel represented politically. A great debate has ensued about the political or proto-political nature of this eruption (Lagrange and Oberti 2006; Mauger 2006; Mucchielli and Le Goaziou 2006).

More recently, a wave of plant closures elicited violent reactions from furloughed workers, such as Cellatex workers, who threatened to pour acid into a river in 2000 (Vanommeslaghe 2009). In 2009, many managers were taken hostage by their workers, and this boss-napping found support in French public opinion: in April 2009, 45 percent of a national representative sample judged these sequestrations "acceptable," versus 50 percent who deemed them "unacceptable."[7] This spectacular type of violence remains rare (Giraud 2009), but it is reminiscent of poor people's movements, in which those who do not feel represented by existing organizations have their "moments of madness" (Piven and Cloward 1977) because they feel this is the only way to attract media attention and to be heard. The current context of global recession might kindle such revolts.

Politics in the Marketplace

Social movements do not only take place in the streets. There is a form of action that protest events and rally surveys do not catch: political consumerism, or what Micheletti (2003) has called an "individualized collective action" that brings "politics in the supermarket" (Stolle, Hooghe, and Micheletti 2005), thus developing a new form of political participation. Pairing the Political Action Survey of 1974 with the World Values Survey, Stolle and colleagues show that in comparison to demonstrations, petitions, and the occupation of buildings, boycotts are the form of participation that has experienced the strongest growth, having become more than four times as likely in 1999 as in 1974 (247; see Polletta et al., chapter 2, for a discussion on consumerism).

The very detailed research of Dubuisson-Quellier (2009) shows that consumer protest is also developing in France. Indeed, French consumerism has shed its prewar patterns and developed an anticapitalist and sometimes radical posture (anti-ads, anti–growth networks, various forms of fair trade, Local Exchange Trading Systems, community-supported agriculture, etc.). Some of these protests bypass the market, whereas others use it to their own ends. In either case, the economy becomes a political arena, and this trend is gaining traction. The current recession seems to be encouraging economic austerity and antimarket action, as illustrated by the latest results from the CREDOC survey on consumption and living conditions. In 2007, 44 percent of the adult population claimed to take into account the "citizen commitment" of the firm from which they buy a product (as compared to 38 percent in 2002) (Delpal and Hatchvel 2007). Between June 2008 and 2009, the share of consumers who said they cared about environmental guarantees increased by 9 percentage points; those who gave preference to regional products increased by 10 points; and those who were concerned about the company's workers' rights and product origins also saw a 10-point increase.[8] This form of protest is less visible than large marches and demonstrations. It is also not necessarily directed at the state. Rather, by influencing consumption, this form of protest forces firms to change (Balsiger 2010, 2011).

Transnational Politics

The antiglobalization movement is a good example of the way activism now crosses borders. Thus the survey conducted among the French protesters gathered at the anti-G8 mobilization in Evian and/or the Second European Social Forum of Saint Denis (2003) shows that they travel more, have more ties to other countries, have lived abroad, and speak and read foreign languages far more often than the average French person. Yet they remain well anchored in the nation-state, they are overrepresented in the civil service, they are politically overintegrated (voting habits, party proximity), and they are as mobilized nationally (on issues such as unemployment and the defense of the public service) as they are on antiglobalization issues (Gobille and Uysal 2005; Fillieule and Blanchard 2008). National and transnational activism feed off each other.

Conclusion

The French case is thus characterized by a "double exceptionalism," in its social movement sector as well as in the research devoted to the sector. France combines an above-average propensity to protest and to take to the streets with a political opportunity structure that is, at first sight, more conducive to short-lived disruptive actions than to full-fledged social movements. Yet, since the 1990s, the social movement sector has thrived. New networks have appeared and are more active than ever with the current Sarkozy government and context of global recession. At the same time, the gap between the social movement field and party politics is increasing, and it would be interesting to see if this same process is occurring elsewhere.

Meanwhile, the French approach to social movements invites a different perspective that would pay more attention to the local scene and micro-mobilizations that are overlooked in national press data and an approach that would not underestimate the role of the labor movement and unions. As exemplified by the global justice movement Attac, new movements are not created from scratch; rather, they build on existing ones and combine old and new types of engagement (Trautmann 2001; Agrikoliansky, Fillieule, and Mayer 2005). The French approach blurs the distinction between materialist and postmaterialist claims: like the working-class movement of yesterday that defended the dignity of workers in addition to their wages, the mobilizations of the have-nots—those without a job, without official papers, or without a roof—call for respecting their rights as people (Walgrave, chapter 10, comes to the same conclusion based on Belgian data). Finally, the French approach deemphasizes the rise of transnational social movements; however cosmopolitan they may be, they still are firmly rooted in the national context (Tarrow 2005).

Notes

1. See the Contester series (Presses de SciencesPo) for the comparative approach of these different modes of protest (http://www.pressesdesciencespo.fr/en/collections/contester/).

2. However, these only asked about boycotts, demonstrations, and petitions.

3. On this basis, one-quarter of the protest events in France between 1975 and 1989 can be labeled as ones of "extreme violence," compared to 9 percent in West Germany, 6 percent in the Netherlands, and 3 percent in Switzerland (Kriesi et al. 1995, 253–73).

4. Demonstrations are defined here as "any temporary occupation by several people of an open space, public or private, and which involves directly or indirectly the expression of political opinions" (Fillieule 1997, 4), and strikes are defined as a collective and concerted stoppage of work by employees (Groux and Pernot 2008).

5. The figures are debatable, given that the police tend to lower the number of participants and the organizers tend to raise it. On the basis of the Agence France-Presse dispatches, the newspaper *Le Monde* presented daily maps of the mobilization with both figures city by city: http://www.lemonde.fr/politique/infographie/

2010/11/06/la-carte-des-manifestations-du-6-novembre_1436305_823448.html.

6. According to the CSA Social Movements Barometer, "sympathy" and "support" rose from 68.2 percent between October 1995 and December 2002 (thirty-four social movements) to 61.2 percent between January 2003 and April 2009 (thirty-three social movements): http://www.csa.eu/fusioncharts/mvtsoc/mvtsoc-f9502.html. One should note that all but two of these social movements are about "materialist" issues (wages, working conditions, pensions).

7. Opinion poll CSA, April 2009.

8. http://www.20minutes.fr/article/562243/Economie-La-consommation-engagee-se-developpe.php, Conference on Consumption, October 26, 2009.

References

Agrikoliansky, Eric. 2005. "Du tiers mondisme à l'altermondialisme." In *L'altermondialisme en France: La longue histoire d'une nouvelle cause,* edited by Eric Agrikoliansky, Olivier Fillieule, and Nonna Mayer, 43–72. Paris: Flammarion.

Agrikoliansky, Eric, Olivier Fillieule, and Nonna Mayer. 2005. *L'altermondialisme en France: La longue histoire d'une nouvelle cause.* Paris: Flammarion.

Agrikoliansky, Eric, and Isabelle Sommier. 2005. *Radiographie du mouvement altermondialiste.* Paris: La Dispute.

Armstrong, Elisabeth A., and Mary Bernstein. 2008. "Culture, Power, and Institutions: A Multi-institutional Politics Approach to Social Movements." *Sociological Theory* 26:74–99.

Balme, Richard, and Didier Chabanet. 2008. *European Governance and Democracy: Power and Protest in the EU.* Lanham, Md.: Rowman and Littlefield.

Balsiger, Philip. 2010. "*Making Political Consumers*: The Tactical Action Repertoire of a Campaign for *Clean Clothes.*" *Social Movement Studies* 9:311–29.

———. 2011. "Campaigning for Clean Clothes: How Producing and Consuming Clothes Become Political Issues." PhD diss., University of Lausanne, SciencesPo Paris.

Barnes, Samuel, and Max Kaase. 1979. *Political Action: Mass Participation in Five Western Democracies.* Thousand Oaks, Calif.: Sage.

Béroud, Sophie, René Mouriaux, and Michel Vakaloulis. 1998. *Le mouvement social en France.* Paris: La Dispute.

Billordo, Libia. 2005a. "Publishing in French Political Science Journals: An Inventory of Methods and Subfields." *French Politics* 2:178–86.

———. 2005b. "Method Training in French Political Science." *French Politics* 3:352–57.

Boumaza, Magali, and Philippe Hamman. 2007. *Sociologie des mouvements précaires, espaces mobilisés et répertoires d'action.* Paris: Harmattan.

Braud, Philippe. 2004. *Violences politiques.* Paris: Seuil.

Carlier, Alexandre, and Elise Tenret. 2007. "Des conflits de travail plus nombreux et plus diversifiés." *Premières synthèses* 8, no. 1: 1–6.

Cefaï, Daniel, and Dany Trom. 2001. *Les formes de l'action collective: mobilisations dans des arènes publiques.* Paris: EHESS.

Collovald, Annie. 2002. "Pour une sociologie des carrières morales des dévouements militants." In *L'humanitaire ou le management des dévouements,* edited by Annie Collovald, Laurent Willemez, Sabine Rozier, and Marie-Hélène Lechien, 177–229. Rennes, France: Presses universitaires de Rennes.

Crettiez, Xavier, and Isabelle Sommier. 2006. *La France rebelle.* Paris: Michalon.

Crozier, Michel. 1970. *La Sociéte bloquee.* Paris: Seuil.

Curtis, Russell L., and Louis A. Zurcher. 1973. "Stable Resources of Protest Movements: The Multi-organizational Field." *Social Forces* 52:53–61.

Dalton, Russell. 2008. *Citizen Politics: Public Opinion and Political Parties in Advanced Industrial Democracies.* 5th ed. Washington, D.C.: Congressional Quarterly Press.

della Porta, Donatella, and Olivier Fillieule. 2006. *Police et manifestants: Maintien de l'ordre et gestion des conflits.* Paris: Presses de SciencesPo.

Delpal, Franck, and Georges Hatchvel. 2007. "La consommation engageè safferme comme une tendance durable." *Consommation et Modes de Vie* 201:1–6.

Dorronsoro, Gilles. 2005. *La Turquie conteste: Mobilisations sociales et régime sécuritaire.* Paris: CNRS.

Dubuisson-Quellier, Sophie. 2009. *La consommation engagée.* Paris: Presses de SciencesPo.

Duclos, Nathalie. 1998. *Les Violences paysannes sous la Ve République.* Paris: Economica.

Duyvendak, Jan W. 1995. *The Power of Politics: New Social Movements in France.* Boulder, Colo.: Westview.

Favre, Pierre, Olivier Fillieule, and Nonna Mayer. 1997. "La fin d'une étrange lacune de la sociologie des mobilisations: L'étude par sondage des manifestants: fondements théoriques et solutions techniques." *Revue française de science politique* 47:3–28.

Fillieule, Olivier. 1997. *Stratégies de la rue: Les manifestations enfranca.* Paris: Presses de SciencesPo.

———. 2007. "On n'y voit rien." In *L'atelier du politiste,* edited by Pierre Favre, Olivier Fillieule, and Fabien Jobard, 215–40. Paris: La Découverte/Pacte.

Fillieule, Olivier, Eric Agrikoliansky, and Isabelle Sommier. 2010. *Penser les mouvements sociaux: Conflits sociaux et contestations dans les sociétés contemporaines.* Paris: La Découverte.

Fillieule, Olivier, and Mounia Bennani-Chraibi. 2003. *Résistances et protestations dans les sociétés musulmanes.* Paris: Presses de SciencesPo.

Fillieule, Olivier, and Philippe Blanchard. 2008. "Individual Surveys in Rallies (INSURA): A New Tool for Exploring Transnational Activism?" In *Transnational Challengers: How Activism beyond Borders Changes the Face of Protest,* edited by Simon Teune, 186–210. Oxford: Berghahn Books.

Fillieule, Olivier, Lilian Mathieu, and Cécile Péchu. 2009. *Dictionnaire des mouvements sociaux.* Paris: Presses de SciencesPo.

Fillieule, Olivier, and Danielle Tartakowsky. 2008. *La manifestation*. Paris: Presses de SciencesPo.

Gamson, William, and David Meyer. 1996. "Framing Political Opportunity." In *Comparative Perspectives on Social Movements: Political Opportunities, Mobilizing Structures, and Cultural Framings*, edited by Doug McAdam, John McCarthy, and Mayer N. Zald, 275–90. Cambridge: Cambridge University Press.

Giraud, Baptiste. 2009. *Faire la grève: Les conditions d'appropriation de la grève dans les conflits de travail en France*. Paris: Université de Paris 1.

Gobille, Boris, and Aysin Vysal. 2005. "Cosmopolites et enracinés." In *Radiographie du mouvement altermondialiste*, edited by Eric Agrikoliansky and Isabelle Sommier, 105–26. Paris: La Dispute.

Goodwin, Jeff, and James M. Jasper. 1999. "Caught in a Winding, Snarling Vine: The Structural Bias of Political Process Theory." *Sociological Forum* 14:27–54.

Groux, Guy, and Jean-Marie Pernot. 2008. *La grève*. Contester. Paris: Presses de SciencesPo.

Hoffmann, Stanley, Charles P. Kindleberger, Laurence Wylie, Jesse R. Pitts, Jean-Baptiste Duroselle, and François Goguel. 1963. *In Search of France*. Cambridge, Mass.: Harvard University Press.

Inglehart, Ronald. 1977. *The Silent Revolution: Changing Values and Political Styles among Western Publics*. Princeton, N.J.: Princeton University Press.

Inglehart, Ronald, and Gabriela Catterberg. 2002. "Trends in Political Action: The Developmental Trend and the Post-honeymoon Decline." Paper presented at the Annual Meeting of the American Political Science Association, Boston. http://www.allacademic.com/meta/p65433_index.html.

Ion, Jacques. 1997. *La fin des militants?* Paris: Atelier.

Klandermans, Bert, and Dirk Oegema. 1987. "Potentials, Networks, Motivations, and Barriers: Steps towards Participation in Social Movements." *American Sociological Review* 52:519–31.

Kriesi, Hanspeter. 1995. "The Political Opportunity Structure of New Social Movements: Its Impact on Their Mobilization." In *The Politics of Social Protest*, edited by Craig J. Jenkins and Bert Klandermans, 167–98. Minneapolis: University of Minnesota Press.

———. 2004. "Political Context and Opportunity." In *The Blackwell Companion to Social Movements*, edited by David A. Snow, Sarah A. Soule, and Hanspeter Kriesi, 67–90. Oxford: Blackwell.

Kriesi, Hanspeter, Ruud Koopmans, Jan Willem Duyvendak, and Marco Giugni. 1995. *New Social Movements in Western Europe*. Minneapolis: University of Minnesota Press.

Lagrange, Hugues, and Marco Oberti. 2006. *Emeutes urbaines et protestations: Une singularité française*. Paris: Presses de SciencesPo.

Mathieu, Lilian. 2001. *Mobilisations de prostituées*. Paris: Belin.

———. 2007. "L'espace des mouvements sociaux." *Politix* 77:131–51.
Matonti, Frédérique, and Franck Poupeau. 2004. "Le *capital militant*: Essai de définition." *Actes de la recherche en sciences sociales* 5, no. 155: 4–11.
Mauger, Gérard. 2006. *L'émeute de novembre 2005: Une révolte protopolitique*. Bellecombe-en-Bauges, France: Croquant.
Mayer, Nonna. 2010. *Sociologie des comportements politiques*. Paris: A. Colin.
McAdam, Doug. 1982. *Political Process and the Development of Black Insurgency: 1930–1970*. Chicago: University of Chicago Press.
McAdam, Doug, Sidney Tarrow, and Charles Tilly. 2001. *Dynamics of Contention*. Cambridge: Cambridge University Press.
McCarthy, John D., and Mayer N. Zald. 1973. *The Trend of Social Movements in America: Professionalization and Resource Mobilization*. Morristown, N.J.: General Learning Press.
———. 1977. "Resource Mobilization and Social Movements: A Partial Theory." *American Journal of Sociology* 82:1212–41.
Micheletti, Michele. 2003. *Political Virtue and Shopping: Individuals, Consumerism, and Collective Action*. London: Palgrave.
Mouchard, Daniel. 2001. *Les exclus dans l'espace public: mobilisations et logiques de représentation dans la France contemporaine*. Paris: IEP.
Mucchielli, Laurent, and Véronique Le Goaziou. 2006. *Quand les banlieues brûlent . . . Retour sur les émeutes de novembre 2005*. Paris: La Découverte.
Neveu, Erik. 2002. "Trend Report: The Contentious French." *Mobilization* 7, no. 3: 325–34.
Norris, Pippa. 1999. *Critical Citizens: Global Support for Democratic Government*. Oxford: Oxford University Press.
———. 2002. *Democratic Phoenix*. Cambridge: Cambridge University Press.
Péchu, Cécile. 2010. *Les squats*. Contester. Paris: Presses de SciencesPo.
Penissat, Etienne. 2009. *L'État des chiffres: Sociologie du service de statistique et des statisticiens du ministère du Travail et de l'Emploi (1945–2008)*. Paris: EHESS.
Piven, Francis Fox, and Richard Cloward. 1977. *Poor People's Movements*. New York: Vintage Books.
Reynié, Dominique. 2004. *La fracture occidentale: Naissance d'une opinion européenne*. Paris: Table Ronde.
Rosanvallon, Pierre. 2006. *La contre-démocratie: La politique a l'age de la defiance*. Paris: Seuil.
Shorter, Edward, and Charles Tilly. 1974. *Strikes in France: 1830–1968*. Cambridge: Cambridge University Press.
Siméant, Johanna. 1998. *La cause des sans-papiers*. Paris: Presses de SciencesPo.
———. 2009. *La grève de la faim*. Contester. Paris: Presses de SciencesPo.
Sinigaglia, Jérémy. 2009. "The Mobilization of Intermittents in the Entertainment Sector in France." *French Politics and Society* 7:294–315.

Sommier, Isabelle. 1998. *La violence politique et son deuil.* Rennes, France: Presses universitaires de Rennes.

———. 2003. *Le renouveau des mouvements contestataires à l'heure de la mondialisation.* Paris: Flammarion.

Sommier, Isabelle, Olivier Fillieule, and Eric Agrikoliansky. 2008. *Généalogie des mouvements altermondialistes en Europe: Une perspective comparée.* Paris: Karthala.

Stolle, Dietland, Marc Hooghe, and Michelle Micheletti. 2005. "Politics in the Supermarket: Political Consumerism as a Form of Political Participation." *International Political Science Review* 26:245–69.

Tarrow, Sidney. 2005. *The New Transnational Activism.* New York: Cambridge University Press.

Tartakowsky, Danielle. 1997. *Les manifestations de rue en France: 1918–1968.* Paris: Publications de la Sorbonne.

———. 1998. *Le pouvoir est dans la rue: crises politiques et manifestations en France.* Paris: Aubier.

———. 2004. *La manifestation en éclats.* Paris: La Dispute.

Taylor, Verta. 1989. "Social Movement Continuity: The Women's Movement in Abeyance." *American Sociological Review* 54:761–75.

Tilly, Charles. 1986. *The Contentious French.* Cambridge, Mass.: Harvard University Press.

Tilly, Charles, and Sidney Tarrow. 2007. *Contentious Politics.* Boulder, Colo.: Paradigm.

Touraine, Alain. 1968. *Le Mouvement de Mai ou le Communisme utopique.* Paris: Seuil.

———. 1969. *La société post-industrielle.* Paris: Denoël.

———. 1978. *La voix et le regard.* Paris: Seuil.

———. 1980. *La Prophétie antinucléaire.* Paris: Seuil.

———. 1982. *Solidarité: analyse d'un mouvement social, Pologne 1980–1981.* Paris: Fayard.

Touraine, Alain, and François Dubet. 1981. *Le Pays contre l'État, luttes occitanes.* Paris: Seuil.

Touraine, Alain, François Dubet, and Michel Wieviorka. 1984. *Le mouvement ouvrier.* Paris: Fayard.

Traïni, Christophe. 2008. *La musique en colère.* Contester. Paris: Presses de SciencesPo.

Trautmann, Flore. 2001. "Internet au service de la démocratie? Le cas d'Attac." *Cahiers du Cevipof* 30:1–108.

Vanommeslaghe, Laurence. 2009. "Les stratégies d'action ouvrières face aux menaces sur l'emploi en France et en Belgique (1996–2003)." PhD diss., SciencesPo Paris.

Waters, Sarah. 2003. *Social Movements in France.* Basingstoke, U.K.: Palgrave Macmillan.

Wilson, Frank L. 1987. *Interest-Group Politics in France.* Cambridge: Cambridge University Press.

Discussion: Meaning and Movements in the New Millennium: Gendering Democracy

Myra Marx Ferree

With so many dimensions to the changes in the terrain of political contention today, it is hardly surprising that each essay in part IV identifies these central challenges differently. Yet all focus fairly narrowly on material conditions and organizational actors. Della Porta (chapter 17) argues that state institutions, and thus mobilizations, are eclipsed by transnational ones that address the seat of real power, in her view. McCarthy, Rafail, and Gromis (chapter 18) see the terrain as shifting down rather than up, with national institutions less targeted than local ones in the United States, because American domestic politics has transferred power to the individual states. Mayer (chapter 19) stresses the extent to which change in level depends on context: France has a strong national social movement tradition that is regularly evoked for mobilizations, especially by labor. McAdam and Tarrow (chapter 16) address the relationship between national state institutions and proclivity to mobilize by showing how contending political parties within national party systems operate variously as partners for and alternatives to social movement organizing.

These essays indicate that a major part of what alters movement dynamics is the changes in states and what they do, as Koopmans suggests in his introduction to part IV (chapter 15). Unquestionably, shifts in power between states and transnational economic actors like the World Bank, CitiBank, and Toyota matter; so do regional shifts of political power such as supranational policy integration by the European Union (EU) and the ascendancy of states' rights in the United States. Politics responds to such institutional shifts, as governments, parties, and movements all compete for power in a context in which the stakes are high, the rules are uncertain, and alliances are in flux.

Still, the general principle seems stable: follow the money. The flows of money and thus power are changing, all authors agree, reconfiguring the material terrain of opportunity.

The essays also emphasize that macrolevel strategic situations affect both sides of any struggle. Rises in corporate power combined with declines in corporate accountability make banks and transnational corporations targets of global justice movements, as della Porta shows, while corporate funding of parties (both Democratic and Republican) explains some of the shift to the right in U.S. politics since the 1980s, including the increase in surveillance and repression directed at protest mobilizations on the left, as McCarthy, Rafail, and Gromis note. Party structures, and their potential funders and allies, also respond to movement mobilizations, as McAdam and Tarrow emphasize. Indeed, the EU's control over currency may affect the national strategic situations for Greek, French, and other European mobilizations more similarly than Mayer's comparison of different cultures of contention suggests.

Still, political culture matters. The "Frenchness" of the French includes a willingness to resist state actions that impoverish ordinary citizens, an attitude toward the welfare state that European social movements have cultivated over generations. Conversely, U.S. right-leaning movements, from the John Birch Society in the 1950s to Focus on the Family in the 1990s to the Tea Party in the 2010s, have cultivated an attitude of anxiety about the welfare state. The perception—constructed over time by movement framers—that the EU is itself a unitary, neoliberal actor helps to mobilize national resistance movements in many contexts at various times: in Denmark in the accession process; in Ireland, in rejecting the proposed constitution; in Greece about the euro; in Poland about gender equality directives. The single-minded focus on institutions, whether economic or political, as shaping the context for mobilizations leaves out the discursive frames that give meaning to politics. This essay attempts to bring meaning back in.

The Politics of Discourse

Issue framing, along with institutional situations, defines the terrain on which movement mobilizations take place. I define *framing* as an interaction in which actors with agendas meet discursive opportunities as structured in institutionally authoritative texts. Frames that resonate with particular populations pick up and adapt ideas that are part of their (still predominantly national) discursive frameworks. Movements on the left and right do discursive politics with the cultural tools available to them in that time and place. They are not the only actors with agendas. As della Porta argues, institutional actors promote a minimalist and procedural conception of democracy that is challenged by movements pressing for a broader inclusion of issues and voices. How democracy works depends to a large degree on what democracy is framed as *meaning*, both in terms of the specific institutional arrangements that texts authorize and the disputed frames that are in play.

Unlike the other authors in part IV, I suggest that the changing terrain of movements today may have less to do with the scale or locus of material power than with the unresolved issues of democracy raised by movements of the past, especially, but not only, the position of women as citizens. The institutionalization of procedural democracy went hand in hand with the exclusion from institutional access to politics of certain kinds of issues and constituents in specific ways in different countries. Universal suffrage was not part of the American Revolution, for example, but needed a civil war, a women's suffrage movement, and an African American civil rights movement to include the majority of the U.S. population. Exclusion remains an issue: some portions of U.S.-controlled territory (the District of Columbia and Puerto Rico) have limited access to formal democracy, and new voter identification measures threaten to reexclude challenger groups.

In other words, democracy itself remains a contested term. The struggle over what democracy means is not limited to states that are losing openly autocratic regimes, such as Egypt and Libya, but is overt in places such as Wisconsin and Ohio (where it particularly involves the right to collective bargaining), New Hampshire and Indiana (where disenfranchisement is at issue), and Greece and Germany (where national financial commitments to the EU are seen as undemocratic as well as costly). Whether these movements succeed in shifting the meaning of democracy remains to be seen, but the tension between a view of democracy as institutional, representative, and achieved and a framing of democracy as participatory, discursive, and aspirational is still very relevant.

Redefinitions of democracy reform institutional arrangements, but they also transform the substance of political struggles. When politics is defined through exclusions built on race, gender, sexuality, and national identity, there are different forces aroused than when politics is defined merely by reference to partisan competition or economic resistance to corporate globalization. Although democracy is defined as the power of people, the question still arises, which people?

The terrain of contentious politics shifts when conflicts focus on political issues framed in ways that offer opportunity for new collective identities to emerge. Adams and Padamsee (2001) discuss this in terms of the "signs" that regimes use to invoke various "subject positions," speaking to people in terms of their religions, genders, racialized communities, family values, or other potential identities. To illustrate, consider McAdam and Tarrow's story of how electoral activity is intertwined with movement mobilizations. They stress the parties and movements as actors; the discursive model looks instead at systems and values.

In the case of U.S. civil rights mobilization, the nature of the electoral system was itself at issue. As the links among movements, parties, congressional debate, and social policy were profoundly transformed, the "solid South" shifted from alignment with the Democrats to Republicans electorally, without changing its states' rights discourse, a resonant framing about whiteness and power. Republicans could appeal to portions of the white electorate with racially coded social issue campaigns (including the War on Drugs and welfare reform) without fear of electoral consequences from black voters. This reframing of U.S. politics, which Bonilla-Silva (2003) calls "racism without racists," also produced changes in voting districts, electoral laws, and taxation that restructured the institutional terrain, including where money flowed. Movements and parties are not just related to each other; both are sited in a broader field of political discourse.

Similarly, the deparliamentarization of politics in Europe reflects not only shifts in the locus of corporate power vis-à-vis the state but also changing definitions of what politics is supposed to be about. As the classic left–right alignment of political conflict in European welfare states was disrupted by "new" movements, space opened for contestations over precisely those issues on which left and right had agreed. As the voluminous literature on new social movements shows, the issues of environmental destruction, inadequate investment in higher education, and the exclusion and devaluation of women citizens challenged an institutional political system that defined such concerns as "not political."

Feminism and the Changing Framework of the Political

This reframing of democracy in the 1960s and 1970s changed the relationship between institutions and formerly marginalized populations. This is especially evident in the transformation of global norms to encompass women's citizenship more fully. Feminism—the revolutionary demand for women's autonomy, gender equality, and political solidarity among women (a radical extension of *liberté, egalité, fraternité*)—has now become a discursive framework with institutional anchors creating resonance for a variety of claims (Liu 2006; Jenson 2008). Women's interests were reframed from being apolitical needs to being politically charged demands. Political systems—from conservative parties to leftist movements—were challenged as antidemocratic because they offered no formal avenues for including these concerns in the institutionalized framework of "politics."

Changes ensued as women became visible as citizens and voters. In Germany, for example, the politics of feminism flowed into movement organizations and new political parties such as the GREENS but also transformed old parties such as the German Christian Democrats (CDU) and the Social Democrats (SPD). The SPD, long beholden to the unions, dropped its long-standing objections to part-time work and longer shopping hours; the CDU, which had long seen itself as reliant on women's votes, modernized its family-friendly image by invoking women's rights discourse in restructuring parental leave policy (Von Wahl 2006; Wiliarty 2010).

German feminists speak of "gender democracy," meaning the equal sharing of political power by women and men and women's empowerment to raise issues of gender justice (Ferree 2012). This is a challenge to both the *gender of governance,* the sex composition of decision makers, and the *governance of gender,* state policies that subordinate women (Brush 2003). Understanding gender relations as being about democracy is a global phenomenon, expressed variously in different local and regional strategic situations. The variety of outcomes of these struggles highlights how pervasive the reframing of gender as a contestable political issue has become (Friedman 2009).

Claims about human rights are a global discourse of immense power for bringing democracies into existence, empowering specific groups, and setting limits on what concerns are legitimate (Markovitz and Tice 2002; Maddison and Jung 2008). Across Europe, gender and democracy are connected in policy challenges to the public–private divide, such as quotas for women in political offices and "daddy days" for men to provide child care at home (Hobson and Fahlen 2009), but also in the repression of Muslims in the name of defending gender equality as a democratic value (Korteweg and Yurdakul 2009). The discourses of European welfare states are open to both types of challenges, supporting active state intervention against socioeconomic inequality and recognizing the state as having religion, in ways the United States does not.

Within the framework of "women's rights are human rights," women are still struggling to realize full citizenship. The strategic situations they confront include Central American democracies (particularly Nicaragua and El Salvador), where left parties returned to power through alliance with the Roman Catholic Church and in return introduced both generous state investments in education, health care, and nutrition and draconian penalties for women suspected of abortion (Heumann 2010; Viterna 2011). These states imprison women who miscarry but turn a blind eye to incest, domestic violence, and rape, yet these left-leaning, Catholic-supported governments are not subject to the transnational scrutiny directed at Islamic-supported governments in Turkey or Indonesia, nor does their credibility as leftist seem impaired. So the question of whether democracy actually includes women's citizenship remains part of the unsettled discursive terrain of politics.

The political salience of women's rights and women's bodies indicates a larger shift in terrain for movement mobilization, one Foucault called "biopower": the governance of life itself, with political debates being framed as being about the regulation of birthrates, immigration, sexualities, pensions, nutrition, and health care. Issues of surveillance and demands for self-discipline, two aspects of such governance, follow from biopower debates and make claims for freedom resonate even within formal democracies. Issues where bodies and their management are central are not easily aligned on the classic left–right dimension, as movements and states struggle over the parameters of privacy, security, and sexual autonomy for both women and men. The personal domain, long identified with women, is now incontrovertibly political for both women and men, whether current local contestations are about food or sex, keeping secrets or giving care.

It is not trivial that Western states have changed their understanding of politics to include women. Women holding public office are not now radically disruptive, even when they are as powerful as Angela Merkel or Hillary Clinton, but the discursive terrain for criteria has widened. Politics appears less than democratic when more than 60 percent of the decision makers are men. Parties, legislatures, and executives, and even courts, are increasingly vulnerable to a perception of illegitimacy if they fail to be "inclusive." The institutional norm of gender equality in the public sphere is hard for even relatively conservative parties to challenge. Yet the discursive terrain in the domain defined as "private" tilts more toward "family" than gender equality. Indeed, U.S. family-value activists have been influential globally in seeding and supporting antiabortion campaigns in Latin America, antihomosexuality campaigns in Africa, and anti–birth control campaigns in the United Nations (Buss and Herman 2003; Hassett 2007; Heumann 2010).

The larger strategic situation that this creates for contentious politics in the twenty-first century is one in which the discursive framework of the Cold War has been replaced by a "clash of civilizations" (Huntington 1992). In both conflicts, the norm of gender equality helps define a dichotomous discursive field. In the Cold War, the East claimed the achievement of women's emancipation as its own, while the West embraced religious authority, patriarchal families, and legal repression of homosexuality as counters to the threat of "godless communism" (Moeller 1993). In the postsocialist era, a new polarity with discursive mobilization potential was discovered. In the so-called War on Terror, Western countries congratulate themselves on achieving women's liberation and castigate the Islamic East for being religious, patriarchal, and antigay. The continuing inequality of women in the West is obscured by pointing East and framing Islam and Middle Eastern states as the oppressors of women, just as the continuing inequality of women in communist states was formerly obscured by their governments during the Cold War. Although the polarities have reversed, the broad discursive battle between East and West over appropriate domestic gender relations remains. This terrain, not merely a material shift in power among levels and types of institutional actors, shapes present and future movement outcomes.

Conclusion: Using Feminist Experience to Reframe Political Terrain

A focus on the discursive context for movement mobilizations as a significant, locally variable, and geopolitically shifting terrain also reconstructs the meaning of radical and reformist politics. Because feminists (as well as other challengers to biopower such as disability activists, gay rights groups, and environmentalists) have taken movement claims quickly from the streets to the executive levels of government, the question of how movement success actually transforms societies arises. Perhaps deeply transformative—radical—changes need not be associated with large or long-lasting protest demonstrations. Institutional blockages may force challengers onto the streets, but global-level shifts in discursive opportunity at specific historical moments (such as the inversion of Cold War gender politics in the War on Terror) may also open doors to radical change. The diffusion of antiauthoritarian movements in Eastern Europe, Latin America, and, most recently, the Middle East and North Africa suggests that geopolitical flows of ideas and inspiration shape the terrain for movement mobilizations and confront specific national conditions that shape developments in particular countries. Truly radical transformations may come from the intersection of discursive with material institutional opportunities at the transnational, national, and local levels.

Even so-called radicals may prefer reform strategies when discursive as well as material blockages fade and shifts in discourse open up opportunities to use more conventional tools. As once with working-class men, feminists now have become insiders in parties of various hues worldwide. This "NGO-ization" of the women's movement shifts the reasons, repertoires, and resources for feminist struggles, with outcomes that are quite diverse in how states respond (Lang 1997; Liu 2006; Maddison and Jung 2008). For example, the technocratic expertise in women's networks becomes a tool in competitions among states to show statistically that they are achieving gender equality (Markovitz and Tice 2002). Such competitions are set off by global policy norms institutionalized in everything from the Millennium Development Goals of the United Nations to the parental leave and part-time parity measures of the EU and are actualized by the "audit culture" of global governance through measured outcomes (Power 1994).

State pledges to embrace gender mainstreaming as a tool and gender equality as an objective may be hollow unless external activists hold states accountable (Woodward 2004), but the fact that states self-define as accepting norms of gender equality is still an important achievement of feminism and continuing political opportunity (Ramirez 2012). Feminist movements have become creative in finding ways to hold national governments accountable. Their networks of mobilization mix movement and state resources into tools usable at multiple scales. For example, impoverished, undocumented women immigrants claimed domestic violence as grounds for asylum in Canada; women's groups then mobilized to modify national refugee rights and subsequently succeeded in bringing gender-based violence into international treaties (Alfredson 2008). The porousness of states to transnational discourses is matched by activists' abilities to use the resources of the national state to shift transnational norms, procedures, and legal regulations. Kathrin Zippel (2004) points to the "ping-pong effect" between member states and the EU as feminist activists turn back and forth to spur action where it is lagging.

In sum, feminist experience shows that the future of social movement research is not well conceptualized only as a shift in institutional opportunity structures—whether in state–society relationships, such as states downloading, offloading, or laterally shifting power to others, or within states, by centralization of authority in the executive, or in the growing power of corporate interests at national or transnational scales. The dynamics of contention are discursive as well as institutional, and movements themselves matter in changing discourses. A particularly important change is in the meaning of democracy to include formerly disempowered groups and contentious struggles over concerns that have been formerly defined as private and apolitical.

Movements, however, are not the only sources of discursive change. Global polarizations and national interests in legitimacy steer states' embrace of particular discourses. The rapid reversal of polarity on gender, sexuality, family, and religion between West and East is an indication of how the strategic situation facing movements is reshaped by discourses outside their individual control. State interests drive discursive transformations in nationally and regionally specific directions, too. EU gender policies seen as serving European integration are on a different track than those of the United States, which are hostage to "American exceptionalism." Within Europe, the sense that gender is part of the "EU agenda" means national feminist mobilizations have not moved at the same speed or even in the same direction.

Although feminist challenges to the meaning of democracy illustrate how frameworks of discourse are both elements of opportunity and also malleable objects of political struggle, gender politics is by no means the only case in which meaning matters. The successes of feminist movements have won more public, political space for women but have also changed the dynamics of contention for all movements, making gender issues intertwine with other claims and conflicts. Not only because of neoliberalism and its consequences in shifting opportunities for holding and exercising material power but also because of biopower and its claims on human values, such discursive understandings of democracy constitute important parts of the terrain on which the struggles among states, movements, and transnational actors will be fought in the decades ahead.

References

Adams, Julia, and Tasleem Padamsee. 2001. "Signs and Regimes: Rereading Feminist Work on Welfare States." *Social Politics* 8:1–23.

Alfredson, Lisa S. 2008. *Creating Human Rights: How Noncitizens Made Sex Persecution Matter to the World*. Philadelphia: University of Pennsylvania Press.

Bonilla-Silva, Eduardo. 2003. *Racism without Racists: Color-Blind Racism and the Persistence of Racial Inequality in the United States*. Lanham, Md.: Rowman and Littlefield.

Brush, Lisa D. 2003. *Gender and Governance*. Walnut Creek, Calif.: AltaMira Press.

Buss, Doris, and Didi Herman. 2003. *Globalizing Family Values: The Christian Right in International Politics*. Minneapolis: University of Minnesota Press.

Ferree, Myra Marx. 2012. *Varieties of Feminism: German Gender Politics in Global Perspective*. Palo Alto, Calif.: Stanford University Press.

Friedman, Elisabeth Jay. 2009. "Re(gion)alizing Women's Human Rights in Latin America." *Politics and Gender* 5:349–75.

Hassett, Miranda. 2007. *Anglican Communion in Crisis: How Episcopal Dissidents and Their African Allies Are Reshaping Anglicanism*. Princeton, N.J.: Princeton University Press.

Heumann, Silke. 2010. *Sexual Politics and Regime Transition: Understanding the Struggle around Gender and Sexuality in Post-revolutionary Nicaragua*. Amsterdam: University of Amsterdam.

Hobson, Barbara, and Susanne Fahlen. 2009. "Competing Scenarios for European Fathers: Applying Sen's Capabilities and Agency Framework to Work–Family Balance." *Annals of the American Academy of Political and Social Science* 624:214–33.

Huntington, Samuel P. 1992. "The Clash of Civilizations." *Foreign Affairs* 72:22–49.

Jenson, Jane. 2008. "Writing Women Out, Folding Gender In: The European Union 'Modernizes' Social Policy." *Social Politics* 15:131–53.

Korteweg, Anna, and Goerkce Yurdakul. 2009. "Islam, Gender, and Immigrant Integration: Boundary Drawing in Discourses on Honour Killing in the Netherlands and Germany." *Ethnic and Racial Studies* 32:218–38.

Lang, Sabine. 1997. "The NGOization of Feminism." In *Transitions, Environments, Translations: Feminisms in International Politics,* edited by Joan W. Scott, Cora Kaplan, and Deb Keates, 101–20. New York: Routledge.

Liu, Dongxiao. 2006. "When Do National Movements Adopt or Reject International Agendas? A Comparative Analysis of the Chinese and Indian Women's Movements." *American Sociological Review* 71:921–42.

Maddison, Sarah, and Kyungja Jung. 2008. "Autonomy and Engagement: Women's Movements in Australia and South Korea." In *Women's Movements—Flourishing or in Abeyance?,* edited by Marian Sawer and Sandra Grey, 33–48. New York: Routledge.

Markovitz, Lisa, and Karen Tice. 2002. "Paradoxes of Professionalization: Parallel Dilemmas in Women's Organizations in the Americas." *Gender and Society* 16:941–48.

Moeller, Robert. 1993. *Protecting Motherhood: Women and the Family in the Politics of Postwar West Germany.* New York: Cambridge University Press.

Power, Michael. 1994. *The Audit Explosion.* London: Demos.

Ramirez, Francisco. 2012. "From Citizen to Person." Paper presented at the University of Wisconsin Sawyer Seminar on Globalization and Women's Rights, Center for Research on Gender and Women, Madison.

Viterna, Jocelyn. 2011. "The 'Pinking' of Latin American Politics." Presentation at the Eastern Sociological Society, Philadelphia.

Von Wahl, Angelika. 2006. "Gender Equality in Germany: Comparing Policy Change across Domains." *West European Politics* 29:461–88.

Wiliarty, Sarah. 2010. *Bringing Women to the Party: The CDU and the Politics of Gender in Germany.* New York: Cambridge University Press.

Woodward, Alison. 2004. "Building Velvet Triangles: Gender and Informal Governance." In *Informal Governance in the European Union,* edited by Thomas Christiansen and Simona Piattoni, 76–93. Cheltenham, U.K.: Edward Elgar.

Zippel, Kathrin. 2004. "Transnational Advocacy Networks and Policy Cycles in the European Union: The Case of Sexual Harassment." *Social Politics* 11:57–85.

Afterword

Bert Klandermans

Have the dynamics of contention changed? This is the question that the social movement scholars who contributed to this volume were asked. The easy answer is that we don't know, as we haven't done the proper longitudinal research. At the same time, it is hard to believe that the dynamics of contention have not changed. Over the past years, the world has seemed in constant turmoil, whether we look at China, the Arab world, the African continent, Latin America, Central Europe, or the Western world. Our "all-star team," including "some of [today's] most influential scholars in the field" (to cite our two external reviewers), was asked not only to reflect on our focal question but also to respond to each other's answers. The result is a rich compendium of answered and unanswered questions, of challenges and provoking thoughts, and of directions recommended to take.

Reading through the various contributions, I made the final notes that I present in this afterword. I arrange them according to the four concepts that framed the discussion: demand, supply, mobilization, and context. However, I want to start with a comment about dynamics per se. McAdam, Tarrow, and Tilly (2001) first started discussion about dynamics and mechanisms, as explained in the introduction by Jacquelien van Stekelenburg and Conny Roggeband. I second McAdam, Tarrow, and Tilly's argument that we must think more in terms of dynamics, mechanisms, and processes. Understanding movement activities, whether contentious or not, is about understanding the processes that generate these activities. This is important as movement activities are the visible aspects of movements. Seeking to understand the dynamics that produce those activities and their consequences is what the study of social movements is all about.

When we were revising and finalizing our essays, the world exploded into what we began to call "Contentious 2011." Many of the questions we formulated appear even more relevant in view of actual political events. We asked our authors to form a commentary on the events. The last section of this afterword is based on their responses.

Demand, supply, and mobilization are inherently dynamic concepts. For demand to translate into action, supply is needed, and vice versa. Mobilization is the process that brings the two together. I will argue that the formation of demand and the construction of supply are processes that do not get the attention they deserve individually, let alone their interplay. Studies on movement participation are predominantly about mobilization; hence mobilization is the process we know much more about. Yet, as we will see, there is still much to be learned even about the process of mobilization, especially regarding the rise and impact of new information and communication technologies (ICTs). Demand, supply, and mobilization evolve in a context that varies over time and place. Contextualization of the dynamics of demand, supply, and mobilization is therefore crucial, as evidenced by the differences and changes in social and political opportunities in the parts of the world mentioned earlier and by the rise and fall of regimes and the economic and financial crises that recently lashed the world. The contributions to this volume exemplify that the study of movement activity requires a constant interplay of the micro-, meso-, and macrolevels of analysis.

The Dynamics of Demand

Dynamics of demand are the most psychological of the dynamics of contention. Key processes are grievance formation, identification, emotion work, and empowerment. As we are studying social movements and collective action, we are dealing with *shared* grievances and emotions and *group* identification and empowerment. How are such feelings formed and shared? Van Doorn, Prins, and Welschen (chapter 4) suggest that they are socially constructed in interpersonal interactions among people who share a fate. They report findings from focus group discussions of Moroccan youth engaged in identity talk. In earlier work, I coined the term *consensus formation* for this process of unplanned convergence of ideas. Shared grievances and emotions, group identification, and empowerment imply fundamental psychological processes, but as Van Zomeren (discussion to part I) observes, not many studies of movement participation show awareness of the psychological fundamentals underlying these processes. Van Zomeren urges us to open the black box of dynamics and build into our models of individual participation what we know from social and political psychology about individual behavior. The models he proposes are tested in experimental studies; this confirms the presumed causal mechanisms. The problem with such experiments is their ecological validity—would the experimentally manipulated situation work similarly in the real world? Nonetheless, experimental studies help to sharpen our models, and in any event, Van Zomeren is right: we should design research accounting for the fundamental psychological processes that underlie the dynamics of demand.

People want to influence politics because they want to promote or protect their interests or principles. In doing so, they may find that access to politics is denied and that they are excluded from the political arena. This was, for instance, the case for blacks in South Africa and for both blacks and women in the United States, as Myra Marx Ferree (discussion to part IV) memorializes. Under those circumstances, people have no choice but to resort to contentious politics, as blacks in South Africa did in their struggle against apartheid and as American blacks and women did during the civil rights movement and the suffrage movement, respectively.

The Dynamics of Supply

Dynamics of supply are about organizations and their appeal. What exactly do movement organizations offer in terms of opportunities to participate, and why are their claims appealing? Who is making the strategic choices about what to offer and what to aim for? Movement organizations can take a variety of forms and offer a wide range of opportunities in which to participate. Comparisons to assess which forms of organization and which activities are effective are rarely made, if at all. Yet these are important questions to study.

Seeing the fuzzy boundaries between movement and nonmovement organizations, one may wonder what exactly *is* the movement, where does it begin, and where does it end? Coalitions come and go; networks expand and fall apart. Social movement organizations are embedded in multiorganizational fields, as various authors emphasized. Such fields are divided into allies and opponents and structured by the social cleavages in a society. Movements and countermovements, political parties, governmental and nongovernmental organizations alike occupy the organizational fields in society. Sometimes they build coalitions; oftentimes they compete. In any event, they try to disseminate their views of the situation, and as they are divided, the dynamics of supply are very much a competition for people's hearts and minds, while perceived credibility and trustworthiness make those people believe one actor more than another. Future research into the dynamics of supply should give attention to these persuasion processes in the context of the noisy environment in which people are embedded.

Within the multiorganizational field, movement organizations and political parties encounter one another. Ferree makes the observation that movements and parties are not just related to each other but that both are related to a broader field of political discourse. Citizens who want to influence politics can choose to engage with a movement organization, a political party, or both. Which way they go if they want to influence politics, and why, are important topics for future research.

The Dynamics of Mobilization

Basically, dynamics of mobilization involve convincing and activating, in other words, consensus mobilization and action mobilization. Obviously, one needs communication channels for that, but one also needs a susceptible audience, that is, a demand.

The communication channels employed these days are both real and virtual. The effectiveness of either is a subject of fierce debate. No doubt present-day mobilization campaigns are inconceivable without virtual channels such as the Internet and social media. The differential effectiveness of traditional media, such as newspapers, leaflets, and posters; face-to-face interaction; and the Internet is far from clear, however. Comparative studies of means of communication in the context of mobilization campaigns are difficult as it is virtually impossible to isolate the impact of one specific channel. Experimental designs could help, but as mentioned, they may labor on validity.

It is often forgotten that mobilizing structures are not given but rather must be assembled. This is where the process of mobilization begins and often falters. Coalitions break down or fail to come along; potential allies engage in mutual fighting and fail to collaborate. In this stage, abeyance structures appear extremely important, as mobilizing structures are seldom built from scratch. Systematic knowledge about this phase of the mobilization process is largely lacking.

Susceptibility affects the dynamics of mobilization as highly susceptible people are easy to mobilize. A simple announcement might suffice to get them onto the streets, as the White Marsh in reaction to the murder of young women by Dutroux in 1996 in Belgium illustrated. Indeed, people were so upset by the murders and the way the authorities dealt with them that they needed very little to be mobilized. Similarly, in countries where indignation about the imminent war in Iraq was strong, information in the newspapers simply sufficed to bring people onto the streets in large numbers. Organizers may try to affect people's susceptibility through identity work and emotion work. *Identity work* is meant to draw boundaries so that people are made aware of with whom they share fate; *emotion work* is meant to raise people's anger and explain why people should be angry.

The differential workings of real and virtual media, the assemblage of mobilizing structures, the role of abeyance structures, identity work, and emotion work should all be high on our research agendas for the future.

Contextualization

In her discussion of part IV of the volume, Ferree argues that much of the turbulence and change in the context of contention stems from the fact that *democracy* remains a contested term. Major movements in Western democracies—the labor movement, the civil rights movement, the women's movement—were movements to claim citizenship rights for people who were excluded from the democratic process. And indeed, these days, the global justice movement and the Occupy movement, but also the colored revolutions and the Arab Spring, can be seen as recent examples of movements that address the unresolved issues of democracy.

Demand, supply, and mobilization and the movement activity resulting from them develop in an ever-changing social and political context—state formation and modernization in the past and globalization in the present. Political systems and movement sectors differ between countries and are subject to change. The interplay of demand, supply, and mobilization is influenced by such contextual variation. Contextual changes can be both institutional and cultural. In the words of Ferree, "transformations may come from the intersection of discursive with material institutional opportunities at the transnational, national, and local levels." Politically active citizens take these opportunities and stage instances of contentious politics. Do we know how these processes work? Do we understand how and why people take the political and discursive opportunities they encounter to influence politics? Not really. To be sure, we know that people perceive the macrocontext in which they are embedded and that this affects the way they take part in party politics and/or movement politics, but how exactly that works is much less clear.

Investigating Dynamics

Our research designs are part of the problem. Investigating dynamics requires comparisons of time and place. Of course, we can conduct in-depth single case studies, which will tell us how specific cases evolved, but these will not tell us whether our findings are unique to a specific case or can be generalized to other cases or other configurations of demand, supply, mobilization, and context. Debra Minkoff, in her discussion of the changing dynamics of supply (discussion to part II), touches on some of the issues to be solved in comparative research. Obviously, our findings are determined by the comparisons we make. Do we compare campaigns? Do we compare movement organizations?

Do we compare events staged by the same movement at different points in time or at different places? Do we compare individuals and assess how levels of involvement change over time? Many more comparisons can be made and, in fact, are made.

One of the problems we are faced with when it comes to comparative research is the lack of standardization. Comparisons of time and place would be so much easier if the same measures and designs were employed everywhere. In an ideal world, we would be able to download the data set of our Italian colleagues and compare that to our Dutch data. This is less utopian than it may seem. In a comparative study of street demonstrations in eight different countries, we worked very hard to secure that designs, samples, and questionnaires employed were identical.[1] All data are stored in a single archive, which can be approached from wherever scholars are in the world. I know this is still rare, but these days, we have the techniques that make such collaboration possible; we must now build the networks we need to realize it.

Contentious 2011

The times of contention may not have begun and terminated in 2011, but they seemed to culminate during that year: protests against austerity measures all over the Western world, the *indignados* in Spain, the Arab Spring, the urban camps in Israel, the Occupy movement spreading over the world. Perhaps the most striking aspect is the fact that everything came together in so many parts of the world. Obviously, there is an element of imitation to it in which new communication technologies played a crucial role, but imitation is not a blind mechanism. Rather than mindless copying, people choose to adapt action strategies to their situations because the sentiments resonate with their feelings. In this ever more globalizing world, the sociopolitical context in which social movements operate is no longer simply national, or only supranational, but a mix of supranational, national, and local influences. Consequently, the targets of social movement organization are more and more beyond the focus of the state. To fully understand this, Sarah A. Soule, in chapter 6, advises social movement scholars to seek collaboration with students of organizations that have focused on movements directed at corporations, firms, and industries.

Globalization changes contentious politics not only in terms of *targets* but also in terms of *claims,* claims directly concerned with the functioning of democracy and the political outcomes it generates (Offe 2011). Beginning with Iceland, and moving to Spain, Portugal, and Greece, indignation has been expressed regarding the corruption of the political class, the privileges granted to lobbies, and the close connection between public institutions and financial powers. It is this corruption of democracy that is held responsible for the economic crisis and the inability to manage it. Both Occupy ("the democratic deficit") and the Spanish *indignados* ("*Democracia real ya!*") have placed this metaquestion of democracy at the center of their action.

Much has been written about the role of the Internet and social media in this respect. ICTs influence mobilization; they seem capable of getting large numbers of people onto the streets, both in repressive and democratic societies. It is plausible that ICTs help in bringing together (often geographically dispersed) critical communities; however, the extent to which this matters is disputable. The Arab Spring offers mixed evidence on this point. It seems clear that new and old ICTs were critical in spreading the word, making *diffusion* central to the 2011 wave of protests in the United States, Europe, and the Middle East. The same can be said for *brokerage*. In fact, Arab activists who translated tweets from Arab into English operated as virtual brokers, relating the Middle East to the rest of the world. Focusing only on the role of ICTs, however, deflects attention from identifying activists (or, more likely, activist cadres) who are sufficiently connected and embedded so that they can be quickly activated. This is precisely what Suzanne Staggenborg shows in chapter 7. She reveals how the movement community that was important for the G20 protests was also supporting the Occupy camp and movement in Pittsburgh. Notice that, despite the emphasis on ICT, organizing on the ground remains of central importance. The mobilization of the crowds in Tahrir Square, for instance, was happening on the ground through traditional word-of-mouth communication channels. Most people in the square were not plugged into new media. This does not make ICTs unimportant, however, if only because ICTs help to draw international attention and support along with old media by activating diasporas. When the authorities shut down the Internet, people used land lines to call friends and relatives outside the country, who would then relay information via ICTs to international networks.

In our ever more liquefying and virtual world, the assemblage of mobilizing structures is changing. Sometimes mobilization takes place in networklike structures without much coordination because events unfold so fast and in so many different ways that they are hard to coordinate. Other times, mobilization employs a coordination structure. Occupy, for instance, was coordinated by a website that relayed information on where what activities were staged and how many squares worldwide were occupied. Although we see more and more networklike and coordination-structures, the role of community-based networks, movement organizations, and coalitions between movement organizations cannot be underestimated. In fact, in addition to articulating multiple issues, the signs at the Occupy camps were full of names of formal organizations involved in the protest. One important point is whether more liquid mobilizing structures will be able to develop communitarian, subcultural action, or simple coalitions into long-term, sustained social movements. Indeed, Occupy faltered without taking the steps to greater formalization even of a decentralized, nonhierarchical type. In the Middle East, where networklike mobilization appeared incredibly effective in the first instance, it would be a mistake to see organizations as a legacy of the past, to be replaced by virtual and nonvirtual informal networks. In fact, the final outcome in Egypt and Tunesia reveals that grassroots work still pays off. The Islamists did that in local communities, while the modern progressives surfed on the Internet. We know who won the elections. If anything, these changes in mobilizing structures reveal that protest mobilization is not the same as building an enduring movement that stays around to strive for substantial change.

The protests have taken not only politicians but also social movement scholars by surprise. It put the "why now" question high on the agenda. Indeed, one of the most difficult problems in contentious politics is predicting protests. To be sure, real-world consequences of the worldwide economic recession (e.g., foreclosures, personal bankruptcies) were building up, but why did Occupy not explode on the scene earlier? The same can be asked regarding events as they unfolded in the Middle East. When events actually start cascading and escalating, they tend to catch people by surprise. Dynamics of contention are seldom just a matter of static structural conditions but imply contingency and the impact of events on other events over time. Moreover, people were protesting on a smaller scale and laying the groundwork for large-scale protest a long time before the eruptions that captured the attention of international media and social movement scholars. The Tunisian story is one of protests going on for quite a while but being ignored by outsiders, until they finally started getting international notice by the tweets that were spread. The events in Tunisia inspired the Egyptians, but the Egyptians had already had years of protest going on. The April 6 movement of 2008 was an example in which activists experimented with using Facebook to help publicize and coordinate a strike. These are examples that further illustrate that social movement studies tend to concentrate on mobilization and neglect the development of demand and supply factors. Yet neither can be taken for granted. Indeed, grievances abound, but we must still explain how grievances develop and transform into a demand for protest. Similarly, the presence of organizations staging protests cannot be taken for granted, while their formation and the creation of opportunities to participate must be accounted for as well. This process, by which supply factors in a society transform demand for protest and willingness to participate into action, is a thorny but underexposed issue in the literature.

Explaining or predicting outcomes of protests is an equally prickly undertaking. After all, the protests are only one among many factors influencing the course of events. The Arab Spring certainly changed the political scenery in the Middle East, but which way it will go and what impact the protest will eventually have are difficult to predict. Similarly, Occupy has changed public discourse, but whether it will have any long-term impact on public policy, inequality, media coverage, and so on, remains to be seen. To be sure, Occupy's message brought the discussion of inequality back into mainstream conversation, but its tactics and organizational forms have led commentators to conclude that its impact on politics and public policy will be limited.

Finally

The authors of *The Future of Social Movement Research* have all positioned themselves vis-à-vis the current state of the field of social movement studies. They have discussed changes they witness, unanswered research questions they signal, weaknesses and strengths they observe. Dynamics of contention are about the processes and mechanisms that make people engage in politics. The various essays in this volume are a gold mine for students of such political engagement. They formulate questions to be researched and point to possible directions our research could, or even should, take.

Note

1. See http://www.protestsurvey.eu/.

References

McAdam, Doug, Sidney Tarrow, and Charles Tilly. 2001. *Dynamics of Contention.* Cambridge: Cambridge University Press.

Offe, Claus. 2011. "Crisis and Innovation of Liberal Democracy: Can Deliberation Be Institutionalised?" *Czech Sociological Review* 47:447–72.

Contributors

MARIJE BOEKKOOI is assistant professor of sociology at VU-University, Amsterdam.

PANG CHING BOBBY CHEN is a lecturer in sociology at the University of California, Merced.

DONATELLA DELLA PORTA is professor of sociology at the European University Institute.

MARIO DIANI is professor of sociology at the University of Trento, Italy, and ICREA Research Professor at the Universitat Pompeu Fabra, Barcelona.

JAN WILLEM DUYVENDAK is professor of sociology at the University of Amsterdam.

MYRA MARX FERREE is Alice H. Cook Professor of Sociology and director of the European Union Center of Excellence at the University of Wisconsin–Madison.

BETH GHARRITY GARDNER is a PhD student in sociology at the University of California, Irvine.

ASHLEY GROMIS is a graduate student in sociology at the University of California, Los Angeles.

SWEN HUTTER is assistant professor of comparative politics at the University of Munich.

BERT KLANDERMANS is professor of applied social psychology at VU-University, Amsterdam.

RUUD KOOPMANS is director of the research unit Migration, Integration, and Transnationalization at the Social Research Center Berlin (WZB) and a professor of political science at the University of Amsterdam.

HANSPETER KRIESI is chair of comparative politics at the University of Zurich.

NONNA MAYER is research director at the Centre for European Studies (SciencesPo–National Centre for Scientific Research).

DOUG MCADAM is professor of sociology at Stanford University.

JOHN D. MCCARTHY is Distinguished Professor of Sociology at The Pennsylvania State University.

DEBRA MINKOFF is professor and chair of sociology at Barnard College, Columbia University.

ALICE MOTES is a PhD student in sociology at the University of California, Irvine.

PAMELA E. OLIVER is a Conway-Bascom Professor of Sociology at the University of Wisconsin–Madison.

FRANCESCA POLLETTA is professor of sociology at the University of California, Irvine.

JACOMIJNE PRINS is a PhD student at VU-University, Amsterdam.

PATRICK RAFAIL is assistant professor of sociology at Tulane University.

CONNY ROGGEBAND is associate professor of political studies at FLACSO, Ecuador.

CHRISTOPHER ROOTES is professor of environmental politics and political sociology and director of the Centre for the Study of Social and Political Movements at the University of Kent at Canterbury.

DIETER RUCHT retired in 2011 as professor of sociology at the Free University of Berlin and as codirector of the research group "Civil Society, Citizenship, and Political Mobilization in Europe" at the Social Science Research Center Berlin.

DAVID A. SNOW is Distinguished Professor of Sociology at the University of California, Irvine.

SARAH A. SOULE is Morgridge Professor of Organizational Behavior at the Stanford Graduate School of Business.

SUZANNE STAGGENBORG is professor of sociology at the University of Pittsburgh.

SIDNEY TARROW teaches in the Department of Government at Cornell University.

VERTA TAYLOR is professor of sociology at the University of California, Santa Barbara.

MARJOKA VAN DOORN is a PhD student in sociology at VU-University, Amsterdam.

JACQUELIEN VAN STEKELENBURG is associate professor of sociology at VU-University, Amsterdam.

MARTIJN VAN ZOMEREN is associate professor of social psychology at the University of Groningen.

STEFAAN WALGRAVE is professor of political science at the University of Antwerp, Belgium.

SASKIA WELSCHEN is a PhD student in sociology at VU-University, Amsterdam.

Index

Abortion, 4, 25, 269, 295n7, 423
AC! (Acting against Unemployment), 398
Accountability, 172, 321, 353, 356, 420, 426; electoral, 352, 354
ACORN, 383, 384, 391
Action, xviii, 155, 182, 249, 254, 267, 305; antimarket, 412; globalization and, 302–3; Internet-based, 221; local, 226–27; mobilization, 11, 97, 172, 173, 206, 268, 382, 432; networks of, 229; political, 26, 30, 97, 198, 257, 287, 293; potentiality and, 192; social, 29–30; social movements and, 412–13; violent, 211; virtual, 220. *See also* Collective action; Field of action
Activism, 20, 30, 117, 128, 207, 294n5, 340, 384, 385, 390, 391, 398, 412; black, 337; career, 276; Internet, 18, 26, 48, 219; model of, 409; online, 48, 108, 305; political, 31; post-it, 321, 409; social, 26; student, 380; transnational, 412. *See also* Grassroots activism
Activists, xiv, 30, 100, 139, 141, 146, 147, 173, 178, 185, 316, 357, 372, 382, 383; authorities and, 135; collective identity of, 140; deliberations of, 155; identities of, 43, 49; media, 186; transnational, 265
Activities, xiv, 38, 66, 172, 198, 271, 332; civic/social, 32; movement, 187, 192, 327, 340, 429, 433; organizational, 133; repression of, 371–72; supply of, 191
Actors, 256, 257, 272; claim making by, 319 (fig.); collective, 23, 183, 281; globalization and, 302–3; group meaning and, 65–66; mesolevel, 64–65; mesomobilization, 185; mutual reputation of, 158; social, 264, 382; social movements and, 158, 160; typology of, 238–42
ACT UP, 343n1, 398, 408
Adbusters, 387

443

Afghan War, protesting, 378
African Americans, 246; drug war and, 241; incarceration rates for, 236, 243
Age, 4, 100, 291, 401
Agence France-Presse, 403, 413n5
Agendas, 140, 147, 207, 256
Air Lib, 402
Airline Passengers' Bill of Rights, 20–21
AIVD (Dutch security agency), 68
Alliance for Climate Protection, 20
Al Nisa (Muslim women's organization), 69
Al-Qaeda, 270
Alterglobalization, 302, 400, 410–11
American Airlines, 20, 21
American Civil Liberties Union, 392
American Family Association, 386
American Federation of Labor, 161
Amnesty International, 372
Anger, group-based, 85, 86, 89
Animal rights, 20, 24, 147, 153
Anti-AIDS movement, 398, 408
Anti-birth control campaign, 424
Anti-Castor campaign, 175–88, 193, 194; coordination of, 182–83; groups/activities on transportation route, 181 (fig.); recognition for, 185–86; structural elements of, 180–81; tactics of, 184–85
Anticopyright mobilizations, 29
Anticrime movement, 248, 250
Anti–drunk driving movement, 248, 249
Anti-G8 campaign, 186, 412
Antiglobalization, 302, 408, 409, 412
Anti-health insurance reform groups, 240
Antihomosexuality campaigns, 242, 424

Anti-immigrant movements, 5, 110, 240, 242, 254, 255, 283, 316, 332
Antiminority movements, 240, 255
Antinuclear movements, 179, 185, 398
Antiracist movements, 317, 407
Antislavery, 334
Anti-War Committee (AWC), 137
Antiwar movement, 115, 226, 240, 247, 301, 332, 390
Apartheid, struggle against, 431
April 6 movement, 436
Arab European League (AEL), 68–69
Arab Spring, xi, 156, 160, 230, 342, 433, 434, 435, 437
Armey, Dick, 386
Attac, 159, 398, 408, 413
Austerity measures, 408, 409, 434
Authenticity, 113, 114, 118n3
Authoritarians, 156, 287–88, 399
Autonomy, 230, 406, 410

Baader Meinhof Gang, 270, 276
Banaszak, Jane, 315, 316, 318, 320, 322n1
Barnes, Samuel, 400
Basic action groups, 171, 176–77, 182
Bauerliche Notgemeinschaft (Farmers Emergency Alliance), 177
Bauman, Zygmunt, 40, 95, 97
Beck, Ulrich: individualization of class thesis and, 98
Beckwith, Karen, 315, 316, 318, 320, 322n1
Beissinger, Mark: elections/opposition movements and, 326–27
Bernstein, Mary, 39, 399
BILD, 179
Biographical availability, 288, 289
Biopower, 247, 424, 425
Black Bloc, 221

INDEX 445

Black box, opening, 80–84, 86–89, 90
Black Panthers, 276
Boekkooi, Marije, xviii, xix–xx, 410; formal coalitions and, 223; ICTs and, 304; mobilization and, 212, 300
Boundaries, 39, 61, 65, 130, 146, 399; class, 98; cultural, 281, 282, 292; drawing, 61, 64, 69–72; economic, 281, 282; ethnic, 98; gender, 98; group, 69; national, 281; negotiations on, 75; organizational, 151, 154; political, 281, 282; sexual, 98; social, 241; transcending, 47
Boundary construction, 150, 153, 160, 193, 194
Boundary definitions, 146, 151, 154, 155, 162n1, 399; active, 192; identity and, 153; mechanisms of, 152; shared, 161
Boundary work, xvii–xviii, 69, 154
Bourdieu, Pierre, 398, 408
Bove, José, 397
Boycotts, 11, 26, 29, 30, 288, 363, 411, 413n2
Bread and Roses March, 135, 136, 140
Bureau of Justice Statistics, 236
Bürgerinitiative Lüchow-Dannenberg (Regional Citizen Initiative, BI), 177–78, 185
Bush, George H. W., 333
Bush, George W., 199, 331, 334, 371
Buycotts, 29, 363

Campaigns, 68, 186, 187, 196, 227, 242, 330, 383, 412, 424; alliances, 172; civil rights, 337; collective, 126, 133; communication, 363; corporate, 383; mobilization, 152, 218, 226, 432; movement, 126, 127, 129, 131–33, 134, 141, 185, 193; networks, 172; political, 334, 341; social issue, 151, 170, 422; transnational, 362
Canadian World March committee, 135
Carmichael, Stokely, 118n3
Case studies, xvii, xx, 127, 148, 433; qualitative, 148
Castells, Manuel, 40, 99, 102
Castor transports, 175, 176, 177, 178, 179, 180, 181, 184
Catholics for a Free Choice, 114
Catholic Workers, 276
CBOs. *See* Community-based organizations
Centre for Political Research of SciencesPo (Cevipof), 400
Change, social movements and, 39, 147, 363
Charter of Amiens (1906), 406
Chen, Pang Ching Bobby, xviii
Cheppih, Mohammed: AEL and, 68
Christian democrats, 288, 423
Christian right, 332, 333
CitiBank, 419
Citizen involvement, 171, 382, 412
Citizenship, 241, 295n6, 317, 411, 423; rights, 352, 433; transnational conception of, 352; women's, 424
Civic engagement, 31, 370, 385, 386
Civil disobedience, 27, 42, 187, 250, 375, 377, 390
Civil rights, 128, 335, 337, 338, 353, 361, 422; forces, 339, 340
Civil rights movement, 23, 29, 42, 44, 110, 118n3, 128, 195, 196, 197, 241, 246, 328, 336, 337, 338, 340, 431, 433; African American, 251, 252, 421; confrontational tactics of,

114; mobilization of, 335; tactical/goal diversity of, 111
Civil Service Commission, 335
Civil society, 148, 222, 300, 317, 351, 356, 359; transforming, 39, 96
Civil War, 334, 343n2
Claim making, 317, 320; by collective actors, 319 (fig.); protests in, 319 (fig.)
Class, 4, 41, 44, 50, 64, 100, 239, 308–10, 309; differences, 252, 253; Marxist concept of, 39; struggle, 98
Class movements, exclusionary, 254–55
Clinton, Bill, 333
Clinton, Hillary, 424
Coalition against the New War, 225
Coalitions, xix, 132, 155, 161, 183, 196, 223, 225, 226, 408, 435; building, 160, 224; community-wide, 385; as independent variable, 115; instrumental, 160; movements and, 154; organizational learning via, 114–15
Cold War, 317, 335, 424, 425
Collaboration, xv, 99, 150, 193, 220, 434; generative effect of, 195; interorganizational, 151, 152; organizational, 115, 116; sustained, 160, 161; unwillingness for, 197
Collective action, xiii, xiv, xx, 5, 6, 10, 24, 49, 61, 63, 65, 68, 80, 81, 85, 89, 90, 97, 125, 126, 128, 129, 131, 132, 146, 148, 158, 199, 200, 211, 213, 244, 269, 325, 363, 374, 386; challenging, 245; collective disadvantage and, 79; consumption-based, 30; continuity of, 194; coordination of, 145, 149–56, 155 (fig.); coping and, 88; demonstrative forms of, 303; effective, xix, 307; emotions and, 83; ethnic minorities and, 255; mobilization and, 205, 306; motivation for, 84, 86; participation in, 8, 11, 47, 74, 153, 300, 382; predicting, 84; promoting, 149, 151; resource mobilization theory of, 171; shared identity and, 307; single-issue, 147; social movement and, 87, 193; social/psychological dynamics of, 33, 37–38; student, 380; sustained, 192, 194; transnationalization of, 304

Collective identity, xviii, 3, 6–7, 18, 19, 21, 22–24, 38–42, 43–50, 83, 95, 96, 98, 99, 102, 125–28, 129–31, 133, 136, 139, 140, 141, 161, 162, 195, 199, 267, 273, 275; alignment of, 276; concept of, 37, 38, 63; constructing/maintaining, 38, 39, 40, 100, 276; expression of, 196, 274; formation of, xvii, 45, 60, 131, 198, 358; fundamental aspects of, 194; importance of, 263–66; long-term, 351; negotiation and, 67; perspectives on, 63–64; politicization of, 8, 9, 11, 38, 46, 48, 49, 59, 60, 62, 63, 66, 69, 73, 75; promotion of, 198, 220, 221; rituals/narratives and, 130; shared, 151, 193; social cleavages and, 64–65; social movements and, 41, 61; transformation of, 46, 47; transnational, 265

Collectivity, 48, 62, 150, 171–72, 267, 270, 273; identification with, 151, 265

Commitment, 24, 225; distant/individualized, 409–10; identity, 268; moral, 270; political, 30, 31, 32

Committee on Civil Rights, 335

Communes, 155, 276, 406
Communication, xv, 25, 42, 101, 102, 125, 173, 180, 257; channels, 10, 11, 242, 304, 432; costs of, 220; electronic, 31; flows of, 358; many-to-many, 219; online, 87; opportunities for, 187
Communication Rights in the Information Society (CRIS), 159
Communism, 317, 326, 424
Communist Party (CP), 129–30, 304, 407, 409, 410
Communities, 155–56, 245; centralized, 129; closed, 100–102; decentralized, 141; discursive, 10, 42–46; fragmented, 95; identity and, 50, 114; imagined, 187; media-generated, 45; online, 31; student, 380; transnational, 316; virtual, 24
Community-based organizations (CBOs), 192, 383–84, 391
Community organizations, 134, 136, 196, 244
Comparative research, xx, 199, 210, 433
Comparative Studies of Electoral Systems, 294n6
Conceptualizations, differences/similarities between, 63–66
Confédération Paysanne, 408
Conflicts, 132, 141, 161, 209, 270, 357, 383; cultural, 238; ethnic, 236, 238; over globalization, 282, 283, 285–86; intergroup, 60, 65; intramovement, 252–53, 256; political, 359; triangulation of, 62–63; workplace, 404–5
Congress of Industrial Organizations, 161
Consciousness, 48, 62, 65, 240, 252
Consciousness raising, 46, 62, 65, 69, 72–74

Conseils Sondages Analyses (CSA), 402, 414
Consensus formation, xix, 4, 5, 8, 10, 11, 206, 430
Conservatism, 288, 340
Consumerism, 26, 29, 412; political, 363, 399; social movements and, 411
Consumption, xvii, 18, 412; public use and, 26–29
Contention, 320, 331; dynamics of, xi, xii, xv, xvii, 49, 426, 429, 436, 437; electoral, 326, 328; racial, 334, 340; social change and, 95; supply side of, 95, 200
"Contentious 2011," 430, 434–37
Context, changing, 405–12, 429, 433
Cooperation, 152, 224–25, 227, 320
Coordination, xix, 139, 145, 149–56, 155 (fig.), 157, 193, 197, 199, 320; centralized, 182; costs of, 220; lack of, 133, 140; mobilization and, 227; modes of, 145, 149, 152, 154, 155, 156, 159–62, 200; networks and, 157; overarching, 182–83; structures, 224, 225, 226–28, 230, 435
Coping: collective action and, 88; dual-pathway model of, 84, 86–87; emotion-focused approach to, 85, 86, 87, 88; problem-focused approach to, 85, 86, 88
Copyright, 18, 27, 28, 30
Countermovements, 111, 273, 339, 431
Counterpublics, 359, 360
Creative Commons, 28
Crime, 41, 238, 243, 246, 248, 327; drugs and, 247, 249
Crime control, 244, 246, 247, 250, 253, 269

Criminal justice, 246, 251; disparities in, 236–38, 247–48, 249, 252
CSA. *See* Conseils Sondages Analyses
Cultural changes, 49, 50, 410
Cultural context, 43, 406
Cultural diversity, 42, 44, 47, 50, 236, 252
Cultural groups, 43, 125, 134, 141, 239 (fig.)
Cultural integration, mobilization and, 238–42
Cultural issues, 149, 283, 294n4, 360
Cultural liberalism, 283, 288, 289, 292, 295n7; immigration and, 286; salience of, 284 (fig.)
Cultural practices, 38, 128, 130
Culture, 136, 310; Dutch, 71; organization and, 126, 127–29; structure and, 206; understanding, 242
Cyberoptimists, 101

Daewoo, 402
Dahl, Robert A., 356, 361
DAL (The Right to Housing), 398
Dalton, Russell J., 288, 327, 397
Data, 97, 208, 294n1, 321, 399, 403; collecting, 148; diachronic, 161; police, 404; press, 407; protest, 291, 374; sources, 374; storing, 434; survey, 282
David, Françoise, 135
Decentralization, 101, 318, 329, 408, 409
Decision-making, 5, 25, 159, 170, 183, 209, 213, 281, 316, 355, 360, 423; consensual, 362; democratic, 388; downloading power of, 317–18; liberal–deliberative quality of, 362
Defense of Marriage Act, 41, 48
Della Porta, Donatella, xiii, 316, 322, 420; democracy and, 320–21; GJM and, 98; multiple belongings and, xiv; transnationalization and, 282, 419
Demand side, xvi, 17, 19, 26, 32, 79, 200, 429, 433; dynamics of, xvii, 3, 8–10, 430–31
Demobilization, 44, 305, 331, 332, 333, 340; movement, 328, 386; national-level, 316
Democracy, 238, 281, 288, 295n6, 321, 410, 433; challenges for, 352, 353 (fig.), 426–27, 434–35; conceptions of, 320, 347, 348–49, 353–54, 355–61, 357 (fig.), 363, 420–21; constitutional formalities of, 310; crisis of, 352–53; deliberative, 321, 358–59, 360, 385; gender and, 423; Globalized Space and, 352; as global phenomenon, 423; institutional, 361, 421; minimalist form of, 321, 420–21; models of, 348, 356, 358–59; opportunities for, 353 (fig.), 354; participatory, 356, 357, 358–59, 421; practices of, 347, 354, 360, 362; procedural, 352, 420–21; radical, 357, 360; real, 355, 361; redefinitions of, 421, 422; representative, 286, 320, 348; social movements and, 321, 347–49, 351–52, 355, 360, 361–64; transformations in, 348, 349–52, 352–55; understandings of, 427
Democratic National Convention, 333, 340
Democratic Party, 23, 256, 330, 333, 334, 337, 339, 420, 422; black voters and, 335, 338; CBOs and, 384; domination by, 331–32; transformation of, 335

Democratization, 326, 327, 347, 352, 353
Demographics, 3–4, 38
Demonstrations, xv, 20, 22, 147, 210, 225, 227, 228, 294n5, 373, 400, 402, 406, 411, 413n2; approval of, 401, 401 (fig.); defining, 413n4; increase in, 405; lawful, 392n1; mass, 371, 372; mobilizing, 17; number of, 403–4; participants in, 375, 378; peace, 226, 288; politically oriented, 403; self-policed, 304; street, 359, 401, 401 (fig.), 404; studies of, 400
Demos project, 362
Denationalization, 209, 316, 317
Department for Public Order and Traffic, 405
De Weerd, Marga: collective identity/social identity and, 39
Diallo, Amadou, 375, 392n4
Diani, Mario, xvii, xix, xx, 102, 191, 195; on boundary construction, 194; coordination and, 138, 200; networks and, 192; SMOs and, 193; social movements and, xx, 126, 127, 197, 200
Diasporas, 305, 435
Differentiation, 157, 238, 270; double, 286, 293
Digital Future, 31
Disability rights movement, 264
Disadvantaged, 79, 90, 240, 241, 243, 254, 255, 257, 300, 310
Discrimination, 68, 253; gender, 362; racial, 237, 238, 244, 248
Discursive fields, 272–75, 420
Discussion, xvi–xvii; multiple contributors to, 358
Dissent, 243, 244, 246
Distrust, 354, 410

Diversification, xi, xiv, xv, 50, 100
Diversity, 111, 160, 195, 210
Dixiecrats, 335–37, 339
Domination, 246, 252
Downloading, illegal, 27, 28, 30
Droits Devant!! (Rights First), 398
Drugs, 247, 250, 251; crime and, 249
Drug war, 241, 244, 246
Dutch farmers, 265, 267
Dutch Moroccans, 72, 73, 81, 87
Dutch Muslims, 45, 48, 81
Duyvendak, Jan Willem, 194, 196, 198, 406–7; mobilization and, 199; organizations and, 191, 192; social movements and, 210
Dynamics, 50, 79, 89, 90, 195, 246, 292, 343; black box of, 11, 80–84, 86; collective, 328; exogenous/endogenous, 196, 197; field-level, 197; investigating, 433–34; macrolevel, 67–68; mesolevel, 68–69; microlevel, 69–72; mobilization, xvii, 82, 207, 213, 220, 283, 430, 432–33; movement, xii, xiv–xvi, 148, 247, 294n3, 327, 419; protest, 217, 218, 235; social, 37; social movement, 50, 107, 161, 195; supply-side, 197

Earl, Jennifer, 29, 30, 33n1, 199, 372, 374
Ecology movement, 99, 431
Economic issues, 241, 257, 286, 288, 410, 430, 435
Economic liberalism, 286
Education, 228, 295n8, 300, 310, 317, 328, 379, 380, 401, 422; poor-quality, 4; science, 330
Efficacy, 6, 8, 85, 221
Eisenhower, Dwight, 332
Elections, 321, 347; movements and,

326–28, 328–30, 334, 340, 341–43; participation in, 352, 355; social movements and, 316, 327
Electoral regimes, 331–32, 334–36, 339–40
Electronic Frontier Foundation, 28, 29
El Yaakoubi, Naima, 69
E-mail, xiv, 17, 20, 21, 22, 29, 221, 253, 304
Embeddedness, 116, 229, 275; mobilization and, 222; network, 42–46; organizational, 228; virtual, 3, 221, 222, 228
Emotions, 5–7, 7–8, 50, 79, 80, 85, 87, 221, 326; collective action and, 83; expression of, 48; power and, 46; regulation of, 46; shared, 430; subordinate, 47
Emotion work, 430, 432, 433
Empirical phenomena, xvii, 145, 146
Empirical research, xvi–xvii, 112, 192, 196
Environmentalism, 147, 153, 242, 425
Environmental issues, 31, 44, 148, 149, 153, 362, 412, 422
Environmental movement, 109, 147, 148–49, 153, 301, 307, 371, 403
Environmental organizations, 109, 110, 295n8, 320
E-petitions, 24, 30, 33n1
E-tactics, 24, 33n1
Ethnic diversity, 235, 237, 238, 242, 245, 252, 264
Ethnic groups, 136, 239, 240; integration with, 239 (fig.); majority, 235–36
Ethnicity, xv, 4, 44, 50, 64, 101, 237, 241, 269, 283, 308–10
Ethnic majorities, 236, 255; disadvantaged, 240, 254; protests by, 256

Ethnic minorities, 238, 242, 248, 251, 253, 267, 301, 302, 308, 309; collective action and, 255; hostility for, 255; imprisonment of, 237; Internet and, 100; mass mobilizations and, 240–41; movement, 307; opportunities for, 236
EU. *See* European Union
Eurobarometer, 265
European Social Survey, 403
European Union (EU), 97, 267, 315, 316, 318, 349, 350, 403, 404, 408, 409, 419, 420, 421, 425; agenda of, 426; farmers, 265; policy field, 317
European Values Survey, 397, 402–3
Exceptionalism, 412–13, 426

Facebook, 10, 20, 21, 23, 24, 30, 97, 199, 218, 219, 221, 227, 228, 229, 306, 436; flash mobs and, 304; friendship and, 18; reach of, 305
Farmers Alliance, 177, 178, 182
Fear, dangerous other and, 309
Fédération des femmes du Québec (FFQ), 135, 136, 140, 141
Feminism, 44, 59, 99, 134, 136, 265, 426; framework of the political and, 422–25
Feminist movement, 42, 46, 197, 264, 407, 425–27; Muslim, 99
Feminist organizations, 44, 97, 114, 135, 149
Feminists, 128, 129, 137, 156, 425
Feminists for Life of America, 114
Ferree, Myra Marx, 431, 432, 433
FFQ. *See* Fédération des femmes du Québec
Field-net, 158, 159
Field of action, 235–36, 246–52
Fillieule, Olivier, 400, 403, 404, 405

First Hire Contract (CPE), 405, 407
Flash mobs, 304, 308
Focus groups, 67, 75, 76n1
Focus on the Family, 420
Foucault, Michel: biopower and, 424
Fox News, 293n5, 386, 388
Fragmentation, 98, 210, 410
Frame alignment, xix, 211–12, 275
Framing, 20, 21, 65, 187, 275, 420; collective action, 24–25
Fraser, Nancy, 359
Freedom Summer, 23, 337–38, 339
Freedomworks, 386
Free Press, 29
Free Software Foundation, 28
Free spaces, 43, 128
Fukuyama, Francis, 317
Futrell, Robert, 130–31

G-6 Billion, 137, 140
G-7, 350, 407
G-8, 186, 350
G-20, 193
Gamson, Joshua, 4, 131, 243, 399
Gardiner, Beth Gharrity, xviii
Gay and lesbian movement, 40, 42, 44, 45, 47, 80, 113, 129, 131, 149, 195, 242, 264, 371
Gay men, shared identification among, 265
Gay rights, 111, 252, 425
Gender, xv, 4, 44, 45, 46, 50, 64, 98, 100, 239, 266, 269, 270, 362, 401, 421, 425, 426, 427; democracy and, 423; divisions, 264; justice, 423; studies, 101
Gender equality, 67, 420, 422, 423, 424, 425, 426
General Agreement on Tariffs and Trade, 349
General Confederation of Labour, 404

Gerlach, Luther, 151, 182
German Aryan Nation, 130, 131
German Christian Democrats (CDU), 423
Giddens, Anthony, 188
Giugni, Marco, 364
GJM. *See* Global justice movement
Globalization, xi, xiv, xv, 40, 42, 44, 48, 50, 97, 100, 101, 196, 199, 209, 213, 238, 421, 433, 434; actors/forms of action and, 302–3; affluent societies and, 299; conflicts over, 281, 282, 283, 285–86; economic, 285, 352; immigration and, 293; individualization and, 95; migration and, 308; mobilization and, 302–3; neoliberal, 37, 294n2, 282, 283, 285, 302, 303, 349, 350, 408; networks and, 96; politics and, 286, 292–93, 349–50; processes of, 4, 96, 125, 265; protests and, 283, 292, 302, 303; social divisions and, 310; social movements and, 282; transnationalization and, 308
Globalization losers, 294n4, 309; nationalist-defensive mobilization of, 286, 293
Globalized Space, 352
Global justice, 285, 292–93, 294n2, 372; protesting for, 398; salience of, 284 (fig.); social movements and, 360
Global justice movement (GJM), 98, 100, 102, 133, 154, 173, 187, 193, 200, 213, 302, 303, 348, 372, 413, 419, 433; contemporary, 294n2; extraparliamentary, 342; French, 397
Global South, 351
Goals, 131, 224, 227, 238, 252, 268, 270; collective, 81, 158, 171–72;

movement, 130, 131; social change, 249
Gore, Al, 329, 331
Gorleben, 175–80, 183, 184, 196
Governance, 408–9, 423
Governments, 315, 318, 329
Grassroots activism, 24, 132, 155, 160, 182, 193, 250, 304, 386; lobbying and, 384–85, 391
Green parties, 225, 288, 329
Greenpeace International, 177, 178, 183, 184, 185
Green Revolution, 230
Greensboro lunch counter sit-in, 41–42
Grievances, 5–7, 9, 17, 32, 64, 68, 69, 88, 221, 245–46, 253, 309, 406; advocacy groups and, 310; class-related, 98; collective, 38; communication of, 310; emotions/perceptions of, 46–48; formation of, 11, 430; politicization of, 8, 79; shared, 3, 38, 62–63, 74, 75, 89, 268, 430
Gromis, Ashley, xx, 316, 321, 362, 419, 420
Group consciousness, 37, 62
Group efficacy, 85, 86, 88, 89
Group identity, 7, 38, 66, 74, 79, 81, 83, 84, 86, 430
Groups, 39, 81; networks and, 224; online, 31; social conceptions of, 49

Habermas, Jürgen, 101, 359
Hacktivism, 17, 26, 221
Hare Krishna, 270, 272
Have-nots, 398, 399, 408
Headscarf Brigade, 69
Health care, 31, 424
Heterogeneous groups/organizations, 152, 161, 209, 210
Homogenization, 42, 100, 210
Homosexuality, 67, 295n7, 424
Hoover, Herbert, 335
Human rights, 362, 423
Human rights movement, 109, 248, 316, 251
Humphrey, Hubert, 340
Hurricane Katrina disaster, 273
Hussein, Saddam, 226
Hutter, Swen, xx, 299, 309; mobilization and, 213, 302; populist right and, 302; social movements and, 213

ICTs. *See* Information and communication technologies
Identity, 3, 5–7, 11, 32, 63, 66, 79, 128, 130, 140, 156, 193, 198, 223, 224, 227, 430; activist, 199, 272, 307, 308; boundary definition and, 153; building, 64, 99, 150, 154, 192; category-based, 113, 266, 276, 277; change in, 80; claiming, 272, 273; clarity of, 113; class, 269; communities and, 50; competing, 7, 64, 308; comprehensive, 269; concepts of, 265, 268; crises, 264, 266; cultural, 309; dual, 7, 44, 49; entrepreneurs of, xix, 65; established, 80, 81, 84, 85, 87, 273; ethnic, 7, 67, 68, 71, 73, 266; fluid/fragmented, 306–8; gender, 45; importance of, 115, 263–66; Internet and, 17; local, 265, 266; mission and, 330; mobilization and, 235, 263; movement, 19, 98, 131, 154, 185, 212, 263, 264–65, 266, 270, 272, 276, 277, 301; national, 265, 266, 308, 421; networking and, 364; organizational, 98,

109, 112–14, 117, 154, 194; participation and, 276; personal, 46, 84, 100, 266, 267, 277; pervasive, 269–72, 308; politicization of, 23, 30, 42, 43, 61, 64–65, 68, 79, 80, 89; power of, 351; processes of, 8, 45, 357; protecting/maintaining, 80; public, 48; religious, 67, 68, 71; self and, 80, 81, 87, 90; sexual, 44, 45; shared, 8, 38, 40, 74, 300, 307; single, 268, 306; social, 39, 40, 266, 267, 274, 355, 410; social movements and, 19, 41, 43, 46, 49, 98, 131, 210, 212, 263, 276, 277, 300, 307; social/technological change and, xviii; subordinate/supraordinate, 7; sustaining, 273; tactics and, 49; tolerant, xix, 184; transforming, 81, 87; transnational, 276; understanding, 242; utilization of, 272; utopian, 270

Identity fields, 274, 275

Identity formation, 81, 307; collective, xvii, 45

Identity hierarchy, 268

Identity politics, 45, 49, 95, 264; light identities and, 98–100

Identity salience, 263, 268–69, 272, 276

Identity talk, 130, 274

Identity work, 40, 263, 274, 276, 277, 433; dilemma of, 272–75; emotion work and, 432

Ideology, 5, 126, 128, 140, 149, 187, 270, 273; importance of, 65, 115; neoliberal, 350; right-wing, 287

IGOs. *See* International governmental organizations

Immaterial service structures, 172–73

Immigrants, 7, 66, 237, 320; hostilities for, 255; illegal, 241, 253, 399, 405; insurgency/violence by, 241

Immigration, 19, 38, 44, 209, 236, 242, 252, 282, 288, 295n7, 317, 318, 320; as culture issue, 238, 286, 292; ethnic relations and, 283; focus on, 285; globalization and, 293; integration and, 4; mobilization against, 289; populist right and, 303; salience of, 284 (fig.)

Incarceration, 238, 244, 245; disparities in, 237, 246–47, 249, 251; minority groups and, 236–37

Income inequality, references to, 388, 389 (fig.), 390

Indigenous spaces, transmovement spaces and, 130

Indignados, 434, 435

Individual identity, 45, 49, 89, 95, 99, 130, 267, 307; alignment of, 276; fragmentary natures of, xiv

Individualization, xi, xiv, xv, 98, 102, 195, 196, 199, 221, 229, 230, 328; globalization and, 95; process of, 218–19

Industrial Areas Foundation, 383

Indymedia, 139, 173, 305

Inequalities, 10, 238–42, 425; class, 300; distributional, 307; economic/class, 39; gross, 310; illegitimate, 62; income, 388, 389 (fig.), 390; reproduction of, 95, 200; social, 359; socioeconomic, 423; structural, 37, 46, 360

Informal structures, 154, 176, 197, 225

Information, 29, 44, 199; democratization of, 101; exchange of, 157; proliferation of, 220

Information and communication technologies (ICTs), 198, 199, 207,

212, 217, 220, 221, 229, 299–300, 304, 306, 308; impact of, 219; mobilization and, 305, 430, 435; social movements and, 305
In-groups, 61, 64, 66, 85
Injustice, 6, 43, 47, 68, 245, 246, 274
Institutionalization, 283, 328, 364, 369
Integrated framework, 8, 9 (fig.)
Integration, 80; cultural, 241; differentiation and, 157; ethnic, 254; European, 282, 283, 285, 317; immigration and, 4; international, 350; political, 239; social, 239, 241
Interactions, 25, 75, 199
Interest groups, 149, 210, 213, 320; characteristics of, 160
International governmental organizations (IGOs), 316, 349, 350, 352, 362
International Monetary Fund, 182, 349
International Socialists, 225
International Social Survey Program, 295n6
Internet, xi, xiv, xviii, 10, 11, 20, 23, 25, 38, 40, 45, 79, 82, 101, 102, 173, 186, 304, 384, 432, 435, 436; activism and, 18, 26, 48, 219; contention and, 49; ethnic minorities and, 100; governance, 156; grievances and, 32; identity and, 17, 32; mobilization and, 88; participation and, xv, 96; private property and, 28; proliferation of, 95; protest and, 19, 26–27, 86; role of, 19, 50, 221; social bonds on, xv; social cleavages and, 100; transformative power of, 17, 33n1; use of, 29, 31; virtual actions and, 220
Interorganizational relations, 116, 153, 159

Intervention, 194, 253, 353, 355; social movement, 320
Intragroup relations, 66, 253
Ion, Jacques, 409
Iraq War, 115, 225, 273, 390; protesting, 9, 137, 371, 372, 377, 378, 409
Islam, violence/intolerance and, 67
Islamic movement, 343, 436
ITCs. *See* Information and communication technologies

Jasmine Revolution, 220
Jasper, Jim, 39, 46, 399
Jenkins, Craig, 70, 113–14, 327, 343
John Birch Society, 420
Johnson, Lyndon B., 337, 338, 340
Jones, Jim, 270
Juppé Plan, 402, 404, 405, 406, 407
Justice: distributive, 5–6; economic, 410; procedural, 5, 6; racial, 334; social, 5, 100, 248, 352, 362, 410

Kaase, Max, 400
Kennedy, John F., 337
Killian, Lewis: on social movements, 169
King, Braydon, 110, 118n2, 195
Klandermans, Bert, xvii, 19, 23, 37–38, 45, 48, 61, 66, 69, 79, 89, 187, 200, 235, 268, 276, 343, 363; collective action and, 307; collective identity and, xviii, 39, 59, 60, 63, 65, 67; emotions and, 82, 88; entrepreneurial effort and, 364; identity/networking and, 364; mobilization and, 10, 43, 206, 382; model of, 84, 85, 86–87; motivation and, 9; out-groups and, 64; politicization and, 12, 62; psychological process model and, 8,

83; retirement of, xii; triangulation and, 74; virtue of comparison and, xx
Koopmans, Ruud, 197, 283, 392, 419
Kopecký, Petr, 342
Kriesi, Hanspeter, xiii, xvi, xx, 287, 299, 309, 321; mobilization and, 213, 302; political context/opportunity and, 326; popular mobilization and, 326; populist right and, 302; social movements and, 213

Labor movement, 98, 99, 136, 161, 300, 301, 350, 361, 363, 392, 413, 433; influence of, 383; institutionalization of, 351; Obama and, 383; organization by, 383
Lazarus, Richard S., 84, 88, 89
Leach, Colin W., 85–86, 156
Leadership, 132, 150, 169, 228; avant-garde/elitist, 182; charismatic, 282
Lecomte, Josée, 41, 134
Left, 138, 285, 343n1, 410; collective identity of, 130; different logics on, 289, 291–92; progressive, 332; radical, 288, 291, 292
Legal status, 20, 27
Le Monde, 403, 411, 413n5
Le Pen, Jean-Marie, 294n5, 403
Lesbians, 42, 113, 156
Liberal democracy, 299, 306, 310, 360, 361, 363; conception of, 356; ethical-political principles of, 358; participation and, 309
Liberal Democrats, 339
Liberals, 288, 335–36
Libération, 403
Libertarianism, 287–88, 293, 301, 303
Liberty and Responsibilities of the Universities law (2007), 409

Lifestyles, 173, 230, 410
Light communities, 100–102, 207; emergence of, 95–98
Light identity, identity politics and, 98–100
Lincoln, Abraham, 334, 335, 339
LinkedIn, 219
Lipsky, Michael, 348, 357
Listserv, 228
Lobbying, 328, 355, 384–85, 386, 391
Local Exchange Trading Systems, 412
Local movement community, 127, 130, 134, 148
Lunch counter sit-in, 41–42
Lutheran Social Services, 253

Macrocultures, 157
Macrosocial indicators, 66, 75
Mair, Peter, 342
Majorities, disadvantaged, 240, 255
Manin, Bernard, 354
Mansbridge, Jane, 48, 360
March for Jobs, 137, 140
Marginalization, 310, 338, 350
Markoff, John, 352
Marriage counter protest, 41–42
Marriage Equality California, 41
Marx, Karl, 269, 308, 398
Marxists, 225, 226, 270, 407
Materialism, 413, 414
Mayer, Nonna, 321, 322, 362, 370, 419, 420
McAdam, Doug, xi, xvi, 146, 292, 316, 429; collective actors and, 23; DCA data set and, 374; movement mobilizations and, 420, 421–22; national state institutions and, 419
McCarthy, John D., 252, 316, 321, 362, 419, 420; DCA data set and, xx, 374; formal organizations and, 109; movement studies and, 145;

SMOs and, 125, 126
McGovern, George, 339
McGovern Revolution, 333
McKibben, Bill, 226
Meaning-making, 15, 60, 67; processes of, 64–65, 66, 75, 273
Media, 26, 32, 45, 70, 212, 226, 273, 274, 304, 386; attention from, 5, 388–89, 389 (fig.); classical, 219; commercialization of, 353; digital, 24, 433; international, 436; mainstream, 180; mass, xv, 180, 185, 186, 187, 208, 242, 302, 305, 318, 322; protest and, 50; social, xi, xiv, 79, 219, 221, 228, 306, 432, 435; unfriendly, 275
Medicaid, 256
Melucci, Alberto, xvi, 7, 39, 99, 126, 156, 265
Merkel, Angela, 424
Mesomobilization, 222–23
Metal Europ, 402
Meyer, David S., xiii, 48, 115, 289, 399; movement society and, 19; political protest and, 3–4
MFDP. *See* Mississippi Freedom Democratic Party
Micromobilization, 19–25, 37, 413
Migration, 68, 285, 308
Millennium Development Goals, 425
Milošević, Slobodan, 331
Ministry of Labor, 404–5
Minkoff, Debra, 110, 145, 289, 433
Minorities, 240, 253; disadvantaged, 241, 243, 257; disadvantaged majorities and, 255; incarceration rates and, 236–37; intervention/rehabilitative programs for, 253; mobilized movement, 329; repression of, 245–46, 247 (fig.).

See also Ethnic minorities; Racial minorities
Mississippi Freedom Democratic Party (MFDP), 337, 339, 340
Mitterand, François, 407
Mobilization, xii, xiv, xix, 38, 41, 44, 95, 125, 133, 140, 200, 217, 211, 221, 228, 252, 255, 257, 331, 383–84, 408, 413n5, 429, 436; antecedent of, 308; anti-pension, 405; bottom-up, 207; campus, 379–81, 381 (fig.), 390; changing, 207–10, 333; channels of, 205–6, 282, 292; coevolution of, 243–45; collective, 192, 205, 241, 299, 300, 309; community, 244; conducting, 88, 151, 240; consensus, 4, 8, 43, 45, 172, 173, 206, 268, 275, 276, 432; consequential, 302; contemporary, 229, 282; context of, xvi, 10, 11; coordinated, 161, 227; costs of, 18; course of, 308; cultural, 206; cultural integration and, 238–42; decentralized, 182; decisions, 213; decrease in, 220, 229, 235, 405; demographic characteristics of, 4; digital, 17; dynamics of, xvii, 38, 82, 213, 220, 281, 292, 310, 430, 432–33; effective, xvi, 305; electoral, 293, 329, 330–31; embeddedness and, 222; ethnic diversity and, 235, 242; evoking, 419; extreme right, 309; forms of, 220, 306; globalization and, 302–3; goal of, 222; grassroots, 304, 306; have-nots and, 413; ICTs and, 305, 430; identity and, 41, 235, 263; impacts of, 245; inequality in, 238–42; informal, 156; intermittency of, 308; Internet

and, 88; labor, 383, 385; landscape of, 96; level of, 9, 283, 316, 321, 385, 386; literature on, 206; maintaining, 306; mass, 240–41, 245, 318; mechanisms for, 211; models of, 19; movement, x, xvi, 3, 47, 125, 126, 192, 238, 267, 274, 301, 316, 321, 328, 342, 343, 371, 382, 422, 424, 425; networks and, 235, 304; nonprofessional, 248; online, 82, 87, 88; organization and, 108, 235, 404; participant, 226, 227, 263, 265, 266, 277; political, 43, 159, 199, 235, 244, 285, 303, 310, 420; popular, 248, 326, 332; proactive, 330, 337–38, 339; protest, 213, 241, 289, 293, 371, 382, 386, 420; reactive, 330–31, 333, 334, 339, 342; recruitment to, 304; relationships of, 289; research on, 205, 212, 265; resources for, 240; rhizomatic, 228, 229; social, 100; spontaneous, 306; strategy and, 139, 210, 227; successful, 230, 332; supply side of, 99, 191, 195, 198, 199; sustained, 24, 306; technology and, 304–6, 384; theory, 209, 211, 212; top-down, 206–7, 209; transnational, 265, 267, 303; types of, 211, 213; understanding, 18, 194; youth, 408–9

Mobilization, 108

Mobilization potential, 117, 226, 228, 244; formation of, 3, 4–8, 10, 11

Mobilization processes, 11, 208, 209, 239–40, 391; comparing, 210; fundamental, 382, 387; supply-side, 387

Mobilization structures, xiii, 140, 194, 196, 206, 218, 222–29, 230, 432, 433, 435; building, 217; concept of, 212; continuum of, 223 (fig.); types of, 25, 225

Moderate left, 291–92

Moderate right, 289, 292

Modernization, 95, 270, 299, 433; discontents and, 300–302

Monitoring the Future, 381

Moral standards, 84, 130, 157

Moroccan Dutch identity, 12, 60; collective action and, 67, 68; focus groups and, 69; identity of, 67–68, 73, 75; Muslim community and, 67; native Dutch and, 70–71, 72; nonpoliticization and, 66–67; politicization of, 74, 75

Motes, Alice, xviii

Motivation, 9, 18, 21, 86, 87, 89, 90; collective action and, 84; identity-based, 82; ideological, 9, 83, 187, 224

Mouffe, Chantal, 357, 360

Movement communities, 127–29, 131–32, 137, 138, 140; changes in, 126, 132; cultural practices and, 128, 129; diversity/heterogeneity in, 195; international/national, 141; overlapping, 136; studying, 133–35

Movement organizations, 114, 115, 117, 126, 127, 161, 172, 182, 196, 327, 329, 330, 334–35, 386, 432, 433; coalitions between, 435; intervention by, 194; lobbying by, 384; long-standing, 140; mobilization by, 329, 339; nonmovement organizations and, 431; policy change and, 111

Movement participation, 7, 26, 208, 430; instrumental pathway to, 6; networks and, 43

Movements, 4, 114, 117, 152–53, 209, 239, 422, 425; aims of, 333; building, 19, 194; coalition of, 154, 408; collective properties of, 146–47; concept of, 48; definition of, 329; elections and, 326–28, 334, 340, 341–43; influence of, 44; integrated, 148; levels, 194; literature on, 327; macrolevel of, 217; network underpinnings of, 242; organizational characteristics of, 40; political, 141, 308; professionalized, 252; religious, 136, 308; structures of, 125, 130, 141; student, 301, 379, 381, 398; tactics of, 29, 328–30; third-party, 329, 338; working-class, 242, 406, 413

Movement society, 19, 32, 147, 161, 369; thesis, 148, 293

MoveOn.org, 102, 198, 199

MSN instant messaging, 228

Mubarak, Hosni, 220

Mugabe, Robert, 331

Multiculturalism, populist right and, 303

Multilevel process, 64–66

Multiorganizational fields, 11, 126, 169, 410

Multiple identity, 19, 42–46, 139, 263, 269, 272, 306–8; dilemma of, 212, 266–68; question of, 49

Mur des Fédérés (Wall of the Federals), 406

Music, 399; downloading, 27, 28, 30

Muslim identity, 67–68, 68, 74, 76n1

Muslims, 4, 7, 67, 68, 99

MySpace, 21, 219, 221, 227, 228

NAACP. *See* National Association for the Advancement of Colored People

Nader, Ralph, 329

National Association for the Advancement of Colored People (NAACP), 23, 251, 335

Nationalism, 255, 282, 317

Nationality, xv, 4, 44, 50, 237

Nation-state, xiv, 216, 320, 347, 349, 351, 408; character of, 315; repressive, 317; rise of, 315

Native Dutch, Moroccan Dutch and, 70–71

Nativism, 240, 255

"Negotiated management" era, 372

Negotiations, 62, 65, 66, 69, 74–75, 152

Neoliberalism, 350, 355, 408, 410, 427

Netherlands Institute for Social Research, 67

Network governance, 145, 157, 160

Network organizations, 158, 159

Networks, xx, 21, 50, 89, 102, 130, 137, 138, 182, 305, 383; activist, 198; advocacy, 135; business, 158; civic, 148, 162; centrality of, 116; community-based, 435; composition of, 160; coordination and, 157; developing, 101, 220; digitalization/hybridization of, 97–98; displacing, 306; diversity of, 48–49, 307; enduring, 172; face-to-face, 192; globalization and, 96; identity and, 364; informal, 100, 101, 109, 198, 223, 224, 225, 228–29; international, 133, 141; interorganizational, 146, 150, 152, 155, 192; mobilization and, 180, 304; movement, 43, 130, 158, 159, 193, 196; offline/online, 219; organizations and, xvi, 145, 157, 158, 159; personal, 153, 227, 228,

304; social movement, 42, 47, 159, 178–80; submerged, 43, 126, 134; transnational, xiv, 97; types of, 192, 223; virtual, 192, 198, 221, 224, 225, 228, 230, 306; women's, 425
Network society, 42, 50, 199
New Deal, onset of, 335–36
New Handbook of Political Science, A, 327
New Left, 130, 287, 332, 333
New social movements (NSMs), xii, 99, 208, 398, 404, 406, 407
Newsome, Gavin, 41
New York City, protests in, 374–75, 375 (fig.), 376 (fig.), 377–81, 377 (fig.), 387, 388, 390
New York Police Department, 392n4
New York Times, xx, 369, 372; protests and, 374, 375, 377–78, 380
NGOs. *See* Nongovernmental organizations
Nichiren Shoshu-Sokagakkai, 270–71, 272
Nixon, Richard, 333, 338, 339, 340
Nongovernmental organizations (NGOs), 251, 317, 320, 425, 431; environmental, 303; humanitarian, 303; international, 132
Nonpoliticization, dynamics of, 29, 66–67
Nonprofit organizations, 192, 253
Nonviolence, 178, 180
NSMs. *See* New social movements
Nuclear energy, 153, 176, 177, 179, 180, 187, 188n1
Nuclear waste, 175, 179, 187

Obama, Barack, 329, 330, 341, 383, 384
Oberschall, Anthony, 356

Occitan movement, 398
Occupy movement, xi, xv, xix, 23, 24, 42, 96, 254, 257, 390, 391, 433, 434, 435; faltering by, 436; media attention for, 388–89; public discourse and, 437
Occupy Pittsburgh, 140
Occupy Wall Street, 42, 140, 256, 369, 386–88, 390, 392n8; media attention for, 389 (fig.)
Oegema, Dirk, 45, 48, 206, 286; collective action and, 307; peace movement and, 11
Old Left, organizational centralization of, 129
Oliver, Pamela E., 4, 300, 309, 310; mobilization and, 213; social carriers and, 209
Olzak, Susan, 111, 112, 118n2, 374
Opposition, 9, 43, 348; elections and, 326–27
Organizational affiliations, 222, 288
Organizational categories, 109, 112–14
Organizational ecology, 110, 116, 118n2, 195
Organizational fields, 146, 147, 148, 159, 386; diversity/heterogeneity in, 195
Organizational forms, 116, 152, 196–97; conceptualization/identification of, 112
Organizational learning, 109, 114–15, 116
Organizational membership, 151, 205
Organizational populations, 107, 109, 110–12
Organizational processes, 107, 155
Organizational sociology, 109, 112, 113
Organizational structures, xix, 126, 131, 132, 156; centrality of, 171;

mobilization and, 235
Organizational studies, 108, 112, 116–17, 145; social movement and, 146
Organizational survival, 111, 195
Organizational theory, 99, 108, 116, 194; resource mobilization in, 363; social movement theory and, 156–59
Organizations, 107, 136, 153, 155, 159, 206, 211, 306; community-based, 385; culture and, 126, 127–29; defined, 170–71; development of, 140, 196, 386; eschewing, 109; formal, 96, 192, 193, 198, 222, 224, 225, 227; governmental, 431; hierarchical forms of, 158; independent, 158; integrated, 158; meaning/conceptual status of, 191; mobilization and, 108; movement, 382; multi-issue, 115; national, 97; networks and, xvii, 157, 158, 306; news, 159; old-fashioned, 310; participatory forms of, 197; political, 282, 301
Organizers, xvi, 217, 227; consequences for, 219–22
Other Summit (1989), 406
Out-groups, 64, 66, 75

Palin, Sarah, 330
Parisian Commune, 406
Participants, xvi, 134, 200, 291; mobilization of, 29, 205, 217, 222, 224, 226, 227, 229, 263, 265, 266, 277; movements by, 239 (fig.); nonparticipants and, 211; SMOs and, 208; social movement, 108
Participation, xv, 5, 18, 22, 24, 98, 175, 226, 268, 276, 318, 352, 356, 362, 369; changing forms of, 409–12; consequence of, 308; conventional forms of, 353; cultural paths to, 206; decrease in, 391; democratic, 101, 359; demographics of, 300; effective, 400; extensive, 385; identity and, 276; increase in, 229, 362; individual, 50; minimal, 355; motivation for, 18, 21, 82; national movement, 386; political, xiv, 99, 300, 301, 308, 309, 351, 356–57, 378, 411; protest, 8, 20, 46, 208, 288; rates of, 373; risks/costs of, 220, 276; social movement, 6, 40, 42, 44, 45, 49, 50, 80, 84, 300, 361, 391, 400, 409–12; sociopolitical, 96; specialization of, 210; structural preconditions of, 205; types of, 211, 220, 300; victims of, 356, 360
Peace movement, 11, 24, 44, 99, 109, 128, 172, 225, 301, 307, 320, 371, 378
Peasant's Confederation, 408
Penn State University, sit-in at, 371
People's March, 137
People's Summit, 137
People's Uprising, 137, 138
Performances, xix; contentious, 38–42, 46; cultural, 132, 133; identity, 39; interactive, 40; postelectoral, 352; ritual, 130, 131
PETA (animal rights group), 20
Petitions, 405, 413n2; e-mail, 22; online, 30, 82, 221; signing, 86, 211
PGRP. *See* Pittsburgh G20 Resistance Project
Pirate Party, xviii, 28, 29
Pittsburgh G20 protests, 126, 134, 137–40
Pittsburgh G20 Resistance Project (PGRP), 138, 139

Pittsburgh Principles, 138, 141
Polarization, 9, 48, 343, 426; movement-induced, 328, 340
Police, 243, 244, 246, 251, 266, 304; brutality, 392n4; harassment, 257; infiltration by, 305; Latinos and, 254; professionalization of, 404; protests and, 377, 377 (fig.); white dominance and, 249
Political Action Survey, 411
Political class, 286, 434
Political cleavages, 162, 246
Political consciousness, 30, 62
Political contention, 50, 146, 326, 419
Political engagement, 288, 437
Political exclusion, 308–10
Political institutions, xi, 325, 328, 351
Political opportunity, xiii, 132, 235–36, 327, 371, 433
Political parties, 97, 192, 291, 295n8, 316, 318, 343, 347, 348, 392, 422, 431, 432; class-mass, 342; domestic politics and, 329; electoral preferences and, 355; ideological control of, 354; left, 351; as main actors, 352; mainstream, 341; membership of, 218; movement, 301, 351; polarization of, 332–34; professionalization/decoupling of, 342; rise of, 315; structure of, 387; weakening of, 363
Political process, xii, 6, 38, 88, 99, 325, 327, 361, 375, 388, 391; approach, 347, 349, 351; models, 398; rise of, 37
Political systems, 243, 329, 422, 433
Political terrain, reframing, 425–27
Politicization, xiv, 75, 87; characteristics of, 69; dynamics of, xvii, 9, 64; privatization and, xviii–xix;

process of, 12, 59, 60, 67, 89; as triangulation, 63
Politicized collective identity, 61, 62; as multilevel process, 64–66
Politics, 6, 25, 31, 88, 100, 288, 289, 309, 322, 339, 355, 388, 401, 406, 421, 437; anti-institutional, 330; conception of, 162, 341; consumption and, 18; contentious, xiv, 38, 40, 146, 325, 399; defensive, 303; domestic, 329, 419; economic, 352; education, 320; electoral, 282, 283, 286, 291, 294, 299, 327, 328, 329, 333, 384, 410; European, 318, 341–43; framework of, 422; functioning of, 9; gender, 425, 427; global, 303, 362; globalization and, 292–93; influencing, 431, 432, 433; institutional, 325, 326, 328; marketplace, 411–12; mobilization and, 420; multi-institutional, 399; noninstitutional forms of, 328; party, 257, 288, 341, 410, 413; protest, 282, 283, 285, 286, 293, 294, 315, 321; racial, 249, 425; representative, 282, 293; social movement, 316, 321; transnational, 303, 412; women and, 424
Pollan, Michael, 13
Polletta, Francesca, xviii, 39, 130; Internet and, 4, 10, 11, 79, 82; online mobilization and, 87–88; outside networks and, 128; participatory democracy and, 100
Poor people's movements, 411
Populist radical right, 281–82, 283, 294n4, 294n5; challengers on, 289–90; mobilization and, 293; political paradox of, 286–89

Populist Right, 286, 302, 303; electoral mobilization of, 213
Populists, 281–82, 287, 302, 318, 330, 342
Postmaterialism, 287, 288, 293, 295n6, 404, 406, 410, 413
Poverty, 135, 310
Power, 85, 317–18, 354; black, 264, 338; citizen, 356; corporate, 420; cultural, 357; decentralization of, 351; economic, 243, 357; explanatory, 399; inequalities of, 10, 46; institutional, 333; lateral loading of, 315; material, 421; mobilizing, 320; political, 17, 40, 243, 255, 357; relations, 66, 199; social movement studies and, 347–49; struggles, 59, 66
Prins, Jacomijne, 5, 12, 76n1, 79, 81, 87, 430; identity boundaries and, xviii; politicized identity and, 80
Prison issue, 238, 248, 249, 250
Privacy, xviii, 18, 21, 25, 424; openness and, 28, 29
Private property, 18, 26, 27
Privatization, xvii, xviii–xix, 341, 363
Prodat data, 321
Professional Insertion Contract (1994), 409
Progressive movements, 134, 138, 141, 325, 332, 343n1, 385–86; decentralized structure of, 188
Pro-life movement, 42, 332, 333
Protest behavior, xix, 48, 361, 403, 430
Protestors, 111, 180, 186, 228, 235, 256–57, 287, 305; antiglobalization, 402; bystanders and, 139; social characteristics of, 301; violence and, 179, 377, 381
Protests, xv, 7, 10, 25, 45, 65, 74, 141, 147, 155, 156, 162, 175, 183, 188, 200, 207, 210, 225–26, 235, 245, 249, 274, 282, 309, 322, 331, 348, 369, 403, 420; alterglobalization, 302, 400; antiwar, 226; bread-and-butter, 224; campus, 379–81, 381 (fig.), 390; changing, 405–12; civil disobedience, 250; in claim making, 319 (fig.); coevolution of, 242–43; constructive performances of, 38; cycle of, 47, 377, 392; data on, 291, 378; declared, 402–3; demand side of, 3, 17, 19, 26, 32, 79; dynamics of, 217, 218, 225, 235; ethnic majorities and, 256; expansion of, 378; global, 364, 372; globalization and, 292, 302; grassroots, 250; G20, 126, 134, 137–40; Internet and, 19, 26–27, 86; levels of, 397; local, 385–86, 387; mass, 252, 392; media and, 50; minorities and, 246; mobilization for, 213, 241, 289, 293, 420; normalized, 210, 286; number of reported, 375 (fig.); offline, 199; online, 24, 87, 199; opportunities for, 19, 27, 217; organizers of, 217, 230; participation in, 8, 20, 46, 208, 289, 369, 370–71, 373, 378–79, 379 (fig.), 380; party/electoral strength and, 291 (table); party/issue preferences and, 290 (table); police and, 377, 377 (fig.); political, 3–4; political action and, 287; post-twentieth-century narrative/U.S., 371–72; potential/France, 400–402, 400 (table); psychological motivations for, 82; public, 18, 82, 282, 288, 305, 369, 370, 371–72, 387, 392, 399;

repression of, 176, 371; rhizomatic/ staged, 228; sociable action and, 29–30; social movements and, 186, 321, 376 (fig.), 406–8; sponsorship of, 373; street, 303, 391; student, 378–81; supply of, 17, 207; supply-side understanding of, 382–86; supporting/sustaining, 255; temporally/spatially, 192; transnationalization of, 285, 293; trends in U.S., 372–74; U.S.–European contrast in, 370–71; wedding, 47–48; willingness for, 378–79

Protest survey, 208, 211, 400

Psychological process, 79, 83, 84, 88, 89, 90

Psychological theory, 80, 83, 84, 89, 90

Public interests, 149, 273

Public Knowledge, 28, 29

Public opinion, 249, 316, 321, 354, 411

Public policy, 360, 388, 437

Public services, 350, 405, 412

Public spaces, 25, 359, 360, 361

Public use, 18, 26–29

Putnam, Robert, 95, 97, 385

Quebec Women's March against Poverty, 135

Queer movement, 45

Race, xv, 44, 50, 266, 269, 270, 271, 421; prison sentences and, 238; remarginalization of, 338

Racial disparities, 245, 248, 249, 254, 257; focus on, 255–56; in imprisonment, 246, 251; in prosecution process, 251–52

Racial minorities, 238, 242, 248, 251; imprisonment of, 237

Racism, 4, 30, 41, 248, 252, 253, 254, 264, 287, 422

Radicalism, 9, 23, 48, 161, 197, 404, 425

Rafail, Patrick, xx, 316, 321, 362, 374, 419, 420

Reagan, Ronald, 332, 333, 343n1, 334, 339

Relations, 148, 162; mutual, 108; public/private, 18; social, 222; state-society, 426; systems of, 145

Religion, 4, 44, 64, 136, 264, 269, 270, 308, 326

Repression, 176, 236, 247 (fig.), 255, 371–72; coevolution of, 242–43, 243–45; mobilizing effects of, 245–46

Republican National Convention, 330, 390

Republican Party, 255, 333, 420, 422; abolitionism and, 334; black voters and, 335, 338; civil rights and, 335; domination by, 331, 332; rise of, 338–39; Tea Party and, 256, 387

Research, 102, 196, 208, 289, 364; collective, 192; comparative, 209; cumulative, 235; future, 210–12; longitudinal, 195; organizational, 194; protest-centric, 246; psychological, 23, 80, 83, 87; quantitative, 62; social, 107; sociological, 95, 236

Resistance, 399, 405; democracy and, 360; national, 420; spatial/temporal chain of, 181

Resource mobilization, xii, 6, 25, 38, 101, 107, 109, 150, 217, 356, 398; models, 88–89; movement structures and, 171; rise of, 37; theory, 125

Resources, 6, 85, 217, 245; allocation of, 150, 155, 157; cultural, 188; exchange of, 157; organizational, 150, 188; psychological, 89; social, 89

Responsibility, 128, 218; offloading, 315, 320

Right, different logics on, 289, 291–92

Riots, 309, 322, 411

Rituals, 130–31

Roggeband, Conny, 194, 196, 198, 322n1, 429; mobilization and, 199; organizations and, 191, 192; social movements and, 210

Role identity, 266, 269–70, 276; convert, 271–72; pervasive, 271–72; theory, 268–69

Roosevelt, Franklin D., 335

Rootes, Christopher, xviii, xix

Rosanvallon, Pierre, 354

Rucht, Dieter, xiii, xvi, 96, 97, 192, 193, 195, 197, 316, 318, 320, 321, 322; anti-Castor campaign and, 194; organizations and, 102; politicization and, xix; protests and, 200; state authority and, 315; structure in action and, 198

Same-sex marriage, 41, 42, 132, 330

Sarkozy, Nicolas, 405, 408, 413

Schottern, 178, 179, 184, 185

Seattle protest, 285, 372

Secessionists, mobilization by, 334

Second European Social Forum, 412

Security, 7, 424

Segregation, 25, 42, 241, 243, 335

Self, identity and, 80, 81, 87, 90

Self-categorization theory, 81, 85

Self-definition, 61, 81

Self-expression, 406, 410

Self-help, 41, 47, 149, 399

Self-relevance, 80–90

September 11th, 67, 267, 332, 371, 372

Sexuality, 44, 50, 100, 421, 424, 426

Sexual orientation, 264, 301, 307

Shared interests, 3, 37, 193, 301

Sheehan, Cindy, 371

Shirky, Clay, 20, 21

Simi, Pete, 130–31

Simon, Bernd, 6, 9, 12, 23, 61, 66, 67, 69, 74, 82, 85, 89; collective identity and, 59, 60, 63, 65; model of, 86; out-groups and, 64; politicization and, 62

Sit-ins, 41–42, 359, 371

SIU. *See* Step It Up

Skocpol, Theda, 95, 385

SMCs. *See* Social movement communities

SMGs. *See* Social movement groups

SMI. *See* Social movement industry

Smith, Jackie, 364

SMOs. *See* Social movement organizations

SNCC. *See* Student Nonviolent Coordinating Committee

Snow, David A., xiii, xvi, xvii, 274; boundary activities and, xviii; collective action and, 307; frame-alignment approach of, 206; ICT and, 300; identity and, 212, 308

Sobieraj, Sarah, 330

Social change, xviii, 63, 88, 242, 249, 300, 373, 410; contention and, 95; macrolevel theories of, 199; methodological innovation and, xx; opposing, 357; preferences for, 126

Social cleavages, 60, 75, 100, 196, 245, 246, 252, 431; boundary drawing and, 64; collective identity and, 64–65; globalization and, 310
Social control, 157, 236, 238, 243, 245, 246, 247, 248, 267; agents, 48, 273
Social Democratic Party (SPD), 181, 423
Social forums, 360, 362
Social groups, 31, 161, 213, 235, 369, 404
Socialism, 410
Socialist Party (SP), 225
Socialists, 301, 407
Social justice, 5, 100, 248, 352, 362, 410
Social life, 150, 269, 359
Social location, 239, 242–43, 243–45, 253–54, 256, 257
Social milieus, 173, 182, 187, 193
Social movement communities (SMCs), 41, 43, 46, 50, 125, 126–33, 139, 141, 192, 198; free spaces and, 128; organization/culture of, 140; structures/cultures of, 132
Social movement groups (SMGs), 320, 330, 372
Social movement industry (SMI), 126, 169, 386, 410
Social movement organizations (SMOs), 48, 97, 99, 102, 108, 109, 110, 112–13, 125, 131, 132, 148, 169, 171, 179, 183, 191, 192, 193, 196, 199, 207, 210, 249, 266, 274, 306, 348, 369–70, 373, 375, 382, 391; antiwar coalitions and, 115; collaboration between, 116; distinctiveness of, 160; diversity of, 111; example of, 177–78; expansion of, 392; focus on, 205; formal, 126, 198; goals of, 222; local, 386; mobilization by, 211; nonparticipants and, 212; participants and, 208; population diversity of, 111; protests and, 376 (fig.); weakening of, 208–9
Social movement process, 112, 114, 117, 149
Social movement research, xx, 37, 107–8, 206, 217, 281, 348, 398–400, 426; future of, xii; modes of, 159–62; trends in, 170
Social movements, xi, xii, xiii, xvii, xix, xx, 11, 38, 44–48, 83, 90, 97, 108, 116, 149–56, 157, 188, 194, 196, 207–10, 220, 238, 240, 242, 243, 246, 264, 273, 287, 292, 306, 308, 317, 320, 322, 325, 332, 359, 371, 382; analysis of, 145, 146, 148; attention for, 49, 403; bureaucracy of, 171; collective, 41, 87, 99, 171, 193; concept of, 146, 399; constitutive elements of, 192, 302, 307; context of, 7; data on, 403; defining, 160, 171, 357; democracy and, 321, 347–49, 351–52, 355, 360, 361–64; demonstrations/strikes and, 404; development of, 155, 159, 170, 197, 257, 315, 351; diffuse nature of, 125–26; framework for, 170; historicization/recontextualization of, 399; identity and, 19, 41, 43, 46, 49, 98, 131, 210, 212, 263, 276, 277, 300, 307; impact of, 98, 107; influence of, 320, 406; insulation of, 326; issues of, 113, 210; mobilization of, xv, 3, 47, 192, 274, 301, 316, 321, 370; models of, 158, 191; new, 283, 410;

opportunities for, 408; organization of, xv, 109, 129, 141, 171, 172, 191, 419; outcomes of, 110–12, 115; political process approach to, 360–61; progressive, 187; questions of, 117; racial/ethnic/class tension in, 255–56; as relational processes, 149; relative autonomization of, 316; repoliticization of, 363; resocialization of, 362; tradition, 80, 419; understanding, 205

Social Movements Barometer, 402, 414

Social movement scholars, 13, 17, 19, 32, 40–41, 102, 107, 108, 109–10, 110, 112, 115, 116, 117, 125, 149, 197, 213, 263, 275, 281, 282, 292; collaboration and, 434; collective identity and, 39

Social movement sector, 102, 116, 210, 391, 410; French, 397–98, 400–405

Social movement society, 369, 373, 378, 390; elements of, 370, 391, 392; thesis, 375, 377, 381

Social movement studies, xii, xx, 48–49, 133–34, 145, 197, 211, 326, 327, 356, 429, 436, 437; alternative conceptions and, 360–61; conceptual innovations in, 362; democracy and, 347–49; engaging in, 116–17; normative theory and, 364; organizational theory and, 116; power and, 347–49

Social movement theory, 19, 20, 37, 99, 107, 108, 116, 191, 328; advances in, xii; collective identity and, 61; organization theory and, 156–59

Social networks, 4, 21, 22, 23, 32, 42, 125, 127, 246, 328, 409; conductive, 205, 206; electronic, 304; formal organizational, 223–29; informal, 223–29; mobilization and, 235; online, 25, 224; virtual, 224, 228

Social psychology, 11, 37, 38, 42, 49, 79, 263, 325, 430; collective action and, 33; group identification and, 7; literature, 5

Social Psychology of Protest, The, 5

Social *relais*, 173, 180, 182, 193

Social Security, reforming, 402, 404

Social structure, 146, 171, 239

Societies, xii, 46, 60, 73, 218; changes in, 299; diversification of, xii; organization/structure of, xi, xiv

"Sociological intervention" methods, 398

Sociological theory, 95, 102, 188

Sociology, 7, 263, 264, 340, 398

Sociopolitical context, 18, 64, 73

Sokagakki International, members of, 271

Solidarity, 21, 37, 45, 47, 150, 154, 197; exchange of, 157

Solidarnosc, 398

Sommier, Isabelle, 398

Soule, Sarah A., xvii, xviii, xix, 113, 375; boundary construction and, 194; collaboration and, 116, 434; DCA data set and, 372, 374; interorganizational competition and, 110, 118n2; organizational theory/research and, 194; social movements and, 99, 118n2, 148, 195

SPD. *See* Social Democrats

Spears, Russell, 5, 85–86

Spontaneity: routine–organization–institution versus, 183–84

"Spread of Protest Politics, The" (Rucht), 321

Staggenborg, Suzanne, 96, 102, 156, 191, 195, 200, 435; centralization and, 193; politicization and, xix; social movement community (SMC) and, 41
State Department, 335
States General, 406
Step It Up (SIU), 226–28, 229
Stop Global Warming, 20
Strategies, 98, 125, 132, 210, 223, 227, 242; collective, 73; "coming out," 45; electoral, 329, 333–34; identity, 41, 42–46, 48, 143; lack of coordination on, 133; mobility, 73; mobilization and, 139; movement, 19, 39; reform, 425; social movement, 126
Strikes, 375, 402, 404, 405, 406
Structural availability, 288, 289
Structural basis, 169, 170, 187
Structural changes, 50, 141
Structural components, 170, 173, 176
Structure, 38, 139, 194, 209, 225; in action, 188, 198; culture and, 206; duality of, 188; loose, 230; social, 146, 171, 239; social movement, 146–49, 169–70, 173, 174 (table), 175, 187, 192, 193, 307; social/nonsocial phenomena and, 170
Student Nonviolent Coordinating Committee (SNCC), 337
Students for Free Culture, 28
Subcultures, 99, 155–56, 241
Supply, 191, 429; construction of, 430; dynamics of, xvi, xvii, 430, 431–32, 433
Supply side, 95, 99, 191, 195, 197, 198, 199, 200, 382–86, 387, 391
Support, 173, 181, 183, 402, 414
Supranationalization, 318, 320, 434

Supranational organizations, 97, 315, 316, 317, 349
Survey on Professional Relations and Firm Negotiations, 404
Sweatshops, protesting, 383
Swiss People's Party (SVP), 294n5
Symbols, 43, 65, 147, 177

Tactics, 24, 29, 33n1, 111, 114, 116, 162, 184–85, 328–30; expansion of, 220–21; identity and, 49; movement, 275
Taliban, 270, 272
Tarrow, Sidney, xi, xii, xiv, xvi, 126, 187, 265, 292, 316, 322, 419; GJM and, 372; movement mobilization and, 420, 421–22; movement society and, 19; multiple belongings and, xiv; political participation and, 356; political protest and, 3–4; protest behavior and, 48; social movements and, 51, 363; transnationalization and, 282
Taylor, Verta A., 5, 12, 67, 69, 79, 156, 399; collective identity and, xvii, xix, 59, 60, 61, 62, 63, 65, 129; discursive communities and, 10, 11; emotions and, xviii, 46–47, 82, 88; negotiation and, 62, 66; out-groups and, 64
Tea Party, 4, 273, 330, 334, 341, 369, 386–88, 390, 391, 392, 420; ethnic majorities and, 255; Fox News and, 388; mobilization of, 254; newspaper coverage from, 389 (fig.); protest by, 48; Republican Party and, 256, 387
Technology, xviii, 101, 102, 199, 300, 350; communication, xiv, xv, 42, 45, 50, 101, 102, 126, 133, 219,

310, 434; digital, 17, 18, 19, 20, 32; information, xiv, 102, 133; mobilization and, 304–6, 384; web-based, 45

Terrorism, 273, 276, 364

Theories, xi, xvi–xvii, 196, 205, 242; top-down, 209

Thimbl, 305

Thomas Merton Center (TMC), 137, 138–39, 141

Three Rivers Climate Convergence, 137

Tilly, Charles, xi, 17, 50, 151, 315, 321, 325, 326, 348, 361, 429; on social movements, 357

TMC. *See* Thomas Merton Center

Tonry, Michael, 236–37

Touraine, Alain, 99, 398

Toyota, 419

Trade, 320, 350

Transformation, 46, 47, 196, 292, 335, 348, 349–52, 352–55, 433; social, 361, 436; social movement, 161, 197, 349

Transgender movement, 264

Translocal movement, 266

Transmovement spaces, indigenous spaces and, 130

Transnational corporations, xiv, 420

Transnationalization, 285, 292, 308, 362

Transnational markets, regulation by, 320

Transnational movements, xiv, 265, 266, 277, 282, 308, 413

Transparency, 352, 358, 360

Treaty of Maastricht (1989), 408

Trotskyists, 407

Truman, Harry: civil rights reform and, 335

Twitter, 17, 24, 32, 97, 185, 199, 304, 305

UK Uncut, 305

Unemployment, 350, 408

Unions, 97, 98, 208, 295n8, 301, 304, 316, 320, 383, 410, 413; action by, 399; dissident, 408; revolutionary, 406

Union Summer, 383

United Nations, 97, 133, 135, 315, 424, 425

United Nations Millennium Summit, 375

United Nations World Women's Conference, 135

University of Alabama, Wallace and, 338

University of Pittsburgh, 139

Urban League, 251

U.S. Supreme Court, liberalism of, 335–36

Van Doorn, Marjorka, xviii, 5, 12, 79, 430; identity and, xix, 81, 87; politicized identity and, 80

Van Dyke, Nella, 115, 380

Van Stekelenburg, Jacquelien, xviii, xix–xx, 45, 48, 96, 207, 300, 410, 429; ICTs and, 304; mobilization and, 10, 212; model by, 8; motives and, 9

Van Zomeren, Martijn, 11, 86, 430, 431; collective identity and, xviii; group efficacy and, 86; relative deprivation and, 5

Velvet Revolution, 156

Vera Institute, 251

Verizon workers, strike by, 375

Vermeulen, 109, 110

Victim's rights movement, 248

Vietnam War, 338, 377, 378

Violence, 184, 188, 331; domestic, 25, 423, 426; ethnic, 240–41, 411; extralegal, 246; gender-based, 426;

interpersonal, 375; mass collective, 255; poverty and, 135; protestors and, 179, 377, 381; return of, 410–11
Virtualization, xii, xiv, xv, 220, 229
Voluntary associations, 151, 155, 244
"Voters and Parties" (Wren and McElwain), 327
Voting rights, 302, 331, 337, 338, 354

Walgrave, Stefaan, 283, 299
Walker, Edward T., 109, 374, 392n6
Wallace, George, 329, 338, 339, 340
Wal-Mart stores, protesting, 385
War on Drugs, 422
War on Terror, xiii, 371, 378, 424, 425
Washington Post: Tea Party and, 387
Weather Underground, 276
Web 1.0, 219
Web 2.0, 212, 219, 220, 224, 229
Welfare, 309, 350, 361, 422
Welfare state, 286, 315–16, 347, 348, 349, 355, 422, 423
Welschen, Saskia, 5, 79, 81, 87, 430; identity boundaries and, xviii; politicized identity and, 80
Western democracies, 318, 349, 405–6; collective action in, 398; empirical research in, 351; multicultural nature of, 42; pacification in, 404; political life in, 390
White Marsh, 432
White power movement (WPM), 130, 131
White supremacists, 337, 338
Whittier, Nancy, 39, 65, 67, 69, 129, 156; collective identity and, 59, 60, 61, 62, 63; identity strategies and, 43; negotiation and, 62, 66; outgroups and, 64
Wikileaks, 28
Wilson, Woodrow, 331
Win without War coalition, 115
Wisconsin Uprising, 254, 257
WMW. *See* World March of Women
Women: inequality of, 425; politics and, 424; quotas for, 423
Women's centers, 134, 136
Women's movement, 41, 44, 45, 98, 109, 110, 113, 129, 133, 140, 149, 247, 307, 320, 371; international, 135; organizations, 134; transnational, 47
Women's rights, 423, 424
Women's Tent City, 137
World Bank, 182, 349, 419
World March of Women (WMW), 126, 133–34, 135–37, 140, 141
World Social Forums, 133, 200, 409
World Trade Organization (WTO), 315, 349, 350
World Values Survey, 288, 370, 373, 397, 402, 411
Wuthnow, Robert, 43, 95, 97

Xenophobia, 4, 242
X-signs, 177
X-tausendmal quer, 179, 183, 185

YouTube, 23, 227, 228, 304

Zald, Mayer N., xiii, 125, 252
Zippel, Kathrin, 426

(continued from page ii)

Volume 29   Paul D. Almeida, *Waves of Protest: Popular Struggle in El Salvador, 1925–2005*

Volume 28   Heidi J. Swarts, *Organizing Urban America: Secular and Faith-based Progressive Movements*

Volume 27   Ethel C. Brooks, *Unraveling the Garment Industry: Transnational Organizing and Women's Work*

Volume 26   Donatella della Porta, Massimiliano Andretta, Lorenzo Mosca, and Herbert Reiter, *Globalization from Below: Transnational Activists and Protest Networks*

Volume 25   Ruud Koopmans, Paul Statham, Marco Giugni, and Florence Passy, *Contested Citizenship: Immigration and Cultural Diversity in Europe*

Volume 24   David Croteau, William Hoynes, and Charlotte Ryan, editors, *Rhyming Hope and History: Activists, Academics, and Social Movement Scholarship*

Volume 23   David S. Meyer, Valerie Jenness, and Helen Ingram, editors, *Routing the Opposition: Social Movements, Public Policy, and Democracy*

Volume 22   Kurt Schock, *Unarmed Insurrections: People Power Movements in Nondemocracies*

Volume 21   Christian Davenport, Hank Johnston, and Carol Mueller, editors, *Repression and Mobilization*

Volume 20   Nicole C. Raeburn, *Changing Corporate America from Inside Out: Lesbian and Gay Workplace Rights*

Volume 19   Vincent J. Roscigno and William F. Danaher, *The Voice of Southern Labor: Radio, Music, and Textile Strikes, 1929–1934*

Volume 18   Maryjane Osa, *Solidarity and Contention: Networks of Polish Opposition*

Volume 17   Mary Margaret Fonow, *Union Women: Forging Feminism in the United Steelworkers of America*

Volume 16   Bert Klandermans and Suzanne Staggenborg, editors, *Methods of Social Movement Research*

Volume 15   Sharon Kurtz, *Workplace Justice: Organizing Multi-identity Movements*

Volume 14   Sanjeev Khagram, James V. Riker, and Kathryn Sikkink, editors, *Restructuring World Politics: Transnational Social Movements, Networks, and Norms*

Volume 13   Sheldon Stryker, Timothy J. Owens, and Robert W. White, editors, *Self, Identity, and Social Movements*

Volume 12   Byron A. Miller, *Geography and Social Movements: Comparing Antinuclear Activism in the Boston Area*

Volume 11   Mona N. Younis, *Liberation and Democratization: The South African and Palestinian National Movements*

Volume 10   Marco Giugni, Doug McAdam, and Charles Tilly, editors, *How Social Movements Matter*

Volume 9   Cynthia L. Irvin, *Militant Nationalism: Between Movement and Party in Ireland and the Basque Country*

Volume 8   Raka Ray, *Fields of Protest: Women's Movements in India*

Volume 7   Michael P. Hanagan, Leslie Page Moch, and Wayne te Brake, editors, *Challenging Authority: The Historical Study of Contentious Politics*

Volume 6   Donatella della Porta and Herbert Reiter, editors, *Policing Protest: The Control of Mass Demonstrations in Western Democracies*

Volume 5   Hanspeter Kriesi, Ruud Koopmans, Jan Willem Duyvendak, and Marco G. Giugni, *New Social Movements in Western Europe: A Comparative Analysis*

Volume 4   Hank Johnston and Bert Klandermans, editors, *Social Movements and Culture*

Volume 3   J. Craig Jenkins and Bert Klandermans, editors, *The Politics of Social Protest: Comparative Perspectives on States and Social Movements*

Volume 2   John Foran, editor, *A Century of Revolution: Social Movements in Iran*

Volume 1   Andrew Szasz, *EcoPopulism: Toxic Waste and the Movement for Environmental Justice*